# Recollections in Tranquillity

# Recollections in Tranquillity

Maurice B. McNamee, S.J.

2001
ST. LOUIS UNIVERSITY PRESS
St. Louis

All photos are from the author's collection.

**Library of Congress Cataloging-in-Publication Data**

McNamee, Maurice B., 1909–
    Recollections in tranquility / Maurice B. McNamee.—1st ed.
        p.   cm.
    Includes bibliographical references and index.
    ISBN 0-9652929-5-9 (alk. paper)—ISBN 0-96529296-7 (pbk. : alk.
    paper)   1. McNamee, Maurice B., 1909–   2. Catholic Church—
United States—Clergy—Biography.   I. Title.
BX4705.M47656 A3   2001
271′.5302—dc21
[B]                                                     2001041663

Printed in the United States of America
01   02   03   04   05      5   4   3   2   1
First Edition

# CONTENTS

# LIST OF ILLUSTRATIONS

The following are abbreviations of the actual captions.

Following page : 182

My parents, me, and brother Fran.

The house where we lived before I joined the Jesuits.

St. John the Baptist Church, Montello, Wisconsin.

Traf Maher and me at the Villa of Waupaca, Wisconsin.

My mother, sister Marcella, and my father on the day of my First Mass.

The Rock Building, Jesuit Novitiate, Florissant, Missouri.

Father Henry Riordan, my English teacher.

My Tertian class.

My class in the Juniorate.

Our class's Golden Jubilee, Cupples House.

My nephew, Rev. James McNamee.

My niece Jean and me.

My niece Marie Iwanski and me.

My brother Howard, sister Laura, and me.

With friends in Killarney, Ireland.

At the *Fountain of the Rivers* in Rome.

With Father Terrence Dempsey in Florence.

With Verner Burks.

Father Edward Mathie presenting me with a gift at my Golden Jubilee.

Jim and Martha Jane Soltow.

Sarah Harriman White, John White, and me at a book signing.


Following page : 374

Former pupils Professor Clarence Miller and Sister Una Hayes.

Entrance to the McNamee Gallery, Cupples House.

On the steps of Cupples House.

Admiring glass collection donated to Cupples House by Mrs. Eleanor Turshin.

Cupples House board members, 1995.

Former English Department colleagues help me celebrate my ninetieth birthday.

Miss Mary Bruemmer and Kathleen and Tyron Winter at my ninetieth birthday celebration.

Father Ray Tully, me, and Father Paul Reinert, 1999.

Charles Cuttler, me, Carolyn Valone, and Terry Dempsey on my ninety-first birthday.

Margaret Anthony and Ginny Bartling on my ninety-first birthday.

Sherry Linquist and Peter and Pamela Ambrose on my ninety-first birthday.

Dale and Carol Boggs on my ninety-first birthday.

With Trudy Busch at Grant's Farm on my ninety-first birthday.

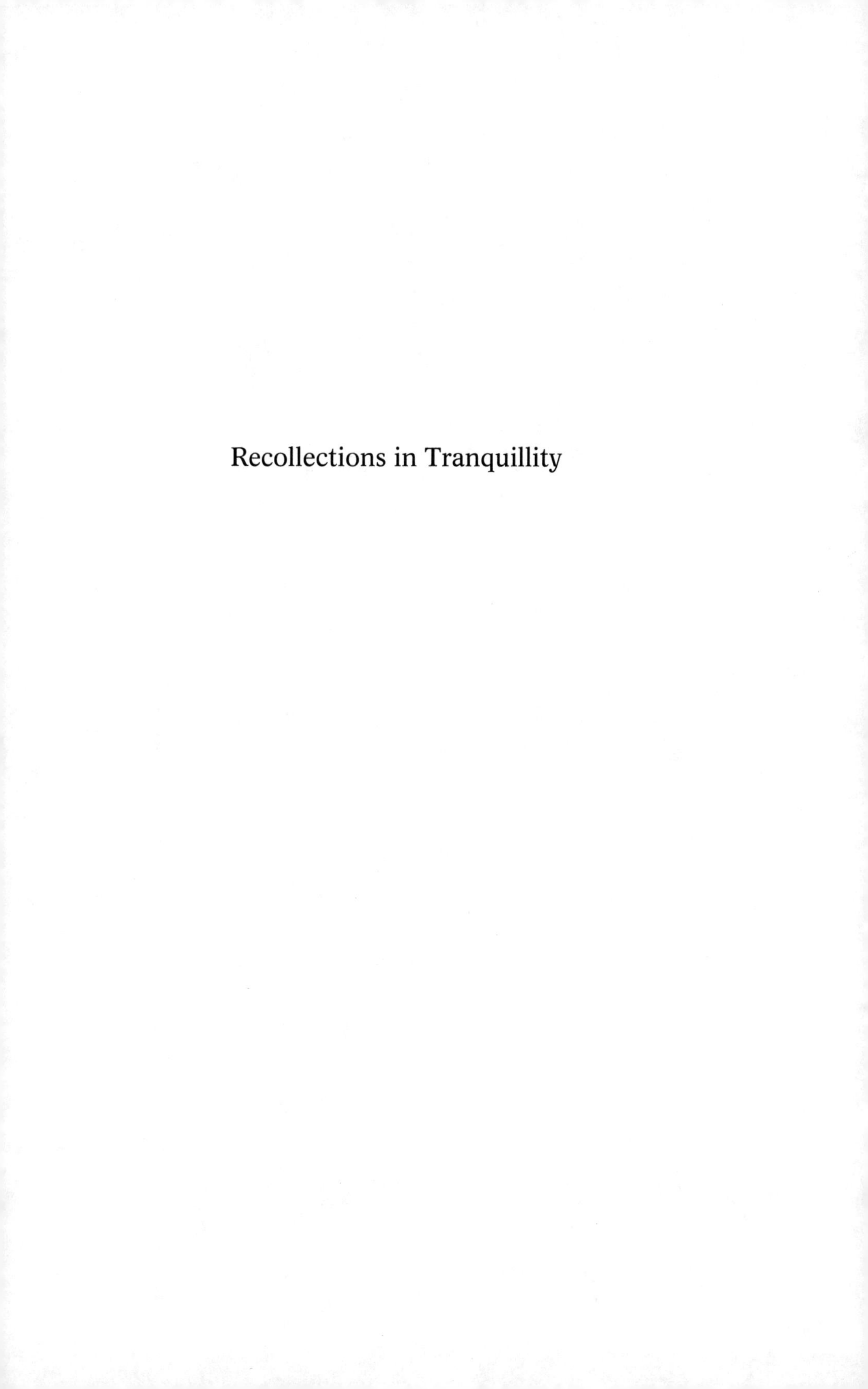

Recollections in Tranquillity

# 1

# Pastoral Beginnings

I HAVE BEEN PERSUADED TO write my memoirs not because I have any particular importance in the world, but because a whole series of accidental circumstances in my life provided the opportunity for special experiences that might be interesting to some readers. As I set out to respond to requests from inside and outside the Society of Jesus to share some of those experiences, I am reminded of the title of one of Maurice Baring's books, *In My End Is My Beginning*. As I look back on my life from the perspective of ninety years, I realize how much of my end was in my beginning.

It all began on June 5, 1909, in Montello, Wisconsin. It was a fairly prodigious beginning. I weighed thirteen pounds when I was born and almost killed my mother in her birth pangs. I was so overweight that I looked for all the world like an Olmec baby, so fat that my arms seemed to be bound in rubber bands with layers of fat dangling over them. A few months after birth I caught the whooping cough and whooped off most of the excess fat, but the horror of my baby pictures (which my vanity later induced me to destroy) gave me the lifelong motivation to watch my diet so that I would never again present to the camera anything like what my babyhood did.

A tale hangs about the name of my hometown—Montello, Wisconsin. It was named, according to a very old tradition, by the famous Jesuit explorer and missioner, Père Marquette. In the part of Wisconsin around Montello a glacier had deposited along the Fox River a huge chunk of red granite that rose several hundred feet above ground and extended at least that much below. When Marquette and his companions canoed their way down the Fox en route to the Wisconsin River and ultimately to the Mississippi, they were impressed with the picturesque sight of the "little mountain" of granite rising above the waters of the Fox and stopped there. Father Marquette said Mass there and named the place Mont de L'eau (Mountain of Water). In time, the French name was corrupted on English tongues into Montello. So, in a way, there was a kind of Jesuit hex on my career from the beginning, although in my boyhood I didn't know a Jesuit from a hacksaw. I did, however, remember that every August a day was set aside called Marquette Day. One of the celebratory floats in the town parade always carried an individual decked out in a Jesuit cassock and biretta to commemorate Marquette's association with the naming of the site. Years later, when I had learned more about Jesuits and had become one, I mentioned in a Jesuit dining room this legend about the naming of my hometown. Father Joseph Donnelly, a well-known Jesuit historian, was at the table. He had just completed a biography of Père Marquette. His rejoinder to my proud recounting of the naming of my home town was, "There is not a shred of historical evidence that Marquette ever stopped at the site, much less that he named it." So much for my happy legend. I asked Joe whether he had ever heard of oral tradition as a legitimate source of historical truth. A very long oral tradition told how Montello got its name, and the town itself is the county seat of Marquette County. I'll continue to hug my happy legend. Some historians, of course, will not accept anything as historically true for which they lack documents signed and sealed, but to insist on this, I believe, robs us of a great deal of historical truth.

There are other things about Montello that, in a sense, are a microcosm of the whole American experience. In my youth, it had a population of only twelve hundred, and, in fact, its population is still about the same. But making up that population was the kind of ethnic, religious, and cultural mix that has made America what it is. There were Lutheran Germans and Irish Catholics, both of which, for the most part, were farmers. A quarry had been opened to exploit the deposit of beautiful red granite; many of the quarry workers were Polish Catholics, and many of the stonecutters were Welsh. A great many of the tradesmen and shopkeepers were also Welsh Methodists. Punctuating the main street were the steeples of the Methodist, Catholic, and Lutheran churches that gave visible testimony to the diversified ethnic and religious backgrounds of the townspeople. The Catholics and Lutherans had their own schools, and there was some friction between them, but the various groups in general worked well together. All thought of themselves as Americans. Life in Montello was a tiny example of the American miracle of the amalgamation of many diverse peoples into a new unity. There eventually was a good deal of intermarriage between members of the different groups that helped to strengthen that unity. I myself am a duke's mixture. My father was full-blooded Irish and Catholic, but my mother was half Welsh and half German and a convert from Lutheranism. So within my own family I saw a good deal of the diversity that went into the making of America.

I was born in a little house that had been built on a sliver of land at the edge of the farm that my great-grandfather had homesteaded. The land was there for the taking on condition that it was homesteaded and brought into production, which was easier said than done in my part of Wisconsin. The whole area had been produced by the glaciers that had moved south from Canada as far as the northern Illinois border. What they left near Montello was very unpromising for agricultural development. Any acreage that a pioneer might homestead was apt to be a combination of blow sand, peat bog marshes, gravel pits, and forests heavily wooded with oak and hickory. The land was free to homesteaders, but hardly a square foot was arable. What the homesteaders did to hew out a bit of usable farmland from this unpromising terrain is a very interesting example of sheer necessity creating a means of survival. No one could raise a bean on the sand dunes or on the gravel deposits left by the grinding action of the glaciers. There were fertile stretches of better land, but they were covered with thick stands of oak and hickory trees. The only way of developing any arable land was to clear some of the forests, which had to be done by backbreaking hard labor with saws and axes. When the trees were down and sawed up for firewood, the stumps had to be grubbed out by hand before there was any clear land for planting. The homesteaders would begin by purchasing a team of oxen or horses to help with the work and a cow to provide milk and butter for the family. But the animals had to be fed. They could graze in the woods in the summertime and survive, but what was to be done for feed in the long winters?

Luckily the work of the glaciers in the area had not all been malignant. As they ground their way south, they drove huge icebergs into the soil and created numerous small spring-fed lakes and acres of marshes. Over the centuries, these grass-topped marshes deposited layer after layer of vegetable matter that became peat bogs. They were not as compacted as the Irish peat bogs; they were much more loosely fibered, saturated with water, and covered with light moss. But on these bogs flourished a fine waist-high stand of wild grass. It would provide fodder for horses and cattle if it could be mowed. The trouble was that heavy horses and mowers would mire in six feet of muck if they ventured onto the marsh grass—a challenge that the resourceful homesteaders met with a solution that, as far as I know, was unique to this part of Wisconsin.

The farmers took their horses to the blacksmith and had clogs made for each of their hooves. The blacksmith first fashioned special horseshoes with inch-long iron corks at the front and rear. The clog itself was really a wooden snowshoe the size of a dinner plate. Holes were drilled in the clog, and the corks on the metal shoe fit snugly in the holes. The blacksmith then had to custom make a clamp that snapped over each hoof to keep the clog firmly attached. With the clogs in place, and gunnysacks wrapped around the wheels of the hay mower and rake, the farmer and his horses could safely venture onto the marshes without miring. It was comical to see the horses learning to walk with these clumsy clogs on their feet, but they soon managed. Holes were bored through the wooden clogs to create less pressure on the marsh surface. I can remember seeing water spurting up to the bellies of the horses through these holes in the clogs as they plodded on in front of the mower. Although arable fields had been cleared before my time, the farmers still used this ingenious method of mowing. I can still remember going as a boy to the blacksmith shop to have the horses clogged before hay season. It was frequently my job to pinch the horse's nose as the blacksmith was going about the long process of fitting the shoes and clogs for each of its feet. The pinch was a sufficient distraction from all the uncomfortable manipulation of its feet to prevent the horse from kicking the black-smith into kingdom come.

In those clogging sessions, I learned to admire the blacksmith's dexterity. It was a wonder to me how he could take an unlikely bit of iron, bring it to red-hot heat in his blow furnace, then with a few twists of his pincers and some deft blows of his hammer fashion it on his anvil into a shoe that would exactly fit the horse's hoof on which he was working. In fact, my admiration for his ability was so great that, at that time of my callow youth, I thought I might like to become a blacksmith myself when I grew up. We were reading Longfellow's poem "The Village Blacksmith" at the time in school, and I shared the poet's admiration for the blacksmith:

> Under a spreading chestnut-tree
>   The village smithy stands;
> The smith, a mighty man is he,
>   With large and sinewy hands;
> And the muscles of his brawny arms
>   Are strong as iron bands.
>
> Week in, week out, from morn till night,
>   You can hear his bellows blow;
> You can hear him swing his heavy sledge,
>   With measured beat and slow,
> Like a sexton ringing the village bell,
>   When the evening sun is low.
>
> And children coming home from school
>   Look in at the open door;
> They love to see the flaming forge,
>   And hear the bellows roar,
> And catch the burning sparks that fly
>   Like chaff from a threshing-floor.

I so admired Basil the Blacksmith in Longfellow's "Evangeline" that when I was confirmed, I took Basil for a middle name because I had not been given one at baptism. I certainly was not thinking of St. Basil, the great eastern doctor of the Roman Catholic Church. I had never heard of him. It was Basil the Blacksmith I was taking as a patron, and, in a way, he remains my patron to this day. I am firmly of the opinion that if you become so intellectual that you forget how to use your hands, you are only half human.

My close observation of the blacksmith at his anvil prepared me, years later, to appreciate fully the forcefulness of an image in Gerard Manley Hopkins's "Wreck of the Deutschland." He is talking of the ways of God with sinners. God can either storm them into repentance or, with His grace, steal through their resistance like a spring breeze.

> With an anvil ding
> And with fire in him forge thy will
> Or rather, rather then, stealing as Spring
>   Through him, melt him but master him still:
> Whether at once, as once at a crash, Paul,
> Or as Justin, a lingering-out sweet skill
>   Make mercy in all of us, out of us all
> Mastery, but be adored, be adored King.

Unless you have watched a blacksmith hammer his idea into a reluctant piece of iron on his anvil, I don't think you are quite prepared to see the forcefulness of the image of God forging His will on the heart of a reluctant sinner: "With an anvil ding / And with fire in him [forging His] will."

But now back to the marshes. One of the peat bogs near the Montello area stretches for at least ten miles along the Fox River. The homesteaders early realized what a resource of free fodder these marshes were, so they took out claims of forty-acre plots in them. With their horses clogged and the wheels of mowers and rakes properly padded, they would go to their plots in haying season and "put up the hay." Putting up hay began by mowing it, raking it into windrows, hand-cocking it, then pitching the cocks onto wooden sleds that would not cut through the soft moss into the muck below, and finally stacking it into Monet-like strawberry-shaped stacks weighted down by wooden blocks so the wind wouldn't blow them apart. I can remember that when haying season was over, we could see hundreds of these stacks stretching out to the horizon. In winter, when the marsh was frozen solid and covered with snow, the farmers would go in with bobsleighs and haul the hay home, thus providing a large part of the fodder for the horses and cattle during the winter. In homesteading days, before the land was cleared for other crops, putting up hay was an absolute necessity. In later years, it provided a crop of wild hay for the taking, before modern chemical fertilizers enabled farmers to raise tame hay such as alfalfa on the not too fertile cleared land.

The haying of the peat bog marshes has long since ceased. The peat bogs are still there, but the ability to raise tame hay on the cleared land has made the difficult job of haying the marshes unnecessary and unprofitable. More modern technology has put some of the bogs to other good uses. They have been turned into what are called muck farms because of the six feet of the mucky peat bog. Entrepreneurs have come in with heavy equipment and cut deep ditches that drain off some of the excess water. The partly dried out peat deposit provides a fertile soil for crops such as carrots that are harvested for canning factories and especially great quantities of mint. Pressing machines press out the mint juice and barrels of it are shipped all over the country. In recent years, the muck farmers have brought in itinerant Mexican laborers to plant, cultivate, and harvest the crops. This influx has very much changed the ethnic nature of the little community, at least during the summer. But it was these peat bog marshes and the ingenious method of harvesting the hay that flourished on them that made the settlement of the homesteaders in this part of the country possible in the first place.

The glaciers were benevolent to the Montello area in other ways. The area got its name from Marquette because of the picturesque scene of the Fox River meandering around the huge red granite deposit from northern Canada. Very early in the history of that little mountain of red granite, some far-sighted entrepreneurs saw its potential and proceeded to quarry it. Much of it was fashioned into pavement blocks and shipped to the burgeoning cities. A great deal of the pavement between the old streetcar tracks in Milwaukee and Chicago was made of Montello granite. The beautiful red granite was very fine grained and was reported to be some of the hardest granite in the world. When polished, it became a handsome material for fine graveyard monuments. Cemeteries all over the Midwest boast of beautiful headstones made of Montello granite. The entire first floor rotunda of the state capitol in Madison is decorated with Montello granite. The sarcophagi of Ulysses S. Grant and his wife on Riverside Drive in New York are also made of Montello granite. The granite quarry in many ways affected the visible appearance and economy of the town. It provided jobs for many of the townsfolk and particularly attracted a group of Polish Catholic and Welsh Methodist immigrants, which somewhat changed the ethnic nature of the community. Quarrying the granite also changed the physiognomy of the town. A stream fed by springs to the north of the site ran through the town and emptied into the Fox River, which circled the town to the south. The quarry company dammed up the stream at the quarry site, thus forming a small lake just north of the city. A generator was put in at the dam site, which generated enough electricity to run the derrick and other machinery at the quarry. The Fox River itself had been dammed up on the south side of the town, which created a lake stretching some twenty miles west. The Fox River at the time was kept navigable as far as Montello for small boats hauling freight and some passengers. But in preparation for making the river navigable beyond Montello, a canal was dug around the dam by dredging. But the advent of the railroads made river traffic less practicable, so the Fox never became a boatway beyond Montello. Thus, Montello was practically surrounded with lakes. Segmented by the little Montello River that flowed from the quarry dam and by the canal that skirted the dam on the Fox River, the town was punctuated by a series of bridges. The ubiquity of water made it feel a little like Venice. All these rivers, canals, and lakes were to play an important part in its much later development as a tourist center, but in the early days tourism was no part of its life.

Some of the granite from the quarry was shipped by boat, but a more efficient means of shipping had to be devised. The Canadian Sioux Railroad had a line that ran from Canada to Madison. It passed through Portage, Wisconsin, just eighteen miles from Montello. So a spur was built from Portage to Montello that enabled the quarry company to ship out the granite by train. Because there was no turn-about in the town, the train *backed* the eighteen miles into town in the morning, loaded up the granite, and steamed back to Portage, head first, in the evening. As you saw the train chugging backwards through the countryside in the morning, you got the impression that you might have had too much to drink the night before. The train had one passenger coach, which provided a means of public travel out of the town. You could connect at Portage with the main Milwaukee line that ran from Chicago to Minneapolis.

The little Sioux line train was the first means of my escape from the very circumscribed horse-and-buggy world in which we all lived in Montello. There was only one automobile in the town, owned by the family doctor. He used to take people out riding on Sunday, as pilots later took people for a ride on a plane for a Sunday thrill. The doctor's car, I recall, was an early Maxwell. You climbed up two steps of the running board to get into the high leather-upholstered seats. There were no top and no side doors. The windshield was a straight-up affair fastened to the fenders with brass ropes. A horn, mounted on the fender, was sounded from a rubber ball next to the driver. One Sunday, I recall, Doc took a pair of elderly spinsters out driving all wrapped up in their dusters and hat veils. He went over a high culvert in the dirt road, and the ladies were thrown out the side openings. Doc was as deaf as a post and, what with the loud noise of the engine, he never missed the ladies until he got back in town. Meantime, they trudged their way home. But it was a thrill for all of us to ride for the first time in a horseless carriage.

But back to the quarry. It impinges rather importantly on my boyhood memories. In his early married years, my father worked in the quarry as the operator of the derrick that lifted the huge cut pieces of granite out of the quarry pit. Quarry lore forms a large part of my earliest memories. My dad had been raised on the farm homesteaded by his grandfather. He was the only boy in a family of four, so he learned early all about farming, and the farm remained in his blood. As a matter of fact, in the wintertime, he ran the farm because Grandpa worked in the lumber camps in northern Wisconsin to augment the family income. But when Dad married, there was no way Grandfather's farm could support two families. It was then that my father bought the little house on a seven-acre splinter of the homestead and went to work in the quarry. But the farm still called. He was hesitant about working indefinitely in the quarry because many of the quarry workers developed silicosis—a disease caused by the heavy stone dust produced by drilling, shaping, and polishing the granite. When I was about four years old, he decided to go farming again. There was no more homesteading, so the only way he could do it was by purchasing or renting a farm. Dad had an unconquerable dread all his life of going into debt, so he opted for rental. His first move was not really renting a farm, but managing a large farm for a successful farmer who was prevented from working it himself because of a sudden illness. We moved into the upper floor of a country store on the edge of the farm. Our house was across the tracks from Glen Oak Depot. Glen Oak was three miles from town on the main Northwestern line between Chicago and Minneapolis. Some of my most vivid childhood memories came from our brief residence there. The lonely whining of the monstrous big steam engines at night as they pulled long freight trains through the countryside was a fascination to me. And even more fascinating were the passenger trains filled with finely dressed passengers in coaches and diners. They could not have been more impressive to me if they had come from Mars. And Chicago to me at that time was about as remote as Mars. We knew that our Mars was inhabited because we had some rather well-to-do relatives in Chicago. They made an appearance occasionally on these magic wheels, and every Christmas they shipped us a literal barrel of clothes that they had discarded for newer ones. My mother was a marvelous seamstress, and out of the contents of these magic barrels she fashioned all our clothes for the next year. I never had a "store bought" suit until I started high school, but nobody knew it because what came from my mother's hands was as finely tailored as any suit we could have bought in the store. Mother could look at a suit or dress in the Sears and Roebuck catalog (our other contact with Mars) and reproduce it exactly on her sewing machine without benefit of any other pattern.

Another new experience for us at the Glen Oak habitat above the country store was tuning in on Edison's invention. Jennie Cotter, the proprietress of the store, had an Edison phonograph with the old tubular records and the morning glory–shaped speaker. It bore the authentic mark of the dog sitting in front of the phonograph enraptured at the sound of his master's voice. I, too, sat for hours delighted with the sound of old familiar songs wafting out of the horn. It was my first experience of artificial sound reproduction, and I never ceased wondering at the miracle of the thing. I learned by heart the words and melodies of the songs pealing off the wax tube and still know most of them.

Many of the songs on the records I already knew because I had learned them from my father, who was something of a folk singer. When he was growing up on Grandpa's farm, he used to cut firewood, haul it to town, and sell it to augment the family income. One day when Dad was delivering a load of wood to a customer in town, he saw one of the young lads of the family dragging a violin around as a toy. Dad had decided he wanted to learn to play the violin, and here was his chance to get one. The McGloughlins, his mother's family, had music in their blood. His granddad, Tom McGloughlin, was an excellent violinist, and his mother, our grannie, played the cello. They used to give duet performances, and Dad had decided he wanted to emulate them, so he offered to give the family the load of wood for the violin that the kid was dragging around the house. They agreed, and Dad went home elated with his coveted instrument. It turned out to be a very good instrument, and Dad soon had it restrung and in tiptop shape. He went about teaching himself to play it and before long became a proficient violinist. He also eventually learned to play the guitar and banjo, and formed his own little combo that played at barn dances and other social events. He had an excellent voice and a facile memory and developed a limitless repertoire of folk songs. So folk music was an important part of my young days. In fact, before radio and television, it was our chief form of home entertainment. Dad sang his endless repertoire of folk songs so often that we all learned to sing them with him. When the evening chores were done, we often spent the evening singing. Those sing-alongs provided some of my happiest boyhood memories, giving me first-hand experience of an oral culture. Some of the songs were very familiar ones, popular ones at the time, but some Dad had picked up from his Irish grandfather and mother, and they smelled of the old sod. Some were happy or humorous, and some were sad. I can still remember the words and tunes of many of them. A Christmas never came around that Dad didn't sing "Miss Fogarty's Christmas Cake," and I have been known, seventy-five years later, to inflict it on some gatherings myself. The words run something like this:

> As I sat by my window last evenin'
>     The postman he brought unto me
> A fine gilt-edged invitation
>     Saying, McFadden, come over to tea.
>
> I knew that Fogarty sent it
>     So I went over for auld time's sake.
> And the first thing they gave me to tackle,
>     Was a piece of Miss Fogarty's cake.
>
> There were plums, and prunes, and cherries
>     Lemon and oranges, citron too.
> There were nutmeg, raisins, and berries,
>     And the crust it was nailed on with glue.
>
> McFadden began to shiver and shake
>     And Paddie had took to the sofa.
> It would kill a man twice if he ate but a slice
>     Of Miss Fogarty's Christmas cake.

Some of the songs had a slightly racist tone to them that was entirely lost on me at the time. There were no African Americans in our part of the country; I never saw one until I went to Milwaukee for high school, so I caught none of the racist humor in the following song about a black minister in the South.

> A preacher went out a-hunting
>     'Twas on a Sunday morn;
> Of course it was against his religion
>     But he took his gun along.

> He shot himself a very fine quail
>   And one little miserly hare;
> But on his way returning home
>   He met a great big grizzly bear.
>
> The bear stepped out in the middle of the road
>   Right up to the coon, you see.
> And the coon got so excited,
>   That he climbed up a sycamore tree.
>
> He cast his eyes to the Lord in the skies
>   And these words he said to Him:
> "O Lord, you delivered Jonah from the belly of the whale
>   And the three Hebrew children from the fiery furnace
> As the Good Book doth declare
>   O Lord, if you can't help me
> For goodness sakes, don't you help that bear."

There were songs to fit any occasion or mood. Mother sometimes controlled the program. When Dad would start off on one of the sad Irish songs, she'd say, "No, Dad, you can't sing that song tonight; it's too sad." I was reminded of this many years later when I encountered a line in one of Chesterton's poems, referring to Irish songs, where he says: "All their wars are gay wars / And all their songs are sad." A good many of them are.

But the music was not only a part of the home experience at that time; it was important in the social life of the community as well. Dad's little orchestra provided some of the fun. I can recall that on many Sundays the whole family would be piled into the surrey with fringe on top, and we'd take off to a neighbor's homestead for a barn dance. Dad's little combo would provide the music, and Dad would often call the square dances. Mother loved to dance, and these dances were literally barn dances. The driveway floor between the haymows or an empty haymow provided the dance floor. The adults danced the night away, while the youngsters played games in the haymows, where, before the evening was over, most of them would be asleep. When the dance was over, the parents would gather up their kids and carry them over their shoulders fast asleep to the buggies or surreys for the trek home. There was a great deal of such simple self-entertainment. In fact, that was all there was before radio and television. It was always participatory and created a wonderful community spirit. All of this reminiscing about the folk singing and self-made music in my youth was inspired by my first experience of the phonograph, which was the very beginning of the technological developments that would soon make obsolete such simple pleasures as folk song and community dance.

Another form of self-entertainment in this pretechnological age was storytelling. The Irish have always been great storytellers. My granddad was the great storyteller in our family. We kids often spent an evening sprawled on the floor around his chair listening to his tales. He had a neat little white goatee. I always enjoyed watching it bobbing up and down as he told his stories, which frequently had to do with his boyhood experiences in Ireland. He came to this country at the age of seventeen. His father had come over first and homesteaded the farm, then he brought over his wife and later his eight children. Three boys came over together, but were separated in New York and never saw one another again. Grandpa's two brothers went south and eventually joined the Confederate army and lost their lives in the Civil War. Grandpa came west and lived with his parents on the farm. He was old enough before he left Ireland to have intense memories of his experiences there and had the ability of making them very vivid to us. Ireland was still under the thumb of England at the time, and the Catholic Church was severely outlawed. One of the most vivid experiences of Grandpa's youth that he often repeated for us was his standing watch at a wood site to give a signal to the little "hedge church" gathered secretly along a creek beyond the woods for a Sunday Mass. It was his duty to keep a lookout for the government soldiers on horseback who might show up to stop the Mass and arrest the participants. If the lookout detected their approach early enough, he could warn the gathering, and they could flee before the soldiers got there. Grandpa said that when a warning was given, the priest would quickly take off his vestments, give them to a member of the hedge church, and flee. Priests were not numerous, and everyone agreed that it was important for him to flee first so he could provide the sacraments for other hedge congregations in the future.

This story came vividly back to me recently when I visited the site of one these hedge churches near Cork. My guide was Sister Una Hayes, whose doctoral dissertation I had directed at St. Louis University. Her father was a schoolteacher and an actual member of the group who had worked secretly, and ultimately successfully, for the revolution led by Daniel O'Connell that finally won southern Ireland its freedom from the civil and religious oppression of England. Sister Una and her family had experienced firsthand a great deal of that oppression, as had my grandfather. Her experiences and those of my grandfather have enabled me to understand some of the deep-felt antipathy of the Irish for the English. On a recent visit to Ireland, I visited Sister Una, and she took me to see, among many other fascinating things in the Cork area, the site of one of the hidden hedge churches. It was very much as my grandfather had described the one for which he had stood "lookout." A dense stand of trees hid a winding creek that had hollowed out a little clearing in a rocky section of the terrain. A ledge jutted out from the side of the rock that was used for an altar. There was sufficient flat space in front of the rock for the small secret congregation to assemble for Mass. If a warning of advancing soldiers came from the lookout, the congregation could hastily disperse across the creek and into the woods beyond.

The terrible oppression that the Irish experienced for centuries at the hands of the English was expressed in some of the Irish popular songs. All kinds of oppressive laws kept the Irish subdued and dependent. Any improvement on their modest property would slap an increase on their taxes. Just adding a window to the cottage would mean higher taxes. The injustice and irrationality of these kinds of laws are the theme of one of the songs that Dad used to sing for us.

> O Paddy dear, and did you hear
> The news that's going round.
> The shamrock is forbid by law
> To grow on Irish ground.
>
> St. Patrick's Day no more we'll keep
> His color can't be seen.
> For there's a bloody law
> Agin' the wearin' o' the green.
>
> Sure, I met with Napper Tandie
> And he took me by the hand,
> And he says, "How is old Ireland
> And how does she stand?"
>
> I say, "She's the most distressful country
> Me eyes have ever seen

> Sure they're hangin' men and women there
> For wearin' o' the green."
>
> "When the law can stop the blades of grass
> From growing as they grow
> And when the leaves in summertime
> Their colors dare not show,
>
> "Then I'll change the color
> That I wear in my gobeen,
> But til that time, please God,
> I'll stick to the wearin' o' the green."

Some of the burdensome laws that the English pressed upon the helpless Irish were, indeed, as senseless and unjust as forbidding the shamrocks to grow. My grandpa's tales and the experiences of Sister Una's family gave me a feeling, early and late, of what it was like to live under such an oppressive regime.

When Sister Una was working on her dissertation and would come to my office for a conference, she would walk in and turn over an ashtray on my desk that bore a map of England. She said she couldn't sit down in peace before a map of England. This was, of course, half jest—*but only half.*

Many of Grandpa's tales were about the fairies, the "wee folk," and leprechauns that populated the Irish countryside. Children always like to believe in fairy stories, and Grandpa's tales were so vivid and detailed that we were always sure he had experienced every one of them. Years later, when I took a jaunting-car trip through the Lakes of Killarney and was enwrapped in the lush green of the woodlands, feet thick with moss blanketing the ground and fallen trees in the forest, I knew these places *had* to be inhabited by leprechauns. If they didn't exist, your imagination would put them there.

No matter what the story was, Granddad always told it as if everything in it had happened to him personally. I remember one story that he said had happened in his neighborhood in Ireland. It occurred at the very special wake for Pat, an elderly neighbor. The custom in many wakes was to lay out the deceased on a simple cot with a sheet draped over the body. It so happened that Pat in life was very crippled and stooped over with a hunched back. To get his body to lie flat on the cot they had to tie it down with a rope. At the wake, one of the rascal lads in the family slid under the sheet and cut the rope. When Pat sat up on the bier, consternation reigned. Grandpa went on to say that a young girl was frightened into such hysteria that she ran out into the farmyard and stumbled over a sleeping donkey. In fright, it stood up and brayed loudly, terrifying the girl so much that she had a heart attack. Grandpa told all of this as if he had experienced every bit of it. Years later I discovered that he probably hadn't experienced any of it. It was a tale he had picked up from others and had handed on to us only slightly embroidered.

On my first trip to Ireland, I did the jaunting-car tour of the Lakes of Killarney. I was a Jesuit priest by that time, and when I, dressed in clerics, came out of the little hotel where I was staying to engage a jaunting-car driver, the young driver waiting at the door said, "Oh, Father, you deserve a better driver than me. I'll get you one of the best around." At that he reined his horse around and rode off to the Grand Hotel up the hill to fetch what turned out to be indeed one of the most practiced jaunting-car drivers and raconteurs in the business. As we made our way through the beautiful woods that surround the sparkling Lakes of Killarney, Pat regaled me with one story after another—and told them all as if every detail of them had happened to himself. As we drove on, we began to experience what the Irish call a "soft mist," which sometimes means it is raining like hell. When the "mist" got a bit too thick to go on in comfort, we'd stop under a tree, and Pat would continue to reel out his endless stories. On one of these stops, he said, "Now I want to tell you about a special wake I experienced as a boy," then went on to tell exactly the same story that Granddad had told about the wake of the crippled Pat. Everything was the same except for the donkey and frightened girl—an embroidery my granddad added, no doubt, to the well-worn tale. Many years later I caught another recording of the story from a very different source. When I joined the English department at St. Louis University, Father Norman Dreyfus, the chairman of the department, had a program of visiting speakers. One year Sir Sean Leslie was on the list. We went down to Union Station to meet him. He was dressed in stripes and tails, and the only luggage he had with him was a lap robe. He stayed with us in the Jesuit community, and we discovered that all he had in the lap robe was a straight razor, a small shaving mug, a stub of a shaving brush, and a hand of fresh bananas. We had to supply him with a fresh hand when he left. He gave a fascinating public lecture on Irish literature, but we had also heard that he was an incomparable storyteller, so we invited him to give an evening of storytelling to the English Club. He was happy to do so. We engaged the newly decorated Campus Club in Chouteau House, an old mansion on campus, got a supply of port and English biscuits, and thought we were ready for the evening. But we soon discovered we weren't. When Sir Sean arrived, he wanted all the lights out with only a candle burning on the table next to him, and he wanted all of us seated on the floor—to provide the proper atmosphere for his evening of stories and Irish lore. So we sat on the floor and looked at Sir Sean's goatee bobbing up and down in the flickering candlelight. We were enchanted with his ghost stories—all of which, of course, he assured us he had experienced himself. This to me was all a flashback to my boyhood days of sitting listening to my granddad unwinding his endless tales as his goatee bobbed up and down in the light of the kerosene lamp. And when Sir Sean began to tell some of the more personal experiences of his life in Ireland, I was amazed that one of these tales was the exact same story that Granddad had told about the wake of humpbacked Pat, minus the girl and the donkey.

I recount all this because it is an interesting example of how an oral tradition works. Here was the same story told by three different individuals from widely different parts of Ireland and containing almost identical details, with an embroidered addition by one of the narrators.

How true a purveyor of fact and fiction a strictly oral tradition can be was borne home to me by another speaker in the speaker's cycle of the English Club at the university. The speaker was Seamus McManus from Donegal. He had just published a gathering of legends and folk tales from Donegal that had never before been published. When the book first appeared, he was accused of plagiarizing the legends of the Near East, from which the Celts originally came. Apparently, legends that had developed in the East had been handed down orally generation after generation for centuries by the Celtic people in the West with so little change that their modern publication in the West would look like plagiarism. In a semi-illiterate and a preprinting culture, the oral tradition, of course, is the chief means of transferring any knowledge from generation to generation.

Because of the proscription by the English against schools and education for the Irish, many of the Irish were illiterate and lived in an almost entirely oral world. That is why storytelling and folk song were so important to them. My grandfather himself was illiterate. He could neither read nor write until he was well into his old age. Grannie finally taught him to read. He preened himself on the new accomplishment. When he and Grannie had retired from the farm, he'd sit in his old rocker in the evening reading the newspaper out loud. Both he and Grannie were deaf as a post by this time, so it was no disturbance to Grannie. He'd read every line in the paper, the advertisements included, proud as a peacock that he could read the lines on the paper. He read the family Bible through from cover to cover three times.

But I've wandered far afield from Glen Oak. We lived there only one year. Dad was just farm manager there. He was anxious to get on a farm that he could work for himself, but his horror of going into debt induced him to rent one rather than buy one. The Barrett farm southeast of the town was up for rent. Deaths in the Barrett family had put the farm into the possession of a widow and her daughter Anne, so we rented the farm on halves and began farming in earnest. It was a dairy farm. This was my first experience of the fact that when you are running a dairy farm, you are all indentured servants to the cows. They have to be milked twice a day, every day, Sundays as well as weekdays, summer and winter. The cattle can graze in the woods and meadows in the summer, but you work in the fields all summer to raise the fodder to keep them alive in the winter. Mechanization has lightened much of the labor in all of this since I was a boy. The cows are milked by machines now, but you still have to be there twice a day to do it. And it's still true that a great deal of the year's work in the fields—all highly mechanized now—is expended to provide feed for the cattle in the winter.

When we moved onto the farm, I was too young to be milking or working in the fields, but I had my chores. The farm was situated right on the Fox River. Across from it was the famous Puckaway peat bog stretching for miles. The Barretts, like the other families who had homesteaded here, had staked out a claim to about forty acres of the peat bog marsh across the river. Here I got my first experience of "clog" haying. To get to the marsh with horses and mower we had to ferry across the river on a barge. Because I was too young to be engaged in the hard work of haying itself—that was my dad's and my two older brothers' job—haying season was a literal picnic for me. Mother used to cook up a good hot meal for the hayers and pack it in heavy milk pails to keep it warm. We would hitch up a horse and buggy, and drive the mile or so to the marsh, where we and the hayers would spread out a tablecloth on the grassy bank of the river and enjoy a picnic dinner. The dinner always included a freshly baked pie—blueberry, huckleberry, or blackberry—all of which grew wild on the farm. Sometimes it was apple made from fresh apples from the orchard. This was to me a real daily picnic.

My chore on the farm turned out to be almost as much of a picnic. When the Barretts had homesteaded the farm, they also laid claim to a twenty-acre marshland on the near side of the river. It was not peat bog, but a regular marshland meadow that provided excellent grazing for the cattle. But it was not contiguous to the rest of the farm. To get to it we had to go down the public road for a quarter of a mile and about a mile down a public country lane that gave access to the river. It was my job, after the morning milking, to drive the cattle down the public road and the country lane to the meadow where they grazed all day. I had to fetch them back in the afternoon for the evening milking. It took all my puny skills and the more adept ones of Rover, our cattle dog, to get the cows to the pasture and back again. There were always individualists in the herd that resented being herded anywhere, but a few nips by Rover on the heels of these loiterers would get the whole herd moving together. On the trip back from the pasture in the morning and down to it in the afternoon, Rover and I had the lane all to ourselves. It was these daily trips through the beautiful country lane that developed my lifelong love of nature. There was so much to observe. Beautiful weeping willows grew plentifully in the damp soil. Their graceful pendant twigs waving in the breeze reminded me of a young girl tossing her long hair in the wind. Birch trees are native to this part of Wisconsin, and their white-barked beauty punctuated my lane.

Along the fences, there was an array of bushes and plants that had been seeded by the birds perching on the fence. There were elderberries—high bushes that flaunted coronas of white blossoms in the spring that became clusters of purple berries in the late summer. Large sections of the fences were entwined with wild grapevines. Both the elderberries and wild grapes made excellent wine. When they were ready for pressing, the entire family would gather them on a Sunday afternoon for our wine press. Another bounty the bird droppings provided were patches of asparagus. In early spring, when the lush shoots were just poking their heads a few inches above the ground, I'd bring a wicker basket with me on the way to the pasture and come home laden with fresh asparagus for the family. But that was not the end of the asparagus for me. I enjoyed watching it growing to its full height as the summer advanced until it was peppered with red berries in the fall. Its green ferny splendor was then a haven for wild goldfinches that feasted on the berries. With their lemon-yellow feathers and velvety black wings, they were a beautiful sight against the fluffy green fern of the asparagus plant. The whole sight looked like a Japanese print.

In other ways, the lane was a kaleidoscope of changing beauty. There were flowers for every season. The earliest to appear were the mayflowers, which were really wild crocuses. They poked up their bluebell heads on their fuzzy stems before all the snow was melted. The next in line were the buttercups that looked like little fallen stars. My favorites were the birdfoot violets, which were more like pansies than the summer violets. They got their name from the leaves that lay close to the ground and are shaped exactly like birds' feet. Their bright blue, flat faces bunched together created patches of blue along the lane, looking for all the world like a cloud fallen from the sky. There was another fascination about them, too. In the patch of light-blue violets, I would occasionally find one that was deep purple, with a velvety surface, in contrast to the more silken surface of the rest. Finding one of the purple ones was supposed to bring good luck—like finding a four-leaf clover. You may be sure that I looked diligently for that good omen and generally found one. Later on in the summer, the lane was fringed with delicate white Queen Anne's lace, bright goldenrod, and blue asters.

There was plenty of animate life to observe along the lane, too—especially bird life. A family of orioles always wove their nest on the outermost twigs of a great fan-shaped American elm. Because I went down the lane twice a day, I could watch the astounding process of the construction of the little baglike nest delicately stitched onto the twigs—and all of this done while the oriole was fluttering in the air. That experience prepared me to appreciate years later a passage in Chesterton's *Orthodoxy* in which he is discussing art as the real sig-nature of man, between the amazing patterns that appear in nature and those that appear in man-made artifacts. The latter are the product of free choice and vary infinitely from artist to artist. The former are instinctual and remain pretty much the same or evolve only to meet natural needs. He illustrates the difference by saying that an artist would probably be hard put to weave a nest as delicate as that of an oriole, but the difference is that oriole nests remain always pretty much the same. There are not Romanesque and Gothic periods of oriole nests; and, says Chesterton, an oriole has never been known to paint a portrait of great orioles of the past for the edification of its young. Chesterton, of course, is perfectly right, but I was always astonished at the sheer achievement of *my* orioles weaving their nest in *my* elm tree. Other birds that impressed me along the lane and in the pasture beyond, as they perched atop waving cattails, were the red-winged blackbirds. The little red spot on their black velvety wings gave them their name. They nest in the marshes, which are their favorite habitat, and have a short treble song that is rather sad. Whenever I hear it, waves of memories of my life in the marshes come rushing back to me.

Rover and I developed a close bond in our daily treks to the pasture. We had our little games to play to while away the time. One of them involved the habits of the killdeer. Killdeers make their nest on the ground and are open there to all kinds of disturbances. When anything threatening the nest approaches, the mother killdeer will fly off the nest, land at some distance, and put on an act simulating a broken wing, all the while emitting squawks of distress. This act is supposed to distract any intruder and lead him away from the nest, and it generally succeeds. There was always a killdeer nesting somewhere along the lane, and I used to get Rover to sneak up on the nest to inaugurate mother killdeer's little dramatic performance.

All this little play world along my country lane rushed back to me years later when I read "Birches" by Robert Frost, who must have experienced birches along a country lane like those that graced my lane. Here is part of the poem:

> When I see birches bend to left and right
> Across the lines of straighter darker trees
> I like to think some boy's been bending them.
> But swinging doesn't bend them down to stay.
> Ice storms do that. . . .
> I should prefer to have some boy bend them

> As he went out and in to fetch the cows—
> Some boy too far from town to learn baseball,
> Whose only play was what he found himself,
> Summer or winter, and could play alone.
> One by one he subdued his father's trees
> By riding them down over and over again
> Until he took the stiffness out of them,
> And not one but hung limp, not one was left
> For him to conquer. He learned all there was
> To learn about not launching out too soon
> And so not carrying the tree away
> Clear to the ground. He always kept his poise
> To the top branches, climbing carefully
> With the same pains you use to fill a cup
> Up to the brim and even above the brim.
> Then he flung outward, feet first, with a swish
> Kicking his way down through the air to the ground.
> So I was once myself a swinger of birches.

I, too, was that boy—a country boy "whose only play was what he found himself."

All this intimate communion with nature in its variegated beauty and moods—all these sights, smells, and tastes—eventually gave me a simple feeling that there was something divine behind it all.

The poet Gerard Manley Hopkins expresses this perception beautifully in his little poem "Pied Beauty," which is a kind of hymn of praise to God for the very special hints of divinity that suffuse all the very individual, variegated, and contrasted beauties of creation:

> Glory be to God for dappled things—
>     For skies of couple-colour as a brindle cow;
>         For rose moles all in stipple upon trout that swim,
> Fresh firecoal chestnut falls; finches wings,
>     Landscape plotted and pieced—fold, fallow, and plough;
>         And all trades, their gear and tackle and trim.
>
> All things counter, original, spare, strange;
>     Whatever is fickle, freckled (who knows how?)
>         With swift; slow; sweet; sour; dazzle; dim;
> He fathers-forth whose beauty is past change:
>                     Praise him.

And Francis Thompson puts the same idea very succinctly in these lines: "The world's unfolded blossom / Smells of God." When you live intimately with the constantly changing pageantry of the beauty of God's world, you don't have to be argued into a belief in the existence of God. You have *felt* God's presence long before you *knew* what you were feeling.

Another pleasure I had in my daily treks to the pasture came from a very different source. Anchored on the riverbank in the pasture was a houseboat that a man named Jack Smith inhabited. Jack had lived in Chicago but had grown tired of the urban world, and, like Thoreau, had picked up and left the city to take on a simple life close to nature. He bought a houseboat and anchored it on the riverbank in our pasture. When Rover and I had put the cows to pasture, we frequently went over to Jack's houseboat and soaked up details of his very interesting way of life. He had made himself almost entirely self-sufficient. There were plenty of fine fish—perch, bass, bluegills, and sunfish in the river for the taking—and clams galore in the riverbed. He had made a little flat boat from the sides of which he could submerge racks strung with fishhooks that scraped the sandy bottom of the river and came up with dozens of clams. Jack ate some of the clams or made clam chowder out of them, but they served him in more important ways. He occasionally found natural pearls in their shells, which he extracted and sold to a jeweler in Chicago. Jack was a rather talented painter, and he spent a great deal of his time painting landscapes on the insides of the shells, which he'd send to a souvenir shop in Chicago for sale. There was no end to the beautiful scenes he could paint in all seasons by just looking out from the deck of his boathouse. The interior of his little two-room house was lined with shelves of these little painted vignettes. It was a fascination to me to watch Jack evoke little nature scenes on the clam shells with the deft touches of his brush. It was my first introduction to an artist at work.

Jack had left the big city for the pleasures and independence of a life in the country, but he still had all kinds of connections with the city. Besides the occasional pearls and the many clamshell paintings he sold there, he had other market connections with the city. He always had two large wooden barrels sunk into the edge of the river full of turtles that he had gathered up from the river and the marshes. He shipped them to a Chicago hotel to make turtle soup. In wintertime, he trapped muskrats, whose fur was in demand at the time for making fur coats. The fur wasn't mink, but the pelts made presentable women's coats. Muskrats were also edible, so Jack peddled them to a restaurant in Chicago that billed them as a delicacy under the title "marsh rabbit." They actually tasted like rabbit. I had some intimation of life in Chicago from our well-to-do relatives there and from the apparition of the well-heeled patrons of the great passenger trains that puffed by the Glen Oak railroad station headed for Minneapolis, but a place that was inhabited by people that could indulge in turtle soup and wear strung pearls and fur coats was still a very foreign country to my young imagination. Jack preened himself on his relative self-sufficiency in the country, but he could not have existed there in his leisurely life without his mercantile connections with the big city. With fishing in the summer and hunting in the winter, he managed to provide the staples of his diet. He subscribed to a Chicago newspaper and had it delivered in our mailbox. He'd come up every other day to pick up his mail. Not exactly accidentally, he'd frequently come about suppertime because he knew that Mother would always ask him to eat with us. In the summertime, Mother also supplied him with vegetables from the garden, so he made out rather well. We eventually realized that we were supplying Jack with more than we knew. Dad discovered that one of our cows regularly turned up at the evening milking with one quarter of its bag dry. Jack was helping himself to the milk, and Dad mentioned it to him one day. Jack said he knew exactly what was happening. He said he had seen a milk snake following the cow, and he was sure it had stripped the quarter of the bag that was dry. Neither Dad nor the rest of us ever let on to Jack that we knew that the snake that was milking our bossy walked on two feet. A couple of quarts of milk a day was a small price to pay for the diversion that Jack's presence brought to our lives.

The two-year interlude on the Barrett farm was a delight to me. Close to the river and close to the ever-changing pageantry of nature in my private lane, I developed an undying love of nature that has remained with me throughout my life. Those early brushes with the constantly changing panorama of beauty in the natural world also prepared me to savor to the fullest the power of language in the great poets of nature, such as William Wordsworth and Gerard Manley Hopkins, to create marvelously detailed and evocative images of the outside world.

But for Dad and Mother and my two older brothers and sister, the experience was far from unalloyed pleasure. The two ladies who owned the farm turned out to be very difficult landladies. In the first place, they had pressed for a very oppressive rental arrangement. It was half of absolutely everything on the farm: half of the crops, half of the milk check; half of the egg money; and half of the sale of chickens and pigs. That was bad enough, but besides that they were forever getting into their horse and buggy in town and driving out to see that they were not being cheated out of their half. They'd count the chickens and calculate how many eggs they ought to lay, and if their half didn't jibe with what they thought the hens ought to lay in the month, they would accuse us of eating the lacking eggs. We ran the farm as a dairy farm, separated the cream from the milk, sold the cream to the butter factory, and fed the skimmed milk to pigs (where to this day I still think skimmed milk ought to go). On the forays out to the farm, the grim ladies (we kids dubbed them "the witches") would examine the pig troughs to make sure that we weren't feeding whole milk to the pigs and cheating them out of some of their milk money. Dad was one of the most intelligent farmers I ever knew, and neither Mother nor he ever cheated anyone out of five cents in their entire lives, so this kind of interference and suspicion was utterly intolerable to them. They began looking for a different farm to rent where life would be less stressful.

Our next-door neighbors, the Roits, were quite well off. They had come down from the northern Wisconsin lumber camps to take up farming, and our two families had become very close. Mr. Roit tried to persuade Dad to buy the Barrett farm. He offered to loan him the money at very low interest with a very long-term return payment arrangement. But Dad had that insuperable horror of going into debt and refused the offer. He continued looking for another farm to rent and eventually found one. The rental arrangement could not have been better.

It was the Kane farm on a road seven miles north of town. Every farm along that seven-mile stretch had been homesteaded by settlers before the Civil War. Most of the homesteaders were Irish Catholics, as names such as Riordon, Curley, Flynn, Collins, Maloney, Gibbons, Calnin, and Kane would suggest. But this string of Irish homesteaders was punctuated by three German Lutheran families—the Schumans, the Hoffmans, and the Hellmers. Just north of the Kane farm, two Polish Catholic brothers, the Ruziks, owned two farms. So this rural stretch illustrated the same kind of ethnic and religious mix that made up the town of Montello itself.

The Kane farm had been homesteaded by the original Kanes who had come from Ireland. It was an extensive holding of more than 500 acres. When the Kanes got it, the whole acreage was wooded with a dense stand of several kinds of oak trees and a generous sprinkling of hickory. By the time we moved there, all but 150 acres of it had been cleared for cultivation. As was the case with most homesteaders in the area, the original Kanes had staked out a 40-acre claim in the Puckaway peat marsh ten miles to the south, and two other separate marshlands of about 20 acres each within a mile or two of the main homestead.

The farm had come into the possession of the last male member of the Kane family, bachelor Billy. He had no interest in farming himself, lived with a niece on a neighboring farm, and had rented out the old farmstead. The previous renters had overcropped the fields, and the land was very rundown. Billy was looking for a renter who would respect the land and bring it back to better productivity. He knew Dad was the man to do it, so he gave him a very advantageous rental arrangement. Billy would take half of only the grain crops (corn, rye, and oats for the most part), but we could have our own herd of cattle and get the entire cream check, as well as any income we made from pigs and chickens. Billy was fairly well off independently of income from the farm. He just wanted enough from the farm to pay the taxes on it with a little margin of profit. Half share in the grain crops did that nicely. He was more interested in seeing that the land was restored to better productivity. Dad set out about doing that immediately.

He knew all about the necessity of rotating land usage and crops themselves in order not to exhaust the land, but as the farm was laid out, that was difficult to do. The fields were all large 80-acre plots, and there weren't enough of them to facilitate rotation. So the first thing Dad did was to work up fence posts from the oak trees in the woods and, at his own expense, to install four-strand barbed wire fences down the middle of all the fields. Some fields would be allowed to lie fallow for a year or so; others would be sown with clover, the roots of which enriched the soil. These plots would then be used for pasturing the cows, whose droppings provided some additional natural fertilizer. The plots that remained were ploughed and seeded. They were fertilized before sowing with the natural fertilizer of the manure that accumulated throughout the long winter from the cleaning of the cow and horse stables. Through this respectful rotation of land usage, Dad soon had a greater yield from a third less acreage than the total acreage had provided before. Billy was very happy about it, and so were we all.

When Dad had reshaped the farm, it was a very different looking place than when all the fields were uniformly planted with the same crops. From some of the hills, you could get an overview of pretty much the whole farm. It looked like a crazy quilt made up of irregular shaped and variously colored patches. Gerald Manley Hopkins must have had just such a view of the Welsh countryside from his perch at St. Beuno's, the place where he did his tertianship, the last year of spiritual training for a Jesuit. He speaks of his vantage point as "a pastoral forehead in Wales." And in "Pied Beauty," the poem I quoted above, he speaks of the countryside itself as "A landscape, plotted and pieced / Fold, fallow and plough." He sees it as a crazy quilt pattern made up of green sheep*folds,* gray green land lying *fallow,* and brown corduroy stripes of freshly *plowed* fields. That would exactly describe our farm after Dad had gotten his rotation of usage and crops under way. It is a landscape we are all very familiar with today as we look at the countryside from the vantage point of an airplane.

I lived on the Kane farm for the next twelve years. It was more home to me than any place I ever lived. When the past comes up in my dreams in my old age, as it does increasingly, it is the part I spent on the Kane farm. I was old enough there to join the workforce, and I soon learned all about farming. I learned what a backbreaking job it was. It was certainly not the picnic it seemed when all I had to do was see the cows to the pasture and bring them home at night. It was a different story when I had to crawl out of bed every morning at five, stumble half asleep out to the barn to help with the milking and the other morning chores, and, after breakfast, take to the fields all day to work on the crops that would keep the cows alive and giving milk in the wintertime. In time, I came to hate cows. They were the real leisured class in the establishment. After morning milking, they strolled out to the pasture, where they grazed leisurely for a part of the day, filling their four stomachs with fresh grass. But they spent a great deal of the day lying in the shade, regurgitating the grass from one or other of their stomachs and quietly chewing their cuds, while we were out in the field slaving in the heat of the day to provide their fodder for the winter. They knew that in the evening after the long day's work in the fields, we'd come to fetch them home for the evening milking, and they seemed to take perverse delight in having a late afternoon siesta as far away from the barn as possible. It was still Rover's and my job to do the fetching, and after a hard day's work in the fields, traipsing a mile and half to the end of the woods to get the cows didn't have quite the delights I had felt fetching them down the country lane from the pasture by Jack Smith's boathouse. I also learned at this time what I didn't know before: that cows demand not any kind of pasture to graze on; they need something special. They have no front teeth. They don't bite off the grass, but wrap their tongues around it, pull it loose, and then swallow it whole. They later regurgitate it, and chew it as a cud with their back teeth before re-swallowing it. This means that they have to have a pasture where the grass is high enough to get their tongues around it. That's why you can't graze sheep and cows in the same pasture: the sheep nibble the grass down so low that a cow would starve on the pasture the sheep leave behind them.

But horses were a different matter. This is the time, I think, to record my youthful love affair with Bess. She was a horse. We were born on the same day. Among all his eight children, Dad could remember my birthday most easily because something important happened on that day: a horse was born. Bess and I grew up together. When I was old enough to toddle around, I used to go out to the pasture where Bess was running loose as a foal. She would come running and give me a couple of hairy nuzzles on my face. I'd put my arms around her front legs and we'd sashay about the pasture in perfect contentment. When she got old enough, Dad broke her into harness as a buggy horse. She seemed to love it. When she got in the fills, she'd raise her head in a graceful curve and prance off proudly as if she were born to the buggy. She was our main source of transportation into town when we still lived on the little sliver of land carved out of Grandpa's farm. But when we moved to the Kane farm, her buggy days and my picnic of a life were over. We both had to work in the fields, plowing in the spring and cultivating corn all summer. Bess became one of my team. I think she resented being demoted from the buggy to the plow. She became either the laziest or the wisest horse on four feet. When cultivating corn, she'd lag behind and let poor Ted, her gelding partner, pull most of the load. In fairness to Ted, I'd keep nipping her with a whip all day to get her to pull her share. But when we'd turn off the last row in the evening, she'd practically pull my arms out of their sockets to get home because she knew that the work was over. On Sundays, Bess became a buggy horse again to get us to the church on time, and in between the fills of the buggy she was her old prancing self again. The buggy is where she felt she belonged. Bess had to continue this schizophrenic life for the rest of her days. When she had outlived her usefulness on the buggy and in the fields, she met the fate of the domestic animals that could no longer contribute to the workload of the farm. She was taken to a sand dune in the woods, shot, and buried there. Little sentiment was shown on the farm at the death of domestic animals that could no longer work. Bess died when I was away at high school in Milwaukee. I confess that I had enough of the sentimental about me to visit her grave when I came home, decorate it with a few flowers, and shed a quiet tear. I didn't say any prayers for her because I knew she wasn't in purgatory—or in heaven either, for that matter—and didn't need them. I wasn't *so* sentimental that I didn't recognize there *is* a difference between animals and humans when it comes to a life hereafter.

Bess was not the only domestic with whom I had an affair. There was also a goose in my life. We didn't have geese. With a large family to feed, Mother was very careful about the domestic fowl she would admit to the place. She had a wonderful flock of Rhode Island Red hens that she nurtured carefully. They supplied a constant source of both revenue and food. We had all the eggs we wanted for our own table and for cooking; the rest were carefully crated and bartered at Smart's general store in town, which is the way we paid for practically all the groceries we needed. Some eggs were, of course, reserved for hatching new chicks. Some of these chicks were raised to maturity to augment or renew the flock, but most of them were sold to butcher shops when they had grown to a good frying size. The income from these sales financed practically everything that was bought for the house, so, for Mother, raising fowl was a very bread-and-butter affair. She would have no ducks around because they ate their weight in food every day; and when they themselves were served up, they provided only a tiny smidgen of breast meat. Geese she considered a noisy aggressive nuisance in the chicken yard.

But in spite of Mother's proscriptions against ducks and geese, I decided I wanted a goose, so I went to the neighbors, who had a gaggle of geese, and got a goose egg. I set it under a hen that, I presume, was surprised at the size of the egg she was asked to hatch. She was probably even more surprised when she saw her hatchling, but she mothered it enthusiastically. In fact, she became the proudest mother hen in the chicken yard. She'd strut around with the little gosling in her wake as much as if to say to the less-favored hens: "Look at the marvel I've produced." She continued to mother her gosling until it was bigger than she was. At night, she'd work her wing around it, and the gosling's head would poke up over the top of that mothering wing. So I had my goose. When it was full grown, it waddled its way around the chicken yard, eating twice as much as any of the chickens and becoming the aggressive kind of noisy nuisance Mother said it would be. But I enjoyed my purloined goose until Christmas time, when Mother served it up as part of our Christmas dinner. I must say that I didn't enjoy the meal. I hated to see *my* goose served up, like the head of John the Baptist, on a platter.

Living on a farm in those premechanized days, a family could have a pretty complete larder just from the farm itself, and much of it came without planting. Our part of Wisconsin was famous for its wild berries. They grew so plentifully that in the early days the indigenous people of the area practically lived on them. They ate them fresh in the summer and dried them, like raisins, to provide much of their food for the winter. There was an abundance of them on the Kane farm. Wild red and black raspberries, wild currants, and gooseberries flourished in the woods. Blueberries and huckleberries grew along the edges of the marshland, and big lush blackberries flourished in the marshes themselves. A smaller, harder type of blackberry grew on the sand dunes left by the glaciers. In some of the peat bog marshes, there were beds of wild cranberries, which provided a wonderful variety of fresh dessert in the summer and, canned in Mason jars, a sauce for supper all winter. The woods were also well stocked with hickory trees and hazelnut bushes, making the woods a squirrel's heaven. But the little furry rascals had the bad habit of chewing the hickory nuts off the trees before they were ripe and eating them on the spot or storing them in hollow trees or burying them for food in the winter. For this reason, the homesteaders, when they were clearing the land of trees for cultivation, left one or two choice hickory nut trees in the middle of the cleared field. They hoped that the squirrels would be content with the cornucopia of nuts in the woods and not take the trouble to travel a half-mile across the open field to the few trees sequestered there. The scheme worked. There were several such trees in our fields. We'd let the nuts ripen fully. When they dropped off the trees they bounced on the ground and cracked open their rough husks. There would be a blanket of the white nuts under the tree. All we had to do was gather them up in gunnysacks to provide hickory nuts all winter to crack around the heating stove. Mother, of course, worked them into tasty hickory nut cakes and cookies. The squirrels seemed not to be interested in the hazelnuts—perhaps because they were wrapped in prickly husks that looked like little ruffled cabbage leaves. They grew in clusters on the bushes. We'd gather bags of the clusters and spread them on the roof of the machine shed to dry out. It was then easy to loosen the nuts from their husks.

A great deal of the food for our table was raised on the farm. The main grain crops were corn, rye, and oats, which supplied food for the livestock in winter. Ripe hard corn on the cob could be hand fed to the horses, but they preferred oats. Corn and rye had to be ground at the mill and mixed to provide feed for the cows in the winter. With no front teeth, they couldn't handle hard corn on the cob. None of these grains would do much for us humans. When the First World War came along and everything was tightly rationed, the farmers in the area became very resourceful in creating substitute sources for what we couldn't get easily in the stores. Wheat flour and sugar were almost impossible to get in any quantity. Wheat does not do well in Wisconsin, but the farmers planted a few acres of it anyway. The yield was sufficient to supply wheat flour and bran when it was milled. An acre or two of buckwheat provided enough grain to be milled into buckwheat flour, giving us the makings for buckwheat pancakes, the staple of hearty breakfasts all winter. Sugar was even a greater challenge. It was almost entirely unavailable in the wartime stores. But, undaunted, the farmers planted a couple of acres of sugarcane. It certainly didn't do in Wisconsin what it would in Mississippi, but it did well enough. Stripped, headed, cut, and bound into bundles, the stalks were hauled to a central press, and the juice boiled into sorghum. Five-gallon crocks of it would supply a substitute for syrup on the hot pancakes all winter, and it was good for a snack spread on slices of hot homemade bread. The housewives devised recipes for molasses cakes and cookies that didn't need sugar. And if the sorghum gradually evaporated in its crock containers, it would crystallize into brown sugar that could also be used for sweetening. Honey provided another natural sweetener. We often found wild beehives in hollow trees when we were getting up our firewood in the woods. The farmers became adept at enticing the queen bee into a domestic hive, and the rest of the swarm would follow. The hive would be placed in the apple orchard, and each family would have its own honey makers. The bees particularly liked the nectar from the buckwheat blossom, and the honey made from the buckwheat nectar had an especially pleasing flavor. So a combination of sugarcane, bees, buckwheat, and human ingenuity got around the sugar shortage very neatly.

On the farm, of course, there was never any lack of fresh milk, cream, and butter, and the garden provided an ample supply of fresh vegetables. Mother was a genius in the garden and loved working there. Her garden was always a picture that would grace even the most beautifully illustrated seed catalog. It was right across the driveway from the house and abutted the main public road. It was such a model of what a good garden should be that people passing by on the road would frequently stop to admire it. Long rows of red raspberry and red currant bushes grew down one side. A large section was devoted to vine plants, including watermelon, muskmelons, Mother Hubbard squash, and cucumbers. There were neat rows of lettuce, radishes, onions, and carrots. Peas, green and golden string beans, cabbage, and cauliflower were also always part of the planting, and Mother raised her own dill for dill pickles.

Mother always had a large strawberry bed. We covered the bed in the spring with a light layer of straw so that when the strawberries ripened on the short plants that pushed up through the straw, they would be protected from the raw earth below, which kept them clean and fresh and ready for the table. In season, they provided one of our favorite country delights and often constituted our Sunday dessert—strawberry shortcake. It was the good old-fashioned strawberry shortcake. Mother would whip up the batter, approaching the quality of baking powder biscuits. She'd spread it into big cake pans for baking.

When it came out of the oven, she'd slice it into serving sizes, add a generous helping of fresh creamery butter, and then smother it with an avalanche of fresh-sliced, sugared strawberries swimming in their own juice. A puff of fresh whipped cream completed what was about as ambrosial a dessert as you could imagine. We enjoyed the short-cake with free-hearted impunity because we had not yet heard of cholesterol.

On the north side of the house was the orchard. It climbed up the side of a gentle hill. When the trees were in bloom in the spring, it looked all the world like the orchards that Van Gogh painted in the south of France. Along the top of the hill, silhouetted against the sky, was a row of Lombardy poplars. Their plumelike shapes looked a bit like the cypress trees that Van Gogh worked into so many of his paintings in a kind of flamelike pattern. He said they were *laudate psalms* singing a hymn of thanksgiving to God for the fruitfulness of the earth. I felt a little like that myself about our poplar trees. There was always a nest of robins in them, and often, as the sun was setting, a robin perched on one of the branches and sang its heart out. It was always a little sad in the fall, when all of the poplar leaves had turned yellow and were about to fall, to realize that the robins would soon be flying south, and we wouldn't be hearing them again until the spring. But while they sang, we did have much to be thankful for right there in the orchard, with its great variety of apple trees: crabapples for crabapple pickles, yellow harvest apples and red russets that ripened early and made delicious eating. We also had the harder and larger varieties that were best for baking, apple pie, and applesauce. Others ripened quite late in the summer, firm and hard; they snapped when we bit into them. If we wrapped them carefully, packed them in barrels, and placed them in the cool cellar, they would provide good eating well into the winter. They went well with the hickory nuts and hazelnuts around the winter's fire. The work in getting the apples safely stored in the cellar for winter eating prepared me years later to empathize with Robert Frost in his meditative poem "After Apple Picking":

> My long two-pointed ladder's sticking through a tree
> Toward heaven still,
> And there's a barrel that I didn't fill
> Beside it, and there may be two or three

Apples I didn't pick upon some bough.
But I am done with apple-picking now.
Essence of winter sleep is on the night,
The scent of apples: I am drowsing off.
I cannot rub the strangeness from my sight
I got from looking through a pane of glass
I skimmed this morning from the drinking trough
And held against the world of hoary grass.
It melted, and I let it fall and break.
But I was well
Upon my way to sleep before it fell,
And I could tell
What form my dreaming was about to take.
Magnified apples appear and disappear,
Stem end and blossom end,
And every fleck of russet showing clear.
My instep arch not only keeps the ache,
It keeps the pressure of a ladder-round.
I feel the ladder sway as the boughs bend.
And I keep hearing from the cellar bin
The rumbling sound
Of load on load of apples coming in.
For I have had too much
Of apple-picking: I am overtired
Of the great harvest I myself desired.
There were ten thousand thousand fruit to touch,
Cherish in hand, lift down, and not let fall.
For all
That struck the earth,
No matter if not bruised or spiked with stubble,
Went surely to the cider-apple heap
As of no worth.
One can see what will trouble
This sleep of mine, whatever sleep it is.

There was, of course, also a plentiful source of meat on the farm—beef, pork, and fowl. The chickens were no problem. One could always be killed and plucked whenever needed. We favored using full-grown hens for baking, rather than the younger chickens for frying. In fact, they frequently provided our Sunday dinner. Mother would prepare one on Saturday night, stuff it with a fine bread-and-sage dressing, put it in the oven of the wood stove in the morning, bank the fire, and when we got back from church in the surrey with the fringe on top, it would be done—browned to perfection and ready for carving. No turkey I have ever eaten matches the savory taste of a well-baked full-grown hen. It's a delicacy impossible to get in these days of force-fed fryers.

But before refrigeration, a supply of other meat when we wanted it was a problem. A young steer and a pig were often butchered late in the fall. We could thus freeze the sections of beef or pork, hang them in the smokehouse, and thaw them out in the wintertime as needed. Butchering day was always an event—especially the butchering of a hog. Elaborate preparations had to be made. A gibbetlike contraption, with a pulley on the crossbeam, was built. A wooden barrel was propped up on stones beneath it and the barrel filled with water. A charcoal fire was lit below the barrel, which brought the water in the barrel to a boil. At this point in the venture, the hapless pig selected for the slaughter was brought to the scene with its feet "hog-tied" together. It was dispatched with a deft plunge of a knife in its jugular vein. The blood was not wasted. It was caught in a basin. Some of our German neighbors made *Blutwurst* with it, which was not something we fancied, so we mixed the blood with ground grain and fed it to the chickens. This was the opening step of the age-old ritual of butchering. Bruegel, the sixteenth-century Flemish genre painter, has pictured it, along with many other details of everyday Flemish life, in his famous painting of Joseph and Mary being turned away from the inn. The Flemish painters had the habit of juxtaposing the sacred with the secular to suggest that the two worlds coexisted side by side.

The English poet W. H. Auden also makes much of that juxtaposition in his poem "Musée des Beaux Arts," which is the title of the museum in Brussels where Bruegel's *The Enrollment at Bethlehem* hangs. Here is part of Auden's poem:

> About suffering they were never wrong,
> The Old Masters: how well they understood
> Its human position; how it takes place
> While someone else is eating or opening a window or just walking
> dully along;
> How, when the aged are reverently, passionately waiting
> For the miraculous birth, there always must be
> Children who did not specially want it to happen, skating

On a pond at the edge of the wood:
They never forgot
That even the dreadful martyrdom must run its course
Anyhow in a corner, some untidy spot
Where the dogs go on with their doggy life and the torturer's horse
Scratches its innocent behind on a tree.

In Bruegel's painting, the little first act of hog butchering is pictured right in front of the figures of Mary and Joseph, who are seeking a room in the inn. The actors in the life drama are too busy catching the blood of the just stuck hog to notice another couple in the crowd that has come to Bethlehem to register in the census. Bruegel was probably right. That's doubtless the way it did happen. There was not very much about Joseph and Mary that made them stand out from the crowd.

But back now to the rest of the ritual of butchering. When the central character in the little drama had shed its last drop of blood, it was hoisted up back legs first by a rope and pulley onto the gibbet. It was then sloshed up and down in the barrel of hot water to loosen its bristles so that they could easily be removed with a sharp metal scraper. That done, the barrel was removed, and the hog was strung up head down on the gibbet, then sliced open from tail to head and its innards removed. The liver and heart were carefully set aside for almost immediate consumption because they wouldn't keep well. The rest of the carcass was carefully cut up into sections that would provide roasts, chops, and barbecued ribs. The muscles and gelatinous material in the head of the hog were set aside to make head-cheese: the lean parts were cubed; spices, vinegar, and the gelatinous material were added; and the whole mixture was boiled and then allowed to cool in cake pans. The result was a gelatinous brick of headcheese that, sliced and eaten with rye bread, was a great delight. The rear flanks of the hog were separated, rubbed with salt, boiled, encrusted with brown sugar, and then hung over a hickory fire in the smokehouse to become homemade country hams. Slabs of bacon were prepared in very much the same way. This done, all the sections of the hog, along with the hams and slabs of bacon, were hung up in the smokehouse, where the severe winter froze them solid. They were there all winter as a source of fresh meat as long as the cold lasted, and it lasted a long time in Wisconsin.

Butchering a young steer followed pretty much the same procedure, and a hog and a steer were almost always butchered at the same time. There were variations of the ritual for a steer. He was knocked dumb with a strike of a mallet to the head and then had his throat cut to yield up his life's blood. The whole carcass was then skinned, and the body gutted and dismembered on the ground without benefit of the gibbet. The flesh was scraped off the hide and sent to a tannery, either to be made into a lined cowhide lap robe or to be kept at the tannery for shoe leather. The steer, like the hog, was dismembered into its component parts suitable for the table—roasts, steaks, and short ribs. Much of the carcass was ground into hamburger meat, and all of it was again hung in the smokehouse to freeze. The smokehouse really was a kind of primitive freezer.

Some of the details of this butchering ritual sound savage, but people now forget that something like them still has to happen to put pork chops and steaks on our tables. People today are, of course, not as aware of this as we all had to be on the farm.

I was early impressed with how little was wasted in the butchering process. As the hog and steer were cut up for freezing, much of the excess fat was trimmed off and thrown into a huge iron kettle perched on a few field stones. When the butchering was done, some lye, borax, and a little water were added to the kettle. A wood fire was built under it, and the whole thing brought to a kind of boiling witch's brew. When the brew was finished and cooled, the water would sink to the bottom, and the fat, transformed by the lye into a smooth texture, would come to the top, leaving a primitive form of soap. Cut into bars, it was used the year round for washing clothes. The upper level of this congealed brew was fluffier in texture and lighter in color than the bulk of it below. Some adventuresome brewers used to slice off this upper level, reheat it, and add perfume to it. When cooled again and sliced into small bars, it was used as a facial or hand soap.

The product of this butchering ritual provided fresh meat throughout the winter as long as the deep frost lasted, but providing meat for the summer without ice or refrigeration was more difficult. Ways, however, were invented to do it. Late in winter, the entire butchering ritual was repeated but generally confined to a hog. When the butchering was finished, some of the meat was immersed in a salt brine in big earthen crocks and stored in the cool cellar. When needed, the meat could be taken out of the brine in the summer, parboiled in water to get out the excessive salt, and then fried or roasted. It was a long way from fresh or frozen meat, but it was a tolerable substitute. There were two other means of preserving meat for the summer that left it much closer to fresh meat. It was completely cooked and then put up in Mason jars or packed in large earthen crocks sealed in its own natural fat. The crocks were then stored in the cool cellar. Meat preserved in either of these ways could just be warmed up when needed, and it pretty closely approached the taste of freshly cooked meat.

A supply of water for drinking, cooking, and washing for humans and for drinking for the livestock was always a problem on the farm. Before rural electrification and gasoline engines, the problem was solved by the windmill. Every farmstead had one. Ours was just a few steps from the back door of the house, and it was pretty central to the life of all of us—cattle and humans alike. It kept running almost constantly as long as there was wind to drive it. Right next to it was the milk house, very important on a dairy farm. The milk was brought there to be put through the separator that separated the cream from the milk. The cream was kept in large metal cream cans to be brought to the creamery for making butter. The cream check was the main cash income each month on a dairy farm. It was imperative that the cream accumulating from the daily milkings didn't sour before it was taken to the creamery. That's where the windmill was pressed into service. In the milk house was a sizable cement tank that was kept full of cold water freshly pumped by the windmill. The cream cans were immersed in it. The water flowed continually out of this tank into a large galvanized drinking tank in the yard beyond the milk house for the cattle and horses. The windmill was a pretty important link in the chain of life on the farm. Once the windmill was installed, it worked on forever free of charge. It is interesting that today the old-fashioned windmill is being increasingly used once more as a source of free and nonpolluting energy.

The cooling tank in the milk house served other purposes besides keeping the cream fresh for the creamery. It also kept butter, milk, and cream fresh for our table before the advent of iceboxes and re-frigerators. The butter in earthen crocks and the milk and cream in glass jars would be suspended in the cold water to keep them fresh. Sometimes the same end could be achieved just by placing the butter and milk and cream pitchers in the cool cellar.

As used to inside plumbing as people are now, they little realize what work went into supplying the water needs of a family before its invention. The windmill again figured prominently in filling those needs on the farm. A pail of drinking water always stood on the kitchen table with a drinking dipper hanging on the wall above it. Everyone drank from the same dipper. With the windmill constantly pumping just outside the back door, there was always a source of fresh cool water. But if you really wanted it cool, you had to keep refilling the pail. There was no ice to cool it for you. Water for cooking had to be lugged in from the same source. For hand and dish washing, we had a different arrangement. A cistern under the kitchen was filled by rain water draining from the roof of the house. A cistern pump at the end of the wash sink in the kitchen gave access to the water. Some of it was used to fill the reservoir on the end of the wood range. We used this hot water for washing our hands and faces in a graniteware basin and for washing dishes in dishpans on the kitchen table.

For bathing—which was only a weekly event on Saturday in preparation for church on Sunday—we carried water in from the windmill in buckets, heated it in a big copper boiler on the kitchen stove, and transferred it to the bathtub. On many farms, the wash water from the kitchen hand sink and from the bathtub had to be carried out in slop buckets. We had the luxury of a drain from both the kitchen hand sink and the bathtub to a cesspool, so some of that drudgery was eliminated.

To get water for the Monday laundry was a laborious task. Water had to be carried in buckets from the windmill to fill the large copper boiler on the kitchen stove. Laundry started with the clothes rubbed clean with homemade soap on a washboard in a tub of warm water from the copper boiler. When wrung out, the white clothes were put in the copper boiler, boiled to get them whiter, and rinsed in another tub of water. They were then sent through a second rinsing of water with bluing in it, which helped bleach them. When they were finally wrung out through the hand wringer, they were hung out to dry on clotheslines. The sight of clothes flapping and billowing in the wind came to be pretty much a signature of a country homestead on Mondays. Laundering consumed the better part of a day, and ironing the clothes a half part of another. Some of the drudgery was removed by the advent of the gasoline Maytag washer, but before interior plumbing, washday still needed a bucket brigade from the windmill to get the water.

In those early days without indoor plumbing, everybody was a member of the privy and potty club. The privy in summer was a relatively comfortable place to take care of one of the universal human needs, but in below-zero winter temperatures it was a challenge few people wanted to meet, so they took to the potty. There was a chamber pot in every bedroom. Their use added another drudgery to housekeeping because they had to be emptied and cleaned every morning. Some of us actually preferred the shivering challenge of the privy to the humiliation of using the potty. When I think of this, I realize that there was a kind of leveling social effect in the necessity of using the privy and the pot: prince and peasant alike had to use them. The chamber pots of kings and queens might be of porcelain and be emblazoned with their coats of arms, but the fact that their majesties, like everyone else, had to use them was a gentle reminder that they and the rest of humanity were all akin.

This little meditation on the leveling effect of privies and pots reminds me of another form of meditation enshrined in a popular medieval and early Renaissance motif—the Dans Macabre or Dance of Death. It appeared in many book illuminations and panel paintings. In it, there appeared a procession of human beings from king and pope down through the whole human hierarchy to peasant and country pastor. Beside each one of them was the skeletal figure of Death with his bony hand resting on their shoulders—a grim reminder that, high or low, they would all alike one day have to confront death. One of the most famous examples of the Dans Macabre was painted, life-size, on the outside walls of the Holy Innocents Cemetery in Old Paris. Ironically, right in front of it was the common farm market. When marketers from all walks of life jostled one another to get the cabbage and cheese they needed to help keep body and soul together, they were reminded that death might be lurking just around the corner. Holbein rendered the same motif in a famous set of woodblock prints. If you cross the covered bridge spanning the river in Lucerne, you can still look up and see another version of it painted on the roof beams. The lesson that common humanity makes the whole world one was taught us less artistically in our preplumbing days by the fact that prince, priest, and peasant all had an equal need for the privy and the pot.

Before rural electrification, having some light at night was another problem. For years, kerosene lamps provided light. They were everywhere—small glass ones in each bedroom and others perched on wall brackets in the kitchen. There was always a fancy one with porcelain globe and shade in the parlor, not much used. In fact, the parlor itself was not much used. It was generally closed off, with the shades drawn except when guests came. The women then sat and gossiped in the parlor, while the menfolk smoked and "chewed the fat" on the front porch or under a tree in the yard. The room that was best lit was the dining room, frequently by a double kerosene lamp that pulled down on a chain from the ceiling, which shed a pretty even light over the whole table. It was around that single well-lit spot in the house that most of the evening activity of the family took place. If we had school homework to do, that's where we did it. If there were letters to write, that's where we wrote them. Mother would pull up to one side of the table to do her sewing or mending, and Dad would frequently be there smoking and reading one of his farm magazines or mending a harness. The nightly scene under the lamplight around the dining room table was almost exactly like that pictured in Van Gogh's famous *Potato Eaters*. The artist depicts three generations—grandpa and grandma, dad and mother, and a little girl—all circling a dining room table lit by an overhanging kerosene lamp. The lamp lights up their simple peasant faces and the circle of their callused hands all reaching for the potatoes on the platter at the center of the table. One year during the First World War, the night scene around our dining room table would have matched that of Van Gogh's *Potato Eaters* almost exactly. Because of food rationing, navy beans were much in demand and brought high prices on the market. So Dad put in some acreage of navy beans to augment our income. If we sorted the beans and culled out all the dark or misshapen ones, we got a higher price for them. When supper and the barn chores were done, we'd frequently dump out a twenty-five pound sack of beans on the dining room table, and the whole family would gather around to do the sorting. Grandma Wolsey, my mother's mother, was staying with us at the time. So there it was—a Van Gogh genre scene—not the *Potato Eaters*, but the *Bean Sorters*, three generations of sorters, lit by a kerosene lamp around a dining room table, with hands all stretched out toward not a platter of potatoes, but a pile of beans. But the same kind of family solidarity that had brought the potatoes onto Van Gogh's platter had put the pile of beans on our table. We had planted them in the spring, hoed and cultivated them all summer, helped harvest and hull them in the autumn, and were now preparing to reap the fruit of our labor.

Deep winter always brought a considerable change of pace on the farm. I looked forward to the first snowfall when I would wake up some morning to a work-a-day world suddenly transformed into a white wonderland. I don't know of anybody who has better caught the sense of smothered silence and magical beauty that envelopes a world blanketed with new-fallen snow than has James Russell Lowell in his poem "The First Snowfall." Mother taught it to me before I could read, and whenever or wherever I experience the transforming beauty of a first snowfall, the words always come back to me:

> The snow had begun in the gloaming
>    And busily all the night
> Had been heaping field and highway
>    In a silence deep and white.
>
> Every pine, and fir, and hemlock,
>    Wore ermine too dear for an earl;
> And the poorest twig on the elm tree,
>    Was ridged inch deep with pearl.
>
> From sheds new roofed with Carrara,
>    Came chanticleer's muffled crow.
> And the stiff rails were softened to swan's down
>    But still fluttered down the snow.

That poem admirably captures the beauty of the first snowfall. But as snowfall followed snowfall, and the sharp winds of winter blew the snow into huge drifts, the prospect was less lovely. The drifts were sometimes so high between the house and the barn that we had to cut tunnels head high through them to move from one to the other. But we kids made sport even of the drifts. The snow had been ground into such fine powder by the wind that the drifts were like light marble. We used to saw them into blocks and build castles and fortresses out of them.

The winter snow changed our mode of travel. The buggy and surrey were put away for the winter. If only two were traveling, they traveled in the one-horse sleigh with its curve-backed dashboard. The outfit looked like the conch-shaped sleigh in which Santa Claus rides. Bess was the sleigh horse, and with the sleigh bells jingling on her harness, she seemed to be as content with the sleigh as she was with the buggy. But when the whole family was going somewhere, as was always the case on Sunday for Mass, another conveyance had to be contrived. It was the bobsleigh—two sets of snow runners surmounted by a double wagon box. Mother and Dad sat on a spring seat mounted high at the front of the box and drove the team. They were insulated from the cold by sheepskin-lined overcoats, fur caps, woolen mittens, and warm blankets. A light layer of straw was strewn on the floor of the box and covered by blankets, where we kids would sit, also wrapped in woolen coats, hand-knit stocking caps and mittens, snugly warm while the cold wind whipped over our heads above the sides of the wagon box. The roads were so drifted at times that they were impassable. We then took out into the open fields wherever we could find passage. Even there the drifts were sometimes so high and so hard packed that we could sleigh right over four-foot fences and not know they were there. When that wasn't the case, we might have to snip a farmer's barbed wire fences to get through. That was all right with the farmers because they all knew that they had to do the same thing to get anywhere. The fences could be easily spliced together again in the spring.

Getting to Mass and back on Sunday in winter as in summer consumed most of the morning. And in Lent, after the chores were done and we had an early supper, we all piled into the bobsleigh again and returned for evening devotions. It was always dark before we started home. Those homeward winter treks at night provided me with one of my most memorable impressions of the majesty of the night skies. It was a silent world broken only by the crunch of the horse's hooves and the squeak of the sleigh's runners on the hard frozen snow. With all the world around us cut out by the high wagon box, we could look up at the dark blue velvety sky arched by the sweep of the Milky Way and spangled with a million stars. It must have been an experience of the night sky like this that prompted the poet Hopkins to pen his beautiful "Starlight Night." In it, he strains to come up with images that suggest the magic of a star-studded night sky. Listen to him:

> Look at the stars! look, look up at the skies!
> O look at all the fire folk sitting in the air!
> The bright boroughs, the circle citadels there!

> Down in prim woods the diamond delves! the elves' eyes!
> The grey lawns cold where gold, where quick gold lies!
> Wind beat white beam! airy abels set on flare!
> Flake-doves sent floating forth on a farmyard scare!
> Oh well! it is all a purchase, all is a prize.

He has re-created here the shifting, mysterious beauty of the Milky Way. He sees it as a kind of paling, or fence, enclosing "Christ and His Mother and all His hallows (saints)!" The Milky Way here becomes the outskirts of heaven. I think that anyone looking at the glory of the wintry night sky alone has a feeling somewhat akin to this. I know I did as I sat in the bobsleigh box, snug in my sheepskin-lined coat, looking up at the sky.

But there were less-poetic things to be done on the farm in the winter. Although we had a reprieve from the hard work in the fields, the aristocratic cows still demanded their tribute. They had to be fed and milked twice a day. Some of the time saved from the fields was devoted to refurbishing the wood supply. Dead or dying trees in the woods were felled and the trimmed logs gathered together in one pile. Our German neighbor had invested in a buzz saw powered by a gasoline engine, which he moved from farm to farm for a fee. The neighbors pooled their labor and moved from farm to farm to help saw the logs into stove-length blocks. These blocks still had to be split with axes into sizes that would fit the kitchen range and the heating stoves. The split wood was then hauled to the farmstead and either corded up outside or put into a wood house if one was available. The wood house on our farm was an extension of the kitchen wing itself. The firewood was thus available without going outside. Our woodshed served several purposes. A kind of mezzanine stretched over about half of it on the same level as the kitchen floor. This space became the laundry every Monday, and all summer it functioned as the summer kitchen. The cooking was done on an oil stove there to eliminate the added heat of the wood range in the kitchen in the hot summer.

Almost everything I have been recollecting here had to do with the main business of a farm—putting food in the mangers of the cattle or on the plates of the farmers. I had no quarrel with that, but I was ever a maverick, and I decided that I'd like to have something that was not good to eat, but merely good to look at. Mother's garden was good to look at, but that's not why she planted it. It supplied much of the food for our table. She liked flowers but didn't have time to fuss with them. So, like my purloined goose, I decided to purloin some flowers. A synonym for purloin is "steal" and that's what I did. I stole some irises from the graves in a nearby country cemetery. It didn't do much damage to the irises there because irises multiply quickly, but I did steal them. I planted them along the fieldstone wall that edged the lane, and we soon had an array of beautiful white irises every spring. I don't know whether it is to remind me of this little felony of my youth, but irises have punctuated my life ever since. Mother came to love them, and she herself planted great varieties of them, as did my older sister Laura. In her retirement, Laura developed one of the most spectacular flower gardens in all of Montello, and a great variety of hybrid irises were always featured in it.

Years later, in one of my several incarnations, irises again figured prominently. In my work on Flemish painting, I discovered that in their religious paintings the Flemish artists frequently used the iris as a symbol of Mary's suffering. It got that meaning in a roundabout way. The Latin name for iris is *gladiolus* (sword flower) because of the swordlike shape of its leaf. That shape was associated with the incident in Mary's life when she presented the Christ child to Simeon in the temple. He took the child in his arms and said: "This child will be set for the rise and fall of many," and looking at Mary, he added, "and your heart a sword shall pierce." Thus, the iris (sword flower) became a symbol of Mary's suffering.

Most of my active life has been spent at St. Louis University, named after the great St. Louis IX, king of France. His symbol, and that of the university, is the fleur-de-lis, an abstraction of the iris. And as I am writing this book in the 175th year of the university, I am surrounded with banners all over the campus bearing three white irises. That's the number and the color of those I stole from the grave in the little country graveyard. Have they come back to haunt me? Perhaps. I am also surrounded with real irises of many colors that I have planted in beds surrounding the old mansion I have spent a quarter of a century restoring. But that's a story for later.

In all this work and some play on the farm, where did formal schooling fit in? If I am honest, I would have to say it was rather peripheral. It was certainly very peripheral to all my four brothers. Except for my oldest brother and sister, who had a couple of their early years of schooling in the parochial school in town, we all received our elementary schooling in a one-room country schoolhouse. My brothers weren't much interested in formal schooling and left it after the eighth grade. What they needed for the careers they followed was mostly self-taught. None of them chose farming as a career. My oldest brother, John, worked for a while as a farmhand on a farm near Fondulac and in the Nash car factory in Kenosha, but he finally decided to go into interior decorating back home in Montello. Mother had taught him how to wallpaper, and he had learned carpentry from Dad. Because there were no unions in Montello, the interior decorator could do anything that was required to remodel or decorate the house. So when John took over a job, he could do everything: remodeling, electrical wiring, and plumbing, as well as plastering, cabinet making, wallpapering, and painting. With the burgeoning development of summer and year-round homes on the surrounding lakes, he never lacked work for the rest of his life. What he didn't know how to do, he taught himself. He was a perfectionist, and whatever he did, he did extremely well. But, as is often the case with perfectionists, he was very impatient with anyone who didn't come up to his standards—which was most of us. I preached the homily at his funeral, and I remember saying that John might at last be entirely happy because he had hopefully gone to a place where everything was perfect. But I added that if heaven wasn't perfect, God would have already heard about it.

My brother James also worked for a while as a farmhand but eventually married and managed a dry-cleaning establishment for a time. Then he and his wife finally settled into running a restaurant very successfully. Francis, after a stint in the South Pacific during the Second World War, worked for a while with John in interior decorating, but being much more casual, he couldn't put up with John's perfectionism and went to work for an interior-decorating group in Madison. He commuted the forty miles every day for the rest of his life. Howard, my youngest brother, was something of a mechanical genius. As a teenager, he'd buy an old secondhand car, take it completely apart, and then rebuild it. If he didn't have the right spare parts, he'd make them. He eventually joined the marines, who immediately put his mechanical skills to good use. He was put in charge of an engineers' unit and taught them their engineering skills. He was sent into active duty, and his unit was the first to land on Guadalcanal and Guam before the combat soldiers. They had to be there to repair gear that might be put out of commission in the landing. Only sixteen of his unit survived these landings. He was one of the survivors, but he was peppered full of shrapnel. Sent back to the States, he was discharged. He has continued mechanical work in various ways ever since he left the service. None of what my brothers did needed much schooling. They learned most of their self-sufficiency from Dad. He used to insist with all of us, "If you have something that has to be done, and you don't know how to do it, learn how and do it." Another equally wise bit of advice: "If you have a problem, analyze it, and go ahead and solve it. Don't wait for someone else to solve it for you." I think we all benefited by those wise bits of advice. I know I have.

The three girls in the family and I were the only ones who went on to schooling beyond the grades. My oldest sister Laura finished high school at the top of her class, went on to teacher's college, earned her teacher's certificate, and taught elementary school before she married and began to raise her family. She was a very good teacher. I can personally testify to that because she taught me for a year in our little one-room country school. The two youngest members of the family were girls, Marcella and Mary. They were late arrivals and were just beginning their elementary schooling when I left home to begin my long career of higher education. Marcella went on to high school and finally became a nun in the Teaching Order of St. Francis. She was extremely successful in the classrooms, but was stricken by a heart attack, the result of rheumatic fever in her childhood. She was sent to the order's nursing home and feared she would have to remain there for the rest of her life. But a young doctor, substituting for the regular doctor who was on vacation, examined her and said he thought she would respond to a new technique at the time, the insertion of an artificial valve in the heart. Marcella (Sister Mauritia was her name in religion) said she had nothing to lose. She had the operation. It was very successful, and she returned to more than twelve years of active work inside and out of the classroom. Mary, my youngest sister, finished high school, married young, and spent the rest of her life raising her six children. She loved children and cared for more than thirty-five foster babies until each of them in turn was adopted. She had a wonderful sense of humor and needed it to get her through physical ailments that she suffered all her life. She eventually died of cancer of the brain. When she wrote me telling me that the doctors had diagnosed terminal cancer, she said she and her husband Adam had gone for an autumn ride. Autumn can be beautiful in Wisconsin with its orange-red splash of hard maples, the shimmering gold of birch trees silhouetted against dark-green pine trees, and the flash of fiery red sumac bushes along the roadside. Mary said in her letter that what all this rush of autumn beauty told her was that death could be beautiful. Her death a few months later was beautiful. She discontinued therapy and went into a nursing hospice, where she died quietly and *beautifully* surrounded by her whole family.

In education, as in a good many other areas, I was the maverick in the family. Education became my whole life. My own education began literally in a little red one-room country schoolhouse near the Barrett Farm. I spent one year there, then, except for part of one semester, the rest of my grade school education occurred in another little one-room country schoolhouse (white this time) just a half mile across the woods from the home farm. I saw a turnover of five teachers in my seven years there, so it didn't have much continuity, but the teachers were devoted to their job and were good teachers (one was my sister Laura and another my cousin Gerald Collins). It was pretty difficult to teach much to eight grades in the same room, in fifteen-minute classes. About all I learned in the seven years was how to read and write. I never did learn how to add well and still rely on a calculator and a good secretary to do my adding. But what I did get out of the experience was an unquenchable desire to learn and a love of reading. The frustrating fact was that in my world there was nothing to read. In an age when we are so flooded with books and the printed page, it is difficult to realize that there is anyone still living who grew up in a totally bookless world. But that was my world. The only books in the country schoolhouse were the textbooks we were using. There was no library. The only books in our home were a Bible and a Bible history book. There were times when we didn't even have a subscription to a newspaper. Dad had a subscription to a couple of farm magazines, but they were of little interest to me.

Then into this bookless desert there fell some manna from heaven. We were assigned a new pastor from Milwaukee, Father Henry Velte. He took pity on his bookless flock, installed a large bookcase in the vestibule of the church, and filled it with books. Some of them were religious, but many of them were not. No matter what their content, I read them all. They included all the novels of the Jesuit Father

Finn. The stories were set in a boys' school run by the Jesuits in St. Mary's, Kansas. Starved as I was for anything to read, they were exciting to me. In that same year, more manna fell into my literary desert from a very unexpected part of the sky. A couple miles down the road from us, a bachelor and maiden sister ran a farm. In their middle age, they decided to adopt a boy from an orphanage. When John Ward came, a boy about twelve years old, he arrived with boxes of books. They included all the novels of Dickens and Thackeray. The Israelites with their manna from heaven in the desert couldn't have been any more delighted than I was at this unexpected windfall. I borrowed the books in succession and read every one of them. I was so eager to get through one of them that I took it out in the field with me, propped it up on my cultivator, and tried to read it as I was cultivating. When I started to cultivate out some of the corn along with the weeds, Dad put a stop to that venture into learning.

Father Velte, who had done so much to satisfy some of my thirst for reading matter with his little library in the church, did much for the parish as a whole. He was a very edifying and dedicated priest. He revitalized the parish Holy Name Society, and, before long, almost all its members made an annual closed retreat. He inspired the Women's Sodality to take on the task of raising funds to support the seminarians from the parish. During his regime, seven young men went to the seminary and persevered, and approximately nine young girls joined seven different religious orders. It was all largely the result of Father Velte's edifying example.

Father knew our family very well, and for some reason he decided that I ought to complete eighth grade in the parochial school in town to deepen my knowledge of the faith. I had never had any formal catechetical instruction except what Mother taught us at home. Her approach was not memorizing the catechism (I never did memorize it) but rather reading it with us and trying to tell us what it meant to her. We read Bible history the same way. The Old Testament was a story of a people and the New Testament the story of Christ. Moses and David became real people to us and so did Christ and his Apostles. Mother was a convert from Lutheranism. When she came into the Roman Catholic Church, she pretty much stuck to the essentials, and for her *the* essential was the Mass. She made that the focus of her religious practice and made it the focus of ours. She probably didn't have a very specific theological reason for that focus, but the focus was there. I didn't know until years later how right she was in putting the emphasis there, but the Mass has remained the central focus of my spiritual life ever since. Nothing was ever made of some of the more superficial religious practices—medals, indulgences, novenas, devotion to the calendar of saints, except for devotion to our Blessed Mother. We always said the rosary together as a family during Lent. The mysteries were a way of again moving through the life cycle of both Christ and Mary—joy, suffering, and triumph. To me, at the time, this seemed religious instruction enough, but it didn't seem so to Father Velte. He persuaded Mother and Dad to send me to the Sister School for my last elementary school year.

Father Velte had recommended that I transfer to the parochial school with the sincere hope that there my intellectual horizons would be broadened and my faith deepened. Actually, neither of these hopes was realized. The experience for me turned out to be a nightmare. A little country bumpkin thrust into the midst of these town kids, I was soon the object of their ridicule and practical jokes. Youngsters, left to themselves, have a streak of cruelty in them. They can, in fact, be a bit savage. I was to experience some of that savagery in the few months I stayed in the Sister School. We all had to participate in the yard games at recess, and for two reasons I was ill equipped to be good at any of them. On the farm, I had had no opportunity to play games, and even if I had, I probably would not have done very well in them. I was born with a physical difference that prevented me from ever developing the kind of physical coordination needed for adeptness in athletic sports. One of my legs is longer than the other; one of my hips is bigger than the other; and these two defects have given me a slight curvature of the spine that makes graceful physical coordination difficult. This difficulty showed up conspicuously in my attempts to join in the games, and I was the immediate butt of my playmates' hooting ridicule. Everything in the school was run in a rather military manner. Sister Thecla, a Dominican nun who was the teacher of the seventh and eighth grades—my room—was the sergeant at arms. We marched everywhere. When the bell rang at the end of recess, we lined up and marched up to our classroom to a tune wheezed out from a foot-pedaled organ played by one of the pupils at the head of the stairs. Sister Thecla reviewed the troops from the landing. We were all supposed to keep in perfect step with the music. One of the marchers would deliberately trip me up, so I would get out of step, an intolerable disruption of order to the troop marshal on the landing. When we went by, she would give me a good strong-armed cuff on the ear. This happened fairly regularly. When it did, I could always expect a cuff from Sister Thecla and generally got it. I simply would not become a tattler; I decided I'd put up with it if it killed me. But Sister Thecla's cuffs became so ingrained in my subconscious that years later, when, as a priest, I would be distributing Communion and came to a Dominican nun at the railing, I would almost instinctively hesitate, expecting that I might be due for another cuff on the ear.

My new schoolmates showed a bit of barbarism in other ways as well. Bess and I had come to school together. Bess, you remember, was my horse. She rather liked the idea because it meant that she could munch hay all day in Grannie's barn, just across the street from the school, instead of laboring in the fields. Grandpa and Grannie had by now retired from their farm. These were still horse-and-buggy days, and everybody in town had a horse barn behind the house. After school, when I had hitched up Bess and we were starting home, some of my charming schoolmates would wait along the street with sticks and try to whip Bess into running away. Skittery horses that were frightened sometimes did take off at breakneck speed that even a strong adult had difficulty restraining. That's what the attackers were trying to whip Bess into doing, but they didn't know that Bess and I had a lifelong concordat of loyalty. She had nothing but contempt for their shenanigans. She would turn and nip at them and try to kick them from behind the fills. They eventually would be frightened away, and Bess and I would go on home in the even tenor of our ways. But all this didn't add up to a very pleasant educational experience.

Other things that happened at the school made me aware that it was no Garden of Eden. Some of the boys approached me one day and asked whether I would like to join a little club they had formed. To enter it one had to steal five dollars or its equivalent in merchandise. I didn't get a rundown on what privileges membership in the club entitled one to because I said I'd have nothing to do with it. It wasn't so much out of a sense of superior virtue that I refused to join, but out of the very real knowledge of what other kind of club might be waiting for me if my parents found out about my joining. I didn't tell Sister Thecla about this incident either. There is a kind of camaraderie and loyalty that binds youngsters together even when they don't like one another: they will not tattle on one another. But the club was eventually exposed. We were all surprised one day when the county sheriff appeared in the classroom and took away the ringleaders. He brought them down to the courthouse to answer for some of the petty thievery that had been occurring in the local stores. The culprits were put on probation, and I presume that was the end of the club. I didn't stay around to find out. Exercising the kind of independence that has characterized me most of my life, without anybody's permission or advice, I picked up my books, hitched up Bess, and went home. In spite of my parents' attempt to get me to go back, I refused. I returned to the one-room country school, finished the eighth grade there, and graduated as a member of a huge class of three.

Father Velte's well-intentioned attempt to broaden my educational experience and deepen my faith had not worked out as he intended. My experience had indeed been broadened, but not in the way either he or I expected or wanted. Very little had been done to deepen my faith. But, by this time, Father Velte himself had affected me in a very profound way. It was his example as a very selfless devoted priest that brought me to the conviction that what I really wanted to be was not the blacksmith of my serious boyhood ambitions, but a priest. Late in the year, I divulged that desire to my parents. They were simply elated. Mother immediately hitched up Bess and drove me down to the rectory to tell Father Velte. When she broke the news, Father looked at me quizzically for a long time. He was probably thinking, "I'm not sure that this lad with his minimal schooling and country background can make the grade at a seminary full of boys from sophisticated urban schools." He finally said, "All right, if that's what you want. You will come in here every day this summer, and I'll teach you Latin." That seemed to be an astounding prescription, but I learned, when I went to the seminary, what an utterly wise thing it was for him to do. Father knew that if I went to the seminary with my meager country schooling and bumped up against the competition of vastly better-prepared students, I'd probably be so discouraged that I'd do what I did in the Sister School—pick up my books and go home. He figured that if I had a start in Latin, which none of the others would have, I might have enough confidence to compete in the rest of the course. That's exactly the way it worked out. So Bess and I went to school again that summer, she in Grannie's barn and I in the rectory. By the end of the summer, I did have a good introduction into the mysteries of Latin and was eager to be off to the seminary.

There is one aspect of my upbringing that I want to record here before I go on to something else because it prepared me very well for the artistic and restoration work to which I have devoted the last quarter of my life. I never was very active in sports, in part because, like Robert Frost's lad in "Birches," I lived too far from town to have the opportunity of playing baseball and in part because my two older brothers were too old and my two younger ones too young for me to become very much involved in their sports. That left me isolated in the middle of the tribe. My older sister, Laura, ten years older than I, was similarly isolated in a passel of boys. My two youngest sisters didn't come on the scene until much later, so that threw Laura and me together most of the time. She actually became and, until her death at the age of ninety-four, remained a second mother to me. Under her tutelage, I learned to help around the house. Mother was a very good housekeeper and had taste in what she did. She had developed sensitive feelings for domestic refinements as a young girl. Her father, our Grandpa Griffith, a Welshman, had died of pneumonia as a very young man. Pneumonia was a death sentence in those days before antibiotics. We knew him only from his oval portrait that hung in the parlor. When he died, Grandma was left with three little girls to raise. She couldn't manage the farm alone, so she sold it and moved into town. She bought a tiny house with the income from the farm and tried to make a living by taking in washing. That didn't easily fill four mouths, so as straitened families often did at the time, she put two of her daughters "into service." Mable and Ida were the ones chosen to go. Ida was my mother. Mable and my mother both spent years in that service, which meant working as maids for wealthy families. Mable spent so many years "in service" at a distance that Grandma didn't even recognize her the first time she came home. Mother worked for a successful doctor and his wife in Portage, Wisconsin. It was in those years of service that she developed what I think she had instinctively—a sense of design, color, and composition in the arrangement and decoration of a home and a skill in cooking and baking. She never lost these skills and made good use of them in our home. She didn't have much to arrange, but what she had was always arranged tastefully. She did much of the decoration herself—which included wallpapering, painting, and restoring and reupholstering furniture—the skills of an interior decorator. My brother John, who later became a professional interior decorator, learned many of the tricks of his trade from her, as did my sister Laura.

Mother also had something of an artistic flair herself. I've already referred to her skill with the needle and the sewing machine, making practically all our clothes. But she was also skilled with a crochet hook. Tables in the parlor and dressers in the bedrooms were decked with runners and doilies that she had crocheted. But her favorite creations were braided rugs. They were made from strips of old woolen clothes, braided and sewed together in oval or circular shapes. To get the right blend of colors, old woolen blankets would be dyed (blues, reds, greens, and yellows) to make strips that would contrast with the grays, browns, and blacks of the braids from old clothes. It took a real sense of color and design to make a good braided rug. And Mother's were beautiful. She made dozens of them. Almost every room in the house boasted of one. My sister Laura developed a similar skill. She made more than a hundred braided rugs. I have a large one in my office at present, a beautiful blend of grays and blues. A recent commercial cleaner who worked on it said, "You have here a real collector's item." So, humble as our circumstances were, there was an element of taste and refinement in our household. Being poor does not mean that one's world *has* to be ugly.

Being somewhat isolated from my brothers and growing up close to my sister Laura meant that I, willy-nilly, gradually learned to be helpful with work around the house. When Laura started high school and boarded with Grandpa and Grannie in town, then went off to teacher's college and a teaching job, and then later married, Mother was left with no help in the house at all. She relied on me more and more to pitch in. When she contracted an illness that kept her bedridden for almost a year, I did more than pitch in: I kept house. Dad said that because I was pretty handy around the house, he would excuse me from the fields to do the housework. That meant doing everything! Cooking, baking, marketing, gardening, taking care of the chickens, cleaning, washing, and ironing. Some of it I already knew how to do; the rest I had to learn. Under Mother's guidance, I learned it well. I little dreamed then that this stint at housekeeping was preparing me for what I'd spend the last quarter of my life doing—"keeping house" in an elegant forty-two-room mansion. But that story will have to wait for later. Here again, in my end is my beginning.

# 2

# A German *Gymnasium*

During that last summer before going to the seminary, I was working as usual in the fields—that is, when I wasn't studying Latin. Finally the day came for my departure. Mother was to take me to Milwaukee. Dad drove us out in horse and buggy to Glen Oak, where we had lived for a year and had watched the great passenger trains from Chicago come to a huffing and puffing stop at the little station. It was exciting to be boarding the train for the first time instead of just gawking at the passengers from the station platform. I had ridden the little one-coach train from Montello to Portage, but this was the first time I had ever been on one of the main passenger trains. It was a sudden wrench out of my horse-and-buggy days. I was all decked out in my first "store-boughten" suit, and Mother was in her Sunday best.

Aunt Mame, one of my father's sisters, met us at the train in Milwaukee, and for a day or two showed us something of the city. It was my first experience of a big city and full of surprises. Everything seemed so big—beginning with Lake Michigan. I was used to lakes; Montello was surrounded by lakes. But I had never imagined that there could be such a big body of water as that which stretched out from the shores of Lake Michigan. Skyscrapers, actually not that skyscraping in those days in Milwaukee, looked positively immense to me. We got onto one of the clanging streetcars (another first for me) to go to Aunt Mame's apartment. She reminded us on the way that the cobblestones between the streetcar tracks were all made of Montello granite. The car passed through what people then called a "colored" section of town, and I was utterly amazed to see people walking on the street who were actually black. I had never seen an African American before. There were none in Montello and probably none in the whole of Marquette County at that time. My horizons were being expanded in many directions. After a couple of days of sightseeing, we boarded the streetcar and went out to the seminary. It is dedicated to Saint Francis De Sales and is beautifully situated right on the shore of Lake Michigan. The sad moan of the foghorn on the lake was going to become an integral part of my new environment. We were welcomed by Father Huepper, the master of discipline, which sounded a bit forbidding. After a tearful farewell, Mother and Aunt Mame left. As the umbilical cord to family and home was suddenly cut for the first time, such a wave of homesickness swept over me that I thought I would die. I had never been away from home before. There wasn't any shoulder to cry on. Father Huepper's were big ones, but they did not invite tears. Father unceremoniously marched me off to show me my bed and locker in a huge dormitory and my desk in an equally huge study hall. I was then thrust into a clack of freshman seminarians, a motley crew from all over the Midwest. I didn't know a soul. My experience in Sister School didn't give me much hope that I'd fare any better here. But I did. Once the ice was broken, I found my new confreres much more receptive than those in my own hometown. In fact, I soon struck up a friendship with one of them, Ed Stumpf by name, that was to last until Ed died a few years ago. Our backgrounds could not possibly have been more unlike. He came from a well-placed family in Milwaukee. His father owned an exclusive men's clothing shop. Ed had had a year of study at a Jesuit school, Marquette High. What I liked about Ed from the beginning was his dry sense of humor. We soon learned that we needed a sense of humor, dry or wet, to survive the life into which we were being inducted.

St. Francis Seminary at that time was run like a military academy. It resembled a German *Gymnasium* and that wasn't entirely accidental. It was founded by German-Swiss diocesan priests, and, when I was there, it was still headed by one, Monsignor Breig, who spoke broken English. The bishop of the diocese at the time, Archbishop Messmer, was also a Swiss German. He wore a white beard, and when he made his appearances at the seminary for ordinations or to celebrate St. Francis De Sales Day, we always felt as the Israelites must have felt when Moses appeared at their tent door. He had been an Alpine mountain climber back home in Switzerland. He would be driven out to the seminary for his visitations, but he always walked home (some fifteen miles) to show that he retained some of his Alpine vigor.

The German-Swiss founders had brought with them some of their notion of how a prep seminary should be run, like a German *Gymna-*

*sium,* and it was. Discipline was the order of the day. We rose at five in the morning, and after a brief half-hour's toilet, we went to our desks in the study hall for an hour of study—all of this in complete silence. We then lined up in alphabetical order and marched to chapel for Mass and Communion. Thanksgiving prayers over, we marched to the refectory for breakfast. Two long tables stretched the length of the room. There were no chairs; we pulled out our stools from under the table. The whole place looked like the boys' dining room Dickens describes in *Oliver Twist.* And what was on the table looked like what was served there, too. It consisted of a plate of sliced bread and a gray granite pot, not of coffee, but of some kind of malt drink with milk and sugar already in it. There was no butter and no jam for the bread, so we didn't need any utensils. We just dunked our bread in our cups of malt brew. To all of us young hungry Americans, used to hearty American breakfasts, this was extreme austerity. The only redeeming feature was that the bread was good—baked by the Sisters from the neighboring convent in big old-world stone ovens. We used to say that we were sure the superior at the convent sent over all the hatchet faces in the community to do our cooking in order to strengthen our vocations. On feast days, there was a big concession to our appetite—bread with a powdered sugar frosting on it. If one of us found the breakfast too severe, he could buy a can of cocoa and give it to the sisters. He would then find a cup of cocoa at his place when he came to breakfast. When his can was empty, he would find a note at his place reading: "Your cocoa is all." We wanted to ask—all what? The sisters were just translating the German *"Das ist alles,"* which meant, of course, it's all *gone.* Our diet in general was wholesome enough but completely lacking in any kind of inventiveness. We managed, however, to relieve the monotony with boxes of food from home and with food that we purchased on our Thursday walks. This latter was a bit *ex lex,* of course, and the discipline fell heavy on us if we were caught.

One of the most irksome features of the Germanic passion for order was that we were lined up alphabetically for everything—in the study hall, dining room, chapel, and dormitory. So if one of us got next to a lemon, he was with that person from morning until night. I did. The lemon I drew reminded me of a ditty my Dad used to sing.

> A million peaches round me
> Yet, I would like to know

> How I picked a lemon in the Garden of Love
> Where they say only peaches grow.

My lemon was a sort of a wild man from a farm in a German community in Iowa. He spoke English with difficulty and was irritatingly crude in some of his habits. He chewed tobacco. He'd buy a box of Cracker Jack and use the wax box as a spittoon in the drawer of his study hall desk. It wasn't a pleasant sight or sound to have just at arm's reach away from my desk. He was next to me in the dormitory as well, and because he never took a bath, his body odor used to be oppressive. In winter, I would wait until he had gone to sleep, and then get up and crack the big French windows to let in some of the icy air off of Lake Michigan to relieve the malodorous scent.

The establishment at the seminary was quite serious about preserving the military atmosphere of the place. How serious they were I discovered a couple of times when I stepped out of line. After the night study hall and the evening visit to the chapel, we were supposed to keep complete sacred silence and go to bed. We had a candy store in the building, and some of us used to buy some *dulcia* to munch in bed. One night I brought up a box of Cracker Jack, and when I opened it, my prize was a big metal marble. Some of my confreres dared me to roll it down the deep groove in the grand stairs banister. That sounded like a good idea to me, too, sacred silence or not. I tiptoed out to the grand stairwell and sent the marble rolling down the railing. We were on the fourth floor, so as it descended, it kept picking up momentum and racket. It slipped the track on the second floor and crashed into the door of none other than Father Huepper, the master of discipline. This egregious breach of discipline and sacred silence summoned the Discipline Committee into plenipotential session the next day, and the culprit was asked to appear before it. Some of the more rigid of its members insisted that the blatant offense I had committed against the tradition of sacred silence merited my dismissal from the seminary. Most of the less Gestapo-ish members disagreed. Father (later Bishop) O'Connor spoke up in my defense. He said: "It was a boyish prank, and I'm glad he did it because I hadn't thought he'd have the gumption to do it." So with a sharp reprimand, my case was dismissed.

Later I was involved in another episode that was a more serious infraction of sacred silence and physically more destructive. On one of our Thursday hikes into town, a few of us had decided to get some snacks and soda for a little secret party in our dormitory after night prayers. This was in our junior year. Juniors and seniors were housed in smaller dormitories with no resident prefect, so we thought we could have our party undetected. There was a row of sinks for our morning ablutions at one end of the dorm. We put our soda bottles in the sink and turned on the water to keep the soda cool for our evening soiree. Unfortunately, the paper labels came off the bottles, clogged up the sink, and the water avalanched over the rim of the sink onto the floor. When we came up after night prayers, the dormitory was afloat. We desperately pressed our bed sheets into service to mop up the water, not realizing that the water had soaked through the floor and collapsed the plaster ceiling in Father Ziegler's study just below us. This was a serious infraction of sacred silence and good sense, and we knew we were in for the worst. This time the Discipline Committee pretty generally thought we ought to be dismissed. But amazingly, Father Ziegler, whose ceiling had collapsed, came to our defense. He had us all in his German class and knew us all very well. He put up such a persuasive defense for us—in English, I presume—that the committee relented. They prescribed a public reprimand to be read in our presence before the whole school, but allowed us to stay. We certainly were grateful for this reprieve. We all did stay, and we all went on to the priesthood. I was particularly grateful to Father O'Connor for saving my neck the first time. Years later, after he had been made a bishop, I encountered him at the tomb of St. Peter in Rome. I took the occasion of telling him that but for his interventions, I probably wouldn't have been making this pilgrimage to Rome as a priest.

Athletics were a very important part of the *Gymnasia* in Germany, and so were they at the seminary. We had regular compulsory gymnastic exercises every week in the gym, and there was plenty of opportunity for competitive sports as well: baseball, football, and basketball. I didn't get involved in any of these because of my lack of experience and my physical limitations, but for the first and last time of my life I did get interested in the games as a spectator, probably because I knew all the players. I got so interested that I became one of the official cheerleaders. The only game I participated in physically was volleyball, in which my lack of good physical coordination was less of a handicap.

No part of our makeup was neglected at the seminary. Our spiritual needs were met by a regular prayer life centered around the daily Mass. On Sundays and feast days, the Liturgy was always a Solemn High Mass. We joined in the Gregorian chant for which we had been prepared in our weekly class in Gregorian. As part of our spiritual training we were all assigned a spiritual director. I was fortunate in being assigned to Monsignor Rainer, who was by this time retired from active duty. He was a classical scholar and, in fact, had authored the text we used in our Latin classes. He had also been rector of the seminary for a time. He was a learned, refined, and gentle old man, and I couldn't help thinking that the ship must have been less militaristic when he was at the helm. Be that as it may, he provided for me a haven of warmth and understanding. I used to look forward to our visits, and that's what they were. Going to his study was like stepping into a little tropical oasis. It was full of potted palms taller than I or even than the tiny little monsignor himself. Among the palms were cages of canaries. It was a pleasant relief from the starkness of the rest of the seminary environment. And he always accidentally on purpose had some candy for me to take along when the visit was over. As a classicist, he was interested in how I was doing in Latin, and I was doing very well because of the head start Father Velte had given me back home. In every way, Monsignor became a kind of father figure for me. He also provided me with another new experience. Every Sunday evening in the chapel, he would conduct a little devotion in honor of Mary that replaced our regular night prayers. He selected me to be one of his acolytes for the ceremony. I had never before had the opportunity of functioning as an acolyte. I loved the new experience of donning the red cassock and white lace surplice, and then, with lighted candle, accompanying Monsignor in his monsignorial robes to the Blessed Virgin's altar for the Sunday-night devotions. He always gave a little talk in which he was able, in very simple language, to bring alive the humanity of Mary and make us youngsters realize how grateful we should be in knowing that we had such a considerate mom pleading our cause in heaven.

But all of this lockstep routine inherited from the German *Gymnasium* was but a frame for what turned out to be a first-rate liberal education—also an inheritance from that form of schooling. The curriculum was solid, broad, and balanced. It included four years of Latin, two years of Greek, and two years of German; courses in European and American history; religion and Scripture courses; training in Gregorian chant each semester; and four years of English literature. Mathematics and science were represented by courses in algebra, geometry, and physics. We were also given training in debate and an opportunity to participate in dramatic performances.

Perhaps even more important than the balanced offerings in the courses themselves was the quality of most of the teachers. Some of mine were outstanding both as scholars and teachers. "Doc" Johnston, as we called him, had published widely in U.S. history and had the knack of bringing history alive for us. We loved Father Ziegler, our German teacher; he made learning to speak German fun. To this day, when I use in Germany the little German I have retained or picked up since, I'm told I speak German like a native. It's because Father Ziegler made the learning of German not a dry study of *grammar* but a means of *verbally communicating* in a foreign language. He took a personal interest in each of us and was careful to correct our pronunciation until we got it right.

St. Francis Seminary educated seminarians through high school, two years of philosophy, and four years of theology. We were all housed in the same impressive old building, but the groups were strictly segregated from one another. The faculty, all diocesan priests, were also housed in the same building, which meant there were some talented and well-trained teachers available for the high school religion and Scripture classes. I was fortunate in having several of the best: Father Muench, who later became bishop of Fargo, South Dakota, and world renowned for his work in the rural life movement; Father O'Connor, who later was the first bishop of the new Madison diocese; and Father Haas, noted historian and sociologist who also later became a bishop. Their well-prepared classes were a particular delight to me because I had never before received any formal instruction in religion. I had learned the essentials from my mother, but none of what I had learned had ever become a memorized catechism. It was really an enlightening experience to be getting from these authorities an expansion and explanation of the little I knew.

For Scripture, we had a very fine teacher, Father Schulte. He had published widely in his field, but probably more interesting to us were some of his achievements outside the classroom. He was hefty and burly, and his bulk, combined with his eccentricities of dress, would remind you of Sam Johnson. He always wore a huge black frock coat and an immense black felt hat. He was quite a sight as he strolled around the grounds with his frock coat flapping in the breeze. Frequently he would be carrying a shotgun: he loved to shoot blackbirds. The grounds were extensive—more than two hundred acres of wooded land—so there were always enough blackbirds around for him to shoot. When we'd hear the "bang, bang" of his shotgun, we'd say, "Bye, bye, blackbird." In fact, that's what we came to call him. We heard one day that "Bye, Bye, Blackbird" had had a car accident. He had just bought a new four-door sedan and was examining it inside and out before he drove away from the dealers. He neglected to close the rear door before he drove off; when he did, he ripped the whole door off its hinges.

Although my preparation in mathematics was dismal, my teacher in algebra made it so interesting that I did pretty well in it, so well, in fact, that I used to tutor my good friend Ed Stumpf before examinations because he found it very difficult.

But any proficiency in mathematics I might have achieved was nipped in the bud by my experience in geometry. The teacher I had in that subject ran a close second to a teacher I had years later in chemistry: he was perhaps the worst teacher in my long educational career. He was Father Hans Reis, a wonderful old gentleman, but a terrible teacher. His name appeared for decades on the frontispiece of books printed in the Milwaukee diocese because he was the *censor librorum* for the diocese. He was an emanation from another age. He wore a long black French soutane, with a long line of buttons down the front and a cape flapping over his shoulders at the top. In places, it was green with age. He had a heavy shock of long white hair. He must have always combed it just before he came to class because there were always loose hairs clinging to his soutane. My friend Ed picked them off over the semester, wove them into a little wreath, mounted them, and presented them to me at the end of the semester, marked "First Class Relic of Hans Reis." Hans had won this accolade by demonstrating all semester how not to teach a course in geometry. He never gave any homework; he never sent anyone to the blackboard; and he never used it himself. He would sit on one of the student desks in the front of the room and chalk out the theorem on the desk as he talked about it. One of the students near him might rub out one of the letters, and he would spend the hour trying to figure out where his calculations went wrong. Meantime, the class would be in pandemonium. Hans was almost stone deaf, but his deafness was odd. If we whispered he could hear us; if we talked out loud, he couldn't. So everybody talked out loud about things other than geometry, while Hans worked out or didn't work out his theorem on the front desk. One day he came into class and almost caused a cataclysm. He sent somebody to the blackboard: my friend Ed Stumpf. He told Ed to draw an isosceles triangle. Ed hadn't a ghost of a suspicion of what an isosceles triangle was, so he drew an arbitrary construction on the board. Hans looked at it and said: "Oh, my boy, sit down, that isn't an isosceles triangle—it looks more like a bathtub." Hans then drew an isosceles triangle for us himself, so that was one exact detail we carried away from the class in geometry, but not much else. We learned later that the reason for the extraordinary incident that day was that Hans's mother had died the night before.

I had more than the usual number of good teachers and one of my worst at St. Francis Seminary, but I also had what was unquestionably the very best teacher I have ever had anywhere. He was my English teacher, Father Henry Riordon. I don't know whether he ever knew that we called him Hank. He had an enormous influence on the later direction of my life. When I came to the seminary from my bookless world at Montello, I was amazed to find that there were enough books in one spot that a separate building had to be built to house them. The seminary's library was heaven for me. My country schooling had given me an insatiable appetite for reading, but there had been no way of satisfying that appetite. The De Sales Library was arranged on the old closed-stack system; we could not browse in the stacks. But that did not deter me. The card catalog was an open sesame—scribble down the name of the book you wanted, and in a few minutes you had it in your hands. Father Riordon thought we might be intimidated by the big library and the closed stacks, so he withdrew the books he thought we might like or ought to read and installed them in an antechamber outside his study. He was there almost every afternoon on class days to discuss our reading with us. He'd suggest a book and then discuss it with us when we had finished it. He'd say, "If you liked that one, you'd probably be interested in this one." In this way, he led us from book to book and gradually expanded and deepened our appreciation of what we read. It wasn't the assignment of books for book reports, but a personalized guide through some of the best of English and American fiction—an incomparable educational experience.

He was equally stimulating and challenging in his work in the classroom. We wrote a theme every week (for four years) in old-fashioned bound notebooks. We wrote on only one side of the page so that the opposite page would always be free for making our corrections. I never remember the theme books not coming back with his corrections the day after we handed them in. Spelling mistakes had to be corrected, and the word we had misspelled written five times on the blank page. Grammar mistakes also had to be corrected, and the grammar rule we had offended against written on the blank page. If there was disorder or lack of logic in our organization, we would be asked to rewrite the whole theme and correct the sloppy logic or loose organization. If the piece just needed strengthening in its rhetorical effectiveness, Father would suggest some ways in which it might be done—more varied sentence structure, parallel structure for parallel ideas, more concrete examples of what we were discussing, more effective imagery, or a better choice of words. We would be expected to take the hint and try to improve our piece rhetorically. He made it quite clear that our theme might be grammatically correct but still be dull as dishwater. He expected us to make the necessary corrections of the old theme in our notebooks before we began a new one. Failure to do so would dock fifteen points off our new theme. We took care: we did not just look at our mark and throw the theme away. We actually couldn't do so because they were all in the bound notebook—a permanent record of our successes and failures.

We spent a great deal of class time reading and discussing literature—poetry, short stories, and essays. In discussions of essays, we paid considerable attention to how the author had achieved his effective expression—how he organized his material or how his imagery added to the effectiveness of what he had to say. We might be asked to express the main ideas without the imagery to see how bland the expression became without it.

Father made much of the interpretative reading of literature. He was an excellent reader himself. After we had come to understand a poem, he would read it dramatically for us. He trained us to do the same and would often call on us to read in class—helping us to use our voices to express our feeling for what we were reading. He used to say that being content with just the poem on the printed page without its coming alive in our ear would be like being content with the score of a great operatic aria instead of enjoying it sung by a great opera singer.

We read and discussed a Shakespearean play each year. We had to memorize the most important speeches. When we had worked through the play rather thoroughly in class, we would read it together. Father always read the lines of the leading character. Because we knew the play pretty well by this time, we would really relish his impressive reading of the main speeches. We were asked to read the lesser parts, which were rotated around the class. I still know most of the important speeches in *Hamlet, Julius Caesar, Macbeth,* and *King Lear,* which were the plays we read in the four years at the seminary. The theologians usually put on a Shakespearean play toward the end of every year, and they tried to do the play we were studying during the year.

I am very grateful for another of Father Riordon's teaching devices. He made us keep a commonplace book. We had to put down a brief passage from something we had read or a favorite stanza from a poem every week, and we had to memorize our entries. He would frequently come into class, point a finger at one of us, and ask that person to get up and recite what he had put in his commonplace book and tell the class why he had put it there. Father Riordan also pretty regularly put on the board something that he wanted us to add to our books—generally a stanza from a poem he happened to be reading at the time—he seldom told us where they came from—and we had to memorize his as well as our own. At the age of ninety, I can still recite almost all the entries either he or I made in my commonplace book. I don't know whether or not he was consciously following Mathew Arnold's advice on how to develop a sense of taste in literary neophytes, but in our commonplace project he was doing exactly what Arnold recommends—filling our minds with touchstones of literary excellence. We were becoming familiar with the best that had been thought and said in the past and were developing a sensitivity to how it had been said. We did gradually sense the difference between the quality of the things that struck us in our own reading and the superior quality of many of the things that Father added. We were beginning to develop almost subconsciously some discrimination between the good and the better in literary expression. One of the added pleasures that came to me down through the years is the discovery of the sources of the literary gems that Father had us memorize. In my later literary studies, I was frequently surprised by those sources: *The Faerie Queene* or a poem by one of the metaphysicals or a poem by Keats, Shelley, or Emerson. Occasionally I discovered that what Father had entered in our commonplace book was a complete poem by a poet such as Emily Dickinson. It was always a joy to greet these old friends in their original settings.

Father also participated in some of our outside activities. Our free day was Thursday rather than Saturday, in accordance with another feature of the German *Gymnasium*. We were frequently taken for excursions into the city to a site of historical importance or an interesting factory. I particularly remember a visit to the Johnston Chocolate Factory in which we saw the whole process of making chocolates, but particularly interesting to us was the little box of free chocolates that awaited us at the end of the tour. Hiking was always part of the outing. We would take the streetcar to our destination and hike back—generally about a fifteen-mile walk. The administrators of the seminary were at pains to see that our *mens sana* would be incorporated *in corpore sano*. I little suspected as we were hiking back from the Johnston Chocolate Factory that some four years later I would be led by Bob Johnston, the son of the owner of the chocolate factory, over hill and dale on a hike through the Florissant Valley in Missouri, both of us as Jesuit novices.

Father Riordon would sometimes choose the objective for our Thursday excursions and come along as our guide. To me, the most memorable destination was the Milwaukee Art Museum. At that time, it was just a wing of the City Central Library. It housed a conglomeration of stuffed animals and a small collection of sculpture and painting. This was my first experience of a museum of any kind, and it left a lasting impression on me. I was particularly fascinated by the landscape paintings. I had previously come to admire Jack Smith's little landscapes brushed into his array of clamshells, but here were beautiful glimpses of the outside world I had come to love blown up in large scale on canvas. It was my first serious exposure to the world of the fine art that later absorbed a very large part of my personal and academic life.

Another aspect of Father Riordon's life that impressed me was the way he combined his academic life and his devotion to his students with his priesthood. I am sure he looked on his work with us in the classroom and outside of it as a very important part of his priestly apostolate, but he combined all of that with a more direct apostolic activity. All the four years I knew him at the seminary, he drove a hundred miles every weekend to serve the needs of a little community of farmers in their little country church built on a country road in the middle of a cornfield. Father never allowed his academic life to obscure the fact that he was a priest.

Father Riordon's example of combining the two vocations so admirably convinced me that this was what I would like to do. My desire to be a priest had not at all diminished, but his example led me to think that I might be able to combine teaching with the priesthood. I told Father what I was thinking, and he said if I prepared myself well, I might be able to achieve that ambition by teaching in a seminary, as he did, or elsewhere. It is very ironic that Father Riordon himself was to determine where I was to realize that ambition and that it was to be in a place not at all to his liking.

Our heroes all may have their Achilles' heel. Father Riordon's was his strong dislike of the Jesuits. He had received his master's degree in English from the neighboring Jesuit Marquette University, but for some reason he had developed a deep-seated dislike of Jesuits. He was always referring to them as self-satisfied and arrogant. Moreover, his dislike of the Jesuits was not unique at the seminary. We always had an order priest give our annual retreat, but in the previous thirty years a Jesuit had never been invited to give it, in spite of their proximity at Marquette University. Father Riordon's frequent jibes at the Jesuits piqued my curiosity. I knew practically nothing about them at this time except that one of them, Father Marquette, had named my hometown. I went to the library and checked out Campbell's *History of the Society of Jesus* to find out who these Jesuits were who had become such a burr in the side of my hero. I was amazed to find that one of their chief concerns was education. I also discovered that they had an array of high schools, colleges, and universities all across the country, including a high school and university, Marquette, in Milwaukee, named after the Jesuit who named my hometown. I felt that this information could bear further investigation. Perhaps becoming a Jesuit would give me a better opportunity of realizing my new ambition of combining the priesthood with a career in teaching.

I didn't dare reveal my "temptation" to anyone at the seminary, least of all to Father Riordon, so I took the streetcar to Marquette

University and asked to see one of the ogres. Father Magee, rector of the Jesuit community, responded. Neither he nor the other examiners he sent me to were very encouraging. They did not want to leave the impression that they were enticing anybody away from the seminary. But I persevered and after a few more visits made my formal application to enter the Society. This was late in the last semester of my senior year, so I had to inform the authorities at the seminary of my decision. It met with a very mixed reaction. Some tried to dissuade me, but good Monsignor Breig, the Swiss-German rector, called me in and said in his broken English: "Ja, ja, boy; don't worry. Dis speaks gut for da seminary." Father Riordon didn't think so. He called me down and said that he just wanted to warn me that, three years hence, when I was trying to get out of my vows, he wanted me to remember that someone had warned me of what I was getting into. In spite of my great admiration for Father, which I never lost, this warning seemed to me to be an outrageous interference in my free choice. I decided I'd go to the Jesuit novitiate and stay if it killed me. His disdain for the Jesuits puzzled me because, in spite of his frequent jibes against them, he had all of us subscribe to the Jesuit-edited *America* magazine. He wanted us, he said, to be informed on what was going on currently in the country and in the Church. The magazine at that time was more literarily oriented than it is today. Father would sometimes use articles in it as a take-off for some of our own writing. He'd say: "This is a very good article, but it does show some of that narrow Jesuit rut." It is ironic that his frequent barbs against the Jesuits were responsible for my becoming one.

But that does not end my story of Father Riordon and the Jesuits. I did not keep up my contact with Father Riordan after I joined the Jesuits, but thirteen years later, when I was ordained, I sent him an invitation to my First Mass. He was then a monsignor and pastor of a parish in Fondulac, not far from Montello. I did not expect he would come, but, when I looked down from the sanctuary, I saw Monsignor with a young boy in tow in one of the pews. He had come late, so he wasn't in the ceremony. He came up to me at the reception, congratulated me warmly, and said, "I want to introduce you to this young man, John Blewett. He is a straight 'A' student who has just graduated from Mount Calvary High School, and I have recommended that he become a Jesuit." I couldn't believe my ears. I have no idea what had changed his attitude. John did become a Jesuit, taught for many years in the Jesuit University of Sophia in Tokyo, and eventually became an assistant to the general of the Society, Father Arrupe, in Rome. After I later became chairman of the English department at St. Louis University, Father Riordon never stopped bragging about one of his boys who had made good, and he had some right to do so. I did become rather successful in the classroom, eventually receiving an award for my teaching. It was Father Riordon's example that inspired me to want to become a teacher of English, and almost everything I did that made me a successful one was in emulation of his good example.

When I had signed up to join the Jesuits, I told my good friend, Ed Stumpf, about my decision. I was amazed to discover that he had also already signed up to do the same. Neither of us had ever confided to one another that we were thinking of making this move. His decision was good news to me because, considering Father Riordon's warning of what an insane thing it was to do, I thought I'd at least have company in my misery. We later discovered that a third member of our class, Harold Gibbons, had also decided to join the Jesuits. I'm sure Father Riordon must have thought that a really bad virus had infected our class.

The four years I spent at the diocesan seminary were divided into academics in winter and farmwork in the summer. I returned every summer to the usual routine on the farm, and because my two older brothers had left home by this time, the farm work fell squarely on me and my two younger brothers. It was still the hard work of a premechanized age, but things happened during those years that were to yank rural life out of its horse-and-buggy condition. First came the multiplication of automobiles. During those years, we purchased our first car—a simple Ford Tin Lizzy. It was something like a glorified coffee grinder, but it greatly facilitated travel to and from town. And we were no longer confined to the space we could cover, going and coming, in a day in the horse and buggy. All the farmers soon had cars, as did most of the townsfolk, which put a lot of automobile traffic on the roads. They were just dirt roads—a space fenced off to keep the cattle out. You could see the approach of cars on these "roads" a half-mile away because of the clouds of dust they stirred up. The roads became deeply rutted, and in wet weather the cars frequently got stuck in the mud. Farmers would have to come to the rescue and pull the cars out with a team of horses, which soon became a nuisance to both drivers and farmers. It became evident that something had to be done to provide a better roadbed. I don't know how widespread this situation was, but the solution in our part of Wisconsin showed a considerable amount of ingenuity. The glaciers had left behind whole hillsides of gravel fashioned into rounded pebbles by their grinding movement. This ready-made gravel was there for the taking. The farmers devised a clever way of taking it. They covered their wagons with what were called dump planks—four-by-four oak planks—and laid them next to one another on the wagon bed. Within the high side and end boards, they would fill the box with gravel shoveled in from the gravel pit, then proceed to the road, lift the side and end boards and shift the loose dump planks until all the gravel had fallen on the road. This would deposit gravel about a foot thick on a piece of the road the size of the wagon. This process was repeated until the entire surface of the road was covered. A grader drawn by a team of horses would level out the gravel. This work was hard and slow. The farmers did it in the off season—early spring or late fall—and paid off their taxes by doing so. Each farmer was responsible for graveling the road in front of his farm. Later, these gravel roads were covered with a mixture of oil, sand, and tar to create the grandfather of the blacktop roads that now web the whole country.

With mechanization came the tractor, which was to simplify farmwork and eliminate a great deal of its drudgery. It would also eventually eliminate the horse. There is no question that tractor-drawn combines are a more efficient and labor-saving means of harvesting crops, but a certain personal element vanished from the farm with the disappearance of the horse. Farmers did develop something of a personal relationship with their horses that they do not with their tractors. Of course, one of the advantages of the tractors is that they don't have to be fed when they are not working.

I had learned in my several trips a year on the train back and forth from the seminary what train travel had done to break the bonds of the circumscribed world of the horse and buggy. And the automobile had done it even more effectively. During those four last summers on the farm, I was also to experience for the first time the vision of a technological advance that was to make the whole world one. I saw my first airplane. In from the fields, I often spread out on the lawn under a huge elm tree after our dinner for a nap before returning to the fields. One day as I lay there looking up through the network of the elm twigs, there flew into my ken what looked to me like a giant mosquito. I was looking for the first time at a little biplane flying low at almost treetop level. This sight was in many ways more exciting to me than the later spectacle of astronauts landing on the moon. What the astronauts did was just a continuation of what I saw happening above the twigs of my elm tree—my first glimpse of a man in flight. I little thought then that on the giant successors of that little biplane I would myself fly to almost every continent on the globe.

Another technological innovation that I was to experience during these four years was eventually to annihilate that distance even more. We had always had a telephone that provided some contact with the outside world. We were on a party line, so when we cranked out the number we were calling, we could hear the "click, click" of the phones of the other parties on the line who were intruding on our conversation. If we counted the clicks, we could tell how many were listening in. It was the standard way of keeping in touch with some of the affairs of our neighbors. When there were too many clicks, communication to the other party was sometimes dimmed. If there was an emergency, we might have to ask the partyliners to hang up so we could get our message through clearly. But the phone was a means of communication with parties at a distance.

During my high school years, a new invention made distant communication much more possible. The radio had arrived. There still was no rural electrification, so for farmers to enjoy the new invention, they again had to be resourceful. The solution was to mount a small windmill on the roof of the house, which generated enough electricity to charge a battery that would power a small radio. It was magical to sit and listen to broadcasts from ever more distant places. At first, the reception was so poor that we got little more than an identification of the station where the broadcast was coming from. Everyone kept a log of the stations they had tuned in during the evening and exchanged reports with their neighbors the next day. The number and distance of the stations tuned in was the achievement, not what we heard on the program. But soon the reception improved enough that we could begin to benefit by programs of local, national, and world news and by musical programs. This was just the tiny beginning of the technological evolution that would end in the radio and later the TV programs that would knit the world into what Marshall McLuhan later called the global village. As we listened to our squeaky little radio, we had very little suspicion of these communication wonders of the future. And I certainly had not the remotest idea that Marshall McLuhan, who did so much to analyze the effects of this communication miracle that I was experiencing in its absolute infancy, would come into my life as a teacher and the director of my doctoral dissertation.

I spent the last two weeks of my life on the farm in a much more primitive technological task before I left Wisconsin to go to the Jesuit novitiate in Missouri: working on a threshing crew. In those precombine days, threshing was the last step in the long process of harvesting the grain crops. In Wisconsin, that crop was rye because wheat did not do well there. The process started with cutting the rye with a horse-drawn binder, which cut the rye and bound it into neat bundles. These bundles had then to be set up in the field in shocks by hand. At threshing time, the threshing rig, powered by a steam engine, was brought to the farmstead. Neighboring farmers came together to cooperate in the threshing. Some came with teams of horses and hayracks. The shocks of rye in the field were pitched onto the hayracks, brought to the thresher, and pitched by hand into the threshing machine. The thresher separated the grain from the straw and blew the straw into large straw stacks, and the separated grain would then be funneled down into grain sacks. The sacks of grain were hauled directly to market or stored in the granary for winter feeding of the cattle or saved to go on the market when the price might be better. The threshing operation took many hands and was always a communal effort. Neighboring farmers pitched in to supply the manpower and moved from farm to farm with the threshing rig until the threshing was done. My job on the threshing crew during my last two weeks on the farm was working one of the teams and hayracks that brought the bundles in from the field and fed them into the thresher. Threshing was hard work, but it was also a kind of a communal gathering where everybody pitched in to complete the harvest. A very important and pleasant part of the threshing experience was the lavish dinner that the housewives prepared for the threshers. The women vied with one another in providing a cornucopia of home-cooked meals. The wonders of technology that were just beginning when I left the farm would soon eliminate practically every step of the harvesting process I have just described. The tractor-drawn combine would soon cut the grain, thresh it immediately, deposit the grain in a tender, and distribute the straw on the land to fertilize it. The entire process could be accomplished by one man sitting on the tractor. There would be no need of the thresher or of the type of threshing crew in which I spent my last two weeks on the farm.

# 3

# From the Frying Pan
# into the Fire

In 1927, when the threshing season was over, I made final preparations for my departure to St. Louis, Missouri, where I would begin my training as a Jesuit. I was to go to Milwaukee on the Northwestern train for the last time and depart from there with Ed Stumpf and Harold Gibbons for St. Louis. I made a very tearful farewell to Mother and Dad. None of us quite knew what the future would bring. My oldest brother, John, drove me to the Glen Oak station, where I boarded the train for the last time to Milwaukee. As the train pulled out from the station, I felt as if my entire life was slipping away behind me. In a way it was, but in another way it wasn't. The world I was leaving has remained very much with me in the whole of my subsequent life. "In my end *is* my beginning."

I joined Ed Stumpf and Harold Gibbons in Milwaukee for the trip to St. Louis. A fourth young man, Harold McManus, joined us there. He was a graduate of Marquette High School and was also headed for the Jesuit novitiate. His father was the engineer for the great transcontinental luxury train, the *Hiawatha,* on the Milwaukee line between Chicago and the West Coast. He had arranged to be the engineer on the train that took us from Milwaukee to Chicago, where we would catch a Pullman car to St. Louis. The McManus tribe had turned out in huge numbers to bid farewell to Harold, who, in the excitement, almost let the train pull out without him. He ran and hopped onto the platform of the observation car just in time. Mr. McManus had arranged for a late dinner for us in the famous Harvey's Restaurant in Union Station in Chicago. Then it was a night of fitful sleep on the Pullman. We woke up in St. Louis and had breakfast in another Harvey's Restaurant in the St. Louis Union Station. I was immensely impressed with the station, which at that time was one of the busiest in the country. More than two hundred trains a day came and left from it. I had never seen anything like the grand spaces of its interior, especially the magnificent Romanesque Grand Hall, which you could see from Harvey's Restaurant. That impression has not dimmed with the years. After its recent complete restoration, it remains one of the most magnificent Romanesque interiors in the country.

But that impression of magnificence faded quickly once you stepped outside the station into one of the most wretched slums in the whole United States crowding right up to the station. There was no Milles Fountain of the Meeting of the Waters to greet the visitor then. A down-at-heels heavily populated slum stretched uninterruptedly for eighteen blocks all the way out to Grand Avenue. At the turn of the century, this had been the elite residential district in the city. The old houses had Brownstone fronts. But the more affluent residents had moved west and had left behind a clutch of run-down boarding houses. St. Louis at that time was also one of the most polluted cities in the country because of the cheap soft coal available from strip mines in nearby Illinois. Every house and factory in the city belched clouds of pitch-black smoke, and most of the buildings had been blackened with soot. This sight was a disillusioning shock to me, coming as I did from the rural beauty of Wisconsin and from a village that echoed Venice with its lakes, rivers, and canals, all without a smidgen of soot. From the hints of life in Chicago gathered up from the stories of our relatives there and from Jack Smith's accounts, I had built up a rather idealized picture of a city as a kind of beautiful Eldorado. This first glimpse of the heart of one of the big urban centers was certainly a letdown. The disillusionment did not lessen as we drove by taxi through the blocks of slums to St. Louis University, situated on the western end of this slum area. The university, as it was then, did little to dispel the disillusionment. It was a pretty grim-looking institution—and certainly not very extensive. All that was there was the College Church, an impressive Gothic structure, but blackened with soot; what came to be called Dubourg Hall, the administration and classroom building; and Verhaegen and De Smet Halls, which then housed the Jesuit seminarians, all of them also darkened with decades of St. Louis soot. There was no semblance of a campus, no grass, no trees. The community had been founded by Belgian Jesuits, and they had built very much in the manner they were accustomed to in Europe. Buildings were constructed right up to the street, and with only a quadrangle space behind them.

Here the quadrangle was enclosed by a high cement wall, and the space inside the wall was black topped. It looked for all the world like a prison yard. The whole appearance of the place was depressing. Some wags used to say: "St. Louis University is the oldest university west of the Mississippi, and it looks it." It *is* the oldest. It was founded in 1818 by Bishop Dubourg. And the wags were right; it did look its age and then some. Coming from the years at St. Francis Seminary, beautifully situated right on the shores of Lake Michigan on a wooded property of more than two hundred acres, I found my first glimpse of St. Louis University to be something of a shock. My initial thought was, "Maybe Father Riordon was right. If this is the kind of surroundings the Jesuits are content with for their university, perhaps there is something wrong with them." I little thought then, as I stood disheartened at what I was seeing, that I would live to see this university expand its campus to cover more than a hundred acres and, through the vision of several Jesuit presidents, become one of the real beauty spots of the city. I recently spoke to a prospective student who had decided to come to St. Louis University because she thought the campus was so beautiful. I would not have dreamed back in 1928 that anyone would ever be able to say that of this campus.

We were met inside Dubourg Hall by a Jesuit scholastic who was finishing his theological studies at the university. Paul Smith was from Milwaukee. His warm welcome, good nature, and sense of humor were a pleasant diversion from the grimness of the surroundings. He was to be our guide until we arrived at the novitiate in Florissant about twenty miles outside the city.

Paul volunteered to give us a little tour of the city before we went out to Florissant. The one thing we wanted to see was the Mississippi River. We were surprised to find that at that time there was absolutely no place where we could do that conveniently. The city had literally turned its back on the river. The riverfront was a clutter of old factories, warehouses, and run-down business buildings. The actual river's edge was made up of the old cobblestone frontage from steamboat days, and railroad tracks cut right through the frontage. Undaunted, Paul wove his way through the clutter to the cobblestone frontage so we could get our first glimpse of the mighty Mississippi, and in doing so we also saw for the first time the famous and beautiful Eads Bridge. Paul told us it was historical in many ways: it was the first bridge built across the Mississippi carrying both rail and automobile traffic, and the first bridge anywhere built with large sustaining steel arches spanning the space. There was no question about its beauty. I learned much later that Eads, the famous engineer who designed it, had patterned its aesthetic form after a bridge over the Rhine at Koblenz, Germany, which was later destroyed in the Second World War. I also learned later that the double-tiered Romanesque stone arches of the approach to the bridge on either side of the river were inspired by the double-tiered Roman bridge and aqueduct of Pont du Gard in southern France. We didn't need all that information to recognize and enjoy the sheer beauty of the way Eads Bridge leaps across the river in graceful curves.

While we were in the area, Paul struggled through the maze of warehouses to let us see the Old Cathedral, the oldest church in continuous use west of the Mississippi. At the time, it, like St. Louis University, looked it. Architecturally, it is a building that echoes the style of many New England churches, which in turn echo some of those built by Sir Christopher Wren in old London. It is fundamentally done in the Greek Revival style with four massive stone pillars in the Roman Tuscan style supporting a triangular pediment surmounted by a pointed central steeple. The interior is also in the simple Greek Revival style, employing the Roman Tuscan version of the Greek Doric columns in the nave, Ionic columns on the side altars, and Corinthian on the main altar. All these architectural refinements were lost on me at the time, but I did perceive that the design was relatively simple and chaste in contrast to the more exuberant Gothic style with which I was familiar from my home parish church in Montello.

Over the years, the church had been garishly decorated and cluttered with loads of statues. Tasteless stained glass windows had replaced the original clear glass ones. Bishop Rosati had initially chosen the New England style of church as the model for the first cathedral in St. Louis to give it something of an American flavor. Much of that flavor had been lost through the accretion of the years, and the building itself was half hidden in a maze of warehouses and city clutter. At this first glimpse of the down-at-the-heels area and of the Old Cathedral itself, I could not have dreamed in my wildest imagination what this area would become. All of the space between Eads Bridge and the new Poplar Street Bridge—about six blocks long and three blocks wide—has been entirely cleared to make way for the beautiful Federal Park fronting on the river and dominated by what is undoubtedly the most beautiful city monument in the world—the Saarinen Arch, Gateway to the West. The only old building retained in the area is the Old Cathedral. It has been restored to its primitive simplicity and beauty by another famous architect, Joseph Murphy.

The other stop on our little tour of the city that simply awed me was the New Cathedral on Lindell Boulevard. I had certainly never seen anything remotely like it, with its wealth of massive domes on the interior, creating a truly awesome space. It had been dedicated in 1916, but still lacked most of its mosaics, so the interior was largely a vast expanse of raw concrete. The only mosaics were those on the Arch of Triumph, on the arcade around the main altar, and in the Blessed Virgin's Chapel, the All Saints' Chapel, and the Blessed Sacrament Chapel. It would have been inconceivable to me at the time to think that I would live to see every inch of this raw cement space (a space the size of two football fields) completely covered with splendid mosaics. Covering half that much space in St. Mark's in Venice took more than three hundred years. And it would have been the most irresponsible kind of fantasy on my part to have thought that one day I would be on the committee that planned the iconography of the last of the mosaics to be installed and that for seven years I would help to oversee their installation. Nor could I have thought then that I would plan a museum in the basement of this great cathedral that would demonstrate for visitors the process of making mosaics from the design of the artist, through their fabrication and final installation and that would help visitors better understand what they are looking at. What they are looking at is the largest collection of mosaics in any one building in the world. They were all installed in my lifetime. The later educational opportunities that prepared me, a teenager just detached from a threshing crew in Wisconsin, to cooperate in the completion of this great artistic venture is part of my later story.

Sightseeing over, we finally boarded the streetcar for Ferguson, where we transferred to a Toonerville Trolley that rattled through miles of lush farmland to the little depot in Florissant, a small Frenchified village in the middle of the Florissant Valley. At that time, this valley was one of the most fertile stretches of farmland in the country. There was good reason for the name the French villagers gave their town—Florissant (flowering or flourishing). At the time we arrived, it was still a small town, very French in feeling, overlooking the rich Florissant Valley from a little promontory, and dominated by the steeples of its two churches, Sacred Heart and St. Ferdinand's. Both of these churches were still served by Jesuit pastors at the time of our arrival.

We were met at the trolley station by Brother Louie, dressed in his black clericals and driving a primitive Ford Tin Lizzy with straight fenders and a brightly polished brass radiator. We were still about two miles from the novitiate across the Florissant Valley, and we had one more adventure before we arrived there, a blowout. We had to wait while Brother Louie did what everyone had to do in those days when he had a blowout. He removed the inner tube from the tire, vulcanized it, and replaced it. The operation completed, we rattled on and finally arrived at the novitiate compound. It was the closest thing I was ever going to experience to what a traditional medieval monastery must have been like in full swing.

Central to the compound was its oldest building: a handsome, three-story, solid limestone structure with walls three feet thick, pierced by windows shaded with green shutters. The front entrance was a flight of stairs leading up to the second floor, in the European manner, culminating in a Palladian-like porch. The building was topped by an open-domed bell tower in which the bell was mounted that would soon be summoning us from morning to night to our regimented duties. As we pulled up to the picket fence in front of the old building, Father Krenz, the master of novices, was there to greet us. He identified himself and said presciently to the three of us: "Welcome, and I am glad that you are all now in the right place." We only later understood what he may have meant by that. He, like us, had had his seminary training at St. Francis Seminary. He had actually gone on through the complete seminary program and was ordained a diocesan priest, but then decided to become a Jesuit. His Jesuit training was very much shortened. After his novitiate and a few years of teaching, he was made novice master. I presume he felt he was in the right place and was suggesting that we had finally arrived there, too. What we soon discovered was that he had carried a great deal of the *Gymnasium* atmosphere of St. Francis Seminary with him and superimposed it on the stringent regimen developed by the Belgians who had founded the Missouri Province of the Society of Jesus. The result was every bit as militaristic a way of life as the one we had left at St. Francis. Father Krenz's first name was Leo (lion), and we soon found out the appropriateness of that name. We augmented it later to read Leo the Lionhearted, a sobriquet that perhaps suited him even better.

I soon discovered that I had left a five-hundred-acre farm in Wisconsin to take up residence on an eleven-hundred-acre farm in Missouri. That's what St. Stanislaus Novitiate was. It came into the possession of the Jesuits in a very interesting way. The diocese of Bishop Dubourg, centered at New Orleans, extended over the entire area of the Louisiana Purchase. St. Louis was at its northern extreme. Bishop Dubourg, back in 1818, recognized the future importance of St. Louis in the development of the Midwest and in the whole westward movement, so he took up residence in the small village for two years and replaced the little chapel that had been built near the river with a large church that became the first cathedral of the burgeoning city. It was built on the exact site where the Old Cathedral stands today. There were still many Native Americans in the area at the time, so Bishop Dubourg decided to build a school next to his church for the Native American children. But very soon they were pushed westward by the French settlers, and there were no Native American children to teach. The school became available for the children of the French settlers, but the bishop had no teachers for his school. He had heard of a group of Belgian Jesuits who had set up a school in Maryland to train young Belgian Jesuit seminarians for work among the Native Americans. He invited them to come out and take over his school. If they agreed, he said he would give them the farm he had acquired near the village of Florissant, where they could set up their training center for young Jesuits. It was an offer the Belgian group in Maryland could not turn down. All eleven of them packed up their belongings on wagons and started the long trek by foot, wagon, and river barges to Missouri. They took possession of the farm and built a little log cabin on the premises as the first novitiate. While that was in the building, they were given hospitality by Mother Philippine Duchesne, a religious of the Sacred Heart who had established a convent of her order in the little village of Florissant. The small log cabin was soon supplanted by the fine Old Rock Building, in front of which Father Krenz had just welcomed us to the novitiate. It was built in the 1840s, long before the Civil War and, we were told, with the assistance of slave labor. In fact, we were also told that the little hotel-like building, which in our time housed the lay workmen, had been the slave quarters before the Civil War.

This eleven-hundred-acre farm that Bishop Dubourg had given to the Jesuits was laid out in the French manner—with long and narrow lots. It was only about a half-mile wide but about four miles long, stretching from what is now Lindbergh Boulevard all the way to the Missouri River. The reason for this odd shaping of French farms was to cut down the distance that farm villagers would have to walk to their fields. French farmers did not live on their farmlands. They lived in villages and went out to their fields to work. The Jesuits at St. Stanislaus, of course, lived on the land, but they also positioned their residence in the center of the long strip of land to cut down the distance of going out to work in the fields. From the beginning, the farm provided the largest part of the income for their support. And that was still true when I arrived there.

Some of the land had been set aside as woodlands and grazing land for the large herd of dairy cattle. A great deal of it was taken up with grain crops—wheat and corn—and in the fifty acres immediately adjacent to the living quarters was a grape vineyard that provided the grapes for the winery where both Mass and table wine were made. There was a large orchard of apple and peach trees. I had never seen a peach tree before, and never since have I seen anything like the huge, lush peaches that these well-tended trees produced. Adjacent to the orchard was a large five-acre vegetable garden that provided vegetables of all kinds for the community. This setup looked pretty familiar to me, but on a much larger scale than I had experienced before.

The buildings, as I said, had been placed in the exact center of the long strip of farmland. A public road cut through the middle of the compound. On one side were the farm buildings: a huge dairy barn, silos, machine shops, and the workmen's hotel. Towering up on that side of the road was the huge water tank, filled by pumping water from a creek in the nearby woods. This tank supplied most of the water needs of the community. Across the road were the novitiate buildings themselves. I have already described the oldest and most attractive one—the Old Rock Building. Behind it was the main novitiate building, connected to the rock building by a long bridge. To the right of the novitiate building was a building that housed the infirmary and rooms for the faculty. To the left of it was the building that housed the juniorate that provided the living quarters and class-rooms for the juniors, or Jesuit collegiate students, for their two years of college work after completing the novitiate. The newest building was adjacent to the old novitiate and contained the beautiful chapel with the refectory below it and an auditorium or little theater below that. All these structures were connected to one another by bridges, so in our regimented life we were crossing bridges all day. To one side of this central compound of buildings was a grouping of auxiliary structures that included a creamery, a laundry, a cobbler's shop, a carpenter shop, a printer's shop, a blacksmith shop, and, most promi-nently, a winery where the grapes were pressed, the juice fermented, and the wine bottled for marketing. In the next two years, we were to become very familiar with all these places and buildings because a great deal of our time in the novitiate was spent in manual labor.

After Father Krenz welcomed us to the fold, he turned us over to our guardian angel, a second-year novice appointed to be with us for the next seven days to familiarize us with the physical layout of the institution, to explain the order of the day we would be following once we had been formally admitted, and to begin following some of that order on a kind of dry run. During these preliminary days, Father Krenz gave us several conferences in which he outlined for us the spiritual, apostolic, and educational aims of the Society. He made it perfectly clear that if we did not feel that we could willingly dedi-cate our lives to fulfilling those objectives, we were at perfect liberty to pick up our things, right then, and go home. I don't recall that any of the sixty-five neophytes did so right then, although approximately fifteen of them did pull up stakes before the two years of the novitiate were completed.

Those introductory days over, we were given our cassocks, full-length black gowns bound by a cincture at the waist. They were not habits; Jesuits do not wear distinctive habits as Benedictines, Domin-icans, and Franciscans do. St. Ignatius suggested that his followers adopt whatever form of garment diocesan priests wore in the country or area in which they worked. This simple cassock became a kind of second skin for us. We wore it continually, except when we were doing manual work inside or outside the house—when we donned a company issued *manualia* jacket. In recreational games, we could wear more casual clothing. And there were a variety of games—softball, soccer, and especially handball. Both soccer and handball were new to me. I avoided softball and soccer because of my physical disability, but I learned to like handball and did fairly well playing it.

Play, however, was a very small part of our day—in fact, no part of many days. We had a rigid daily regime that was very much like the one with which I had become familiar in the seminary. We arose at five o'clock, had a half hour for our morning toilet and a first visit to the chapel, then an hour's meditation at our desks in the study hall, daily Mass and Communion in the chapel, and then breakfast— almost the same regime as at St. Francis Seminary. My biggest surprise was our first breakfast. In the first place, it was not in a barrackslike refectory, as at the seminary, but in a large lightsome dining room with tables *and chairs* accommodating the whole community of novices, juniors, brothers, faculty, and administrators— more than two hundred at the time. The room was attractive, light, and airy, decorated with a fine large oil reproduction of Leonardo da Vinci's *Last Supper* stretching all across the wall behind the faculty head table and two very fine full-length oils of St. Ignatius and St. Francis Xavier. But remembering our austere breakfasts of dry bread and malt drink at the seminary, I was amazed at what was wheeled out for our first breakfast—generous slices of watermelon, huge pieces of hot cornbread, and bowls of fresh beef stew. I learned that the latter combination was almost a signature of Jesuit cuisine in the Missouri Province. That was just an introduction to what would prove to be a very substantial, varied, and well-cooked diet at St. Stanislaus. Most of the food came from the extensive novitiate farm itself. We were to become very familiar with where it came from because in our *manualia* (hand work) periods, which took up about a third of each novitiate weekday, we helped produce it.

A second-year novice was appointed beadle or prefect of the group, and one of his chief duties was assigning us to our daily duties. The novices did a lot of work that helped get the food on the table, including labor in the creamery, in the bakery, in the kitchen, in the vegetable garden, and in the dining room itself—washing dishes and resetting the tables. The novices also did much of the daily cleaning. There were hierarchies in these daily tasks. The least-dignified task was cleaning the many toilets. Because of the importance of keeping these toilets really clean, an individual novice was appointed for an extended time to oversee that work. We called him *rex castellarum* (king of the castles—because "castles" is what we called the cans).

When he was appointed, we had a coronation ceremony at evening recreation in which he was crowned with the top of a chamber pot and given a rubber plunger as his scepter. His permanent assistants we dubbed *principes castellarum* (princes of the castles). Their insignia were scrub brushes and a can of Old Dutch Cleanser. If the *rex castellarum* was at the bottom of the hierarchy of permanent appointments, the sacristans were at the top of it. The necessity of preparing for some twenty private Masses in side chapels each day as well as for the community liturgies at the main altar and of decorating the altar for Sundays and feast days demanded considerable continuity, so the novices appointed to the sacristan's duties escaped the constant shifting from one *manualia* task after another and from some of the harder work that many of the other assignments entailed. For some reason unknown to me, I landed the head sacristan's job.

We soon learned that the novitiate was run in a rather militaristic manner under Leo the Lionhearted as commander in chief. His own German background and personality gave him a very militaristic view of life. I always presumed that he had been born and raised in Prussia. I asked him one day what part of Germany he came from. "What do you mean?" he snapped back. "Germany! I come from Peoria." Peoria or not, he had all the qualities of a German army officer. He lived in a world of absolutes. He could and did make perfectly clear what the ideals of Jesuit spirituality and living were, and he expected us to accept them and live up to them without question. There was very little coddling of the individual. His own native instincts had been reinforced, I think, by his training at St. Francis Seminary, and he stepped into the Missouri Province of the Society of Jesus, which had also been formed by a rather militaristic regime imported from Europe by its Belgian founders. Because Father Krenz had such a short number of years in the Society before he was made master of novices, he never had the opportunity of having his hard corners rubbed off by some of the realities of life in the Society. It was said of Father Krenz that he was so severe in the way he presented his view of life that he could make a meditation on devotion to the Sacred Heart sound like a meditation on hell. It was true. But we soon learned to laugh off his thundering pronouncements. They were sometimes so exaggerated that they became ridiculous and therefore humorous, and for that reason ultimately bearable.

I remember that I was occasionally the object of one of his blasts.

One of our spiritual exercises was a quiet reading of Rodriquez, a classical writer on the spiritual life. His work combined a rather thorough discussion of certain principles of the spiritual life with a list of events supposedly from real life that confirmed the principles. The examples were sometimes hilariously unlikely and provided a little comic relief in our lives. One day, perched up on the back porch of the novitiate and leaning against a post four feet off the ground, I fell asleep reading my Rodriguez, tumbled off the porch, and almost broke my neck. I thought that this fall might have been punishment enough, but the novice beadle (or prefect) who was reading his Rodriquez in the neighborhood didn't think so. He reported my delinquency to Father Krenz. I received a note that read *"Pater Krenz vult loqui tecum."* I went to his room in fear and trembling. He looked up at me over his glasses and said: "I understand, *carissime,* that you fell asleep this morning during Rodriquez." "Yes," I said, "I have that difficulty." "Difficulty!" he snapped back, "You don't even try. You say 'All for the greater honor and glory of God' and then go to sleep. I see you, even in my conferences, sometimes nodding off to sleep." He was right on all counts, but it was an example of his no-compromising approach to all situations in the spiritual life. And, incidentally, the term *carissime* (dearest)—used in greeting one another in Latin in the novitiate—always sounded a little strained on the lips of Leo the Lionhearted.

Latin was the language we had to use if we addressed one another during the day—when we were supposed to be keeping silence. We could speak English during recreation periods, but some evenings the beadle would break into our conversation and announce, *"Separatio Latina"* (Latin separation), which meant that we had to separate into groups of three and converse in Latin for the rest of the recreation period. This emphasis on Latin was, of course, a preparation for our many years of the study of philosophy and theology in Latin texts. The examinations in these subjects would also be in Latin. So, willy-nilly, we had to learn to communicate in Latin. You may be sure, however, that Cicero would not have recognized the Latin spoken on these *separationes Latinae.*

I have noted previously that I thought the severe militaristic regime that we were subjected to in our novitiate was an inheritance of Father Krenz's own training at St. Francis Seminary and a tradition that had been imported from Belgium by the Belgian Jesuits who founded the province. One indication of the latter influence was the customs book, which was read to us periodically. It was meant to give us helpful hints about the proper conduct of a Jesuit in all kinds of circumstances. Some of the helpful hints were such that we knew they were translations of pointers meant for young Jesuits in Belgium. For instance, there were very exact instructions on how to eat an artichoke. I don't think any of us had ever seen an artichoke, but if we ever did, we knew how to eat one. There was also a caution to be observed in going on long walks. We were not to climb big trees or bend down small ones. There was a long list of things about which we might talk during recreation, but we were not to talk about the virtues or vices of other Jesuits unless they were dead or absent. Some of these suggestions seemed so odd to us that they generated a giggle when we first heard them—a levity not appreciated by the powers that were.

Father Krenz, Leo the Lionhearted, was rigid, stern, and unremitting in the way he enforced the rules or customs. And his assistant, Father Zamiara, or *socius*, as he was called, was equally so. We had no refuge to fly to. Father Zamiara hewed to the letter of the law with a stoutness that matched that of the master. He had his rules to follow, too, and he followed them strictly. One directive for the *socius* to the master of novices indicated that if he found one of the novices guilty of some aberration, he should exercise him in actions that would counteract it. I have mentioned that I had been appointed head sacristan, which was considered one of the most privileged appointments a novice could get. It excused him from many other *manualia* tasks that were much more difficult physically and often rather messy. I was glad to have the position because it acquainted me intimately with the liturgy and with every detail of the liturgical vestments and vessels. I had no idea then how important this knowledge would be much later in my adopted second career as an art historian.

My intimate knowledge of the liturgical vestments learned in my sacristan days prompted me to call attention to the ubiquity of vestments of the subministers of a Solemn High Mass as the garb of angels in Early Netherlandish paintings and their eucharistic significance there—a detail that has changed the interpretation of many Early Netherlandish paintings. It is a detail that art historians had missed in the past and that I would probably have missed, too, had I not become so familiar with them in my work as sacristan. This is another example of how much of my beginning remains in my end.

But in my beginning Father Zamiara thought my position as head sacristan might have gone to my head—that I might be getting a little vain or proud—so it was his duty, he felt, to see to it that I would be practiced in the opposite virtue of humility. That virtue might be achieved by some humiliation. He called me to his room one day and said, "Will you please kneel down and kiss the floor?" A little amazed, I did so. When I stood up, he went on: "I am afraid that you may be getting a little vain about your position as head sacristan, so I have decided to remove you for a time from the office and send you into a second probation in the scullery." Probation was an exercise that all novices went through to test their adaptability to change of assignments. The probation, or "proving," consisted in the novice's being taken out of his regular routine and being sent to live with the brothers for a week or two and assigned to work for one of them in some capacity.

The *probatio,* as it functioned in the novitiate in my time, I really believe involved a kind of class distinction in the community that was a leftover from the European background of the Belgian founders of the province. The large community was divided into several segments: the faculty, the juniors (or collegiates), the novices, and the lay brothers. Each division was physically separated from the others. There were special days during the year when there was a *fusion* of the several groups, but other than that they worked, recreated, and slept separate from one another. All came together in the same dining room for meals, but each group in their separate assigned places. Father Rector had his reserved place at the head of the head table.

This hierarchical order was much more exaggerated in Europe than it was here in the States. I recall coming down to breakfast the first morning as a guest at the Collège St. Michelle in Brussels in 1955 and entering through the first of the three doors of the dining room—the one nearest the stairs I had just descended. One of my Belgian confreres reminded me there that we didn't enter through that door; it was reserved for Father Rector. And when I was a guest for a year in the English Jesuit novitiate at Roehampton in London, I noticed that the lay brothers didn't eat in the same dining room with the rest of the community, but in a room by themselves. On feast days, the father minister (a kind of plant manager in a Jesuit community) would eat with the brothers as a special favor to them. There really was something of that old-world class distinction that still remained in the novitiate in the segregation between the various groups in the community and especially in the attitude toward the brothers. Hence, separating a novice from his own group and sending him to live and work with the brothers all day were meant to be a *probatio* or trial in humility. I don't think any of us novices thought of it that way. I know I certainly didn't.

The brothers were doing wonderful work of all kinds that made the institution function very efficiently. One brother oversaw the extensive farm and dairy herd, and others completely manned or managed the orchard, the vineyard and winery, the vegetable garden, the extensive landscaped grounds and greenhouse, the kitchen and bakery, the dining room, the laundry, the print shop, and the cobbler's shop. They all came from very different backgrounds and brought considerable know-how and skills to their various tasks. So working, living, and conversing with the brothers for a spell was a very interesting diversion for us novices. Only a class-oriented viewpoint would consider it a *probatio*, a training in humility, but I'm sure that is what Father Zamiara considered he was sending me into when he assigned me to kitchen *probatio* during the Christmas holidays, especially because kitchen *probatio* involved washing all the pots and pans accumulated in the big kitchen every day. What Father Zamiara did not know was that I didn't consider washing pots and pans very humiliating. I had spent a great deal of my life at home washing pots and pans, and hadn't found it particularly humiliating. Nor did I find it humiliating to associate with Brother Alex, the jolly, roly-poly, Polish head cook, and his German assistant, Brother Housman, a former engineer. It was fun.

Another thing that Father Zamiara had not taken into account was the fact that in the kitchen Bill Ulrich and I would have access all through the holidays to the walk-in refrigerators packed with candy, nuts, and other *dulcia* sent to the community for the holidays. I don't know what virtue Bill Ulrich was supposed to be developing in his second *probatio*, but I know that we both had a great Christmas vacation together there.

Under a later administration, a new type of probation was introduced: hospital probation. One or two novices at a time were sent into old St. Mary's Hospital in St. Louis, managed by the St. Mary's nuns, to function as orderlies. The hospital was run for the care of the very poor, so here the novices had the opportunity of combining the spiritual prayer life in which they were being trained with a real-life active service of the sick poor, the kind of combined prayer life and activity they would be expected to carry on in their later lives. This kind of probation was more meaningful than the kind of artificial probations that were created for us in our novitiate days. It also was much closer to the probations the very early Jesuits experienced. The Jesuit St. Stanislaus Kostka, now patron saint of all novices, died of the plague, which he contracted while nursing the plague stricken in Rome.

I had another experience with our *socius*, Father Zamiara, which I thought revealed a strange bias on his part. Someone usually read aloud at table during lunch and dinner—a rather helpful custom. It eliminated the necessity of *making* conversation at table, and the books were very informative. Some of the most important ones read during my stay at Florissant included a discussion of the Jesuit missionary activity in Zambizi, Africa; a life of Mother Cabrini; Father Broderick's *Life of Cardinal Bellarmine;* Evelyn Waugh's *Life of Edmund Campion;* and a volume of Pastor's *Lives of the Popes.* The juniors (collegiate students) did the reading. Another benefit of this public reading was what it did to improve our pronunciation. One of the fathers was appointed as official *repetator.* If the reader mispronounced a name or other word, the *repetator* would interrupt with his *repetat* (let it be repeated). He would give the right pronunciation, and the reader would have to repeat the sentence with the right pronunciation of the word. This practice educated the whole community in pronunciation. I have known university professors who could have benefited by this kind of training in correct pronunciation. The reading at table was sometimes interrupted by homilies prepared by the juniors on an assigned passage of Scripture or by novices in what was called a Marianum, or an account of an impressive event that had benefited by the intercessory power of the Blessed Virgin. Both the homilies and the Mariana were meant to give the juniors and novices early experience in the pulpit. It was a rather artificial arena for such experience because I cannot think of a more unsympathetic congregation than a dining room full of young Jesuits eating their dinner.

The early Mariana I had experienced were rather conventional timeworn stories about Mary's successful intercession for ardent devotees. When my turn came to write one, I decided to use a little more originality. I remembered a little poem by the actress Cornelia Otis Skinner that Father Riordon had contributed to our commonplace book and had us memorize. Cornelia was not a Catholic, but she had some friends who were. She said she envied her Catholic friends their tender devotion to Mary. In that mood, she wrote this little poem:

> Lady most serenely fair
> Hear an unbeliever's prayer.
> Nurtured in an austere creed,
> Sweetest Lady, she has need
> Of the solace of your love,
> You, whom no one taught her of.

I thought that was a beautiful sentiment, so I invented the conversion of Cornelia to the faith through her devotion to Mary. I wrote up my Marianum and took it over to Father Zamiara to correct. He said it was interesting and well written, but I couldn't give it. I asked why, thinking he might have suspected my invention. But his answer was, "You can't give it because it is about a woman." Amazed at this reason, I reminded Father that Mary, whom we were supposed to be honoring in our Mariana, was also a woman and that Wordsworth had called her "Human nature's solitary boast." But Father was insistent. I tried another tack. I said I could make the main character a man. "That would not do," Father insisted, "because that would be tampering with the historicity of the story." I couldn't tell him that I had already done that with irresponsible abandon, so I agreed to work up another Marianum. Father's strange scruple about delivering a Marianum in which the main character was a woman in the sacred precinct of the cloister *did* save me from flaunting a completely unhistorical episode in the life of Cornelia Otis Skinner. The Marianum I eventually delivered had to do with the powerful intercessory powers of the Blessed Virgin when implored by a convent of nuns in New Orleans, who prayed for the success of a battle led by General Packingham in the War of 1812. Father Zamiara approved my second try. I was rather surprised because some of the main characters in this story were also women. I took my story and ran with it and delivered it in the dining room pulpit with as much verve as I could muster.

I have given a rather negative view of my novitiate experience thus far, highlighting its regimentation. Actually that was only a peripheral element, and we all had a sufficient sense of humor to laugh it off. Beneath that strictly structured surface, however, was the heart and substance of the novitiate training: a very thorough introduction to Jesuit spirituality, which is based solidly on the *Spiritual Exercises* of St. Ignatius. Our two years of novitiate training gave us ample opportunity, with very few distractions, to experience those *Exercises* to the fullest. Early in the first year, we made the thirty-day retreat that embraces the *Exercises* in their entirety. The eight-day retreat in the second year was a condensed version of them; and the several days of recollection and daily meditations throughout the two years were based on sections of the *Exercises*. Father Krenz had a deep knowledge of the *Exercises*, and in the retreats, conferences, and points for meditations he shared with us his knowledge of and enthusiasm for them.

St. Ignatius, at the beginning of the *Exercises*, discusses what he calls the principle and foundation of the spiritual life. A principle is some truth from which everything that follows logically flows, and a foundation is that basic part of a building that supports everything above it. The principle and foundation of our spiritual lives, as St. Ignatius sees it, is the fact of creation—the fact that God created me, personally, and everything in the universe as well. The fact that I owe to God my very existence and all the things that sustain that existence makes me a creature of God, with an obligation to recognize His authority, to show Him obedience, reverence, and gratitude. But also part of the basic truth about God and myself is the fact that God's creation of me was an entirely unselfish act on His part. He had nothing to gain for Himself by creating me. He made me as an intelligent, conscious being in order that He might have someone with whom He could share His infinite truth, goodness, and beauty. He manifests Himself in countless ways in the world He created. He asks us to recognize Him in His creation, to do His will, and thus gain an eternal life with Him in heaven. By creating us as free creatures, He knew He was taking a risk; free creatures can abuse their freedom and make wrong choices for selfish reasons. That's what sin is. That is what Adam and Eve did; that's what we all do when we sin. Given our waywardness and our selfishness, God could have left us to our own devices and given up on us as a bad job. But He didn't. Unbelievably, He sent His own Divine Son down to become one of us, to suffer and die for our redemption, to prove once more the extent and the depth of His love for each one of us. God designed the resurrection of His Son from the dead, His many appearances in His glorified body, and the final Ascension into heaven to make clear to each of us the measure of His love for each one of us, His forgiveness of our sins, and the glorious destiny that is still ours if we will accept His love and forgiveness. This is the almost unbelievable story of God's love and mercy. "Greater love than this no man hath than that a man lay down his life for his friend."

The Incarnation of the Son of God, his becoming one of us from birth to death, creates a new foundation for our spiritual lives. It brings God much closer to us; we no longer look upon God as merely our Creator who rules the world He has created in majesty and power. We now see Him as a loving Father who loves us so much that, even when we have wandered away from Him in sin, He sends His own Son to become one of us and to suffer and die for our redemption. The Incarnation cuts down the distance between ourselves and God. The poet Hopkins says that by reason of the Incarnation the blinding light of the Godhead has been "sifted to suit our sight." Because the Eternal Son of God became man, we can look into the human eyes of Christ and know that we are looking into the eyes of God. We no longer have to think of God reigning in heaven on an eternal throne or appearing amidst thunder and lightning on Mount Sinai or in the burning bush. We see him, a human very like ourselves, being born, being nursed, being rushed off to Egypt to escape Herod's persecution; working in a carpenter shop; eventually preaching to his Apostles, but eating, drinking, and fishing with them like any other human being; and eventually suffering and dying on the Cross. This certainly does cut down the distance between ourselves and God. That is one of the mercies of the Incarnation. It is true, too, of course, that we see this same Christ working miracles, healing the sick, multiplying the loaves and the fishes, walking on the waters, raising the dead to life, and himself ultimately rising from the tomb and ascending into heaven. Coming to grips intellectually and emotionally with this double nature—human and divine—of Christ is what the *Spiritual Exercises* of St. Ignatius are meant to accomplish. That is why two-thirds of the *Exercises* consist of meditations on the life of Christ.

Father Krenz did a superb job of helping us penetrate the significance of the many episodes from the life of Christ that were the subject of our meditations in the retreat and in the daily meditation we made throughout the two years of the novitiate. The purpose of the *Spiritual Exercises* is really to bring the retreatant to a personal knowledge and love of Christ. They conclude with a "Contemplation for Obtaining Love." That contemplation is a recapitulation for the retreatant of all the things that God has done for him in the natural order of creation by bringing him into existence and giving him all that is needed to sustain that life and in the supernatural order of grace: his adoptive sonship in redemption from sin through the Incarnation of God's Divine Son and the whole sacramental system that enables him to overcome his weakness and win him final eternal happiness in heaven. All of this is seen as an outpouring of God's love for each of us individually. Love begets love, so in the face of all this continued manifestation of God's love for us at every turn of our lives we would be strange creatures and strange sons and daughters, indeed, if we did not want to return that love—and with a love that shows itself in deeds and not just words. This is the climax of the Ignatian *Spiritual Exercises*. St. Ignatius meant all of the preceding exercises to be a preparation for it. But we fall in love with people not abstract ideas. The many meditations on the life of Christ that precede the "Contemplation for Obtaining Love" are meant to make Christ as real as possible to the retreatant so Christ will be seen as someone lovable, a person for whom we would like to do something to prove that love. To achieve a sense of reality in dealing with Christ, St. Ignatius devised the three-step meditation: applying first the senses and imagination, then the intellect, and finally the will to the subject being meditated.

St. Ignatius was of the opinion that to make Christ lovable we had to make him as real as possible—hence, the importance of the application of the senses to make any scene from the life of Christ as vivid as possible. St. Ignatius says, for instance, that in meditating on the nativity we should *see* the cave, vividly, and *see* Joseph and Mary preparing the manger-crib for the Christ child about to be born. He pictures a servant girl attending to the donkey on which Mary rode. He also asks us to *feel* the cold and the rough straw of the manger. We are asked to use our other senses as well, to *hear* the song of the angels. When the subject being meditated is an abstract rather than a concrete historical incident in the life of Christ, St. Ignatius asks the exercitant to employ his imagination to make the idea concretely real.

Once the episode from the life of Christ or the spiritual idea being meditated has been made vividly present by the application of the memory or the five senses or both, the exercitant is to proceed to the second step, which is the application of the *intellect* to the subject being meditated upon, and ask himself what is its special relevance to his own spiritual life. And then the meditation moves on finally to some exercise of the *will* in which the exercitant comes to a practical resolution of some kind of action in his own life. The meditation concludes with the exercitant's colloquy or prayer to God for the grace to carry out his resolution into action.

We, as callow novices, knew practically nothing about this programmatic structure of an Ignatian meditation, and Father Krenz spent little time discussing it. What he did was march us through the process over and over again as he guided us through the dozens of meditations during the long retreat.

With details from Scripture, from other literary and artistic sources, and from his own imagination, he brought the scenes from the life of Christ alive for us as we had never experienced them before. In the thirty days of the retreat, the entire range of the episodes from the life of Christ in the many meditations on his life did bring Christ vividly to us as a person. We could see, too, why we needed the extended time of a month to do it. We were learning how to meditate by doing rather than by theorizing about it. What we learned by doing would be a permanent help to us in our prayer life far beyond the novitiate. With Father Krenz's help, we had come to see that the health of our prayer lives and of our religious lives in general would depend on how effectively we kept Christ as the vivid personal focus of our lives.

It was this focus on the place of Jesus in the lives of his followers that induced St. Ignatius to insist on calling the religious order he founded not the Society of Ignatius Loyola, but the Society of Jesus.

The prolonged meditation throughout the novitiate on all that God the Father and His Incarnate Divine Son have done for each one of us naturally induced the desire to make some return to God for all this generosity—the desire to dedicate our lives in some capacity to God. St. Ignatius gives beautiful expression to this generous sentiment in the *Suscipe* prayer he appends to the "Contemplation for Obtaining Love" in the *Exercises*.

"Take, Lord, and receive all my liberty, my memory, my understanding, and all my will—all that I have and possess. You, Lord, have given all that to me. I now give it back to you, O Lord. All of it is yours. Dispose of it according to your will. Give me your love and your grace, for that is enough for me." Love begets love, and the gifts of love inspire gifts in return.

This sentiment that concludes the *Spiritual Exercises* is also the sentiment that fills the heart of a novice at the end of his novitiate. In the vows he takes, he has the opportunity of making a real gift of his future self to God in return for all that God has done for him. His vows of chastity, poverty, and obedience are a complete surrender of his entire self to God. For the Jesuit, these vows are for life. In many orders, the first vows are temporary. Final perpetual vows are taken later. But for the Jesuit, his first vows are for life, perpetual. If he ever wishes to leave the Society later, he has to be dispensed from his vows. St. Ignatius was of the mind that after the training of the novitiate, the novice should be ready to make a final decision and final commitment to Christ in his vows. In the vow of chastity, he gives up the privileges and joys of a family, but his life is not to be without love: he substitutes his love for Christ and his love for the people of God. Free of the obligations of a family, he can serve God's people more completely. In the vow of poverty, he surrenders the right to private property, to money, and to the power and pleasures that money can bring. But freed from the pressure of the business world, he is free to devote all his energies to the service of God and his neighbor. In the vow of obedience, he surrenders some of his freedom of choice in career and activities, but by doing so he makes himself a more malleable instrument for the realization of the apostolic purposes of the Church and the Society.

So in this generous spirit of surrendering our entire selves to God in the Society, I and my fellow novices took our vows during Mass in the chapel of St. Stanislaus Novitiate on December 8, 1930, the Feast of the Immaculate Conception of Our Lady. As was the custom, the *Suscipe* (take and receive) in Latin, beautifully set to music by the Jesuit composer, Louis Lambillotte, was sung by a soloist when we had each pronounced our vows. We were now full-fledged Jesuits.

We soon moved from the novitiate to the juniorate to begin the next step in our Jesuit training.

Our daily order in the novitiate was pretty well confined to prayer, spiritual reading, and manual labor. We had only one academic class—in Latin. Our Latin teacher was Father Mijeres, a Mexican Jesuit exiled from Mexico by the revolutionary government. He himself had been imprisoned for some time. He had many stories about his experiences in Mexico during the revolution before being expelled from the country. In prison, he was permitted visits from some members of his family, but, of course, he was not allowed to function as a priest. His family was allowed to do his laundry for him, so they would bring him a consecrated host hidden in a clean sock so that he could receive Communion himself and, when possible, share a part of the host with a fellow prisoner. Father Mijeres was a delightful, refined individual who enlivened our novitiate experience. We were amused by his pleasant Mexican accent. Because we did not see the newspaper or have access to any other news source, Father Mijeres became something of a weekly gazette for us, providing some news of what was happening in the outside world. One day he came to class and announced that we were going to spend the whole class on a study of the Latin preposition *pro.* He then proceeded to tell us the story of one of his former Mexican students named Father Pro. Since the revolution, which had either executed or exiled Catholic priests, Father Pro, like Edmund Campion and other Jesuits in Elizabethan times in England, had assumed a disguise and continued to administer the sacraments to the faithful in secret. He posed as a traveling salesman. Nattily dressed, he moved about presumably making his sales, but actually offering Mass in hidden places and administering the sacraments. But, as happened to Edmund Campion in England, Father Pro's clandestine apostolate was discovered by the revolutionary authorities. He was apprehended and, Father Mijeres told us at the end of his account, was shot by a firing squad on that very morning when Father Mijeres was telling the story. Father Mijeres ended his story with a prayer not *pro* Padre Pro but *to* Padre Pro. Father Pro has since been canonized as a modern martyr of the faith.

# 4

# College Days—The Juniorate

MOST OF THE YOUNG MEN who entered the Society in my time came directly from high school, so when the novitiate was completed, they began their collegiate training. It consisted of two years called the juniorate, devoted largely to the humanities: Latin, Greek, European history, English literature, and some mathematics. The juniorate was followed by three years devoted to the study of philosophy and the sciences. If an individual scholastic had finished college before he came, he might go directly into the juniorate after the first year of the novitiate. He was called a "skull cap" because he didn't wear the biretta that the juniors wore. In the early Society, he probably would have worn a skullcap at meals. In early days, everyone wore some head covering because of the unheated dining rooms, but skullcaps were the exception in my time. The juniorate years were spent at St. Stanislaus Seminary at Florissant, Missouri, and the years devoted to philosophy and science at St. Louis University in St. Louis.

The juniorate as we knew it was a kind of fossilized remains of the traditional Collegium Jesuiticum. The Jesuit College was not what we think of as a college today but closer to our four-year high school and the first two years of college. Graduates of this *collegium* went on into public careers of various kinds or to the university. The training in this traditional *collegium* was very much centered on Latin. The aim was to produce individuals who could write Latin well and deliver a Latin oration. The rhetoric class was where this training took place, and note—the rhetoric taught had to do with persuasive writing and speaking in Latin. There was no such training in vernacular languages in a Jesuit college or in any other college, for that matter. The vernacular language and literature did not become a part of the curriculum in any of the schools until well into the nineteenth century, so the emphasis on Latin in the Jesuit juniorate as the center of the curriculum had a very old precedent in the Jesuit educational tradition and in educational tradition in general.

This emphasis on Latin, of course, served the practical purpose for us Jesuit scholastics of preparing us for our later study of philosophy and theology, where all the texts and examinations would be in Latin. Another very important benefit of our studying Latin was the confident sense of the exact meaning of the words in our own language that were derived from Latin.

As I look back on the way the Latin literature we studied was taught, I feel that it did not contribute greatly to our literary sensitivities. It was largely a matter of gerund grinding. The works we studied included *Orations* by Cicero, some of the odes of both Horace and Virgil, and the *Eclogues* of Virgil, selections from the historians Livy and Tacitus, and selections from Virgil's *Aeneid,* with an emphasis on the fourth book. We were asked to work out our own translations of the works we were studying. In class sessions, we translated a passage in rotation around the class with the teacher correcting our errors. I do not recall spending a great deal of time discussing the literary qualities of what we were reading. Occasionally in small works, such as the odes of Horace, some attention was given to the importance of the sentiment being expressed by the poet and the appropriateness of the language, imagery, and rhythm by which he expressed it. But for the most part our Latin contact was confined to the humdrum task of translation. In the case of Virgil's *Aeneid,* the approach was such that there was almost a guarantee that we would not get an idea of what Virgil was doing in his great epic poem. We read only a section of book four, which deals with the story of Dido. We had no opportunity of reading the other parts to see how the Dido episode fits into the general theme and dramatic sweep of the epic poem as a whole. No translations were available to us. In fact, any translations that existed were firmly locked up in a room we called Gehenna or the hell of forbidden books: the translations were consigned to hell lest we use them as cribs in our task of translating the fourth book. I'm sure our sympathies were all for Dido, as were those of St. Augustine, who said he wept for her at the cold-hearted manner in which Aeneas left her to her suicidal fate as he went about his business of founding the new Troy. We had no idea that neither Virgil nor the Romans in general would have wept for her. They would have seen her as a serious hindrance to Aeneas's duty to fulfill the commission of the gods to found a new Troy no matter what the cost to himself. That is why Virgil called him *pius* Aeneas—*pius,* a dutiful

Roman, devoted to the service of the gods, the state, and the family. It was only in a later encounter with the *Aeneid* that I discovered what the great Roman epic was all about.

We fared much better from the humane point of view in our study of Greek, although most of us were less well prepared in Greek than we were in Latin. The class was more humane largely because the teacher who taught it, Father Francis Preuss, was unquestionably the most humanely educated individual we encountered in our juniorate experience. He had been prepared specifically to teach in the juniorate and functioned as dean there for many years. His preparation for both his teaching and his administrative work was at Cambridge University. Knowing what he was preparing for, he wisely chose not to do the doctoral program at Cambridge, but rather the undergraduate honors tripos. It is in the tripos that the real humane education is achieved at Cambridge. The doctoral program, in contrast, involved no *required* courses. The candidate prepared for a tough general examination in his area of specialization and wrote a dissertation. That, Father Preuss rightly decided, would be of little help to him as a teacher in the juniorate, whereas the undergraduate tripos would provide him with a top-level education in the very things he would be teaching. Several generations of Jesuit scholastics benefited immensely from his wise decision. He taught my class Greek, and it was a genuinely humane experience from every point of view. We read the first two books of Homer's *Iliad* in Greek and had to translate them, but our study was by no means confined to mere translation. Father did not give us access to translations of the whole *Iliad* because he knew human nature well enough to guess that we would probably use them as cribs for our translations, but he did give us a clear idea of what the *Iliad* was about and how the books we were translating fit into the theme of the epic as a whole. But the most rewarding literary experience with Father Preuss was our introduction to Greek tragedy. We studied *Oedipus Rex* by Sophocles and *Medea* by Euripides. And this study was by no means just an exercise in translation, although it embraced that, too. From his own broad background in Greek culture, Father explained how the theater was intimately related to the political, social, and religious life of the Greek people and then showed us how the subject of both *Oedipus Rex* and *Medea* were related to all of this background. Even more importantly, we were introduced to the Greek theorizing about art in general and about tragedy and comedy in particular through a thorough reading and discussion of Aristotle's *Poetics.* We then wrote papers on how Aristotle's principles of art and tragedy in particular were illustrated in the two plays we were studying. This immersion in Aristotle's *Poetics* and in Greek tragedy planted ideas and raised literary questions for me that I would work on for the rest of my literary career and incorporate into my own later teaching and publication.

Besides the courses in Latin and Greek, the juniorate curriculum contained a fine survey of European history and a program in English composition and literature. The history survey was taught by Father William Padberg, who was the very first Jesuit I had ever laid eyes on. He had taught church history for Mundelein Seminary outside of Chicago at a time when all the faculty at the seminary were Jesuits. One of my aunts lived at the nearby town of Mundelein, and while I was visiting her on an Easter vacation from St. Francis Seminary, she took me out to see the beautiful grounds at Mundelein Seminary. While we were there, she pointed out a priest walking up and down near the chapel saying his office. She said, "That is a Jesuit." It was Father Padberg. With his sharp features and semibald head, he looked for all the world like the ancient busts of Julius Caesar. With the constant drubbing the Jesuits had received from Father Riordon at St. Francis, I *was* a little startled to see an actual Jesuit in the flesh. I looked for the cloven hooves but didn't find them. I little thought then that in three years I'd be a Jesuit myself and have Father Padberg as one of my teachers. He was a very good one. His background in church history enabled him, all through his course, to show us the influence both for good and bad that the Church had in the development of Western culture. He was particularly adept at relating the past to what was going on in our world in the present.

Besides this dip into the history of Western culture, we had a full cycle of courses in English composition and literature. The first course was in rhetoric, the principles of effective composition. For four years under the guidance of Father Riordon at St. Francis, I had benefited by an intensive attention to rhetorical effectiveness in writing. Father Garvey, our teacher at Florissant, approached the subject in a very similar way: weekly themes carefully corrected and a progressive exposure to rhetorical principles. We didn't have a text on rhetoric; Father dictated the most important principles of organization, sentence structure, diction, and imagery, which resulted in a little personal handbook on rhetoric. I think the dictation was a mistake; it absorbed too much of our class time, but the application of the principles to our own writing was invaluable.

I still remember the first writing assignment Father Garvey gave us. We had just come from our two-year novitiate, and he asked us to write about the most impressive part of that experience. I was still aglow with the vision of God's plan for each of us as outlined in the *Spiritual Exercises* of St. Ignatius and the part that a personal love of Christ played in our lives. I wrote a fervent account of what I thought the *Exercises* and Christ meant in my life at the time. When Father returned our papers, I noted he had penned on mine: "Very well done. Wouldn't this be a wonderful subject for an epic?" I had not the foggiest notion of what an epic is at that time, so I hurried to Father Garvey's room and asked him when he wanted me to begin writing the epic. He looked at me indulgently and replied, without cracking a smile: "Now that will take a little time to prepare for. It took Milton half his life." When I later found out what an epic poem is, I was in admiration of the gentle way in which Father Garvey had let me down.

Father had a passion for Shakespeare and read his plays sensitively and with verve, another way in which he reminded me of Father Riordon at St. Francis. We read *Hamlet* (my second go at it) and *Henry V*. We analyzed the rhetorical effectiveness of most of the great speeches in both plays and wrote papers on the characters Hamlet and Henry V.

The second English course was on poetry, taught by Father Francis Yealy, who, like Father Preuss, had received his training at Cambridge. Unlike Father Preuss, however, he had elected to do the doctoral program, which meant that he did practically no course work there but spent several years preparing on his own for the final doctoral examination on the whole field of English literature and writing his dissertation on Emerson. While Father Yealy was at Cambridge, exciting things were going on there in the approach to the study of literature that would revolutionize both the study and the teaching of literature on both sides of the Atlantic. Frank Raymond Leavis and Ivor Armstrong Richards were at work there formulating the principles of what became known as the New Criticism. It really was a very close application of the *old* principles of rhetorical effectiveness to a given piece of literature. By a close scrutiny of the whole text itself, the reader was brought to the discovery of the precise *theme* that was being developed in the piece, the *attitude* the writer was taking toward that theme, and the elements of overall structure, sentence pattern, diction, imagery, and rhythm that he employed to develop and communicate his theme. This method required really digging into the verbal texture of the literary piece being scrutinized to see how it worked. Much of the "new criticism" appeared in a magazine called *Scrutiny* that was published at Cambridge. All of this was blazing at the university while Father Yealy was there, but I do not recall that he ever mentioned it in his teaching the poetry course to us, nor did we approach any of the literature we studied in the manner of the New Criticism. His course proceeded much in the manner of the very *old* criticism, which consisted of a heavy helping of biographical detail of the authors' lives, historical background, and some personal evaluations by the teacher of the poet and the poem being studied. We were never asked to dig very deeply if at all into the verbal texture of the poem nor made to justify interpretations we put on the poem by using text of the poem itself. Our papers, I am afraid, were personal essays written on the occasion of reading the poem but not anything like a close analysis of what the poet had actually done in the poem. It was not until years afterward, when I benefited by the teaching of Marshall McLuhan, who came hot from the ferment of Leavis and the New Criticism of Cambridge, that I learned how much we had missed in our first critical encounter with poetry in the juniorate.

Father Yealy was a delightful gentleman straight out of the nineteenth century. His critical judgments of literature were worth listening to, but he did nothing in his teaching to help us come to like conclusions based on a close scrutiny of the text. Nothing was accidental in his classes. He had almost everything he was going to say written out, and in class he slowly and deliberately read what he had written. I never knew a person who was more deliberate in everything he did. One day in class, he got up from his desk (he always read his literary pronouncements seated at the professor's desk) to write something on the board. Just as he reached up to start writing, a pendulum clock above the board fell off the wall. He caught it, laid it down on the desk, and proceeded to write his *dictum* on the board, as if the clock episode were part of the lesson plan.

He used to take daily walks in the afternoon in the woods and fields of the large seminary farm, and he often took a junior with him as a companion. Conversation didn't flow with Father Yealy; nothing did. Walking with him one day was a young junior who was immersed at the time in reading Homer. The seminary herd was grazing nearby, and young Peterson asked Father Yealy why Homer always spoke of the shambling gait of the cattle. Father didn't say a word; he just picked up a stone and hit the rump of one of the cows with it. The cow "shambled" off across the greensward. "Now do you know why Homer always speaks of the 'shambling' gait of cows?" he asked.

Father had certainly noticed the "shambling" gait of cows before, as well as a thousand other details in nature. He was an inveterate bird-watcher and had totaled up a formidable list of birds he had observed closely. One day in class while he was reading some of his long thought out pronouncements on poetry, he stopped dead and was transfixed as he looked out the window. We followed his gaze and saw a flock of yellow-breasted grosbeaks that had just landed on a mulberry tree laden with fruit. Framed by the window, the scene looked like an Oriental tapestry come alive. We, too, were transfixed with the sight, and when Yealy came out of his trance, he interrupted his lecture long enough to tell us more about yellow-breasted grosbeaks than we really wanted to know. Doc Yealy (we used to call him) had many endearing qualities, but helping us *tear into* the literary texture of a poem was not one of them.

Our second-year curriculum included a survey of English literature. Father Norman Dreyfus taught the course. He had just completed his doctorate in English at Johns Hopkins University, where he had specialized in the eighteenth century. His approach to the study of literature was very different from that of Father Yealy. It was quite close to what the New Critics were advocating, although Father had not studied them at this time. He really did get us intimately into the texts we were studying. Any judgments we made about the works we were studying had to be backed up with precise evidence from the author's text. Our papers were required to be closely argued and well expressed. If they were not, we would find a hemorrhage of red ink on them when they were returned—with a prescription to redo them, which was sometimes painful, but really a tremendous help in learning how to write. Father Dreyfus was a perfectionist. We could hardly ever do anything that *completely* satisfied him. His abundant corrections were sometimes exasperating, but they were very good training.

Father was just as hard on himself. Although he had forgotten more than many eighteenth-century specialists knew about eighteenth-century literature, he never published anything himself. He could not convince himself that anything he had written was good enough for publication. Exaggerated perfectionism can sometimes be paralyzing. I was later to get to know Father Dreyfus much more personally. He was chairman of the English department at St. Louis University when I worked for my doctorate in English there, was still chairman when I joined the department as a faculty member, and remained in the department when I became its chairman. Again—in my end was my beginning.

One of the defects of our English training in the juniorate, as I see it, was the fact that reading fiction was proscribed. In fact, all novels were removed from the library and consigned to "Gehenna," where they were unavailable to us. It was feared, I presume, that we would read too much fiction at the expense of our Latin and Greek studies. We could get permission to read specific novels of our choice during the summer when the regular schedule was somewhat relaxed. The requested book would be sent out of Gehenna on parole, but when completed, it was reassigned to hell. This practice was certainly a far cry from what I had been accustomed to at St. Francis, where Father Riordon checked out all the novels from the main library to make them *more* accessible to us and was himself available almost every afternoon to guide us in our reading of fiction. The policy at the juniorate struck me as being particularly wrongheaded. For approximately 90 percent of the juniors, this would be their last chance to do any extended reading in English literature. They would soon be studying philosophy and theology, and beginning work on their specific areas of concentration. If there was one area of reading that they might be expected to continue along with their specializations later, it was fiction—provided they had developed an interest in it. The proscription of reading fiction at this formative period in their training made that interest an unlikely eventuality.

But the juniorate experience was enriched remarkably through the addition of excellent courses in Greek and Roman architecture and sculpture. These subjects had been a part of Father Preuss's Cambridge tripos experience, and he incorporated them into the juniorate program. He taught the courses himself, and they gave us a thorough grounding in all three orders of Greek architecture and the Roman variations on them. We learned how much the visual arts of a culture can reveal of that culture's spirit and values. The study of Greek sculpture particularly laid the foundation for distinguishing between the two opposite values in art that have created a pendular swing between a more restrained and intellectual approach to artistic design, the style we call "classical," and the more emotional and exuberant approach that we sometimes call "baroque." The difference shows up in Greek culture in the contrast between Hellenic and Hellenistic art. Multiple examples of each style were analyzed in class with the help of slides—until we came to recognize the different effects of the two styles and learned the compositional patterns and dominant lines that help create the contrasting effects. Squares, rectangles, solidly based pyramidal shapes, and horizontal and vertical lines help to create the repose and intellectual control of the classically conceived work. Broken forms, tense activity, and a conflict of diagonals and curves contribute to the emotional quality of the opposite type of artistic creation.

The contrast was made evident when we analyzed the visual qualities of works such as the *Charioteer of Delphi* (all that remains of the horses are the hooves solidly planted on the ground), in which the charioteer is standing immobile in his chariot with the horses at rest and the reins limp, his garments falling in vertical lines almost like the fluting on a column. This work represents the *idea* of a charioteer; it is an image presented to us to *think* about, not an image that invites us to sense the drama, the motion, and the excitement of a charioteer in action. In contrast, the famous *Laocoon* represents the specific episode in the *Aeneid* in which Laocoon has warned the leaders of Troy not to bring the mighty wooden horse within their walls because it is a trap set by the deceptive Greeks. The goddess Artemis, who wants the Greeks to win, is outraged at Laocoon's warning and sends a pair of serpents from the sea to do away with Laocoon and his two sons. It is Laocoon and his sons struggling in the grip of the serpents that the Hellenistic artist represents in his famous sculpture of the subject. The compositional pattern is a broken triangle. The bodies of the father and the sons are represented in tortured diagonals, bound together by the smothering curves of the serpents. There is agony written on their faces and physical tension evident in their strained muscles. We are asked to *feel* the emotion expressed in the whole composition, not just to *think* about it. This approach is the exact opposite of the restrained and intellectual approach of the Hellenic sculptor who did the *Charioteer of Delphi.*

In many contrasts like this, Father Preuss was pointing up the fundamental contrast between two types of art that we would discover had reoccurred all through the history of art: the one restrained, controlled, intellectual; the other exuberant, dynamic, and emotional. It is the difference between fifth-century B.C. Hellenic and fourth-century B.C. Hellenistic art. In the Middle Ages, it is the difference between Romanesque and Gothic; in the Renaissance, the difference between High Renaissance and baroque; in the eighteenth and nineteenth centuries, the difference between the neoclassical and the romantic; and in the twentieth century, it is the difference between the Cezannesque and cubistic approach to the visual experience, culminating in such abstract patterns as the squares and rectangles of Mondrian and the expressionism and surrealism of painters such as Van Gogh, Gauguin, Dali, and Chagall, terminating in the abstract curvilinear pattern and violent color of an abstract artist such as Kandinsky.

What Father Preuss did in his remarkable introduction to Greek and Roman architecture and sculpture provided us with principles of design and style that were perennial and would make us feel at home in the art of any period down through the history of art.

In a strange way, I became very intimately involved in Father Preuss's artistic endeavor. To teach his classes on Greek and Roman art he needed slides. He had excellent illustrated books on the art of both Greece and Rome, but slides were imperative if he was to share his considerable knowledge with us in class. This was before the development of color photography, so what was practicable were black-and-white slides. One of my classmates, and a very good friend of mine, was an excellent photographer and had developed a fine darkroom. We volunteered to make four-by-four black-and-white slides of the architecture and sculpture in Father Preuss's books. "Pop" Warner would take the photographs and develop them, and I would mount them under glass. Father leaped at the idea, so we set to work. But Father foresaw a difficulty with the sculpture slides. Most of the statues were in the nude, and he felt that there would be criticism from some of the powers that be if it were known he was showing slides of completely nude figures to his classes, so to avoid that criticism he asked me to ink in shorts on all the male nudes, which I reluctantly did. Hence, I was one of the few juniors in his art classes who had seen beauty bare. This procedure was rather ridiculous but, I suppose, dictated by the somewhat puritanical and prudish attitude that prevailed in some quarters at the time.

The courses in Greek and Roman architecture and sculpture were formal and were controlled by the sanction of regular examinations. Another formal peripheral course that Father Preuss added and that he taught himself was on heraldry. It was a subject he became very interested in while he was at Cambridge, and when he became interested in something, he pursued it with vigor. We learned all about the physical qualities of a good coat of arms: in the first place, symbols big enough and bold enough in color to carry from a distance. We also learned the laws for arranging symbols and colors. The course included a study of the symbolism of the coats of arms of many distinguished individuals, countries, and cities, with an analysis of how well or poorly the designers had followed the laws of heraldry. This area of concern is certainly rather esoteric, but it added another interesting dimension to my reading and travels.

In a very roundabout way, the course on heraldry was ultimately responsible for St. Louis's getting what is probably the most accurate heraldic city flag in the United States. How it did so is an interesting story. Strangely, up until the 1960s, St. Louis had no official flag. At that time, the mayor and aldermen thought one ought to be commissioned. A local artist volunteered to design one. When his design was submitted to the aldermen, one of them thought it was not acceptable. He didn't think it was heraldically correct. The alderman was Peter Simpson, a poet of some repute in the community who had done his master's work in English at St. Louis University and had taken some of my courses. In one of them, we studied the medieval romance *Sir Gawaine and the Green Knight,* looking specifically at the rich medieval color symbolism that pervades the poem and particularly at the symbolism of Sir Gawain's shield or coat of arms. In that connection, we went into all the requirements of a good heraldic design: that it use symbols rather than photographic scenes to identify the family or place being symbolized, that the symbols be large enough to carry from a distance, and that it employ color symbolism to express some of its ideas. Pete thought the design submitted to the aldermen did none of these things. He called me one day and asked me whether I could help them design a properly heraldic flag. I told him I did not think I could but that I knew someone who unquestionably could: Dr. Theodore Sizer, a history professor at Yale University and an authority on heraldry who actually functioned as the official heraldrist at Yale. I had gotten to know Professor Sizer in Mexico.

It was at the Cortez Hotel that I had met Dr. Sizer. He frequently spent his vacations in Mexico and was an enthusiast for pre-Columbian art. We made many visits to the extensive national collection of pre-Columbian art. During our frequent conversations, I learned of Dr. Sizer's exhaustive knowledge of and enthusiasm for heraldry. When Pete Simpson asked for help in designing a heraldically correct flag for St. Louis, I wrote to Dr. Sizer and asked him whether he would be interested. He replied immediately that indeed he would. He said that he would pay a visit to his very good friend Mr. Charles Nagel, then director of the St. Louis Art Museum, dig into the history of the city, and try to come up with a properly designed flag that would express some of that history. He finally submitted a design that the mayor and aldermen unanimously accepted. It does express much of the story of St. Louis. The heraldic symbol for a river is a blue wavy line. The two sets of wavy lines converging into one on the flag symbolize the confluence of the Missouri and Mississippi Rivers at St. Louis. The city itself is symbolized by the fleur-de-lis because of the French founders of the city. Of course, it also symbolizes the patron saint of the city, Louis IX of France. The three colors chosen for the flag—red, white, and blue—occur in the flags of both France and the United States. As I look at the city flag waving from flag poles all over the city, I am reminded of the fact that, in a way, St. Louis has its heraldically very correct flag in part as a result of the course on heraldry Father Preuss taught in the Jesuit juniorate at Florissant.

Out of the abundance of Father Preuss's heart and knowledge, he extended our artistic horizons in still another way. During the years he was at Cambridge, he traveled widely all over Europe and became very interested in the development of Romanesque and Gothic architecture. Scholastic philosophers have a saying, *"Bonum est diffusivum sui"* ("goodness tends to diffuse itself"), which I think expresses what motivates any good teacher: he or she wants to share the wealth of his or her knowledge with others. Father Preuss wanted to share with us his knowledge of and love for the great contribution that the Middle Ages had made to the history of architecture. But he did not think he could add another course to our curriculum in which to do it, so he offered what he called *illuminabitur* evenings in the auditorium. *Illuminabitur* means "let it be lighted." On rainy evenings, when it was impractical for us to take our evening common recreation outside in the garden, a sign would go up on the board: *"Illuminabitur!"* We would go to the auditorium, where Father showed us slides of Romanesque and Gothic churches from all over Europe, discussing their history and stylistic features. To give these *illuminabitur* evenings, of course, he needed slides, so he put Pop Warner to work making them. He had a wealth of illustrated books from which to draw, but both the photographs in the books and the slides were in black and white. I decided to liven up the slides by tinting them. The skies would come out blue, trees and grass green, and I sometimes enlivened the stone of the buildings a bit, too. Years later, when I saw the original buildings, I realized that my artistic renditions did not always match the color of the originals, but all the detailed work on the slides familiarized me with the structures in a very intimate way. I became utterly fascinated with medieval architecture. I got out Ralph Adams Cram's book *The Spirit of the Gothic* and Henry Adams's *Chartres and Mont St. Michel* and immersed myself in the spirit of the Gothic. My sister bought me the set of Boston Prints on medieval architecture (about one hundred prints). I propped up a little easel on my desk and flipped a print each day on it. The great medieval cathedrals became as familiar to me as the palm of my own hand. In those days of sparse travel, I had no belief or hope that I would ever see any of these buildings themselves. I could not have dreamed then that in a much later period of my life I would spend three summers doing nothing but photographing most of the cathedrals that were on my flip list. Nor could I possibly have imagined that I would one day be master of ceremonies at the dedication of a hospital chapel on the campus of St. Louis University designed by Ralph Adams Cram, who had so stimulated my interest in medieval architecture through his *Spirit of the Gothic.* Much less would I have guessed then that fifty years later I would be on the committee that directed the cleaning and restoration of the same chapel and that I would plan the iconography of the stained glass windows designed by Rodney Winfield, which would finally give the chapel its full Gothic flavor. But here again in my end is my beginning.

Father Preuss was an impressively learned man but by no means a mere bookworm. He loved the outdoors. His knowledge of trees and birds was impressive, and, like everything else he possessed, he loved to share his knowledge with us informally on walks or at the villa on the Missouri River where we spent our Thursdays. He not only loved to look at trees, but also loved to plant them, and he planted dozens of them in the extensive gardens at the seminary itself and at the villa. He elicited our help in his planting sprees. It was always a delight to work with him because he knew what he was doing, and we would learn so much about horticulture in the process. The combination of Father's love for the classics with his love for nature and horticulture was very much like the balance of the two values that characterized Virgil, one of his literary models.

I participated in two of Father Preuss's planting projects. They were both rather monumental. When I first came to Florissant, there was a lovely lane of majestic American elms leading up to the main entrance to the old rock building, the elm disease struck them, and they all died. Father Preuss directed the project of having them felled and sawed up. He then had us juniors help him in replacing the mighty American elms with young English elms that were presumably immune to the elm disease. It was with great sadness that we saw the American elms go, wonderfully graceful even in their death throes. Our sadness at the loss of the particular beauty of the elms joining their graceful branches above the lane like the tracery of a great Gothic cathedral made me empathize years later with the sadness Gerard Manley Hopkins expresses at the felling of the Binsley poplars he had loved:

> My aspens dear, whose airy cages quelled,
> Quelled or quenched in leaves the leaping sun,
> All felled, felled, are all felled;
>   Of a fresh and following folded rank
>     Not spared, not one
>     That dandled a sandalled
>    Shadow that swam or sank
> On meadow and river and wind-wandering weed-winding bank.
>
>   O if we but knew what we do
>     When we delve or hew—
>   Hack and rack the growing green!
>     Since country is so tender

> To touch, her being so slender,
> That, like this sleek and seeing ball
> But a prick will make no eye at all,
> Where we, even where we mean
>     To mend her we end her,
> When we hew or delve:
> After-comers cannot guess the beauty been.
>     Ten or twelve, only ten or twelve
>     Strokes of havoc unselve
>         The sweet especial scene,
>     Rural scene, a rural scene,
>     Sweet especial rural scene.

By planting the English elms, we indeed did try to mend the scene we had hacked and racked. But Hopkins was right; even where we meant to mend her we ended her. The lane never looked the same. The English elms grew up and matured but never created again the "sweet especial scene" that the elm disease and our axes had destroyed.

Father Preuss's other great planting project in which we juniors participated was meant to create "a sweet especial rural scene" where there had been only a bare hill. The hill out at our villa was almost completely bare of any growth at all. Father decided that it should be forested and a gazebo built at its top to command a sweeping view of the Missouri River. So he started a tree-planting program on Thursdays that would eventually enfold the entire hill with a wonderful variety of trees: oaks, maples, ash, hackberries, and Lombardy poplars. Young specimens of all these trees grew wild in the extensive woods of the seminary farm, but they had to be carefully dug up, the roots balled for transplanting, and the holes dug on the hillside to receive them. A wagon and team of horses from the farm were pressed into service to haul the trees to the hill. My familiarity with workhorses and wagons ordained me to the transportation crew. The result of all this labor eventually was a hill pleasantly wrapped in forest green where before there had been only a barren hill. It was the result of the vision and leadership of Father Preuss, an extraordinary human being and classical scholar after the heart of Virgil.

Tennyson catches the two sides of Virgil that were like the two sides of Father Preuss:

> Roman Virgil, thou that singest Ilion's lofty temples robed in fire,
> Ilion falling, Rome arising, wars, and filial faith and Dido's pyre.

But the poet also was, Tennyson says,

> Landscape lover . . .
> . . . that singest
> wheat and
> woodland, tilth and
> vineyard, hive and
> horse and herd.

And so was Father Preuss.

There was one fortuitous happening in the juniorate that I want to record here because it had a lasting effect on the rest of my career. On Sundays, we had free time that we could use any way we wished. One Sunday I decided to do some browsing in the library. As I wandered into the reading room, Joe McCallin, whom I did not know very well at the time, was perched on top of a five-foot library ladder with a book in his hand. He asked me whether I had ever read Hopkins's "The Blessed Virgin Compared to the Air We Breathe." I told him that not only had I not read it, but I had never even heard of Hopkins. He said: "If you've got a minute, I'd like to read it to you." He did. I could not follow all the nuances of the poet's thought and expression at this quick reading, but I caught enough to know that this was not just any pious ditty on the Blessed Virgin. The wonderfully controlled rhythm of the piece struck me immediately, as well as the freshness of the sustained image of the Blessed Virgin as the very air we breathe in our spiritual lives, her presence as mediatrix of all grace that pervades our lives as intimately as the natural atmosphere around us and that

> nestles me everywhere,
> That each eyelash or hair
> Girdles, goes home betwixt
> The fleeciest, frailest-flixed
> Snowflake; that's fairly mixed
> With riddles, and is rife
> In every least thing's life.

This was my introduction to a poet whom I came to admire just this side of idolatry, a poet who I believe was the greatest English poet of the nineteenth century, and possibly the greatest religious poet in any language. And I learned about him from Joe McCallin as he perched on a library ladder in the juniorate library.

I immediately acquired a personal copy of Hopkins's poetry and still have it, thumb worn and almost a loose-leaf edition because I have used it so much over the years. Hopkins has become a lifelong love, and I have given voice to some of that love in several publications that span my career. My enthusiasm for Hopkins was so generally known that when Father Norman Weyand was bringing out his *Immortal Diamond* in 1949, a collection of studies on Gerard Manley Hopkins, he asked me to make a contribution to it. That request generated my chapter "Hopkins, Poet of Nature and the Supernatural." When I had dug more deeply into Hopkins's work of the poet, I was immensely impressed with how closely and accurately he had observed every minute detail of the world around him: "rose moles all in stipple upon trout that swim," "skies of couple colour as a brinded cow," skies full of "cloud puffballs, torn tufts, tossed pillows," "star-eyed strawberry breasted throstle above her nested cluster of bugle blue eggs," "a dare-gale skylark scanted in a dull cage," or the masterful free flight of a wind hover, "thrushe's eggs that look like little low heavens." He had looked at Harry the Ploughman long enough to observe his "hard as hurdle arms," his "rack of ribs," "scooped flank," "rope-over thighs," "knee-nave," and "barrelled shank," and on and on, until Harry stands before us as vividly rendered as the David of Michelangelo. And Hopkins had looked at Harry's plow long enough to notice that the sheer plod of the earth moving across the plowshare had polished it to such mirror brightness that its glint could be caught down the whole length of a freshly plowed furrow ("sillion" he calls it).

Hopkins makes us look at the natural world in a brand-new way, as if it has just been newly created. He sees all this striking detail in the world around us as a harvest in which we reap intimations of God Himself and even of Christ, the *Word of God.* All these things are vocables in which God and Christ speak to us of Themselves. This is Hopkins the poet of nature. He is equally felicitous in bringing about aspects of the supernatural order of grace. Realities in that order that are particularly dear to him are the Pauline idea of the mystical Body of Christ, the fact that through grace we become Christ and Christ becomes us. He returns to that idea again and again in his poetry, nowhere more tellingly than in his sonnet "The Soldier." Central to this aspect of Hopkins's thought on the supernatural is the part the Blessed Virgin plays in our lives as the mediatrix of all grace, which is the theme of "The Blessed Virgin Compared to the Air We Breathe," possibly the most perceptive and finely wrought Marian poem ever written in any language. It was Hopkins as a poet both of nature and the supernatural that I enlarged on in my 1949 essay.

Some critics have lamented Hopkins's entry into the Society of Jesus, where they thought his poetic temperament and talent were not appreciated. They are probably right, but Hopkins himself never regretted it. In fact, it was his experience of the *Spiritual Exercises* in the Society that created the very substance of his poetic vision. It was the attempt to get a medium versatile enough to do justice to the vision of life that opened up before him as outlined in the *Spiritual Exercises* that drove him on to the creative experiments in new imagery and rhythm that make his poetry so distinctive. The whole logical and psychological progression of the *Spiritual Exercises* focuses the structural background of his greatest and longest poem, "The Wreck of the Deutschland," which I demonstrate in an article I published in *College English* in 1962, entitled "Mastery and Mercy in *The Wreck of the Deutschland*."

Hopkins's experience in the Society affected his poetry in another way. He became very aware of the three steps in an Ignatian meditation: an application of the *senses* to the subject of the meditation, an *intellectualization* of the experience in which we consciously relate it to ourselves, and an exercise of the *will* to bring the subject to bear on one's own personal action. Louis L. Martz pointed out back in 1962, in his book *The Poetry of Meditation: A Study in English Religious Literature of the Seventeenth Century*, that some of the metaphysical poets had been affected by the structure of the Ignatian meditation in building the structure of some of their poetry. In a study that appeared in the 1990 *Annual of the Catholic Commission on Intellectual and Cultural Affairs*, I pointed out that this same Ignatian meditation structure is the pattern on which several of Hopkins's poems are built, notably "The Blessed Virgin Compared to the Air We Breathe" and "The Windhover." The Hopkins seed sown by Joe McCallin from the top of a library ladder in 1932 has continued to fructify in my academic career up to the present. "In my end is my beginning."

Mentioning McCallin again prompts me to take time out and do a little sketch of Mac. He was a real "character" in the idiosyncratic acceptance of that term. He was also the paradigm of a certain type of person, of whom I have known several, who start out in life ahead of the crowd, but end up archconservatives, way behind where the crowd has moved. I preface these remarks with the statement that Mac was a dear friend of mine and remained so through thick and thin. His very idiosyncrasies endeared him to me. When I first knew him, he was the embodiment of an avant-garde person who was always ahead of the pack. The very fact that he not only knew Hopkins but knew him so well that he had picked out his favorite poem was a sign of his avant-garde approach to life at the time. I am willing to bet that not another person in our class had ever heard of Hopkins. Another thing Mac prided himself on, I soon learned, was the fact that he had read the complete monumental *Lives of the Popes* by Pastor. I'm sure again that for the rest of us Pastor at that time was completely unknown. We did get to know him eventually because one of his volumes was read to us from the pulpit at meals, but Mac had already read his volumes and in fact took delight in regaling us with some of the less-edifying aspects of the lives of some of the popes. Another way in which he showed his individualistic tendencies was in his dress. When we came to St. Louis for our philosophy, we were still supposed to wear our cassocks everywhere. Mac never wore his; he always dressed in a suit and Roman collar. But later, true to type, when the custom changed and a decree came out that we were not to wear our cassocks in public, Mac put his on and wore it everywhere—along with a large black flowing cape and the biretta. When everyone else was wearing suit and Roman collar or more casual clothes, Mac was floating around the campus in this full regalia. When some of the traditional devotions were becoming less popular, even among Jesuits, Mac was reasserting them. He had a huge Franciscan rosary as big as a logging chain, and he used to go over to the public plaza in front of the Pius XII Library in his full dress of cassock, biretta, and flowing cape, and say his beads with rosary fingered at arm's length. One day when he was returning to the residence, Jesuit Hall, he stopped at the corner for a traffic light. Two little African American lads looked up at the apparition in awe. When another Jesuit came along and struck up a conversation with Mac, the lads remarked: "Oh, it talks." Mac carried this parade of the traditional to a kind of extreme. Garavelli's was a famous and favorite bar-restaurant hangout just a block down the street from the Jesuit residence. Mac would float down the street in all his traditional clerical getup, take his place at the bar for a flagon of beer, and engage in conversation anyone within earshot—much to the admiration of the customers at large.

But with this return to the costumes of old—strangely for this person whom we always thought of as the embodiment of the avant-garde—went an intellectual and spiritual freeze into the most rigid kind of unyielding conservatism. Mac never said anything but the Latin Tridentine Mass. He became frozen in a rigid, unchanging ideology about matters theological, political, social, and spiritual—the very opposite of the avant-garde attitude he had displayed early on. Some individuals are born conservatives and have an innate allergy to any kind of change. Others launch themselves as liberals but, as change passes them by, become arch conservatives. Mac was of the latter breed.

Father Preuss's introduction to Greek and Roman art in the juniorate so impressed me that I thought I might like to go on and specialize in art history with the idea of teaching that subject rather than English literature, much as I loved that prospect. In the courses on Greek and Roman art, I experienced what a marvelous instrument art is for understanding a culture. I thought it would be exciting to do that as a career. I suggested this to Father Mike Mallon, who was in charge of the training of scholastics at the time. His response was that there was no need or place for anyone trained in art in the province because neither studio art nor art history was taught in any of our schools. I was amazed to learn that, but was finally resigned to settle into my first love—teaching English. I made a quiet vow, however, then and there, to go on teaching myself art history and do whatever I could, if the opportunity ever presented itself, to make art a part of the Jesuit curriculum.

# 5

# The Collegiate Tertianship

WHEN WE CAME to the juniorate, the most important elements of our spiritual lives continued. We continued to make the morning meditation, and examination of conscience, and to participate in daily Mass and night prayers. We made our eight-day retreat each year, had two three-day periods of recollection, and had the benefit of a spiritual father's guidance. Our academic studies replaced most of the manual labor of the novitiate. We did just enough manual work to help keep our living quarters clean. But come the late fall, all hands, including those in the juniorate, were summoned into the vineyard to pick the grapes and help press them in the winery. Classes started right after grape season.

Toward the end of the summer following the second year of the juniorate, when we second-year juniors were preparing to make the move into St. Louis to begin training in philosophy, I was informed that I had been chosen to stay on at Florissant for another year of what had come to be called the *tertianship,* a third year of study in the humanities. It was a program Father Preuss had designed to enable a small number of juniors to stay on and benefit from another year of intensive study of the classics or English literature or both. Because I was now destined to teach English, I welcomed the opportunity. At this point, I had a sufficient mastery of Latin and Greek to make further exposure to the classics easier and a real pleasure.

To study the classics under the expert guidance of Father Preuss, who acted as tutor, was an added pleasure. Father Yealy was to be my tutor in my English studies during the year, which I was not all that excited about because his teaching in the juniorate had not been particularly inspiring. But the course in Victorianism he worked out for me could not have been better, and the background material he personally provided for it was superb.

Because I, together with four of my classmates, had been chosen for the tertianship, I remained behind when the rest of the class made the trek into the city. I was about to join the other "hands" in the vineyard for the grape season before the tertian program began when Father Preuss called me to his room. He explained that the coming year was the bimillennial year of Virgil's birth and that he was planning a program to celebrate it. The choir would sing the Cantata arranged around Tennyson's "Ode to Virgil"; there would be a lecture by a visiting scholar on Virgil; and he said he would like to have me write a paper on Virgil's *Aeneid* for the program. I was, of course, flattered at the suggestion but also terrified. I said I didn't see how I could do it considering that I had never even read the whole of the *Aeneid.* He said he'd strike a bargain with me. If I would agree to do the paper, he would excuse me from the vineyard, give me a translation of the *Aeneid,* and sit me down to read it. When I had done so, he would discuss a possible topic for the paper. That sounded like a good idea to me. The bargain was struck. For two weeks, I immersed myself in the *Aeneid* and was perfectly fascinated with the story and what it revealed about the Roman ideal of duty to the gods, the state, and the family. Aeneas has a serious commission from the gods themselves to found a new Troy. He has the solemn duty, no matter at what cost to himself, to fulfill that commission. It is not only a new Troy but a new race he is to establish, which means that his present wife, Creusa, would have to remain behind. He has a duty to his father, the *pater familias,* so Anchises has to go with him as his inspiration and counselor. Aeneas leaves Troy with Anchises on his shoulders and his son Ascanius at his side. Anchises will be there throughout Aeneas's wanderings to prod him on through hardships and dallyings to continue on to fulfill his destiny. Anchises is important to Aeneas even after death. When Aeneas visits the underworld, the ghost of Anchises gives him a vision of the Rome to be, and urges him to brave any hardships to fulfill his commission to found that city. In the light of all this, the Dido episode took on a very different meaning than it did when we read it isolated from the rest of the work. In this context, Dido can be seen as a dangerous hindrance to Aeneas's great destiny of founding a new Troy. She has to be sacrificed to Aeneas's great destiny and commitment. Much as Aeneas and Virgil himself despise *horrida bella* (horrible wars), Aeneas has to fight them to subdue the followers of Turnus, who would prevent him from founding Rome. I saw here for the first time that the Roman ideal, as Virgil penned it, had a certain kind of nobility about it. It was not just self-aggrandizement. It demanded certain limitation on the individual in the interest of the will of the gods, the benefit of the state, and the good of the family. Some of the nobility of that ideal is expressed in the vision of Rome's glory Anchises outlines for Aeneas in the underworld.

> *Excudunt alii spirantia mollius aera*
> *(credo equidem), vivos ducent de marmore vultus,*
> *orabunt causas melius, caelique meatus*
> *describent radio et surgentia sidera dicent:*
> *tu regere imperio populos, Romane, memento*
> *(hae tibi erunt artes), pacisque imponere morem,*
> *parcere subjectis et debellare superbos. (Aeneid,* VI.846–52)

> Others shall beat out the breathing bronze
> to softer lines, I believe it well; shall
> draw living lineaments from the marble;
> the cause shall be more eloquent on their
> lips; their pencils shall portray the paths
> of heaven, and tell the stars in their
> arising: be thy charge, O Roman, to rule
> the nations is thine empire; (this shall
> be thine art), to ordain the law of peace,
> to be merciful to the conquered and
> beat the haughty down.

This passage sounds almost like a line from the *Magnificat*. This social and political ideal has some of the checks on reckless self-aggrandizement that approaches Christian humility and charity. The ideal was never reached and often not even approximated in Roman practice; ideals never are. But the fact that Virgil, the great Roman epic poet, could formulate the ideal in this way is a manifestation that the Roman ideal was quite different from the self-aggrandizement that was so much a part of Achilles, the Greek epic hero, honored for this very self-aggrandizement in the *Iliad*. We had read enough of the *Iliad* for me to make this contrast between the two heroes, and I decided I would write my paper on that subject. Father Preuss agreed. Here, I was taking the first feeble steps toward the development of this theme into a book-length study that appeared thirty years later, in 1960, entitled *Honor and the Epic Hero*. "In my end is my beginning."

Grape season and my venture into the *Aeneid* over, we chosen souls settled into the routine of the tertianship. It was a program of special studies designed by Father Preuss based very closely on the honors tripos program at Cambridge, the program Father Preuss had elected to take there. It consisted of an intensive reading program in the classics directed by Father Preuss himself or, in my case, in English literature by Father Yealy. But I had become so interested in the classics that I decided to do some of the reading program in the classics as well as in English literature. The work in both areas proved to be one of the most enriching educational experiences in my whole career. The private reading program involved written papers that each of us discussed with his tutor periodically. These papers were supplemented twice a week by two-hour discussion sessions of the whole group of five tertians with Father Preuss. Here he provided background for our reading and discussed some of our papers with us or any topic that either he or we introduced that was related to what we were doing in our reading. Those topics ranged widely. It was an incomparably enriching experience to benefit twice a week from Father Preuss's broad background, knowledge, and enthusiasm. The area of special reading in the classics that I chose to pursue was Greek tragedy. We had already read *Oedipus Rex* by Aeschylus and *Medea* by Euripides in the juniorate in Father Preuss's Greek class, which was enough to whet my appetite for more. It was an area that would provide excellent background for the history of the development of drama in the West, a subject I was particularly interested in because of the good introduction to Shakespeare by Father Riordon at St. Francis and by Father Garvey at the juniorate. So with Father Preuss's help I worked out a program of reading in Greek tragedy that included the *Oresteia* trilogy (*Agamemnon, The Libation Bearers,* and *The Furies*) by Aeschylus, *Oedipus Rex* and *Antigone* by Sophocles, and *Medea* and *Electra* by Euripides.

Studying plays from each of the dramatists in close proximity, Father Preuss suggested, would enable us to experience the gradual evolution of the form and structure of Greek tragedy and the very different approaches of the three main tragedians to their work. Aeschylus was the pioneer whose work evolved from the combination of song and dance gyrating around a semireligious ritual in honor of the god Dionysus. The choral odes combining song and dance that were a large part of the rituals constitute a good half of an Aeschylean play, with minimal dramatic dialogue on the stage between just two characters. And the plays themselves had a kind of religious quality about them, as if the playwright was himself a religious seer perpetuating some of the ancient myths about his characters.

Sophocles brought both the form and content of Greek tragedy forward to a more dramatic and intellectual intensity. He introduced the third character on the stage, which enabled him to increase the dramatic tension of his plays, but he still observed all the limitations of the three unities that gave his plays a very restrained, intellectual, and classical quality. Only one plot is developed. The action takes place on one day and in one place. There are never more than three characters on the stage at any one time. No violence is ever represented on the stage; if there is violence in the plot, we learn about it from messengers or the chorus. There is never any admixture of comedy in the tragic presentation. The tragic hero wears buskins (high wooden sandals that give him greater physical height to augment his heroic stature) and a mask with a frozen tragic grimace that eliminates any changing facial expression—a deliberate suppression of strong emotion, which fitted into the Greek, or at least the Platonic, suspicion of the emotions as unworthy of the highly controlled intellectual Greek ideal. Of the three great Greek tragedians, Sophocles undoubtedly best represents that ideal.

When we considered Euripides' plays in contrast to those of Sophocles, we discovered that we were moving into a very different world. Euripides chose subject matter that was much more emotional, such as Medea's violent reaction to being jilted by Jason in favor of Creusa. Medea expresses some of that violent emotional reaction through the murder of her children to wreak revenge on Jason, their father. Euripides' sympathies are with Medea, and in spite of Medea's semi-barbaric origins and her murder of her own children in the play, he manages to win *our* sympathy for her as well, rather than for the self-satisfied, self-serving Jason. This is characteristic of Euripides' approach. Rather than being suspicious of emotion, he uses his considerable poetic ability to arouse it and to direct our sympathies to characters that he thinks have been somehow oppressed in the past, particularly women. The very titles of many of his plays indicate that interest: *The Trojan Women, Hecuba, Andromache, Electra, Helena,* and *Medea.*

Euripides' emphasis on the more dynamic and emotional elements in his plays is in sharp contrast to Sophocles' more restrained and intellectual approach. He is actually moving in the direction of the greater emotion of later Hellenistic art. There is an affinity between Sophocles' restrained approach to his themes and such Hellenic sculpture as *The Charioteer of Delphi* as well as between the plays of Euripides and such a dynamic work as the Hellenistic *Laocoön.* We discussed those analogies in one of our evening sessions.

This program of intensive reading of a few classical masterpieces in their original Greek, with ample time to read commentary on the works and to discuss them from various angles with like-minded confreres and with our tutor, Father Preuss, was an incomparably enriching experience that inspired me many years later to incorporate a similar reading experience into an undergraduate honors program I helped plan at St. Louis University.

This rewarding unit of reading in the tertianship was from the classics program. My own program was in English and was devised by Father Yealy. The very thing that made his class in poetry somewhat dull and uninspiring proved to be the perfect instrument for enlarging my horizons in this tertian program. The area of concentrated reading was the Victorian period. I had had only a minimum of exposure to the background of this period. What Father Yealy proposed to do was give me a thorough summary of the various developments that went into the making of the Victorian mind—what he called Victorianism. He would do it in a series of his well thought out lectures, supplemented by readings in the major works that expressed the Victorian mind. The rest of the time would be spent in reading works of the major critics of Victorianism. It was an admirable plan for digging into what Victorianism was and what some of its chief shortcomings were. This exploration of the Victorian mind in depth was an extremely helpful probe into a period that has greatly affected our own world. One of the main developments Father Yealy outlined in his introductory lectures was the Industrial Revolution, which so completely shifted the center of the world from the farm to the industrial centers, revolutionized work on the farm itself, and changed the whole nature of farming. I had personally seen much of that change in my own experiences on the farm. The emphasis on technology and technological inventions that facilitated production gave rise to the utilitarian outlook. Only that which contributed to this kind of physical advancement was considered valuable. This orientation came to be described as *utilitarianism.* Hand in hand with this idea went the Darwinian theory of evolution and the socially extracted doctrine of the survival of the fittest in the inevitable *evolutionary forward progress* of the human race. Certain people felt that if some individuals or groups of individuals fell by the wayside in this forward progressive sweep, that was unfortunate but inevitable and ultimately contributed to the betterment of the human race as a whole. Along with that idea went the notion of laissez-faire in politics and the social order. Government did not—and should not—interfere in this inevitable progress on behalf of those who might be left behind. Such things as labor unions and strikes were outlawed in this laissez-faire world. Education was to be limited to those disciplines that would contribute to the practical, physical, utilitarian advancement of society. There was also a strong Calvinistic element in the Victorian frame of mind. Monetary success became a sign of predestination. Hence, hard work and financial success became a moral duty. This attitude came to be dubbed the Protestant ethic and was a driving force in the Victorian world.

*Liberalism* was another movement that greatly characterized the Victorian mind. What the Victorians meant by it was complete freedom from any restraints on their own personal pursuit of success and happiness: freedom from the restraints of government and religion, and freedom from the trammels of tradition. The individual was to be left free to pursue his or her own happiness, largely construed in terms of physical and monetary success. Neither government nor religious sources were to interfere with that pursuit. Father Yealy outlined the evolution of all these ideas in the Victorian period in great detail and referred me to some of the original writings that had helped generate them. They included such works as Darwin's *Origin of Species,* Jean Jacques Rousseau's *Emile,* John Stuart Mill's *Liberalism,* and, above all, Thomas Babington Macaulay's *Essay on Francis Bacon,* which probably capsulizes the Victorian mind-set better than any other single work. But the main thrust of the course was the well-planned program of independent reading, reflection, and writing on the response to Victorianism by what Father Yealy called the great Victorian critics. He was not referring to literary critics, but to contemporaneous thinkers who had made thoughtful analyses of Victorianism and found it wanting. These critics included Mathew Arnold,

John Ruskin, Thomas Carlyle, and John Henry Newman. I had to read some of the major works of all these critics and write a paper on each of them explaining how he had reacted to what he considered the limitations of Victorianism. In *Culture and Anarchy,* Arnold saw the contemporary scene as anarchic because the exaggerated individualism, pragmatism, and utilitarianism of the period had narrowed men's visions to what would promote material wealth at the expense of spiritual and cultural values. The remedy, Arnold thought, lay in a broader education, in immersing oneself in the best that had been thought and said in the past. This immersion, he thought, might sensitize the public to values other than the merely material and utilitarian. He elevated culture into almost a religion. However, his remedy for social anarchy, which he analyzed rather accurately, seemed somewhat vague and ineffectual.

John Ruskin was primarily an art critic, who wrote prolifically on architecture and painting. He did much to interest the public once more in medieval Gothic architecture. His *Stones of Venice* captured the aura of that unique city as no one had done before him or has since. His remarkable command of language enables the reader to see in full Technicolor every least detail of what he is describing. I am particularly struck by his marvelously detailed description of the facade of St. Mark's in Venice as it is perceived for the first time from the Bocca di Piazza at the end of a crowded narrow street. It's worth a glance here.

> A yard or two farther, we pass the hostelry of the Black Eagle; and glancing as we pass through the square door of marble, deeply moulded, in the outer wall, we see the shadows of its pergola of vines resting on an ancient well, with a pointed shield carved on its side; and so presently emerge on the bridge and Campo San Moisè, whence to the entrance into St. Mark's Place, called the Bocca di Piazza (mouth of the square); the Venetian character is nearly destroyed, first by the frightful façade of San Moisè, which we will pause at another time to examine, and then by the modernizing of the shops as they near the piazza, and the mingling with the lower Venetian populace of lounging groups of English and Austrians. We will push fast through them into the shadow of the pillars at the end of the "Bocca di Piazza," and then we forget them all; for between those pillars there opens a great light, and in the midst of it, as we advance slowly, the vast tower of St. Mark seems to lift itself visibly forth from the level field of chequered stones;

and, on each side, the countless arches prolong themselves into ranged symmetry, as if the rugged and irregular houses that pressed together above us in the dark alley had been struck back into sudden obedience and lovely order, and as if all their rude casements and broken walls had been transformed into arches charged with goodly sculpture, and fluted shafts of delicate stone.

And well may they fall back, for beyond those troops of ordered arches there rises a vision out of the earth; and all the great square seems to have opened from it in a kind of awe, that we may see it far away—a multitude of pillars and white domes, clustered into a long low pyramid of coloured light; a treasure-heap, it seems, partly of gold, and partly of opal and mother-of-pearl, hollowed beneath into five great vaulted porches, ceiled with fair mosaic, and beset with sculpture of alabaster, clear as amber and delicate as ivory; sculpture fantastic and involved, of palm leaves and lilies, and grapes and pomegranates, and birds clinging and fluttering among the branches, all twined together into an endless network of buds and plumes; and in the midst of it, the solemn forms of angels sceptred, and robed to the feet, and leaning to each other across the gates, their figures indistinct among the gleaming of the golden ground through the leaves beside them, interrupted and dim, like the morning light as it faded back among the branches of Eden, when first its gates were angel-guarded long ago. And round the walls of the porches there are set pillars of variegated stones, jasper and porphyry, and deep-green serpentine, spotted with flakes of snow, and marbles, that half refuse and half yield to the sunshine, Cleopatra-like, "their bluest veins to kiss"—the shadow, as it steals back from them, revealing line after line of azure undulation, as a receding tide leaves the waved sand; their capitals rich with interwoven tracery, rooted knots of herbage, and drifting leaves of acanthus and vine, and mystical signs, all beginning and ending in the Cross; and above them, in the broad archivolts, a continuous chain of language and of life—angels, and the signs of heaven, and the labours of men, each in its appointed season upon the earth; and above these, another range of glittering pinnacles, mixed with the white arches edged with scarlet flowers—a confusion of delight, amidst which the breasts of the Greek horses are seen blazing in their breadth of golden strength; and the St. Mark's lion, lifted on a blue field covered with stars; until at last, as if in ecstasy, the crests of the arches break into a marble foam, and toss themselves far into the blue sky in flashes and wreaths of sculptured spray, as if the breakers on the Lido shore had been frostbound before they fell, and sea-nymphs had inlaid them with coral and amethyst.

> Between the grim cathedral of England and this, what an interval!
> There is a type of it in the very birds that haunt them; for, instead
> of the restless crowd, hoarse-voiced and sable-winged, drifting on the
> bleak upper air, the St. Mark's porches are full of doves, that nestle
> among the marble foliage, and mingle the soft iridescence of their
> living plumes, changing at every motion, with the tints, hardly less
> lovely, that have stood unchanged for seven hundred years.

This passage of poetic prose pans up the facade of the great cathedral and re-creates it, detail after detail, in full color. It shows the power of language to summon up in our imagination a very real experience of things we have never seen. Later, when I did get to see San Marco, I photographed the facade in the same sequence of detail as Ruskin describes it. By projecting the shots for my students as we read Ruskin's description, I could show them how accurately Ruskin had done in words what the camera did mechanically. Actually, Ruskin does more than the camera in his vivid diction and imagery. He communicates not just the beautiful details of San Marco but his own enthusiasm about it.

Ruskin as an art critic was the first to appreciate what Joseph Turner, his contemporary, was up to: a special interest in the effect of shifting light on objects. Turner had actually anticipated the impressionists in this respect, and Ruskin defended what Turner was doing in the face of many other critics who described Turner's work as uncontrolled smears of color.

But Ruskin was not only an art critic; he became interested in the economic and social conditions of the Victorian period and wrote some perceptive analyses of the situation. In one work called *Unto This Last*, he discusses what he calls "the roots of honor." Here he talks about the basis for the honor we show the professions of the physician, the priest, the lawyer, and the soldier. Members of these professions, Ruskin suggests, profess to be dedicated to the welfare of others rather than primarily to their own. He points out that whenever a prejudice arises toward any of these professions, it is because they have put their own profit before the welfare of their clients. The merchant, in contrast, is conceived as having personal monetary profit as his main concern. But until the merchants (who for Ruskin stand for the whole contemporary industrial and mercantile world) develop some sense of responsibility for the world that is dependent on them for their livelihood, there will be no social justice and no remedy for the irresponsible self-aggrandizement that characterizes the Victorian world. This voice—lifted in the interest of social justice, unselfishness, and concern for others—sounded in Ruskin's time like a voice crying in the wilderness. Making unselfishness the very basis for the honor we pay an individual or a profession sounded to me very similar to the Roman ideal of duty to the gods, to the state, and to the family, incorporated by Virgil in the *Aeneid.* This was another step for me on the way to developing the concept of honor that would be central to my later study *Honor and the Epic Hero.*

Another of the Victorian critics, Thomas Carlyle, discussed the hero as a possible savior of society from the political, social, and economic problems it had created. In his *On Heroes, Hero-Worship, and the Heroic in History,* Carlyle paints an individual quite different from the self-sacrificing hero Ruskin honors. Influenced, no doubt, by his reading of the German romantic philosophers, Carlyle envisions a great noble leader who naturally rises to his position of leadership as cream rises to the top of the pitcher. That leader has an almost intuitive knowledge of what is best, socially and economically, for his people and the innate powers of leadership to induce them to adopt his suggestions. In *Past and Present,* Carlyle narrates the story of Abbot Sampson, who was just such a natural leader. His abbey had fallen into decay in almost every way. It had been impoverished through mismanagement and was in a state of spiritual decline as well. But the monks recognized in one of their number spiritual qualities, good practical sense, and a potential for leadership that led them to think he might help them to come out of their decline, both physically and spiritually. They elected Samson Abbot, and they were not disappointed. By his native goodness and innate powers of leadership, he did succeed in bringing the abbey back to a flourishing condition. Here, Carlyle suggests, is a pattern Victorian England ought to follow. Find a person with the innate ability to teach and give him the authority to lead England out of the selfish, materialistic condition to which it had arrived. In *On Heroes,* Carlyle elaborates further on his concept of the hero and discusses historical figures he thinks illustrate that concept. His list is a rather odd congregation of figures, including Cromwell.

Carlyle's hero is troublingly like the kind of leaders we have lived to see coming to the fore in our lifetime, with disastrous results to their own countries and to the world. Hitler, Lenin, and Stalin come to mind. It is not accidental that Carlyle's *On Heroes* was required reading in pre-Nazi Germany. This is hardly the kind of leadership that Victorian England needed to solve its problems, as was pretty evident even at my first reading of Carlyle's picture of his hero; it became far more evident later as we saw the terrible results of this kind of megalomaniacal leadership in the careers of Hitler and Stalin.

The most balanced and constructive critic of Victorianism in my reading list turned out to be Cardinal John Henry Newman. He was certainly aware of the ravages that the extremes of liberalism, individualism, industrialism, and utilitarianism had made on the Victorian soul, and he felt the very best way to counteract the negative effect of all these "isms" was by a truly liberal education. In his *Idea of a University,* he probably did more to define and illuminate the idea of a liberal education than anyone who has ever written on it. For Newman, a liberal education is one that is respectful of all knowledge, endeavors to embrace as much of it as is possible, and recognizes the interdependency and interrelationship between the various segments of knowledge. He almost defines liberal education as one that enables a person to perceive these interrelationships. It is not the mere accumulation of knowledge, no matter how prodigious, that makes for the educated mind, but the ability to see the proper subordination and interrelationship of the segments of knowledge to one another.

The result of this integrated and ordered view of reality is truly liberating, freeing the mind from the impotence of ignorance, from narrowness and provincialism, and from prejudice. But to achieve this freedom of vision, the content of the educational venture must be broad; it must contain a knowledge of philosophy, of science, of mathematics, of the humanities (literature and art), and above all it must contain theology (the knowledge of God and His plan for the universe) because from theology flows a good many of the principles that help us order all the rest. Knowledge of this kind is worthwhile in and of itself whether it ever results in anything useful or not. Physical utility cannot be the sole driving purpose of an education. It is Newman's contention, of course, that the liberally trained mind is very useful to society and can provide the kind of leaders who will be most beneficial to the best interests of society at large. This is his response to the exaggerated utilitarianism of his age.

This whole body of reading provided me with an admirable understanding of the great advances and physical and scientific changes that took place in the Victorian period and that permanently changed all of our lives. I saw, as I never had seen before, how these very changes and physical advances had generated a kind of hubris in the human mind that had brought them about and a callousness about the needs and rights of individuals who had fared less well from the changes. It was interesting to see some of the great minds and writers of the period struggling to come to grips with the political and social world in which they lived and endeavoring to suggest some possible remedies. It was also exhilarating to be able to disagree with some of their suggestions, given hindsight by what has happened since, but also to recognize the perennial value of some of their suggestions— the validity, in particular, of Ruskin's social consciousness in his definition of what is honorable and of Newman's insistence that the liberally educated mind is truly useful to itself and to society at large.

# 6

# To the City and Philosophy

When the happy tertian year ended, it was a trek into the city for me—my first experience of urban living. St. Louis at that time was the most polluted city in the country. All the factories and homes burned cheap soft coal from the Illinois strip mines across the river and belched forth pitch-black smoke all day and all night. The worst polluters of all were the hundreds of steam engines that puffed day and night in the Mill Creek Valley just a few blocks from St. Louis University. The Terminal Railroad had a monopolistic contract that gave them the exclusive right to move the hundreds of trains that came into the city station each day, doubling the number of engines belching smoke into the air twenty-four hours a day. The result of all this was that most of the buildings in downtown St. Louis were covered with a black shroud of soot. It wasn't until years later that I realized that the city hall, a take-off of the Hotel de Ville in Paris, is constructed of pink stone and buff brick. When I was at the university, it was all a coal-black smudge. The lovely limestone Gothic church on campus was also caked with soot, and it wasn't until some thirty years later that Cupples House, the mysterious old Richardsonian mansion just off campus, which was a black hulk in my college days, would be revealed as made of beautiful purple Colorado sandstone and light-pink granite. Little did I think then that I would one day be responsible for sandblasting it back to its pristine beauty.

In my tertian reading program at Florissant, I had come across John Ruskin's laments about what industrialism and the factory system had done to some of the cities of England. Francis Thompson had also written an essay called "Blackest England," in which he describes cities such as Manchester that had been blackened by what he calls "the satanic mills" of England. Gerard Manley Hopkins lived for a time in Manchester and wrote some of his poetry there. In one of his very famous poems, "God's Grandeur," he contrasts the beauty of God's uncontaminated world with the pall that industrialization had cast over cities such as Manchester.

The world is charged with the grandeur of God.
   It will flame out, like shining from shook foil;
   It gathers to a greatness, like the ooze of oil
Crushed. Why do men then now not reck his rod?
Generations have trod, have trod, have trod;
    And all is seared with trade; bleared, smeared with toil;
    And wears man's smudge and shares man's smell: the soil
Is bare now, nor can foot feel, being shod.

And for all this, nature is never spent,
   There lives the dearest freshness deep down things;
And though the last lights off the black West went
   Oh, morning, at the brown brink eastward, springs—
Because the Holy Ghost over the bent
   World broods with warm breast and with ah! bright wings.

The city all around and St. Louis University itself at that time were, indeed, "seared with trade" and wore "man's smudge" and "share[d] man's smell." There was a packing plant in the neighborhood, and when the wind came from that direction, the smell was almost suffocating. The smoke in the air was so dense at times that we literally couldn't see across the quadrangle at high noon on a sunny day. The air pollution would sometimes be so intense that crisis health warnings would have to be sent out, and people with respiratory problems would be rushed out of the city lest they die of suffocation. All of this was a pretty grim introduction to urban life, and there was not much of an indication that the Holy Ghost was brooding over this bent world with "bright wings." But in a way that Spirit was.

A few years after I came to the city in 1933, Mayor Dickmann inaugurated a cleanup program that started a phoenixlike resurrection of the city from its smudge. He introduced a stiff smoke ordinance that forbade the use of the cheap soft coal, which had to be passed by the aldermen. While in California at a convention, the mayor learned that they had passed the ordinance but had exempted the Terminal Railroad Company, one of the chief polluters. He telephoned the aldermen and told them that unless they reversed that decision, he would make public the amount each of them had received from the Terminal Railroad to exempt the company from the ordinance. The aldermen made the reversal, and there were *no* exceptions to the new ordinance. The mayor then appointed Raymond

Tucker, a professor of engineering at Washington University, as smoke czar with broad authority to enforce the ordinance. And enforce it he did. Tucker appointed block watchers, and if black smoke was seen emanating from a chimney in a home on the block, the owner's furnace would be sealed until the offending smoke was eliminated. So after a few years the smoke problem was solved. But when I came to the city, the cleanup was several years in the future. We were still in "blackest St. Louis." We could brush off our desks in the morning before we went to class, but when we came back, there would be a palpable grit over every flat surface in the room. It was a grim environment.

I soon learned that the academic curriculum I was coming into was almost as smoky as the physical environment. Traditionally, this stage of a Jesuit's education was devoted to the study of philosophy for three years. The curriculum included a thorough course in logic—which comprised a grounding in the methods of argumentation, both inductive and deductive, and the procedure of syllogistic reasoning. This background would be useful for anyone, but it was particularly helpful to us scholastics because our main courses in philosophy were all set up on the thesis pattern and argued syllogistically. The core of the philosophy curriculum was the course in metaphysics, which dealt with the fundamental principles of being in general. It was supposed to supply the metaphysical substructure of all the other philosophy courses such as "The Philosophy of Man" and "Ethics." The texts for these courses were in Latin; the classes were taught in Latin; and both written and oral examinations were in Latin. Traditionally, the text used for the metaphysics course was by the Jesuit scholar Christian Pesch, and the metaphysics it was based on was that of Francisco Suarez, a famous Spanish Jesuit, which differed rather fundamentally from that of Thomas Aquinas.

Just at the time when I was beginning the study of philosophy, there was a great revival of Thomism under way in Europe and America. In Europe, the revival was led by such important thinkers as Jacques Maritain and Etienne Gilson. Gilson also became an important influence on the Thomistic revival at the College of Saint Michael at Toronto University, where he taught one semester a year for a long time. Men trained at Toronto—such as Vernon Bourke, Robert Henle, George Klubertanz, and Linus Thro (the latter three all Jesuits)—were to become important linchpins in the development of Thomism in the philosophy department at St. Louis University. But in my time, Thomism at St. Louis University and in the training of the young Jesuit scholastics was just a slight glimmer on the horizon. The gleam had been lighted by the Jesuit Henry Renard, who had been sent from Rome to teach the young Jesuit philosophers. He was a very enthusiastic Frenchman, and he had developed a passion for St. Thomas. But his assignment at the philosophate was to teach metaphysics, the text for which was the traditional book by Christian Pesch. This was Suarezian metaphysics sifted through Pesch's German consciousness, which did not at all fit in with Father Renard's new enthusiasm for Thomism. So, in his first year of teaching, he simply ignored Pesch and taught St. Thomas. This approach, of course, did not sit well with the powers that be, so he was told, before his second year of teaching—the year I was beginning my study of philosophy—that he had to teach Pesch. Father Renard came into the classroom on the first day of class with a copy of Pesch. He held it up and said: "We are beginning the study of metaphysics, and this is our text by Father Pesch, a Suarezian philosopher. Our adversary in this study is St. Thomas, and any respectable student ought to know something about his adversary." With that, he went on throughout the semester introducing us to Thomism.

This procedure on the part of Father Renard was a classic example of the kind of conduct of some individual Jesuits that prompted one characterization of the Society of Jesus as an absolute monarchy limited only by the insubordination of its subjects. Father Renard's insubordination did give us an introduction to the mind and work of St. Thomas, but it did little to prepare us for the final examination at the end of the philosophate, when we were responsible for defending the Suarezian approach to metaphysics. We had to get that up on our own. This situation was the source of some of the smog that shadowed our approach to philosophy in my years, but I am grateful for Father Renard's surreptitious introduction to St. Thomas, which I followed up in some of my paraphilosophical work.

Besides the core philosophical courses in Latin ("Logic," "Metaphysics," "Philosophy of Man," and "Ethics"), we had several other courses taught in English, including courses in cosmology, theoretic psychology, experimental psychology, and anthropology. In the case of cosmology, experimental psychology, and anthropology, the texts for the courses were by the teachers who taught them, all Jesuits—

James McWilliams, Hubert Gruender, and Albert Munsch. They knew their subjects well and taught them well.

One of the reasons for separating the study of philosophy from the study of the humanities, which was the concentration in the juniorate, was to give the young Jesuit students the chance to immerse themselves more completely in each area. That separation obviously had some advantages, but it also had some disadvantages. It precluded seeing subtle connections that exist between the two areas, which you are more apt to see when you are experiencing them simultaneously. And that, Newman insists, is what education is all about—seeing relationships.

There was an attempt to round out the educational experiences of us young Jesuits during the years devoted to philosophy. Up to this point, our education had been totally devoid of science. The location of the philosophate on the university campus made it possible to fill in that lacuna. Individuals who planned to go on into a science as a specialization could and did begin their full-fledged science courses on the side at the university during their philosophate, but that left the rest of us without any real experience of the scientific approach to learning. It was thought that this lack had somehow to be remedied. The remedy devised was at its best far short of satisfactory and at its worst a sheer disaster. It consisted of two courses for the nonscience majors, called "Quaestiones Scientificae" (Scientific Questions). They were to be devised by two science teachers, one in physics and the other in chemistry. Each teacher was to select a principle or problem specific to his area, explain it thoroughly to the class, and then perform experiments before the class that would illustrate the principle or solve the problem. This presentation was supposed to acquaint us with the scientific approach to learning, but it actually made no attempt to give us anything like an overview of either physics or chemistry. Father Shannon, who taught physics, was a superb teacher, and the few *quaestiones* he taught he handled extremely well. Father Cooney, the chemistry teacher, on the other hand, was a disaster. A very good chemist himself, with a doctorate in chemistry from Johns Hopkins, he simply could not communicate what he knew even about these limited *quaestiones scientificae,* much less make his demonstration experiments meaningful. So his class was almost totally useless, and neither of these courses gave us any real experience of the scientific approach to the world. Science is not a spectator sport, and unless you get into the laboratory and apply a hands-on approach to the problems of the various sciences, I don't think you really learn what science is all about. I certainly learned more physics and chemistry in my high school courses, which included laboratory work, than I did in either of these truncated courses in *quaestiones scientificae*. The fact that these courses were ultimately dropped from the scholastics' curriculum is probably a sign that we were used as guinea pigs for an unsuccessful experiment.

But another educational experiment introduced into the philosophate schedule in my time was extremely successful. We had the first lay teacher to be introduced into the program. Dr. Vernon Bourke came from Canada, fresh from his doctoral program in philosophy at Toronto University. He taught us a course in the text of Aristotle, quite an innovative course at the time. From the Middle Ages on, the method of teaching both philosophy and theology worked out by the Scholastics in the medieval universities was the thesis method. In that method, the truths you were trying to prove were stated in an introductory thesis. You then listed the adversaries' opposite ideas. You next proceeded to what was called the *corpus* or body of your proof, which generally consisted of a carefully worked out rational proof of your thesis with citations from other authorities or from Scripture if you were proving a theological thesis. Then, in light of the reasoned proof of your thesis, you gave a response to the objections of the adversaries listed at the beginning of the discussion. This method was all very orderly and logical, but it did nothing to get you inside the mind and texts of philosophical or theological writers. You never actually saw any of their writings, so you had no way of following the nuances of their thinking. The author of the text you were studying might quote Aristotle, but you never saw that quotation in the full context of the work by Aristotle himself. When you did, you were sometimes surprised to see that in its original context the quotation might not have quite the meaning the author was putting on it. Hence, for us, it was a brand new experience, and a refreshing one, to be reading the whole *texts* of Aristotle's *Metaphysics, Nicomachean Ethics,* and *Politics,* and to be seeing how the ideas expressed in these several works were related to one another and how, taken together, they provided a rather full view of Aristotle's impression of reality in general. It showed us how in Aristotle's thought we get to know whatever we do know through our sense experience of the visible world around us. We also saw the practical effects of that knowledge on our personal lives (ethics) and on our social lives (politics). I had already had a good introduction to the text of Aristotle's *Poetics* in the juniorate.

Dr. Bourke also taught a course on the text of Thomas Aquinas pretty much based on the *Summa contra Gentiles.* I was so much impressed with Dr. Bourke's ability to help us get inside a philosophical text that later on when I was looking for a subject for a master's thesis in English, I decided to work on St. Thomas's idea of beauty and compare it with Francis Thompson's view and with the illustration of this view in some of his poetry. Dr. Bourke directed the thesis and guided my reading through all the *loci* in St. Thomas where he discusses the concept of beauty. My approach involved an interesting broad scrutiny of the original philosophical text of an author in contrast to the more usual and traditional thesis approach to a subject. There was certainly nothing world-shaking in my conclusions about either St. Thomas or Francis Thompson, but the way of getting at them was a very important educational experience for me.

Mentioning the master's thesis in English reminds me of the distinct advantage of doing the philosophy course in the context of a university. It enabled us to take academic work in the university related to our area of specialization. Mine was English, and so all during the three years of the philosophy program I took the usual courses in English covering all the major periods, authors, and movements that would count for a master's degree in the subject.

The English department at the time was chaired by Father William McCabe, who had done his doctoral work at Cambridge University. He had assembled some impressive faculty members, including Leo Kirschbaum, a specialist in Shakespeare and Elizabethan drama who had done his doctoral work at Columbia University; and Kirby Neill, who had just completed his doctorate at Johns Hopkins under the famous Spenser scholar Edwin Greenlaw. But the two most important influences on my own development were Father McCabe himself and Marshall McLuhan, whom Father had brought to the university from Cambridge.

One of Father McCabe's central interests corresponded to one of my own, Aristotle's theory of tragedy as illustrated in the tragedies of the great Greek dramatists and in Shakespeare. I had become interested in the subject in the juniorate through my first exposure to

Aristotle's *Poetics* in Father Preuss's class. We had discussed there the notion of a catharsis or purification of the emotions of pity and fear as one of the purposes of the tragic spectacle on the stage, but I had to confess that the purification of the emotions did not make much sense to me. I could see no reason why they needed purification, and I thought that everything Aristotle said about the requirements of the tragic character would seem to suggest that the purpose of the tragic spectacle was to arouse the emotions of pity and fear rather than to assuage them. Father McCabe called attention to the fact that nowhere in the *Poetics* does Aristotle say anything about catharsis or the assuaging of the emotions, but rather uses the term in an aside in his *Politics* in a completely different context. What he does say in the *Poetics* is that a tragedy, like all other forms of literary expression, is meant to provide a *specific* pleasure. This idea is part of his emphasis on teleology, the idea that every action is aimed at achieving a specific purpose or end. Tragedy provides a pleasurable insight into the human situation in that it shows that the tragic catastrophe is owing, in part at least, to a character flaw or misjudgment on the part of the tragic character and is not entirely the result of blind fate. In the downfall of the tragic hero, we are not overwhelmed with a surge of pity for a blameless victim; we realize that he is to some extent responsible for his own downfall. This responsibility does not eliminate our pity and sympathy for him, but it is a pity commingled with some criticism of his erring judgment or character flaw. The commingling of compassion for and criticism of the tragic hero gives us some slight insight into the problem of evil in human life, and any kind of illumination in that mysterious area is uniquely pleasurable.

In order to achieve that mixed emotional pleasure, Aristotle insists that the tragic character cannot be a complete villain: if he were, we would not pity him but be outraged at his villainy and feel that his catastrophe is what he deserved. Nor can he be completely innocent: if he were, we would be outraged at the injustice of his fall and get no insight into his own partial responsibility for it. That insight does not eliminate the pity we feel for the tragic hero, but it does reduce it. This does not mean that there are not individuals in life and literature whose catastrophes are in no way a result of any mischoice or flaw in their own character. Their situation is not tragic, but pathetic. They, of course, elicit our sympathy but no criticism. They are innocent victims and not what Aristotle meant by tragic heroes. This approach to Aristotle's analysis of the tragic situation gave us students endless opportunities to argue its validity by applying it to the great Greek tragic heroes, those of Shakespeare, and those of such modern tragedians as Eugene O'Neill and Arthur Miller. It was an approach that I, much later, found immensely helpful and stimulating in my courses on tragedy both on the undergraduate and graduate levels. Again in my end was my beginning.

Another of Father McCabe's courses exposed an entirely new horizon for me. It was a course on the Jesuit theater as it had developed at St. Omers, a Jesuit school on the continent for English Catholic students during the years of persecution in England. It revealed to me for the first time what an important part the Jesuits played in the cultural life of the continent before the suppression. The course was the fruit of Father McCabe's doctoral dissertation at Cambridge. He showed that the theaters were an integral part of an education in the traditional Jesuit *collegium*. They centered specifically on the annual production of a spectacular dramatic performance, which sometimes involved most of the students in the college and many of the city population. It was the duty of the rhetoric teacher to write the text of the play and to oversee its production. The settings for these plays were elaborate, demanding the work of expert designers in the baroque manner. Andrea Pozzo was a Jesuit brother and a world-famous theorist on perspective, as well as an accomplished baroque artist himself. Among other things, he designed the fabulous baroque fresco *St. Ignatius in Glory* on the ceiling of the San Ignazio Chapel of the Roman College. He devoted some of his time to designing sets for the spectacular Jesuit theater productions. The performances included musical accompaniment and formal dance, so training in both areas was part of the curriculum in the presuppression Jesuit schools. I was to learn later how completely involved the early Jesuits were in promoting the arts. They commissioned churches all over Europe designed in the elaborate baroque style, so much so that baroque is sometimes called the Jesuit style. The Jesuits certainly did not invent it, but they used it so extensively that it became identified with them. Some of their baroque churches were designed by Jesuit artists such as the famous Brother Andrea Pozzo, mentioned above, and others by some of the great baroque masters such as Lorenzo Bernini, who designed San Andrea in Quirinale, the chapel of the

Jesuit novitiate in Rome, which he considered his masterpiece, and Peter Paul Rubens, who designed the facade and the interior decoration of the Jesuit church in Antwerp.

The discovery of this early Jesuit involvement in the arts was amazing to me because I had observed no involvement whatever in the arts at St. Louis University. The courses at Florissant on Greek and Roman art and Father Preuss's *illuminabitur* evenings on medieval architecture had whetted my appetite for more art history, but, to my surprise, I found nothing was offered at the university to slake that appetite—no formal courses whatever in music, art history, or studio art. The only brush with the world of art at all in the institution was a not-for-credit series of lectures on symphony music by the psychologist Father Hubert Gruender. He had concocted a high-fidelity player that looked like a huge Rube Goldberg invention but that anticipated some of the sophisticated sound reproducers to be perfected later. He would set up his contraption in one of the physics laboratories, lecture on the structure of a symphony, and then play it on his elaborate phonograph. He gave these performances on Thursday evenings, and he usually lectured on the symphony that the city orchestra would be playing on that weekend. Father Gruender's symphony lectures were the only bow the university made in the direction of the arts.

In my first year in the city, however, there was an academic art relic left in the Jesuit scholasticate, the separate program for young Jesuits preparing for the priesthood. The Jesuit theologate had just moved to St. Mary's, Kansas, to occupy the famous old St. Mary's College campus that had just closed. The theologians, the theological library, and the faculty had all been transplanted, but one faculty member, Father Francis X. Manhardt, had remained behind. He had taught a course on the history of Christian art to the theologians and continued to offer the course for any Jesuit scholastics studying philosophy who might be interested. It was the only course available in art, so I signed up for it. The course was almost exclusively devoted to architecture and was delivered from notes in Father Manhardt's broken Germanized English, but it was better than nothing. Some of Father's evaluations and remarks were hilarious. We could not tell whether he meant them to be funny or that they just struck us as funny. I remember his remark on King John's making a strategic retreat from a battle he had lost: "It was such a pitiful sight to see poor King John in the woods endeavoring to cover his rear." Another time he was contrasting the French and German use of flying buttresses. "The French," he said, "exposed their buttresses quite boldly; the Germans were much more delicate about the matter." But our glimpse of art and our enjoyment of Father's idiosyncrasies were not to last; he died in the middle of the course. He had been using old-fashioned four-by-four black-and-white slides to illustrate his lectures, which were filed in cases in the philosophers' library. I was librarian at that time and had access to them, so I got the idea of getting together a small group from the class and finishing the course ourselves. I suggested this to about six of my good friends, and we launched out on our own. Father Manhardt had given us an outline of the course. We divided up the topics, researched them, and took turns giving illustrated lectures. It was a good experience in self-education. We even brought in guest lecturers. I remember Dr. Coulson, a native Englishman in the history department, lecturing for us on "the ruined abbeys of England." We even reached out to the staff of the art history department at Washington University. Frederick Harrt lectured on Michelangelo, and Horst Janson on Flemish painting. I little realized then what an important part both of these scholars would play in my later career as a self-taught art historian.

It occurred to me that we might enrich our little "do-it-yourself" course in art history by visiting the St. Louis Art Museum to study the artwork there related to our home discussions. I was aware that there was a prohibition in our province customs book against visiting art museums, but, having a fairly elastic conscience in such matters, I suggested it anyway. Thursday was our day off. We would pack a bag lunch, eat it in the park, and then spend part of the day enjoying the relevant paintings in the museum. All went well until one of the group, with a more delicate conscience than mine, had scruples about our visitations because they were explicitly forbidden in the customs book. I took it upon myself to get what the moralists call a *sanatio in radice* (a remedy at the root) or retroactive permission. I went to the father minister, Father Eugene Murphy at the time, and asked him for permission to visit the museum in connection with our self-taught course in art history. He threw up his hands and said such visits were explicitly forbidden in the province customs book. I said I knew that, but a custom was a custom, and a superior was there to dispense from a custom when there was good reason for doing so. I asked him if he had ever been to the museum himself. He said no, he hadn't. I remarked that if he went, he'd see that a very large number of the works were on a religious subject matter—which actually was an exaggeration because, strangely, the St. Louis Art Museum all through its history has rather systematically avoided adding paintings with a religious subject matter to its collection. But the ploy worked with Father Murphy, who said: "If that's the case, it will be all right for you to go." With this positive approval, I told Father Murphy that we had been going to the museum for weeks, and the only reason I was asking permission to go was to lighten the burden on the more delicate conscience of my confrere. Father Murphy laughed this off in good spirit and did not rescind his permission. I cite this incident to indicate how far American Jesuits had departed from the position of patron of the arts they had held in the earlier history of the Society. It was another experience that confirmed my intention of eventually trying to do something about bringing back the arts as a part of Jesuit education at St. Louis University. It was Father McCabe who first alerted me to what an important place they had once held in Jesuit policy.

Father McCabe had other very important influences on the direction in which my life in the Society would move. As I indicated above, he had done his doctoral dissertation at Cambridge University on the Jesuit Theatre at the College of St. Omer. While researching that topic, he became aware of how important the Jesuits' influence was on the formulation of eighteenth-century literary criticism, especially on the rather straight-jacketed interpretation of Aristotle's *Poetics,* in which the three unities governed the writing of much dramatic literature in eighteenth-century France and England. Father was aware that this Jesuit influence had never been studied, and he thought it should be. He suggested the topic as a possible subject of investigation for me in a doctoral program at Cambridge University. He indicated that if I would take on this research project, he would recommend that I be sent to Cambridge for my doctoral work immediately after completing my philosophy studies, instead of doing the usual years of scholastic teaching. The idea sounded good to me at the time, so I began building a bibliography on the Jesuit critics involved and continued to build up the course work for the master's in English at St. Louis University. But the plan was not to be fulfilled.

World War II broke out, and there would be no possibility of going to Cambridge for anything. Father McCabe recommended instead that I take a year of special studies in English at St. Louis University and complete my master's degree in English, which I did. This degree program actually was a far better preparation for my teaching career in English at St. Louis University than years of research and writing at Cambridge on a subject very peripheral to English literature would have been.

The war, however, actually brought one of the most important influences of my entire academic career into my life in the person of Marshall McLuhan. Father McCabe had kept in touch with Cambridge, and he knew about McLuhan's work there. Because McLuhan was a Canadian citizen, if he had stayed on at Cambridge, he would have been drafted into the Canadian air force. Father offered him a teaching position at St. Louis University, which he accepted. He arrived during the year of my special studies for the master's degree. He had been working at Cambridge on his own doctoral dissertation on the prose style of Thomas Nashe. The analysis of what lay behind Nashe's various self-conscious styles had plunged him into a study in depth of ancient classical and medieval traditions. He had come to see the dichotomy that existed between two educational traditions in the Middle Ages—the scholastic tradition of the universities, with its heavy emphasis on dialectics, and the more humane tradition of the cathedral schools (such as Chartres and Orleans), which put very much more emphasis on a humane grammatical and rhetorical approach to learning. Marshall was to deepen his understanding of this dichotomy at St. Louis University, where, under the influence of Bernard Muller-Thym, he learned a great deal more about the scholastic tradition and method. Until then, he did not know Latin, but he taught himself the language so that he could read the sources in the original.

Marshall's chief mentor at Cambridge had been F. R. Leavis, who more than any other one individual was responsible for the New Criticism. I had heard a great deal about the work of Leavis and the "modern" criticism at Cambridge, and here was McLuhan hot from the heart of the movement on campus. I did not need the credit for my master's degree, but I decided to sign up for his course in the practical criticism of poetry to see what this "modern" criticism was all about. In a very short time, with all my course work completed for the master's degree in English, I realized I did not know how to read. I had never been made to dig into a text and see precisely how it worked to achieve its theme. McLuhan was singularly sensitive to every verbal nuance of the poem he was analyzing, but it soon became apparent that his analyses were an application of the age-old principles of rhetoric to the piece in hand. We were asked to read the piece carefully as a whole to catch the general theme the poet was endeavoring to communicate; we tried to see how he divided or structured the development of his theme; and then we scrutinized the propriety of his diction or choice of words, of his imagery, and especially of his rhythm for communicating his theme effectively. This sounds like a banally obvious way of approaching a work of literature *now,* but it was a very new approach at the time. Modern critics such as F. R. Leavis and I. A. Richards in England and Robert Penn Warren and Cleanth Brooks in this country gave the approach its currency; and Marshall McLuhan domesticated it at St. Louis University. Later on, when I became chairman of the English department at St. Louis University, courses in the practical or rhetorical criticism of both poetry and prose became required courses for every English major, and this method of criticism affected the teaching of much else in the department. Marshall McLuhan was later to influence my academic formation even more broadly as the director of my doctoral dissertation, but I am eternally grateful to him for initiating me and the university into the empowerment of the New Criticism.

Catastrophes sometimes work to good ends. The catastrophe of World War II certainly worked to my advantage in bringing Marshall McLuhan into my life and thinking. It also worked to my advantage in another strange way. The young Jesuit scholastics studying philosophy in the Midwest had for years been sent to a lake villa in Wisconsin in the summer, where they studied modern languages, took required courses in education, and enjoyed the pleasures of the lake villa. As seminarians, we were excused from the military service during the war, but it was thought inappropriate for us to be enjoying a Wisconsin villa when the draftees were in training or in battle. So, instead, we were sent out to St. Mary's College in Kansas, newly transformed into a theologate, where we helped the neighboring farmers in the harvest work and pursued our own summer studies. The theologians left during the summer for Wisconsin.

The first year I went to St. Mary's, Father Charles Clark, a newly ordained priest, remained behind to help in parish work in the Jesuit church at the village of St. Mary's. Father Clark was later known as Dismas Clark for his wonderful work in developing a halfway program for recently released prisoners. He was an ebullient enthusiast for anything he took up. During his theologate, he had, on his own and not as part of the regular curriculum, become very well informed on the theory of the Mass as developed by the French theologian Maurice de la Taille. De la Taille's theory at that time was available only in the monumental volume in Latin entitled *Mysterium Fidei* (The Mystery of Faith). But Father Clark had assimilated it completely and was, as usual, burning with enthusiasm for his new insight and eager to find a public with which to share it. There was not that much to do on the plains of Kansas, and so in the hot summer a half dozen of us decided to benefit by Father's enthusiasm and discover why he was so excited about his new understanding of the Mass.

The old explanation of the Mass as an unbloody repetition of Calvary had never made much sense to me. De la Taille points out that this notion was the result of scholastic theologians working out a rational definition of the essentials of a sacrifice and then, at all costs, finding those essentials in the sacrifice of the Mass. They insisted that when the thing being offered in the sacrifice is a living creature, one of the essential features of the sacrifice is the slaying of the victim, what they called in Latin a *mactatio.* Unless there was a slaying, a *mactatio,* as part of the sacrificial act, it wasn't a genuine sacrifice. In the case of Christ's sacrifice, there obviously was a slaying on the Cross. There were also a priest making the offering and a victim being offered, both in the person of Christ. Some of the theologians spoke of Christ's action at the Last Supper as also a complete sacrifice. The priest was there as well as the victim in the person of Christ, but there was no actual slaying of the victim, no *mactatio.* They posited a mystical or symbolic slaying in the distinct and separate consecrations of the bread and wine into the Body and Blood of Christ. And when they spoke of the Mass, they spoke again of a mystical or symbolic slaying of Christ through the separate consecrations. So, in this view, the Mass is a mystical reenactment of Calvary—in spite of the fact that the Letter to the Hebrews states over and over again that Christ was slain only once and that what is repeated in the Mass is Christ's *offering* of himself to his Heavenly Father as a sacrificial victim. De la Taille sees Christ's sacrifice as comprising both the Last Supper in which Christ makes the solemn offering of himself to death on the Cross and Calvary, where this offering is actually carried out. Christ tells us at the Last Supper, as he institutes the Eucharist, that he wants us to do in the Mass what he did at the Last Supper. What he did was make a solemn offering of himself to the sacrificial death that would take place on Calvary on the morrow.

So what we do in the Mass is repeat that *offering* of Christ's having been sacrificed in death on the Cross. There is no new slaying of Christ in the Mass, mystical or otherwise. That took place only once, as Letter to the Hebrews reminds us; what we repeat is the offering that Christ made of himself to his Heavenly Father at the Last Supper and still makes in heaven. So what *we* bring down on the altar and offer to our Heavenly Father is not a dead or dying Christ, but the resurrected living Christ as he is in heaven today. There is no new slaying or *mactatio;* that took place only once on Calvary. And there is no need of it because it is eternally true that Christ as he is in heaven was slain for us on Calvary for our redemption. What Christ offered at the Last Supper and bade us to offer in the Mass was his total self from the Incarnation to the Last Judgment. That gives a eucharistic relevance to every mystery of Christ's life because it was all part of what Christ offered at the Last Supper and bade us offer in every eucharistic offering of the sacrifice of the Mass.

This explanation all made eminent sense to us neophytes as Father Clark expounded the theory to us with his usual emotional intensity and enthusiasm. It was an interpretation of the Mass that de la Taille showed, by an exhaustive historical survey of the writings of church fathers and theologians, was much more ancient and persistent than that of the medieval scholastic theologians. One of the additional bits of evidence that de la Taille gives for the persistence of this interpretation of the Mass is the fact that this theory is illustrated in the ubiquitous eucharistic allusions in the Early Netherlandish painters, the most profoundly and consistently religious school of painting in the history of art. In his original Latin volume, he includes an illustration of Jan van Eyck's famous *Adoration of the Lamb* and shows in his analysis of the work how perfectly it expresses his theory of the Mass. I knew very little about Flemish painting at this point in my life and so the importance of the witness of the Flemish painters for de la Taille's theory was lost on me. I little realized then that some of my own work in art history would one day reveal an important eucharistic symbol in Flemish painting: the vested angel, which all the art historians had missed and that helps express this theory of the Mass in work after work of almost every one of the important Flemish artists of the fourteenth and fifteenth centuries. The story of how I came to make that discovery is the subject of a later chapter, "In Pursuit of Angels." But if it were not for Father Clark's introduction to de la Taille's theory of the Mass, there on the hot plains of Kansas, I might never have found myself in pursuit of these vested angels.

After the usual three years of philosophical studies, I was given an additional year of special studies in English that enabled me to complete the requirements for a master's degree in English. This extra year also gave me the opportunity to accumulate additional course work for the doctorate in English at St. Louis University because the war made it impracticable for me to go to Cambridge.

With the three year's philosophy course finished and the requirements for the master's degree also completed, I was assigned to teach English at the Creighton University Prep School in Omaha, Nebraska. Jesuit scholastics, at this juncture of their training, were usually assigned to three years of high school teaching, called their regency. But because I had had two years of special study, one at Florissant in the tertian program and one at St. Louis University in English, I was to have only one year of regency. I am grateful for that year because the challenge of teaching young high school students is a unique one that I would not have wanted to miss entirely. Creighton Prep, at the time, was a comparatively small school still tucked physically into a corner of the main building at Creighton University. The principal at the time was the legendary Heine Sullivan, who was a kind of a mystery wrapped in an enigma. He had everybody, faculty and students alike, so baffled that he was able to keep everybody guessing about what he would do next. The result was that he ran a very tight ship and was a very successful principal. He held the position longer than any principal in the history of the province.

I was assigned to teach classes in sophomore literature, which at the time was devoted to American literature. It was my first experience in the classroom, and I loved it. It gave me the opportunity of putting into practice for the first time some of the teaching methods of Father Riordon, my old high school teacher: the weekly composition in a composition book, the commonplace book of memorized entries, and especially the guided outside reading program. I also incorporated trips to the art museum and introduced many of my students to the area of art, which was not too difficult because the Joslyn, which was just being developed at that time, was within easy walking distance of the campus.

I suspect that what one learns in one's first year of teaching is largely what not to do. As I look back on that one year of high school teaching, I'm sure I could have and should have done many things better, but on the whole it was a very challenging year's experience that I would not have missed for the world. The year was filled, of course, in the same way every regent's was, with all kinds of extracurricular activities that occupied a great deal of time: prefecting, working with the debate teams, attending athletic events, and directing a literary club. In connection with the latter project, I recall an episode that brought out for me one of the endearing qualities of Heine Sullivan as a principal. Some of the senior students in the literary club decided that they would like to revive the publication of an annual that had been defunct for several years before my advent on the scene. They came to me with the idea. Because I did not think it practicable, I suggested a plan I thought would effectively put an end to it without my telling the students they couldn't do it. I told them if they could come up with a promise of enough ads to pay for the publication of the annual, we would go ahead with it. I did not think they could get any, yet in a month they had a promise of more than enough ads to cover the printing. I had not said anything to Heine about my suggestion, but some of the subscribers to the ads had mentioned the project to him. He called me into his office one day and said: "I hope you will give me a copy of the annual when it comes out. I'm getting money from subscriptions of ads for it." This enigmatic but benign comment was typical of Heine. Another principal would have blasted me off the face of the earth for having made this suggestion without consultation. Heine gently let me know that I should have consulted him, but he let the project go on, and we did publish a revived annual that year.

If Heine's performance here was typical, I'm afraid mine was, too. I've always had the reputation of anticipating the will of superiors— which not all of my superiors have reacted to as benignly as did Heine Sullivan.

7

# Back to the Farm and Theology

AFTER THE ABBREVIATED REGENCY, it was back to the farm for me, this time on the plains of Kansas. In 1931, the theologate had been moved to St. Mary's, Kansas, to the campus of what had been the Jesuit boarding high school and St. Mary's College. St. Mary's was for decades a very popular school for boys all through the Midwest. It was familiar to many readers through the boys' novels of Father Finn, for which St. Mary's College provided the setting. The novels had been part of the library that Father Velte had set up in the vestibule of my parish church in Montello. I little thought as I read the tales of Percy Wynn and the other heroes of the Finn novels that I would be spending four years of my life on the St. Mary's campus and be ordained to the priesthood there.

The extensive property of St. Mary's College, more than two thousand acres, had come into the possession of the Jesuits through their missionary work among the Pottawatomie. That part of Kansas had been Pottawatomie territory, and the Missouri Jesuits had opened St. Mary's missionary center and school for the tribe. It was a very successful missionary venture for decades. The Religious of the Sacred Heart conducted a school for Pottawatomie girls side by side to the school for boys run by the Jesuits. Government agents and prominent visitors to the mission regularly commented on the high quality of both schools and on the success of the Jesuits in helping the Pottawatomie adapt to life on their fertile lands. But eventually the government decided to break up the reservation and give citizenship and pieces of land to individual Pottawatomie. Those who did not want this arrangement would be moved to new reservations farther west. The schools for the Pottawatomie were to continue, and in the new arrangement St. Mary's Mission was assigned approximately a thousand additional acres of land, which brought its holdings up to about two thousand acres. The schools continued to flourish for a while, but in a short time this new arrangement proved disastrous to the Pottawatomie. Most of those who had taken up private land and citizenship lost the land through mismanagement and the machinations of unscrupulous whites so that the enrollment in the schools began to decline steadily until it was no longer feasible to continue to operate them.

The Religious of the Sacred Heart closed the school for girls and withdrew from the mission. It was then that the Jesuit Missouri Province began to develop the site as a boarding school for boys, which evolved into the very successful high school and college of St. Mary's. The school flourished into the 1920s, when it, like similar boarding schools throughout the country, began to lose its popularity. The enrollment plummeted to such an extent that it was no longer practical from a financial viewpoint to keep it open. It was closed in 1930. At the same time, the Jesuit theologate at St. Louis University had become so crowded that it was imperative to find other quarters for it. The decision was made in 1930 to move the whole theologate to the vacated campus of St. Mary's College.

It was to St. Mary's that I went in 1936 to begin my four years of theological studies. I began them in what was called "the long course," which was a relic of a kind of class distinction in the Society that always seemed to me a bit irrational. What it was will need some clarification for some readers, and I confess that its origin has needed a good deal of clarification for me as well. From the beginning, the Society always included *coadjutors* (helpers), lay brothers who contributed to the work of the Society by exercising the skills they brought with them. They usually received no further education in the Society, but without the contribution of their various physical skills, the many institutions of the Society could not have operated. Some of the brothers had remarkable skills. I referred to one previously. Brother Andrea Pozzo, who was an outstanding architect and artist, brought a great deal of prestige to the order by the quality of his accomplishments in architecture, painting, and writings on the principles of perspective. But, for the most part, the skills of the brothers were on humbler but very useful levels. In my time at the Florissant novitiate, at least thirty brothers managed the extensive farm, dairy herd, and creamery; the orchard, vineyard, and winery; the vegetable garden, greenhouse, and landscaped park; the bakery, kitchen, and dining room; the laundry, tailor shop, and cobbler shop.

They also oversaw maintenance of the entire extensive physical plant. There was no way in which the institution could have run without them. The brothers, in all periods of the Society, took the three vows of poverty, chastity, and obedience, and they were in every way considered genuine members of the Society.

The other major group of the Society from the beginning were those who were destined to become priests and whose main work as Ignatius originally conceived it would be catechizing and preaching the Word of God to the faithful. To do that well, St. Ignatius realized they would have to be well grounded in theology. For that reason, he prescribed, from the beginning, that their training culminate in four full years of theology. He was particularly insistent on this prescription because he was aware that one of the serious problems of the Roman Catholic Church at the time was the dismal condition of many of the clergy who had little if any formal education in theology. So he insisted that the candidates successfully complete a full four year course in formal theology in order to become full-fledged professed members of his Society. Because he at first envisioned their chief work to be catechizing and preaching the Word of God, he wanted them to be as mobile as possible so that they could catechize and preach anywhere in the world that the holy father might need them. For that reason, he had those who had successfully completed the course in theology take the special vow of availability to the pope for evangelical work anywhere in the world that the pope might designate. Those who had completed the full four years of theology and had taken this additional vow of availability to the pope were considered the fully professed members of the Society. This arrangement worked well for a time. It did provide a body of clergy well grounded in theology, who were not tied down to a specific monastery by a vow of stability but who had vowed themselves to be available to go anywhere in the world where their services, knowledge, and expertise might be needed.

But the Society grew and spread at a rate far beyond what either St. Ignatius or the other founders could ever have dreamed of, and its work fanned out into education in schools that were soon established in every major city in Europe. Just taking care of the ever-increasing spiritual needs and administering the sacraments to so many more of the faithful was far more time-consuming than those who had benefited by the four years of theology and had taken the fourth vow of special availability could handle. So St. Ignatius petitioned the pope to allow him to accept priests into the order who were less well trained in theology and candidates for the priesthood who might be less capable of benefiting by the full four-year course in theology in order to have sufficient numbers who could do minimal catechetical work and administer the sacraments to the faithful. For this work, less theology would be needed, and what was needed would be given in a shorter course (one or two years) with the minimal content for simple catechetical work.

Both St. Ignatius and the pope who approved the plan envisioned this arrangement to be temporary. According to an extended study of the matter by Father Ladislas Lukocs after the Thirty-first General Congregation of the Society and summarized at length by Father George Ganss in his edition of the Constitutions of the Society, during St. Ignatius' lifetime there were sixty-three priests in the Society with theological learning and sixty-one without it. By 1600, the proportion was 70 percent with and 30 percent without theology; and by 1650, 91.8 percent with and 8.2 percent without. It is obvious that St. Ignatius's emphasis on the desirability of a thorough theological education for full-fledged members of the Society was having its effect. Had things been allowed to progress naturally, the position of spiritual coadjutors in the Society would have lapsed. But St. Ignatius had said that he wanted the professed in the Society to be *conspicuus* (conspicuous) for their knowledge of theology. They would be conspicuous, he felt, if they had had the four years of theology he had prescribed, in contrast to many of the contemporary secular clergy who often had none. St. Ignatius was not thinking of extraordinary proficiency in theology as part of the requirement of profession in the Society. But as time went on, under the leadership of Jerome Nadal and the Generals Mercurian (1573–80) and especially of Aquaviva (1581–1615), the concept of conspicuousness in theology as a requirement of profession was interpreted as meaning an unusual proficiency in theology sufficient to teach the subject.

Gradually the test of whether that was the case was tied to passing a comprehensive examination on the content of the entire four-year course in theology, called the *ad grad* examination, an examination to determine your grade in the Society. Only those who passed this *ad grad* took the fourth vow of availability to the pope and were considered full-fledged *professed* members of the Society. Those who failed it took only the usual three vows of poverty, chastity, and obedience, but not the fourth vow of special availability to the pope. They were not *professed* members of the Society, but spiritual coadjutors. As time went on, the testing for sufficient proficiency to warrant profession in the Society was pushed all the way back to the years of philosophical training. An examination called the *de universa* (concerning the entire content of the philosophical course) was introduced at the end of the third year of philosophy; it covered the material studied in all three years of the philosophical program and was an oral examination in Latin before three examiners. You had to pass this examination in order to enter the *long* course in theology. If you failed this examination, you went into the *short course,* which originally was two or three years rather than four. This meant that you might be effectively excluded from the profession in the Society by the end of your philosophical studies. But even if you made the long course, you still had to face the hurdle of the *ad grad* exam before you qualified for profession.

This procedure effectively created a class society in the order: the professed at the top, with the spiritual and lay coadjutors beneath them. This hierarchy was obviously not what St. Ignatius intended. It may have fitted a European context, but it always seemed incongruous in the more egalitarian American milieu. And the method of determining who would be professed always seemed irrational to me. I am not speaking out of a feeling of sour grapes; I did pass the *de universa* and the *ad grad* examinations and was professed. But determining grade by achievement in these two examinations was not very fair. So much depended on whom you got on your board of examiners and the specific areas on which they happened to examine you, and also how proficient you were in Latin. Some individuals in my own year who failed one or the other of the two examinations and were not professed knew a great deal more theology than some who passed and were professed. And certainly some who were not professed went on and did outstanding work that was a great credit to the Society. Another absurdity of the procedure was the fact that actually in practice there really wasn't a short and long course in theology. Everyone took four years of theology and the same courses, but with different teachers. The absurdity of the situation became so apparent that the delegates to the Thirty-first General Congregation made the resolution to abandon grades in the Society, but Pope Paul

VI vetoed their idea because he said that it would be too radical a change in the order's constitution, not realizing that the procedure of grades had in the first place been a very radical departure from St. Ignatius's original intention. So the procedure remains legally in place, but it is, at least in the United States, more honored in the breach than in the observance. There certainly is no longer any distinction between a short and long course in theology. All candidates for the priesthood take pretty much the same courses in theology and are professed of the four vows.

And what was the difference between the "short" and "long" courses in theology in my time? Actually very little. They both extended through four years, and there were courses in the same subjects in both programs. The only real difference was that they were taught by different teachers. In my time, some of the teachers in the short course were better than those teaching in the long course. Those students registered in the short course did not have to face the trauma of preparing for the *ad grad* examination at the end.

And what was the content of these theology courses? In my work with Marshall McLuhan, I had learned about the two contrasting approaches to theological learning in the Middle Ages, the scholastic dialectical approach on the one hand and the more grammatico-rhetorical and historical approach on the other. The latter is sometimes called positive theology; it is based on a careful reading of the texts of Scripture and of the writings of the church fathers in their broad historical context, thus tracing the evolution of theological ideas. The scholastic dialectical approach was quite different. It started with a statement of theological theses, which were then demonstrated logically and reinforced by citations from Scripture and the writings of the church fathers. The whole purpose was to prove the thesis against the objections of adversaries, whose ideas were refuted in the light of the logical and scriptural proof developed for the thesis statement. It was all very argumentative and aimed at refuting one's adversaries, as opposed to the more historical and analytical approach of positive theology.

This contrast of theological approaches had been largely theoretical in my education prior to this point. I was now to experience it directly. The main courses in the theological curriculum, the ones on which we would be examined in the *ad grad,* were all built on the scholastic thesis method. They were taught in Latin, largely from the prepared notes of the professor of each course, and were meant to cover the important content of dogmatic theology. They began with an introductory course, "De Revelatione" (Concerning Revelation), which was meant to establish the validity of the sources of revealed truth in Scripture and tradition. This first course was followed by a sequence of courses that provided a survey of the whole content of revealed truth. "De Deo Creante et Elevante" dealt with the fact and purpose of creation and with the elevation of humans to a supernatural condition of divine adoption here and in eternity. "De Verbo Incarnato" dealt with the fact and consequences of the Incarnation of the Second Person of the Blessed Trinity, and "De Gratia" dealt with the nature of grace and the nature of the supernatural life it initiated in the human soul. Much attention was given in this last course to reconciling God's omnipotence and humans' freedom as handled by the Dominican theologian, Domingo Banez, and by the Jesuit Luis de Molina. All of these courses were built up strictly on the scholastic thesis method. The texts consisted of a series of thesis statements followed by short summaries of the adversaries' positions and then long proofs of the thesis statements. The proof consisted of what reason itself could provide in explication and defense of the thesis statement, followed by quotations from Scripture and the writings of the church fathers that would bolster the idea. The treatment generally ended with a refutation of the adversaries' ideas in the light of the proof just elaborated. This method was all very neat and orderly, and was supposed to provide a fair degree of certitude about the truth of the theological idea enunciated in the thesis statement. In fact, the *degree* of certitude one might claim for each of the theses was carefully tabulated at the head of each thesis. These tabulated degrees of certitude were part of what you were expected to indicate to examiners in the *ad grad* examination. The problem was that, in some instances, after weighing all the dialectical proof and scriptural quotations, we sometimes felt that we did not have much certitude at all about the truth of the thesis and certainly could not measure the degree of our certitude. We were never asked to read the works of the adversaries to see how they came to the conclusions that were attributed to them in the list of adversarial opinions at the head of the thesis. Nor were we sent to Scripture or to the writings of the church fathers to see the quoted texts in their original context and to test whether they actually could bear the interpretation put upon them in the argument of the thesis. Father Mark Haworth, a cohort of mine, told me that when he and some of his classmates were preparing for their *ad grad* examination, they asked Father Gruenthaner, who was unquestionably the most enlightened Scripture scholar at the theologate, to go over the scriptural texts contained in the theses listed for the *ad grad* exam. He did so, and except for those cited for the Eucharist, not one of them, when read in their full context, really proved what they were meant to prove in the theological theses. This was the problem of the thesis approach to theological learning. The endeavor to find proof for the thesis statement in Scripture meant that we looked at Scripture as a mine from which we could extract nuggets that would enhance our theological position—but, when read in full context, they might not have the meaning put on them at all.

The material for the *ad grad* examination was a selection of some fifty theses taken from these dogmatic courses. We were expected to be able to defend any one or several of them orally in Latin before three examiners. We were given four months free of classes to prepare, and I'm afraid that most of us spent those four months memorizing the proofs and the degree of certitude possible for each of them, and polishing our Latin so we could whip off all this information to impress our examiners. We did have the opportunity to review the whole content of dogmatic theology but not in an atmosphere that induced much deepened appreciation of or insight into the dogmas we were defending. And the *ad grad* examination did not prove very much. It didn't prove that we knew very much theology because so much chance was involved: how the examinee related to the examiners on his board, and what they happened to ask him. I drew a very congenial board, and they asked me to defend a thesis concerned with the purpose of God's creation, a subject I was particularly interested in because it related to many ideas that had been important to me in my study of literature and art. I waxed eloquent on the unselfishness of God's creating anything because as an infinitely perfect being, He couldn't do it to augment in any way His own well-being, even by receiving the recognition and honor and glory. He could do it only for the unselfish motive of sharing Himself with us. All creation manifests Him, and I quoted St. Paul to the Romans to the effect that "From the visible things of this world we come to know the invisible things of God." God did not create in order to receive this recognition; He created only to give and share Himself. Everything in creation acknowledges God just by being; but man, as an intellectual being like God Himself, recognizes God consciously and freely acknowledges God's goodness and beauty, and honors Him. I referred to the poets Wordsworth, Thompson, and Hopkins, who express this idea beautifully in verse, and to the Laudate Psalms, many of which express the same idea. And I said all this in fairly creditable Latin. The examiners were impressed, and I passed with flying colors. I was lucky. There were dozens of other theses on which I probably would have floundered. My examiners were a benign lot, and the thesis on which they chose to examine me was one about which I could be eloquent. Passing the examination did not mean that I knew much theology.

This just again points up the absurdity of the *ad grad* examination and of determining one's rank in the Society by it. I suspect that this matter will be brought up in some future General Congregation in the Society and be eliminated from the books as it has been eliminated from practice, at least here in the United States. Incidentally, there no longer is a "short" and "long" course in theology in present Jesuit practice in this country. Theology is taught in the vernacular and certainly not in the thesis method. Changes do come if you live long enough.

Actually some changes were under way while I was in the theology course. Father Clem De Muth had organized his course on the sacraments along the historical lines of the positive theologians. He traced the evolution of each sacrament from what scriptural references were available for it and found that for some there are no scriptural foundations. The idea of marriage and viaticum as sacraments, for instance, seem to have evolved by practice as time went on. When he discussed the Eucharist, Father De Muth alluded to the *Mysterium Fidei* of Maurice de la Taille, to which I had been so enthusiastically introduced by Father Dismas Clark at St. Mary's when I summered there during my philosophy years. It is, of course, an outstanding example of the fruitfulness of the positive theological approach to a theological subject. Father De Muth built his general course on the sacraments—not just on quotations from Scripture and early patristic writings, but on actual reading assignments in the original texts so that we could follow the elaboration of the idea of each sacrament as it evolved in practice and the written word.

Father Gruenthaner took the same historical and analytical approach in his teaching of Old Testament Scripture, especially in a graduate seminar I took from him on the Psalms. Each of us in the class was assigned an individual psalm, which we had to analyze completely in its total historical and literary context. That meant discussing its author, his audience, the purpose and theme of the psalm, the literary type it represented, and then its literary effectiveness in the diction, imagery, and rhythm it employed. This assignment put into practice in the analysis of Scripture all the methodology that the contemporary modern critics were advocating for a thorough analysis of a poem or any other literary composition. When Scripture was read this way, it yielded a very different harvest than when it was farmed only for quotations to bolster a preconceived thesis. As I look back on my theological training, mainly the *Treatise on the Sacraments*, especially the section on the Eucharist, and the broad analytical approach to Scripture as exemplified by Father Gruenthaner's courses have had a lasting theological and spiritual influence on my life. Most of the content of the straight-jacketed thesis courses in dogma has slipped away.

There were, however, some other academic oases in the St. Mary's years. The four-semester course in moral theology was outstanding, made so by the caliber of its teachers. The course was taught in my years by Father Stephen Boyle, who was bowing out at the time, and by Father Gerald Kelly, who was just beginning his teaching career. In his many years of teaching, Father Boyle had earned the reputation of being the most insightful, balanced, and humane moralist in the country. He kept his balance by taking a confessional every summer in the College Church in St. Louis to keep in touch with the real problems and needs of penitents, and he continued to do so even after the theologate was moved to St. Mary's. Father Kelly had very much of the same balanced and humane approach to moral theology. He eventually became one of the most respected moral theologians in the country and published widely in the field. So we were singularly blessed in our moral mentors at St. Mary's.

Another very special academic oasis was Father Gerald Ellard's course in the nature and history of the Liturgy. He was tied into all the forward-looking experiments in the Liturgy at the time, especially those recorded by Maurice Lavanoux in the distinctive magazine *Liturgical Arts* and the actual experiments in the Liturgy conducted by Monsignor Martin Hellriegel at the Precious Blood Convent at O'Fallon, Missouri. Many of these experiments at the O'Fallon Convent anticipated the liturgical reforms of Vatican II and were much encouraged by Father Ellard. His course on the history and evolution of the Liturgy was the only brush we had with the visible manifestation of the faith during our theology years. The course in the history of Christian art taught by Father Francis X. Manhardt at St. Louis when the theologate was there was never replaced at St. Mary's, so, unfortunately, the theologians at St. Mary's learned nothing about the rich history of Christian art down through the centuries.

This all may sound as if the St. Mary's years were all work and no play, which was not the case. There was plenty of opportunity for physical exercise: hikes in the countryside, swimming in the Kaw River when the water was high enough or in the large outdoor pool supplied with water from an underground stream coming all the way from the mountains in Colorado; tennis or golf on an extensive course on campus; or baseball, basketball, or soccer in season. Some less athletically inclined got their exercise by helping keep the landscaped gardens in trim.

When I was at St. Mary's, the Second World War was in full swing, and many goods were difficult to come by in quantity. Besides this, the father minister in charge and his lay assistant were rather penurious, so the result was that the food was rather sparse and of poor quality. Some of the theologians who helped in the kitchen said that they saw signs on some of the canned goods that said "Not Fit for Human Consumption." Whether that was true, I don't know, but I do know that the quality of the food was pretty bad. The theologians managed to make a joke of it. One morning we came out of the dining room, and the whole herd of pigs from the farm were grunting at the door. When asked what had happened, one of the theologians remarked that the prefect of the pigs was leading a protest march against the quality of their food. We sympathized with their protest.

But the theologians, being a resourceful lot, got occasional relief from the austerities of the table at home by building a series of little shacks in caves, ravines, and the woodland that surrounded the college, in which they cooked meals of their own on Thursdays, their day off. They could get some of the substantials from the community kitchen, but they augmented these essentials with food mailed to them by relatives or purchased in the village. Some even took to hunting and added wild game to their cuisine. One adventurous and rather amoral group was known to have purloined a piglet from the community herd, butchered it, and served up a roast piglet with an apple in its mouth. When the theologate was eventually moved back to St. Louis, the shacks fell to ruin and some of them burned down in brush fires. I can see archaeologists, some hundreds of years hence, puzzling over the remains of these reversions to Bronze Age living that developed right next to a highly developed village in the middle of the twentieth century. I confess that the attraction of this escape to the caves and the woodlands was a little difficult to explain rationally even at the time.

During my years at St. Mary's, the theologians still spent their summers in Wisconsin at the Lake Beulah villa near Milwaukee. But after my first year of theology, Father Mallon, the prefect of studies, asked me to go to Campion, a Jesuit boarding high school at Prairie du Chien, Wisconsin, to teach some of the Jesuit scholastics who summered there. I was to teach those who were assigned to teach English or American literature in high school. I had had various education courses in teaching methodology but never found them particularly helpful in my own teaching. So what I decided to do for these eager young prospective teachers was give them an opportunity to study in detail the actual works they would be teaching. The high school syllabus was carefully worked out and published, so we knew what works they would be teaching. Some of the students had not read many of the works on the syllabus, and I thought that even those who had would benefit by a close study of the works before they taught them. In the hurly-burly of the first year of teaching, they would have little time to do so on the job. The work was really a course in practical criticism on the precise works listed in the high school syllabus. The plan worked out very well. Many of the scholastics told me afterward that they were grateful for this nontheoretical but "practical" preparation for their teaching.

Because I was going to be in an academic milieu in the summer, I decided to make the most of it. I had completed all the requirements for the doctorate, but still had to face the comprehensive written examinations. There would be four of them in areas of my own choosing. The Renaissance was the area in which I had the largest course concentration and in which I felt most confident. So I made a proposal to Father Norman Dreyfus, who by that time had become chairman of the English department at St. Louis University, that I would prepare for the comprehensive in the Renaissance during the summer and would stop at St. Louis on the way back to St. Mary's to take it. He agreed to the arrangement, and that's what I did.

The arrangement was so satisfactory that I decided to use the rest of my summers during theology to complete the written comprehensives in the other areas I had selected: Old and Middle English, eighteenth-century, and nineteenth-century literature. Dr. Millet Henshaw, from whom I had had much of my work in Old and Middle English literature at St. Louis University, was to be teaching a graduate course in Chaucer at Creighton University during the summer following my second year of theology. He had his degree from Columbia University and was a walking encyclopedia on the whole world of Old and Middle English literature. He was not a particularly inspiring teacher, but I thought that the graduate course in Chaucer would get me back into the medieval milieu and be a help in reviewing for the comprehensive in that period. So I arranged to go to Creighton for the summer, wait table in the Jesuit community room to pay for my keep, and register for the graduate course in Chaucer. It turned out to be a perfect arrangement. Millet was stimulated by being in a new setting and positively scintillated all summer. He was also flattered that I had come to register for his course and gave me limitless time outside of class to discuss Old and Middle English literature. He was unquestionably very well informed and was very helpful in a one-to-one situation. It was the perfect preparation for the written comprehensive that I took at the end of the summer.

Because ordination at St. Mary's and my First Mass at Montello and all the social and religious obligations that were related to those great events in my life followed the third year of theology, I spent a more relaxed summer at the Lake Beulah villa in Wisconsin that year.

The summer after my fourth year saw me back at academics again, this time at Marquette University working on eighteenth-century literature under Dr. Victor Hamm. I had had courses in the eighteenth century and in the history of criticism from him at St. Louis University just after he had completed his doctoral work at Harvard. Working with him again was excellent preparation for the comprehensive examination in the eighteenth century, which I took at the end of the summer.

After the fourth year of theology, it was usual at the time to proceed to a tertianship to complete this final step in a Jesuit's training. It is a year devoted completely to reassessing one's spiritual life and includes making once again the thirty-day *Spiritual Exercises* of St. Ignatius. It gets its name *tertianship* from the fact that it is an additional *third* year of spiritual training added to the two years of the novitiate with which the Jesuit's life begins. The powers that be decided that because I was so close to completing my doctorate, my tertianship would be delayed and that I would be given time in special studies to complete the doctorate. So it was back to St. Louis University to take the last written comprehensive in the nineteenth century and do the dissertation.

The last comprehensive was no problem, but I had not as yet even chosen a subject for a dissertation. Back at the university, I found Marshall McLuhan at a high pitch of enthusiasm about his own dissertation on Thomas Nashe, which he was preparing to defend at Cambridge. He had done a great deal of research on the rhetorical background of Nashe's writings and had greatly clarified for himself the contrast between the two approaches to learning in the late Middle Ages and the early Renaissance: the dialectical method of the Scholastics as opposed to the grammatico-rhetorical method of the positive theologians. He had also clarified for himself the effect this dichotomy in the approach to learning had on prose style, and he had demonstrated that influence on Nashe's multiple prose styles.

In his research on his own dissertation, McLuhan had observed the new light that the two approaches to learning had on Francis Bacon's thinking and prose styles and suggested that this topic would be good for a dissertation.

I had just completed four years of theology in which I had had a firsthand experience of the difference between these two approaches to theology, so I leaped at the suggestion and began my research under Marshall's guidance. His direction of my work consisted pretty much in his coming to my room once a week, throwing himself on my bed, and talking for a couple of hours about his dissertation. But what he had done on Thomas Nashe's background and on the consequences of this background on Nashe's several prose styles was precisely what he wanted me to do on Francis Bacon. It worked out perfectly. I followed up on the primary and secondary sources he recommended, and he came back each week for another chat on what I had absorbed.

One of the things that Marshall suggested I look into more closely was how the purpose and works of the Christian humanists at the time were related to this opposition between the two approaches to theological learning. The Christian humanists he was referring to were John Colet, Bishop John Fisher, Erasmus, and Thomas More. He said he thought I would find a striking parallel between their critical attitudes toward the traditional dialectical approach to theological learning at the universities, along with what they suggested should replace it, and Bacon's criticism of the traditional learning of the universities and his suggestions for changes in the disciplines, or "the advancement of learning," which Bacon used as the title of one of his most important works.

The purpose of all the Christian humanists, I discovered, was to bring about a rekindling of real devotion to Christ based on a first-hand knowledge of his person and his values as derived from a first-hand experience of him revealed in Scripture and in a reading of the early church fathers. They did not feel that the dialectical and argumentative thesis method of teaching theology that obtained in the universities achieved this purpose at all. Hence, they were all antischolastic. What they wanted was a method of preparatory education that would teach students to read Scripture and the writings of the church fathers as they would read the text of any work of literature in a broad historical and contextual manner—the approach of the traditional cathedral schools in the Middle Ages as opposed to the dialectical approach of the Scholastics in the universities. The Scholastics had come to dominate medieval education so completely that dialectics pervaded it from top to bottom. John of Salisbury, one of the traditional positive theologians in the Middle Ages, had remarked that students had come to drink in dialectics with their mother's milk. Dominated by it, the curriculum of the prep schools was still made up of the trivium: grammar, rhetoric, and dialectics. But dialectics was in control. Grammar, in this atmosphere, was no longer the broad contextual study of literature that it had been traditionally, but merely the close study of the logic of languages. Rhetoric had traditionally been made up of four parts: *inventio,* the discovery of the substance of one's discourse by broad reading around the subject; *dispositio,* the effective arrangement of one's material; *memoria,* committing to memory the material to be communicated; and *eloquentia* or style, which had to do with elements of language. Under the influence of the scholastic dialecticians in the Middle Ages, whose main purpose was effective argumentation, the first two parts of rhetoric, *inventio* and *dispositio,* were turned over to dialectics because the main substance of their proofs of any thesis was rational argumentation, and the main method of organization was by deductive and syllogistic proof. For both argumentation and proof, dialectics was a better preparation than the rhetorical invention and organization of rhetoric. All that was left to rhetoric in this approach was ornamentation or style, a study of the figures of speech and the figures of sound that give ornateness and grace to one's expression. The Scholastics, however, were not much interested in this aspect of communication. They communicated in Latin, but the humanists thought the Scholastics' Latin was a rather barbarous butchering of the language, lacking any of the grace and flow of Ciceronian Latin.

In this situation, the Christian humanists thought the only solution was to build a new approach to education that would train students not in dialectics but in the broader grammatico-rhetorical methods of analyzing a literary text that would prepare them to read and analyze Scripture in the same way. This approach, they thought, would give the students a better and more intimate knowledge of Christ and his values, and thereby induce a deeper and more personal devotion to him.

The first of the English Christian humanists to do something practical along these lines was John Colet. He had been educated at Magdalen College, Oxford, where he had become very familiar with the traditional dialectical and thesis approach to the theology of the Scholastics, but he also had the good fortune of encountering William Grocyn, who taught divinity there with a perspective that was a little broader than the traditional scholastic approach. Grocyn had studied Greek in order to be able to read the New Testament in the original. Erasmus, the great Christian humanist, described him as "holding the first place among many learned men of Britain." Grocyn himself says: "To put the Sacred Scriptures before the world in their original tongue is a divine work—a most arduous work, and one most worthy of a Christian man." It was through Grocyn that Colet developed his interest in a new approach to Scripture as an aid in developing the devout life of a Christian. After graduating from Oxford, Colet was ordained and became dean of St. Paul's Cathedral. Upon the death of his father, he inherited a substantial sum of money and decided to use it to found a school at St. Paul's that would have as its main purpose training in the more historical, grammatico-rhetorical reading of Scripture precisely to build up a fuller knowledge of and devotion to Christ. Because of this purpose, Colet did not want the early training in the grammatico-rhetorical analytical method to be expended on pagan classical authors lest the students absorb the pagan contents of what they were studying, so he suggested that the writings of early churchmen such as Lactantius, Prudentius, and Sedulius be used. But the point is that he wanted the students to be trained in the grammatico-rhetorical approach in reading so they could apply it to their reading of Scripture. They were to be taught Latin and Greek and, where possible, Hebrew, so they could read Scripture in the original languages. He himself spent some years in Italy perfecting his own Greek, and his lectures on Romans and Corinthians I were examples of the fruit of the kind of scriptural scholarship he was advocating. There were no texts available that would assist students in developing this approach to the study of Scripture, so he invited Erasmus to compose texts for his school. The texts that Erasmus wrote, *Institutum Christiani Hominis* and *De Copia Verborum et Rerum,* became the standard textbooks for all the grammatical schools founded for purposes similar to those of Colet at St. Paul's. Colet had said that it was his purpose "by this scole specially to increase knowledge and worshipping of God and our lorde Crist Jesu, and good Cristen lyff and maners." The children were to learn "good litterature both laten and greke, and good auctours such as have veray Romayne eloquence joined with wisdome." But recall that for Colet these "good auctours" were not the pagan writers, but Christian writers such as Lactantius and Prudentius.

There were other Christian humanists in England at the time who were interested in promoting this new grammatico-rhetorical approach to learning not only in prep schools such as St. Paul's but also in the universities themselves. Bishop John Fisher was one of them. He was chancellor of Cambridge University and wanted to promote the new learning there, but he knew that the dialectical approach of the Schoolmen was so entrenched in the universities that he would have no chance of getting the new program introduced into any of the existing colleges at Cambridge. So what he did was found the new College of St. John the Evangelist, over which he would have complete control. He invited Erasmus to help him plan the curriculum, which would be oriented around the grammatico-rhetorical approach to the interpretation of Scripture. Erasmus did so and took up residence at the college for a time. He worked on his edition of the Greek New Testament and on the works of St. Jerome while there. Bishop Fisher knew that if the new learning was to prevail at St. John's, students would have to be prepared for the new approach by their literary studies before they came to the university, so he founded a prep school where they would get this training.

Richard Fox, bishop of Winchester, was a Christian humanist of like mind to Bishop Fisher. He founded Corpus Christi College at Oxford to promote this new approach to Christian learning and a grammar school at his native Grantham to prepare students for the new approach at Corpus Christi. He commanded that at his new college the early church fathers be taught rather than the scholastic doctors and that all students be obliged to take Greek as well as Latin.

Cardinal Wolsey founded Christ Church College at Oxford in 1524, with a like purpose of promoting the new grammatico-rhetorical approach to learning, and founded a new grammar school at Ipswich to prepare students to benefit by the new approach.

It is in this educational milieu that Francis Bacon grew up. He was educated at Cambridge at a time when the curriculum was still very much dominated by the study of theology as developed by the Schoolmen. It was not the balanced theology of a great Schoolman such as Thomas Aquinas, but a debased Scotism and the empty nominalism of the Ockhamites, so we can understand why Bacon disliked it. "This degenerate learning," he said, "developed a kind of quickness of life and spirit, but no soundness of matter or goodness of quality."

Bacon was not opposed to the theological knowledge of the Schoolmen; "it had been a good and sound knowledge," he says. But what he rejected was the corruption of that knowledge by the dialectical method into "subtle, idle, and vermiculate" questions, spun out and argued about forever. He agreed with the Christian humanists that the best remedy for this dialectical aberration was the kind of educational reformation that would put emphasis on the broad grammatico-rhetorical analysis of Scripture in order to deepen Christian piety.

But Bacon's discontent with contemporary university education ran deeper than that. He thought that there was too much concentration on theology and not enough on the scientific study of the physical universe, and that in what was taught about the physical world there was too much reliance on the authority of Aristotle and on the observations of other past scholars about the outside world. He thought what was needed was a method of observation that would expand man's knowledge of and power over his physical world. He set about devising that method, the *Novum Organum,* he called it. It would avoid anything like preconceived conclusions, what he called the scholastic "anticipations of Nature," and content itself with what was justified by a very close scrutiny of the phenomena of nature themselves. He was, of course, working out an elaboration of the whole process of induction, which is the heart of the scientific method. His doing so has won him, perhaps undeservedly, the title of the father of modern science.

But what is interesting in the present context is that Bacon's concept of scientific induction as he elaborates it turns out to be built on the method of the grammatico-rhetorical critics of literature and Scripture. The critic does not approach the work he is to analyze with any preconceived idea of what the theme of the work is. He arrives at that idea from a very long, careful scrutiny of the text itself. The true scientist, Bacon insists, does the same. He approaches the Book of Nature (and this is Bacon's phrase) just as the critic approaches the written book. It is only after this very careful scrutiny of nature that he is in any position to begin to jot down preliminary notions about the meaning of the phenomenon he is studying. It is only after he has done this repeatedly and jotted down his disparate observations that either he or someone else can put together and formulate something of a general principle or law similar to the final conclusion that the critic comes to about the general meaning of the text he is studying. Bacon is so opposed to the scholastic method of starting a discussion with the thesis statement that he does not want his scientific grammarian to begin even with an hypothesis. The scientist must rely solely on what the scrutiny of the natural phenomenon prompts him to record. This method of induction would have been so disparate and dispersed that it would probably never lead to a legitimate scientific conclusion. Fruitful scientific experiments almost always begin with a hypothesis that is tested by specific repeated experiments.

All I wish to do here is call attention to the fact that very much of Bacon's notion of scientific induction and the language in which he expresses it were derived from the contemporary grammatico-rhetorical reformers in theology. I discovered that he was not the only one to have made this transfer of method. Juan Luis Vives (1492–1540), the Spanish humanist who was tutor to Princess Mary of England and contemporary and friend of Erasmus and Thomas More, had made the same transfer of the grammatico-rhetorical method to the area of scientific induction and in an even more sustained way than Bacon. It is possible that Bacon may have gotten the idea from Vives; he does not say so, but he seldom indicates the sources of his ideas.

Bacon's attitude toward and practice of prose style were very much affected by his own educational experience and by his ideas about what he felt was desirable for the advancement of learning in the future. When the purpose was to persuade someone to accept an opinion on something, he felt that all the traditional elements of rhetoric were appropriate. The first part of *The Advancement of Learning*, where he is trying to persuade King James I to do something about the education procedures in the universities, is structured just like a classical oration, with all the emotional appeal of rhythmic sentence structure, effective diction and imagery, and literary and scriptural allusion. But in his semiscientific writings in both Latin and English that flow out of his scientific explorations in his new inductive methods, he employs brief, simple, curt, almost aphoristic statements to frame the results of his scientific observations. He wants their very curt and disparate nature to suggest the disparate nature of the observations they express.

The light I was able to throw on Francis Bacon's contribution—philosophically, educationally, and stylistically—by placing it in the context of the contemporary conflict between the two approaches to the study of theology was well received. The section on Bacon's own reaction to these two traditions and its effect on his prose style was published in *Saint Louis University Studies* (edited by Norman Dreyfus, March 1950), and my discussion of Vives's anticipation of Bacon's use of humanistic grammar in scientific induction was included in a symposium, *The Legacy of Bacon,* published by Georgia State University Press in the series Studies in the Literary Imagination. It was picked up and republished later in the *Bacon Journal* in London.

But whether my work on Bacon did or did not add much to a better understanding of his work, I am very grateful to Marshall McLuhan for pushing me into the study and guiding me throughout it. The work gave me a key to a better understanding of much that transpired in theology, education, and literary prose style in the Renaissance period itself and much that has transpired in all these areas in the centuries since, including our own.

The educational changes made by the Christian humanists really amounted to a reform movement within the Roman Catholic Church. Its aim was to develop a genuine devotion to Christ based on a personal knowledge of him drawn from a close reading of Scripture and of the writings of the church fathers. It was the movement within the Church comparable to the contemporaneous Protestant Reformation going on outside the Church. The close reading of Scripture in the broader grammatico-rhetorical manner was essential to both movements. But the official Catholic Church at the time grew fearful of too much individual reading and interpretation of Scripture lest they aid and abet the multiplication of the Protestant sects, so in the Council of Trent the Church retreated into the old approach to the study of Scripture and canonized the scholastic thesis method of teaching theology in the seminaries. From then on, the general public got its theology in catechisms faithfully memorized, and seminarians got it in the straight-jacketed thesis form. The thesis pattern in theological courses continued on through the post-Tridentine centuries down to our own time. The bulk of my own dogma courses were still built on that pattern. In fact, in that tradition, personal reading of Scripture was actually discouraged lest there be too much unguided private interpretation that might become heretical. The result was that the general Catholic public had very little firsthand knowledge of Scripture. When I started teaching English literature in college, I could easily separate the Catholic from the Protestant students: the Protestants knew Scripture; the Catholics usually did not. In England, the scriptural revival instigated by such Christian humanists as John Colet, Erasmus, and John Fisher in such schools as St. John's at Cambridge was carried on by Protestant divines after Henry VIII's split with Rome and the suppression of the Catholic Church. Two of the great Catholic humanists, Bishop John Fisher and Thomas More, were martyred in defense of their faith. So the hoped for Catholic revival of learning and a more Scripture-related theology leading to a renewal of fundamental Christian piety were nipped in the bud by the decrees of the Council of Trent and by the Henrican break with Rome.

The people who were to benefit by what the Catholic humanists in England had started were the Protestant divines because the humanists' approach fitted the Protestants' emphasis on Scripture and on the witness of the early church fathers as the source of true doctrine. Richard Hooker's *Of the Laws of Ecclesiastical Politie* and the Scripture-laden sermons of great Protestant preachers such as Sandys, Jewel, Henry Smith, Launcelot Andrewes, John Donne, and Jeremy Taylor were the direct result of that influence.

In the nineteenth century, it was the continuation of the historical approach to positive theology that brought John Henry Newman into the Roman Catholic Church. It was his broad reading of the works of the church fathers in historical sequence that enabled him to see that it was the teaching deposit of Roman Catholicism rather than his native Anglicanism that rang true. As a result of this approach, he elaborated his theory of "the development of doctrine," which takes account of the evolution of doctrine under the influence of changing historical circumstances. In Vatican I, he was almost condemned as a modernist for this theory. It is an index of how much the Church itself has changed since Vatican I that Newman was practically the patron saint of Vatican II and that his theory of the development of doctrine became a rather central guiding principle of its decrees. And it is interesting that right now Cardinal Newman's cause for beatification is being promoted. The Vatican II position on the necessity of a more vital Christian practice with a more enlightened theology solidly based on a *personal* knowledge of Scripture and susceptible to some evolution and a more personalized use of the Liturgy is a development that sounds like a long-delayed fulfillment of what the early Catholic humanists were striving for back in the sixteenth century.

Certainly one of the most positive effects of Vatican II is the emphasis it has placed on the importance of a firsthand knowledge of Scripture as the basis of one's spiritual life. Ordinary Catholics today are exposed to very much more Scripture than they ever were before. The expanded scriptural readings in the Liturgy of the Word at Mass acquaint them with a considerable amount of both Old and New Testament readings. But many Catholics today do much more extended personal reading in Scripture than they ever did in the past. I have been counselor myself to a group of eleven laymen for the last thirteen years who meet every month to read and discuss passages from Scripture. In that time, they have read and discussed a considerable amount of Scripture. The group is made up of a doctor, two lawyers, an engineer, a chemist, and several successful businessmen. Christ has become very familiar to these men as he has revealed himself to them in the pages of Scripture. I am impressed with how they carry him and his values with them into their everyday lives and how they translate what they have learned about him into social work for others in their families and outside their families. That is what Christian humanism was meant to do. And that is what the changes in church practice in Vatican II were meant to do and to some considerable extent are doing.

I devoted the entire year of special studies and the following summer to researching the Francis Bacon topic and writing the dissertation, both under the close scrutiny of my mentor, Marshall McLuhan. I completed typing the final copy of the dissertation just a week before I took off for the West Coast, where I was to complete my next assignment, the delayed tertianship.

# 8

# Go West, Young Man

THE FARTHEST WEST I had ever been was Denver, so I was rather excited about the assignment of making my tertianship at Port Townsend on the West Coast. Port Townsend is almost as far northwest as you can go in the United States. It is situated on the Olympic Peninsula at the juncture of the northernmost part of Puget Sound and the Straits of Juan de Fuca. Because it was so far north, I expected it to be almost Alaskan in its temperature, so I equipped myself with long underwear and a leather jacket to be prepared for the worst. No one had told me about the Japanese current that keeps the climate relatively temperate in the winter. Camellias thrive in the gardens there as comfortably as roses in the Midwest, and banks of wild rhododendron fifteen feet high stretch for miles along the highways, a blaze of blossom in the springtime. The rhododendron is actually the state flower of Washington. I was to find myself picking wild violets on Christmas day, so temperate is the climate. And because of the acidity of the soil, all flowers are very intense in color. In the garden at the tertianship was a fence laden with beautiful perennial sweetpeas. They were so brilliantly red that the color almost hurt my eyes. My sister Laura was a flower lover, so I gathered some seeds from the sweetpea vines and sent them to her. They grew and flourished, but their color in the Wisconsin soil was an anemic washed-out pink. The climate was my first surprise in the Northwest. There were many other surprises to come.

I had finished typing my dissertation just days before I took off for the West. I dropped off at Montello for a home visit first and then at Portage caught the fabulous cross-continental *Hiawatha* train on the Milwaukee line to Seattle. Another thing no one had told me about was the fog of the Northwest. Father Dick Porter had arranged for his sister, who lived in Seattle at the time, to pick me up and show me around the city before I took off for the tertianship at Port Townsend. But when I arrived in Seattle, the whole city was wrapped in an impenetrable fog. I could sense that the city was very hilly and situated on water, but I could see practically none of it. Miss Porter would stop on a promontory and say, "On a clear day, you get a beautiful view of Mount Rainier from here"; or from another vantage point, "On a clear day, this provides a spectacular view of the Cascades and Mount Baker." I had to take it all on faith because all we could see was the white veil of fog. Miss Porter finally deposited me at the ferry landing, and I was off on the final leg of my journey to what seemed like the end of the world. And it turned out to be almost that. To get to Port Townsend from Seattle at that time, you took a bus to the ferry landing (where Miss Porter had deposited me) and a ferry across part of Puget Sound to Whidbey Island. A bus brought you across the island to another ferry landing, and a final ferry got you over the last stretch of the Sound to a landing on the Olympic Peninsula, where you caught a final bus to Port Townsend. I was managing all of this trip in a dense fog, so it had some of the aspects of a nightmare journey. I had no idea where we were going and no idea at all of the beauty of the surroundings we were passing through on the way. I took a taxi from the bus station at Port Townsend to Manresa, the tertianship. It finally loomed up out of the fog, a towering, turreted old mansion that looked like Hawthorne's House of Seven Gables. It was to be home, off and on, for the coming year. The tertian master, Father Leo Martin, had a warm greeting for all of us incoming tertians. His simplicity, genuineness, solid spirituality, and common sense were to endear him to all of us as the year wore on.

I was assigned a second-floor room on the front of Manresa Hall. I looked out at the fog before retiring and was not at all prepared for what met my eyes when I looked out the window again in the morning. The fog had lifted, and I now realized that Manresa Hall was situated on the shore of a little bay in Puget Sound. The front lawn ran right down to the water's edge. Across the Sound were the snow-capped Cascade Mountains, with Mount Baker towering to the north. As I looked out that first morning, the sun was just coming up behind the mountains, irradiating the whole range in a soft rose light. As the sun moved higher, the mountain range shifted in color tone as if a rheostat were gradually being moved across the board. The light caught the many pine-clad islands in the Sound and the mists of fog between them, so the whole scene looked like a delicate, shifting Japanese print.

A line of Hopkins's sprang to my mind: "The world is charged with the grandeur of God." I thought what a wonderful way to begin this year of spiritual renewal. This sight was only a tiny sampling of the inspiration that this little corner of what I think is one of the most beautiful parts of the United States was to provide for me that year. I had never before lived this close to the sea and mountains, and both were a constant source of inspiration for me. But they did not seem to be that for everyone. I recall one of my fellow tertians who hailed from the area remarking to me one day: "I feel sorry for you three Missourians. You were parked in a Kansas cornfield for four years, and now you have to come out here and live next to the stinking sea." It was not *stinking* to us at all. It did have a distinctive smell generated by the kelp thrown up on the shore and by the salt breezes, but it was not an unpleasant odor. In fact, I can understand that when you get used to it, you might miss it if you move away from the sea. I later met a young man in Victoria, Canada, who had been raised in Scotland right on the seashore. When he came to Canada, he settled first inland and was very restless and did not know why. He kept moving farther and farther west until he got a whiff of the sea again in Vancouver and knew that he was home. He settled down in Victoria and said he was content to stay there forever breathing the familiar scent of the sea.

We had a few days of leisure before we settled down to the serious schedule of the tertianship, so most of us did a little exploring of our new environment. Manresa Hall was on the outskirts of Port Townsend. The site of the town is quite picturesque, a very hilly terrain stretching along the beautiful bay. It reminded me of San Francisco. In fact, when the town was founded, some thought that it would become the San Francisco of the north, but that never happened. It was actually a city built as a ghost town. It was laid out in paved streets with lighting and sewage pipes to accommodate forty thousand residents. All the downtown structures were built four stories high. But the city, up to the time I was there, never had a population of more than four thousand. The paved streets ran out into uncut forests, and only the first floors of the downtown buildings were ever occupied. Port Townsend was on the wrong side of Puget Sound. Because it had no railroad connections and no easy access by road, it never developed into an important mercantile or maritime center in spite of its strategic position on the juncture of Puget Sound and the

Straits of Juan de Fuca. Since my time, bridges have been built from the mainland to Whidbey Island and from the island to the Olympic Peninsula, which now makes Port Townsend quite accessible by car and truck. It has become a rather active tourist and mercantile center. But in my time, it was still the planned ghost town.

Thursday was the day off for the tertians, as it was for young Jesuits everywhere at any point of their training. So on our first Thursday, we all piled into the back of a truck and drove to the tertianship villa on Discovery Bay, a picturesque inlet off the Straits of Juan de Fuca. To the south of us loomed the northern shoulder of the Olympic range of mountains. They were so close that we always felt that they were looking over our shoulders. But in between them and the Straits stretched virgin evergreen forests of majestic Douglas fir and cedars, some of them rising to heights of 150 feet or more. Great diagonal shafts of sunlight cut down between their majestic trunks, dimly illuminating the moss-covered logs at their roots. It all looked like the forest world pictured in the Bambi movie. The road to the villa cut through this primeval forest, and one often saw entire families of Bambis on either side of the road. The villa, a small cottage, was perched on a high bluff overlooking the whole of the elongated Discovery Bay, stretching off to the Straits of Juan de Fuca. When the tide was coming in, its wrinkled surface made the whole bay look like a giant monster crawling toward us as we were perched like an eagle on the high bluff. It brought vividly to my mind a little poem, "The Eagle" by Tennyson, which must have been inspired by a similar experience of seeing a moving body of water from a height:

> He clasps the crag with crooked hands;
> Close to the sun in lonely lands
> Ringed with the azure world, he stands.
>
> *The wrinkled sea beneath him crawls*;
> He watches from his mountain walls,
> And like a thunderbolt he falls.

It was a sight we were to enjoy every Thursday from our eagle's perch on the bluff above Discovery Bay. And the bay had other favors to offer us. Father Pete Halpine, the father in charge of Manresa House, went deep-sea fishing in the bay every Thursday, and he always succeeded in catching a sizable salmon or cod fish big enough to supply a meal for the whole community on Friday.

But what about the main business of the Port Townsend sojourn? It was, after all, my final year of spiritual training as a Jesuit: the tertianship. St. Ignatius had incorporated it into the training of his followers as a result of an important personal experience in his own development. He had planned at first to go with his first companions to the Holy Land to do apostolic work there, but he and his companions had failed to get passage and had been holed up at Venice working in the Hospital of Saints John and Paul there. St. Ignatius himself and those of his companions who were not yet priests were ordained at Venice. Because they could not go to the Holy Land, it was imperative that a decision be made as to what direction the little group would go. In preparation for this important decision, St. Ignatius decided he needed some time for quiet prayer and thought, so he withdrew to a Franciscan monastery near Vicenze, a few miles away from Venice, and remade the month-long *Spiritual Exercises*. That completed, he and his companions continued to work in the hospital and did catechetical work, but they eventually came to the decision to go to Rome and petition to be recognized as an apostolic order offering their services to the pope in whatever capacity he chose to use them.

This year of prayer and apostolic work before coming to the very important decision about the future of his little band of followers was so helpful to St. Ignatius that he decided to make a similar combination of the long retreat and a year of combined prayer and apostolic work an integral part of every Jesuit's training.

Father Martin, the tertian master at Port Townsend, was very much in agreement with St. Ignatius that the tertianship should combine a renewal of prayer life, a repetition of the long retreat, and some public apostolic work. There was plenty of opportunity for apostolic work in this remote peninsula at the time. The Second World War was raging in the Pacific, and the whole area was alive with navy and marine bases, army posts, and ammunition dumps of various kinds. Baby flattops came from the Pacific almost weekly and anchored in the little harbor right in front of our house to be degaussed. Plowing through the seas, they built up a magnetic charge on their surface, which attracted Japanese torpedoes and mines. They had to be brought back periodically and desensitized (degaussed). In the process, they were surrounded by floating metal nets through which current was passed that removed the magnetic charge from their surfaces and made them less attractive to Japanese torpedoes. When they were in harbor, some of the tertians functioned as chaplains on board ship. We said Mass for the sailors and administered the sacraments to them. They were a mighty serious congregation. Besides this work on the baby flattops, we served at a half-dozen or more permanent army, navy, marine, and air corps posts on the peninsula. My assignment was Indian Island, an assembly point for marines headed for active duty in the Pacific. It was a sobering experience to be saying Mass and hearing the confessions of these young men who knew that their next move was into the thick of the battle in the Pacific. A good half of the men shipping out every week would not return alive. The marines were in the forefront of the fighting in the Pacific Islands. Homilies delivered to this congregation in these circumstances held pretty close to the core of the faith. The marines were very interested in clearing their spiritual decks through a good confession before they pushed off to sea. Their Communions were for many of them a real viaticum. Never before or since have I experienced what an empowering force the sacraments can be.

I had one experience on Indian Island that I will never forget. A young black marine came into the sacristy one Sunday and said he would like to be baptized. I asked him if he had had any instruction in the faith. He said: "Yes, indeed, back at St. Ignatius Jesuit Church in Baltimore." I quizzed him on the essentials and found that he had been very well instructed. He was about to be baptized back in Baltimore but had been shipped out to Indian Island for duty in the Pacific before he could arrange for the ceremony. I planned his baptism for the next Sunday as part of the Liturgy of the Word. His name was Luther Shaw. I asked him whether he would like to take a saint's name when he was baptized. He said he would and that he'd like to take the name Bernard. I thought he might have known of Bernard Shaw and that was why he had chosen Bernard to be his name, but that wasn't it. To my inquiry of why he had chosen that name, he replied: "Because I have a great devotion to St. Blase." "Why not take Blase for a name, then?" was my next question. "Because if I do," he said, "the boys will call me 'Blazes,' so I'll take Bernard for a name because it begins with a 'B,' but I'll have it in mind that St. Blase is my real patron in heaven." When I asked him how he had come to know about St. Blase, he said he had happened into St. Ignatius Church on St. Blase's Day, when they were blessing throats, and he was so impressed with the candle ceremony that he went to the rectory and asked to learn more about the Catholic faith. God certainly works in mysterious ways. Who would have thought that this very peripheral ceremony of the blessing of throats in the name of St. Blase would have been the instrument of the grace of faith for this young man? So Luther Shaw was baptized Bernard Shaw on the next Sunday. I leave it to the bookkeepers in heaven to sort out who his real saintly patron is. Luther-Bernard-Blase was shipped out to the Pacific, and in a few months I received notice that he had been killed in action. I know now there is another St. Bernard or St. Blase in heaven to pray for me, and when I remember, I say a prayer to him. He and countless others like him are commemorated at least once a year on the Feast of All Saints.

The regular order of the tertianship was similar to that of the novitiate: a routine of quiet prayer, instructions on the Constitutions of the Society, spiritual reading, and physical labor. Besides the regular chores involved in maintaining the house and helping in the kitchen and garden, we did special assignments to augment our food supply because so many goods were rationed during the war. Washington State, like Oregon, is famous for its apple orchards. The owners of these orchards allowed us to come after the first picking and gather the less-prized fruit that was left. We would come back with a truckload of apples, which we peeled and prepared for cooking and canning as applesauce. The father minister occasionally bought dozens of large fresh salmon from the fisheries, and a clam chowder factory in town allowed us to use its facilities on Saturday to can the salmon for our own use.

But this work was interrupted on rotation by stints as hospital chaplains. With these projects and a Victory Garden, which had been developed by plowing up the front lawn and planting it to vegetables, we were able to provide a good amount of the staples for our table. The only problem at Manresa was that Brother Ryan, the cook, seriously considered it his vocation to spoil the food in order to provide what he considered the necessary mortification of the tertians. And I must say, it was a vocation that the brother realized completely. The food was terrible. There was no redress because Father Martin, the tertian master, was so abstracted that he could have been served asbestos, and he would not have noticed. I recall one occasion when the brother served small squash harvested from the garden. They should have been baked, of course; he had cubed them and boiled them, so they tasted exactly like lye. The tertians would take one bite in their mouths and immediately replace it on their plates. We looked up at the head table, and Father Martin was eating the bitter bits as if they were ambrosia.

Work in the Hospital of Saints John and Paul had been an integral part of the year in Venice that St. Ignatius used as the pattern for the final year of spiritual training for his followers. Our tertian master, Father Martin, also tried to make a stint as hospital chaplain an integral part of the tertian's experience. In my year, he had added a new hospital to the list where the tertians might be sent, Mount Saint Grace Hospital in Victoria, Canada. I was one of the first to be sent there on what was called hospital probation. It was to prove to be in many ways the most profound spiritual experience of my whole year there.

Victoria itself was very rewarding. It is situated on the southern tip of Vancouver Island, which in size is about the same acreage as England and is in many ways an echo of England. A kind of oak tree thrives on the island that grows nowhere else except in England. Many of the inhabitants of Victoria are of English descent and have brought some of their customs with them. There are many lanes instead of streets in the residential areas, and often, instead of street numbers, the houses are identified by quaint names. Bowling greens are a prominent feature of the great Princess Hotel that fronts the harbor. Victoria is definitely a little bit of England away from England.

Because Mount Saint Grace Hospital was a new hospital on the list for tertian chaplaincies, Father Martin decided to check it out. He announced his coming the first weekend I was there. He had told us in one of his conferences that when we stayed in a convent, we should be sure to have a key for our luggage because the nuns would go through it. We thought that an unlikely story, but I was to find out that it was true. Father had a thing about poverty and certainly squandered nothing on himself. He arrived at the hospital just before dinner with an unpretentious handbag that looked like the little satchels that country doctors used to carry. We deposited it in his room and went down to dinner. When we came back to the room, the nun in charge of the room had not only gone through his satchel, but also had thrown away his very battered pajamas and his worn-out stub of a shaving brush and replaced them with new ones. Father turned to me and said: "You see what I mean, Father?" I did, indeed. But this invasion of his privacy did not prevent him from giving his enthusiastic approval to Mount Saint Grace as a very fine place for the tertians to do their hospital probation.

I am certainly glad that it was at Mount Saint Grace that I had my assignment early in my priesthood. I learned things there that have been greatly helpful in my later career as a priest. It was the function of the chaplain, of course, to visit the patients each day. The hospital specialized in caring for the terminally ill or completely disabled patients. I had never seen before nor have I seen since so many patients suffering from so many terminal diseases—such as cancer and heart ailments—or so many disabled from strokes, diabetes, Parkinson's disease, and arthritis gathered under one roof. It was my job to bring them Communion in the morning and to visit them during the day to cheer them up, but it soon became apparent to me that they didn't need a lot of cheering up. In spite of their many terminal illnesses and their many crippling disabilities, they were almost to a person the most cheerful lot of human beings I had ever encountered anywhere. Our functions had almost been reversed. They were cheering me up rather than I cheering them up. I tried to analyze what accounted for this extraordinary phenomenon. I came to the conclusion that it was largely the result of one person—Sister Mary Grace. It seemed not accidental that her name was Sister Mary *Grace* and that she was head of Mount Saint *Grace* Hospital. I have never been in a place where the effects of God's grace were more palpable than at Mount Saint Grace Hospital, and I believe that Sister Mary Grace was the channel of much of that grace. I'd like to tell her story.

Some years before, she had herself become critically ill with a tumor on the brain. She had been taken to a hospital in San Francisco for surgery, and five of the best brain surgeons in the area were assembled for the operation because the case was such a special one that they all wanted to witness the operation. It seemed to have progressed successfully, but after hours on the operating table she suddenly went into shock and seemed to have died on the table. No signs of life were apparent; the doctors declared her dead and began a verbal postmortem on what had gone wrong. But she wasn't dead. She said she heard their conversation. Because they had declared her dead, she presumed that she was on her way somewhere, and she would have given her immortal soul for someone to have breathed a prayer to speed her on her way. All she heard was the postmortem. Then, to the astonishment of the assembled doctors, her pulse came back, and she began to breathe. Her postoperative recovery was complete.

The result of all this experience was that she resolved to spend the rest of her life caring for the terminally ill. There was no question in my mind that the marvelous spirit I found in all the suffering patients at Mount Saint Grace Hospital was the result of the peace and graciousness that radiated from Sister Mary Grace. If there was a dying patient who had fallen into a coma, Sister, remembering her own experience on the operating table, would stay up all night, vocalizing prayers for them and occasionally touching them to let them know that there was someone there who cared. It was the sort of loving concern that had transformed this house of suffering into one of the most peaceful domains I have ever been privileged to experience. While I was there, a rough customer from the labor union of the harbor shoremen had been admitted to the hospital in the last stages of cancer of the abdomen and liver. He was a fallen away Irish Catholic who had become a leader of the Communist Party in the region and had the utmost contempt for anything associated with the Church. This attitude was in almost diabolic contrast to the whole spirit of the place. When he saw me coming down the corridor, he would burst into shouted profanities against me and the Church. Nothing I could do would calm him down. But Sister Grace, by extra kindnesses to him, wore down his antipathy until he ceased his rages. Eventually he was reconciled to the Church and died a happy death. This was another example of the grace that radiated from Sister Mary Grace.

During my six-week stay at the Mount, I was to learn a bit more about the background of this extraordinary person. One wing of the hospital building was really a retirement home for elderly people who did not need nursing care but did need some supervision. Sister Mary Grace's mother lived there. Sister told me a good deal about her mother's background. She was English and Anglican, and ran a bookstore in Oxford, England. One day a young man came into the store looking for a copy of Newman's *Apologia pro Vita Sua*. She did not have a copy, but she told the young man she would search out one for him, which she did. Before he returned to pick it up, she read it herself. She was much impressed with the conclusion that Newman drew from his reading of the church fathers that the Roman Church rather than the Anglican could make the best case for being the true Church of Christ. When the young man came back, she talked with him, also an Anglican, about her reactions to the book. When he read it himself, he returned and discussed his similar reactions with her. To make a long story short, they both were eventually received into the Church, fell in love, and were married. An early business assignment saw them in Northern Wales, where their first daughter (Sister Grace's older sister) was born. She contracted a very stubborn throat infection, which no form of doctoring or medication could seem to cure. The doctors thought the baby's power of speech might be permanently damaged. Her parents were in the neighborhood of Holy Well, a famous place of religious pilgrimage in Northern Wales.

The story of its origin was familiar to me. It is near St. Beuno's, where the English Jesuit tertianship is located. Father Gerard Manley Hopkins made his tertianship there on what he calls "a pastoral forehead of Wales." He became very familiar with the legend about St. Winefrede and her uncle, St. Beuno, the Benedictine abbot of an abbey in the neighborhood. In fact, Hopkins began writing a play on the subject, a fragment of which remains. One of his most beautiful poems, "The Leaden and the Golden Echo," was to function as a choral ode in the play. According to the legend, Caradoc, a Roman legionnaire, became enamored of Winefrede, the beautiful Christian niece of Beuno, and attempted to seduce her. She steadfastly resisted him, and in a fit of frustration he whipped out his sword and lopped off her head. Her uncle, the saintly Beuno, heard of it, came to the scene, picked up his niece's head, and replaced it, miraculously restoring her to life. According to the legend, where her head had landed, a clear stream of water sprang up, and a well was formed. The place was named Holy Well. It became a place of pilgrimage, and many miraculous cures were recorded of pilgrims who had bathed in its waters. Hopkins says of it in his unfinished play on the legend,

> Here to this holy well shall pilgrimages be
> And not from purple Wales only nor from elmy England,
> But from beyond seas, Erin, France, and Flanders,
>     everywhere.
> Pilgrims, still pilgrims, more pilgrims, still more
> pilgrims.

My father, James P. McNamee Sr., and me at age four, and my mother, Ida McNamee, and my brother Fran at age one.

The house in which I lived until I left to join the Jesuits.

Right: St. John the Baptist Church, Montello, Wisconsin, where I was baptized, confirmed, and offered my First Mass. Below: Traf Maher (right) and I, as cooks, with a pie and salad at the Villa of Waupaca, Wisconsin. Bottom: Mother, my sister Marcella (Sister Mauritia), myself, and Dad at the reception on the day of my First Mass.

Upper left: The Rock Building, Florissant, Missouri, the Jesuit Novitiate where I began my training as a Jesuit. Above: Father Henry Riordon, inspired English teacher who got me hooked on teaching English and who disliked the Jesuits. It was his criticism of them that led me to look up their history and become one. Below: the Tertians in front of the Old Juniorate. Front row, from left: myself, Father Preuss, Henle. Back row: Barnett, Corley, Arnold, Wetmore, Stauder.

My class in the Juniorate: First row (from left): P. Reinert, Casper, Luebke, Hockhouse, Bishop, Barnett, Murray, Tully. Second row: Warner, Wernert, Corley, Stumpf, Schenk, Wetmore, Rochel, me, Ulrick, Stauder. Third row: Arnold, Stockhousen, Rahn, Poeches, Freeman, Henle, Gibbons, Flannery, Kessler, Bruckner.

My class at Golden Jubilee Celebration in Cupples House. First row (from left): Henle, Barnett, Kessler, Murray, Barton, me, Linz, Bushman, Goodenow, Willmes. Second row: Gibbons, Adams, Ulrick, a visitor, Sedlack, Tully, Stumpf, Casper, Campbell, Luebke, Stockhousen, Bishop, Hogan, P. Reinert.

Above, left: Rev. James McNamee, my nephew. Above: with my niece Jean at the Missouri Botanical Garden, St. Louis. At left: with my niece Marie Iwanski at the Garden. Below: my brother Howard and sister Laura (and me, standing).

Above: with friends on a jaunting car in Killarney, Ireland. At left: At the *Fountain of the Rivers* by Bernini in the Piazza Navona, Rome.

At left: Father Terrance Dempsey and me in the Boboli Gardens, Florence. Below: in a festive mood with Verner Burks.

Above: Father Edward Mathie presenting me with a gift on the occasion of my Golden Jubilee, at Marquette University. At left: Jim and Martha Jane Soltow. Below: Sarah Harriman White, John White, and me on the occasion of signing my *Vested Angels* book.

> What sights shall be when some that swing,
> > wretches, on crutches,
> Their crutches shall cast from them, on heels
> > of air departing,
> Or they go rich as rose leaves hence
> > that loathsome came hither!

This was all to me only a legend that Hopkins had picked up and woven into verse. A legend was a legend and no more. The word *legend* comes from the gerundive form *legenda,* from the Latin verb *legere,* to read, so it merely means something to be read but not necessarily to be taken too seriously. At least, I had not taken the legend of St. Winefrede and St. Beuno seriously, but the rest of the story of Sister Grace's mother forced me to do so.

When everything else had failed to help their ailing daughter, Sister's parents decided to go to Holy Well and bathe their infant daughter in St. Winefrede's Well. They did so, and the child was completely healed immediately. According to the legend, on the throat of patients who had been healed at the well a scar would appear that resembled the scar of St. Winefrede herself when her uncle had miraculously reattached her head. Sister's older sister lived in Victoria and often came to visit her mother at Mount Saint Grace Hospital, and I myself saw the scar that completely circled her neck. This sight certainly yanked me up short and shook my previous skepticism about all such tales of miraculous cures as *mere* legends. It was a humbling experience and suggested to me that it was what Christ may have meant when he remarked to some of his skeptical followers that "faith can, indeed, remove mountains."

I introduced Sister Mary Grace to Hopkins's dramatic fragment on St. Winefrede's Well. It was, of course, very meaningful to her. She became enamored of Hopkins's poetry in general, and before I left the hospital, we had read a great deal of his poetry together. I must say that never in my whole teaching career have I ever shared Hopkins with anyone who was more attuned to the spiritual depth of his poetry than was Sister Mary Grace.

With my human and spiritual horizons broadened and deepened in many directions by the hospital experience, I returned to Manresa to begin the long retreat. St. Ignatius was certainly right to include a repetition of this month-long pursuit of the *Spiritual Exercises* as an integral part of this final year of Jesuit spiritual training. The *Exer-*

*cises* are approached much more maturely at this point in one's training, after about a dozen years of life in the Society. But our year was not to have the luxury of a completely leisurely experience of the long retreat. It was interrupted by an extremely bizarre episode. One week into the retreat, the retreatants are always given a break day on which they can talk and relax. On our first break day, we all went out to the villa on Discovery Bay. We noticed that one of our group, a Father Murphy from the California province, spent the better part of the day violently thrashing around in the high surf in the bay. This was particularly significant in light of what happened, or what we thought happened, the day after we resumed the long retreat. Our retreat master, Father Martin, came in for our first conference looking rather sober and troubled. He announced that Father Murphy was missing. He was not in his room or anywhere in the house. Father Martin had already inquired at the bus station, the only mode of exodus from Port Townsend at the time. The people at the bus station were very familiar with the goings and comings there and said that only one unfamiliar person left on the bus that day, a gentleman with a very strong southern accent. Father Murphy didn't have any such accent. Father Martin had concluded that Father Murphy, whom he knew well, might have become mentally disoriented and might have just wandered off on the peninsula somewhere, so he said he thought we had to disrupt our retreat and try to find him.

We all fanned out and began a three-day manhunt. Our efforts were augmented by state police with bloodhounds and by a hunting party scanning the terrain from a helicopter. The search went on to no avail for two and a half days—certainly a tense and emotional interruption of the peace and meditative quiet of a retreat. In the afternoon of the third day, the group I was with was looking along the shore of the bay in the neighborhood of a paper mill where a large cache of logs floated in the bay waiting to be processed in the mill. Remembering Father Murphy's very energetic swimming in Discovery Bay on our break day, it occurred to us that he might have gone swimming off these logs in the daily afternoon rest period on the day following our break day and might have drowned while doing so. We had hardly finished voicing that thought when we ran onto a pile of clothes on the shore just in front of the floating logs. They proved to be indeed Father Murphy's clothes. On top of them was his breviary. During the war, it was difficult to get new breviaries, so some of the tertians were using secondhand breviaries of individual Jesuits who had died. The breviary that Father Murphy was using had belonged to a young California Jesuit who had drowned at a California beach a few years before. This all suggested that our surmise was correct. Father had probably drowned while taking a swim near these logs. Both we and the police authorities conducted a prolonged search for the body among the logs to no avail. Father Murphy was declared dead. A solemn requiem Mass was offered for him at the Jesuit university church at the University of San Francisco, where he had been teaching very successfully the year before he came to the tertianship. Needless to say, we tertians resumed our retreat in a very sober mood. The meditation on death occurs at just this juncture of the retreat, and we all felt we had had a stunning confirmation of one aspect of death: the fact that we never know when or how it is coming. We completed the retreat in a sobered mood and went on about the usual routine of the tertianship.

But in mid-December Father Martin came to one of our conferences again in a very troubled mood. We could always read his countenance like a book. He said: "Fathers, I have some very troubling news to bring you this morning. We have just discovered that Father Murphy is not dead. He is alive and is functioning as a guard in one of the winter skiing lodges on Mount Rainier." This news was a bombshell for all of us. The drowning scenario had been staged. In retrospect, some of the pieces of the act fell together. The conspicuous floundering through the surf on our break day at Discovery Bay was to induce us to think of him swimming and to convince us, when we found his clothes, that he had drowned while taking a swim near the floating logs. I had been waiting table with him during the first week of the retreat, and I recalled that he had spoken with a marked southern accent—which I didn't know he was feigning. When the agents at the bus station said the only stranger leaving on the bus that day had a heavy southern accent, it threw Father Martin off the track because he knew that Father Murphy had no such accent. I didn't put two and two together myself until after the event. We then recalled that one of the shrewd locals who was on the scene when we discovered the clothes on the shore had said: "I wouldn't be too sure he has drowned. His wrist watch isn't here." Right he was. It was almost the perfect disguised exodus, but he forgot one thing: his clerical draft deferral card. The draft board finally caught up with him.

He was drafted into the navy as an ordinary gob and did his boot camp with some of the students he had taught the year before at the University of San Francisco. What the motive was for all this mysterious contrivance we could never figure out. Sex was not involved. He never married. As far as I have been able to determine, he went into a business career after he got out of the navy. But he certainly managed to shake all of us up mightily during our tertianship.

The locals at Port Townsend, who for the most part were of fundamentalist Protestant persuasion, could never understand who and what we tertians were—thirty full grown men living by themselves with nothing very obvious to do, taking hikes through the neighborhood, and piling into a truck every Thursday for an outing on Discovery Bay. They were convinced that Manresa was a mental institution and that we were there for a cure. The Father Murphy episode was bound to convince them that they were right.

In the spell after the long retreat, we settled down to a routine schedule again. Although the temperature doesn't drop very low in the Port Townsend area in the wintertime, it does get chilly and damp, and because of fuel rationing during the war we had little or no heat. I caught a bad cold, which turned into pneumonia. I had to go to the hospital next door for almost three weeks to be nursed back to health. Antibiotics were not yet very effective. Father Martin could not have been more solicitous. He visited me every day. He was not much of a conversationalist; he would sometimes just come and sit without saying anything. But I very much appreciated his presence; it indicated that he cared.

I was dismissed from the hospital three days before Christmas, and I presumed that I'd be staying at Manresa during the holidays. All year Father Martin had deliberately sent us inlanders from Missouri to very special places to broaden our exposure to the Northwest. He put me on the Christmas list for Friday Harbor, which was on a little island just off of the Canadian Island of Vancouver. On a clear day, from my window I could see the little island across the Straits of Juan de Fuca. But to get to it you had to take the string of buses and ferries down to Seattle, then a bus north to Everett along the Sound, and then a three-hour ferry weaving among dozens of islands in the Sound until you reached Friday Harbor. All that was there was a small marine research center manned by the University of Washington, a post office, a general store, and a drug store. I was to stay with the druggist. He drove me out to a little clapboard church in the middle of the pine forest for Midnight Mass. The church was heated by a little pot-bellied wood stove in the corner, and the only source of light was from candles stuck on the ends of the pews. The congregation was made up of fishermen and their families, who trudged through the woods from their fishermen's cottages along the shore. Midnight Mass there in that little humble clapboard church in the woods with the simple fishermen as my congregation was the closest thing I have ever experienced to that first Christmas in the cave of Bethlehem with the simple shepherds in from the hills adoring the newborn infant. The weather was so mild that, although it was a bit chilly, wild violets bloomed alongside the little chapel. This was a Christmas I will never forget.

When we tertians were all back in the routine at Manresa, we became more and more aware of what a strategic part our Puget Sound and Olympic Peninsula area were playing in the Pacific War. After Pearl Harbor, it was very much feared that the Japanese might make a sneak attack on Bremerton, where so much shipbuilding was under way. The baby flattops built there were a very important element in the Pacific War. The whole Olympic Peninsula and the islands in the Sound had been heavily armed. All the services had forts or centers there. One day we learned how close some of the armament caches were to our backyard. One of the tertians, Andy Vashon, was an artist with a physical disability; he had a defective leg and had to take extra exercise for therapy. He got some of it by biking. One day we heard he had been picked up by the military police and was in their custody until someone from Manresa could properly identify him. He had biked out into the wooded hinterland and seated himself on a mound to do some sketching. He was actually sitting on an ammunition dump. When the military police saw him, they presumed he was a spy making sketches for the Japanese. We had other reminders of where we were because there was a strict blackout every night all along the West Coast, so conscious were we of the Japanese threat.

I was soon to have another reminder of the same thing. I was assigned to help out during Lent in the parish in Astoria at the mouth of the Columbia River. The river is seven to eight miles across at its mouth; it is like an arm of the sea and deep enough to accommodate seagoing ships. During the time I was there, the navy was equipping and taking on the crews for the new baby flattops manufactured at the Bremerton naval center in Puget Sound. They commissioned one a week, which shows the breakneck speed with which we were trying to build up a resistance to Japan after the disaster of Pearl Harbor. Astoria was abuzz with activity and navy personnel, which meant that there was also a flurry of activity at the parish. There was a great demand for baptismal records. Because no index had ever been made of the records, locating a specific entry was very time-consuming, so the pastor gave me the job of working up an index of the records. The parish is quite old. When I got back to the first volume, I found that all the entries were in French. One in particular popped out at me: three baptisms by Pierre De Smet, S.J.

I recalled then that Father De Smet had preceded me at Astoria by a century. He had in fact sailed around Cape Horn at the tip of South America three times, terminating each journey at Astoria. One of these terminations was almost final. The ship on which he was sailing was shipwrecked on shoals at the mouth of the Columbia River, and he was almost drowned. But the baptismal records showed that he had remained at Astoria long enough on one of his trips to record three baptisms in the parish records.

Astoria was the terminus of another famous journey, the overland trek of the Lewis and Clark expedition. Lewis and Clark, like Father De Smet, began their journey in St. Louis. The fact that they terminated it at Astoria is commemorated by a monumental column patterned after the Column of Trajan in Rome. It towers up on the high bluff overlooking the mighty mouth of the Columbia. Spiraling around the column is a low relief sculpture detailing the journey of Lewis and Clark's intrepid crew all the way from the banks of the Mississippi to the mouth of the Columbia.

My Lenten pastoral experience at Astoria was unbelievably busy but immensely rewarding. I also had time to explore some of the environs, especially the Columbia River itself. A hundred-mile drive along its shores impresses you with its might. In some places, it has ground its way through solid granite, creating a gorge with walls rising more than a hundred feet. A road winds its way through the gorge at the water's edge, and you encounter occasional streams that empty their water into the river by means of waterfalls tumbling down the side of the granite wall. They are called horsetail falls; and that's what they look like—great tails trailing down the side of the bluff. These horsetail falls are truly spectacular. They fan out plumelike as they fall, and they drop into the great polished basins they have worn into the granite. The water finally gushes out of the basins into the river. Bridges have been built across the streams that flow from these basins to carry the traffic along the riverside road. The drive terminates at the great dam that has been built to contain the might of the Columbia, to convert it into electric power, and to provide a source of water for irrigating some of the many apple orchards in the neighboring states of Washington and Oregon. Here for the first time I experienced the fascinating sight of salmon leaping from one step to another as they made their way up the salmon ladders built on either edge of the dam

When the Lenten experience was over, I returned to regular order at Manresa, but the order was not to last very long for me. About a month later, I received word that my mother had had a serious heart attack and stroke, and was not expected to live. Father Martin, with his usual very human concern, told me to stay at home as long as I was needed, and then, instead of returning to Manresa, to go home to my own province and make the eight-day retreat that terminates the tertianship under the guidance of someone appointed by my provincial.

So home I went to find Mother in a very serious condition, completely bedridden, but her condition not immediately terminal, which meant she needed a great deal of care. At that time, there was no nursing home in the area where Mother could be placed. All the members of the family had their work to do, and some of them had their own considerable family obligations. When I had finished the tertianship, I had been assigned to the English department back at St. Louis University, but that assignment would not begin until September, so I asked permission of the provincial to remain at home to help take care of Mother. The permission was readily granted. I found myself back in the same position I had been in years earlier when Mother had had an incapacitating illness. I was again housekeeper and nurse. I worked in that double capacity until I had to leave to take up my duties in the English department at St. Louis University.

Mother lived longer than the doctors said she could. She actually died in mid-December of 1944. I went up from St. Louis to conduct the funeral. A heavy, fluffy snow fell the night before, blanketing the whole world with a cover of white down. It was so cold that the individual snowflakes did not melt. We could see them in their beautiful filigree patterns sparkling in the sun as we laid Mother's remains to rest in the snowy cemetery. I thought that this was just the right atmosphere for her funeral. She would have enjoyed the sight. That day, in the cemetery magically transformed by the fall of snow, I remembered James Russell Lowell's lines that Mother had taught me years before.

> The snow had begun in the gloaming
>     And busily all the night
> Had been heaping field and highway
>     In a silence, deep and white.
>
> Every pine, and fir and hemlock
>     Wore ermine too dear for an earl,
> And the poorest twig on the elm-tree
>     Was ridged inch deep with pearl.
>
> From sheds new-roofed with Carrara
>     Came Chanticleer's muffled crow.
> The stiff rails were softened to swan's-down,
>     And still fluttered down the snow.

We left Mother that day folded fast under *sparkling* snow. I felt very grateful for all that she had taught me over the years by word and example. And I was grateful, too, that I had had the opportunity of returning some of her loving care in the last months of her life.

# 9

# A Homing Pigeon

MY LIFE up to this point had been a series of comings and goings to and from St. Louis University, but my assignment to the English department in 1944 was a permanent homecoming. Except for a few sabbatical leaves, I have spent the rest of my life here. I had one opportunity to move to Wisconsin when the Jesuit Wisconsin Province was formally constituted in 1954, but by that time I had so identified with St. Louis University that I chose to remain and have been active here ever since. Most of my activity has been in the English department as a professor and as chairman of the department for seventeen years.

Becoming an English teacher was the fruition of a life's ambition that had been planted years before by my high school English teacher, Father Riordon. My teaching career has been all that I had ever hoped it would be and more. I have loved every minute of it, and judging from students' reactions, I think I can say that I have been successful in the classroom. Among the awards I have received, the one I cherish most is the Nancy McNeir Ring Outstanding Faculty Award, which I received in 1973, because the students themselves nominate the awardee.

In my fifty years of teaching since 1944 at St. Louis University, I have seen remarkable growth and change physically and academically at the university. During the first years I was here, the war was still going on, and the enrollment was rather small and consisted mostly of young women. There were actually only three sections of Freshman English in my first year in the department, but with the end of the war we immediately experienced the flood of G.I. students. In a very few years, there were more than forty sections of Freshman English. Physical space was at a premium. To accommodate the greater numbers in the swollen enrollment, seven Quonset huts were constructed in the Dubourg quadrangle to provide additional classroom space. I actually spent many years of my early teaching career in the Quonset huts—not the most pleasing ambiance for teaching the beauties of Chaucer, Shakespeare, Spenser, Wordsworth, and Hopkins.

Because the Quonset huts did not provide sufficient classroom space for the burgeoning student body, the president at the time, Father Patrick Halloran, decided to build a new classroom building. Building material was almost impossible to come by at the time, but Father Halloran was a person who would not take "no" for an answer. He decided in January that, come what may, he would have a new classroom building by the end of the summer. He found a contractor in East St. Louis who assured him he could deliver the building by that deadline if he could build it without an architect. It was to be just a two-story series of identical classrooms with a full open basement. That seemed extremely simple and perhaps possible without an architect, so Father signed the contract for the work to proceed. What he did not know was that the contractor was hooked into the East St. Louis Eagan Gang and was looking for an outlet for some of his gang-related laborers. They went to work on the building and worked round the clock to get it done in time. But what they built was a concrete structure with continuous concrete walls instead of with supporting pillars filled in with concrete blocks or brick. It had 75 percent more cement in it than such a building needed, much to the financial benefit of the Eagan Gang, who commandeered the material. When the structure was up, it was discovered that the contractor could not get brick to finish the exterior, and it also was soon discovered that the cement leaked and had to be coated with tar. The classroom building *was* finished by the end of the summer, but it looked like a German pillbox or a Nazi execution chamber. It was not until several years later, when brick became available, that the architect Preston Bradshaw designed a skin of brick and limestone for it that made it somewhat more presentable. When the campus buildings were later all given names, this one was named Des Peres Hall to commemorate the disastrous decision of one of the fathers to rush through the construction of a classroom building. It has been facetiously known ever since as Despair Hall or Eagan's Haul—the despair of generations of faculty and students who have had to use it for classrooms. It is no longer used for classes; refurbished on the inside, it has become a computer center.

But important as attractive buildings for educational endeavors may be, what goes on inside them is much more important. When I joined the English faculty at the university, Father Norman Dreyfus was chairman of the department. He put me in complete charge of the freshman and sophomore program. With the hordes of G.I. students pouring in, it was a large and ever-growing program because all students took Freshman and Sophomore English. I was soon discontented with the existing program and the texts for it. The freshman program consisted of critical reading and the study of grammar. The text for reading was a selection of essays, evidently selected by the editor rather randomly, with very little relationship to one another in subject matter, and the exercises attached to them were rather haphazard questions about content. The kind of questions asked at the end of the semester were pretty much the same as those asked at the beginning; there was no progression in the reading experience and practically no attention given to principles of rhetorical effectiveness. The other textbook was a straightforward grammar concerned merely with elements of correct expression rather than with rhetorical effectiveness. Correctness, of course, is a minimal necessity in any writing program, but I felt that a college course in writing ought to aim at something beyond that.

I had come to agree with Cardinal Newman that the educated mind is the mind that sees relationships and that can organize its disparate knowledge into some kind of an organized pattern. To see relationships, you have to have something to relate, but you also have to have some principles of organization and subordination in order to see some pattern in what you know. I thought it would be helpful to have the freshman readings illustrate Newman's idea of education by presenting information on a series of related topics and at the same time provide some of the principles by which the subjects could be seen to be related to one another. But beyond that the essays themselves should be well written and illustrate the rhetorical principles of effective communication. They should be well structured and developed, and employ the devices of varied and effective sentence structure, effective diction, and imagery that enlivens the subject discussed. The exercises accompanying the readings should be a progressive introduction to these principles of effective expression as illustrated in the essays being studied. And the students, at the same time, ought to be encouraged to imitate some of these devices of effective composition in their own writing. In other words, both the analysis of the readings and their own writing assignments ought to be a progressive training in rhetoric. My study of practical criticism under McLuhan, which was really the application of the old principles of rhetoric to a piece of writing, and my work on the history of rhetoric, also under his guidance, had shown me the important place rhetoric had played in the grammatico-rhetorical educational traditions of the past. I had become convinced of the central place rhetoric ought to have in any humane educational program.

Because I could find no freshman text that did any of these things, I decided to construct one on my own. I put together a collection of well-written essays by important traditional and contemporary writers on a progression of subjects that included the nature and purpose of a college education; the nature and purpose of literature and art; the use of the rhetorical principles of effectiveness by the propagandist and the advertiser; and the nature of history, science, philosophy, and theology and their place in a complete education. John Ruskin, Cardinal Newman, J. W. Mackail, Christopher Dawson, G. K. Chesterton, Robert M. Hutchins, Wilson Follett, Sir Richard Livingstone, Leonard Feeney, and Jaime Castiello were some of the writers I included in this collection.

The written exercises accompanying the readings progressed from mere grammatical questions to rhetorical concerns, including paragraphs and overall structure, effective diction, variety, sentence structure, and imagery. I titled the collection *Reading for Understanding*.

The book was published by a local press in St. Louis and used at first only at St. Louis University. Both student and faculty satisfaction with it soon came to the attention of an agent for the Rinehart Publishing Company. He asked whether his company might bring it out as an experimental edition, try it out in a couple of other Jesuit universities, with the intention of issuing it for more general consumption if it proved to be successful in the two experimental universities. That question, of course, was music to my ears, and I readily assented. The two experimental universities chosen were Santa Clara in San Jose, California, and Loyola in Chicago. The book was very well received in both places, and the Rinehart Company issued the first formal edition of it, already considerably revised and augmented, in 1950. It went through three later editions, each substantially revised and expanded. The last edition was published by the newly amalgamated press Holt, Rinehart, and Winston. It was adopted by colleges and universities, mostly Catholic, all over the country and eventually sold more than a million copies. No other freshman text then was organized quite like it, and for many years it served a very good educational purpose. Some of the students who used it seemed to think so, too. I have often encountered them in various parts of the country years after they graduated, and many of them have told me they still have the text and still refer to it.

Another problem in freshman composition classes is getting challenging topics for term papers in which the students can demonstrate not only the necessary mechanics of a term paper, but some of the rhetorical expertise they have learned during the year. They frequently lack anything serious to write about. I recalled what a thrill it had been for me in my collegiate days at Florissant to have been let loose to read the whole *Aeneid* of Virgil for the first time and how easy it was in that new enthusiasm to write the essay that I composed on Virgil for the two thousandth anniversary of his birth. It occurred to me that a program of outside reading in the great classical epics of Homer and Virgil for the freshmen would do something similar for them, so I put in the reading of the *Iliad,* the *Odyssey,* and the *Aeneid* as a requirement for the freshmen with the proviso that their term paper topics be related to that reading. The rhetorical principle of comparison and contrast could be easily employed in drawing contrasts between the exaggerated individualism of Achilles and the more social consciousness of Aeneas: there are many examples of the action of the two heroes exemplifying these traits. Admiration for the intelligence of the Greeks could be illustrated in a discussion of the way various aspects of intelligence are embodied in Achilles, Agamemnon, Nestor, and Odysseus, but completely lacking in the mighty but dumb Ajax. Topics of these kinds would not only focus the students' reading but would give them concrete topics to write about, provide the materials to develop their chosen topics, and, incidentally, introduce them to two of the most important roots of their own culture—the Greek and the Roman. It would also, as a matter of fact, do the same thing for some of the teachers, who, I discovered, had never read through the Greek and Roman epics. We did this program for several years with a considerable amount of success. We later added the epic *Beowulf,* which enabled us to contrast the self-centered and exaggeratedly self-seeking pagan Achilles with Beowulf, built on the self-sacrificing pattern of a Christian hero who ultimately, like Christ, lays down his life for the redemption of his people.

Father Dreyfus eventually turned over to me the direction of the entire undergraduate program, retaining for himself only the direction of the substantial graduate program. Father had worked out a very integrated program of required courses for the English major covering the history of English and American literature and a schedule of written and oral examinations required for the B.A. in English. The only required course I added was one in practical criticism. The course as taught by Marshall McLuhan had been so helpful to me in improving my critical reading ability that I thought it ought to be a part of every English major's experience. I myself taught it for years, but several other teachers in the department became proficient in it, and the critical analytical method taught there was employed in teaching many of the period courses as well. The course in practical criticism focused on poetry and used the text *Understanding Poetry* by Cleanth Brooks and Robert Penn Warren, which went through several editions and was widely used throughout the country. It did more than any other single book to domesticate in this country the best features of the Cambridge school of criticism. It certainly was my *vade mecum* in all my years of undergraduate teaching. I eventually worked up a parallel course in the analytical approach to prose called "The Practical Criticism of Prose," which was equally well received. Some of the students who took that course went on to do some significant writing on their own. The most recent example is Richard Dooling, who was nominated for the 1994 National Book Award for his second novel, *White Man's Grave*.

An educational venture that had been inaugurated in the School of Arts and Science some years before I returned to the university was the honors program. It was inaugurated by Dean Wilfred Mallon and had been presided over by Father Paul Reinert, Father Robert Henle, and Dr. William Korfmacher. The chairmanship for the program was turned over to me in 1950. I discovered that it was a rather simple and minimal program, consisting merely of a modification of the great books program. For the small group that joined, less than a dozen, the program included the study of four great books, one in each successive semester of the students' junior and senior years, and a public oral examination on these books at the end of their senior year.

I felt immediately that two things were wrong with the program. In the first place, not enough was required of the students in merely the study of these four books—which, incidentally, were not pursued in sufficient depth. First, there was too much lecturing about the authors and their books, instead of the students' grappling firsthand with the texts themselves. And second, the program started too late. Really talented students should be challenged the moment they step in the door of the institution in their first year. I set about making some changes in the program that would remedy these deficiencies.

In the first place, I began the program in the freshman year and established a series of courses in several cooperating departments (including English, history, and philosophy) which would be open only to honors students and in which they could be pushed to the edge of their capacity. I taught the English course myself and soon found that there were individual students in the classes who could do considerably more than was required even in these special classes and who wanted to do it. I took them on almost as a personal tutor and sometimes found that work I was requiring of graduate students, in the same area at the same time, they could do as well or better. This program was what was needed to give them a challenge right from the beginning. In their junior and senior years, the students registered for some of the special courses provided by several departments—especially in philosophy and theology.

The courses in various departments that the honors students took in common developed a sense of community among them that enabled them to exchange ideas with one another on many topics in a way that is impossible when individuals are lost in a mass of students. To foster this sense of camaraderie, we set aside the library room in the old Chouteau House (now Cupples House) for the exclusive use of the honors students. We stacked the bookcases in the room with books related to their various courses. It was a place where they could read quietly and engage in discussions with one another. Some of the honors classes were also held there because the group was small enough to be accommodated in the room. We named the room the Thomas More Room because the great Christian humanist had become a kind of saintly patron of the program. A fine copy of Holbein's portrait of the chancellor, the original of which is in the Frick Gallery in New York, graced one wall of the room.

But something had to be done with the traditional honors great books courses in the junior and senior years to make them more of a challenge. We decided on four great books that would become the core of these four courses: *The Republic* by Plato, *The Divine Comedy* by Dante, *Utopia* by Thomas More, and *Principia* by Sir Isaac Newton. A whole semester would be devoted to each. Each work would be placed in its historical context, but the text of each would also be explored minutely. Each student would also be expected to give an oral and written report on some work analogous to or relevant in some way to the text studied in class. For many years, Dr. Leonard Eslick from the philosophy department taught *The Republic,* and I taught *Utopia.* A succession of teachers from the English and physics departments taught Dante and Newton.

The students were challenged in this revised program. Most of them accepted the challenge, performed with distinction, and went on to distinguished careers. When I have encountered them later in various parts of the country, I have found them uniformly grateful for what the program did for them.

The students worked in various departments and went on to achieve in various areas of specialization. I would like to call attention here to two who achieved particular distinction in the English area. The first was Richard Sylvester. He was one of the first students to enter the expanded program. He was an outstanding athlete who was so proficient in baseball that scouts encouraged him to think of pursuing a professional baseball career, but Dick had other ideas. He had an instinct for the intellectual and cultural life that he had probably inherited from his grandfather, an accomplished artist who produced some of the most sensitive paintings ever done of the Mississippi River. The artist was something of a transcendentalist in philosophy, and his notion of the divine spirit immanent in nature showed through in much of his painting of external nature. His grandson Dick inherited some of that sensitivity. Dick was in the first course I taught on Thomas More's *Utopia,* and it was love at first sight for Dick. He spent almost the remainder of his relatively short life promoting Thomas More. He wrote his paper in the course on George Cavendish's *The Life and Death of Cardinal Wolsey,* More's unfortunate predecessor as chancellor of England. Dick eventually received a Rhodes scholarship to Oxford, the first St. Louis University student to receive one.

At Oxford, among other things, Dick learned textual criticism and applied it to a further study of the original text of Cavendish's *The Life and Death of Cardinal Wolsey.* Upon returning to the States, Dick did his work for the doctorate at Yale University. His training in textual criticism at Oxford led him to submit as his dissertation a detailed textual edition of Cavendish's work. It was done so well that it was accepted not only by Yale but also by the Early English Text Society for publication. The authorities at Yale University were so impressed with his ability as a textual critic that they asked him to stay on and undertake the editorship of *The Complete Works of Thomas More,* which they were about to launch. Dick did so, and he spent the rest of his short life editing approximately half of the twenty-one volumes of the complete works of Thomas More. Dick was prematurely carried off by cancer in 1978. It is an interesting coincidence that the editing of the final volumes of the More edition was carried on by another student from my Thomas More class at St. Louis University, Dr. Clarence Miller. Here is some of his story.

Clarence came to St. Louis University in 1947. He had just graduated from Rockhurst High School in Kansas City and had won the National High School Latin Contest. I counseled him during freshman week and, on the basis of his distinguished high school record, suggested that he go into the honors program. He said he didn't think he could because time was of the essence for him. I said that the quality of his expenditure of that time might be equally important and that I still thought he ought to go into the honors program. He did so, and I soon found that he was one of the students who needed individual tutorial attention to challenge him to his capacity. He eventually took the junior course in the *Utopia,* and he chose to investigate and report on Challoner's translation of *The Praise of Folie* by Erasmus, the great humanist friend of Thomas More. *The Praise of Folie* is, as a matter of fact, a kind of ironic companion work to More's own *Utopia.* Clarence finished the undergraduate course in English with top distinction and won a scholarship to Harvard from the American Council of Learned Societies, where he completed his doctorate in English. He returned to the English faculty at St. Louis University, where he had a distinguished teaching and publishing career. He completed an authoritative edition of the text of Challoner's translation of *The Praise of Folie,* which, like Dick Sylvester's edition of Cavendish's *The Life and Death of Cardinal Wolsey,* was published by the Early English Text Society in 1965. After Dick's death, Clarence also took Dick's place as executive editor of the More edition, which he brought to its completion in 1997.

Both Dick and Clarence give me credit, in their introductions to these works, for having introduced them to this area of study. If I in any way had anything to do with the accomplishments of these two scholars, it is a proof that water *can* rise higher than its source. I do not think I would have had the patience to do the painstaking work it takes for this kind of scholarly textual study.

I would like to call attention to one other of the many remarkable students who were part of the honors program in these days. His name is Clyde Cahill, an African American. African American students had an interesting history at St. Louis University prior to Clyde's arrival. The university president, Father Patrick Halloran, had integrated the school back in 1944, ten years before the federal mandate of integration. He was not particularly interested in doing so himself, but he did it at the urging of his board of trustees, the members of which, incidentally, were still all Jesuits. But he only went halfway. African American students were admitted to all the academic programs in the university, but social functions such as school dances were not to be open to them. Some of the trustees and other individuals in the university community were highly critical of this policy. Father Claude Heithaus, who was moderator of the *University News,* published an article in the paper severely condemning the policy. The president told Father Heithaus that he was to make no further comment on the matter either in print or in speech. Father Heithaus took this injunction as an unwarranted intrusion into what he considered a matter of personal conscience, so he preached a famous homily to the entire student body in the College Church, in which he advised the students not to consent to do anything that would injure the sensitivities of the newly admitted African American students. His talk was a highly ironic presentation of the subject that might be compared to Jonathan Swift's famous *A Modest Proposal,* in which Swift, the dean of St. Patrick's Cathedral in Dublin, suggested that to solve the Irish problem the English government might fatten up Irish children and sell them in the meat market for food. He said they were already being killed by starvation and oppression, but that his suggestion would make their elimination profitable and would also supply a new delicacy to the table. Father Heithaus's similarly ironic presentation of the situation of the African American students at St. Louis University precipitated a thunderbolt from on high: Father was publicly reprimanded in the community dining room and sent packing to Marquette University. He taught there for several years and functioned as chaplain in one of the hospitals there. The social ostracism of the African American students was soon ended at the university, and, in calmer days, Father Heithaus returned to the university and spent his latter years developing the very important museum of Jesuitana in the Old Rock Building at Florissant. All of this fracas about integration was happily a thing of the past by the time Clyde Cahill arrived.

Clyde was born and raised in a very poor part of the city near the old St. Mary's Infirmary on the near south side, where the residences did not even have interior plumbing. Clyde was a bright boy and made good use of his early educational opportunities in grade school and high school. He joined the Air Corps and eventually rose to the rank of first lieutenant. During part of his service, he was located in the South. The services were still segregated, and each night he was driven thirty miles to a segregated camp for blacks. As a black, he was not allowed to sleep in the camp for white servicemen where he worked during the day. What I found remarkable about Clyde from the beginning was his lack of bitterness in spite of the deprived circumstances of his upbringing and the many ways in which he had personally experienced racial discrimination.

When Clyde left the service, he made use of the G.I. bill and registered at St. Louis University. His superior record in all his previous schooling entitled him to join the honors program. He did so, and he showed up in my Freshman Honors English course. One of his first papers showed a clear indication that he had a very inquisitive mind, but also that he was confused about some fundamental religious and ethical problems. I suggested that he drop by my office to talk over these problematic questions. He did so, and this first meeting inaugurated a series of regular weekly Saturday visits that continued for almost a year. He was definitely interested in religion, but he had a very probing mind and would accept nothing from anyone without a thorough explanation. I was fresh out of four years of theology and thought I knew all the answers. I have never been so pushed to come up with right and satisfying answers to questions of religious dogma and ethical practice as I was in those sessions with Clyde. As a result of it all, he finally accepted the Roman Catholic faith and was baptized. I can say of Clyde what St. Ignatius said of Francis Xavier, his confrere at the Sorbonne: "He was the hardest mettle I ever tried to mold." But Clyde was very much worth molding. He graduated from the university in the honors program. He went on to the Law School of the university, where he also distinguished himself, and then on into the practice of law. There was in St. Louis at that time a successful businessman and something of a political entrepreneur who had the habit of equipping office space for young African American lawyers when they started practice, in the hopes, I presume, that they might prove helpful to him in some of his wheeling and dealing. He offered to do so for Clyde, but Clyde said, "No, thank you." He set himself up in a two-by-four office on Jefferson Street and began to serve some of the legal needs of his own people for nothing. He worked nights in the post office sorting mail to pay his expenses. He continued this pro bono work until his reputation as a lawyer and his genuine desire to be helpful became so well known that he could begin to charge for his services. His reputation grew so that he ultimately received an appointment as a federal judge. He distinguished himself in that position for the quality and utter fairness of his judgments, which he managed to keep completely color-blind. He was given an Alumni Merit Award from St. Louis University for his equitable and exemplary performance as a federal judge. I was at his table at the dinner when he received the award, surrounded by his sons and daughters, all distinguished professional people. He was kind enough to say in his acceptance speech that he owed a great deal to me for having counseled him in his early days at the university. He said that if the truth were known, he probably spent as much time in my office as he did in the classroom during that first year. He was probably right. But as I looked at Clyde that night, flanked by his wife and successful children, I realized that no hours of my life had been better spent than those I had given to Clyde in his early career.

My directorship of the honors program also enabled me to make good on a vow I had taken when I was assigned to the university—to do what I could, when I could, to bring some attention to art into the curriculum. I thought it was a pity that the honors students, who would probably be going into professions that would put them in the forefront of the cultural milieu, were leaving without a smidgen of art in their college experience. So I added to the honors curriculum a four-semester course—one hour a semester—in the appreciation and history of art. I made it a four-semester course deliberately. I wanted the students to be exposed to the experience of art over an extended period of time. I did not want it to be a three-hour course that they could do in a semester and have done with it. There was no one to teach the course, so I taught it myself, which gave me the opportunity of broadening my own reading in the theory of artistic design and in the history of art. The students liked the course. Many of them have told me that it added a new dimension to their own personal lives and later to the lives of their families. It enriched their travel experience because they brought something with them that made what they saw much more meaningful. A fine arts component has become a permanent part of the honors curriculum.

The honors art course was also the catalyst that eventually stimulated the development of the art department. Some of the students who were not in the honors program complained that they were being discriminated against; the honors students were being given an introduction to art, and they were not. I agreed, but I had no control over the general curriculum. Back in 1950, I could not offer a straightforward course in art appreciation or art history to the general student body. What I could do, though, was construct a course in the English department that would indirectly serve the purpose. I devised a course called "Parallel Themes in Literature and Art," which was offered under an English course number. The course consisted of literary selections from the Renaissance, romantic, Victorian, and modern periods, with parallel treatments of the same values or themes from the visual arts. There was no one to teach this course, either, so I took it on. It was not difficult for me to do because I had always made a connection between the verbal and visual arts in all my teaching of literature.

The course had a sizable enrollment the first time it was offered (more than 50 students), but the second time it appeared in the syllabus more than 150 students signed up for it. It was obvious that a sizable group of students had an interest in receiving some exposure to the visual arts, and it was also obvious that I could not go on stealing time from the English department to satisfy the need. We were allowed to hire our first art instructor. We hired not an art historian but a practicing artist. We wanted the students to know that art was not something that happened in the past that you merely talked about, but a creative activity still going on. Tom Toner was the artist we hired. He had just completed his M.F.A. at the Art Academy at Philadelphia and came to the job with a good deal of youthful enthusiasm. We were told by the administration that all we had permission for was an introductory course in art appreciation. We were not to think of a studio art program or of a full-fledged art history program, but I confess that I did continue to think of both. Tom Toner had a studio on campus, and many students flocked to it to watch him work. He soon gathered some of them together in the evening and taught them, how to paint—without a fee and without credit. The registration for the course in art appreciation drew such large numbers that it was soon obvious to everyone, including the administration, that we would need an additional teacher to accommodate the burgeoning enrollment. Some of the students who took the introductory course were interested in additional courses in art history and wondered whether a sufficient number of courses could be offered to build a minor in art history. Because the real demand was there, we were allowed to hire an additional teacher, this time a trained art historian. There was still no art department; the courses were listed as a program, and I administered the program. Eventually the demand for art history courses was such that it was deemed possible to create an art department and to increase the faculty. An additional teacher in art history, David Ramsey, was hired, and he became the first chairman of the fine arts department. Permission was also finally given to offer formal courses in studio art—and a full-fledged Department of Art was finally in place.

There had always been an interest in theater in the university, and Father Robert Johnston developed the theater program into a formal department. Music at the university for years had been confined to a chorale directed by Professor Gainer in the English department. It was through Father Francis Guentner's activity and perseverance that an academic program was developed and that a Department of Music was finally established.

In 1973, all of these departments were integrated into a new fine and performing arts department that embraces art history, studio art, music, and theater, but the department actually evolved from the introduction of the courses in art appreciation in the honors program. This development is at least a partial fulfillment of my vow to try to do something to bring art into the curriculum of St. Louis University.

In spite of these diversions into the honors program and art, my main responsibility remained teaching in the English department, my first love. In my first years in the department, besides the Freshman Honors English course, I taught in rotation a variety of upper-division courses, including courses in Shakespeare, Spenser, Milton, romanticism, Victorianism, and practical criticism in poetry and prose. I enjoyed the variety of subject matter, and it helped me expand and deepen my own appreciation of the whole expanse of English literature. The courses in practical criticism were my favorites, and they were probably the most helpful to a wide variety of students. I was able there to communicate what I myself had learned from Marshall McLuhan about coming to grips with the actual verbal fiber of a literary text.

In the graduate program, I gravitated to teaching Spenser; a course on tragedy that included the Greek tragedians, Shakespeare, and modern tragedy; and a course on mannerism in literature and art. Besides teaching, the graduate work, of course, included the direction of master's theses and doctoral dissertations. Many of the doctoral dissertations I directed focused on the parallelism between literature and art; one, for instance, was entitled "The Baroque Elements in Spenser's *Faerie Queene*"; another, "Mannerist Elements in Faulkner's *Absalom, Absalom*"; and still another "The Technique of Impressionism in O'Casey's Tragedy." But two of the very first master's theses I directed were to have lasting effect on the direction of my own later research and writing. Mary Elizabeth O'Connor, a young woman in my Spenser course, decided she would like to write her master's thesis on some aspect of Spenser's work. I suggested that she write on his *Prosopopoia; or Mother Hubbard's Tale.*

In the poem, Spenser pictures himself as ill and being distracted from his illness by his friends' narrating various stories to him. Some tell tales of knights and ladies, some of squires, some of fairies and giants, but a simple old lady, Mother Hubbard, tells the tale of the ambitious Ape who, with the connivance of the wily Fox, usurps the throne of the Lion, the King of the Beasts. The tale is a *prosopopoia,* or a rhetorical personification. The Ape personifies the exact opposite of magnanimity, or the balanced and rational attitude toward honor, which Spenser develops in the Red Cross Knight in Book One of *The Faerie Queene.* Because what is personified in the tale is the opposite of true magnanimity, I suggested that Miss O'Connor look up Aristotle's definition of magnanimity in his *Nicomachean Ethics* and use that as the norm from which the Ape in the tale has departed. She did so and came back to say that what Spenser pictures in the ambitious, self-seeking ape comes pretty close to what Aristotle's magnanimous man would have sought and been honored for. I had not read Aristotle on this point for years, and when I did reread him, I was surprised to find that Miss O'Connor was right.

Aristotle defines all virtues as a mean between two extremes—an excess on one hand or a deficiency on the other—a mean between too much or too little. Courage, for instance, is a mean between brashness on the one hand (too much action in the presence of threat) and cowardice on the other hand (too little or no action in the presence of threat). Magnanimity (the virtue that has to do with the rational attitude toward personal honor) is the only virtue in Aristotle's list that, according to him, has no possibility of excess. The magnanimous man or hero, according to Aristotle, excels in all the virtues and deserves the highest honor. He cannot claim more than he deserves; and, as a matter of fact, being superior to others in all respects, he has the right and even the duty to claim the highest honor and respect for his excellence. There is no limit on his claim for recognition. He can, however, neglect to demand the honor he deserves; he can, in other words, fail in the matter of personal honor by deficiency. He then becomes the pusillanimous or small-souled individual who does not have the gumption to claim what he deserves. To Aristotle and the Greeks in general, the pusillanimous man would be despised. This whole Greek attitude toward the pursuit of personal honor, as Aristotle formally defined it, looks exaggeratedly self-centered and lacking in social consciousness. It is essentially pagan. It is the very self-seeking attitude that Spenser presents in an unsympathetic ironic light in the story of the Ape and the Fox in *Mother Hubbard's Tale*.

When I thought of it, I realized that it was this very self-centered and self-seeking attitude toward personal honor that Homer makes the center of his story of Achilles in the *Iliad*. Achilles is represented as by all odds the bravest and most intelligent of Greek warriors. He has been dishonored by Agamemnon, who has robbed him of Briseis, the damsel awarded to Achilles in recognition of his success in a previous battle. Achilles withdraws from battle and lets the Greek cause languish until Agamemnon humbles himself and recognizes Achilles' superiority. Achilles' position is recognized by the gods, by

Agamemnon, by the wise old Nestor, and by Odysseus as justified in his claim for honor. In the eyes of any of his fellow Greeks, there is no possibility of Achilles' being excessive in his claim for recognition and honor. What Homer plays out in the story of Achilles corresponds exactly to Aristotle's definition of the magnanimous man, the hero with no possibility of an excessive claim for personal honor. The correspondence is so great that one might suspect that Aristotle may have had Achilles in mind when he constructed his definition of magnanimity. It was interesting to reread the *Iliad* from this point of view and to see how the action of the epic gyrates around this push of Achilles to get the honor he is convinced he deserves.

The correspondence between the Greek philosophical theorizing about the heroic or the truly magnanimous or great-souled man and the concrete image of him in the epic emanating from the same culture prompted me to think this might be a fruitful approach to all the major epics. I began looking at the Roman theorizing about the virtue of magnanimity or the honor due the truly great man or hero of Roman culture. I found that Cicero had written a whole treatise on the subject, which has been lost. But in another work, the *De Officiis* (Concerning Duties), he discusses it at some length. It is typical of the Roman view of human greatness that the basis of the honor paid the hero or a great man is his fulfillment of his duty to the gods, to the state, and to the family. The Roman ideal is much more social minded. The hero has an obligation to the gods, to the state, and to his family that puts a check on his pursuit of personal honor and self-aggrandizement. He may, in fact, have to sacrifice some of his own personal ambitions to satisfy these other social obligations. For the Roman, then, magnanimity or the pursuit of honor does admit of an excess. The hero can so pursue it as to neglect his duty to the gods, the state, or the family. This Roman philosophical analysis of magnanimity with its emphasis on social duty proved to be the perfect background for the Roman values dramatized in the action of Virgil's *Aeneid*. It is not accidental that Aeneas's epithet in the epic is *pius*, which means "devoted" or "dutiful." The whole epic narrative shows what sacrifices of his own pleasure and well-being Aeneas has to make in his many wanderings and in the warfare that he hates in order to fulfill the commission of the gods to found a new Troy and to establish a new family. His pursuit of his own pleasure, reputation, and honor is severely limited by his duty to found the new Troy.

I came to agree with C. S. Lewis, who said that, after Aeneas, the only possible forward movement in the development of the hero is in the direction of the Christian hero. As a matter of fact, in the Roman emphasis on duty as the most important element in the hero's makeup, one had almost arrived there already.

I began to examine the writings of St. Paul, especially his Letter to the Corinthians, to assemble the specifically Christian idea of human greatness or the heroic. The Letter to the Corinthians was occasioned by a typical Greek hassle. The Corinthian Christians had begun to dispute and quarrel with one another about who was the greater among them—those who had been baptized by Apollo, by Cephas, or by the illustrious Paul. Paul chides them for their idle vanity and takes the occasion of instructing them in the true idea of Christian humility and charity. Whatever they are and whatever they have received, they have ultimately from God and it doesn't matter from whose hands they have received it. Whatever they have received, they have received not for themselves alone, but to share in Christian charity with others. St. Paul here touches on the two bedrock foundational stones of the new Christian ideal of greatness: humility and charity. Pope St. Gregory, quoted by the Venerable Bede in his *Ecclesiastical History of England,* wrote to Augustine, the Apostle of England, who had gained wide recognition for his miracles. The pope commends him for his apostolic zeal but reminds him that the power of working miracles was given him by God not to augment his (Augustine's) own reputation but to assist his apostolic work for others. Here we have them again—the two cornerstones of Christian greatness and honor—*humility,* or a recognition that one's achievements come from God, and *charity,* a recognition that what one achieves is not meant merely for one's own self-aggrandizement but for the benefit of others.

When the epic *Beowulf* is read in this context, it is obvious that the Beowulf poet has taken a traditional pagan Nordic hero and modified his character and his story to fit the new Christian idea of a hero. There is no doubt about Beowulf's abilities and his own self-confidence, but it is also obvious throughout the poem that he is very aware of his dependence on God, for his abilities and his successful use of them in subduing Grendel in the first part of the poem and the Firedrake in the last episode. And the main action of both episodes is a clear manifestation of the Pauline virtue of charity. Beowulf dedicates all his expertise to freeing Hrothgar's subjects from the depredations of Grendel and Grendel's mother, and in the last episode he lays down his life to free his own people from the devastation of the Firedrake. The character of Beowulf from the Nordic myth has been carefully reconstructed to illustrate the less self-centered and self-seeking Christian hero manifesting both Christian humility and charity.

In tracing through how completely this new concept of the hero pervades the action of the poem, I also noted that the action of the old Nordic myth had been constructed in such a way as to image the Christian story of salvation. It actually becomes an allegory of the story of salvation. Hrothgar's kingdom (the human race) is being ravaged by a man-monster (Satan) that the kingdom is powerless by itself to overcome. Beowulf, a powerful and generous leader from outside (Christ), comes and defeats Grendel (Satan), thus freeing Hrothgar's kingdom from his depredation. Beowulf provides a similar saving action for his own people, suffering from the destructive incursions of the Firedrake that they, like Hrothgar's people, are unable to overcome themselves. But this time it costs Beowulf (the Savior) his life (an analogy to Christ's sacrificial death on the Cross). None of this is stated explicitly, as it usually is not in a good allegory. But the poet gives enough cues for the reader to catch the analogy and to read the narrative as the Christian story of Christ's saving the human race from the depredations of Satan. This parallel seemed so obvious to me that I determined to research the subject and publish my findings.

But meantime I followed through on the magnanimity theme. One of the great achievements of St. Thomas Aquinas was his integration of the philosophy of Aristotle into the Christian theological tradition. Among other things, he adopted Aristotle's concept of virtue as a mean between the two extremes of excess and defect. But it is clear that in his discussion of magnanimity, the virtue that has to do with the rational attitude toward the pursuit of personal honor, he does not go along with Aristotle's idea that in this one case there is no possibility of an excess—the idea that the truly great man cannot be excessive in his demand for honorable recognition. Like St. Paul and St. Gregory before him, St. Thomas very emphatically asserts that even the great man can be excessive in his claim for honor in a twofold way: (1) if he does not humbly recognize that whatever his achievements are, he has received them from God, and (2) that whatever he has was given not merely for his own self-aggrandizement but also for the benefit of others. In other words, the Christian virtues of humility and charity put a definite limitation on his pursuit of personal honor.

Aristotle's concept of magnanimity or the pursuit of honor has undergone a substantial change in St. Thomas under the influence of values derived from Christian revelation. It occurred to me that it might be interesting to trace the shifting attitude toward magnanimity or the pursuit of honor from Aristotle to St. Thomas and make a book-length study of the way that shifting idea was embodied concretely in the characters of the great epics in succeeding Western cultures. The epics would include Homer's *Iliad* and *Odyssey* from Greece and Virgil's *Aeneid* from Rome (from the shifting pagan tradition), as well as *Beowulf,* Spenser's *Faerie Queene,* and Milton's *Paradise Lost* (from the Christian tradition).

I suggested the idea to Father Norman Dreyfus, chairman of my department, and he was enthusiastic about it. He suggested that I take a sabbatical for a semester and get away to work on it. He further suggested that I go to England to do it. He said this sabbatical would in part make up for the fact that I had not been able to do my doctoral work at Cambridge because of the war. The sabbatical was, of course, a very delightful prospect for me. With my teaching responsibilities and administrative duties in the department and in the honors program, I had little leisure to do much writing. I was very familiar with all the epics; I had studied them and taught them for years; and with a little leisure I was sure I could reexamine them from this new focus of the shifting concept of magnanimity and write the book. I already knew what I'd call it: *Honor and the Epic Hero.* The prospect of England was also exciting to me at that precise time because, as I mentioned before, in my work on Beowulf as a Christian hero I had become convinced that the poem was an allegory of the Christian story of salvation. In that context, I thought there was good evidence in the poem that the Beowulf poet intended the episode in which Beowulf descends into the mere to register his victory over Grendel, who had slunk away after their battle in the hall of Hrothgar, to symbolize Christ's descent into hell, or what the medieval dramatists called "the harrowing of hell." The mere is represented in *Beowulf* as a man-monster-infested lake. I wondered whether the lake was an

Anglo-Saxon method of representing hell. I thought that if I could examine some Anglo-Saxon illuminated manuscripts in the British Museum and elsewhere, I could find out.

Another thing that made the prospect of a tour of the continent and a sojourn in England a particularly exciting prospect to me was that it would give me my first opportunity to see the great cathedrals of Europe. Father Preuss's slide lectures on the European cathedrals had sown the seed of that interest years before, but I had fostered the seed by my own continuous reading over the years until I knew the details of almost every major cathedral like the palm of my hand. Now I would have the opportunity at last of seeing them in reality. I promised myself not only to see them but to photograph them in detail for use in our art history course. So with the funds secured from the university in the fall of 1955, I was off for a sabbatical semester in England.

# 10

# An Innocent Abroad

Some of my confreres might question the accuracy of the "innocent" epithet in the chapter title, but there is no doubt that, if not innocent, I was very naive as I set off for my first trip abroad in the summer of 1955. I was to go by ship, of course, because transatlantic air travel was still not very common. I was booked for the fastest ship on the seas at the time, the *United States*. It made the trip to England in four days. I was traveling alone, so I did not have a cabin partner. When I got to my cabin, I found the luggage of the person I presumed had been assigned as my partner, but the luggage tag indicated that person was a woman. I knew that cabin partners were assigned to individuals traveling alone, but I did not think that they would be assigned quite this casually. I betook me to the purser to inquire, and by the time he and I returned, the lady had come back to the cabin. She was in a state of alarm when she saw the luggage with my name on it, but was appeased by being assigned to another cabin, and the pleasant upshot of the confusion was that I had the cabin to myself for the whole trip. The cabins on the *United States* were quite large, so I luxuriated in one that was almost as ample as a first-class stateroom.

As we were pulling out of port in New York, I was at the rail on deck with many others watching the New York skyline recede and giving our farewells to Lady Liberty as we passed her statue. While we were leaving the port, we were favored with an impressive water display by the harbor tug boats. We knew that Cardinal Spellman was on board in first class with a group of pilgrims he was taking to Europe and presumed that the display was for him, but that night in the second-class dining room a lady from New York at a table adjacent to mine told us the display was for her. Her brother was a captain of one of the tugboats, and he had persuaded his fellow tugboat captains to put on the display for his sister. Cardinal Spellman may also have thought it was for him.

I drew an interesting couple as my table companions, a father and daughter. The father was a skilled cabinetmaker from Harrisburg, Pennsylvania, where he did fine cabinetwork for Pullman dining and club cars for the Pennsylvania Railroad. He was German by nationality and was born and raised in Alsace-Lorraine. Alsace had in its history been intermittently under German and French rule. Although it had been under French rule since the First World War, German is still the dominant language there. It is still more German than French. He had learned his trade there before he emigrated to the United States. This was his first trip back to his homeland since he had emigrated. Upon the death of his first wife, an Alsatian who had emigrated with him, he married an American woman who had no interest in seeing Alsace-Lorraine, so he was traveling with his married daughter from Hackensack, New Jersey. She was the daughter of his first wife and, like her father, had been born in Alsace. It was with a great deal of emotional anticipation that the father and daughter were going home to their roots.

The sea voyage was tremendously pleasing to me. I never wearied of standing at the railing and contemplating the immensity of the sea in all its moods. No wonder it has in all cultures become the symbol of the awesome majesty of God. I soon learned that the ship was also awesome in its own way, a veritable city afloat. By a happy circumstance, I had the opportunity of exploring it to its bowels. The head engineer on the *United States* was a McNamee from upper New York. He made a habit of looking up any McNamees booked on the boat and offering to give them a tour of the whole working part of the ship, which he did for me. I was amazed at the extent and complexity of the engine rooms, big enough to service a whole city, and at the vastness of the kitchens, laundry, and other service facilities. The ship also had an interdenominational chapel that a cabin boy prepared each morning for my Mass, which drew a sizable congregation from the passengers.

We docked early in the morning at Le Havre. The *United States* made a call there to let off passengers headed for Europe before steaming across the Channel for England. As we skirted the south coast of England and passed the great shipyards of Portsmouth, we encountered small freighters chugging off to all sorts of commercial destinations. I was reminded of the last stanza of John Masefield's "Cargoes":

> Dirty British coaster with a salt-caked smoke stack,
> Butting through the Channel in the mad March days,
> With a cargo of Tyne coal,
> Road rails, pig lead,
> Firewood, iron ware, and cheap tin trays.

I don't know what the freighters' cargo was, but there they still were, "the dirty British coaster[s] . . . Butting through the Channel." As we pushed into port at Southampton, I recalled that it was in these very waters that Tennyson wrote his poem on death, "Crossing the Bar," as he rode the ferry from Southampton to the Isle of Wight, where he had a summer home. This was just the beginning of my rich experience of the next few months in England, when every turn was to stimulate a literary or historical memory.

I boarded the boat train for London. As we rode through the beautiful English countryside, I was impressed with the shapely chestnut trees in full bloom; they punctuated the landscape with clusters of white blossoms that looked like inverted chandeliers. This was my third spring that year. I had experienced one in Missouri with its flood of dogwood, Judas trees, and magnolia, and a second one later in Wisconsin with its splash of lilac and bridal wreath, when I made a home visit before taking ship for Europe. Here was my third one, in England, dotted with blossoming chestnut trees. At this first glance of rural England, I was struck by its freshness and seemingly unravished condition in spite of the fact that it has been inhabited and cultivated for thousands of years. I was to find that to be true of the landscape in every European country.

When I arrived in Victoria Station, I began to discover how naive I had been in planning my trip. It was my intention to go on immediately to Rome and then see a little of the rest of Europe before settling down in England. I thought I could make an immediate transfer to a train for Dover, then take the ferry to Calais, and finally go on by continental train to Rome. I presumed I could check my steamer trunk at the station until I returned. (You traveled with steamer trunks in those days, not with the light luggage of the air age.) I went to the information desk and stated my plans. The attendant looked at me in astonishment and said there was no way in which I could get immediate accommodations for Rome; it might take a couple of days to pin them down. He asked me whether I had reservations in London. When I said I did not, he assured me I might have real difficulty finding a place to stay because they had done no rebuilding of commercial or public buildings since the war. All their limited resources had gone into private housing. He made some calls to no avail, so I decided to go up to the Jesuit residence on Farm Street in the Mayfair area and throw myself on the mercy of my Jesuit confreres. The information agent did help me get my trunk checked in the baggage room until I returned from Rome. I took a taxi out to Farm Street.

As we drove through the city, I noticed block after block fenced off by high wooden fences to hide the huge bomb craters that still pockmarked the city almost ten years after the war. I understood what the man in the information booth had meant when he said they had done no rebuilding of commercial and office structures. I was later to see the bombed out acres that still surrounded St. Paul's Cathedral in the old city, punctuated here and there by what remained of the famous Sir Christopher Wren churches in the area, sometimes no more than the side walls and the steeple. These raw traces of the constant bombardment of London in the war made one admire the courage, stubborn perseverance, and even sense of wry humor with which the Londoners bore this nerve-wracking ordeal month after month.

I finally arrived at the Jesuit residence on Farm Street and rang the doorbell. A quaint little brother, who could have stepped right out of one of Dickens's novels, appeared at the door. When I told him my predicament, he said the whole community was out seeing a special movie and that the only one home, besides himself, was the rector, and he was in the bath. I said I'd wait until he got out of the bath, which I did. When the rector appeared, he couldn't have been more considerate. He said they had been hard hit by bombs in the war and were very short of rooms. They actually had only one extra one at the moment, and the only reason they had that was that Father Darcy, whose room it was, was lecturing in America. He went on to say that I was particularly lucky because the room had been occupied until that morning by an African bishop who had thrown himself on their mercy, as I was doing at the moment. Happily, the rector's mercy had not dried up, and I had the room as long as I needed it—the two days that the information person at the station had said it would take to get my reservations for transportation to Rome.

More of my naïveté was evident in the fact that I had not settled ahead of time with the English provincial about where I would live during my stay in England. He would have been utterly justified had he been upset by my coming without making previous arrangements for residence, but actually he was not. He said he did not know immediately where he could place me, but that I was not to worry. I was to go on to Rome, enjoy what I planned to see in Europe, and he would have a place for me when I returned. He surprised me by saying that one place in Italy I must not miss was Perugia. With all of Italy and the rest of Europe before me, I confess that Perugia was not high on my list, but he had been so kind and considerate to me, bursting in on him unannounced, that I put it on my list. After I visited Assisi, I took the bus to Perugia and certainly did not regret it.

Perugia is one of the very charming hill towns in central Italy, perched on its mesalike rocky promontory overlooking plains and rolling hills in all directions. It was the home of Perugino, under whom Raphael apprenticed and from whom he learned the gentle classical formality that characterizes both his and Perugino's works. The city is also world famous for its chocolates. I stayed overnight, and as I sat on the terrace of my hotel sipping some ambrosial Perugino chocolate at breakfast in the morning, I was struck by the idyllic views of the surroundings. It was what both Perugino and Raphael had frequently painted into the backgrounds of many of their compositions: a gentle plain in the foreground, rolling hills in the background, with slender alder trees on the horizon stitching the hillside into the sky, and all of it bathed in a golden sunlight. The artists painted exactly what they saw, idealizing it only slightly. I knew now why the provincial had suggested that I come to Perugia.

But to get there or anywhere else on the continent, I had to make my arrangements to get to Rome. The train trip from Calais to Rome would be overnight, so I made a Pullman reservation for that part of the trip—the usual way we traveled overnight in trains at home. When I got to Calais, I realized that what they had reserved for me was a large bedroom that practically nobody but the very wealthy used. It was too late to make other arrangements. I was traveling in clerics, and so, in order not to scandalize the public by my luxurious accommodations, I would pull down the shades when we stopped at a station. I had not suspected what I was getting in the way of accommodations because the monetary exchange was so favorable to

Americans at the time that the cost of the reservation was only a tiny fraction of what we would have paid for a simple Pullman berth at home. In any event, I got safely to Rome. It was a thrill to be approaching the Eternal City for the first time, with the shades up, and get my first glimpse of the dome of St. Peter's silhouetted against the morning sky.

I had arranged to stay at the Bellarmino in Rome, an old palace converted into a residence for young Jesuits studying in Rome. As soon as I had checked into my room, I took to the streets to begin my exploration of the city. One of the first things I wanted to see was the ancient Roman Pantheon. It is just two blocks away from the Bellarmino. In no time at all, I was seated on the edge of the fountain in the piazza in front of the Pantheon, studying what is perhaps the best preserved of all ancient Roman buildings and certainly the most impressive. Its plan, combining a domed structure with the facade of a classical temple, has probably inspired more great structures than any other single building in the whole history of architecture. Stepping inside it, I was awed, as anyone must be, by the majestic uninterrupted circular space topped by the mighty dome. The awesome space is defined by the wide diagonal shaft of light always moving with the sun that originates in the broad open oculus at the apex of the dome. This is the only source of light in the interior. When I stepped into the space for the first time, this shaft of light was focused on the tomb of Raphael. My instinctive thought was: an appropriate place for Raphael's tomb—here in the greatest relic of ancient classical Rome—because he had done so much to incorporate the spirit of ancient classicism into the art of the High Renaissance.

As I admired this great open interior space, I recalled that two Roman inventions had made it possible: the perfecting of the dome as an architectural principle and the development of poured concrete as a building material. The great dome is a poured cement structure resting on massive walls thirteen feet thick. The dome itself was lightened by filling the forms with pottery and pouring the cement around them, resulting in a honeycomb-like structure. It was further lightened by the fact that its inner surface was all coffered, thus again vastly reducing its weight.

With this great architectural achievement before me, I realized that nothing like it occurred again until Justinian commissioned the even greater dome of Hagia Sophia in Constantinople in the fifth century. Centuries later, the great Renaissance architect Filippo Brunelleschi designed the great dome of the Duomo in Florence; and, in the late Renaissance, Michelangelo, in partial emulation of Brunelleschi's achievement, designed the great dome of the new St. Peter's. The combination of a domed structure with the facade of a classical temple that characterizes the Pantheon became a pattern architects around the world emulated for centuries. It became stock in trade for Palladio, one of Italy's most famous architects. Witness his Villa Rotonda in Vicenza and the two churches he designed in Venice: San Giorgio and Il Redentore. The Pantheon in Paris also employs the pattern, as does St. Paul's Cathedral in London. And in the United States, Jefferson employed it in his home at Monticello and in the library he designed for the University of Virginia. We are all familiar with its variation in the National Capitol Building in Washington and in many state capitol buildings throughout the country. In St. Louis, the pattern is repeated in the design of the old courthouse.

I knew that in the short time I was to be in Rome I would have to make a selection of what I wanted to see. High on my list were some of the sites associated with the roots of the Society of Jesus. I discovered that most of them were within easy walking distance of the Bellarmino, where I was staying. Foremost among them was the Gesu, the Jesuit residence on the site of the very first Jesuit residence in Rome, where St. Ignatius lived after the Society of Jesus had been approved as a religious order. In fact, the three simple rooms in which he lived and in which he wrote the Constitutions of the Society that have guided its development through five hundred years are preserved intact within the larger present Gesu residence. When I saw them there, back in 1955, they had been gussied up with a great deal of fussy decoration. Years later, in 1990, in the Ignatian year commemorating the five hundredth anniversary of St. Ignatius's birth, I was to see these rooms brought back to their original stark simplicity by Father Thomas Lucas. At the same time, Father Lucas also uncovered the remarkable frescoes by Brother Andrea Pozzo in the gallery outside St. Ignatius's rooms. These frescoes are an impressive baroque tour de force in trompe l'oeil design by Brother Pozzo, who was a great master of perspective and the baroque style. I was soon to experience two of his greatest masterpieces in the Gesu church and the Church of San Ignazio nearby. The frescoes in the gallery at the St. Ignatius Rooms were still mostly plastered over in 1955. Father Lucas was responsible for discovering them and restoring them in 1990. One of the rooms that St. Ignatius occupied had a little balcony, and legend has it that he used to sit there of an evening and contemplate the stars. The balcony is still there. As I sat there on a bench looking up at the heavens, a small patch of which can still be seen, I recalled the beautiful poem "Nox Ignatiana" that the Missouri Province Jesuit poet, James J. Daly, penned on the legend of Ignatius as a star watcher:

> His vigil was with the stars; his eyes were bright
> With radiance of them. Mystically slow
> Was their processional, while far below,
> Rome's quick and dead slept—fellows in the night.
> These very stars had marched in cryptic rite
> For Virgil in clear evenings long ago,
> Gliding, like motes, athwart the overflow
> Of splendor from immortal tides of light.
>
> "What is this ant-life on a sphere of sand
> That it must drive, with ant-like cares my soul
> Than all the stars together more sublime?"
> So in the spacious night Ignatius planned
> His spacious morrows—centuries his scroll
> Upon a background of Eternal time.

St. Ignatius, very early in his plans for the future of the Jesuits in Rome, realized that the Jesuits would need a church in which to carry on their apostolate of preaching and administering the sacraments. He set about planning one and worked for a while with Michelangelo on a design. He was not to live to see it realized, and when it was built, it was designed by other architects, Vignolla and Giacomo della Porta. It is the Jesuit mother church and an early example of baroque design, a style so much used by Jesuits in structures all over Europe that it is sometimes called the Jesuit style. Its interior is an example of what is called "the hall church," a space without side aisles, which gives everybody in the congregation a clear unobstructed view of the altar. The pulpit is placed halfway down the nave and raised high above the congregation, again to facilitate an unobstructed view of the preacher and to make his message more audible to the whole congregation. These features of design, I was to learn, were repeated in later churches designed by or for Jesuits all over the continent.

But what I was most interested in on this first visit to the Gesu was one side chapel and the famous altar and tomb of St. Ignatius. The former housed the little painting of Madonna della Strada (Our Lady of the Way), St. Ignatius's favorite Madonna. It had decorated the facade of the little chapel that Pope Paul II had turned over to St. Ignatius when he gave him permission to establish the first Jesuit residence and apostolic center on this very spot. So, while kneeling before this simple little Madonna of the Way and saying a few thankful Ave Marias, I felt drawn very close to the Ignatian roots of the Society.

Just a few feet away from the little chapel of the Madonna della Strada is the tomb and the altar of St. Ignatius, a striking contrast to the stark simplicity of the rooms in which the saint lived. It is perhaps the most lavish example of baroque design in the history of art. Designed by Brother Andrea Pozzo, it fills the whole north transept of the Gesu. The tomb of St. Ignatius, of wrought bronze, rests beneath the altar table. The upper structure of the altar is made up of a cluster of great blue-marble Corinthian pillars decorated in the fluting with bronze and topped with bronze capitals. These pillars are topped by a marble pediment broken open to house a huge lapis lazuli globe surmounted by a bronze cross. All of this frames the impressive full-length silver statue of St. Ignatius in the full ecclesiastical vestments of the celebrant at Mass. He is looking up to heaven as if in ecstasy, which recalls the fact that he is said to have frequently experienced a vision of the Trinity while offering Mass. Very early in his spiritual career, he had been favored with a vision of the Trinity. I arranged to offer Mass myself at his tomb and altar, and as I elevated the Sacred Host heavenward and caught a glimpse of the great baroque figure of St. Ignatius above me and was conscious of the mortal remains of the little limping soldier from Loyola at my feet, I felt very grateful for being a member of the company he founded.

My next stop on this Ignatian pilgrimage was San Ignazio, the former chapel of the original Jesuit College in Rome. The college building is still there, functioning now as a public library, but the chapel still functions as a public church. On its ceiling, Brother Pozzo painted what is unquestionably his masterpiece and one of the greatest baroque compositions in the history of art. It is reproduced in all major books on the history of art. It represents St. Ignatius in glory contemplating the Holy Trinity. In the four corners of the composition are allegorizations of the four continents to which St. Ignatius sent missioners and educators. The composition is an astounding baroque tour de force, which displays Brother Pozzo's extraordinary command of the laws of perspective. He was an authority on the subject and wrote books on it, some of which are still in print. The composition covers the entire ceiling of the chapel, which is a continuous barrel vault. On it, Brother Pozzo has painted a whole second church in perfect receding perspective. Its roof is open to the skies, and St. Ignatius, contemplating the Trinity, is seen amidst floating clouds against a clear blue sky. The allegorical figures of the continents float on clouds at the corners of this structure projected on the vault. It is an astounding piece of work, one of several masterful baroque designs Brother Pozzo executed in various parts of Italy. It was a surprising manifestation to me of the importance of art in the early history of the Society of Jesus.

This importance was manifested not only in baroque works of art such as Brother Pozzo's, but also in the work of the important baroque artists that the early Jesuits patronized. Gian Lorenzo Bernini was unquestionably one of the most talented of all baroque artists anywhere. It has been said of him that he found Rome a classical city and left it a baroque city. You feel the truth of this when you move around Rome and encounter one great work after another by him. These works include the famous baroque *Fountain of the Rivers* in the Piazza Navona, the marvelous *St. Theresa in Ecstasy* in the Cornaro Chapel in Santa Maria della Vittoria, the sculptures *Apollo and Daphne* and *David* in the Borghese Gallery, and, of course, the great bronze baldachino, the Altar of the Chair, and the massive colonnade at St. Peter's. But what Bernini himself considered his masterpiece is the Chapel of San Andrea on the Quirinale, commissioned by the Jesuits as the chapel for the Roman novitiate. It is a highly successful baroque building. Baroque artists frequently take a traditional static, classical, highly segmented form and break or stretch it into a fluid and broken pattern in which part flows into part. They thus create a sense of movement through the whole composition, which San Andrea illustrates admirably. Bernini has taken the static, segmented, and circular pattern of the Pantheon and stretched it into an oval. The flat, segmented temple facade has become semicircular and is surmounted by a broken semicircular pediment. Little arms reach out from each side of the building inviting the public into the space within. The semicircular steps move out from the doorway like a lava flow. When you step inside, movement again is dominant. St. Andrew in the painting above the main altar, suspended on his X-shaped cross, is looking up to the figure of the Dove of the Holy Spirit, suspended in a flood of amber light in the cupola at the apex of the oval dome. Winged putti fringe the base of the dome like figures on a carousel. Dynamism and motion seem to pervade every element in the building. But San Andrea had other associations for me on that first visit. It was here that St. Stanislaus Kostka had come from Vienna on foot to beg to be admitted into the Society by the then father general, St. Francis Borgia.

I was to encounter other examples of the Jesuit preference for the baroque in other cities during my little grand tour of Europe, notably in Venice in the Church of the Assumption, where a splendid baroque altar was designed by a secular blood brother of the Jesuit Andrea Pozzo. Talent must have run in the family. Another example was the Jesuit church of St. Charles Borromeo in Antwerp, the facade of which was designed by Peter Paul Rubens, the consummate baroque artist of the north. He also painted more than two dozen baroque paintings to decorate the interior—all but two of which were destroyed in a disastrous fire. As I perused for the first time these baroque creations designed or commissioned by Jesuits, I little suspected I would be returning in 1990, the Ignatian year commemorating the five hundredth anniversary of his birth, with two professional photographers in tow to photograph these great Jesuit baroque monuments for a photographic show at St. Louis University entitled "The Influence of the Jesuits on Baroque Art," as part of the jubilee celebration.

On this first visit to Rome, I was also interested in the monuments that showed the apostolic beginnings of Christianity there. That meant to me the presence of Saints Peter and Paul. This pilgrimage took me first to the Mamartine Prison in the ancient Roman Forum just yards away from the House of the Senate, in front of which Julius Caesar was assassinated. It was intensely moving to stand within the walls of the prison in which Peter was incarcerated and from which he was miraculously released by an angel. Next stop was the *tempietto* on the Janiculum Hill, a perfect little jewel of a round and domed temple, designed by the Renaissance architect Bramante. It is said to mark the spot where St. Peter was crucified upside down at his request because he did not consider himself worthy to emulate his master, crucified head up on the Cross. There is some evidence that both Peter and Paul were at first buried for a time in the catacombs of Saint Calixtus. The larger carved-out burial place that probably housed their remains for a time struck me as perhaps a more appropriate resting place for the remains of these simple apostles than the impressive basilicas that Constantine built to house them, outside the walls for Paul and on Vatican Hill for Peter. It is certainly more appropriate than the present gigantic St. Peter's Basilica that now towers over the remains of St. Peter. I finally got to the basilica and have to say that its overpowering vastness, an adaptation of the pantheon formula of dome and temple facade, exploded to gigantic proportions, is the extreme opposite of what I would have thought appropriate for Peter, the simple fisher of men. I had that feeling of inappropriateness even more when I stood at the Bernini baldachino that towers over the crypt of St. Peter below. Something simpler might be more appropriate. But at the same time, you cannot help being impressed by the sheer artistic achievement of Bernini in what is undoubtedly one of the most awesome baroque creations in the world. As you gaze up the serpentine form of one of the gigantic columns towering more than two hundred feet up into the dome, you feel as dwarfed as you do in a redwood forest. And the sense of a living twisted organic form is intended; it is augmented by the fact that the whole surface of the twisted columns is covered with a bronze fretwork of a vine pattern as a great tree in a jungle might be; and amidst the vines are bronze images of bees. All of this is the baroque opposite of the formal staid verticality of a Greek classic Doric or Ionic column.

The bronze bees on the columns reminded me of the Barberini family coat of arms, where they also appear. It was a Barberini pope, Pope Urban VIII, who commissioned Bernini to design the baldachino. He also ordered the bronze for it to be stripped from the portico and dome of the ancient Roman Pantheon. This act prompted a much circulated quip in Latin: *Quod non fecerunt barbari, fecerunt Barberini* (What the barbarians had not done, the Barberini did). It refers to the habit of the Barberini pope and other popes of making the ancient Roman monuments quarries for building material for new papal buildings. It was at this time, too, that half the stones of the ancient Colosseum were hauled away and incorporated into new papal projects.

I decided to offer Mass in St. Peter's as part of my pilgrimage to Christian roots. I made the arrangement with the little monsignor in the sacristy who was in charge of such things and asked to say Mass at the altar at the rear of the basilica, above which the famous early *Pietà* of Michelangelo was mounted. The *Pietà* was originally executed by Michelangelo for the private chapel of a French cardinal who resided in Rome; hence, it is in more human scale than the immense sculptures in some of the other chapels in St. Peter's. When the appointed day and time came for my Mass, I was led the literal half mile through the basilica to the altar. I confess that as I proceeded through the liturgy of the Mass, I was somewhat distracted by the presence of this great world image of the Sorrowful Mother gazing in sorrowful resignation at the limp body of her Son in her lap. But in a typical Roman fashion, I was yanked from my aesthetic ecstasy by Roman reality. At the lavabo when I had washed my hands and waited for the acolyte to give me the finger towel, he reached down and held up the end of the altar cloth for me to dry my hands. When I looked at the cloth, I saw that many others before me had already used it as a towel. But the whole experience of getting that intimately close to one of Michelangelo's greatest creations was a great privilege that can no longer be had since the madman attacked the great masterpiece with a hammer. It is now enwrapped in bullet-proof glass and can be contemplated only from a distance.

I set aside a day to experience another of Michelangelo's creations, the overpowering Sistine Chapel frescoes. The visit would include, of course, the Raphael frescoes in the Stanze of the Vatican Museum. To get to the Stanze or to the Sistine Chapel, you wind your way through endless galleries of classical sculpture, which very few visitors have time to observe closely. But there were two statues in the maelstrom of classical art that I wanted to see very particularly. I had used slide reproductions of them for years to illustrate the dichotomy between the classical and the Hellenistic styles. The *Apollo Belvedere* is a good example of the former, and the *Laocoön* of the latter. I had used these two works to familiarize my students with the aesthetic qualities of these two artistic tendencies and was eager to see the originals. I sought them out amidst the literally hundreds of other

Greek and especially Roman sculptures that surround them. The *Apollo* with its strong vertical lines, its repose, its restrained emotion, and its relaxed physical anatomy was all that I would have expected it to be from the photographic reproductions of it I had studied. Michelangelo knew it in his early days, and it inspired the similar kind of repose and controlled emotion that characterizes his *David* and the early *Pietà,* in the presence of which I had just said Mass.

The original *Laocoön,* on the other hand, was something of a surprise to me. I had envisioned it as at least life-size if not of heroic proportions. But in reality it is considerably less than life-size. That is one limitation of studying art work in a slide reproduction. Everything comes out on the screen as of the same scale. But after I got over the shock of the small scale of the original, I was impressed all over again with its baroque quality. The broken triangle of its whole composition with the violent diagonals of the agonizing bodies of Laocoön and his two sons all bound together by the twisting curves of the entwining serpents, the signs of physical tension in their contorted bodies, and the contrasted emotions expressed in their faces create a dynamism and emotionalism that is the exact opposite of the static repose and emotional restraint of the *Apollo.* Michelangelo was present when the *Laocoön* was dug up in the excavation of a Roman villa. It had an effect on the dynamism of his later sculpture and painting, which is much more mannered or baroque than his earlier work.

Just down the hallway from the endless sculpture halls are two great series of frescoes that again exemplify this contrast between the classical restraint of the High Renaissance and the emotional power and dynamism of the mannered and baroque styles. They are the frescoes of Raphael in the Stanza della Segnatura and those of Michelangelo in the Sistine Chapel. The Stanza della Segnatura (Room of the Signature) got its name because it was a square vaulted room, a quasi-library, in which some of the popes signed important documents. Giovanni Sodoma had begun to decorate it, but eventually Pope Julius II turned over the project to Raphael.

Raphael planned a decorative scheme that was a typical example of High Renaissance synthesizing. The frescoes on the four walls were to represent the major disciplines that entered into the Renaissance view of a balanced human life and education: theology, philosophy, literature, and law. It is typical of the new Renaissance glorification of Greek culture that philosophy is represented exclusively by Greek philosophers in the School of Athens fresco. Plato and Aristotle, the greatest of them, stand in the center of the composition—Plato pointing to the heavens, the realm of his eternal ideas and the source of all truth for him, and Aristotle pointing to the earth, the realm of sensible reality and, for him, the source of all knowledge. Many of the other Greek philosophers are scattered to the sides of the composition: Epicurus, Diogenes, Socrates, and the Sophists. Representatives of all the disciplines of the quadrivium and trivium are also assembled in animated discussion in the incomplete structure of St. Peter's Basilica.

On one wall, literature is represented by Mount Parnassus, on which are assembled Apollo, the three Muses, and individuals representing pastoral, lyrical, epic, and tragic literature. On the opposite wall is law, represented by the seated figures of Justinian, who codified Roman law, and Pope Gregory the Great, who codified canon law. They are accompanied by figures allegorizing the three of the cardinal virtues that should guide the practice of law: prudence, temperance, and courage. Justice is suggested by the figures of Justinian and Gregory, who codified secular and ecclesiastical law.

On the wall opposite the School of Athens is the most impressive of all the four frescoes. It is perhaps the most important example of High Renaissance composition in the history of art. It is the *Disputa*, representing theology. *Disputa* might be loosely translated as "Witness," an earthly and heavenly witness to the truth of the presence of Christ in the Eucharist. At the very center of the composition is the Eucharist in a small monstrance on an altar. Many Protestants in the north at this time were denying the presence of Christ in the Eucharist, so Raphael is making a dramatic reassertion of the truth of that dogma in this composition. He exploits the shape of the wall on which it is painted to give central importance to the eucharistic presence. The wall is semicircular. He paints in perfect perspective, a receding semicircular apsidal space in which he positions on earth a semicircle of great doctors of the Church who have written on the eucharistic presence, joined by artistic geniuses such as Dante, Bramante, Fra Angelico, and himself, who have written, designed buildings, or created paintings to enhance belief in the eucharistic presence. In the heavens above, he pictures God the Father at the apex of the composition, with arms spread above the figure of Christ enthroned in a cloud and displaying the wound in his Side. Below Christ hovers the Dove of the Holy Spirit, through whose instrumentality the Son of God was incarnated and by whose power the Bread of the Eucharist is transubstantiated into the Body of Christ. Mary is at the right of Christ and St. John the Baptist at his left. Choirs of adoring angels fly in receding semicircles to each side. The whole thing is a very ordered, centralized, and symmetrical divine tableau presented for our thoughtful meditation. We are not invited into the space, nor are we expected to be very emotionally involved. We are expected to *think* about the subject of the Blessed Sacrament in a very quiet meditative way, which everyone in the composition seems to be doing. The uniform golden light that pervades the composition helps to induce that meditative reaction. That is the whole purpose and method of a classically conceived High Renaissance painting. It was one thing to have been told of this purpose and method and to have experienced it to some extent in small colored reproductions or slides. It was quite another thing altogether to stand in the Raphael Stanza for the first time surrounded by his great compositions, every one of which instinctively induced that quiet contemplative mood.

And what a contrast it was to follow the crowd through narrow back corridors, down winding precipitous steps into the Sistine Chapel. The barrel-vaulted ceiling of the chapel had originally been painted blue and spangled with gold stars. Pope Julius II decided to add some figurative decorations to bring it into harmony with the large frieze of paintings on the lower walls by such outstanding artists as Perugino, Botticelli, and Ghirlandaio. What Julius had in mind was some medallions representing the twelve apostles. Michelangelo at first demurred. He said he was a sculptor, not a painter, but Julius was a person who would not take "no" for an answer. He urged Michelangelo to take on the project, and the artist finally agreed to do so but only on condition that he could decorate the ceiling in a way that he considered worthy of the space. What he came up with is one of the most astounding compositions in the history of art. When I first stepped into the chapel, fresh from the contemplative mood of Raphael's Stanza, I was simply overwhelmed by the cosmic majesty and power of Michelangelo's conception. Unfolded before me on the vault and east wall was a cosmic panorama stretching from the creation of the universe to the Last Judgment. It sweeps through the creation of Adam and Eve; their temptation, fall, and expulsion from paradise; the tortured maelstrom of the flood. And it ends in the terrifying giant figure of Christ as Judge in the immense rendering of the Last Judgment. Christ is otherwise alluded to in the figures of his ancestors in the gables above the dormer windows along the side of the chapel and in the colossal figures of the prophets and sibyls between the windows, who, in their various ways, gave prophetic intimations of the coming of Christ. And all of this is rendered very expressively through mannered distortion and baroque exuberance. There are no quiet closed tableaus here, but open dynamic action scenes that flow out into our space and invite us to become part of the action. God hovers over the world He has just created like a great bird separating the land from the sea. In the creation of Adam, the majestic figure of God the Father rests on a cloud supported by angels. His beard is blown back by the wind; He stretches out His strong finger toward the limp finger of Adam just beginning to waken into life. We imagine the spark of life actually leaping from the strong Finger of God to the limp finger of Adam. And so it is throughout this dynamic composition: energetic action and powerful emotion. The first glimpse of this astounding artistic achievement is almost overpowering. It made very understandable to me the appropriateness of the epithet often given Michelangelo: the Titan. His achievement here and elsewhere is truly titanic, gigantic, gargantuan.

What I was looking at back in 1955, of course, were the frescoes before they were cleaned. There was considerable difference in the visibility of various parts of the ceiling. The relatively small figures of the ancestors of Christ on the spaces above the dormer windows were quite dim; the gigantic figures of the prophets and sibyls in the curved spaces between the windows were much brighter; and the panoramic scenes of the Creation and the Flood at the apex of the vault were brightest of all. I was aware that some art historians had made a great deal of this variation in brightness in the composition. They saw in it an influence of Platonism on the thought and work of Michelangelo and had written extensively on the subject. The distant ancestors of Christ, who were only dimly aware of the Christ to come, were partially in darkness, paralleled in the Platonic view of things by those who were partly buried in the material world and only dimly aware, if at all, of the enlightenment of the eternal ideas. For these scholars, the better-lighted prophets and sibyls paralleled those in the Platonic world who had some glimmer of the eternal ideas from the philosophers with their firsthand intuition of the eternal ideas. And the best-illuminated central compositions, detailing the revealed knowledge of creation and fall of man, paralleled the full enlightened vision of the philosopher king of the eternal ideas. This was a nice theory, but it did not stand up under the facts about the frescoes that the modern thorough cleaning revealed. What I and the art historians were looking at in 1955 was five hundred years of candle grease. The cleaning revealed that the figures in all three sections of the vaulting are equally well lighted and show remarkable nuances of color and chiaroscuro (light and shadow) that had been entirely obscured by the coats of candle grease and smoke accumulated over the centuries and by crude restorations that had been attempted in the past. Some of the art historians had also said that Michelangelo was not a colorist, that he had the imagination of a sculptor even when he was painting, and lacked a delicate sensitivity to color. The cleaning has revealed him as a marvelous colorist. In fact, the nuances of color in the drapery of the ancestors of Christ, obscured before the cleaning, are very much like the subtle off-tone color that we associate with the work of mannerist painters such as Parmigianino and Russo Fiorentino.

The rediscovery of these color tones in the frescoes of Michelangelo and in the attitudinizing poses of some of the ancestors, sibyls, and prophets makes understandable why mannerism itself was early on called *la maniera di Michelangelo* (the manner of Michelangelo). The cleaned frescoes reveal clearly what that manner was. Neither mannerism nor what the cleaned frescoes would reveal about Michelangelo's part in the development of the style was any part of my first experience of the Sistine frescoes, but my first vision of them even in their uncleaned condition was a pretty heady experience. I knew that I had to return. The morning had been exhausting both physically and emotionally, so I decided to return to the Bellarmino for lunch and an afternoon siesta.

I picked my way down from the Sistine Chapel and through St. Peter's Basilica only to find that it was raining. I made use of the protection of Bernini's great colonnade and worked my way along a neighboring street toward the bus line. The street was Borgo Santo Spirito. That name pulled me up short. It was the street on which the headquarters of the Jesuit Generalate was located. That realization reminded me of a fact I had almost forgotten in my excitement of experiencing the historical and artistic treasures of Rome for the first time. My being there was really illegitimate. At the time, Jesuits had to have the permission of Father General to come to Rome. They applied for that permission through their own local provincials, who procured it for them. I had applied to Father Conway, my local provincial, for the permission well in advance of my departure, but Father was ill at the time, and when I was about to leave, I discovered he had not applied for the permission. With my somewhat lax conscience, I was not much troubled by that. Rome is a big place, I thought, and there would be hardly any likelihood of my running into Father General there, so I went on to Rome without the permission.

But here I was today on the street where the general lived. As this fact dawned on me, the rain began to come down in torrents. I stepped into a doorway to get out of the deluge. I looked up at the number on the door—Borgo S. Spirito 5—the address of the general. Just then the father minister of the house, the man in charge of the physical needs of a Jesuit community, stepped into the doorway and stopped to fold up his umbrella. He introduced himself, and when he found out who I was, he invited me to lunch. My heart skipped a beat. If I accepted, I might run into the general. Then I thought, "No, they will have reading at table, and I will be lost in the crowd." I was right. They did have reading at table in Italian, and I was lost in the shuffle. But what I did not know was that it was the custom at the time to have the national assistants to the general line up outside the dining room to meet visitors. Then the visitor joined his own assigned assistant and sat down with the general for recreation, so I found myself taking recreation with the general, Father Janssens. The first thing he asked me was, "How long are you staying in Rome?" I told him a week. He said: "A week isn't enough to do justice to Rome; stay a month if you can; and if you do, you can be here for the canonization of the Jesuit Father Joseph Pignatelli, our second founder." So I stayed a month. I couldn't have a more direct sanction of my stay than the firsthand word of the general himself. I am certainly glad I did. It gave me the chance to revisit some of the important things I had already seen and to enjoy many others that I had not seen. And I also managed a quick trip to Naples, Pompeii, and the Amalfi Drive. But most of all it gave me the opportunity of attending the canonization of Father Pignatelli and Pope Pius X, which had to be the most impressive experience of my stay in Rome.

Father Pignatelli was a link between the old and new Society of

Jesus. He came from a prominent wealthy family from central Italy but spent a great deal of his active life in Spain. He was in Spain when the Society was suppressed by Pope Clement XIV in 1773. He and thousands of Spanish Jesuits were exiled from Spain. They actually became "boat people," set adrift without a place to land. Father Pignatelli used his family influence to obtain permission for them to land in Italy, and he also, with the help of his family's wealth, supported them in Italy until they could become incorporated into the work of the diocesan clergy there. Although they were no longer a religious order, the exiled Jesuits did keep some kind of loose affiliation with one another, and Father Pignatelli helped them in that effort. These years were very difficult for all the former Jesuits and for Father Pignatelli among them. When Pope Pius VII restored the Society of Jesus in 1814, Father Pignatelli was elected the first general of the new Society. It was no doubt his heroic and saintly life during these difficult years that tested his dedication to his religious life and that ultimately won him the great honor of canonization. It was that canonization that I was to have the privilege of witnessing.

Pope Pius X was canonized on the same day in the same ceremony. Pius was well known for his strong stand against modernism but also for his defense of the rights of the poor, his advocacy of frequent Communion, and the reception of Communion by children. As patriarch of Venice, before he was elected pope, he had become very popular with his people in Venice and throughout Italy. Because of his popularity and the fact that Jesuits and friends of Jesuits from all over the world would be coming to Rome for his canonization, it was thought that not even St. Peter's Basilica could accommodate the crowd. So for the first time the canonization ceremony was scheduled in St. Peter's piazza in front of the basilica. The place was jammed for the ceremony, which was scheduled for the late afternoon. A great red velvet canopy had been erected over an altar on the steps of the basilica, and huge portraits of Pius X and Father Pignatelli were suspended from the balcony on the facade of St. Peter's. At that time, Pius XII was the reigning pontiff. He was carried from the Bernini colonnade on the *sedia gestatoria,* accompanied by uniformed papal guards carrying the *flabella,* ceremonial fans made of peacock feathers. It was all very princely, almost imperial, a relic of the old courtly Byzantine religious ceremonies from the East. And Pius XII in his bearing was every inch the prince, but there were a few circumstances on the occasion that reminded him of his mortality. He was already quite ill at the time and could not go through the long ceremony of the canonization and Mass that followed without the relief of restroom facilities, so behind the impressive velvet canopy that covered the altar they had constructed a velvet tent that housed temporary restroom facilities to which his holiness retired in solemn procession twice during the ceremonies to take care of some of his human needs. But this did not detract from the solemnity of the occasion. By the time the ceremony was over, it was getting dark. Before the recessional, the *petrini* (workmen associated with the material fabric of the great basilica) began lighting the flaming oil torches that had been attached to the whole outer fringe of the basilica. They started at the top of the Cross on the very tip of the great dome and gradually slid down the cables holding the torches, lighting one after another until the outline of the great structure was alight with flaming torches. When the last one was lit, the great bell, visible at the top of the facade, began to boom; and it was soon joined by the clang of the more than four hundred church bells all over Rome. It was an overwhelming experience of light and sound joining in the declaration of faith expressed in the voices of the thousands of faithful singing the Te Deum in thanksgiving for the lives of Saint Pius X and Saint Joseph Pignatelli as Pope Pius XII was carried out through the immense crowd on his *sedia gestatoria.*

The sound of all the bells of Rome chiming together their great hymn of thanksgiving brought to my mind some lines of a poem by the New Zealand poet Eileen Duggan. She is talking about a pilgrimage of church bells from countries all over the world to Christ's tomb on Easter morning to pay homage to the Risen Christ. Each of the bells has the tone and character of the country from which it comes.

She speaks of "the queenly, weary din of Notre Dame"; the bells of Spain, "the Moors still moaning through the saint"; "the frosty fiery bells of Germany"; the Irish bells "jesting all the way"; and the English bells " slow bosomed as a swan." But on before them all, she says, are the bells of Rome, "baying, sweeping down the heavy joyful pack of thunder jowls that tongue hosannas from the leash of Rome." Miss Duggan's lines are exactly right for the sense of majesty and controlled power that we associate with Christian Rome, a feeling that certainly washed over me at the end of this canonization ceremony when I listened to the peals of church bells from all over Rome.

This was an experience I will never forget and certainly a dramatic way to end my stay in Rome. It was also an experience I would not have had if I had not taken refuge from the rain in the doorway of Borgo Santo Spirito, *numero quinto.*

Because my stay in Rome was longer than I had originally planned, I had to cut short my tour of the rest of Europe before returning to England. But there were certain places I wanted to get to even if only briefly. In Italy, two of them were Assisi and Venice. I always had a special affection for St. Francis of Assisi because of his simplicity and his warm love of nature, something I shared with him ever since my early days on the farm. And a dog-eared print of *The Grand Canal* that hung in my little one-room country schoolhouse had early kindled my desire to see one day the city of canals. I took the local bus to Assisi, and as we approached the town and could glimpse the monastery perched on its hill ahead of us, I was delighted to see whole fields of bright sunflowers in full bloom nestling on the monastery hill. What an appropriate setting for the monastery that contains the remains of St. Francis who so loved his brother, the sun. The monastery itself is also very appropriate, a simple plain stone Romanesque structure. And the Saint's tomb could not be more appropriate—a very simple stone tomb surrounded by a wrought iron grate. Anything more would be wrong for St. Francis, who made so much of poverty in his life. I enjoyed the Giotto frescoes on the life of Francis, especially the one in the upper church picturing Francis preaching to the birds. Legend has it that a bevy of birds one day set up a racket at the window of a church where Francis was preaching. He told them that if they would be quiet, he would preach them a sermon of their own after the one he was giving was finished. They piped down immediately, and when he had finished preaching, he kept his promise and went out and preached to the birds. He told them to go on singing because their song was a hymn of praise and thanksgiving to God. They, of course, immediately broke forth in song. Giotto has caught the disarming simplicity of that legend in his fresco on the subject. I said a few prayers to Francis at his tomb for my sister Mauritia, who was a member of the Teaching Sisters of St. Francis, and then took the bus to Perugia, the stop recommended to me by the English provincial. I have already given my impression of that charming hill town so rife with reminders of the artists, Perugino and Raphael. I stayed the night in Perugia and then went on to Venice.

I had made arrangements to stay at the Jesuit house in Venice, but I had no idea of how to get there. As we crossed the long causeway connecting the island of Venice to the mainland, the fabulous city ahead of us seemed to rise from the sea like an apparition in a dream. When we got to the vaparetto station (vaparettos are the boats that substitute for buses or taxis in Venice), I gave myself over to a porter and commissioned him to get me to the Jesuit residence on the Fondamento Nuovo. He was a big strapping individual. He looped a leather strap through the handles of my luggage, threw it all over his husky shoulder, and told me to follow him. The vaparetto took us down the whole length of the Grand Canal to St. Mark's Square. The little oleotype of the canal in my country schoolhouse had not prepared me for the ever-shifting panorama of marble-faced palaces, with arcades of oriental ogee-shaped arches, domed churches, and numerous bridges leaping across the canal, including the famous Rialto. We docked at the vaparetto station at St. Mark's Square amidst a cluster of gondolas. Here I got my first glimpse of the Doge's Palace, with its walls of diaper-patterned, rose-colored marble made more roseate in the soft dusk light, and towering up beyond the palace were the golden onion-shaped domes of St. Mark's. We transferred here to another vaparetto that wound its way under the Bridge of Sighs, down a long canal that passed the Hospital of Saints John and Paul, where St. Ignatius had worked as an orderly during his stay in Venice, and finally stopped at a vaparetto station on the Fondamento Nuovo less than half a block from the Jesuit residence. I was warmly welcomed there, but I did not realize until the next morning, when I went down to the church to say Mass, that the Jesuit Church of the Assumption is possibly one of the most beautiful baroque structures ever commissioned anywhere by the Jesuits. The whole interior is of white Carrara marble with a magnificent floral inlay of green marble that creates the impression of a rich damask. The glorious baldachino with its serpentine pillars of green marble and its dome of white-and-green pattern resembling the scales of a fish was designed by the brother of the famous Jesuit architect, Brother Andrea Pozzo. A Venetian canal flows just to the rear of the sanctuary of the church; a window is strategically placed above the altar so as to catch the reflection from the surface of the water in the canal and cast it down on the altar in a shimmering flood of light. It almost dematerializes the twisted serpentine pillars of the baldachino, a typical baroque effect. The whole church inside and out is a splendid example of baroque design. I little suspected then that thirty-five years later I would return here with professional photographers to photograph this church and the Church of San Giorgio, a classical High Renaissance building designed by Palladio, in every way the complete opposite of the Church of the Assumption. I was immensely impressed with the beauty of the Church of the Assumption at my first glimpse of it. No one had led me to expect that anything of this quality was here.

There was much else in Venice that was a surprise to me. When I looked out my window the first morning, what I was seeing across the water was the Island of the Dead or the Venetian cemetery, and I was later to witness funeral processions making their way to the island in which the hearse and all the mourners' vehicles were gondolas. But, of course, the greatest revelation to me in Venice was my first close view of St. Mark's. It was my first experience of a truly Byzantine structure. The Jesuit residence is on the opposite side of the island from St. Mark's, so to get to it I had to wind my way through narrow streets, along numerous canals, through tiny, tucked away piazzas, and over a half-dozen bridges spanning the maze of canals. As I was doing so, I recalled the beautiful passage in Ruskin's *Stones of Venice*, in which he describes his first approach to St. Mark's through the maze of back streets and then re-creates the vision of St. Mark's itself as it is revealed when he steps through the last arch and its full glory bursts upon him. I used the passage for years in my Freshman English classes to show the power of well-chosen words to summon up a visual experience in full form and color. I was anxious to see how the reality would compare with the vicarious experience I had had of St. Mark's from Ruskin's beautiful word picture. It compared well, so well that I am including the passage here because it captures so perfectly the beauty and variety of one's first glimpse of St. Mark's from the Bocca di Piazza (the Mouth of the Piazza). I was to experience later the English cathedrals in their closes, with which Ruskin contrasts this first vision of St. Mark's. The English cathedral that he describes here is almost certainly a composite of Salisbury and Winchester.

> I wish that the reader, before I bring him into St. Mark's Place, would imagine himself for a little time in a quiet English cathedral town, and

walk with me to the west front of its cathedral. Let us go together up the more retired street, at the end of which we can see the pinnacles of one of the towers, and then through the low grey gateway, with its battlemented top and small latticed window in the centre, into the inner private-looking road or close, where nothing goes in but the carts of the tradesmen who supply the bishop and the chapter, and where there are little shaven grassplots fenced in by neat rails, before old-fashioned groups of somewhat diminutive and excessively trim houses, with little oriel and bay windows jutting out here and there, and deep wooden cornices and eaves painted cream colour and white, and small porches to their doors in the shape of cockle-shells, or little, crooked, thick, indescribable wooden gables warped a little on one side; and so forward till we come to larger houses, also old-fashioned, but of red brick, and with garden behind them, and fruit walls, which show here and there, among the nectarines, the vestiges of an old cloister arch or shaft, and looking in front on the cathedral square itself, laid out in rigid divisions of smooth grass and gravel walk, yet not uncheerful, especially on the sunny side, where the canon's children are walking with their nurserymaids. And so, taking care not to tread on the grass, we will go along the straight walk to the west front, and there stand for a time, looking up at its deep-pointed porches and the dark places between their pillars where there were statues once, and where the fragments, here and there, of a stately figure are still left, which has in it the likeness of a king, perhaps, indeed a king on earth, perhaps a saintly king long ago in heaven; and so higher and higher up to the great mouldering wall of rugged sculpture and confused arcades, shat-tered, and grey, and grisly with heads of dragons and mocking fiends, worn by the rain and swirling winds into yet unseemlier shape, and coloured on their stony scales by the deep russet-orange lichen, melan-choly gold; and so, higher still, to the bleak towers, so far above that the eye loses itself among the bosses of their traceries, though they are rude and strong, and only sees like a drift of eddying black points, now closing, now scattering, and now settling suddenly into invisible places among the bosses and flowers, the crowd of restless birds that fill the whole square with that strange clangour of theirs, so harsh and yet so soothing, like the cries of birds on a solitary coast between the cliffs and sea.

Think for a little while of that scene, and the meaning of all its small formalisms, mixed with its serene sublimity. Estimate its secluded, continuous, drowsy felicities, and its evidence of the sense and steady performance of such kind of duties as can be regulated by the cathe-dral clock; and weigh the influence of those dark towers on all who have passed through the lonely square at their feet for centuries, and on all who have seen them rising far away over the wooded plain, or catching on their square masses the last rays of the sunset, when the city at their feet was indicated only by the mist at the bend of the river. And then let us quickly recollect that we are in Venice, and land at the extremity of the Calle Lunga San Moisé, which may be considered as their answering to the secluded street that led us to our English cathedral gateway.

We find ourselves in a paved alley, some seven feet wide where it is widest, full of people, and resonant with cries of itinerant salesmen—a shriek in their beginning, and dying away into a kind of brazen ringing, all the worse for its confinement between the high houses of the passage along which we have to make our way. Overhead an inextricable confusion of rugged shutters, and iron balconies and chimney flues pushed out on brackets to save room, and arched windows with projecting sills of Istrian stone, and gleams of green leaves here and there where a fig-tree branch escapes over a lower wall from some inner cortile, leading the eye up to the narrow stream of blue sky high over all. On each side a row of shops, as densely set as may be, occupying, in fact, intervals between the square stone shafts, about eight feet high, which carry the first floors; intervals of which one is narrow and serves as a door; the other is, in the more respectable shops, wainscotted to the height of the counter and glazed above, but in those of the poorer tradesmen left open to the ground, and the wares laid on benches and tables in the open air, the light in all cases entering at the front only and fading away in a few feet from threshold into a gloom which the eye from without cannot penetrate, but which is generally broken by a ray or two from a feeble lamp at the back of the shop, suspended before a print of the Virgin.

The less pious shopkeeper sometimes leaves his lamp unlighted, and is contented with a penny print; the more religious one has his print coloured and set in a little shrine with a gilded or figure fringe, with perhaps a faded flower or two on each side, and his lamp burning brilliantly. Here at the fruiterer's, where the dark-green water-melons are heaped upon the counter like cannon balls, the Madonna has a tabernacle of fresh laurel leaves; but the pewterer next door has let his lamp out, and there is nothing to be seen in his shop but the dull gleam of the studded patterns on the copper pans, hanging from his roof in the darkness.

Next comes a "Vendita Frittole e Liquori," where the Virgin, enthroned in a very humble manner beside a tallow candle on a back shelf, presides over certain ambrosial morsels of a nature too ambiguous to be defined or enumerated. But a few steps farther on, at the regular wine-shop of the calle, where we are offered "Vino Nostrani a Soldi 28 32," the Madonna is in great glory, enthroned above ten or a dozen large red casks of three-year-old vintage, and flanked by goodly ranks of bottles of Maraschino, and two crimson lamps; and for the evening, when the gondoliers will come to drink out, under her auspices, the money they have gained during the day, she will have a whole chandelier.

A yard or two farther, we pass the hostelry of the Black Eagle; and glancing as we pass through the square door of marble, deeply moulded, in the outer wall, we see the shadows of its pergola of vines resting on an ancient well, with a pointed shield carved on its side; and so presently emerge on the bridge and Campo San Moisé, whence to the entrance into St. Mark's Place, called the Bocca di Piazza (mouth of the square); the Venetian character is nearly destroyed, first by the frightful façade of San Moisé, which we will pause at another time to examine, and then by the modernizing of the shops as they near the piazza, and the mingling with the lower Venetian populace of lounging groups of English and Austrians. We will push fast through them into the shadow of the pillars at the end of the "Bocca di Piazza," and then we forget them all; for between those pillars there opens a great light, and in the midst of it, as we advance slowly, the vast tower of St. Mark seems to lift itself visibly forth from the level field of chequered stones; and, on each side, the countless arches prolong themselves into ranged symmetry, as if the rugged and irregular houses that pressed together above us in the dark alley had been struck back into sudden obedience and lovely order, and as if all their rude casements and broken walls had been transformed into arches charged with goodly sculpture, and fluted shafts of delicate stone.

And well may they fall back, for beyond those troops of ordered arches there rises a vision out of the earth; and all the great square seems to have opened from it in a kind of awe, that we may see it far away—a multitude of pillars and white domes, clustered into a long low pyramid of coloured light; a treasure-heap, it seems, partly of gold, and partly of opal and mother of pearl, hollowed beneath into five great vaulted porches, ceiled with fair mosaic, and beset with sculpture of alabaster, clear as amber and delicate as ivory; sculpture fantastic and involved, of palm leaves and lilies, and grapes and pomegranates, and birds clinging and fluttering among the branches, all twined together into an endless network of buds and plumes; and in the midst of it, the solemn forms of angels sceptred, and robed to the feet, and leaning to each other across the gates, their figures indistinct among the gleaming of the golden ground through the leaves beside them, interrupted and dim, like the morning light as it faded back among the branches of Eden, when first its gates were angel-guarded long ago. And round the walls of the porches there are set pillars of variegated stones, jasper and porphyry, and deep-green serpentine, spotted with flakes of snow, and marbles, that half refuse and half yield to the sunshine, Cleopatra-like, "their bluest veins to kiss"—the shadow, as it steals back from them, revealing line after line of azure undulation, as a receding tide leaves the waved sand; their capitals rich with interwoven tracery, rooted knots of herbage, and drifting leaves of acanthus and vine, and mystical signs, all beginning and ending in the Cross; and above them, in the broad archivolts, a continuous chain of language and of life—angels, and the signs of heaven, and the labours of men, each in its appointed season upon the earth; and above these, another range of glittering pinnacles, mixed with the white arches edged with scarlet flowers—a confusion of delight, amidst which the breasts of the Greek horses are seen blazing in their breadth of golden strength; and the St. Mark's lion, lifted on a blue field covered with stars; until at last, as if in ecstasy, the crests of the arches break into a marble foam, and toss themselves far into the blue sky in flashes and wreaths of sculptured spray, as if the breakers on the Lido shore had been frost-bound before they fell, and sea-nymphs had inlaid them with coral and amethyst.

Between the grim cathedral of England and this, what an interval!

There is a type of it in the very birds that haunt them; for, instead of the restless crowd, hoarse-voiced and sable-winged, drifting on the bleak upper air, the St. Mark's porches are full of doves, that nestle among the marble foliage, and mingle the soft iridescence of their living plumes, changing at every motion, with the tints, hardly less lovely, that have stood unchanged for seven hundred years.

This, of course, is only the exterior of St. Mark's; the interior is equally impressive with its march of domes, great arches, and pendentives, all emblazoned with golden mosaic. It was my first experience of the splendor of Byzantine architecture. I little realized then that much later in my life, back in St. Louis, I would work for more than seven years planning the completion of the mosaics in the Byzantine cathedral of St. Louis, which now houses the largest collection of mosaics of any building in the world. Some of them, especially the arch of creation, are patterned after the mosaics in St. Mark's.

I did explore a few other haunts in Venice, notably the Frari

Church, where one enjoys Titian's splendid *Assumption,* still gracing the main altar for which it was painted, and the magnificent array of paintings by Tintoretto that enhance the Scuola di San Rocco next door. I also enjoyed a visit to Murano, the little island made famous for its glass making, although it is something of a tourist trap. It is fascinating to watch the fabricators, with a few quick deft twists and turns, fashion beautiful objects out of the freshly blown glass. Then regretfully, I vaparettoed to the railroad station and took the train to Paris.

I was to stay at the Jesuit residence on the rue de Grenelle in Paris, but I didn't have the exact address for it—some more of my naïveté. Father Dick Smith, who was studying theology in Rome at the time and lived at the Bellarmino, had volunteered, on one of my last days in Rome, to take me out to Tivoli to see the Villa d'Este with its fabulous display of fountains. On the way I told him I would be staying at the rue de Grenelle residence in Paris and asked him where I could get the exact address. He said I wouldn't need it. "The rue de Grenelle is a very short street," he said, "and any taxi driver will know where the Jesuit residence is." Well, when I got to Paris, I found that he was wrong on both counts. The rue de Grenelle is one of the longest streets in Paris, and my taxi driver had not the remotest idea where the Jesuit residence was. When we had cruised up and down the street vainly, I finally had the driver pull up to the office of Air France and went in to see whether someone there could help me. When I posed my question, the man at the front desk said, "I know exactly where the Jesuit residence is. I am taking instructions from one of the fathers there." Clutching the number of the residence, I was driven there and discovered that that's all it is—a number 42 on a large door in a blank wall. I rang the door bell and was buzzed into a little lane leading to a gate with a receptionist, who admitted me finally to a little courtyard at the back of which is the Jesuit residence. It is so well hidden that although it is only a few blocks from the hotel that the Nazis made their headquarters during the occupation, the Nazis never knew it was there, in spite of the fact that the residence was something of an underground passage for Jews fleeing the Nazis. It is no wonder that my taxi driver did not know where it was.

The residence is very conveniently located for the things I had time to see in Paris. It is in easy walking distance of the Louvre, Notre-Dame, and the Sainte Chapelle. I spent what time I could in the Louvre, but what I wanted most to savor were Notre-Dame and the Sainte Chapelle. Father Preuss had kindled my interest in Gothic architecture in his *illuminabitur* evenings on rainy nights at Florissant, and I had kept the flame alive by reading, especially *The Spirit of the Gothic* by Ralph Adams Cram. I had familiarized myself with all the major Gothic cathedrals of Europe and England with the packet of Boston prints that I had rotated on my desk every day, but I had not yet seen a single original genuinely Gothic structure. In Italy, there are buildings that are called Gothic, but they really remain dominantly Romanesque in feeling. The Italians did not very much approve of Gothic. They considered it a product of the Nordic imagination and dubbed it *Gothic,* a product of barbarian Nordic taste, and they did not mean it as a compliment. The name stuck. Gothic came to its fullest flowering in France, so here in Paris I had my first opportunity of experiencing it firsthand.

I went first to the Sainte Chapelle. It is a gem of a little Gothic chapel commissioned by King Saint Louis IX, to house the relics he brought back from the Holy Land during his crusade. It is raised one story above a crypt, and you have to go up narrow, winding, stone stairs to get into the main chapel. When you get there, what is revealed is one of the most intact and beautiful examples of French Gothic in the history of the style. It is an aisleless nave created by slender Gothic piers reaching up to the vaulted ceiling. But the walls in between the piers have been completely replaced by continuous stained glass windows, creating a veritable jewel box of color. The light transfused through the thousands of little facets of colored glass creates a subdued, meditative, even mystic atmosphere. When the sun is shining, you see an ever-changing kaleidoscope of color shifting from blue where the sun is indirect to red where it is striking the glass directly and to tones of purple or violet in between where the eye is mingling the blues and reds into shades that are not in the glass itself. When the sky is overcast, the hue of the windows is predominantly blue, in an unchanging color tone. Varied patterns in the leading—round-, oval-, ogival-, and diamond-shaped medallions—float in fields of reticulated metal holding together the scintillating fragments of colored glass. The windows look like a great transparent paisley shawl. One is aware that the medallions contain representations of religious subject matter, but the representations are too small to be read easily, if at all. You are subconsciously aware that there is a religious subject matter, but the marvelous religious effect of these medieval stained glass windows is achieved not by their subject matter, but by the transcendent beauty of their color and of the colored light they transfuse throughout an interior. To achieve this effect best, the windows must all be stained glass. One window glazed in plain glass can destroy the effect. It is like having one unshaded window in a darkened room in which you are projecting slides. The effect of the stained glass windows at the Sainte Chapelle is perfect because they are all there. Chartres Cathedral is one of the few other places where you can experience a similar effect.

As I sat on the stone bench that circles the periphery of the chapel, in a semitrance at the beauty that surrounded me, I began to recollect why stained glass windows developed so successfully in the north and were not an important part of church decoration in Italy and in the Mediterranean area in general. It was largely a matter of climate. In the south, where there is an abundance of constant sunlight, they wanted to cut down some of the light and create a darker meditative atmosphere that would contrast with the blinding light outside. They preferred Romanesque with its massive walls, which served their purpose better than the Gothic. Windows were kept small, even when they ultimately adopted the pointed Gothic pattern, to keep out some of the bright light rather than transmit it. This design left large bare wall spaces on the interior that cried out for the mosaic and fresco decoration that had such a rich history in the south. In the north, it was just the opposite: long winters during which they saw little of the sun and a fair amount of overcast and rainy weather the year round. What was wanted in a church interior was as much light as they could get—hence, the evolution of stained glass windows in the north. The architectural principles of the Gothic enabled the builders to dispense with continuous sustaining walls and to replace them with a continuous apron of translucent glass that provided light and color. I was experiencing the happy result of that northern evolution here in the Sainte Chapelle in a perfect state of preservation.

My next stop was Notre-Dame Cathedral, my first experience of a great French Gothic cathedral. It dominates its site on the Ile de la Cité. When you glimpse it from the bridge that spans the Seine to the east of the Isle de la Cité, it looks like a great ship plowing up the waterway. When you move around to the west facade, you realize how much it owes to its Romanesque predecessors. In spite of its height, it has a massiveness and a kind of ground-hugging quality that is more Romanesque than Gothic. There are strong horizontal elements, such as the sculptured gallery of the kings and the upper horizontal arcades that interrupt the upward sweep of the buttresses and split the facade into evenly divided horizontal segments, creating the exact opposite effect of the sweeping verticals that carry your eye in a rushing movement upward and off into infinity in masterful Gothic structures such as the south tower of Chartres and the whole facade of Rheims. I was not to experience these Gothic masterpieces until many years later. To see where Notre-Dame succeeds in catching the true Gothic feeling on the exterior, you have to go into the bishop's garden behind the cathedral and take in the full splendid Gothic beauty of the chevet, that combination of apse and irradiating corona of chapels that is characteristic of French cathedrals. Here in Notre-Dame, the chevet is a delicate corona of chapels on the ground story surmounted by tall slender lancet windows leading up to a high-pitched roof and framed by the most slender and delicate flying buttresses in the history of Gothic art. The whole rear structure seen from the vantage point of the bishop's garden looks like a great galley with its oars extended in motion. Completing the silhouette is the delicate *flèche* rising above the top point of the pitched roof like an arrow (that's what *flèche* means) shooting off into infinite space. Here is Gothic lightness, movement, and aspiration at its best.

Inside Notre-Dame, you experience that same leap for infinity in the upward movement of the supporting piers that combine with ribs of the vaulting and carry your eye up to the very apex of the vaulting. But you are aware, too, of the roots of the structure in its Romanesque forbears. The supports of the upper vault begin not in Gothic piers but in fat round columns much as they would in a Romanesque structure. The vertical piers begin only above the capitals of the columns. Even so, the sheer height of the vaulted interior and the array of stained glass windows—especially the great rose window in the west facade and those in the two transepts—give the whole interior a distinctive Gothic quality. It was only years later—when I was able to enjoy the interior of Chartres, Amiens, and Rheims, where the vertical shafts of the supporting piers leap up from the very floor and flow into the ribs of the vaults at the very top—that I would experience the complete realization of Gothic aspiration. But I was awed and grateful for this first taste of it in the inchoate Gothic of Notre-Dame.

Sainte Chapelle and Notre-Dame are largely what remains of the medieval city of Paris. A few patches of it remain here and there on the left bank, but what surprises a visitor is to discover what happened to Paris after the Middle Ages. In the eighteenth century, hundreds of acres of the old city were torn down and replaced by what is undoubtedly the most neoclassical city in the world. Stand in front of the Arc de Triomphe de l'Étoile, which is itself a Brobdignagian adaptation of the classical Arch of Triumph of Titus in Rome, and look about you. You become vividly aware of how neoclassical Paris really is. Look down the long stretch of the Champs de Elysée, one of the most handsome planned boulevards in Europe; through the grand oval Place de La Concorde, with its massive formal sculptures representing the French provinces; through the geometricized walks and flowerbeds of the Tuillerie gardens, and your eye comes to rest at last on the Arc de Triomphe du Carrousel of Napoleon, an adaptation of the three-arched triumphal arch of Constantine in Rome. It is on an exact axis with the great Arc de Triomphe de l'Étoile a couple of miles to the west. Look out again from the Arc de Triomphe de l'Étoile down the streets that radiate from it like the spokes of a wheel, and you see that they are all fringed on each side with buildings uniformly four stories high. There was a law forbidding the construction of buildings any higher in neoclassical Paris. You will also notice that all the buildings are finished off with curved roofs of gray slate with dormer windows in them, called Mansard roofs. They were designed by the architect Mansard to provide an attic that, with its dormer windows, actually was a fifth floor of occupiable space within the law. The facades of the buildings are all of a neutral-colored, gray-white stone or are painted to simulate such stone. So whatever street you look at in central Paris, your eye is met with an endless procession of gray-white buildings of an identical height always topped by slated Mansard roofs.

Vistas down side streets off the main boulevard axis terminate in architectural quotations from classical antiquity. Stand in the center of the Grand Place de la Concorde, which is marked by an Egyptian obelisk, and look north. Your eyes rest at the end of the formal street on the Church of the Madeleine, a perfectly rendered Greek Corinthian temple. Look south, and your gaze terminates on the facade of the House of Parliament, an adaptation of a Roman temple facade. Walk a block east and stroll up another very formal street fringed with the ubiquitous four-story structures, and you come to the completely circular Place Vendôme, also fringed with the four-story buildings. In the center of the Place is a bronze adaptation of Trajan's Column in Rome, surmounted by a bronze statue of Napoleon. The low-relief sculptures spiraling up on the column itself detail all Napoleon's battles—except Waterloo. Through all this formal emulation of the classical past meanders the Seine, but it is the most corseted river in the world. It is hemmed in on both sides with stone banks that go down to the very water's edge, and above, along the formal stone esplanades, stone railings fence it in. These railings support endless wooden booths displaying old books and even older prints of every kind for sale. These booths are almost a signature of Paris. It is all very civilized and formal.

Abutting one of the many stone bridges that stretch across the Seine in elongated arches, like the many bridges that span the Tiber in Rome, is the building that houses L'Academie Française. Like everything else in neoclassical Paris, it is an echo of the classical past—this time of the combination of the dome and Greek temple facade of the Pantheon in Rome. There is something symbolic about the French Academy, that institution designed to guard the integrity of the French language and French values in general, being housed in this adaptation of the best-preserved building from Roman antiquity. Stand on the bridge that leads to the French Academy building and look up to the horizon on the hill on the left bank that leads up past the Sorbonne. What meets your eye is another French emulation of the Roman Pantheon—which is actually called the French Pantheon. It shows the same adaptation of dome and classical facade that characterizes many of our state capitol buildings and may very well have provided the inspiration for some of them. The accumulation of all these visual classical details in the cityscape of Paris makes you realize how overwhelmingly neoclassical the city is. Nowhere else is there such an intellectualized, geometricized, preconceived pattern imposed on a city. Washington, D.C., has some of this pattern, but by no means to the extent that you experience it in Paris. This impression seems even more obvious when you come to Paris for the first time, as I did, fresh from experiencing the broken patterns of ancient Roman ruins and the exuberance of baroque Rome. Even nature in Paris has been pressed into mathematical shape. The chestnut and mulberry trees that line the boulevards are trimmed into uniform shapes and kept that way. The all-pervading colors of the city are a neutral gray-white and the dark gray or black of slate roofs.

You wonder what the basis is for the epithet that is often used to describe Paris, "Gay Paree." It is certainly not the visual appearance of the city. *Grisaille Pari* (or Gray Paree) would be more accurate. The gaiety of Paris has to be a thing of the spirit, not of the eye. Gaiety, if it exists, must be found in the café life, in the bars, in the haunts of Montmartre, in the Moulin Rouge, in the dance halls, in the Folies Bergères. But, strangely, even the French artists who concerned themselves with these elements of Parisian life did not succeed in making them appear particularly gay. Toulouse-Lautrec devoted many of his paintings to the subject, but his pictures of prostitutes and bordellos, even his dancers from the Moulin Rouge, often suggest the sadness of the exploitation of women rather than any gaiety in the underground world. Degas had a fascination for the ballet and ballet dancers, but his paintings of dancers more often than not catch them in an off-stage moment when they are practicing their dance; or, when they are on stage, the paintings capture a fleeting glimpse of a fluttered movement, gaslighted in a dark environment, suggesting the fleeting nature of the moment, rather than any particularly light, gay activity. Manet did a famous painting called *Bar in the Folies Bergères*, which now hangs in the Courtauld Gallery in London, but there is nothing very gay about it either. A lone client in a black top hat stands at the bar with his back to us. The full-bosomed barmaid stares at us from behind the bar; other indistinct patrons are reflected in the mirror behind her. But again there is nothing very gay about the representation. Whatever justification there may be for speaking of the spirit of Paris as gay, the sight of the city itself is anything but gay. It is beautiful, but in a very restrained, intellectualized, and neoclassical way. Regretfully, I left Paris after a *very* short visit by way of the Gare du Nord, which, incidentally, I observed was constructed with some neoclassical grandeur. I was headed for Brussels, where a very different experience awaited me.

I arrived at the Gare Sud in Brussels about noon. I had made arrangements to stay with the Jesuit community at the Collège St. Michel, but because it was located rather far out from the center of the city, I decided to go up first to the Grand Place, which I had been told was one of the most impressive city squares in all of Europe. I engaged a taxi, but the driver told me that delivering me at the Grand Place might be difficult because the famous parade, which is staged only every three years in Brussels, was just about to begin in the Grand Place itself. The parade is part of a grand cultural festival that is a very old tradition in Brussels. I frequently have more luck than sense in my travels. Here I was arriving at the Grand Place just as this spectacular parade was about to begin. The taxi driver got me within a block of the Place, and I pushed my way through the crowd to the square itself. The Grand Place, I discovered, was all it was reputed to be. It is rimmed on one side with the great Gothic Hôtel de Ville, with its graceful Gothic tower pushing up into the sky. An impressive array of guildhalls, some with typical Flemish step-gabled facades and many with later Renaissance detailing, lines the other three sides. The Hôtel de Ville and many of the guildhalls have spacious balconies, and on this day all the balconies were filled with representatives of the old Belgian families, decked out in their elaborate ancestral dress to view the parade that was just beginning. It was a three-hour spectacle that brought to life everything I had ever read about medieval and Renaissance pageantry or seen illustrated in book illuminations. It began with heralds in doublet and hose sounding fanfares from their brass trumpets. Some of the Belgian nobility followed on horseback, riding mounts beautifully caparisoned, and themselves garbed in their impressive ancestral best. They were followed by a continuously changing procession of participants that included musicians of various kinds playing medieval and Renaissance music on antique instruments; stilt-walkers, jugglers, and clowns; actors performing religious skits on moving wagons; city magistrates in their full regalia; and clerics in elaborate liturgical vestments. The official garb of the magistrates and clerics provided the opportunity of highlighting the magnificent woven textiles for which Flanders has always been famous. What a marvelous introduction for me to the rich history of the Low Countries.

When I finally arrived at the Jesuit residence at Collège St. Michel, it was approaching suppertime. It was Sunday, and I knew they would have talking at table. I had not yet perfected my French well enough to feel comfortable conversing in it, so I decided to seat myself at the Bollandists' table in the dining room. I knew that they would be able to speak Latin, a language in which I was at ease because of all the years of using it during my training. But who are the Bollandists? They are a changing group of Jesuit scholars located at Collège St. Michel who for more than a hundred years have devoted themselves to the revision of the lives of the saints, sifting legend from historical fact to come up with something like historically accurate portraits. They are versed in many languages, including Latin, and when I suggested that we converse in Latin, they acquiesced readily. I had experienced in the parade in the Grand Place a beautiful survival from the Middle Ages. In my early conversations with the Bollandists, I was to experience a little less beautiful survival from the past—my first personal experience of what social class distinction meant in the past and to some extent still means in some places in Europe. We began our conversation with the usual starter questions. They asked me who I was, where I came from, what I was doing in Europe, where I had had my education. And then one of them asked, "What was your father?" When I said he was an *agricola* (a farmer), I could see their eyeballs roll. They were wondering, I am sure, what this peasant was doing in their midst. Peasants in their experience did not often become university professors. At that moment, I quietly thanked God for America, where, if you are intelligent, diligent, and persevering, you can become anything you want. This emphasis on class distinction may have changed in Europe since then, but it was a reality then, and this was not the only time I was to experience something like it in my travels in Europe.

I had allowed myself only one day in Brussels. I spent it visiting the beautiful Gothic Cathedral of St. Michel, perched on a slope not far from the Grand Place. What I remember most about it on this occasion was the impressive display of great Flemish tapestries on religious subjects that hung in the choir. They were part of the festival display in which I had participated the day before. Flanders has always been world famous for its textiles and its tapestries; Brussels in particular has been known the world over for its carpets. I can remember when we measured some of our own prosperity on the farm by the fact that we had graduated from a rag rug in the parlor to a Brussels carpet.

I spent most of the rest of the day in the Musée des Beaux Arts on the rue de la Regence. Here, for the first time, I was to encounter a large collection of Flemish or Early Netherlandish painting, a school that fascinated me, but one about which as yet I did not know a great deal. I little dreamed then, in this cursory encounter, that it was a school to which I would devote many years of study, one of them in this very city, supported by a Fulbright research grant. From my study would come publications that have changed the interpretation of many Flemish paintings.

I confess that one of the reasons I was anxious to visit the Musée des Beaux Arts was that one of my favorite poems by W. H. Auden has that name as its title. I had taught the poem for years and had studied copies of *The Fall of Icarus* by the Flemish painter Pieter Bruegel to which Auden refers in the poem. Icarus, in Greek legend, was the son of Daedalus. He escaped from Crete on wax wings made by Daedalus, but he flew too close to the sun (against his father's warnings). His wings melted, and he plunged to his death in the sea. That is the subject of Bruegel's painting, but the painter subordinates this classical legend to other values that he typically considers very much more important. All that we see of the unfortunate Icarus are two helpless legs kicking above the water. No one in the painting notices him. A fisherman is bringing in a fish a few yards away from the kicking Icarus, but pays no attention to him. A ship is going out to sea but passes him by. A shepherd on shore is guarding his sheep with his back turned on the floundering Icarus. And the plowman who dominates the center of the composition is moving on in his labor with no thought of the tragedy in the sea.

The whole thing illustrates the general idea that Auden develops in his poem: that ordinary life goes on while great and sometimes tragic events transpire unnoticed within breathing distance of them. This idea is typical of Bruegel, who is sometimes dubbed "Peasant Bruegel," not because he was a peasant himself, but because he was so interested in the simple life of the peasants and painted them so well. It is said of him that he used to disguise himself as a peasant, sit with them in taverns, and join them in their village festivals to observe them closely. Although he lived in the period of the Renaissance, he was not caught up in the heady glorification of pagan mythology. He did honestly feel that the work of the plowman, the herdsman, fisherman, and merchant sailor were more interesting and perhaps more important to society than the fanciful tales of pagan legends, such as the fall of Icarus. That's part of what he is saying in this marvelous painting of that title. It was a great thrill to see the original painting that inspired Auden's poem:

> About suffering they were never wrong,
> The Old Masters: how well they understood
> Its human position; how it takes place
> While someone else is eating or opening a window or just walking
> dully along;
> How, when the aged are reverently, passionately waiting
> For the miraculous birth, there always must be
> Children who did not specially want it to happen, skating
> On a pond at the edge of the wood:
> They never forgot
> That even the dreadful martyrdom must run its course
> Anyhow in a corner, some untidy spot
> Where the dogs go on with their doggy life and the torturer's horse
> Scratches its innocent behind on a tree.
>
> In Breugel's *Icarus,* for instance: how everything turns away
> Quite leisurely from the disaster; the ploughman may
> Have heard the splash, the forsaken cry,
> But for him it was not an important failure; the sun shone
>
> As it had to on the white legs disappearing into the green
> Water; and the expensive delicate ship that must have seen
> Something amazing, a boy falling out of the sky,
> Had somewhere to get to and sailed calmly on.

Another painting by Bruegel that hangs in the same gallery in the Musée des Beaux Arts, *The Enrollment at Bethlehem,* certainly illustrates the point the poet is making: that some of the greatest events of history happen unnoticed by those who surround them. In Bruegel's painting, you have to look in the motley village crowd to find Mary and Joseph searching for a place to stay the night. Right in front of them a group is butchering a pig. They have just stuck the hog and are catching its blood in a pan to make into *Blutwurst.* They are totally unaware that the Mother of God is about to be turned away from the inn. And, yes, there are indifferent "Children . . . skating / on a pond at the edge of a wood." I spent a lot of time with both Bruegel paintings.

The other painter in the Musée des Beaux Arts who riveted my attention was Peter Paul Rubens. One large gallery is exclusively reserved for several of his immense paintings. One's first glimpse of Rubens's vast canvases can be a bit overwhelming, as they were meant to be. Rubens is, of course, the best example of the baroque sensitivity in the north. Part of the awesomeness of his works is achieved by their sheer size. But beyond that, he mastered the techniques of a baroque artist to perfection. His figures are frequently much bigger than life-size; they are swathed in opulent bright-colored drapery; and they are presented in sweeping dramatic poses. They are part of an open composition; the action spills out of the frame and draws us into the composition. The two paintings in the Musée des Beaux Arts that particularly impressed me with all these baroque qualities were *The Adoration of the Magi,* one of the many versions Rubens did of this subject, and the *Assumption.* In the latter, the Virgin, in an ample, flowing, satin garment, is being swept up on a diagonal of light shooting down from a heavenly source outside the painting. It is a dramatic, awesome presentation of the subject in a truly baroque manner.

I also visited the simple tomb of Pieter Bruegel with its simple inscription in a side chapel in the church of Nôtre Dame-de-la-Chapelle, just a few blocks away from the Musée des Beaux Arts. It struck me that this very simple tomb and inscription were most appropriate for "Peasant Bruegel." They would not have done for the more princely and flamboyant Rubens.

Several years later I was to see the Italianate palazzo that Rubens built for himself in Antwerp, where he lived like a prince. He actually was used to consorting with princes and kings all his life. In his early life, he spent some years at the court of the Gonzagas in Mantua and helped the duchess of Mantua develop her impressive collection of paintings as, in our own century, Bernard Berenson did for Helen Gardiner. Rubens later spent productive years painting great canvases for the courts in Madrid, Paris, and London. His patrons became so princely and demanding that he had to employ a whole bevy of great apprentices and assistant painters (Van Dyke worked for him in this capacity for a time) in order to fulfill the demand.

My first continental excursion was coming to an end. I was told by some of the Jesuit community at Collège St. Michel that I should not miss seeing Bruges on my way to Ostend to catch the boat for England. How right they were. Bruges is a charming Flemish town in which time has stood still. It is today almost exactly as the bevy of

Flemish painters, merchants, and Medici bankers would have known it back in the fourteenth and fifteenth centuries. It was the cultural, economic, mercantile, and banking center of all of Flanders at that time, but the River Gand on which it is situated silted up and could no longer accommodate seagoing ships. Thus, Antwerp, with its immense open harbor, became the mercantile center of the country. Bruges remained just as it was in a kind of suspended animation; hence, a visit to the city today is like a step back in time to the late Middle Ages or early Renaissance in a more complete way than any city I have ever visited. The city is small enough so you can experience all of it conveniently on foot, as I did. I started walking to the center of the city from the railroad station and hadn't gone two blocks before I came to a charming little family hotel that looked like one of the step-gabled houses in a David Teniers painting. It was located on one of the many canals in Bruges, with swans swimming on the canal and white geese and ducks waddling on the canal's edge. I brushed through the gaggle of geese and engaged a room with Bruges lace curtains on the windows and an elephantine down quilt on the bed. I was then off for an unencumbered stroll through the town. The street that led into town was lined by charming little brick houses built right up to the sidewalk with their tiny windows covered with Dutch half curtains decorated with the beautiful Bruges lace for which the city is famous. All through the city, you still see ladies sitting on stools in front of their houses busily fabricating the lace. In the first turn off from this residential street, I came to the old Church of Our Lady, which is particularly famous for displaying on one of its side altars the only major sculpture by Michelangelo outside of Italy. It is a Madonna and Child in the reserved early classical manner of the *Pietà* in St. Peter's. The seated Madonna intently observes the rather mature Christ child standing between her legs. I did not know that the statue was here and was very pleasantly surprised to have it greet me as soon as I stepped inside the rather somber brick Church of Our Lady.

I had another equally pleasant surprise in the building just across the street from St. Mary's. You enter it through a Gothic archway in a high brick wall. The archway gives entrance to the courtyard of the ancient Hospital of St. John, strung in step-gabled brick buildings around the courtyard. One of these buildings—what was originally the chapel of the hospital—has been turned into a museum housing

some very impressive Flemish paintings, in particular several outstanding works by Hans Memling. They include his "Jean Floreins"
triptych *The Adoration of the Magi,* several important portraits, the
incomparably beautiful triptych *The Mystical Marriage of St. Catherine,* and the unique reliquary decorated with scenes from the life
of St. Ursula. This was my first encounter with important works by
Memling, and what a marvelous setting in which to encounter them,
here in this chapel in which he himself may have prayed and in
Bruges, where he spent the greater part of his productive life. Memling was not a Fleming himself; he was German. But he came to
Bruges at the height of its cultural supremacy, settled down there,
absorbed the best that the Flemish school had to offer, and became
more Flemish than the Flemish themselves. He was the last great
master to make Bruges his headquarters before the mercantile and
cultural center shifted to Antwerp. He paints in a quiet, reserved,
classical manner that has sometimes been compared with that of Raphael in the south. I was to see all these paintings here in St. John's
Hospital many times in the future, but I don't think I ever recovered
the quiet meditative experience of encountering them almost entirely
by myself this first time.

Leaving the hospital, you meander past little step-gabled buildings,
with statues of the Virgin tucked neatly in corner niches, that look
exactly like cityscapes painted by Vermeer or DeHooch. You come to
one of the charming little stone bridges that span the many canals
threading through the city, with ivy-clad houses and shops reaching
down to the very water's edge. There is a good reason why Bruges
has been called the Venice of the north. Across the bridge a few steps
to the left, you find yourself in the courtyard of the Palace of the
Griuthuse, a mansion built by one of the successful Bruges merchants. It hugs the north side of St. Mary's Church. In fact, one of
the upper rooms of the mansion opens onto the sanctuary of St.
Mary's itself, which enabled the family to attend Mass without leaving
their home. The mansion is furnished with traditional Flemish furniture and contains every conceivable amenity that went into a wealthy
Flemish burgher's home life. A visit there is like walking through the
Flemish interiors that you see pictured in so many of the paintings of
Steen or of David Teniers or, for that matter, of Dutch genre painters
such as De Hooch and Vermeer because the Flemish and Dutch
domestic habits were very similar. Just a half block from the Griu-

thuse is a cluster of small museums, including a carriage museum and the main Fine Arts Museum of the city. The latter has a rich collection of Flemish painting, including the famous *Madonna of the Canon Van der Paele* by Jan van Eyck and that same artist's portrait of his wife. Also on display is the excellent *Baptism of Christ* by Gerard David and a very distinctive *Last Judgment* by Jan Provost. Of course, I did not have an inkling on this first visit to the museum that the Provost painting would play an important part in one of my later studies of Early Netherlandish painting.

Not because it is necessary, the city being so compact, but because it is such a pleasant way of experiencing the ever-shifting medieval vistas in the city, taking a boat ride on the canals is a must for visitors to Bruges, and it was so for me. I got off the boat at a dock near the central square. The square is dominated by the medieval brick Hôtel de Ville with its disproportionately heavy and very high bell tower. Bell towers on churches and city halls in Belgium tend to be disproportionally bulky and very high, deliberately. The country is very flat so this is a way of giving some vertical lift to a cityscape. The bell tower of the Hôtel de Ville in Bruges also manages to dominate the entire city; you can see it from almost anywhere in town!

Close to the Hôtel de Ville is a little Romanesque chapel dedicated to the Precious Blood of Christ. The natives make the unlikely claim that they possess some of the Sacred Blood of Christ. It is kept in a reliquary in this chapel, but on the Feast of the Precious Blood it is carried through the streets in a grand procession preceded by wagons on which scenes from the life of Christ are reenacted for the public, strung all along the route of the procession. The crowd is made up of citizens from Bruges itself, but also of visitors from all over the world. Some years later, I myself was in the crowd, so I can testify that it is an impressive experience indeed. I was particularly struck by the public's devout manifestation of faith on the occasion. However ill-authenticated the relic that is the center of this impressive spectacle may be, there is no doubt about the authenticity of the devotion and reverence of the people who participate in it, townspeople and visitors alike.

Before returning to the hotel, I made a stop at the beguinage, which is not far from the hotel. Listed as adversaries to the Roman Catholic Church in one of our theological texts were the Beguine and *beguardi.* They were both semimonastic groups, female and male, in the Middle Ages, who had fallen afoul of Church teaching in some way. I didn't know during my theology studies and don't know now precisely what their theological errors were, but both groups were particularly widespread in the Lowlands. The Beguine were a group of rather socially well-placed and fairly well-educated women who lived in a loosely organized society for loosely defined religious work. Each had her own little house in the beguinage. The women maintained themselves by making lace or other marketable objects, prayed together in a common chapel, and engaged in social work of various kinds. The movement flourished from the twelfth century on through the Middle Ages into the Renaissance period. When it lost popularity, many of the beguinages were taken over by regular nuns, especially the Benedictines. The beguinage in Bruges is one of the largest and best preserved. I thought it would be interesting to see how some of our "adversaries" had lived. They lived rather well. On an extensive wooded property, the beguinage itself consisted of a long row of separate step-gabled row houses in which the individual Beguine would have lived, worked, and prayed. At present, a considerable section of the beguinage functions as a Benedictine convent, but the nuns have preserved a row of the old houses pretty much in their original condition as a museum where you can see how the Beguine lived. The interiors of the houses were furnished very much as a home of middle-class people would have been furnished and look for all the world again like those interiors painted by genre painters such as De Hooch and Vermeer. With this last nod to the past of Bruges, I wove my way back to its present in my little hotel along the canal.

There I enjoyed a typical Flemish supper of endive salad, seafood crepes, apple strudel, and, of course, a stein of beer. In the morning, after a hearty breakfast of Belgian waffles and bacon, I took off for Ostend, where I was to catch the ferryboat for Dover. From the porch of the hotel, the proprietor of the little hotel and his wife waved me good-bye as warmly as if I were a member of the family, and the ducks waddled up from the canal to bid me a quacking good-bye at the gate of the white picket fence that surrounded the hotel.

The trip from Ostend to Dover was smooth and uneventful, although it can be anything but. Some years later, I was to make the same trip, which should take about three hours but actually took five wild hours.

The sea of the channel was vicious; the ferry was tossed about like a cork; everybody on board got seasick, some so severely that they had to be carried off the boat on stretchers. But on this crossing, the Channel behaved itself; we all disembarked on our own power. I had been traveling on the Continent for about six weeks. I took the boat train to London, went on to the Jesuit residence on Farm Street, and immediately to the provincial's office there. I was delighted to find that he had kept his promise and did have a place for me to stay. It was to be the novitiate at Roehampton, a suburb of London. I was happy about that because Roehampton had pleasant associations for me. It was where my favorite poet, Gerard Manley Hopkins, had made his novitiate as a Jesuit. When I got out to the Roehampton novitiate, I was even more delighted because I found that the original building of the novitiate was a famous Palladian mansion that had made some of the art history books. It was situated on what had been a large, beautifully landscaped country estate. The grounds showed the result of some decades of Jesuit wear, but they were still beautiful. The old mansion faced right on the grand Regents Park, what had once been one of the royal hunting areas but was now a public park. There was an opening in the woods in front of the mansion that provided a sweeping view of the park. I almost always saw deer grazing on the greensward in the distance. It was that kind of park.

Additions had been made to the mansion—a residential wing and a chapel wing—but I was assigned a room on the very tiptop of the old mansion. It sat above the roof of the mansion like a widow's walk, commanding a beautiful view in all directions. I wondered why it had not been assigned to anyone. When the cold weather came, I knew why. It was like an igloo. But meantime it was a very pleasant place to work, so I got to work almost immediately on the manuscript for the book *Honor and the Epic Hero.* I did not have to do much additional research for the book; what I needed was some uninterrupted time to write it, which is why I was given the sabbatical leave. To have this time, free of teaching and administration, just to write was a sheer luxury for me. I made very good progress on the manuscript for the next two months. Then, before the winter months set in, I decided to take a ten-day bus tour of England to get a general overview of the country.

I eventually traveled in Europe more than twenty times, sometimes with a companion and sometimes without one. I find that I usually have more interesting and rewarding experiences when I travel alone. When you're by yourself, you are apt to meet new, interesting people more readily than when you have someone with you. I met one of the most interesting people I have ever come to know anywhere on this quick bus tour of England. The tour was routed up the east coast, through southern Scotland, and on down the west coast through the Lake District, Stratford-upon-Avon, and back to London. We were a couple days out of London and were touring Lincoln Cathedral with the warden of the cathedral as our guide. When we came to the empty space in the choir behind the main altar, the warden said: "This space was once occupied by the tomb of St. Hugh, the second most beautiful tomb in England after that of Thomas à Becket in Canterbury, until that skunk, Henry VIII, stripped it bare." I was still traveling in clerical garb at the time, so my identity was very obvious. At this remark of the warden, a lady, whom I had already observed as probably more sensitive to everything we were seeing than anyone else on the bus, glided over to me, poked me in the ribs, and said: "I am a relative of the former Bishop O'Hare of Kansas City; and he [pointing to the warden] is talking about the founder of his Church." That was my introduction to May O'Rourke Jay. I came to know her very well before the bus trip had ended. She turned out to be one of the most intelligent, sensitive, and interesting women I have ever met. She had a marvelous sense of humor and a healthy curiosity. I noticed that whenever we made a rest stop, she would get into a conversation with one of the locals, and when we got back on the bus, she would know more about the local lore than the guide did. This behavior was probably a carryover from her early days as a journalist. When she learned of my interest in art and art history, she had found a new source of satisfying her curiosity. She was staying all summer at the Gloucester Hotel in London, and we toured the museums and some of the cathedral towns together. I admired her eager desire to learn and her ability to retain what she had learned. Before the summer was over, our acquaintanceship had grown into a friendship that continued until her death. I think some of her background deserves recording here.

May's father, John Matthew O'Rourke, was an internationally prominent engineer. He designed the famous Roosevelt Dam near Phoenix and the Galveston Sea Wall. As a girl, May attended the Visitation Academy in Washington, D.C., and then went into journalism. She married rather young and had one son. Unfortunately, the marriage was something of a disaster. Her husband was a hopeless alcoholic, and they were eventually divorced. She took great consolation from her son, John O'Rourke Mehlig, who had a successful career as an officer in the navy. He was killed in action in the Second World War and was given a posthumous citation at Annapolis. (May later erected a plaque there in his memory and asked me to give the benediction on the occasion.) In her work as a journalist, she met a prominent engineer who had invented a device used in all steam engines at the time and had made a fortune from the patent for it. It was love at first sight for both of them; they were soon married, although without the blessing of the Roman Catholic Church because May was divorced and her first husband was still alive.

Webb Jay, her new husband, had another engineering feat up his sleeve. He and one of the Fisher brothers (of Fisher Body) got the idea of developing the swampland north of Miami into a viable beach and residential and hotel area by dredging up sand from the sea and creating land for building purposes and a beach. They translated their dream into reality, and the result is Miami Beach as we know it today. Part of the development was Treasure Island, a luxurious residential area where Webb and May had their own home. The Jesuits had developed a parish church in nearby Miami, and May became a devout parishioner there, although she could not take communion because of her marriage problem. Her previous husband had died by this time, and one of the Jesuit pastors of the Gesu Church told her there was nothing to prevent her from having her marriage to Webb blessed by the Church, so that she could receive the sacraments again. May was delighted, and she did so. As a result, she always had a soft spot in her heart for Jesuits, which immediately endeared me to her when she discovered on the bus trip that I was a Jesuit.

Incidentally, that was the only time in her whole life that she ever took a trip on a bus. She always rented a car and engaged a private driver for her trips. When I met her, her husband Webb had died, and she was a widow. I kept in touch with May regularly for years afterward. I used to visit her in her Miami Beach condominium in the Imperial Complex, in which she was the only gentile resident. The rest were all prominent Jewish people, most of them from New York. May, as one might expect from her background and social position, was a confirmed Republican, and, as one might expect from my much more humble origins, I am a confirmed Democrat. We had lots of disagreements on politics and engaged in many heated arguments. What I admired about May was that she had an open mind and could change it. After an evening of heated discussion, she would sometimes say when I visited her the next day: "I was thinking of some of the things you said last night, and, you know, you were right as rain."

One night, at midnight, I got a phone call from May. She said she was changing her will and wanted to leave some money to help students save their faith in college, because some of her relatives had lost theirs in college. I told her that right off I could not think of anything that would guarantee their faith could be saved in college, but that I would think about it and get back in touch with her. I did think about it and recollected that many honors students in the troubled sixties had told me that my course in the introduction to the history of art had anchored them in their faith. The panoramic view of the history of art, which for so many centuries was inspired by religion, made them feel that there might be something to religion after all. They hung on to their faith when everyone around them was denying everything. I told this to May and suggested that she might endow a professorship in art history in which art and theology would be taught together. Teaching the two together actually is not difficult to do because you can't teach the first seventeen centuries of art history in the West without teaching the theological truths that inspired so much of it. May said my suggestion was interesting, and she would think about it. That ended our discussion of the matter. I did not know until after she died that she had not only thought about it, she had done it. She left a million dollars in trust to some of her relatives, who receive the income on it for life. When they die, the capital comes to St. Louis University to finance a professorship in art history and theology permanently. Some of that capital has already come and has been invested to support the professorship in art history. (Father Terrence E. Dempsey, S.J., was appointed to the May O'Rourke Jay Chair in Art History during the first part of 1995.) May also left all her beautiful period furniture and art work to the university. It now graces some of the rooms in Cupples House, which May, before she died, knew I was restoring. And all of this came as a result of my casual encounter with her on the only bus trip she ever took in her life. The administration at St. Louis University suggested that I go on more bus trips.

After the overall tour of England and Scotland, I was able to settle down again in my rookery on top of the Roehampton mansion and get back to work on the manuscript of the book on the hero. As long as the warm weather lasted, it was an ideal place to work. I kept at it pretty steadily there for a couple of months, interrupted only occasionally by excursions to some of the cathedral towns. The train service in England is excellent. I would wait for a sunny day, of which there are not that many in England, take an early train to the targeted site, spend the better part of the day exploring and photographing the cathedral, and then return to London on an evening train. By doing this systematically, I built up a collection of slides on the English cathedrals with detailed views of their whole structures such as I have seen nowhere else. Nothing like them is available on the market. Commercial offerings are usually content with a slide or two of the facade and a general view of the interior, but what you want for teaching purposes are slides that show the whole evolution of the building. The builders of the English cathedrals, particularly, had the habit of making additions in the style that was regnant when the addition was made. Any given cathedral is apt to have sections manifesting Norman (the English term for Romanesque because the Normans brought the style to England), early English Gothic, late English Gothic, and sometimes even perpendicular Gothic, in different parts of the same building. To do justice to this interesting variety, you need a whole series of slides; a few general exposures do not do the job. I was able to procure such slides by these leisurely photographic excursions to the cathedral towns. The only English cathedral that does not show this wide variety of styles is Salisbury, which was built in its entirety in one generation. It is a good example of early English Gothic throughout. But its beautiful setting in its expansive cathedral close and its splendid slender central spire reaching up to the heavens above the bishop's garden also cry out for multiple exposures. It is the subject of several of Constable's best paintings and of a good many of my own slides.

Some of these cathedral excursions also gave me the opportunity to meet some very interesting English people. Durham Cathedral, almost on the Scottish border, is too far from London to go and come back on the same day, so I planned on an overnight stay there. On the train trip up, a middle-aged couple and a young man of about thirty shared my compartment. All the way from London to Oxford, no one said a word. When we pulled out of the Oxford station, I decided to see whether I could thaw the ice. I started asking questions about Oxford, and my companions freely shared what they knew about it. That did it. We never stopped talking until we got to Durham. By the time we arrived, I knew more about their families than I did about my own. When we got off the train, the young man, who traveled for the railroad, asked me whether I had reservations for the night, which I didn't. He said I might have trouble finding accommodations because, he reminded me, nothing but private residences had yet been rebuilt since the war. He walked all the way across the town in the opposite direction of his destination to be sure I found a place to stay. I had the luck to find a little inn. But before he left, the young man suggested that, as I would be going through York on my way back to London, I stop off there, where he lived with his married sister, stay with them, and learn how an ordinary middle-class English family lived. I thanked him profusely but had no intention of accepting the invitation. He insisted that he meant it and said he knew that his sister and brother-in-law would enjoy having me come. I finally agreed to do so and am forever grateful that I did. I *did* learn a lot about how ordinary English people live, made friendships that endured until the death of all three of my hosts, and eventually made other contacts in York that were tremendously helpful and enriching for me.

But in the meantime I reveled in the beauty of Durham itself. The massive towering cathedral sits high up like a fortress (which it actually became, at times, during some of the wars between Scotland and England) on a peninsula that is almost like an island. Much of it is built in the heavy Norman style, but later parts, including the dominating massive central lantern, are in the perpendicular Gothic style. The interior of the nave is perhaps the most impressive Norman interior in all of England. Great plump massive Norman pillars, with deeply incised chevron- and diamond-shaped patterns on their surfaces, alternate with massive piers to create an incomparable impression of massive strength. Vertical shafts spring up from the massive capitals and join the ribs of the vaulted ceiling, which is the closest reproduction in England of the vaulting system introduced by William the Conqueror's architects in the Abbaye aux Hommes and the Abbaye aux Dames in Caen, William's headquarters in Normandy. The vaulting in Durham may very well have been designed by William's architect himself. William brought him to England after the Conquest to help plan many of the Norman structures he initiated there. After luxuriating in the severe beauty of the cathedral all day, I took the train for York, and as the train pulled out on the promontory across the river from the cathedral, the late afternoon sun piercing some lowering clouds momentarily illuminated the massive structure. I caught that fleeting glimpse of the cathedral with the mists rising from the river gorge below in one of the most dramatic architectural shots I have ever taken.

It was dark by the time I arrived at York. The railroad station is just outside the walls of the city, but there was enough light that evening to see that long stretches of the ancient walls are still intact, so I did get the impression of what a medieval walled town looked like. Dominating the dark silhouette of the city is the great Gothic cathedral or minster as it is called there. It is unusually high and wide. English cathedrals, in general, as compared to the French, are lower and narrower but stretch off in great horizontal vistas. The extraordinary width of the nave of York Minster, I was told, is in part the result of the fact that it was constructed right over the old Norman cathedral that preceded it, using the old cathedral as a partial scaffolding from which to build the new one. These larger proportions resulted in large wall spaces on the west and east ends, which enabled the designers to work in some of the largest stained glass windows anywhere. The window on the east end is bigger than a tennis court, and the rectilinear pointed window on the west fills almost the entire facade.

I would have time to explore the minster inside and out on my meandering through York the next two days, but meantime I took a taxi out to the home of my kind host. He lived with his married sister Margaret in a section of the city outside the walls that had been bombed out during the war but rebuilt with new homes since. My hosts' quarters were a new two-story duplex flat, quite livable but lacking some of the amenities we take for granted. There were a living room, dining room, and kitchen on the first floor. The double glass door in the dining room gave access to a perfectly charming little garden. There were three bedrooms and a bath upstairs. But there was no central heating and no refrigerator in the kitchen. There were fireplaces in the dining room and in the living room, but no source of heat in any of the rooms upstairs except what drifted up from the fireplaces downstairs. My compartment friend John and his brother-in-law both had to go to work in the morning, so I was left with Margaret to see what the day of a middle-class English housewife was like. She spent a good deal of the morning marketing because without refrigeration she had to market every day for the food for that day. I went to market with her and was fascinated by the number of shops she had to go to just to get the groceries for dinner. There were separate shops for fowl and fish; red meat; eggs, butter, and cheese; vegetables and fruit; bakery goods and sweets; etc. It was quite a journey just to put the makings of a meal together. At this time, there were nothing like general stores, much less the supermarkets that have arrived in England now as almost everywhere else.

Margaret was at pains to show me some of the sights of York as well as to do her marketing. The first place she took me to was the shambles. It is a little narrow street, with overhanging second stories dating from the Middle Ages, where the butchering was done. A shambles was an *abattoir* or place for slaughtering animals. It was apt to be a rather messy place. That's where our meaning of the word *shambles* comes from. But halfway down the shambles, Margaret took me to one of the little houses on the street that has been turned into a chapel dedicated to Blessed Margaret Clitheroe, who was martyred for harboring Jesuits in her home here in York during the Elizabethan persecutions. She was placed between heavy oak doors; stones were piled on the top one until she was crushed to death. Margaret, my guide, was an Anglican, and she, too, was harboring a Jesuit. I told her that if we had been living in Elizabethan times, she might have met the fate of Margaret Clitheroe.

With her shopping done, Margaret went home to do her housework and to prepare the evening dinner, and I spent the rest of the day exploring York, especially the impressive minster. When I arrived back at the house late in the afternoon, I found Margaret bundled up in sweaters in the kitchen, where the only source of heat was the kitchen stove. She had laid a fire in the fireplace of the little dining room. That fire was allowed to go out after dinner, when we retired to the parlor for the evening. Margaret kindled a fire in the parlor fireplace in the afternoon to warm it up for the evening. I could actually see my breath in the bedroom upstairs, though. This situation was not unfamiliar to me; it was pretty much the same in my boyhood on the farm, where the only sources of heat were the wood heating stoves in the dining room and parlor downstairs. The kitchen got what heat it had from the wood range. But I was somewhat surprised to see these same limited accommodations in residences built in England after the Second World War.

The meal that Margaret prepared was delicious and different. I found in my experiences in England that the reputation the English have for unimaginative and bland food does not apply to the food they serve in their homes. The meals I have had in English homes have always been tasty and distinctive. Some English restaurants seem to have given English food a bad reputation. When we had finished our tea and tarts, John reminded me that this date, November 5, was Guy Fawkes night, and there was a traditional event that took place every year on this night to commemorate that fact. He said he was sure I would want to see it.

The event was a bonfire get-together outside the old walls in which a Jesuit was burned in effigy. A bit ironic. Margaret had taken me to the memorial chapel of Margaret Clitheroe, who was martyred for harboring Jesuits, and her brother was now inviting me, a Jesuit, to attend the burning of a Jesuit in effigy. I certainly did want to see it. So we climbed up on the wall, and, sure enough, there was the pile of wood ready to be kindled, and from a gibbet above it dangled the effigy of a Jesuit in cassock and biretta ready to be burned. I instinctively pulled up my coat collar over the Roman collar I was wearing lest the crowd waiting for the fire to be lit might prefer a live Jesuit to a mere effigy of one.

Guy Fawkes came from York. King James I had promised some of his Catholic friends that when he came to the throne, he would see to it that the persecution of Catholics would be terminated. When James did not keep his promises after his accession to the throne, Robert Catesby and a small group of his Catholic friends became disaffected and hatched a plot to blow up the House of Parliament when Parliament was in session and the king was present. The plot was well along toward its realization. The gunpowder was in place in the basement of the parliament building. Guy Fawkes, who was in sympathy with the plot, was assigned the task of actually igniting the gunpowder. On November 5, 1605, he was already in place to do so when the plot was discovered. All those involved in it, including Guy Fawkes, were accused of conspiracy and treason, and were executed. An attempt was also made to implicate the Jesuits in the plot. The

Jesuits were a thorn in the government's side because by their clandestine work among the faithful they were, at great risk to their own lives, able to keep the faith alive among a goodly number in England. False testimony was brought against two Jesuits in particular, John Gerard and Oswald Greenway. Both were tried, condemned, and executed. The memory of the Gunpowder Plot and the presumed Jesuit involvement in it has been kept alive in York, the home of Guy Fawkes, by the bonfire gathering on November 5 in which a Jesuit is still burned in effigy.

As I, a twentieth-century Jesuit, stood there on the old wall of York and watched the effigy of one of my sixteenth-century confreres catch fire and drop into the flames, I breathed a quiet prayer of thanksgiving for the lives of Jesuits such as Edmund Campion and John Gerard, who had worked so hard and eventually gave up their lives in the attempt to keep the faith alive in England in the most threatening circumstances. I'm sure that neither my host with me on the wall nor those dancing around the bonfire were really very much aware of what the event was about. I explained some of its significance to John on the way back to the house and told him how grateful I was that he had enabled me to experience this little bit of past York and English history.

I was also grateful to the family for accepting me for a couple of days into their home. I kept up the contact over the years, corresponding at least every year at Christmas and visiting the family on two occasions when I was traveling in England. They persuaded me to come to York one year during the York Festival. I stayed at the railroad hotel outside the old walls and took in most of the important events of the festival. My friends had managed to get a pass that gave me access to a great many of those events.

The York Festival takes place only every three years. Most of the events are religious in character. The one I was most interested in was the York Cycle of Mystery Plays. The dramatic Mystery Cycles were made up of a whole series of little dramatic skits representing the life of Christ from the Annunciation to the Resurrection and Ascension and sometimes to the Last Judgment. They were presented on a long stage with the individual acts presented in spatial sequence one after the other. One of the most important extant sequences is the York Cycle. The text for the cycle was composed in St. Mary's Abbey, which is situated just outside the old walls of York.

The cycle was revived in our time by the well-known English actor and director E. Martin Browne. For years, he directed its staging at York as part of the York Musical Festival. The production was extremely well done. As the directors of the cycle had done in the Middle Ages, Martin trained local people from York to play the parts. The performance became the centerpiece of the festival. Another interesting feature of his presentation was that it was staged in the ruins of the chapel of St. Mary's Abbey, where the cycle had been composed in the first place. All that is left of the Abbey Chapel is the arcade of Gothic arches from one side of the nave. The long stage was built in front of the arcade, and the march of pointed Gothic arches provided a kind of proscenium frame for the series of scenes in the cycle. Heaven was located in the area above the arcade. It was a very moving and special experience to see this faithful re-creation of the medieval cycle performed here on the very spot on which it had originally been composed.

Many other rewarding presentations in the festival were available at other sites in the city, including wonderful Gregorian and polyphonic musical programs in the compelling setting of the great minster. I was particularly interested in a musical program scheduled in one of the smaller churches. It was a presentation of an Easter play that had evolved out of the simple *Quem Quaeritis* mystery play that marked the very rebirth of drama in the Middle Ages. It presents the visit of the Marys to the tomb, but several other episodes are combined with it. Quite sophisticated vocal arias are woven into it, and it actually takes on some of the qualities of a little opera. E. Martin Browne was again responsible for its revival; he directed the performance here at the festival. I learned that he had gathered together a little group of professional opera singers in London who were interested in this medieval music and performed these medieval plays on the side. I was immensely impressed with the quality of the performance and with the performers' dedication.

I made a point of meeting E. Martin Browne after the performance and expressing my enthusiasm for what he had done with his revival of this Easter play and Mystery Cycle. I found him to be a most charming individual with a dedication to many areas of literature in which I myself had developed a considerable interest. I was to be in London for some time, so he invited me to his home to continue our conversation. I did visit him there and discovered that his home was in one of the many mews in London. The mews are charming little streets of human scale, where the houses are adapted from former stables fronting on what had been alleys behind streets of great mansions. These converted stables always have a charming English garden behind them, and the combination provides a very humane dwelling. I also learned on my visits to Martin's home that he was married to a very successful English actress, Henzie Raeburn. I found her to be a very wonderful human being with a disarming sense of humor.

I kept up contact with the Brownes on later visits to England, and years later, when I was chairman of the English department at St. Louis University, I engaged them for a one-night performance at the university when they were doing a swing through the States. The evening consisted of scenes from various plays, especially from some of T. S. Eliot's plays. I learned that Martin had actually directed the first performance of all of Eliot's plays in England. I was much later, at Martin's invitation, to see his production of *Murder in the Cathedral* in Canterbury Cathedral on the occasion of the five hundredth anniversary of the martyrdom of Thomas à Becket. Martin himself performed the part of Thomas à Becket in the production. The presentation at St. Louis University, of course, included excerpts from *Murder in the Cathedral*, but Martin and Henzie on that occasion also did skits from some of the medieval mystery plays. I shall never forget Henzie's pantomiming the very birth of Christ in the cave. All the scenes were done without settings or costumes, with only lighting as an aid, but their acting was so good that they did not need anything else to bring the scenes alive. As we watched Henzie strain in childbirth, pick up the little infant, bathe him, wrap him in swaddling clothes, and lay him in the manger, we really saw the infant that wasn't there.

Much later, during the bicentennial celebration of the city of St. Louis and at the city's expense, I had Martin bring over his entire troupe from England and put on the Easter play I had seen in York in the College Church. It was one of the highlights of the year's celebration. I have outlived both Henzie and Martin, but I kept in contact with both of them until they died. Henzie died first, of cancer, but before she died, she suggested to Martin that when she was gone, he marry the nurse who had taken care of her, a lifelong friend of both of them. A year or so after Henzie's death, Martin did marry the nurse, and I can testify that it was a very happy marriage because I visited them on several later forays into England. On one of those visits, I was able to get some confirmation from Martin of one of my theories about the medieval religious drama as one of the sources of the convention of the vested angel as a eucharistic symbol in Early Netherlandish painting. When I asked him whether in his examination of the texts of these medieval plays, he had found instructions for vesting the angels in liturgical copes or dalmatics, he said that indeed he had and that if I would come to St. Paul's on the next Sunday where he was staging one of these plays, I would find the angels so vested. So the casual stopover in York at the invitation of John, my train compartment friend, and the consequent revisits of York during the festival reaped dividends far richer than I could ever have suspected when I broke the silence in the train compartment on the way to Durham.

I am a little ahead of myself here, but I did want to suggest how much came of my breaking the silence in the train compartment to Durham. When I returned to London from Durham and York, it had turned quite cold. My little eagle's nest on the top of the Roehampton mansion lost much of its charm. The wind whipped in the windows on all four sides, and there was no heat in the room at all. Heating oil was still rationed, and the only parts of the house that were mildly heated were the common rooms— the chapel, dining room, and recreation room—making it very uncomfortable to work in my room. I would wrap my lower extremities in a blanket and try to continue writing. When my fingers were so numb that I could hardly hold a pen, I would go over to the little sink in the corner, which did have a hot-water faucet, and thaw out my hands so I could continue. I was not overjoyed at the prospect of continuing to work in those conditions for the next months, so I went out and bought an electric heater. Its connector had to be screwed into a socket. The only electric socket in the room was the one that dangled on a wire from the ceiling for the light bulb, which, incidentally, was the only source of artificial light in the room. I tried to screw the heater fixture into the socket, but I created a short, which welded the plug into the socket and blew all the lights in the house. I had to confess my crime to the father minister, and that, of course, was the end of my heater.

I did find a solution to the heat problem. Besides working on the book on the epic hero, I had spasmodically been doing some research on Anglo-Saxon illuminated manuscripts in the Manuscript Room at the British Museum. I was trying to find corroboratory visual evidence for the idea that the Anglo-Saxons conceived hell as a man-monster-infested lake. This evidence would bolster my interpretation of the second episode of the *Beowulf* poem as an allegory of Christ's descent into hell and the whole episode as an adaptation of the medieval drama called *The Harrowing of Hell.* I had cleared my credentials with the director of the manuscript room, and he had assigned a desk to me that I could use as long as I liked. In early illuminated Anglo-Saxon Psalters, I had already found some visual evidence that the illuminators had indeed represented hell as a man-monster-infested lake, but I was continuing to examine other manuscripts to see how commonly this was done. I had been rather amazed what easy access you had to the original manuscripts once your scholarly credentials were checked. The only restriction placed on their use was that you had to check any ink or ballpoint pens at the door. You were permitted to use only pencils in the room. But when you put in a call for any manuscript in the collection, in a few minutes it would be brought to your desk. The manuscripts were sometimes worth thousands of pounds, and you could examine the entire manuscript. I confess that I called for some illuminated manuscripts that were not related specifically to my work on *Beowulf* because I knew that I would probably never again have the opportunity of examining these manuscripts from cover to cover. When they are on public display, all you see is the one page that the manuscript happens to be open to on the day you visit the room. I remember one day asking to see the Book of Hours used by Mary Tudor when she was in prison. Some of the illuminations had been so thumbed as Mary said her prayers that they were half rubbed away. For the fun of it, I asked to see a Book of Hours owned by Henry VIII. Not surprisingly, it was immaculately preserved; it had never been touched by human hands.

I had become a familiar patron of the Manuscript Room, and the room was slightly heated. I now became an habitué. I simply took the bus and underground each morning to the British Museum and spent the day at my desk in the manuscript room. I wrote more than half of the book on the hero and all of the article "*Beowulf* as an Allegory of Salvation" there. In riding the double-decker buses on the first leg of the trip to the museum, I would generally take a seat on the upper deck of the bus, from which I got a nice view of the surroundings through which I was passing. The area was a residential neighbor-hood, and I was interested in observing how some of the mothers conditioned their little babies to the cold. They would push them in perambulators outside the doors of the row houses and leave them there for a time. I could see their little mittenless hands purple with the cold, waving in the air. It was a bit like the habit of some Native American women who used to plunge their papooses into the icy streams to condition them to the cold. And it may have worked. I recall now that I never had a trace of a cold that winter. When you are in a continual deep freeze, germs may not have a chance.

The environment of the Manuscript Room at the museum was very conducive to steady work. If I needed a book from the library, it would be delivered to my desk, as well as the manuscripts from the Manuscript Collection itself. The environment was so conducive to steady work that I often skipped lunch and worked straight through until the room closed in the late afternoon. This mode of procedure caused the most embarrassing but, at the same time, the most hilari-ous episode of my whole trip abroad. I received a phone call from Monsignor Curtin one day inviting me to dinner at the Savoy Hotel. I knew Monsignor in St. Louis. He was in charge of the educational program of the St. Louis archdiocese and at the time lived at St. Patrick's Church in the county, where for years I had helped out on Sunday. He was in England with a group of laymen from St. Louis who were inviting the Benedictines at Ampleforth Abbey to start a boys' school and priory in St. Louis. Monsignor told me to meet them at the Savoy Hotel at about seven in the evening. This was one of the days that I skipped lunch and worked straight through, so when I arrived at the Savoy at seven, I had had nothing to eat all day since a light breakfast in the early morning. They plied me with Scotch, which went right to my head from an empty stomach, and when we were ready to move to the Grand Ball Room of the Savoy for dinner, I realized I might black out. I took a deep breath and hoped it wouldn't happen, but as we sat down at the table, it did. I was in clerics, and I am sure that I am the only cleric in full clerical garb who was ever carried out of the grand ballroom of the Savoy by two English waiters in tails. They all thought I had had a heart attack, so they had sum-moned the house physician. He had evidently diagnosed my case correctly. When I came to, I saw this little roly-poly doctor, with his glasses perched on the end of his nose—a character straight out of

Dickens. I heard him say: "It is perfectly obvious. You Americans wear belts and you trap the gas; you should wear braces." Monsignor Curtin had me stay with him in the hotel for the night. But that did not end the episode. We went up to the Jesuit Church on Farm Street to say Mass in the morning, and I spent a leisurely Sunday with Monsignor. I had forgotten about the check-in system back at Roehampton. If a resident were going to be out late in the evening, he left his card at the door. The last one in locked the door when he picked up his card. They found my card in the morning, and the door was unlocked, which told them I had not returned. They became very worried as the day wore on and I did not show up. When I sauntered in about half past four Sunday afternoon, I discovered they were just about to call in Scotland Yard to look for the missing American. They were greatly relieved and were not too harsh with me when I confessed my delinquencies.

I settled down to work again, and the rest of the semester went on rather uneventfully. I finished what I had come over to do—the manuscript for the book *Honor and the Epic Hero,* which Rinehart and Company published during the following year, and the article "*Beowulf* as an Allegory of Salvation." The latter was published in the *Journal of English and Germanic Philology* and has since been anthologized twice in collections of critical essays on *Beowulf.*

I was to return to the States in early January. My sabbatical was only for the first semester. Because I had completed the work I had planned to do by the middle of December, I decided to take a quick trip to Spain during the Christmas season. I had kept in touch during the semester with a former student of mine, Thomas Langan, who was doing doctoral work in philosophy at the Institut Catholique in Paris. We decided to meet in Spain. He had previously traveled in the Madrid area and in northern Spain, so we decided to meet in Madrid and go south immediately to some of the cities he had not seen there. When he had to leave, I would return to Madrid and tour that city, the Escorial, and Toledo. I flew to Madrid on Christmas Eve on a little Spanish plane. The ride was extremely turbulent, and, for the only time in my life, I got terribly airsick. I stayed at a Jesuit residence in Madrid, and I thought I might get sick all over again when I joined the community for their late dinner. They were having what they told me was a favorite Spanish Christmas Eve dinner.

When the soup came out, it looked for all the world like India ink. It was pitch black. I was told it was octopus soup made from the juice the octopus secretes to disguise its whereabouts. I bravely gulped it down, and I would describe it as warm India ink with a mild fish flavor. The octopus itself that constituted the main entry was less threatening. Rice and brussels sprouts were served with it, and a light white wine. The dessert, I recall, was pressed fruit, a kind of baklava.

The museums were all closed on Christmas Day, so I contented myself with strolling through parts of the city. I have never found Madrid a very interesting city, except for the Prado, one of the world's great museums, and the Royal Palace, which is perhaps one of the most beautiful and certainly one of the most livable palaces in all of Europe. In the late afternoon, I joined the daily paseo in the neighborhood of the Prado. The paseo is the very interesting custom of going for a long walk for a couple of hours in the early evening before dinner, which never begins until about nine o'clock. The only other place in the world I have encountered the paseo was in Perugia. If you join it, you have the feeling that all of Spain is out for a walk, and that is not too far from the truth. After the paseo, I joined the Jesuit community for their Christmas dinner, an elaborate seven-course affair that all of the community attended. At that time, members of the community could visit their family during the day, but they were all expected to be home for the evening Christmas dinner. It was quite festive. No more octopus soup.

Tom Langan had visited friends in Madrid on Christmas Day. The next day, we reconnoitered at the railroad station to go to Seville. Tom is a confirmed railroad buff, and we found ourselves out in the yards checking out the running stock before we boarded our own train. We were amazed to find a steam engine still functioning that antedated our Civil War. The only place you would have seen one like it at the time in the States would have been in a transportation museum, and you really would not have found one quite like it there, either. All trains in Spain at the time ran on wide-gauge tracks that were unique to Spain.

We were headed into Andalusia, where we would become very aware of how thoroughly Spanish culture is an amalgam of Moorish and Christian elements. Much of the landscape south of Madrid is rather barren and rocky, but farther south the terrain changes. The soil of the rolling hills is reddish, and the hillsides are dotted with gray-green olive or glossy green orange trees. Both the olives and the orange trees are Moorish imports to Spain. When we arrived in Seville, we found much else that reminded us of the Moorish influence. On the first evening, we strolled through one of the fine residential districts near our hotel and admired the beautiful homes that we think of as typically Spanish: white stucco frontage right up to the sidewalk with red tile roofs, iron gates that reveal a glimpse of the beautiful inner court around which the rooms of the home are distributed. The courtyard and sometimes the exterior facade as well are decorated with *azulejos,* beautiful ceramic tile. Every one of these dominant features of a Spanish home became part of the Iberian peninsular tradition during the centuries when the dominant culture was Moorish.

This same influence was even more apparent in the Alcazar, parts of which were actually built in Moorish times, but most of it by Spanish royalty in what came to be known as the Mudejar style, a Spanish adaptation of Moorish architecture and design. Both are rife with *azulejos,* intricate molded plasterwork, and multiple ogival arches and colonnades. The elaborate meeting and living rooms are organized around inner courts with formal tiled floors, grass plots, and fountains. Some of the inner courts are also planted with orange trees. Although it was December when we visited the Alcazar, the orange trees in one of the courts were laden with oranges. We had always been told how much more tasty oranges are when you pick them fresh off the trees. We were the only visitors in the court, so we took the liberty of picking one and tasting it. To our chagrin, it tasted a little bit like lye. We had forgotten that Spanish oranges are quite tart. Then we remembered the special tart flavor of English marmalade, which the English make out of Spanish oranges.

Wherever the Spanish went, they took their tiles and oranges with them. That accounts for both the ubiquity of tile work in much of Mesoamerican and South American architecture and the prominence of citrus fruit in the same areas. Citrus fruit is not native to either Mesoamerica or South America. In fact, it was first planted there by Spanish sailors and pirates in order to have the acid fruit available in harbors to counteract the scurvy that they contracted while at sea. It is interesting in Spain to experience this westward movement of architectural, decorative, and citrus fruit migration from the Middle East to the West.

The Moorish influence on Spanish architecture is equally evident in the great cathedral of Seville, but in a different way. You are aware of the cathedral's relationship to the Moorish culture before you enter it. The usual entrance is by way of the Patio de los Naranjos (Patio of the Oranges) on the north side of the cathedral. The patio gets its name from the planting of orange trees that graces it. The whole courtyard and patio formed the entrance to the Moorish mosque at this site.

The cathedral itself is actually built on the foundations of the old mosque. An even more evident residue of the old Moorish mosque is the famous Giralda, which forms the campanile or bell tower of the cathedral. It actually is the minaret of the old mosque with its typical geometric ornamentation from the Almohades Moorish dynasty. A gentle ramp on the interior allowed the muezzin to ascend on horseback to the top of the minaret to call the public to prayer. The minaret dates from the twelfth century. The upper story was added in the sixteenth century to provide housing for the bells that call the Christian public to prayer. *Giralda* means "weather vane," and the Giralda gets its name from the rotating weather vane on the tip of its pointed roof: a revolving bronze allegorical figure of Faith. Surmounting the old Moorish minaret with this symbol of Faith was meant, I presume, to symbolize the victory of Christian faith over the Moorish beliefs. The whole tower has been reproduced on a smaller scale in the famous Country Club Plaza shopping center in Kansas City.

When we stepped into the cathedral through the Puerta de los Naranjos, we were immediately aware of the tremendous spatial difference between this cathedral and the great French cathedrals. The space is not really rectilinear as it is in French and most other cathedrals, but closer to square. It was like stepping into a forest of pillars. There are not two side aisles but four, and there is hardly any clerestory, which makes the four side aisles almost as high as the nave. What you are actually looking at is a mosque jacked up 180 feet in the air. Mosques themselves developed from oriental desert tents that were made up of poles at regular intervals in a square ground pattern with woolen cloth draped from pole to pole to create shade from the sun of the desert. The mosque simply translated this square pattern of poles and drapery into permanent stone columns and elaborately worked plaster designs between them. The Spanish cathedral builders at Seville and elsewhere took the square ground plan of the mosque, extended the pillars up 100 feet into the air, and substituted the stone vaulting at the top for the elaborate plaster decor of the mosque. The double side aisles multiplied the number of pillars so that the overall impression you get is of a gigantically elevated mosque or of looking into a stand of majestic redwood trees.

There are also other things that are different about it. You are immediately struck by the two immense square grilles that interrupt the horizontal sweep of the nave. These grilles are thirty or forty feet high. The one in the middle of the nave, called the *coro* or choir, accommodates the wood-carved stalls of the canons who sing the divine office here at the canonical hours. The other one encloses the sanctuary where the sacred Liturgy is performed. It is called the *capilla major* (the chief or main chapel) to distinguish it from the some twenty-four chapels that fringe the outermost side aisles. These giant grilled spaces effectively prohibit anything like a large congregational gathering. They advertise the fact that the cathedral is not a parish church but a place at the center of the diocese where the official canonical prayer of the diocese is sung in the *coro* and the official canonical ritual of the diocese is performed in the *capilla major.*

We attended a Solemn Vespers one afternoon at which the choir and the canons were in the *coro* and the Solemn Vespers were conducted in the *capilla major.* It was *Solemn Vespers coram Cardinali* (Solemn Vespers in the presence of the cardinal archbishop). In such a ceremony, the cardinal is not the chief celebrant but presides from his throne, accompanied by monsignors as honorary assistants. The cardinal of Seville at that time had become somewhat senile, and one of the signs of his senility was that he began proscribing Andalusian dancing and frequently preached against it. Dancing is so much a part of Andalusian culture and tradition that proscribing it in Andalusia was like proscribing breathing. The ridiculousness of this situation was brought to the pope's attention, and he suggested to the cardinal that he no longer speak about it in public. The cardinal took the proscription lightly and, whenever he found an occasion, continued his harangues on the sinfulness of dancing. One of those occasions was the Solemn Vespers we attended. In the middle of the ceremony, in spite of the best efforts of the two monsignori to prevent him from doing so, he ascended the pulpit and launched out on his usual diatribe. The monsignori kept tugging on his surplice, or cotta, to try to get him out of the pulpit and finally succeeded in doing so. This little episode in the midst of the Solemn Vespers turned the solemn event into a kind of opéra bouffe.

Even without this comic interlude, the ceremony had something of the operatic about it. The huge, beautifully grilled space of the *capilla major* had the appearance of a giant birdcage. The richly vested ministers at the altar and their acolytes, dressed in red cassocks and pleated linen and Spanish lace surplices, with pleated ruffs around their necks, looked for all the world like butterflies or tropical birds flitting around in the giant cage. Behind them, filling the rear wall of the cage to a height of eighty feet, rose a giant reredos, characteristic of many Spanish cathedrals. This one is made up of forty-five hand-carved wood panels representing scenes from the life of Christ and the Blessed Virgin. Dominating the center of it is a crucifixion group, with Christ on the Cross and Mary and St. John at either side. Below this group is a beautiful carved image of Our Lady of the Chair. This whole reredos, with its wonderful sequence of scenes from the life of Christ and the Blessed Virgin, reminded me of the similar sequence of representations of scenes enacted in the York Mystery Cycle. In fact, the scenes in the reredos may owe something to such cyclical dramatic representations because the religious drama preceded visual representations everywhere by centuries.

A site of particular attraction to us was the Provincial Museum of Fine Art. Like most museums all over Europe, it specializes in the art of the area. In these museums, you see work by local artists that you are not apt to see represented in museums anywhere else. And some of the artists are very good. This is true of the museum in Seville. It contains first-rate paintings by artists I had never heard of before, but it is particularly noteworthy for its extensive collection of works by Murillo and Zurbarán—artists on the opposite ends of the artistic spectrum. Both were active in Seville for the greater part of their careers. When we mention Murillo, we almost instinctively think of his many renderings of the Immaculate Conception and his many placid Madonnas, which are sometimes compared to those of Raphael. There are two versions of the Immaculate Conception and several Madonnas in the Seville Museum, along with renderings of various saints, including St. John the Baptist, St. Anthony of Padua, St. Augustine, Saints Justus and Rufinus (patrons of Seville pictured with the Giralda tower in the background), and St. Thomas of Villaneuve, which Murillo himself considered his masterpiece. All are rendered in Murillo's rather placid, some would say almost sentimental, manner. But Murillo was equally famous for his realistic and unsentimental genre paintings of ordinary Spanish peasants.

The powerful works of Zurbarán, the other Sevillian master well represented in the museum, creates the exact opposite impression from that of Murillo. Zurbarán's mastery of dramatic chiaroscuro, strong contrasts of light and shadow, and his dramatic presentation of his subjects remind one of Rembrandt in the north. Zurbarán, perhaps better than any other Spanish painter, caught some of the intensity of feeling of the baroque, the exact opposite of the somewhat static serenity of Murillo. All of these more baroque qualities are well illustrated in his paintings in the Seville museum.

The museum itself is the former Merced Monastery. It forms a perfect contemplative atmosphere for viewing these mostly religious paintings. But I was struck once again with how provincial most European museums are in their holdings. Almost all of them concentrate on the art of the area where they are located. This is true even of the major museums such as the Uffizi in Florence, the Louvre in Paris, and the Prado in Madrid. You do not go to any of them for a complete coverage of the history of art. The Uffizi concentrates on Italian and especially Florentine art. It has a couple of outstanding Flemish paintings, such as the *Portinari Altarpiece* by Hugo von der Goes, and a few outstanding canvases by Rubens, but the strength of its holdings are by such great Italian masters as Duccio, Lorenzetti, Giotto, Botticelli, Michelangelo, Parmigianino, and Andrea del Sarto.

In spite of the Louvre's immense holdings, with paintings from many countries, many of them confiscated by Napoleon, the collection does not represent a comprehensive overview of the history of art. Nineteenth-century art and modern art are practically unrepresented there. The New D'Orsay Museum now provides a comprehensive view of nineteenth-century French art, but only of French art. For an experience of modern art, one has to go to the Museum of Modern Art and the Pompidou Center in Paris.

The fabulous Prado in Madrid has the great Spanish painters—Velasquez, El Greco, and Goya are especially represented in astounding depth—and a large collection of Rubens, as well as some of the most important paintings of Bruegel, but it makes no attempt whatever to cover the history of art.

In fact, a museum that has as its objective a survey of the history of art is an American invention. The first one to set out to do that was the Metropolitan Museum in New York. It realized that objective rather early and continues to round out its collection to provide that kind of broad survey of the history of art. Most other American museums such as the Cleveland Museum and the Chicago Art Institute have worked to create this broad historical coverage in their collections as well. Because the National Gallery in Washington was so late in getting started, it is remarkable for having achieved this same kind of historical breadth in its collection. Even smaller museums in the States have achieved a remarkable inclusiveness, such as the Toledo Museum, the Kimbell Museum in Fort Worth, the Nelson Gallery in Kansas City, and the St. Louis City Art Museum. Even some collections in the States put together by private collectors were built with this broad inclusiveness in mind, notably the Frick Collection. In this relatively small collection, you can experience practically the history of Western painting in outstanding examples of each major style. Probably the reason for this development in the United States is the fact that because it is such a young country, Americans were not surrounded with examples of great architecture, sculpture, and painting from various ages of the past, so it was thought desirable that the public art museums provide some of this artistic historical perspective. The National Gallery in London was begun late enough to have adopted some of this same inclusiveness in building its collection. But to this day, late-nineteenth-century and modern art are practically unrepresented in it. One goes to the Tate in London to experience nineteenth-century English art, and to the Courtauld for a taste of nineteenth-century French art. But these periods on an international level are still poorly represented in public museums in London. I had not realized before what an important contribution the United States has made in the development of the really comprehensive art museum.

Tom and I wanted to visit two other sites together before Tom had to return to Paris: the famous Moorish mosque at Cordoba and the Alhambra at Granada. We took an early morning train to Cordoba and went immediately to the mosque when we arrived there because we were going to have only a few hours in Cordoba. The mosque is situated right on the banks of the Quadalquiver River. To get a good view of its exterior we crossed over the river on the ancient bridge.

The foundations of the bridge were built by the Romans and the upper part by the Moors in the twelfth century. From across the river, you get a very good view of the entire mosque, and from there you can appreciate how really big it is. It stretches for the equivalent of two or three city blocks in both directions. Its heavy, windowless, crenellated walls give it more the appearance of a fortress than a place of worship. It is by far the largest mosque built in all of Spain. We recrossed the river and wandered around to the north side, where we discovered the very large Patio de los Naranjos, very similar to the one that forms the entrance to the Seville Cathedral. As in Seville, the patio was planted with orange trees. Although it was December, they were still laden with fruit. We entered the great mosque through the Puerta de las Palmas and were utterly amazed at what we saw. A veritable forest of hundreds of pillars stretch back as far as the eye can see. They support row after row of double-tiered, horseshoe-shaped arches—zebra striped, with alternating pink and dark-red stone. Between these endless tiers of arches, the ceiling of the mosque is covered with elaborate plaster decoration in varied Arabesque patterns. In places, the plaster decoration is suspended downward so it looks like stalactites in a primitive cave. The hundreds of pillars vary in size and color; many of them came from ancient Roman buildings and early Christian churches. It was a way of asserting the Islamic conquest of the cultures on the peninsula that had preceded the Islamic invasion. There are no windows in the side walls; the only source of light comes from irregularly placed skylights in the ceiling, which creates a rather dimly lit interior relieved only by shafts of light here and there. But the thing that most impressed us is the sheer size of the interior. It could accommodate half the population of the ancient Moorish city, all bowed down in the direction of Mecca on their individual prayer rugs. The size did help us to appreciate what an important center Cordoba must have been at the height of its Moorish development. As we looked at these endless lines of pillars supporting long arcades of double-horseshoe arches, we could also easily see how the mosque is just a transformation of the desert tent with its numerous tent poles and inverted arches of cloth coverings.

Like the sheer size of the *mezquita* or mosque, the visitors' brochures reminded us of the importance of Cordoba as a Moorish cultural center. They called attention to the fact that the great Islamic scholar Averroes and the almost equally famous Jewish scholar Maimonides worked at Cordoba. This fact was particularly interesting to Tom, who was working on his doctorate in philosophy in Paris. Both Averroes and Maimonides were very familiar with the works of Aristotle and wrote commentaries on many of his works. Averroes was of the opinion that there was no reconciling the truths of reason, which Aristotle had explored so fruitfully, and those of revelation. They existed as two independent domains. Maimonides, on the other hand, was quite convinced that the truths of reason and those of revelation could be integrated, and he attempted to do so. St. Thomas Aquinas, the great medieval theologian, was familiar with translations of the commentaries on Aristotle by both men. He, of course, favored Maimonides' view, and he himself beautifully integrated the rational views of Aristotle into the body of Christian revelation in his *Summa Theologica*.

As we moved through the immense mosque (the only larger one in the whole Islamic world is the one at Mecca), we were startled to come upon a complete Christian cathedral sprouting up in the very center of it. The cathedral is typically Spanish, with its encaged *coro* and *capilla major*, and much of its decor is in the elaborate Spanish baroque or churrigheresque style. The anomaly of its placement square in the center of the mosque was meant to highlight the replacement of the Moorish culture by the Christian. The Moors were not only conquered by the Christian rulers; they were driven out of Spain. The placing of the image of Faith on the top of the Moorish minaret at the cathedral of Seville; constructing the Seville cathedral itself on the foundations of the old mosque; and, here in Cordoba, constructing the cathedral in the very heart of the great mosque were all visual gestures on the part of the Christians to publicize their effective conquest of the Moors. But you cannot go anywhere in Spain without being aware of the very pervasive influence that the Moors had in shaping the thought, the culture, the architecture, the art, the music, the dance, and the very people themselves of Spain.

Granada was our next stop. If Cordoba possesses the most impressive Moorish mosque in Spain, Granada boasts of the finest secular Moorish palace, the Alhambra. A large rotogravure of the Court of the Lions in the Alhambra hung in the music room at Florissant. It piqued my curiosity about the Alhambra when I was a young Jesuit scholastic and induced me to read Washington Irving's book on the subject. Now at last I was to have the opportunity to see the fantastic building itself. We took a late afternoon train to Granada and arrived after dark. We went immediately to the Washington Irving Hotel just outside the walls of the Alhambra. Cordoba is situated on rather flat terrain, but Granada, we discovered when we arose with the sun in the morning, is situated on a series of hills facing the snow-capped Sierra Nevada Mountains. Granada was the last holdout of the Moors in Spain after the Christians conquered Cordoba. The leaders of the final Moorish kingdom of the Nasrids built their fantastic palace fortress on one of the most commanding hills. Although fundamentally it is a rather poorly built structure of brick and rubble, its stucco, plaster, and tile decoration inside and out make it one of the most impressive examples of Moorish architectural decoration anywhere. Like most Moorish structures, it is made up of a series of inner courts built around beautiful reflection pools and fountains. You are nowhere out of the earshot of running water, sparkling in fountains and running through open, tiled channels in the floor. The lower reaches of these spaces and the floors are covered with beautiful glazed tile of varied geometric patterns. The upper walls are decorated with elaborate molded plasterwork, some of it painted and gilded. In some rooms, an unbelievable maze of suspended plasterwork resembling stalactites in a cave constitutes the whole ceiling. Much of the decoration of the walls is made up of quotations from the Koran, spelled out in beautiful cursive calligraphy. Many ogee- and horseshoe-shaped arched windows and arcaded balconies provide spectacular views of the hills and the mountains in the distance.

Possibly the most impressive space in the whole palace is the Court of the Lions. The arcade of pillars and interlaced plaster decoration that surrounds the court is the most beautiful in the castle. In its center is a fountain with a large stone basin supported on the heads of twelve lions, which give the court its name. Scholars have discovered that the fountain was designed by a Jewish architect and that he designed it from descriptions of a fountain that was supposed to have graced the Temple of Solomon. This story may be a fair index of the harmonious way in which the Moors and the Jews worked together in the period of Moorish dominance on the Iberian Peninsula.

We were visiting the Alhambra in the off season, so we had the place almost to ourselves. We made use of our time to explore every room in detail and to try to picture the very luxurious and leisurely life that must have been led in these beautiful surroundings. Practically no furniture, carpets, or hangings are left in the palace, so we could furnish it in our imaginations as we wished with rich oriental rugs, elaborate woven wall hangings, brass tea and coffee services, and lush silken divans. We enjoyed the incomparable views of the distant snowcapped mountains from the many ogival windows and balconies. On one of the closer hills across a gorge rose the rather idyllic Generalife, the summer villa for the Moorish kings, a combination of Moorish architecture, dozens of fountains, cypress, olive, and orange trees, and oleander bushes.

On an opposite, more barren hillside called the Sacromonte, we could see a network of paths that led to the Gypsy village. On a much later visit to Granada, I would make my way up one of the paths to the village and, seated on the floor of one of their whitewashed caves, enjoy their energetic and fantastic dancing, one of the roots of the dancing that is so much a part of the Andalusian tradition.

A great surprise to any visitor to the Alhambra, I would think, is to find rising out of one of its courts, just inside the entrance gate, a completely classical Renaissance palace, commissioned by Emperor Charles V; its very classical form, a circle inside a square, with very restrained classical decoration, seems utterly incongruous sitting in the midst of all the exotic Moorish exuberance of the Alhambra palace. Pedro Machuca, who had studied under Michelangelo, was its architect. It is said to be the most purely classical Renaissance building erected anywhere in Spain. It was not finished until the nineteenth century because during Charles V's time a final Moorish uprising interrupted construction, but it was no doubt commissioned by Charles V in the first place to celebrate the victory of the Christians over the Moors.

Just down the hill from the Alhambra are two of Granada's Christian architectural treasures, the cathedral and the Capilla Reale. The cathedral, like so many other European cathedrals, is a mixture of styles: Romanesque, Gothic, and High Renaissance. The feature that impressed me most is its great circular cupola that caps the sanctuary or the *capilla major* below. I learned later that it had also caught the eye of the famous nineteenth-century American architect Henry Hobson Richardson. Richardson was from New Orleans but went to Harvard University to study architecture. After graduation, he went to Paris to the Beaux Arts to continue his studies. While he was there, the Civil War broke out at home, and his family persuaded him to remain in Europe until the war was over. He became very well accepted in French architectural circles, worked extremely hard, and became fascinated with Romanesque architecture. He traveled all over Europe sketching Romanesque buildings. He also sketched the cupola of the Granada Cathedral. It became the inspiration for the great central cupola on Trinity Church in Boston, which he considered his masterpiece. Richardson was largely responsible for the Romanesque revival in the United States. It became popular in civic buildings throughout the Northeast and Midwest, and was used widely in impressive domestic mansions of the turn of the century. I little suspected as I was admiring the cupola at the Granada Cathedral, which had caught Richardson's fancy, that I would devote a good many years of my old age restoring one of the most significant mansions inspired by the Richardsonian revival—Cupples House on the campus of my own university.

Cheek by jowl with the cathedral in Granada is the Capilla Reale, the Royal Chapel, commissioned by Ferdinand and Isabella. It houses their impressive marble tombs carved by the Italian artist Domenico Francelli. Like the palace of Charles V within the Alhambra itself, it is done in a reserved, classical High Renaissance style. The sacristy contains a collection of important works by several of the Flemish painters, including Thierry Bouts, Rogier van der Weyden, and Hans Memling. The presence of these works here was rather surprising to me, but less so when I recalled that Flanders for many years was ruled by Spain.

We had time for little else in the fascinating city of Granada. Tom had to return to Paris by train. I had a free plane ticket from Seville to Madrid, so decided to take the train back to Seville and make use of the ticket. I discovered that at that time there were three classes of train travel in Spain. I thought it might be interesting to go third class to see what it was like. I found out. It was like riding in a boxcar, with a few windows, and some movable seats like park benches. It was dirt cheap, something like the equivalent of five dollars from Granada to Seville. It supplied the only means of transportation that many of the poor could afford. The car was soon packed with a motley group of working people. It was a very local train, stopping at small villages all along the way. One elderly gentleman got on at Granada with a goat. He had evidently bought it at a market in Granada and was on his way home with it. He departed with his bleating goat just a few stops out of Granada. I was also interested in the little family group on the bench next to me. A middle-aged mother in a black woolen dress was carrying a large wicker basket half-filled with packages wrapped in newspaper. With her were two little ragamuffins with pitch-black hair and dark brown eyes. They were soon munching brown bread and cheese that their mother retrieved from the basket. Like the old man with the goat, she had been to market. Her wicker basket at this season had probably been full of live chickens when she went to market. It was now half full of items she had purchased with the money she got for her chickens. This little family was a genre scene that Murillo would have enjoyed painting, and there were several others like it in the car.

Halfway to Seville, the lights went out, and we were in almost pitch-black darkness for the rest of the trip. In the darkness, a couple of Islamic soldiers at one end of the car started singing Islamic songs in their high-pitched whining tremolo tone. It was rather weird hearing the Arabic words and the Islamic music there in the darkness, but it should not have surprised me too much to find Arabs here in southern Spain just across the Straits of Gibraltar from Tangiers and Morocco. By the time we arrived in Seville, almost all the passengers in the car had gotten off at little country villages along the way, leaving only the Moorish soldiers and myself in the car.

I stayed in Seville only that night and took the plane for Madrid in the morning. I had a really interesting encounter on the plane. Father Pedro Arrupe, who was then the religious supervisor of the Jesuit mission in Japan, was on the plane, and I had the opportunity of chatting with him en route. Among other things I mentioned casually during our conversation was the fact that we had observed an engine in the rail yards at Madrid that antedated our Civil War. Sixteen years later I found myself in Rome seated at Father Arrupe's table in the Curia for lunch along with four other Jesuit visitors from various countries. He was then general of the Society. He engaged each of us in conversation in our own language. When he came to me, I recalled that I had last met him on a plane in Spain sixteen years previously. He remarked: "Yes, and I remember you told me you had seen an engine still in use in Spain that antedated your Civil War." Father Arrupe had a phenomenal memory for names and faces that enabled him to deal warmly and personally in all his human relations.

When we arrived in Madrid, Father Arrupe suggested that I go with him to the provincial's residence, where he was sure I would receive hospitality. He was right; the community there welcomed me warmly. The residence was not far from the Prado Museum, which I haunted for the next two days. It is certainly one of the great museums of the world. Nowhere else can you experience the work of Velasquez, El Greco, Murillo, Zurbarán, and Goya in such impressive depth and enjoy some of their greatest works. Almost equally well represented are the Flemish painters, Rubens and Van Dyck. Spanish royalty had commissioned many of the paintings by these artists. The Prado Museum, in fact, boasts that Spanish royalty or the museum itself either commissioned or purchased everything in it, and none of it is the result of the spoils of war or confiscation—probably an invidious remark at the expense of the Louvre in Paris, where so many of the holdings are the result of Napoleon's confiscations. The only greater confiscation ever attempted was that by Goebbels and Hitler in World War II, but that was interrupted by the end of the war, and most of the confiscated work was returned to the place of its origin. The fact that all of the masterpieces in the Prado were legitimately acquired makes all the more impressive the extent of the collection of Italian painting, especially works by the Venetian painters Titian, Tintoretto, and Veronese, with very representative paintings by Raphael; and the fine collection of eighteenth- and nineteenth-century French paintings, including works by Lorraine, Poussin, Boucher, Watteau, and Larguillière. Because of Spain's long rule over the Low Countries, it is not surprising that Flemish and Dutch paintings are very well represented in the Prado.

But the presence there of some of the most famous paintings of Hieronymous Bosch, one of the most esoteric of all Flemish painters, is the result of the esoteric personality and taste of one of the Spanish monarchs, Philip II. Philip was half monk and half king. The somewhat misanthropic and pessimistic view of the human situation that Bosch embodies in many of his works appealed to Philip. It is said of Bosch that the theme in many of his paintings is "merrily we go to hell." That certainly is applicable to his most famous painting in the Prado, the triptych entitled *The Garden of Earthly Delights*. The central panel represents a vast bevy of nude individuals and couples enjoying all sorts of sensuous "earthly delights." The upper part of the central panel pictures a carousel or circle of figures representing the seven deadly sins, all mounted on animals appropriate to the individual vices they represent, circling around a pool in which nude figures are cavorting. The whole scene is punctuated by lush fruit and tropical birds symbolizing sensual indulgence. It all looks gay, sensuous, and delightful, but on the right panel is a representation of hell with enough variation in punishments to suit all the varied sinful indulgences represented in the central panel. Bosch does seem to be saying that all the pleasant cavorters of "the garden of delights" are headed for hell. Even the glimpse of paradise in the left panel is not without its evil. The creation of Eve is in progress at the forefront of the panel, but close by is a cat making away with a mouse in its mouth—here in paradise, where the lion was supposed to lie down in peace with the lamb.

In the Escorial palace that Philip built and where he lived, he had the famous *Haywain* by Bosch hung in his bedroom. If anything, that painting is even more pessimistic about the human situation than *The Garden of Earthly Delights*. The central panel represents a couple of lovers dallying on top of a wagonload of hay. They are being encouraged and led on by a winged devil playing a flute, and they are ignoring the kneeling figure of an angel who is praying for them to the figure of Christ in the clouds above, showing the wounds in his side and hands. The dalliers are ignoring him, too. The load of hay symbolizes sensual indulgence, and the motley crowd from all walks of life that surround it are attempting to snatch some wisps of hay as it moves along. They are being run over by the wheels of the wagon or are fighting one another. But the whole wagon, pulled by a mixed gathering of animals representing the various capital sins, is moving, along with the crowd that is snatching at it, ineluctably to hell pictured in the right panel. Sin and evil are pictured even more unambiguously in the paradise of the left panel here than in the paradise panel of *The Garden of Earthly Delights*. It pictures the creation of Eve, the temptation, and finally St. Michael's expulsion of Adam and Eve from paradise. And at the top of the composition, God is represented as expelling the fallen angels from heaven. They are tumbling like a great flock of black bats toward paradise. Bosch is not denying his faith in Christ or the possibility of redemption; he just seems to be saying that too few avail themselves of the redemption that is there. For some reason, this pessimistic and misanthropic view appealed to King Philip II's morose sensitivities.

When I visited the Escorial, I felt that some of Philip's moroseness had also gone into the planning of that building. Toledo had traditionally been the capital of Spain. Philip moved it to Madrid and later decided to build a palace and move the court to a site some thirty miles northwest of Madrid near the little village of Escorial. The town gave its name to the new palace. The local terrain there is bare and rocky, and the palace that Philip planned matches the terrain. It is actually a combination palace, monastery, church, library, and royal burial place. It is built of gray granite in a very severe classical style and is dedicated to St. Lawrence, to whom Philip had a special devotion because it was on August 12, the feast of St. Lawrence, that he had won one of his important battles. St. Lawrence was martyred by being roasted alive on a gridiron, a fact that inspired the gigantic gridiron shape of the Escorial. Pointed-roof towers rise at each corner of the building like the supporting corner legs of a gridiron. Long, flat, granite walls stretch in between the towers like the side bars of a gridiron, their flatness relieved only by strings of uniformly designed windows. Inside the walls, a whole series of rectangular courts resemble the grate of the gridiron. In the exact center of the huge space rises the monastery church on the exact space where the body of St. Lawrence would have rested on the gridiron. The crypt under the church provides the burial place for the royal family.

The monastery church stands free in the middle of the interior space surrounded by the great cloistered courts. The church was designed by Herrera, the most prominent Renaissance architect in Spain, and it is one of the most important Renaissance structures in all of Spain. Philip's apartments were designed to circle the apse of the church. They are very modest in size and are extremely plain and simple, looking more like a monk's quarters than royal apartments. A door in Philip's bedroom opened directly into the sanctuary of the church so that he could attend liturgical services from his own room. By keeping the door ajar, he could also work continuously in the presence of the Blessed Sacrament. When the Bourbons took over the throne of Spain, they adapted space on the second floor for much more elaborate royal apartments. The contrast between the stark simplicity of Philip's semimonastic quarters and the baroque lavishness of the Bourbon royal apartments is striking.

Part of the Escorial was designed as a monastery, and it still houses a monastery and a school. The beautifully designed library has an outstanding collection of rare books. Philip and succeeding monarchs put together a sizable collection of paintings that still hang in some of the corridors and galleries designed to accommodate them. The collection does reflect Philip's taste. I already referred to his particular interest in Hieronymous Bosch's works. Philip's taste is also manifested in one painting now hung in one of the galleries but never hung anywhere in the palace during Philip's lifetime: *St. Maurus, a Roman Legionnaire and Martyr* by El Greco. El Greco had begun his career as an icon painter in Cyprus and then began to move westward. He went first to Venice, where he was much influenced by Tintoretto. He learned from Tintoretto the technique of painting figures in grisaille or gray paint in fully three-dimensional modeled form and then overpainting them in the desired color and rubbing off some of the added color while the paint was still wet to create highlights by the gray showing through. This is one of the ways in which El Greco achieved the kind of unearthly quality in his work that gives his paintings a mystical feeling. The artist then moved to Rome and fell under the spell of Michelangelo. He was particularly interested in the subtle distortions of some of Michelangelo's work, which had come to be called *la maniera di Michelangelo*, the mannered style of Michelangelo. This subtly mannered distortion was to become a dominant feature of El Greco's personal style. El Greco heard of the generous patronage that Philip was providing many artists from several countries, so he decided to go to Spain to benefit by that patronage. Soon after his arrival, Philip did commission him to paint the panel on St. Maurus, but when Philip saw it, he was displeased with it, never had it hung, and never commissioned El Greco to do another painting. Disappointed, the artist made the old capital of Toledo his headquarters. The city and the artist were a perfect fit. Toledo was to be my last stop in Spain before returning to London. I had the opportunity there of seeing firsthand how perfectly suited the city and the artist were to one another. You really can't think of Toledo without thinking of El Greco.

I took a late afternoon train to Toledo and upon arriving had my taxi driver take me across the old Moorish bridge that still spans the Tagus River to the promontory that commands the spectacular view of the whole city climbing up the side of the hill from the deep gorge cut by the Tagus through solid rock. El Greco had caught that view in one of his most famous paintings, now in the Metropolitan Museum. It was all before me now just as he had painted it: the arches of the old Moorish bridge spanning the river in the deep gorge below; sections of the old walls and watch towers climbing up the hill; and, rising into the sky above the towers of the great cathedral and the silhouette of the massive Alcazar that had played such an important part in so much of the history of Spain. It was all there just as El Greco had painted it, but his painting enwraps it all in a strange light, especially reflected on the odd-shaped clouds stretched across the sky, that gives his painting some of the unreality of a dream. It is a quality that characterizes almost all of El Greco's work, a mystical quality that was a perfect medium for expressing the intellectual and spiritual interests of a group of intellectual humanists led by the great humanist Cardinal Ximenes at Toledo.

When Philip moved the royal court from Toledo to Madrid and the Escorial, Toledo continued to function as the primatial ecclesiastical see. A group of humanists and theologians, much influenced by the mystical writings of Theresa of Avila and St. John of the Cross, made Toledo the spiritual capital of Spain. El Greco was an intimate member of that group, and the mannered style he developed admirably expressed some of the otherworldly and mystical qualities of the human experience that were so central to the interests of this small intellectual and spiritual coterie at Toledo.

After my first glimpse of the El Greco view of Toledo from across the Tagus, the taxi driver took me to my little hotel in the heart of the city. I was to have only the one day in the city, so I arose next morning at the crack of dawn to make the most of it. I started walking to the cathedral to say Mass. I could see the towers in the distance, but I was not getting there through the maze of narrow winding streets. The only other living being out this early was a milkman with two wicker baskets containing milk cans flung across his little burro. He was an apparition straight out of a Murillo genre painting. I asked him the way to the cathedral. He told me to follow him, and he would get me there. We wove our way through the twisting byways and finally came out onto the plaza in front of the cathedral. But my milkman guide was not finished with his services. He wanted to be sure I would find the sacristy, so he motioned me across the plaza, parted the heavy red leather curtains that are usual in the doorways of Spanish cathedrals, and preceded me into the cathedral, burro, milk cans, and all. Stepping through the curtains, I was greeted with the same spectacle that amazed me in Seville—a forest of pillars—again a mosque jacked up a hundred feet in the air. The gigantic birdcage grilles of the *coro* and the sanctuary or *capilla major* also here interrupt the open space of the nave. My guide with his milk-laden burro motioned me around behind the immense reredos of the *capilla major* and stopped to point out to me the most lavish baroque structure in all of Spain, the *Transparente* by Narciso Tome. It is a tangled sculpture of clouds and angels soaring up to the very vault of the cathedral and enframing halfway up a representation of the Last Supper and above that a figure of the Virgin afloat in clouds. Light from an invisible aperture in the ceiling pours down from above. You have the impression that you are looking at a dreamlike apparition from heaven. I could tell that my milkman guide was taking a great deal of pride in pointing out this Toledan treasure to the *padre Americano*. But he motioned me on to the door of the sacristy, where there were other treasures to behold. He bowed at the door, kissed my hand, and then he and his burro clattered out of the transept door to continue his milk route. In all my travels, I have never had a more unusual guide nor one who took more pleasure in what he was guiding me to see.

Left alone, I was astonished at the sacristy. It was as big as a small church. Above an altar at the far end of it was one of El Greco's very impressive early paintings, *The Espolio*. It represents the full-length figure of Christ after the scourging, clothed in the red garment of mock kingship put on him by the jeering soldiers. Almost the entire composition is taken up by this brilliant Titian red garment. The garment does not flow naturally over the body of the Christ figure but is displayed prominently as a symbol of the mockery of the soldiers and of the beginning of Christ's passion and death. It is a painting you can never forget once you have seen it. It dominates the whole space of the sacristy. But above the fine wood-carved vestment cases hang panels by El Greco representing all twelve of the Apostles, a *Holy Family* by Van Dyck, *The Taking of Christ in the Garden* by Goya, and a *Mater Dolorosa* and an *Ecce Home* by Morales. This is a collection of paintings that any museum in the world would be proud to exhibit, and here it is hung as a kind of incidental decoration in the sacristy.

Before leaving the cathedral after my Mass in one of the many side chapels, I stopped to study the immense reredos in the *capilla major*.

It is all of beautifully painted carved wood. Dominating the upper center is a Calvary grouping, but the rest of it is made up of carvings in rectangular Gothic frames representing scenes from the life of Christ. I was somewhat amused at the ingenuity the artist showed in coming up with compositional patterns of the scenes that would fit into the confinement of the uniformly sized rectangles. In the scene of the Ascension, for instance, the artist represents the Apostles grouped at the bottom of the composition looking up intently at the ascending Christ figure, but only the feet and the lower hem of the tunic of the Christ figure are represented as the rest of his figure disappears above and outside the frame. One of El Greco's most famous paintings is *The Burial of Count Orgaz,* which was commissioned for the vestibule of the Church of Santo Tome, where it still hangs. It is a painting I was very anxious to see because it represents the artist in his fully developed personal style. The lower range represents a frieze of earthly mourners, all dressed in black, many of them said to be portraits of the count's friends, one of them actually a self-portrait of El Greco himself. They are rendered fairly realistically and in natural proportions. But invading their space are the larger figures of St. Augustine and St. Stephen in full, rich ecclesiastical vestments, St. Stephen's those of a deacon and St. Augustine's those of an archbishop. They have come down from heaven to help lay the body of the count in his tomb. All this, I presume, is to indicate the esteem in which the count was held in the elite Toledan circle. The count's soul is represented in a diminutive wraithlike figure ascending into heaven above the heads of Saints Stephen and Augustine. Heaven itself is represented in the mysterious cloud-filled space above, populated by the elongated figures of Christ, the Blessed Virgin, and St. John the Baptist. Their garments are all rendered in the strange off-tone, mannered colors that El Greco had learned from Tintoretto and Michelangelo and that he combined with a mysterious lighting and flattened space to create successfully an unearthly, spiritual, and even mystical quality in so many of his paintings.

Down the steep hill from Santo Tome is a house advertised as either the actual house and studio of El Greco or one very much like the original. A wonderful painting of the repentant St. Peter is displayed on an easel in what might have been the very studio in which El Greco painted it. He is swathed in an off-color yellow garment, symbolizing his denial of Christ. His tear-filled eyes express his grief at the realization of his betrayal of his master as only El Greco could express it. The house also contains a version of the complete series *Portraits of the Apostles,* with a later and perhaps better version of the series housed in the sacristy of the cathedral.

Not far from the El Greco house is the El Transito Synagogue. It gets its name from the fact that after the Jews were expelled from Spain by Ferdinand and Isabella, it was turned into a Christian church dedicated to the Assumption or *Transito* of Mary into heaven. Its interior is an extraordinarily beautiful example of Mudejar decoration. It combines abstract geometric patterns dictated by both the Moorish and Jewish traditions in several media: cedar wood, molded plaster, and ceramic tile. The windows are covered with white marble perforated in beautiful patterns. A series of trefoil arches rests on delicate alabaster pillars. The fact that the synagogue is now a museum and only one of the two remaining synagogue buildings of the six that once existed in Toledo was a quiet reminder to me of an unhappy period of Christian intolerance in the history of Spain. The Moors seemed to have respected the Jews during the several centuries in which they dominated the peninsula. Jewish scholars such as Maimonides thrived there, and the Jewish community contributed significantly to the intellectual, cultural, and economic well-being of the country. I have already pointed out that the Court of the Lions in the Alhambra, the most Moorish of all palaces in Spain, was designed by a Jewish architect.

After Moorish Toledo was conquered by the Christians in the thirteenth century, early Christian rulers such as Ferdinand III and Alfonso X were quite tolerant. Moors, Jews, and Christians lived and worked together quite harmoniously until Toledo actually was the most important Jewish center in all of Spain. At one time, there were more than eleven thousand Jews there. But gradually a narrow element of intolerance grew up in the Christian community in Spain, manifested within the Roman Catholic Church itself by the establishment of the Inquisition, which enforced a very strict and straightlaced version of traditional dogma. This intolerance manifested itself politically not only by the conquest of the Moors, which was finally completed at Granada in 1492, but by their expulsion from the country. And an equal intolerance was shown toward the Jews. They were given an ultimatum: they could either convert to Catholicism or leave the country. Some few did convert, later married Christians, and continued to contribute to the culture of the country. It is said that both St. John of the Cross and Theresa of Avila had some Jewish forebears. But the vast majority chose to leave the country. The empty mosque at Toledo is a sad monument to all those Jewish exiles.

Much of this intolerance toward both Moors and Jews was implemented in the reigns of Ferdinand and Isabella. They had made Toledo their capital, a function it had served in Visigothic times and eventually in Moorish times as well. They commissioned a church and monastery there, San Juan de los Reyes (St. John of the Kings), where they planned to be buried. This, however, was not to be. After their successful final conquest of the Moors at their last stronghold in Granada, Ferdinand and Isabella commissioned the Capilla Reale there to house their tombs as a visual symbol of this final victory.

San Juan de los Reyes is lavish enough to have become a royal mortuary. It is done in a flamboyant Gothic style with delicate tracery in the two-tiered cloister court. It was the first place in which I became clearly conscious of this two-story pattern of Spanish cloisters, with a second arcaded cloister walk superimposed above the ground-level one. It was a pattern distinctly Spanish. The Spaniards took it with them wherever they colonized. I was to see it later in monasteries all through Mesoamerica and South America. The Portuguese also adopted it. But I never saw an example anywhere as beautifully executed, with its delicate lacy tracery, as here in San Juan de los Reyes.

Before taking the train back to Madrid, I took time to visit the damascene factory. Toledo has always been famous for its fine decorated steel works. Toledo steel became synonymous with a finely wrought steel sword, but we also think of the exquisite inlaid decoration of the steel objects fabricated there: fine arabesque patterns derived from the Moorish decorative traditions. They are created by hammering delicate gold, silver, and copper wire into a steel base. It was fascinating to watch the craftsmen at work. I purchased a little ashtray and a penknife decorated with some of this delicate damascene work. They are still on my desk and remind me pleasantly of this first excursion into Spain, a country so very different from most other European countries, largely because of the enduring influence of the Moors there.

I took the plane back to London from Madrid and spent a few days there preparing for taking ship back to the States.

# 11

# A Plunge into Administration

As I returned home from my sabbatical semester, I little realized what would be awaiting me there. Had I, I might not have returned. The powers that be had become somewhat dissatisfied with developments in the English department. Father Dreyfus as chairman had worked up a set of requirements for the bachelor's degree in English that included an integrated progression of courses, a healthy outside reading list, and oral and written examinations. The graduate program for the master's and doctoral degrees were equally well planned and prescribed. But Father Dreyfus had been administering the programs so strictly and rigidly that he was scaring away possible majors on both the undergraduate and the graduate levels. The length of time and effort it might take to get an English degree of any kind had become something of a joke on campus. When we still had graduation exercises in the old gym on West Pine Street, I remember seeing an old man with a white beard halfway down to his waist standing outside the gym as the faculty marched out after the graduation exercises. Someone asked who he was, and I heard one of the faculty wags say: "He has just received his A.B. in English." The administration felt that something had to be done to change the atmosphere in the English department.

Just when I returned from England, a request came for a teacher of English for the young Jesuit scholastics in the juniorate at Florissant. Father Dreyfus had filled that position with distinction in his early career. He was a very good teacher. I myself had benefited by his teaching during his previous stint at Florissant. It was suggested that he be reassigned to the juniorate position and a new chairman be appointed in the English department. But who was it to be? Father Walter Ong, who had just completed his work for the doctorate in English at Harvard, was a recent addition to the department. His work on Peter Ramus and his early publications on the cultural effects of the printing press had already brought him national recognition. He had also established himself in the department as a very successful teacher. It was thought rightly that his name and reputation would bring added prestige to the department nationally and help attract students, so he was offered the position. After mature consideration, he steadfastly turned it down. He was convinced that the duties of administration would seriously interfere with his planned research and publication, and he was confident that it was in those areas that he could do the most for the reputation of the department and the university. Time has certainly proved him correct in that judgment.

So I was offered the position. I was not at all enthusiastic about taking up an administrative position. I had just experienced the luxury of a sabbatical in which I could devote full time to research and writing and had completed the manuscript for *Honor and the Epic Hero* and the article *"Beowulf* as an Allegory of Salvation." I was almost sure that, with the heavy duties of administration, I would have no time for very much further research and publication. I had also come to enjoy my teaching immensely. It was the final realization of an ambition planted years before by the example of Father Riordon, my high school hero in the classroom. I suspected that the administrative duties might greatly curtail my teaching as well. But someone had to take over the chairmanship, so I consented to take it on temporarily to see how it would go. It went very well, and the temporary assignment stretched into fourteen years. As it turned out, I did not let it interfere very significantly with my teaching either on the undergraduate or graduate levels. I kept my favorite undergraduate courses in the practical criticism of poetry and prose, offered graduate courses in Spenser and the history of tragedy, and developed new courses in the baroque and mannerism in literature and art.

There must have been some satisfied customers because I was eventually given the Nancy McNeir Ring Outstanding Faculty Award, for which the students themselves nominate the recipients. I also continued to teach the course on the introduction to art to the honors students, which was a continual delight and an outlet for my second love. As it turned out, my administrative duties did not entirely eliminate research and writing either. I managed to publish several articles on the poetry of Gerard Manley Hopkins and began a new program of study and research in art history that resulted in significant publications in prestigious journals on both sides of the Atlantic. But that is a story for another chapter.

Meantime my task was to do something to improve the public image of the English department. I did not think the problem had to do with the requirements on either the undergraduate or the graduate level, or with the faculty. Father Dreyfus had worked out a stiff but reasonable program on both levels and had brought together a very respectable faculty. It was rather a matter of publicizing what we had to offer in the university and to the general public. The potential enrollment was there. The general enrollment both on the undergraduate and graduate levels was reaching the highest it had ever been. To begin with, it was a matter of reaching out to the public we already had within our doors. The best way of doing that, I thought, was to be sure that as many of our students as possible benefited by the expert teaching of the faculty we had. As the number of English majors on both levels increased, I was able to expand and diversify the faculty. In our freshman and sophomore English classes, we touched every undergraduate student in the university. I was convinced that if their experience in the lower-division English classes was a pleasant one, we would soon be generating our share of undergraduate English majors. For that reason, I insisted that the sophomore English classes in literature be taught by the senior faculty, who had a wealth of background and experience to bring to their teaching. The freshman classes, for the most part, were taught by teaching fellows, whom we trained in a special course to do the job. And we were fortunate in having a troika of women teachers on the faculty who confined themselves to teaching Freshman and Sophomore English and did it extremely well—Marjorie Moissner, Frieda Murray, and Jett Sullivan. They were all superb teachers, personally devoted to the welfare of their students and spending hours counseling them. Mrs. Sullivan in particular had a genius for bringing literature alive for her students, and I think it can be said that these teachers, especially Mrs. Sullivan, generated two-thirds of the English majors that populated our upper-division courses. The students themselves gratefully acknowledged Mrs. Sullivan's ability as a teacher by nominating her for the Nancy McNeir Ring Outstanding Faculty Award. We did everything we could to emphasize the quality of teaching on all levels in the department. There was some indication that the students appreciated this quality; they nominated four members of the department for the Nancy McNeir Ring Outstanding Faculty Award. I have already mentioned Mrs. Sullivan as a recipient of the award. The others were Dr. Helen Mandeville, Dr. Ray Benoit, and myself.

As enrollment increased on both the undergraduate and graduate levels, I was able to greatly expand the faculty. In doing so, I attempted to hire individuals with varied and prestigious academic backgrounds, who would do significant publishing, but also who had a reputation for the quality of their teaching. I tried to provide in the faculty more than one approach to each area of study. A considerable spread of academic training was evident in the backgrounds of the faculty as these statistics indicate: they had degrees from Cambridge, England (one); Florida (one); Fordham (one); Harvard (two); Iowa (one); Illinois, Urbana (one); Kansas, Lawrence (one); Minnesota (one); Oregon, Salem (one); Pennsylvania State (one); St. Louis University (three); Toronto (two); Trinity, Dublin (one); and Yale (one). I was eventually able to bring Father Dreyfus from the juniorate at Florissant to the department. He taught his eighteenth-century courses with distinction until he retired. Father Yealy had previously joined the faculty from Florissant and taught his superb introduction to Victorianism and its critics and a course in American literature until he retired.

Our work on making the English department more visible both within the university and to a broader public took place just when the overall enrollment in the university was the highest it had ever been and when a large contingent of women and men religious from all over the country were still being attracted to the university. We benefited from the large pool of potential students, and as a result of our publicizing the department widely and the favorable comments of satisfied customers, we soon had students registered in the graduate program from more than twenty-five states and several foreign countries, including England, Ireland, India, Japan, and Taiwan.

I think it is fair to say that Father Walter Ong's presence on the faculty helped make the department widely known nationally and internationally. His broad scholarship and numerous publications, many of them translated into a dozen or more foreign languages, gave the department a very wide visibility. When students came to the department, they were also impressed with Father Ong's teaching ability and his personal and perduring interest in his students. But they were also impressed with the quality of the faculty in general and with the emphasis throughout the department on the quality of teaching and on a personal concern for individual students. So the job of chairman of the department turned out to be not quite the disturbing drudgery that I thought it would be.

I had accumulated other administrative duties besides the chairmanship of the English department. I was still chairman of the committee that controlled the honors program and was still chairman of the fine arts program. The latter had not yet been given the status of a department. By 1958, I began plans to shed some of these administrative duties. My friend and former student, Tom Langan, had completed his doctorate in philosophy at the Institut Catholique in Paris and had returned to St. Louis University to teach in the philosophy department. He had graduated from the honors program and was very interested in it, so I persuaded him to take over the chairmanship of the program. He did so and was doing quite well managing it. He himself offered an honors course in philosophy. He had become quite interested in modern philosophy at the institute in Paris and had written his dissertation on the existentialist Heidegger. He made existentialism his focus in the honors course, but created a furor in the philosophy department by doing so. At that time, the department, under the chairmanship of Father William Wade and with the cooperation of other prominent scholars such as Father Klubertanz, Robert Henle, Linus Thro, and Vernon Bourke, had built up a very strong and coherent program in Thomistic philosophy, probably the best program in Thomism offered anywhere in the country at the time. But it was a fortified city that rather effectively excluded other philosophical approaches. They took a dim view of Tom Langan's injection of existentialism into his teaching and refused to renew his contract. Modern philosophy and existentialism in particular did not become respectable and accepted in the philosophy department until the advent of Dr. James Collins, who was undoubtedly the greatest authority on modern philosophy and on existentialism in particular in the whole country. He published extensively and taught a very enlightening course in modern philosophy. I myself audited the course because I found existentialism a very helpful background for understanding the approach to the writing of many modern authors.

Tom accepted an appointment in the philosophy department at Indiana University and eventually became the chairman of the department there. He later transferred to the University of Toronto, where he has had a distinguished career as a well-published scholar and teacher. Incidentally, his wife Janine, from Paris, taught a course in literature to the honors students while they were at St. Louis University and completed work for a doctorate in comparative literature while they were at Indiana University. She was so impressed with her experience in the honors program here at St. Louis University that she later almost single-handedly introduced a similar university-wide program at the University of Toronto organized around the concept of Christian culture, which she is still directing there.

After Tom left St. Louis University, the chairmanship of the honors program went begging again. Dr. Al Fisher, also from the philosophy department, eventually took it on and provided distinctive leadership for several years. Al, incidentally, was just as interested in modern philosophy and existentialism as Tom was, but he was more cautious about advertising the fact until the area had been given respectability through Dr. Collins's influence.

Another administrative duty that still consumed some of my time was the chairmanship of the fine arts program. The program had grown so large that we had been obliged to hire two additional teachers to supply the courses demanded by interested students. There were enough students who wanted to do at least a minor in art history to justify thinking of elevating the program of courses into a full-fledged department with its own chairman. One of the teachers who was hired was David Ramsey, a practicing painter himself who had taught painting and art history for several years at the American College in Mexico City and had chaired the art department while there. The position of chairman of our budding fine arts department was offered to Dave, and he took it. He simultaneously worked for a doctorate in administration in the education department, which equipped him eventually to apply for an appointment to the chairmanship of the art department at Mercy College in Burlingame Hills, California. Under various successive chairs, the art department at St. Louis University continued to grow. It eventually included a master's program in art history, which functioned very successfully for several years, but was later eliminated in a successful attempt by then-president Father Thomas Fitzgerald to get the whole institution financially in the black. The master's program in art history, together with several other smaller programs, fell victim to that financial crunch. Since then, the programs in art history and studio art programs have been combined with music and theater into a Department of Fine and Performing Arts with the possibility of a major concentration in any of the four component areas. This experiment has worked rather well, and there is now some talk of reviving the graduate program in art history that would cooperate with the theology department, the liturgy program, the Thomas Aquinas Institute, and the new Museum of Contemporary Religious Art in offering a distinctive program in art history. I have kept up an intense interest in all of this development and have continued to teach in the program even in retirement, but I have not had any administrative duties in the program since it became a full-fledged department.

I have a way of getting caught up in activities outside of my special expertise and was gradually drawn into a very important university activity. The late 1950s and the 1960s saw a great many changes at the university. In the first place, it was a period of tremendous growth in enrollment. When I came to the university in 1944, there were only three sections of Freshman English. In the 1960s, midpoint in my chairmanship, the number had grown to forty-seven. To accommodate these hordes of students, the university had to expand its campus physically. When I arrived, the only buildings on campus were the College Church, Dubourg Hall, De Smet Hall (since torn down), the Commerce and Finance School (now called School of Business and Administration), the old Law School, and Sodality Hall (since torn down). Everything else that is now part of the much-expanded campus west of Grand was private residences, and on Laclede a large warehouse and shoe factory. The university was completely hemmed in, so much so that serious thought was being given to abandoning the Grand and Lindell site and relocating in the county. But under Father Paul Reinert's presidency, it was decided to remain at the Grand Avenue site and to expand there to help anchor that midpoint in the city, which meant that property for expansion had to be acquired piece by painful piece. It was a long and expensive process, but gradually most of the property West of Grand Avenue, now part of the campus, was acquired. This acquisition allowed for the construction of some important new buildings: several dormitories and most important of all Pius XII Memorial Library. What was formerly Xavier High School for girls was purchased and converted into a classroom building when the high school closed. The Missouri Jesuit Province purchased property on Pine west of

Spring Avenue and built Fusz Memorial Building as a house of studies for young Jesuits. The university has since purchased the building, and it now serves as a dormitory. The former Melbourne Hotel on the corner of Grand and Lindell was purchased and converted into a dormitory for women and later into the Jesuit residence on campus.

Father Reinert needed advice on the purchase and use of all this additional property, so he established a building and grounds committee, of which I was appointed chairman. It turned out to be an interesting but a somewhat time-consuming assignment because it eventually required me to work on all space allocations on the whole campus.

The greatest opportunity for the expansion of the campus came in connection with the Mill Creek project, which had involved the vacating and demolishing of all the buildings between Grand Avenue and Jefferson, an area of roughly 450 acres, in preparation for the rehabilitation of that area. It was a rather ill-conceived project, and after the buildings had been razed, the property remained vacant, like a bombed-out area, for twenty years before any redevelopment took place on it. But because of the project, 22 acres just east of Grand Avenue were now available for campus expansion. The price was $650,000, reasonable enough for that much property in the heart of the city, but the university did not have the money to make the purchase. Besides that, Protestants United for the Separation of Church and State sued the university in an attempt to prevent it from procuring the property on the basis that for the city to sell it to the university would be an infringement of separation of church and state. The suit was a long drawn out nuisance; the university eventually won the suit, although it still did not have the money to buy the property. Then Father Reinert got a brilliant idea regarding where he might procure the backing. This is a story that deserves telling.

The property that might become available to the university had an interesting history. During the Civil War, it was the site of Camp Jackson, commanded by General Daniel Marsh Frost, a southern sympathizer. It was suspected that he was accumulating equipment at Camp Jackson to make an attack on the arms supply at the arsenal. General Nathaniel Lyon, the leader of the Union sympathizers in St. Louis, determined to find out whether this was true. He disguised himself as a woman, dressed all in black and wearing a black veil, and drove though Camp Jackson in a horse and buggy on a Sunday afternoon. He discovered that General Frost had indeed had quite a bit of equipment already shipped in from the South and was ready to move on the Union arms cache at the arsenal. General Lyon marched on Camp Jackson the next day and took General Frost prisoner. Frost and his followers were marched to the arsenal but were immediately freed as prisoners of war. Frost eventually signed up with the Confederate cause and functioned for a time as commander of the Seventh Division of the Missouri State Guard. He was later commissioned brigadier-general in the Confederate army, but he resigned in 1864 and went to Canada. His wife Lily had suffered a great deal in St. Louis as the wife of a Confederate officer; she had even taken refuge in the South for a time but was eventually given permission to return to St. Louis. General Frost was very anxious to join her there and was eventually able to do so through the intervention of Father Pierre De Smet, who had known Frost for a long time and, in fact, had baptized him in 1853. De Smet had connections in Washington because of his frequent attempts to intercede with the government for the cause of the Native Americans. He succeeded in getting a pardon for General Frost from President Andrew Jackson on condition that Frost take an oath of allegiance to the Constitution of the United States. He did so on August 7, 1865, at the U.S. consulate in Quebec and then rejoined his wife Lily in St. Louis. She lived until 1872. Two years after her death, General Frost married Harriet Marie Chenie. Two daughters were born of this marriage, Edith and Harriet. It is Harriet, the younger daughter, who figures in the story of the east campus at St. Louis University.

Harriet's father, General Frost, had by inheritance and purchase acquired a large country estate called Hazelwood, from which the town Hazelwood near the airport gets its name. Harriet, as his youngest daughter, inherited the estate. The general also had five daughters from his first marriage to Lily Graham. They all traveled to England, met and married English gentlemen, and remained there. To see that this would not happen to Harriet, his youngest daughter, General Frost never let her travel to Europe in her young days. Harriet met and married a young law student at Washington University, Samuel Fordyce, who eventually became a prominent lawyer. During the First World War, he volunteered his services to the government in Washington on the War Finance Corporation. Harriet, to make up for having not been allowed to travel to Europe, volunteered to work as a nurse's aide in France. She spent the war years serving as an ambulance driver at the American Hospital at Nantilly.

After the war, she settled down at the Hazelwood estate, where she developed a fabulous garden known all over the country. She did most of the work of planning and caring for it herself. Meantime, her husband Sam went on to become a very successful lawyer, but they never had any children. Hattie was able to devote most of her time to her fantastic garden. She never forgot what the Jesuit Father De Smet had done for her father in getting him a pardon from the president and what another Jesuit, Father Eugene Murphy, had done for her husband Sam. Father Murphy baptized Sam at his own request on his deathbed. So when Hattie was getting ready to retire from the Hazelwood estate, she decided to give it to the Jesuits at St. Louis University as a place of weekend relaxation, on condition that as long as she was able, she could come out and work in the garden. It was at this juncture of Hattie's life, when she was still living in the Hazelwood mansion, that I first met her. She was beginning to move out of the mansion and was arranging to dispose of some of the things she did not think she would be using in her apartment. One of them was the large collection of her husband's books. She asked that some of us come out to check over the books and see whether they would be a useful addition to the university library. Father Reinert asked Father Yealy—who had known both Hattie and her husband Sam— the head of the university library, and me to go with him to examine the books.

I was certainly not prepared for what I met. The nearest thing to my first impression of Hattie Fordyce that I can mention is Marie Dressler's impersonation of Tugboat Annie. When Hattie greeted us at the front door, she pointed to me and told me to go out in the kitchen and mix some drinks. So I obediently went into a huge, perfectly strange kitchen, found some glasses, and got ice from the colossal refrigerator (converted to the purpose from an old-fashioned wooden icebox), and, with the ice in the glasses, discovered they were the wrong glasses for Scotch, the only liquor I could find. So I transferred the ice into the proper glasses, only to find that the only mix in evidence was one lone bottle of ginger ale, and I couldn't find a bottle opener. I tried to decap the bottle with an ice pick and broke the top off the bottle. Just then Hattie hoved into sight in the door of the kitchen, took one look at the mess on the kitchen table, and said:

"My God, who but an idiot would try to open a bottle with an ice pick?" At that she grabbed the broken bottle, sloshed the ginger ale into one of the empty glasses, handed it to me, and said: "Here, drink this, and I hope it kills you."

That was my introduction to Hattie Fordyce—not, in all conscience, a very endearing one. But we were eventually to become very good friends. With Hattie, you could always expect the unexpected. On a later visit, as we drove up to the Hazelwood mansion, we found her, dressed in a man's overalls and a man's felt hat that she always wore when she worked in her garden, sitting on the front screened-in porch with a shotgun in her lap. Her greeting was: "Well, I have just shot the only able-bodied man on the premises." And she had. She had been pursuing a rabbit that was ravaging her newly planted bulbs. When it dodged into a culvert, she let fly with her shotgun, but the shot ricocheted and went through the wrist of her gardener, Herb Ransom. She had just come back from the hospital, where she had driven Herb. He said later that the drive to the hospital was more of risk to his life than the pellet in his wrist. But when we found Hattie, she was back on her rabbit watch, shotgun in hand. On still another occasion, I dropped by to see Hattie by myself and found her sick in her huge, four-poster bed. By this time, she had agreed that we might use Hazelwood for student closed retreats as well as a place for the Jesuit faculty to relax. I was discussing with her some of the adaptations that we might be making of the space for retreat purposes. She said that the one thing she was rather sad about was what might happen to the four-poster bed in which I found her on this occasion. It was her father's bed, the bed in which he died. As I looked at it, it occurred to me it would make a fine baldachino for the altar in the chapel we were planning to install in what had been her father's library. All we would have to do is turn it sideways, move the head to the rear, and add an altar table. I suggested that to her, and she was delighted. The bed served that purpose for all the years the Hazelwood mansion was used for student retreats.

I have provided all this detail about the background of Hattie Fordyce and her father, General Frost, to show why Father Reinert thought that Hattie might be interested in financing the purchase of the property east of Grand. He went out to see Hattie, who by this time was living in a large apartment in the Montclair. "Hattie," he said, "if you will give us the money to buy the property east of Grand, where your father was taken prisoner, we will rename the north campus the Frost Campus and reverse the Civil War." The idea struck like lightning for Hattie, and without a moment's hesitation she agreed to do it. Her gift of $650,000 enabled the university to purchase the property. But there was still a problem. On the property was a rather unaesthetic bronze statue of General Lyon on horseback, commemorating his victory over General Frost. It would hardly be an appropriate centerpiece for the new Frost Campus. With Mayor Poelker's cooperation, the statue was moved, at night, to General Lyon Park near the Busch Brewery, actually not far from the arsenal that General Frost had intended to capture for the Confederates. The north campus is now known as Frost Campus. Her father's four-poster bed now graces the master bedroom in Cupples House on campus. The estate was so close to Lambert Field, however, that incoming and outgoing planes at almost tree-top level made it anything but a quiet retreat. Hattie had agreed that it could be sold after she died.

In spite of my unpropitious introduction to Hattie over a broken ginger ale bottle, we did become close friends. She used to pick up the phone at any time of the day or night and throw questions at me. One evening she called and said: "I've been doing some spiritual reading. I can take God the Father and God the Son, but who the hell is the Holy Ghost?" Try to answer that casually over the phone. I tried, but I'm sure without much satisfaction to Hattie. In fact, it wasn't with much satisfaction to myself. Hattie's question had, after all, plunged us into the center of one of the greatest mysteries of our faith. Hattie had the habit of doing that.

After the property east of Grand was secured, the next question was what to do with it. We urgently needed upgraded facilities for the physics and chemistry departments, and quarters on the Frost Campus for biology, which was then located on the South Medical Campus, so that arts and sciences students had to commute to that campus ten blocks away. We needed physical accommodations for the well-established Department of Geophysics and for the more recently founded Institute of Technology or Engineering School. It was decided to erect a complex of buildings on the new campus to accommodate all these needs. To design the complex, Father Reinert himself selected the Daly Firm, which was headquartered in Omaha, where Father Reinert had taught as a scholastic and where he got to know the Daly family well. The second Daly son, Bill, had just established an office of the firm in St. Louis. The hiring of Bill Daly created an ironic situation for me. Bill had been in my sophomore English class at Creighton Prep in Omaha, where I also taught as a scholastic. He was such a troublemaker that I had him removed from my class. The irony was that now as a member of the building and grounds committee I had to work with Bill in developing plans for the science complex. Actually, we got along very well.

I think it was probably a mistake to have engaged a mostly unknown architect to design such an important segment of the new campus. In architecture, it does not cost much more to engage the most established and prestigious architect than it does to hire a completely unknown one. It was perhaps a greater mistake to engage even less-prestigious architects for the later additions to the new campus, Ritter Hall and the Busch Memorial Student Union Building. Neither of these buildings is very distinctive aesthetically. The most pleasing building on the new campus is Tegeler Hall, which houses the School of Social Service. It was designed by Bob Enseroth, who designed several other distinctive buildings in the city, including the State Office Building just across the street from Tegeler Hall and Fitzgerald Hall just east of it.

Some people have criticized the Science Complex Bill Daly designed as being rather stark and unimaginative. Actually, it is a fairly good example of the Bauhaus style, and that is not accidental. Bill was trained at the Illinois Institute of Architecture in Chicago, which was a quasi-successor to the Bauhaus in this country after Hitler suppressed the movement in Germany. It had developed at Weimar, Dessau, and Berlin successively. Associated with its development were such important architects as Walter Gropius and Mies van der Rohe. The building that Gropius designed to house the studio and headquarters in Berlin is perhaps his most famous building and one most characteristic of the style. The science complex that Bill Daly designed for the campus here has much in common with it: a series of varied rectangular boxes with strong horizontal ribbons of alternating continuous windows and masonry, interrupted here and there by strong vertical panels of red brick. The buildings, subtly varied in height and size, are organized around a central court. Gropius, I think, would recognize his influence on the complex. Incidentally, Gropius himself emigrated to the United States after the Bauhaus was suppressed in Germany and joined the faculty of the School of Architecture at Harvard, where he designed the famous Harvard Graduate Center. The Bauhaus architects had an immense influence on the development of modern architecture from domestic to industrial buildings, not only in the United States but all over the world.

Mies van der Rohe, another important personality in the Bauhaus development who had an important influence on the development of modern architecture, also emigrated to this country in the Hitler era. He was influential in organizing the Illinois Institute of Architecture in Chicago, where Bill Daly was trained; he designed the buildings in which the institute was housed. So the Daly science center complex on the new campus at St. Louis University owes much to the Bauhaus movement. Even a casual comparison of the complex here to the Bauhaus building designed by Gropius in Berlin, recently restored, and to the buildings of the Illinois Institute of Architecture in Chicago, designed by Mies van der Rohe, will reveal that influence.

Another extremely important building project on campus was the plan for a new central library. This project was also entrusted to Bill Daly, and the story of its planning is bizarre to say the least. A new library building was one of the most important needs of the institution, made even more imperative because of Father Lowrie Daly's inspired idea to seek and procure permission from the Vatican to film the vast manuscript collection of the Vatican Library. Pope Pius XII had finally granted permission for the project, and the Knights of Columbus had agreed to finance the undertaking. The project was under way, so that it became imperative to have a proper place to house the microfilms and a room where they could be projected and studied. Father Joseph Donnelly, head librarian at the time, was commissioned to start planning a new library. Joe was a fine librarian but rather rigid and very traditional in his ideas of how a library should be organized. The plan he came up with for the inner working of the library was the old closed-stack arrangement in which the public had no access to the stacks themselves. That arrangement had already been shown to be educationally ineffective in a university library, but Joe stuck to his guns. This inner organizational and spatial arrangement was given to the architect to incorporate into his physical plans for the new building. That was mistake number one.

Mistake number two was the initial method employed to raise money to pay for the building. A possible unnamed benefactor was approached, who seemed very interested in the project and who was financially capable of contributing substantially. He was made chairman of the fund-raising committee. It soon became apparent that his chief interest in the building was not its function as a library but its presentation as a physical monument to himself. He kept insisting on checking every detail of the external design of the building and kept demanding that it be made more and more monumental; he insisted on grand stairwells that resembled those in old nineteenth-century libraries and museums, which consumed vast amounts of space, and on more and more impressive ornament in the way of mosaics, fancy brickwork, and sculpture on the exterior. As the cost of all this monumentality soared, there was no certainty that the benefactor would really come through with the money to pay for it. Besides that, the gentleman who had been hired to help raise money for the building had turned out to be inept, "full of sound and fury, signifying [and realizing in hard cash] nothing." So it became apparent to Father Reinert and the Board of Trustees that something radical had to be done. The decision of the board was indeed radical. They decided to disengage the chairman of the fund-raising committee, to dismiss the fund-raiser, and to appoint a new librarian.

The new librarian was James Jones, the first non-Jesuit to hold the position at the university. He took one look at the inner plans of the library that had been worked out by Father Donnelly on the old closed-stack plan and said they simply had to go. A new start, he insisted, had to be made using an open-stack plan that would provide airy, light, comfortable reading spaces throughout the library. He and his staff worked long and diligently to come up with an adequate inner plan, which was eventually given to the architect, Bill Daly. Bill's designs provided effectively all the space arrangements suggested by the librarians: a central open-stack area of three floors and two mezzanines, and an open, bright, reading space extending around the entire periphery of these three main floors. The exterior, as Bill originally conceived it, was really a very beautiful example of Bauhaus design. It was a very large horizontal glass rectangle seeming to float in space. It rested on a rather narrow recessed first-floor pedestal covered with tiles in a random blue and white pattern. The only visible sign of support of the glass rectangle box was a row of round columns covered with gray tile that rose from the ground, pierced all three floors several feet behind the glass wall of the rectangle, and terminated at the roof. This design would give the whole structure a light floating appearance. It really was a beautiful design.

When the librarians saw it, however, they said it would not do. They could not have all that uninhibited sun pouring in on the books in the stacks. The glass walls would have to be broken up by some opaque surfaces. This design was a completely new *second* set of working plans for the building, so everybody concerned felt that there was no way that a new start could be made on the design, especially because the demands of the new librarian and his cohorts had been so satisfactorily met on the interior of the building. So the architect was commissioned to provide somehow the amount of opaque surfaces on the exterior walls that the librarians were demanding, which accounts for the alternating large, high, vertical windows and brick panels that now make up what would have been the architect's light floating glass box. But to support the additional weight of the heavy brick panels the architect had to add square columns to the base. These columns do the job, but they destroy the graceful floating impression of the structure as the architect had conceived it. The supports look like what they are: crutches supporting the building. The only redeeming feature of the changed design is that it did provide flat brick wall spaces on the interior that lent themselves to the display of paintings. I recognized that possibility and had the architect build in rods in the brick panels from which paintings could be hung. In time, our considerable collection of modern art was hung on these walls, so that the reading area around the periphery of the building has become an actual art gallery. All the students who use the building are exposed to some worthwhile art here, and some of it rubs off on them, many of whom would not take the trouble to go to an art museum.

A reorientation of the entrance to the building much later added a semicircular projection on the east side of the building that changes and improves the exterior appearance. On the interior, it provides a handsome grand stairwell giving access to all five stories of the building. It was designed by architect Ted Wofford. Frank Peters, a knowledgeable architectural critic, has called it one of the most handsome new architectural spaces in the city.

With the cooperation of the new librarian and the architect, a very satisfactory space arrangement for the interior of the new library was worked out, although the final compromise solution for the exterior leaves something to be desired aesthetically. The fund-raising campaign, however, remained a problem. It was finally decided that a new chairman of the campaign would have to be appointed. The elder Mr. Morton May, president of the Famous-Barr Department Stores, was persuaded to take over the job. In a short while, he succeeded in raising the approximately $4 million that the building eventually cost.

In the course of the campaign, I got to know the young Morton May and learned about his extraordinary collection of German expressionist art containing a very strong representation of the works of Max Beckmann. It occurred to me that it might be interesting to exhibit the collection in the new Pius XII Library on the occasion of its dedication. I suggested the idea to Morton, and he was enthusiastic about it. He said that actually he himself had never seen his collection together because a very large part of it was in storage. So we went to work preparing for the exhibit. The whole collection was moved to the storage vault in the new library, where we could work on it. I organized the exhibit, wrote the catalog for it, and, incidentally, learned a great deal about German expressionism in the process. The Morton May collection still remains one of the most extensive collections of German expressionism anywhere and of Max Beckmann in particular. Mr. May eventually gave the major part of it to the St. Louis Art Museum, where it now ranks as one of its most distinctive collections, but it was seen for the first time in its entirety in the new Pius XII Library.

This opening exhibit created quite a stir in the art world. Morton May invited everybody who was anybody in the area of modern art, including Max Beckman's widow and Alfred Barr, who was curator of the Museum of Modern Art in New York at the time. Mr. May flew all the guests in and entertained them at a lavish dinner at the Trader Vic's Restaurant. The exhibit was given the center spread in *Time* magazine, which brought national and international attention to the collection and, incidentally, to the Pius XII Library. One of the happy benefits of the event for me was getting to know Morton May himself. He became very supportive of our budding art program at the university, contributed some significant art works to our collection, and eventually set up an endowment of $70,000, the income of which was to help finance art exhibits in our gallery.

Speaking of art reminds me that there was a plan from the beginning to commission an important work of art in connection with the library as a memorial to Pope Pius XII. The architect had suggested a fountain in the Lindell Plaza in front of the library. His plan for it included a life-size bronze figure of the pope in full pontificals. I was not very pleased by the suggestion. I did not think it was particularly appropriate to have the pope in his full pontifical robes being perpetually sprayed by the fountain, but I was overruled by the Board of Trustees, who liked the design. I did, however, persuade them to select an important artist, the internationally known Yugoslavian sculptor Ivan Mestrovic, to do the work. Mestrovic has sometimes been called the modern Michelangelo. Some of his work has the same kind of dynamic quality that characterizes the best of Michelangelo's sculpture. At the time, Mestrovic had a studio at Notre Dame University. The architect's suggestion for the fountain was sent on to him, and he began work on the figure of the pope. After several months, he invited someone from the university to come over and check on the to-scale plaster model he had completed. Father Reinert and I went to Notre Dame, and when we arrived in the artist's studio, we were greeted by the full to-scale plaster model of the pope in full pontificals on display at one end of the large studio. It was a good likeness of his holiness, although I still had reservations about this figure eventually to be cast in bronze standing in full pontificals in a perennial shower, but if that is what was wanted, I presumed Mestrovic's work would do. When we had given the artist our not too enthusiastic reaction to the model, he went to the other end of his large studio and drew back a heavy curtain to reveal a completely finished to-scale plaster model of an alternate representation of Pope Pius XII formally seated on a throne. "This is the monument that the pope, the library, and the occasion call for," was the artist's remark. "Pope Pius XII has given the university the permission to microfilm all the manuscripts of the Vatican Library. The films will be housed in the new library, so it is an image of the pope as a teacher that is called for here. The chair or *cathedra* is a symbol of that teaching function, and I have also given Pius the Byzantine gesture of the teacher and enlarged his right hand to call attention to that." He had, indeed.

In the Byzantine gesture of the teacher, the index and middle fingers are held upright, and the little and ring fingers touch the thumb.

The symbol of the rhetorician in old classical iconography, it was taken over by the early Byzantine iconographers as a symbol of Christ the Teacher. Christ as Pantocrator (Ruler and Teacher) was always given this gesture in Byzantine art, as were the four evangelists in their function as teachers.

So Mestrovic was utterly right in giving this symbolic gesture to his image of Pius XII as teacher. What could be more appropriate than that and the *cathedra,* another symbol of the teacher, for a memorial of Pope Pius XII in front of the library dedicated to him, a library housing the films of the thousands of manuscripts from the Vatican Library? The figure that the artist had conceived was so appropriate that Father Reinert and I, then and there, told him to go ahead with this image and forget the other one. Mestrovic had rescued the pope from a perennial shower.

# 12

# In Pursuit of Modern Art

THE SUCCESS of the Morton May Show of German Expressionism prompted us to mount some similar shows in the new Pius XII Library. One of the most important was a retrospective show of the works of Fred Conway, the "Mr. Chips" of the local art community at the time. The show displayed more than two hundred of Fred's works, which we had to assemble from owners who had purchased them over the years. They illustrated all the various styles Fred had employed in his evolution as an artist. There was a huge turnout for the opening because Fred was so well known in the community. One of the pleasant by-products of the project for me was getting to know Fred himself. We developed a firm friendship that lasted until his death. He eventually painted a fine three-quarter-length portrait of Father Reinert, and we acquired several more of his paintings, including an excellent self-portrait. He did a series of impressionistic renderings of various buildings in St. Louis. Washington University, where he taught, commissioned him to do an impressionistic painting of Dubourg Hall and the College Church, which it presented to St. Louis University on the occasion of our sesquicentennial. So, in a way, the Conway show occasioned our first venture into collecting modern art. The university owned a small collection of older paintings, chiefly Flemish, that had been brought here from Belgium by Father De Smet back in the 1830s and 1840s. The Conway paintings were the first modern works to be added to the collection.

The next push in the direction of beginning a modern collection came by way of a gift from Leonard Scheller, a brother of Father Al Scheller in the sociology department. Leonard, who was a staff member of the *Milwaukee Journal,* had become an aficionado of Georges Rouault. He had purchased three copies of the famous *Miserere* and *Guerre* series of original aquatints, with fifty-eight aquatints in each set. Leonard gave a complete set to Marquette University in Milwaukee and one to St. Louis University. Over a period of years, he gave individual lithographs from the third set to Catholic universities and colleges all over the country.

I had our set of aquatints properly matted and framed, and we exhibited the complete set for the first time in the Pius XII Library. I decided to make an occasion of the event and borrowed important paintings by Rouault for the display. They included a beautiful life-size figure of Christ from Morton May's collection and the painting *The Chinaman* from the St. Louis Art Museum. Rouault's ironic inscription on this lithograph reads, *"Chinois inventa, dit-on, la poudre a canon, nous on fit don"* (the Chinese invented gunpowder, they say, and made a gift of it to us). The painting *The Chinaman* is a development in oil of the same image (number 38) in the *Miserere* lithograph series. I had heard that Sam J. Levin and Audrey Levin owned two small gouaches by Rouault: *The Clown* and *The Circus Performer.* The Levins' chief residence was in Miami Beach, but they maintained a modest residence in St. Louis, where they came from originally. The two Rouaults hung in the St. Louis residence. Sam and Audrey readily consented to loan them, and when I arranged to return the paintings after the show, they said: "Why don't you keep them? We are in St. Louis for such a short time each year, and the paintings hang in an empty house for most of the year. They might just as well be where they can be enjoyed by the public the year round." That was the beginning of a relationship that ultimately resulted in gifts of art to our burgeoning collection of modern art that is now valued at more than $2 million.

The Levins were friends of Charles Yalem, a graduate of St. Louis University Dental School. He practiced dentistry for only a year after graduating, then invested his profits for the year in an insurance company, which he eventually took over, and became very wealthy. The Levins got him interested in investing in modern art. To begin with, they persuaded him to buy an abstract gouache by the prominent Russian painter Serge Poliakoff. Dr. Yalem eventually found it not to his liking, so Sam Levin suggested that he donate it to St. Louis University, his alma mater. He did so. His gift established a contact that became very important in realizing a formal program of procuring modern art for the university collection. That program became a possibility as the result of another fortuitous personal encounter of mine.

Steve Vasquez, the dean of the School of Commerce and Finance, had instigated a weekly lunch-hour program for one semester of the students' senior year to broaden their cultural horizons. He invited speakers from various departments in the university to speak on their areas of concentration to the seniors during a brown bag lunch hour. He invited me to speak on modern art, which I did. Dr. Theo Haimann, a professor of business administration in the commerce school, was in the audience. He came up after my talk, thanked me for it, and said that he had a special interest in modern art and had in his home a modest collection of it that he thought I might like to see sometime. I took him up on his invitation and was amazed to discover the extent and quality of his collection. It contained fine examples of first-rate contemporary French and Italian artists who were well represented in most important modern museums in Europe but not well known on this side of the Atlantic. The central treasures of the collection were six paintings by one of the most prominent modern Italian artists, Georgio Morandi, whose works were chosen to represent Italy in the Italian Pavilion in one of the Venetian Biennale Exhibitions. They actually were the most beautiful Morandi paintings I have ever seen anywhere, including those shown in the Biennale, which I had the good fortune of seeing. I discovered that Theo knew Morandi personally; some of his paintings were gifts of the artist, and the others Theo had purchased directly from the artist himself.

I became fascinated with Theo's own background. He was born and raised in Koblenz, Germany, by Jewish parents. His father was in charge of the Jewish cemetery there. Theo had developed an interest in art very early and had some talent as a painter. He thought that he might make painting a career, but he soon decided that he probably did not have sufficient talent to guarantee permanent success as an artist, so he decided to go to Bonn University and begin a doctoral program in business administration. He was working in Bonn during the rise of Nazism in Germany. When the time came to sit for his oral doctoral examination, he had to say "Heil, Hitler" before he sat down to be examined. Theo "heiled" him, passed the examination with distinction, and then left Germany and settled down on the left bank in Paris to write his dissertation. He was living very close to the Academie des Beaux-Arts and in the midst of the most important commercial art galleries in Paris. He haunted the galleries and got to know all the directors personally. Through his own art background,

Theo had developed a sensitive eye, and he began buying small paintings of young artists whose work he liked, but who as yet were not well known. Many of these artists went on to make fine reputations in the art world, and the value of their works increased substantially, but Theo had purchased their work in the first place just because he admired it.

Theo and I kept in contact with one another, and later, when I was asked to plan an exhibit of modern art on the occasion of the sesquicentennial celebration of the university, I recalled Theo's experience on the left bank of Paris. I asked him to help plan the show. We decided that instead of doing a loan show that would leave us only a catalog after the show was over, we would try to get a small donation in order to acquire some modern works of art as a nucleus of our own modern collection. Charles Yalem, the donor of the Poliakoff gouache, came to mind. We approached him with the idea, and he made a gift of $25,000 for the project. We realized that this amount was a ridiculously small sum with which to consider buying any significant modern art, but then we recalled Theo's experience on the left bank buying the work of young artists who appealed to him, before their reputations were made, for little or nothing. We thought it might be interesting to try to duplicate that experience.

When Theo had finished the dissertation for his doctoral program at Bonn, he and his whole family had left Germany and come to America because of Hitler and the Nazis' threats to the Jewish community. He started a very successful leather goods business in New York. Eventually he moved it to St. Louis, where he met his wife Ruth, who with her family had fled from Russia. Although very successful as a businessman, Theo wanted to get back to the academic world. When an opening in the business school of the University of Arizona became available, he applied for it and got it. But Ruth did not like Arizona, so when an opening in the business school at St. Louis University became available, he applied for it and was hired. He had an extremely successful career here at the university as a professor of business administration. He taught in the school full-time and even after he retired continued teaching up until three weeks before he died of cancer. All during his years in business and also during his career as a teacher, he made regular trips to Europe a couple of times a year. On all those trips, he kept up his contact with the commercial art galleries in Paris and Italy, so he still had an easy entrée to that commercial art world.

In 1965, I received a Fulbright research grant for a year of study in Belgium. Theo and I agreed to meet in Paris during the semester break to see what modern art we might be able to procure in the galleries there and in Italy. Theo personally knew most of the directors of all the left-bank galleries. We made a survey of the main galleries and settled on some young artists whose work appealed to us. We told the directors what we were planning: the initiation of a collection of modern art at a midwestern university that had none. They were very interested and cooperative, and agreed that if we were interested in the work of any of the artists they carried, they would not object to our approaching the artists themselves and arranging to purchase directly from them—an extraordinary concession on their part because it cut out their commission. We did that in several instances and bought the paintings we wanted for a very reasonable price because the artists were quite interested in being represented in this budding university collection. We followed the same procedure in galleries in Milan and Rome, and succeeded finally in purchasing more than forty paintings for the collection. Most of the artists whose works we purchased were not well known at the time, but we liked their work. Some of them still remain relatively unknown, but the reputations of others have taken off; they are represented in important museums all over Europe. They include such artists as the Italians Valerio Adami, Piero Dorazio, Livio Marzot, Gastione Novelli, Claudio Olivier, Marino Marini, Achille Perilli, Mario Schifano, and Emilio Tadini; the French Georges Noel and Michel Tyzszlat; the Belgians Pierre Alechinsky and Gustave Singier; the Russians André Lanskoy and Serge Poliakoff; the Germans Horst Antes and Ghislain Uhrey; the Hungarian Lazlo Mohay-Nagy; the Mexican Rudolfo Nieto; and the Chinese Zao Wu Ki. All of these artists are now well represented in important European museums, but with the exception of Marino Marini, none of them were represented at that time in any other collections here in St. Louis. The present appraised value of the paintings of just these artists in our collection is more than $300,000, so financially we did rather well with the meager $25,000 we had to invest in our inchoate modern art collection. The works of the other artists we purchased who are less well recognized have been appraised at \$45,700, so even their work has more than doubled in value since we purchased it.

We also had another financial arrangement that enabled us to purchase some works by artists whose reputations were already well established and whose works were commanding prices that we could not afford on our meager budget. Sam J. Levin and Audrey Levin, who had given us the two Rouault gouaches, had become interested in our endeavor to start a collection of modern art at the university. They agreed to finance purchases of art by some of these established artists if we could succeed in driving a bargain with the gallery directors on the purchases. We would purchase the paintings for the Levins; they would remain on loan from the Levins until their appraised value exceeded the purchase price and the Levins would donate the paintings for a tax deduction. In the process, the Levins actually made money by the donations, and we had the paintings. It was through that procedure that we acquired paintings by this list of important artists: the Italians Enrico Baj, Giuseppe Cappogrossi, Bruno Caruso, Marino Marini, and Mario Russo; the French Gabriel Dachot, Siemes Eppele, Jean Helion, Georges Matthieu, Pincus Kremegne, Mario Laurenciene, Bernard Lorzou, André Marchand, Richard Pousette D'Art, Maurice Savin, and Theo Tobiasse; the Russians Natalia Gontcharova and Mikhail Larinov; the Americans Carlyle Browne, John Massey, Hassel Smith, and Jack Tworkov; the Germans Horst Antes, Hans Hartung, and Ernest Kirchner; the Swiss Leo Leuppi; the Austrian Friederick Hundertwasser; the Dutch Lucebert (van Swaanswijh) and Anton Rooskens; and the Japanese Juro Yashihara. The present appraised value of these paintings is close to \$300,000.

The works of many modern artists, of course, were selling at prices much higher than the Levins wanted to pay, but Theo and I devised a way of having these artists represented in our collection. We could get original lithographs by them, which were selling in European galleries for much less than in any American gallery. This was true even of American artists. The Levins were willing to finance the purchase of the more expensive ones, and we devised a method of financing the purchase of others on our own. Theo made annual trips to Europe. He would canvas the commercial galleries for lithographs we were interested in and purchase what we could with the help of the Levins. Where multiple copies were available, he would purchase several copies. We would keep one for our permanent collection and sell the rest at pre-Christmas sales, which were always well attended. We used the proceeds to purchase additional lithographs for our own collection.

As a result of this maneuver, we were able to add fine original lithographs by a great many outstanding artists to our collection, including the following: the Italians Valerio Adami, Enrico Baj, Giuseppe Cappogrossi, Lucio del Pezzo, Marino Marini, Mario Schifano, and Emilio Tadini; the French Jean Bazaine, Georges Braque, Sonia Delauney, Jean Dubuffet, Maurice Estève, Jean Fautrier, Christian Fossier, Jean Iposteguy, Fernand Leger, Alfred Menessier, Jean Messagier, Georges Rouault, Niki de St. Phalle, Claude Serre, Pierre Soulages, and Gerard Titus-Carmel; the Germans Horst Antes, Jean Arp, Max Ernst, Wolfgang Goefgen, Hans Hartung, and Kathe Kollwitz; the Belgians Pierre Alechensky, Jacharoff Christo, Paul Delvaux, Jean Folon, René Magritte, and Gustave Singier; the British Francis Bacon, Peter Green, Richard Hamilton, and Henry Moore; the Russians Marc Chagall, Wassily Kandinsky, and André Lanskoy; the Spaniards Eduardo Chillida, Antoni Clavé, Salvador Dali, Lucio Feito, Pablo Picasso, and Antoni Tapies; the Americans Joseph Albers, Alexander Calder, Ron Davis, Sam Francis, Frederick Franck, Ellsworth Kelly, Edward Kienholz, Robert Motherwell, LeRoy Nieman, Robert Rauschenberg, Man Ray, Larry Rivers, Norman Rockwell, and Mark Tobey; the Dutch Karel Appel and Bran van Velde; the Swiss Alberto Giacometti and Paul Klee; the Austrians Friederich Hundertwasser; the Danish Asgar Jorn; the Cuban Wilfredo Lam; the Chilean Matta (Matta Echaurren); the Dalmatian Antonio Music; the Argentinian Antonio Segui; the Mexican Rufino Tamayo; the Hungarian Victor Vassarely; and the Chinese Zao Wu Ki. We were more than satisfied with this very good start on a collection of modern art. Additions have been made to the collection since, and very significant examples of art by outstanding contemporary artists are being added to the university holdings through the new Museum of Contemporary Religious Art (MOCRA) organized and managed by Father Terry Dempsey. It specializes in exhibiting the work of artists of any faith from all over the country who have a religious dimension in their work. Several of these artists have donated works to the permanent collection.

As always in such a venture as Theo's and my pursuit of modern art, we had some very memorable experiences. When we were arranging to purchase a painting by Piero Dorazio in the Maeght Gallery in Rome, we were attracted to a beautiful bronze disk by the prominent contemporary Italian sculptor Arnaldo Pomodoro. The gallery was asking $6,000 for it, a price beyond our limited budget, but we thought we might be able to acquire it with the help of the Levins if we could get the gallery to reduce the price somewhat. It finally did. We got it for $5,000 and had it on loan from the Levins for several years. During that time, Pomodoro's reputation soared on both sides of the Atlantic and so did his prices. When the Levins finally donated the piece to us, it was appraised at $35,000 and would probably be appraised today at more than $100,000. Pomodoro for several years split his time between the art department at California, Berkeley, and his studio in Milan. His work became increasingly well received. One of his large spheres is on permanent display just outside the new university museum at Berkeley, and another even more impressive one now graces one of the large courts in the Vatican Museum in Rome.

Because we had just purchased one of his works, Theo and I called on Pomodoro in his studio when we returned to Milan from Rome. We found him in a forest of plaster models of some new commissions on which he was working. He specializes in very large bronze globes, disks, or columns that are mostly made of highly polished bronze surfaces. But these surfaces are broken open by irregular gashes revealing roughly hewn abstract shapes that look rather chaotic in contrast to the highly finished polished surfaces. In discussing his work, he said that in the globe, the circular disk, and the strong polished columns he was trying to express humans' perennial quest for perfection, a quest that is never completely realized. This inhibiting intrusion of rough reality into the striving for perfection he symbolizes by the broken forms disrupting the smooth perfection of the globe, the circle, and the column. I have asked visitors to our gallery, who are sometimes puzzled by Pomodoro's work, to try to express what they think the artist was endeavoring to communicate in the highly polished but fractured disk. After a little concentration, they almost always come up with an idea pretty close to what Arnaldo himself said he had intended—a pretty good indication that the artist was successful in what he had set out to do. Our meeting with Pomodoro was a very pleasant one. When we were getting ready to leave, he reached up on a shelf and handed me a beautiful little silver sculpture he had done that expressed the same idea. He said he wanted me to have it because I was the first priest he ever met that knew anything about modern art, and he wanted me to have a piece of his.

We had an encounter with another artist in Milan that was also very rewarding in many ways. While we were there, a very large retrospective of Lucio Fontana's work was on display in one of the galleries, more than three hundred paintings showing the complete development of the Argentinean artist's work. Fontana, unlike most of the artists whose works we had purchased, was at the end of his career, not at its beginning. We learned that he was actually ill in the hospital at the moment, but we decided to call on him, explain our project, and see whether he would be interested in donating one of his works to our collection or in giving it to us for a nominal sum. We called him in the hospital, and he said he would be glad to talk to us. He was very interested in our project and told us to call his secretary, make an appointment to meet her at his studio, pick out a medium-size painting, which he would let us have at the price we were paying for the works of the neophytes on our list. What he actually charged us was $450 at a time when his paintings were bringing thousands of dollars. We were flabbergasted at his interest and generosity. What we chose was a medium-size painting in the style that Fontana had become famous for—a plain pure white canvas with three razorblade slashes in it—a minimalist painting if there ever was one. By this time, he was famous all over the world for this kind of minimalist design. Dozens of the paintings in his retrospective show were subtle variations on this motif. We were overjoyed in being able to add a Fontana to our collection.

The painting remained in our collection until 1990, when it created an opportunity we could not afford to pass up. That was the period when the art market had gone wild through the irrational activity of the Japanese, climaxed by the purchase of a Van Gogh for $82 million. The Japanese were also purchasing the works of other artists at the time for very inflated prices. I noted that a Fontana painting very similar to ours had been sold by Sotheby's to a Japanese purchaser for more than $100,000. Having a substantial debt to pay off on Cupples House, the mansion I was restoring on campus, I saw in the inflated art market at the time an opportunity to raise a substantial sum to help pay off the debt by putting our Fontana up for sale. I hated to part with it because of all the circumstances that surrounded our getting it and also because it was such a good example of minimalist art. But the market was already plummeting; the bottom had already fallen out of the Japanese boom. However, the Japanese were still buying Fontanas at inflated prices because they found his minimalism much to their taste. I knew that we would probably never again have the opportunity of benefiting by the inflated price of the moment, so I eventually put the painting up for sale at Sotheby's in New York, much to my friend Theo Haimann's chagrin. The board agreed that we should make the sale. It brought $120,000. Five other collectors had also thought this was the moment to sell Fontanas. Five other paintings by him were in the same sale at Sotheby's, and they all brought similar prices.

Theo and I ended our art expedition back in Paris, where we decided to approach another well-established artist to try to interest him in helping us acquire one of his works for our collection. The artist was the Russian painter André Lanskoy. We had become very interested in his beautiful abstractions in our first go-around in the Parisian galleries, but we knew that his works were well out of the range of our meager budget. We thought he might be interested in doing something like what Fontana had done. We called and made an appointment to visit the artist in his combination apartment and studio in the Bois-de-Boulogne. Some of his friends whom we had met in one of the galleries told us that Lanskoy was something of an eccentric. He lived up to his reputation. He met us at the door of his apartment dressed in an approximation of the outfit that I had seen Portuguese fishermen wearing in the fishing village of Nazare when they were ready to leave on a week's fishing trip at sea: a heavy, bright-colored, plaid woolen jacket and trousers, and a stocking cap of the same material falling down to the waist, tapering off to a point, and ending in a red tassel. I don't know where André had gotten the outfit or why he was wearing it, but wearing it he was. He served us vodka and Russian sweets, and then took us into his studio to show us what he was working on at the time—a set of beautiful lithographs illustrating *The Divine Comedy*. They, of course, were representational and very unlike his abstract paintings that had so intrigued us, although they did share the same brilliant color. The artist's abstractions are created by applying bright rich colors to the canvas in broad swaths with a palette knife. This multicolored surface of broad patches of color create something like the effect of an abstract stained glass window. No other artist that I know of has worked quite in this manner. Lanskoy had several of these paintings in various sizes in his studio that he had just finished. We were particularly attracted to a medium-size one. We explained what we were trying to do and expressed our interest in having one of his works in our collection. He seemed interested in our project, and he said he would be willing to sell us any painting we chose for half what he would get for it through a gallery. That price was still well out of the range of our small budget, but we felt we could manage it through the arrangement we had made with the Levins. We purchased it in their name and kept the painting on loan from them for several years. When they finally donated it to our collection, the value had doubled what the artist was asking for it when we bought it. As we were leaving Lanskoy's studio, he brought out a beautiful signed abstract lithograph and inscribed a dedication to me on it. Like Arnaldo Pomodoro, he said he wanted me to have it because the experience of a priest interested in modern art was something new to him. This purchase completed our little commercial venture into modern art. Theo returned to his classes in business administration at St. Louis University, and I returned to my work on the vested angels in Flemish painting at the Institut du Patrimoine Artistique in Brussels. We were both quite happy with the start we had made in those two weeks on developing a collection of modern art at St. Louis University. When the material we had purchased finally arrived in St. Louis, we mounted a show in the Pius XII Library. We also included in it the entire *Miserere* and *La Guerre* series of aquatints by Georges Rouault. Mr. Yalem and the Levins were at the opening, and both they and we were proud of this modest beginning that modern art had at last made at St. Louis University.

# 13
# Vignettes from Foreign Workshops

MY FRIEND and Jesuit confrere, Father Trafford Maher, had for years offered an academic program in human relations. He had also conducted human relations seminars for the staff and personnel of several of the big department stores in the city. He persuaded me to make presentations in his campus academic workshops. In one, I drew on my study of the changing concept of the hero down through the ages and then had the class try to determine what the modern concept of the hero is, if there is one. The discussion brought out many of the shifting attitudes about human greatness in successive ages and different cultures and helped the students become more aware of what their own age and culture deem admirable. I was reminded of those discussions recently by the TV series *Journey: The World of Joseph Campbell,* composed and presented by KPBS, San Diego, on the changing concept of the hero down through the ages. Campbell's conclusion was much like ours. Our age is not one that makes much of heroes; those we have are apt to be examples of what the age admires most, successful business tycoons. The old saw is still true: "Tell me whom you admire, and I'll tell you who you are."

Father Maher also wanted me to draw on my art background to help the students learn what art can reveal about the shifting values of different cultures. I thought the best medium in which to do this for a group of students indifferently prepared in art would be architecture, so I built up a slide presentation featuring Athens, ancient Rome, medieval Chartres, Renaissance Florence, northern Renaissance Ghent, and modern Manhattan. With a fine set of detailed slides of these sites, it was easy to highlight where the values lay in the various cultures. Athens with its high acropolis supporting the temples of the gods and overlooking the agora below—that marketplace of goods and ideas—is a visual image of typical Greek values. The Parthenon is an exquisitely wrought temple to Athena, the goddess of intelligence, and the open colonnades of the agora were the site of both the marketplace and the peripatetic discussions of Plato, Socrates, and Aristotle. Art and philosophy were the Greeks' great contributions to the world. But the Greeks were highly individualistic, a trait revealed in the way the various buildings are distributed on the acropolis—haphazardly, as if they were dropped from the sky and stayed where they landed. The result of this exaggerated individualism is revealed in Greek history. They never succeeded in developing a unified Greece or an empire except for a short spurt under Alexander. Mostly they remained a cluster of separate city-states generally warring with one another. Much of this history is revealed in the picture of Athens.

What stands out in the sketches of ancient Rome are the several highly organized fora, made up of perfectly axialized successive buildings—a great marketplace open court surrounded by storied shops; a great covered basilica or assembly place for large gatherings, with the law courts situated in the projecting apses; a smaller open court with a library on one side and a museum on the other. In two of these fora, we find great triumphal columns recording in low relief the conquest of two great emperors (Trajan and Marcus Aurelius) and beyond that a temple to the gods. The forum reflects most of the values that made Rome great: reverence for the gods; the importance of the emperor or ruler; law; order; conquest and empire; and the subordination of the individual to the gods, the state, and the family. Elsewhere in the sketch are great domineering buildings that helped keep the populace happy and amused: the great public baths, the coliseum, and the theaters. In the market and these places of recreation were supplied the *panis et circenses* that kept the masses happy and contented. Theaters in Rome were open to the general public, which accounts for the violence on the stage that was systematically excluded from the Greek theater. The Greek theater was reserved for freemen, who made up less than one-third of the Athenian population. The rest were all slaves. The Roman sense of organization, law, and order, and the Roman emphasis on duties made possible the building of the far-flung Roman Empire. In the sketch of ancient Rome, the fact of that empire shows up in the several triumphal arches, from that of Titus to that of Constantine, which record the various victories of successive emperors.

Any picture of the city of Chartres, whether it is an ancient sketch or a modern photograph, shows the great Gothic cathedral spires rising above the city and dominating everything below it. That dominance continues no matter where you are in the city: in the marketplace, in one of the side streets or canals, in a residential area, or in the open plaza in front of the cathedral itself. And that dominance is a pretty good symbol of the pervasive presence of religion and the church in the lives of people in the Middle Ages. The cathedral itself was the center of a great deal of that life. The some three thousand sculptures on the exterior were constant reminders to the populace of the truths of their faith and their historical past. The interior, transformed by the miraculous color and light of its great stained glass windows, was a constant refuge from the turmoil and weight of the world outside, a haven of peace and spiritual inspiration. The Liturgy and Latin liturgical drama performed there on great feast days were a source of instruction and emotional uplift the year round. Religion did indeed touch the lives of high and low alike from birth to death: baptism, confirmation, the Eucharist, marriage, confession and reconciliation, and finally extreme unction and viaticum were all sacramental steps on the way. The cathedral was a constant reminder to the often less than edified medieval Christian of where his duties lay.

A shift to a sketch of Renaissance Florence or to a photograph of modern Florence for that matter, considering that the skyline has changed very little, shows the city dominated by the great dome of its cathedral or duomo. But it is significant that we almost always speak of Brunelleschi's dome and Giotto's campanile or bell tower, the great bronze doors of Ghiberti on the baptistery, and the David of Michelangelo when we are talking about Florence. The Renaissance was the age of the individual. We speak of the Renaissance man, and we mean by that an individual genius, a man such as Michelangelo, who was a sculptor, painter, architect, and reputable poet. We are reminded of the achievements of these individual geniuses no matter where we look in a photograph of Florence or in walking its streets. The other thing that stands out in any sketch of Renaissance Florence or in a photograph of the modern city is the fact that it is punctuated by palaces of the great—the Medici, the Pitti, or the Strozzi. The Renaissance was the age of great families who were strong political leaders and great patrons of the arts, and they built impressive palaces to declare publicly their importance to the community; the palaces are still there and continue to make that declaration. The community was ruled by an aristocracy of wealth, power, and taste in the Renaissance. The very structures of Florence make us keenly aware of that.

A picture of the city of Ghent in the northern Low Countries tells a very different story. Cheek by jowl with the tower of St. Bavo's Cathedral is the equally if not more impressive tower of the central meeting hall for the guilds of the city. Here mercantilism is given equal billing with religion. Ghent was ruled not by an elitist aristocracy but by nouveaux riches merchants who had gained their wealth and position by successful mercantile ventures. The warehouse that received the wool from England that was spun into cloth and then merchandized the world over still stands today along the river and is still functioning as a warehouse. Down along the river is a whole series of step-gabled guildhalls that speak eloquently of the craft and merchant guilds that made Ghent wealthy and famous. One of its merchant mayors, Judocus Veyt, added to his fame by commissioning the most prominent Netherlandish painter, Jan van Eyck, to paint what is probably the most famous Flemish painting in the world, the *Ghent Altarpiece* or *The Adoration of the Lamb,* for a chapel in St. Bavo's Cathedral. It is still on display in the cathedral and has unquestionably added to the fame of its donor, whose portrait, along with that of his wife, is displayed on its exterior panels. Unlike their neighbor city, Bruges, which might be compared to Florence in its opulent patronage of artists, Ghent did not have a reputation for patronage of the arts. Only one prominent artist came from there, Justus van Gand. He painted the famous *Triptych of the Crucifixion* for the cathedral and then picked up his brushes and went to the court of the duke of Urbino in Italy, where he remained for the rest of his life. The everyday work of their craftsmen and the success of their merchants were more important to the citizens of Ghent than artistic achievement. That emphasis is apparent in the prominence of the tower of the Central Guild Meeting Hall and of the many smaller guildhalls in the Ghent cityscape.

Our final discussion in this workshop revolved around a wide-angle photograph of Manhattan. From whatever angle you view Manhattan, the dominant element is the array of skyscrapers reaching up into the sky. These boxy towers of steel, cement, and glass define the cityscape. Any other buildings, such as libraries, musea, churches, hotels, private apartment buildings, all cower at the feet of these megalithic giants. They are again a visible symbol of where American values lie. They house the corporate headquarters of giant industries and businesses and great central banks that represent the financial position and power of the country. There seems to be something symbolic in the way St. Patrick's Cathedral is turned into a little toy structure alongside the huge stone-and-glass towers of Radio City. This visual architectural contrast in our cityscape seems to tell us something about our relative values. The church is tolerated as long as it does not get in the way of big business. But at the same time, the soaring skyscrapers also remind us of the industries and businesses that provide work for thousands of citizens and have probably enabled many more people here to lead a dignified middle-class existence than anywhere else in the world. There is much of America, good and bad, imaged in the Manhattan skyline.

Another visual presentation we made to our students involved showing downtown architectural shots of Manhattan, Chicago, Houston, Rio de Janeiro, Mexico City, Tokyo, Hong Kong, Milan, Brussels, London, Rotterdam, and what was West Berlin. You can hardly tell them apart. They all are a cluster of skyscrapers pretty much alike; they all show how universal and central the power of corporate industry and international banking have become in the modern world. Views of central Paris and Rome and cities such as Florence and Sienna, where there are no skyscrapers, raised the interesting question of what there is in the historic, economic, and cultural background of these cities that would lead them to exclude the skyscraper, which led to very healthy discussions of many questions of human values and relationships, questions that were at the center of these workshops on human relations.

My presentations were a very minuscule part of the overall scope of the Human Relations Workshop. Father Maher had a national reputation for his work in human relations. He was appointed by President Kennedy to the National President's Commission on Human Relations, conducted short workshops all over the country on the subject, was very active in the local chapter of the National Conference of Christians and Jews, and was on the Diocesan Commission on Human Relations. His knowledge of the field and his contact with leading authorities on human relations in the area enabled him to bring very important persons into the St. Louis University campus workshops to broaden and enrich the students' experience. He was kind enough to say that my modest presentations added another dimension to the workshops, and he continued to make them a regular part of the campus offering.

The workshops ran through the whole summer session. They proved to be so successful that Father Maher and his assistant in the education department and in the workshops, Theo Shea, had the idea that it might be interesting to offer them in a foreign setting. Working in a foreign culture, it was thought, and observing some of the human relations problems there might induce the students to take a new look at the problems at home. The only time in which such a foreign workshop could be set up was in the break immediately following the summer-school session, which would mean a second summer school for the faculty of the workshops, but the enrichment of the foreign experience seemed very much worth the price. To begin with, it was decided to make Mexico City the site of these foreign workshops. A core faculty was set up for them, consisting of Father Maher himself; Theo Shea, who took care of all the organizational details; Dr. Alice Cochran, a professor of history at Webster College; Myron Schwartz, from the local branch of the National Conference of Christians and Jews; and me. We were to be supplemented with presenters from the Mexican scene itself. Classes ran for five weeks, from 9:00 A.M. to 12:00 P.M. and from 1:30 P.M. to 4:00 P.M., Monday through Friday. The students came from all over the country. They were mostly teachers who were looking for extra credit to upgrade their educational qualifications. They boarded with Mexican families, but the classes were held on the campus of the American College, then located in Mexico City. The registrar there, Elizabeth Lopez, was from St. Louis, which gave us an entrée to the campus.

The workshops proved to be a very rewarding experience for the students, and they certainly were so for me. Besides my presentations on the history of the hero and the architectural survey of cities around the world as indices of shifting human values, I was expected to show what the art of Mexico revealed about Mexican history and social values. It was something I had to learn myself. I knew very little about Mexico, Mexicans, and Mexican art when we made our first foray into the country. The only Mexicans I had ever met were a handful of migrant Mexican workers who came to my part of Wisconsin for a few weeks in the summers to work on the farms. I was not at all prepared for the rich and complex culture that we encountered in Mexico City and its environs. The rich Spanish colonial influence was evident everywhere. The great sixteenth-century cathedral, one of the oldest in the Western Hemisphere, is partly Renaissance and partly baroque on its exterior. On the inside, you are struck by its general classical Renaissance features but in particular by the blazing golden glory of its immense *retablo* (a screen behind the altar) reaching from the floor to the high vaulting. It is done in a rich version of the elaborate churrigueresque style emblazoned with gold leaf, and all of it frames a large oil painting by Murillo brought here from Spain. The famous facade of the Sagrario Metropolitano or Metropolitan Chapel attached to the cathedral on the north is one of the most striking examples of the churrigueresque style in all of Mexico. It has the typical columns of the style called *estipides,* made up of inverted and right-side-up elongated pyramids stacked on top of one another. So here in the cathedral itself, one experiences three of the several distinctive architectural styles that were to develop in colonial Mexico. In our ten years of workshops in Mexico City, we were able to get to all of the most important sites in the country on weekends, and I never ceased to be amazed at the extent, the variety, and the quality of Mexican colonial church architecture.

Some of the early architecture was fairly simple and restrained. That was true of the plateresque style, which developed early in colonial times. This style gets its name from *platera* (Spanish for silver) because of its rather flat, almost two-dimensional carving resembling the low relief on silverware. The carving is generally confined to the margin of the main portal of the facade, which is otherwise left completely plain. There is a very good example of it in the church of the Augustinian Monastery of Acolman not far from Mexico City on the road to the ruins of the pre-Columbian site of Teotihuacán. This church also is a good example of another architectural feature that seems to have been a Mexican invention: the exterior church or chapel. The church building itself at Acolman is rather small and would not hold a very large congregation, but the walled-in courtyard in front of it was built in a series of gently rising terraces that would accommodate large standing or kneeling crowds. To the right of the church facade and on the second-story level of the cloister is a large open balcony plainly visible from anywhere in the courtyard. Mass was said in this gallery, and sermons were preached for the congregation of indigenous people in the courtyard. It was really an outdoor church. In many other places in Mexico, we encountered separately constructed outdoor churches, which consisted merely of a sanctuary with its altar and a large walled-in enclosure for the congregation. This construction seems to be an ecclesiastical development unique to Mexico, working well there because of the rather unusually mild weather. I have seen some modern modifications of the idea in the outdoor church at Our Lady of the Snows at Belleville, Illinois, and in the beautiful outdoor chapel in the restored village of New Harmony, Indiana. The interior of the little church at Acolman illustrates some other typical elements of Mexican colonial ecclesiastical architecture. The entire wall space behind the altar is filled with a *retablo*, made up here of alternating panels of paintings and sculptures reaching up to the ceiling in stacked rectangular spaces, entirely encased by carved, richly gold-leafed frames. The *retablo* becomes a standard feature of Mexican colonial church interiors, though done in various styles. Another feature of the Acolman church is the fresco work of religious scenes that fill the west wall. They are simply black-and-white representations of religious subjects transferred and enlarged from wood-block book illustrations or line drawings. Some of these scenes also occur in other early monastic buildings in Mexico on the inner wall spaces of the cloister arcades. And, incidentally, the cloisters in Mexico generally copy the two-story arcaded walks surrounding the cloistered space developed in Spain.

As I remarked above, Acolman illustrates the rather restrained plateresque style. In some places, as time went on, the architects also imitated the rather restrained classical style of the High Renaissance in Spain. Emperor Charles V had used this style in the palace he built inside the Alhambra, as did the architect Herrera in designing the Escorial for Philip II. A very good example of this restrained architectural design in Mexico is the Church of the Assumption on top of the pyramid at Cholula near Puebla. That church is extremely interesting for a good many other reasons, not the least of which is the fact that it is perched on top of one of the largest pre-Columbian pyramids in Mexico. The pyramid is so large that when you approach it across the plains near the colonial city of Puebla, it looks like a huge hill with a road winding up its sides to the church. What you are actually looking at is the crumbling adobe remains of a second pyramid that was being built over an earlier stone one that was never completed because the indigenous culture collapsed before it was finished. Had it been completed, it would have been enclosed in stone as the earlier one was and thus given some permanence. It was the custom of some of these pre-Columbian cultures to build a new pyramid over the old one every fifty-two years to commemorate their successful survival of the threat of extinction if the sun did not continue to rise. They tried to guarantee its rising by sacrifices to their gods, especially to the sun god. Some of these sacrificial victims were human beings offered on an altar at the forefront of the pyramid. That is the reason why the church was built on top of this unfinished pyramid, to impress on the native faithful that a sacrifice was still being offered there for their salvation through the blood of their Savior, not their own blood. And here at Cholula, that same fact was dramatized in another way—by placing a stone cross in front of the church at the very front edge of the pyramid on the very spot where the hearts were torn out of the human sacrificial victims when they were offered up to the sun god. It is just a cross and not a crucifix, but carved on it are the instruments of Christ's passion, again reminding the native faithful that Christ made a bloody sacrifice of himself for their redemption.

Looking out from the top of the half-finished pyramid today at the plains of cornfields that stretch out in all directions, you can see churches here and there poking up out of the cornfields. Wherever there was a native temple in pre-Columbian times, the Spanish colonists built a church. The variety and beauty of those churches are amazing. The colonial city in the area was Puebla, built on a high hill overlooking the plains below, commanding a beautiful view of the Cholula pyramid and of the beautiful volcanic snow-clad peaks of Popocatépetl and Ishtitihuatl in the background. The Spaniards who settled in the Puebla area came from the south of Spain; hence, they brought with them their love of tile and their expertise in making it. Beautiful and complex tile work is a feature of the arcades of many of the churches that were built in the Puebla area, and this kind of tile work spread to other areas of Mexico as well. A not infrequent feature of Mexican colonial church design was a dome at the east end of the church above the altar. Because of the Puebla influence, the exterior of those domes were frequently covered with bright ceramic tile that shimmered in the bright Mexican sunlight. Under the Puebla influence, tile frequently came to be a feature of some of the interior decoration of the churches as well. Certainly here in colonial Mexico, as it had in Spain, tile also became a prominent feature of domestic architecture.

One year we visited the Puebla area on the weekend of August 15, the Feast of the Assumption of the Blessed Virgin into heaven, a very popular feast throughout Mexico. We took the occasion to observe how the feast is celebrated in a precious little colonial church not far from the Cholula pyramid. In previous years, we had observed how it was celebrated in the Church of San Francisco in the heart of Mexico City. There, on the eve of the feast, a special statue of the Blessed Virgin representing her as dead in a supine position is placed on a bier in the church. Candles are lit around the bier, and the faithful come to pay their respects as you would at a wake. They each bring a green apple (which are stocked in the markets for the occasion) and place it at the side of the bier. The apples are neatly arranged in pyramidal piles just as fruit and vegetables are in Mexican markets. By the end of the day, the reclining figure of Our Lady is surrounded by pyramids of green apples, a reminder to the faithful that the Blessed Virgin was the new Eve, who, by giving Christ the human body in which he suffered and died for our redemption, repaired the damage of the disobedience of the first Eve. At night, the statue of the Blessed Virgin is removed and a beautiful bouquet of flowers is put in its place. Our Lady has gone to heaven. The faithful return on her feast day and pick up an apple, which is now a symbol of their promised share in Mary's joy in heaven. It is a beautiful little dramatization of one aspect of their faith.

We saw the Assumption dramatized a bit differently in the lovely little church at Cholula. The church itself is noteworthy. Its facade is entirely made up of puebla tiles—unglazed red clay tiles creating the ground and glazed tiles in bright blue, white, and yellow creating a checkerboard pattern over the whole surface of the church. The frame of the door and the ogee-arched window above it is made entirely of beautiful bright yellow tile. The interior is one of the most lavishly decorated in Mexico. Every inch of the surface of the walls and even of the interior of the little dome that canopies the altar is covered with a tangle of vine and cloud patterns made of molded and painted plaster and interspersed with angel faces. What is noteworthy here is that all of the faces have native features. The work on this labyrinthine decoration was done by native craftsmen, as was frequently the case in the building and decorating of these colonial structures. Here, they put themselves into their creation. The center-piece of the interior, of course, is the altar with a domed plaster-molded baldachino canopying a beautiful statue of the Blessed Virgin in a rich flowing robe; her features, too, are those of a native. The church is no longer an officially functioning one. There is no resident priest, and there are seldom any official liturgical functions held in it, but the native people from the neighboring farmlands (the cornfields snuggle up to the very walls of the little churchyard) still take loving care of the church and have ceremonies of their own there, as they did for the Feast of the Assumption. There was to be no official Mass in the church, but they wanted to give Our Lady a beautiful celebration for her Assumption anyway. There was a little wall around the churchyard and iron gates in the front wall, with a brick walk leading up to the steps of the church. The local people had covered the brick walk from the gates to the church steps with colored sands laid down in a checkerboard pattern resembling the tile pattern on the facade of the church. From the door of the church to the steps of the altar, the same pattern was repeated, not in sand but in flower petals. The people had laid a rich carpet of honor for Our Lady as she was mak-ing her exit to heaven. Her figure on the altar was covered with a mantle woven of flowers, a special garment for her going home. The local people gathered and sang a Spanish hymn to Our Lady, and I'm sure the idea of Mary's Assumption had a very special meaning to them. They had done their part in wishing her on her way. It was a very moving event.

The interior of the little Assumption Church was definitely ba-roque in feeling because of all of its exuberant decoration, but per-haps not intentionally so. There were, however, many Spanish colonial Mexican churches that were intentionally planned to emu-late baroque architecture as it had evolved in Spain. The touchstone of this baroque character is the use of what came to be called the Solomonic column because it was thought to be the kind of column used in the Temple of Solomon. More realistically, it derived from the serpentine vine-covered columns that Bernini, the great master of the baroque, used in the bronze baldachino in St. Peter's in Rome. It is employed both on the facade sculpture and in woodcarving and plaster molding, which is heavily gold-leafed in most exuberant lush-ness in some churches in Mexico. I am thinking particularly of the

Dominican Church of the Holy Rosary in Oaxaca and the *retablo* of the Church of the Franciscan Monastery in Talmenalco, Mexico.

But where Mexican colonial exuberance reaches its architectural peak is in the adaptation of the churrigueresque style with its multiple *estipides* or pyramidal detailed columns. I have already called attention to this exuberance on the facade of the Sagrario Metropolitano at the cathedral in Mexico City. One of the most exquisite examples of the style is the charming little church of Santa Prisca, which is the centerpiece of the small and even more charming hill town of Taxco. Taxco was made famous and wealthy in colonial times by its silver mines and is still famous for the fashioning of beautiful silver jewelry. But perhaps the most splendid example of churrigueresque architecture anywhere in the world is the chapel of the Jesuit novitiate at Tepozatlán. Its outside facade and the main and side *retablos* on its interior are all noteworthy for their exploitation of the *estipides* or pyramidal column. The style was actually brought to a greater exuberance in Mexico than it achieved in Spain itself. I wondered why the lavishness of the baroque and churrigueresque became so popular in Mexico. When I eventually learned how exuberant pre-Columbian sculpture, painting, and architecture had been, it seemed logical that the Spaniards would have wanted to replace it with something equally colorful and impressive for the indigenous people, who were used to the high-spiritedness and color of their own native art.

It was obvious to me, especially at Tepozatlán, that the Spanish colonists were thinking of the natives when they planned these churches because of the way they oriented them. In the first place, the novitiate at Tepozatlán is not in the center of a city but out in the countryside. It is made up of several large cloister courts that housed the novitiate community. But the chapel is not walled off in one of these courts; rather, it is situated at one corner facing outward into an attractive plaza open to the public and inviting them into the chapel. The public here was the native population, who worked the cornfields that pushed up to the edge of the community buildings. Again, part of the reason for the extravagance of the chapel was to satisfy the taste of the native peoples.

How impressive these rites had been was brought home to us by a visit to Tula, a pre-Columbian archaeological site not far from Tepozatlán. Here we saw the remains of the central pyramid of an entire Toltec city with enough of the painted plaster finish remaining for us to sense what a colorful spectacle one of these pre-Columbian urban centers must have been. It was at Tula that the first truly post-and-lintel structures in pre-Columbian architecture were built. A forest of these posts or columns still exists, once part of a large gathering place in front of the central pyramid, and on top of the pyramid itself some of the caryatid-like figures of warriors, some twenty feet high, still stand: they once held up the roof of the temple itself on top of the pyramid. You have to recall the impressive sophistication and colorfulness of pre-Columbian art, I think, if you want to understand why the Spaniards went out of their way to create a colonial Christian art that would match or surpass it.

I had another particular interest in seeing the novitiate at Tepozatlán. It was, after all, the place where generation after generation of my Mexican Jesuit confreres received their early training as Jesuits. This practice obtained up until the revolution in the 1930s, when Tepozatlán and all the other religious houses and churches in the country were confiscated by the government. At the time of the revolution, the government plundered much of the artwork in the churches and put it up for sale. I discovered and purchased a fine statue of St. Stanislaus Kostka. The antique dealer assured me that the statue had come from the elaborate side *retablo* in the Jesuit novitiate chapel at Tepozatlán. When I got to the chapel, I realized that this story might well be true because many statues were missing on the rich side *retablo*, making my purchase all the more precious to me. The novitiate buildings at Tepozatlán are now a public museum.

The statue of St. Stanislaus itself is a very good example of an artistic technique that had developed in Spain, was brought to Mexico by the colonists, and was taught to the native craftsmen. It produced the hundreds of statues that populate the many *retablos* in the colonial churches and chapels all over Mexico. In this technique, the basis of the fundamental figure was a rough woodcarving. This carving was covered with a thick coat of gesso (smooth plaster), which, as it dried, was molded into the final form of the figure. To achieve refined drapery effects, canvas saturated with gesso was often fastened to the wooden figure. This fabric could be easily shaped into flowing form. When all of this had dried and hardened, the whole draped part of the figure was covered with gold leaf, which was in turn painted the color desired for the drapery and allowed to dry. Then the surface paint was scratched off in specific floral patterns to allow the gold leaf to shine through. The result was a rich damask pattern of gold and whatever color was added over the gold leaf. In the case of my St. Stanislaus statue, it was gold and black. The face and hands of the figure were painted and burnished to a polished surface. The native craftsmen became very adept at this technique and produced the hundreds of colonial statues all over Mexico that were fabricated in that manner. The technique is called *estofado*.

A figure executed in this manner that was very popular all over Mexico was that of St. James of Compostello on horseback. A seventeenth-century statue of the saint, but without his horse, was available in the same shop where I had purchased the *estofado* figure of St. Stanislaus. I purchased the St. James figure and had a leather pedestal fabricated for it to substitute for the missing horse; St. James, brandishing his sword from his improvised saddle, now graces our collection of Spanish colonial art at St. Louis University. In Spain, St. James had become a symbol of the conquest of the Moors under the title of Matamuros (the slayer of the Moors). It seems an ironic twist of history that he would become a popular saint for the native peoples of Mexico, who, after all, were the conquered rather than the conquering. But popular he was and still is among them. His figure on horseback was often carried in procession on his feast day and was not infrequently represented in sculpture on colonial churches. The converts to the new faith looked upon him as their patron in their frequent battles against the savage Chichimecs of the north of Mexico. And perhaps the vision of a saint on horseback was appealing to them in another way. They were genuinely grateful, however, to the Spanish conquerors for bringing the horse and the burro, which had done so much to lighten their own labor.

This Spanish church architecture and sculpture give eloquent testimony to the Spanish influence on Mexican culture. The other even more pervasive element, of course, is that of the native people. In the first place, they make up the vast majority of the population in Mexico. In the ten years we held workshops in Mexico City, we saw the city more than double in population because of the tremendous influx of Native Americans from the countryside. The population is now well more than twenty million and fills the whole valley surrounded by a ring of volcanic mountains. The city was not prepared to accommodate such a huge influx, so the result has been the creation of vast slums with very few amenities. The emissions of millions of cars have now made Mexico City one of the most polluted cities in the world, all the more so because the fumes are trapped by the circle of mountains. The students in the workshop soon became keenly aware of the enormous disparity between the small number of the wealthy in the city living in luxurious homes and the millions of very poor, mostly native people, who lived in the unconscionable slums that stretched in all directions on the outskirts of the city. When the students expressed their shock at these conditions, we showed them a video that pictured homes in Ladue (a St. Louis suburb) and the slums of East St. Louis, Illinois, just across the river from St. Louis, Missouri. The residential area of Ladue is said to represent more concentrated wealth than any similar acreage in the United States, and much of East St. Louis is one of the most blighted slums in the country. Many of our students came from St. Louis, and practically none of them had ever adverted to this vast disparity between rich and poor right in their own home territory. It took the foreign experience to bring it home to them. Most of the poor in Mexico are the native people, and most of the poor in the United States at that time were African American. Now we have huge numbers of poor Latino and Asian immigrants as well.

In Mexico, it is true that the indigenous people, who had been oppressed and exploited by their own leaders before the coming of the Spaniards, were oppressed and exploited by the Spaniards, but there is a vast difference between what happened to the indigenous people in Mexico and in other South American countries and what happened to them in the United States, where they were all but exterminated. In all the Mesoamerican and South American countries, the native people still form a defining part of the population. The population of Ecuador, for instance, is more than 85 percent full-blooded native. You can't go anywhere in Mexico without being aware of how pervasive the native presence is. The native influence is evident in Mexican dress, food, art, and enduring customs. For the most part, the indigenous people accepted the new Christian faith and the Spanish language of their conquerors, but they often also retained their own languages. And even in religion, they retained elements of their old beliefs and religious customs. Anthropologist Anita Brenner of Harvard University wrote a book entitled *Idols behind the Altar* in which she discusses the many elements of the old religions that remained in the minds and practices of native converts to the Christian faith. We had an opportunity of observing some of this mixture ourselves. In the farmland, around the ancient pre-Columbian city of Teotihuacán, the farmers join their pastor in spring in a procession through their fields carrying a statue of the Blessed Virgin, whom they address in song, asking her to bless and make fertile their fields. When the procession is over, they also bury some clay figurines of the old pagan sun and rain gods just to make sure they have covered all the bases. These figurines are frequently made from molds they discovered in the fields, molds from which their pre-Columbian ancestors had made their own fertility figurines.

The most beautiful example of this mingling of native and Christian elements is the widespread devotion to Our Lady of Guadalupe. This dark-skinned image of the Virgin with native features, venerated in the Basilica of Guadalupe on the outskirts of Mexico City, has an interesting history. According to the legend, the Blessed Virgin appeared to Juan Diego, a native convert, in 1531 on the hill of Tepeyac. It was a place where the local people had venerated the mother goddess Tonantzín. The Blessed Virgin directed Juan to tell Archbishop Zumarraga that she wished him to build a church in her honor on the spot where she had appeared. Juan did so, but the archbishop doubted his word. Juan went back to Tepeyac, where the Virgin appeared to him again. Roses had sprung up on the spot where she had appeared. She told Juan to gather some roses up in his cloak and take them to the archbishop. He did so. When he opened his cloak, the roses dropped out and imprinted on his linen cloak was an image of the Blessed Virgin. The archbishop became a believer; the basilica was built; and the framed image of Our Lady of Guadalupe on the linen cloak was hung there for public veneration. It became the most popular image of Our Lady in all of Mexico. The native people took it to their hearts as their very own and have continued to come from all over Mexico in an unending line of pilgrimage.

When you go to this basilica, you cannot help being impressed with the simple faith and reverence of the native pilgrims. From inside the gates of the basilica precincts, they move forward on their knees until they reach the image of Our Lady. Even during the revolutionary days at the beginning of the twentieth century, when churches all over Mexico were closed and clergy were outlawed, the revolutionary government never dared to close the Basilica of Guadalupe or to interfere with the native pilgrims there. They knew it was so sacred to the native people that they would have had a new revolution on their hands if they had closed the basilica or interfered with the pilgrims.

There are raised stone platforms in the plaza in front of the basilica. Much like those in some of the old plazas of pre-Columbian religious sites, they provide platforms on which the pilgrims perform their folk dances in their native costumes, not as entertainment for tourists, but as a sincere tribute to Our Lady. The dances are a strange amalgam of traditional native folk dances and bits of Christian and Spanish lore, but the native people perform them as a sincere offering to their mother, the Lady of Guadalupe. The old basilica was threatening to collapse during the years we visited Mexico City, and a new one was built beside it, but the native pilgrims keep coming and paying their dramatic respects to their new mother.

Another element that we wanted our students to learn about in Mexico was the great achievement of the pre-Columbian native cultures. In the first years, we relied on a professor of art at the American College, where the workshops were held. He was David Ramsey, who, like his artist wife Thea, had a degree in art from the Chicago Art Institute. Soon after graduation, they went to Mexico, fell in love with the country and its ancient and contemporary art and had never left. Dave did a fine job of introducing all of us to the richness of pre-Columbian art—so fine, in fact, that he kindled my permanent interest in the subject. I began studying it in earnest.

During the thirteen years of our workshops in Mexico and South America, we went to most of the pre-Columbian archaeological sites. I photographed them extensively and eventually worked up an academic course on pre-Columbian art and architecture, which I have taught regularly at the university. It has been a fascinating area in which to work because there is so much continuous archaeological discovery going on that it requires continual revision of the "facts." For instance, recent excavations in Mayan sites in northern Belize have pushed back the dating of Mayan culture by a thousand years. It used to be said that the Olmec culture on the east coastal area of Mexico antedated the beginnings of Mayan culture by a thousand years. The present "facts" make it clear that Mayan culture was at least as old as the Olmec.

How I got my start on educating myself about pre-Columbian art is rather interesting in itself. During our workshops in Mexico City, the faculty members always stayed at a famous little hotel facing the Alamedo Park in the heart of Mexico City, actually the oldest public park in the Western Hemisphere. The Cortez Hotel was the cloisters of an ancient colonial Franciscan monastery. The guest rooms of the two-story cloister were the former rooms of the monks, with Spanish tile on the floors and dadoes waist high.

Another very interesting guest at the hotel, Professor Theodore Sizer, became my private tutor in pre-Columbian art. He taught U.S. history at Yale University and was Yale's official heraldrist. He was well versed in pre-Columbian art. When he learned of my budding interest in the subject, he offered to show me the Archaeological Museum. Much of the incomparably rich collection of pre-Columbian artifacts that are now so magnificently housed in the new National Archaeological Museum were then crammed into what had been classrooms and halls of the Jesuit School. It was a strange experience to walk into a room where one of my Jesuit confreres had previously tried to teach Latin or Greek or religion and instead see the sixteen-foot head of an Olmec warrior reigning from its pedestal, or to stand in the courtyard that once echoed with the voices of obstreperous high school students but was now silent and presided over by the towering colossal statue of the Aztec Venus, with her skirt of serpents and her double serpent's head. The artifacts were rather haphazardly displayed and poorly lit, but there were enough of them to amaze me at the number of sophisticated cultures that had antedated the Aztecs (who were latecomers on the scene), cultures such as the one at the nearby ancient city of Teotihuacán; the Olmecs on the East Coast; the Maya in Yucatán and Chiapas; the Toltecs; the Zapotecs in the Oaxaca area; and the Nayarit, the Colima, and Jalisco on the West Coast. Dr. Sizer knew them all and helped me get my first impression of the diversity and sophisticated achievement of these pre-Columbian cultures in architecture, sculpture, ceramics, and gold work.

I was particularly interested in a colored plaster mockup of what Tenochtitlán, the Aztec capital, looked like when the Spaniards arrived. They must have thought they had discovered the mythical city of Eldorado as they saw it gleaming in the valley when they made their way down the surrounding mountainside. It was a city very much like Venice, a city of canals situated in the midst of marshlands and surrounded by shallow lakes. Like Venice, it was built there for safety, for protection against the raids of the northern Chichimec invaders. The Aztecs themselves had been invaders who came south, liked what they saw, and decided to settle down and build a safe haven in the marshes. The only access to the city from the mainland was by two narrow causeways. The city had been built up in the marshes with canals in place of streets. In its civic and religious center, two huge pyramids had been constructed side by side as the bases for two temples, one dedicated to the sun god and the other to the god of war. The two gods were closely connected in Aztec life. They believed that the sun god had to be nourished by human blood to ensure that he would be strong enough to continue his journey across the sky and guarantee the growth and fruitfulness of their crops. To obtain the victims for the continual human sacrifices that were necessary, they had to be in continual warfare with their neighbors. This bloody barbarism at the very center of the Aztecs' life was mirrored by the two huge pyramids painted in bright colors rising up at the very center of the city in front of a huge plaza, roughly where the cathedral plaza or *zocalo* is today.

The rest of the city was probably a more impressive and certainly a cleaner one than anything existing in Europe at the time. It had a huge marketplace in which goods of all kinds were elaborately displayed: a rich array of food—corn, beans, squash, potatoes, tomatoes; wild turkey and rabbits and deer hunted on the mainland; brightly colored cotton clothing; moccasins and jackets made of deerskin, and bright ceremonial garments made of bright tropical bird feathers; pottery of all kinds, some utilitarian and some meant for use in religious rituals and funerary customs; and fine jewelry, some of embossed gold, some of cast gold, some in filigree work, and some fabricated from jade or obsidian. Also available were knives fashioned from obsidian as well as other tools and weapons fabricated from flint and other stones. The Aztecs, like their predecessors, had no metal tools and no domestic animals (except small dogs, which they fattened to eat and which they also revered because they believed dogs conducted their souls into the afterlife). The lack of technology meant that the construction of their buildings had to be done entirely by human labor and all their artwork tranduseful objects had to be made by hand with very simple stone tools. Nor had they discovered the practical use of the wheel, except on some small toys. This lack of technology makes their great architectural and artistic achievement all the more astounding.

The city was divided into work and residential sections related to different activities. The houses were constructed around an open court, much like those in early Rome. The interior rooms of the upper class were frequently covered with frescoes. Fringing the canalled city were artificial fields created by weaving nets from willow twigs, placing them in the marshes, and filling them with a couple feet of soil hauled in baskets from the mainland. The little plots were separated by canals and kept in place by planting willow trees on the periphery. These floating fields (some of them can still be seen in the Xochimilco section of Mexico City) were planted in corn, beans, squash, potatoes, peppers, and berries, providing the city with most of the food it needed. An aqueduct made of clay-tile pipe supplied water from springs in the nearby mountains. The city used a lot of water. The Aztecs had a passion for cleanliness—they had public bathhouses, and some of them bathed three times a day. They also had public toilets on the canals. The excrement was caught in boats under the toilets and every day the boats were rowed out to the mainland, where the contents were processed into fertilizer.

In the light of all these refinements and amenities, it seems strange that the Aztecs retained human sacrifice at the core of their religious practices. The neighboring tribes between Tenochtitlán and the East Coast had grown weary of the Aztec warriors' constant raids to procure victims for the human sacrifice. Their discontent made it easier for Cortés to conquer Moctezuma and the Aztecs because many of the disgruntled tribesmen joined him when they learned he intended to conquer their oppressors. Cortés's first contact with Moctezuma and his followers was also eased by their belief that the ruler Quetzalcoatl—who had tried unsuccessfully to develop a peaceful realm at Tula, the Toltec capital, then disappeared mysteriously—would return one day with a white face and riding a four-footed creature. When the white-faced Cortés appeared riding a horse, the Aztecs presumed it was the fulfillment of the prophecy. They welcomed Cortés's party but soon sensed that their visitors had no peaceful intentions. They were preparing to attack the Spaniards by night, but the Spaniards attacked first, and the Aztecs, with their spears and bows and arrows, were no match for the Spaniards on horseback with their guns and armor. The Aztecs were defeated; Moctezuma was taken prisoner and eventually executed.

The Spaniards wasted no time in trying to eliminate all traces of the human sacrifice and the native pagan religion. They leveled the two huge pyramids and filled many of the canals with the debris and the broken images of the pagan gods. Many of these images were retrieved in the twentieth century when excavations were made to install the underground railroad system in Mexico City, and they are now on display in special rooms in the new Archaeological Museum.

We were at pains to let our students know that, impressive as the achievement of the Aztecs was, it was inferior to that of many pre-Columbian cultures that had preceded it. The Aztecs were Johnny-come-latelies and derived much of what they did from their predecessors. Their sculpture is impressive; the great calendar stone, for instance, is one of the most impressive relics from any of the pre-Columbian cultures, summing up a great deal of pre-Columbian mythology, but there is a crudeness about the massive sculptures of their deities that reveals the barbarism still lurking under the surface of their artistic facade.

The present Maya in the Yucatán countryside are still living in huts that are identical to those in which their pre-Columbian ancestors lived. They are small oval-shaped structures, the oval shape designed to eliminate any corners in which evil spirits might lurk. The walls, slightly more than head high, are made up of stakes driven in the ground and covered with a net woven from twigs, which in turn are covered with adobe plaster and then painted an ochre color. An open entranceway pierces both the long walls of the hut, which allows for cross-ventilation of the interior. There are no windows. Above the wall is a high-pitched thatched roof. Hammocks are swung in the house for sleeping, and corn, dried fruit, and other supplies are hung from the rafters of the roof, but the peasants spend most of their time outside. They grind corn into meal in stone metates outside for the tacos that are the mainstay of their diet, and they cook on a hearth made up of a few stones—again, outside the hut. We saw many of these huts scattered throughout the Yucatán jungle. The life of the modern country Maya is almost identical to that led by their ancestors for hundreds of years on the peninsula.

We were reminded of that similarity when we carefully examined the sculptural detail at Uxmal, which I found to be the most interesting pre-Columbian site on the peninsula. There is a medium-size pyramid at the edge of the site, but the most fascinating structure is the complex that the Spanish dubbed "The Nunnery" because it does resemble a cloister organized around a central courtyard. The buildings may have been the residences of some of the aristocratic rulers of the city. There is a very long building on each side of the courtyard, approximately two hundred feet long and elevated on a platform with steps leading up to the platform, which runs the whole length of the building. I recognized immediately that the buildings themselves are really a magnification of the simple Mayan huts we had been looking at in the bush, here translated into permanent stone. The first floor is a long extension of the wall of the hut, undecorated, but in stone instead of wickerwork and plaster, and broken up not just by one opening but by five distributed symmetrically across the facade. The upper part of the facade corresponds to the thatched roof of the hut, and in place of the texture of the thatch, the surface was made up of an elaborate textured stone mosaic. Most of it is in a kind of checkerboard pattern resembling the pattern on the skin of a snake and possibly meant to symbolize that. But what struck me particularly was that over each of the entrance openings the stone mosaic is a very exact reproduction of one of the little Mayan huts. This reproduction was to remind the native public, I presume, that the inspiration for the whole building was the simple Mayan hut.

The buildings on all four sides of the court are fundamentally the same, but their decoration represents an evolution in Mayan artistic style and sensitivity. The second building shows the same kind of restrained classical sensitivity to design that we associate with the Greek Parthenon; the apex of classical sensitivity and design. I say this not lightly. I was amazed at how much sensitivity to delicate detailing the building manifests. It is built to the same overall pattern as the first building, but all sorts of refinement have gone into the detailing. For instance, the center opening of five openings is slightly larger than the other four so that it automatically draws the eye to the center of the building. All five openings are slightly narrower at the top than at the bottom, and this slight variation from an exact square shape gives a subtle life and vitality to the design. Around each opening, there is an indentation in the masonry that casts a shadow and adds a three-dimensionality to the doorway that it would otherwise not have. The lower wall is relieved of the flatness both at the bottom and the top. About a foot from the bottom of the stone wall, there is an insert of cylindrical vertical shapes about six inches wide running the entire length of the wall between the openings. These shapes are actually stone reproductions of sections of bamboo poles that were used in a similar way in plaster-and-wood buildings. A few inches from the top of the wall, a similar insert is repeated, but here the pattern is not continuous. Undecorated spaces alternate with the cylindrical bamboo-inspired shapes arranged in groups of four or five. This subtle variation from the continuous pattern at the bottom of the wall creates a very pleasing element of surprise in the overall design. Here on the second level, where the textured thatched roof of the hut would have been, we have a beautifully executed checkerboard stone mosaic running the full length of the building. The resemblance to the pattern on the skin of a snake is even more apparent here. The analogy to the snake is emphasized because, instead of the mosaic representations of the Mayan hut above the openings in the first building, what is represented is an elaborate mask of the rain god: possibly the head of the feathered serpent, which, in several of the pre-Columbian mythologies, was associated with the rain god. The masks are done in bold shapes with feathers irradiating in all directions from the face of the rain god. The mosaic sculpture is bold and carries well from a distance, but it is in rather low relief and subordinated to the space it is decorating, in a true classical manner. What is remarkable about all this decoration is that the mosaic-like sculptures have been put together without mortar and have survived earthquake after earthquake, and that the individual pieces of the sculpture were fashioned without benefit of metal tools. The patience and skill it would take to do so is almost unbelievable.

When you turn away from this structure, which would compare well with a classically conceived building anywhere in the world, and turn to the building next to it on the south, you are awed by a facade that is completely baroque in feeling. In the first place, it is considerably higher than its neighbors, and in contrast to the restraint and subtle detailing of the classically conceived building, it relies on size, mass, and exuberant complexity to create a feeling of awe. It dispenses with all the subtleties of design on the first floor and concentrates all its efforts on the elaborate sculpture of the top section of the facade. It retains the checkerboard snakeskin design, but the elements that make up the pattern are larger, bolder, and more three-dimensional, and they project out from the surface into your space. When you come to the accent decorations above the openings and at the corners of the building, all of the stops are open. The composition here is made up not of just one mask of the rain god in low relief, but of three masks piled on top of one another, and all of them thrust out in almost full relief into your space. Besides, they each sport a proboscis like an elephant's trunk that thrusts and dangles even farther into your space. The complexity of the design, the bold three-dimensionality, and the restless curves of the design are all meant to invite participation in a performance. By sheer size and complexity, the composition creates a feeling of awe rather than of quiet thought and contemplation. I had, of course, seen these contrasted modes of approaching artistic design arrived at again and again in the history of European art, but here was the same dichotomy produced in a culture that had no real connection with that European tradition. It was another manifestation of the two sides of the human makeup, the predominantly intellectual on the one hand and the predominantly emotional on the other. These contrasts are apt to show up wherever and whenever you have human beings engaging in creative activity. Art does help us to realize that in spite of all our ethnic, national, religious, and political differences, many fundamental human values still do make the whole world one. The Yucatán experience certainly did broaden and deepen our appreciation of the pre-Columbian achievement and gave us a very good introduction to the achievement of the Maya in particular.

Later, I had the opportunity on my own to visit most of the important Mayan sites all through the Central American area. At the height of their development, the Maya occupied what is now Guatemala, Belize, Spanish Honduras, the whole Yucatán Peninsula, and Chiapas, the southernmost state in Mexico. The Maya never united into anything like an empire; like Italians until the nineteenth century, they lived in many independent city-states, each with its own government and frequently warring with one another. But they did have much in common, and some of that common inheritance is revealed in their architecture. Everywhere, both their religious temples and their domestic and civic buildings were an elaboration in stone of the simple hut that can be seen in the Mayan countryside to this day. And the various cities did maintain constant trade connections with one another: by trails through the jungle, by river where there were rivers, and in some places by canals dug to create a means to carry on commerce by boat. Recent excavation and aerial photography have revealed the existence of a canal that once connected Mayan cities in northern Belize with the great center of Tikal in Guatemala.

Yet another myth about the Maya has been exploded. It used to be said that unlike the pyramids in Egypt, the pre-Columbian pyramids were not used as burial places but just as great pedestals for temples to the gods. That was believed until the discovery was made at Palenque that one of the pyramids there was indeed used as a funerary monument. An elaborate tomb was discovered, not *in* the pyramid as in Egypt, but *underneath* it. And what was found in it revealed that the beliefs of the Maya about the needs of at least their leaders after death were very similar to the belief of the Egyptians. The leader's body was encased in a large stone tomb with his image in full ceremonial costume carved on the large monolithic lid of the tomb. Two very fine clay bust portraits of the leader were also in the tomb. Frescoes on the wall showed him engaged in some of the ordinary activities of his life. There was a deposit, too, of pottery filled with food, jewelry, and utensils of various kinds that he might have use for in the afterlife. This all looks very much as if the Maya thought, as did the Egyptians, that their leaders needed all these things to continue a happy life in the hereafter. Excavations at Tikal have shown that some of the pyramids in that impressive site also cover burial tombs of great civic leaders.

When you see the impressive remains of these great Mayan centers, you cannot help wondering what it was that caused these cities to disappear almost simultaneously several hundred years before the coming of the Spaniards. Several reasons have been suggested; the real explanation may be a combination of all of these reasons. One suggestion is that the Mayan habit of following the slash-and-burn mode of farm husbandry would have depleted arable land close enough to the cities to support an urban center. In this method of husbandry, a section of the jungle is felled and burned and then planted, but the soil is depleted in a few years, and more acreage has to be slashed and burned. Eventually the fertile fields are too far from the city to provide an easy source of food for a large population when the only means of transportation is the backs of people. That this practice may have been one of the reasons for the decline of

Mayan cities seems to be partially supported by recent discoveries made in the excavations at Quello and other northern Belize sites. It has been known before that these Mayan cities continued to thrive more than eighty years longer than Mayan cities anywhere else. Recent excavations have revealed the reason for their long survival. The cities were all surrounded by raised fields fringed by fresh-water canals. The water from the canals kept the soil in the raised fields moist, and three crops a year could be harvested. The fields were all immediately adjacent to the city and were not depleted by the slash-and-burn technique. Besides this, the canals were all stocked with fish, which provided another constant supply of food close at hand. These details may supply a partial explanation of why the other Mayan cities, which were not so supplied, disintegrated.

But there is another and perhaps more convincing reason for the sudden and almost simultaneous decline of these cities. There may have been a peasant uprising that attacked the leaders and destroyed their city headquarters. When you realize how much impressed labor was necessary to build and maintain these large urban centers and to supply their inhabitants with food and clothing, you understand that there would be discontent among the laboring populace, which might lead to revolution, an overthrow of the ruling powers, and the semidestruction of the cities—the symbol of their power and oppression. Recent archaeological evidence shows that fires destroyed many of these centers. When they were gone, the native Mayan population fell back into its earlier mainly rural habits in an attempt to wrest a livelihood from the soil, which they continued to abuse by the slash-and-burn technique. In this context of the past history of the Maya, it is interesting to note what has been going on more recently in Chiapas, Mexico. The modern Mayan peasantry there have risen up in revolt against the oppression and injustices of the landlords. The present Mexican government is attempting to meet the just demands of the revolutionaries lest their discontent spread and more of Mexico be enveloped in a broader revolution. It is highly conceivable that, in a similar discontent, the ancestors of these peasant Maya rose up and threw off the yoke of their oppressors and destroyed the cities that housed them.

Before leaving Mexico, I want to record my impressions of two other things: the bullfight and the American colony in Mexico City. You can hardly say you have been to Mexico if you haven't seen a bullfight there, and a peculiar set of circumstances provided me with a very intimate view of a section of the American community in Mexico City.

We always took the workshop students to see a bullfight because there is something peculiarly Spanish and Mexican about it. I will never forget our experience of our first bullfight. Elizabeth Lopez, our registrar friend at the American College, where we were holding the workshop, invited us to her lovely home for lunch before we went to the bullring. It was a typical Mexican lunch of enchiladas and a salad of cottage cheese, the heart of the maguey plant, sliced green pepper, and red pomegranate seeds. But she had plied us with drinks before lunch, a mixture of fresh pineapple juice liberally laced with tequila. It tasted like a pleasant, sweet, harmless potion; we did not know the punch that tequila can deliver. Father Maher participated too liberally, and by the time we were ready to go to the bullfight, he was high as a kite. We didn't know quite what to do with him, but we all went on together to the bullring. Traf was wearing a big Mexican sombrero he had purchased the day before and a bright sport shirt. With his dark complexion, black hair, and rather rubbery face, he was always mistaken for a native wherever we went. When we got up to our seats in the ring, he refused to sit with us, plunked himself down on the steps of the aisle and proceeded to boo the bull, much to the chagrin of the native enthusiasts. We pretended not to know who he was. We gathered him up when the bullfight was over and he had somewhat sobered up. Meantime, we tried to enjoy the spectacle in the ring.

I must confess that I never have entered into the spirit of the thing. I know that the whole performance is supposed to demonstrate dramatically and beautifully man's superiority over the brute beast. Much about the performance of the toreador was courageous, graceful, and beautiful, but as the picadors prodded the bull from horseback and the banderilleros plunged their barbed banderillas into the bull's neck, I confess that I sympathized with the bull. We were told that the absolute climax of every bullfight is that moment when the bull, exhausted by his contest with the toreador, stands with his head down, his neck muscles weakened by the painful banderillas. He is almost hypnotized by the toreador's stare and stance. It is then that the toreador delivers the expert final thrust of his sword at just the right spot on the bull's neck. Then the bull collapses at the feet of the toreador, who extracts his sword and raises it on high as a sign once more of his superiority over the beast he has been contending with all afternoon. The crowd explodes in admiration of his achievement. That's how we were told the bullfight should end; the ones we saw never did. We were not in Mexico in the high season, when the top toreadors were performing who might have finished the job with this finesse and grace. The toreadors we witnessed in the off-season, the *novilleros,* were not up to this kind of performance. They often fumbled at the end, and instead of a graceful final thrust, where you hardly think of the death of the bull because the whole thing is done so expertly and gracefully, what we saw was an inexpert fumbling of the toreador that often ended up in a very clumsy and bloody spectacle that the crowd often booed.

Father Maher and I were in Mexico by ourselves one time at the height of the bullfight season, so we thought we would take in a fight when one of the top toreadors of the country was performing just to see if an excellent performance might impress us more favorably than the ones we had seen in the off-season. All through the fight, there was no question that we were looking at superior talent in the toreador. We were actually beginning to feel more admiration for him than sympathy for the bull, so we were waiting for that climactic moment of the contest when the toreador would demonstrate the top of his technique and his unquestionable superiority over the animal. Everything went exactly as it should have: the bull was subdued, with neck bowed, and hypnotically staring at the toreador, whose sword was pitched forward ready to deliver the deadly thrust. Then it happened. The bull had ideas of his own. He decided that death was not for him at the moment. He suddenly got up on his feet, turned tail, and started to run down the ring. The astonished toreador stood humiliated, sword in hand with no bull into which to thrust it. He hesitated for a moment, then took out after the bull, grabbed him by the tail, and tried to get him to turn around and take the deadly thrust. But the bull would have none of it. To Traf and myself, this unexpected incongruous sight was immensely funny; it was good opéra bouffe, and we laughed uproariously, much to the Mexican fans' chagrin. They were outraged at the bull, booed him, and cursed him in Spanish for not cooperating in this performance that was supposed to demonstrate his inferiority to the great toreador.

It was not until many years later, when we had had a workshop on the Island of Majorca and stopped for a few days in Barcelona after it was over, that we really experienced a bullfight that ended with the expertise, grace, and finesse that the aficionados of the sport expect. But that experience was more memorable for me because of the circumstances that surrounded it than for the bullfight itself. While in Barcelona, we had the opportunity of visiting Manresa, dear to any Jesuit as the place where St. Ignatius made his long retreat in the cave and penned some of his *Spiritual Exercises*. But Barcelona itself had its fascinations, too, not the least of which for me was the opportunity it afforded of seeing the work of the famous architect Gaudi, who probably produced some of the most mannerist work in the late nineteenth and early twentieth centuries. Barcelona was his headquarters, and some of his most impressive work is there. The most famous, of course, is the still unfinished Church of the Sagra Famiglia. It is fantastic to say the least—it could fit into a Walt Disney World—a strange combination of elongated orientalized spires, a network of sculptured details taken from organic nature mixed with religious scenes in strange and unexpected places. Gaudi's talent is perhaps better revealed in the flowing lines of his somewhat art nouveau apartment buildings in Barcelona. I had determined to get some good photographs of them before we left Barcelona, but had not done so as yet on the day we were scheduled to go to the bullfight. That summer many people all over Europe had contracted a serious bronchial infection that was caused by breathing air impregnated with pigeon dung ground to dust and floating in the dry air. I had the infection quite seriously; I had spells when I coughed so intensely that I thought I might strangle. I had one of these coughing spells at dinner on the Saturday night before we were to go to the bullfight. The group was really worried about my condition, but I wasn't. I went out late Sunday morning to get my photographs of the Gaudi apartments and, while wandering around the city, discovered that there was an American submarine in the harbor for the weekend and that it was open to the public. Never having seen a submarine, I decided to fill that gap and spent so much time in the harbor that I was late getting back to the hotel for the rendezvous for the bullfight.

The group waited as long as it could and then went on. Remembering my coughing seizure the night before, Father Maher, who, like many other Irishmen I know, seemed always able to put the worst possible interpretation on a given situation, was sure that I had

had another seizure and was probably lying dead somewhere in the streets of Barcelona. Some who were with him told me that he was so serious about this fear that he was beginning to wonder how he would get the body back to the States. Well, the body was very much alive. When I got back to the hotel and found that the gang had gone to the bullfight, I decided to follow them so that my ticket wouldn't be wasted. I took a taxi to the bullring. I was sure they would have purchased tickets on the shady side of the ring, so I took my stand across the street on the shady side and waited. I had no sooner done so than I saw my party moving into the ring right across the street. I nonchalantly walked over and joined them. They couldn't believe their eyes. The dead had risen and had found them in a crowd of more than thirty thousand. The resurrection was fake, but it *was* something of a miracle to have found my friends so easily in that kind of a crowd. And the bullfight was the best one I have ever witnessed.

During the summer when we had a workshop in Bogotá, Colombia, we were to witness a Jesuit mockup of a bullfight in the courtyard of the Jesuit high school there. Clerics in Bogotá at that time were forbidden to go to a bullfight, so it was rather surprising that an integral part of the graduation exercises at the Jesuit high school was a kind of mock bullfight right in the courtyard of the school. The whole faculty and student body were seated in the double cloister walks around the courtyard. One of the students stood on a fifty-gallon oilcan painted a bright yellow in the middle of the court. At the proper moment, a bull was released through one of the doors into the courtyard. Attracted by the yellow barrel, he charged down the court and butted the yellow can. The boy flew into the air, and he was supposed to leap on the back of the charging bull, which, we were told, he almost always succeeded in doing, demonstrating, I suppose, the superiority of even a mere Jesuit high school student over the beast of a bull. The bull for these occasions was supplied by a lady benefactor of the school who ran a bull farm. She usually sent a rather unobstreperous animal that had not yet matured enough for the real bullring. But this year she was in the hospital, and, by mistake, the bull that was sent was anything but placid. It charged the yellow oil can with vehemence, sending the boy flying into the air so wildly that he had no chance at all of landing on the bull's back. And then, to everyone's consternation, the bull turned on the prostrate boy and gored him severely. The boy was rescued and rushed to the hospital, where he recovered. The bull was corralled and taken back to the bull farm. He had proven that sometimes a bull can be superior to a human being. And I must say that this little mockery of a bullfight had more emotional intensity about it than any real bullfight I have ever seen.

The other part of our experience in Mexico City that I would like to record here has to do with a little corner of the American colony there. We gained access to it through Mrs. Jett Sullivan, who taught in the English department at St. Louis University for more than thirty years. She was related by marriage to Harry and Bowland Wright, brothers who were, in a way, founders of the American colony. Harry Wright had married Jett's aunt. Jett herself had lived with her aunt in Mexico City in the summers all through her grade school, high school, and college years so that she knew the American colony in Mexico City very well from the inside. Over the years, I got to know the story of the Wright brothers very well from Jett. It is a fascinating story: a Horatio Alger rags-to-riches tale, a Eugene O'Neill tragedy, and a Faulkner novel all wrapped up in one.

The story begins back in Virginia, where the Wright family lived. Unfortunately, the father was a confirmed alcoholic and his alcoholism wreaked havoc in the family. Witnessing what this condition had done to the family, the two boys, Harry and Bowland, promised their mother they would never touch a drop of liquor, a promise they kept. And, considering the world in which they eventually operated, it must have taken considerable stamina to keep that promise. In their teens, the two boys left home and went to Mexico to seek their fortunes. They started off by collecting scrap metal and selling it. When they saw how much of a market there was for scrap metal, they decided to go into the steel business. They were in Mexico just as the country was beginning to industrialize, and there was a great demand for steel, so that their company, Consolidated Steel, prospered. It became the biggest steel company in the country, and Harry Wright became the wealthiest man in Mexico. An article in *Fortune* magazine back in the 1930s estimated his financial worth as approximately $85 million. With that kind of wealth, he and his brother naturally became important figures in the American colony in Mexico City. In fact, they practically organized and consolidated it. They founded the American Country Club and built the club building; they built the

American Hospital and acquired the property for the American Cemetery; and they were heavy contributors to the American College as well as to causes in Mexico City that reached outside of the American community.

Harry Wright came to be known as Mr. Mexico. He helped finance one government after another and was thus able to ride the storms of changing regimes, including the revolutionary governments of Cárdenas and Obregón. One of the ways in which he promoted the American image in Mexico City was by the open house he had every Sunday afternoon in his palazzo-like mansion, beautifully furnished with Louis XV furniture. Everybody who was anybody in Mexico came to the open houses—businessmen, artists, musicians, archaeologists, and writers. Hemingway was a frequent guest when he was in Mexico; and Lindbergh met Anne Morrow, his future wife, at one of the Wright Sunday open houses. The hostess at all these events was Harry Wright's wife (Jett Sullivan's aunt), who was reputed to have been the most beautiful and most gracious woman in all of Mexico. Judging from the portrait I saw of her, I can believe it. Harry Wright took great pride in her gracious presiding over all his social functions. She was a devout Catholic, and after the revolution, when all religious functions were strictly forbidden, she had Masses offered secretly in the Wright home by priests such as the Jesuit Father Pro, who operated in disguise. It was a considerable risk for Harry Wright to take, but either his devotion to his wife or his influence with the government gave him the courage to take the risk. For some reason, the Wrights were unable to have children. Harry's devotion to his wife and his promise to his mother never to touch liquor did not preclude his indulging in some other pleasures on the side, though: he was something of a womanizer. His immense wealth enabled him to command what he wanted, but I learned from a firsthand witness that the command did not always work. A friend of mine at the American College told me on one occasion that when she first came to Mexico and was working as a secretary for a company that occupied a building where Harry Wright had his office, Harry had propositioned her. When she resisted his advances, he considerably upped the ante and was so persistent in trying to break down her resistance that the only way she could counter his pursuit was to go back to the States for a year until his ardor had somewhat cooled.

Mrs. Wright died suddenly of pneumonia while on a visit to the

States, leaving Harry desolate because, in spite of his womanizing, he was deeply in love with his wife. But it also left him wide open to the approach of gold diggers. One soon appeared in the person of a prominent widow with a beautiful daughter. The mother saw in the widowed and wealthy Harry a very susceptible object of prey, and she began weaving a net for him. At all kinds of social occasions, she saw to it that her daughter, alluringly bedecked, was brought to Harry's attention. Because of Harry's propensity for beautiful women, it didn't take much to attract his attention. He fell for the daughter, head over heels, proposed marriage, and went through with it. The new wife wasted no time in becoming pregnant to guarantee an heir for Harry's fortune and then proceeded to have the legal rights to that fortune drawn up formally. This was just the beginning of Harry's tragic fall. He soon realized the folly of what he had done. His actions had estranged his brother, Bowland, who never spoke to him again after the marriage. Harry turned in on himself, became a recluse, and spent most of his time in a darkened room, lamenting his previous infidelities to his first wife and cruelly making invidious comparisons between her and his new one. After a couple of years of this unhappy life as a recluse, Harry died of a heart attack, unreconciled to the rest of his family. The new wife inherited the entire fortune. To her credit, it has to be said that after she moved to New York, she used much of the huge fortune for very good social causes among the poor. But it has also to be said that Harry, in spite of his fabulous rise to fortune and fame, had a tragic ending that it would have taken Eugene O'Neill or Arthur Miller to do justice to on the stage.

Harry Wright was long dead before our foray into Mexico for our first workshop there, but his bother Bowland—"Uncle Bo," Jett Sullivan called him—was still very much alive. Jett suggested that we get in touch with "Uncle Bo." She was sure he would do something interesting for us. In the brother team that had developed the Consolidated Steel Company, he had been the public relations and sales person, while Harry actually ran the business, so Harry had the major financial interest in the company. Uncle Bo had married the daughter of a Methodist minister, and they had had four children, three sons and a daughter. Uncle Bo was disappointed in all of them. As a self-made businessman who had done pretty well, he just presumed that his sons would become interested in his business and carry it on, but, as is sometimes the case with sons of great business tycoons, his sons had no interest in the business at all and went on to do other things that Uncle Bo considered disasters. One of them opened an antique shop in California; another took up teaching English and taught for little or nothing in the inner city of New York; and the third one stayed at home, but was not interested in his father's business and did not do well in any of the businesses in which his father tried to set him up. So, by the standards of his own extraordinary success as a businessman, Bo considered all three of his sons disappointing failures. He took an even dimmer view of his daughter's choices. She married a native Mexican and joined the Catholic Church in doing so. Uncle Bo was convinced she had married beneath her social status, and he completely disinherited her. She was cut off permanently from all contact with the family. She had one daughter, but she herself died rather young of pneumonia. Uncle Bo refused to have her buried in the big family lot in the American cemetery, so she was buried in a grave without a headstone outside of the impressive Wright lot, and none of the Wrights went to the funeral. The Wrights were headstrong people.

Knowing all this about Uncle Bo, I didn't know what to expect. I contacted him after we settled in. Jett had said he would probably do something interesting for us. He did. He invited all of us for dinner and an evening at his beautiful home in the city. When we arrived, he greeted us warmly. He looked like what he fundamentally was, a white-haired southern gentleman from Virginia, sort of like the colonel in the advertisements for Kentucky Fried Chicken. The size of his townhouse (he also had a splendid villa in the beautiful city of Cuernavaca) can be gauged by the fact that all thirty-two of us were seated at the dining room table, with Uncle Bo and his wife presiding at the head of it. The whole setting looked a little like an official dinner in Windsor Castle. The meal was a delicious Mexican repast; remembering Uncle Bo's pledge of abstinence to his mother, we were surprised that it was accompanied by a nice wine, which neither Uncle Bo nor his wife drank. Uncle Bo pretty much dominated the conversation, but he did have many interesting observations about his years in Mexico. He finally got around to talking about his family. Knowing what I did about it, I could tell it was a touchy subject. His ironic observation about the son teaching in the inner city in New York was: "I've got one son who is going to save the world. Jesus

Christ made a stab at that." And gesturing to Father Maher and me in our Roman collars, he went on: "You gentlemen have also given that a try, but I am here to tell you that my son is going to do the job."

Dinner over, we all retired to the theater, an added wing of the house decorated on the interior to simulate an Egyptian temple and full of memorabilia that the Wrights had gathered in their many trips to Egypt, China, and the Orient in general. Cases all along the rear of the theater housed a large collection of movie films; almost any important movie that had appeared in the previous ten years was there. We could choose what film we wanted to see, and Uncle Bo would screen it for us. I forget now which film we chose, but what I can't forget is the documentary Bo showed before he screened the movie. He had taken it himself. He had filmed the whole progression of the eruption of Paricutín, a volcano in Mexico, from the time it started fuming up in a cornfield until it had built up its whole volcanic cone and started pouring out streams of red hot lava down the side of the cone, across the cornfields, to a little village that it completely engulfed. The last shots were of the lava flowing around the gold cross on the top of the steeple of the little village church. It was a spectacular documentary. Uncle Bo had taken miles of film all through the eruption and then turned it all over to a professional, who had edited it into a first-class documentary, which actually won a prize in a film contest at the time, as it should have. Jett Sullivan was right: her Uncle Bo had indeed provided an interesting evening for us. But as I recall his life, it ended on a somewhat tragic note, like that of his brother Harry, in spite of his financial success. That ending didn't have the kind of bizarre glumness that you find in the tragedies of O'Neill, but Arthur Miller could have perhaps lent it something similar to the tragic intensity of *The Death of a Salesman*.

But now for an episode in the Wright saga that is decidedly Faulknerian. It reflects the same kind of compulsiveness to tell the whole story that drove Miss Caldfield to pour out the story of Thomas Sutpen to Quentin Compson in *Absalom! Absalom!* In the years when we had begun to conduct our workshops in South America and Europe, word came to us that Uncle Bo's wife had died. Almost immediately after her death, Uncle Bo arranged to have his widowed sister Mu (I think her name was Margaret, but she never referred to herself as anything but Mu) come to live with him and act as his hostess. I came to know her well and to know Uncle Bo better during two weeks when I lived with them as I was broadening my knowledge of pre-Columbian art in the recently opened archaeological and ethnological museum. Jett Sullivan again made the arrangements for me; it was a very advantageous situation. Bo knew everybody important in Mexico, so he got me easy access to the director of the museum and to several of the curators who had helped plan and arrange the exhibits. The museum is certainly one of the best-planned and most spectacularly arranged archaeological museums in the world. The building itself is a grand enlargement of the classically conceived structure of Uxmal. In the great structure, you walk through the entire history of pre-Columbian art chronologically with outstanding examples of the art of each culture on display, accompanied by plaster models of whole cities and huge photographic displays that enable you to reconstruct the environment from which the objects on display came. It was a marvelous educational experience to be seeing all this in the company of and through the eyes of some of the curators who had helped put it all together.

During the time I stayed at his villa, Bo had to go to his office every day. Even at his age (early eighties), he was working on a new business scheme, a new housing project on the outskirts of Cuernavaca. He commuted between his Mexico City office and an office he had set up at his villa in Cuernavaca to oversee the project, so he was gone all day. But he had arranged for me to see all kinds of places and people that he thought would be valuable because of my interest in pre-Columbian matters. He had instructed his chauffeur to drive me wherever I had to go. On some of these excursions, Mu came with me. She was relatively new in Mexico City, and many of these places were unfamiliar to her, especially those associated with the pre-Columbian cultures in which she had had little interest. I was amazed at how interested in them she became, how eager she was to learn about them from what I could tell her, and how much of what she learned she retained. And on these daytime excursions, I learned a good deal more about her. I learned that her marriage to a nationally prominent engineer had been pretty much arranged for her by her brothers, as had her sister's to the founder of the Pan-American airline. The boys, it seems, looked upon their sisters' marriages as a kind of financial investment, but the marriages seemed to have been happy enough.

Uncle Bo had also bought a ticket to the sound and light performance at Teotihuacán for me and again had arranged for his chauffeur to drive me there. I had seen it before with the workshop group but enjoyed it even more the second time because I brought much more to the experience. Bo, Mu, and I were always together each evening for dinner back at the mansion, and these dinners gave me the opportunity of picking Bo's brain about his experience of more than half a century of Mexican history. I recount the experience of this sojourn with Bo and Mu because, had it not happened, I doubt whether Mu would have made the request she eventually did make for me to participate in one of the most bizarre experiences of my life.

A couple of years after this visit with the Wrights, Bo became seriously ill and died of a heart attack. Mu stayed on in the mansion for a while and reigned there like the queen mother. Eventually Jett Sullivan and I were summoned to an audience with the queen. Mu wrote and said that it was imperative that Jett and I come down to Mexico City at her expense because she had some business to take care of that only I could help her complete. We had no idea what the business was, but we answered the summons. We flew down and took up residence at the Prado Hotel, where Jett and her husband Leon had always stayed when they visited Mexico City. Leon refused to stay with the Wrights; he treasured his independence and did not want to be beholden to anyone. Mu sent the chauffeur to pick Jett and me up the morning after our arrival. When we got out to the Wright mansion, we found Mu ensconced in the upstairs sitting room, dressed from head to foot in black. She had arranged two chairs in front of her, and as soon as we were seated, she said she wanted to give us a complete account of the lives of her two brothers, Harry and Bo.

She immediately launched into a detailed narrative. I felt like the wedding guest in Coleridge's "Ancient Mariner," fixed by the eye of the mariner as he compulsively tells the story of the shooting of the albatross. Mu's narrative was every bit as compulsive. She began with Harry and went through every detail of his life from his boyhood in Virginia, his financial ventures and fantastic financial success in Mexico, his influence in the American colony in Mexico City and his happy marriage. But she was not canonizing him; she was aware of his womanizing and gave some instances of it. Most of what she told us we already knew, but it was a weird experience to listen to her pouring out this whole tale to us. It seemed at times that she was unaware of our presence and that she was driven by a compulsion to get the story out. Her narrative ended with Harry's final infatuation and second marriage, his surrender of his fortune to the new bride, his metamorphosis into a recluse, and his cruel and invidious treatment of his new wife in the years before he died. When she had disposed of Harry, Mu turned to Bo, emphasizing his success as a public relations man and salesman for the Consolidated Steel Company and his final estrangement from his brother Harry. She touched on his disappointment in all his children and finally came to his cruel and unforgiving treatment of his daughter, who he thought had disgraced him by marrying a Mexican and a Catholic, a marriage he considered beneath her status. We finally discovered what all this compulsive narrative was about.

Mu told us that when Bo was alive he worked most of the day in his office, a little building at the rear of the pleasant garden in his residential compound. A dinner bell was mounted on a pole in the middle of the garden. When the time came, the maid would ring the bell to alert Bo that lunch was served. Mu told us that for some weeks prior to our coming the bell had been ringing at precisely Uncle Bo's lunch time without anybody ringing it. She was convinced that this was a sign that Uncle Bo's spirit was not at rest because of his unfortunate treatment of his daughter and that this would continue to be the case until something was done to make reparation to the injured daughter. She was even more convinced when she received news from Bo's son, teaching in the inner city of New York, that he had been having a repeated dream during the same period that Bo's spirit would not find rest until reparation of some kind had been made to the daughter. Mu had the reparation planned, and I was to figure in the plan. What she wanted me to do was conduct a Catholic rite at the grave of the daughter to try to make up for the fact that Bo had refused to allow her burial in the large family plot and that none of the Wrights had attended her funeral. It was a weird request, but one I could see no reason to refuse. I had no sacramentary with me, but I concocted a graveside rite from some Scripture readings and prayers from the funeral Mass in the missal I did have. The long narrative had taken almost three hours. When it was over and we had agreed on the graveside rite, we moved to the veranda for lunch. Happily the dinner bell did *not* sound, but in the strange circumstances I had the odd feeling that Bo's spirit might be occupying the fourth chair at the table. It was not the most relaxed lunch I have ever eaten.

Lunch over, we were chauffeured to the cemetery, picking up Bo's granddaughter and her Mexican husband on the way, neither of whom Bo had ever seen. Nor had Mu had any previous contact with them. The granddaughter was also dressed completely in black. She and Mu looked like the black-veiled queen and queen mother at the funeral of King George VI. It was a strange feeling standing in the cemetery with our backs to the Wright lot with its large ostentatious monument where the unforgiving father was buried and facing the little unmarked grave of the disinherited daughter. I blessed the grave, read the Scripture passages, and recited the prayers for the dead daughter. When I concluded with the prayer, "May her soul and the souls of all the faithful rest in peace," the granddaughter and her husband joined in a hearty "Amen." I couldn't hear whether Mu joined us or not, but we all knew that what she was most interested in was the prospect of her brother Bo's resting in peace. The delayed obsequies completed, we left the cemetery and went to the grand-daughter's house for tea, a very civil and polite event at which gener-alities were exchanged without much meaningful conversation. Mu made her formal adieu; she had no further dealings with Bo's grand-daughter and her great-niece as far as I know. Now that Jett and I had finished our task, we were graciously deposited at the hotel with more adieus. I never saw or heard from Mu again. After a short time, the Wright mansion was sold. Mu's queenly days were over. She moved to a retirement home in New Mexico. My experience of this Wright episode in my life convinced me of the truth of the old saw that "truth is stranger than fiction."

The success of the workshops in Mexico induced us to think of addi-tional ones in South America. Father Robert Henle at St. Louis Uni-versity had participated in organizing some educational programs, especially in nursing, in Ecuador, and he thought we would find the capital city, Quito, an interesting setting for one of our programs. We planned one for Quito and set up headquarters in a hotel there. Father Henle was right: Quito proved to be quite intriguing.

In the first place, we were astonished at the undeveloped state of the country at the time we were there, some thirty years ago now.

For instance, there was no general mail delivery system in the whole city of Quito, the capital. To receive mail you had to go to the central post office, and it was only there that you could purchase stamps. We went there one day to purchase some, and we found them being sold at several booths in the main hall of the post office. The same stamps were being sold at different booths for different prices. In most countries, you are overwhelmed with acres of postcards for sale. We saw none anywhere in Quito except, again, in the central post office, displayed under plastic as if they were relics. It didn't appear that many were ever sold. I bought some, to the seeming surprise of the person at the wicket where I paid for them. While I was addressing some cards at a desk in the hallway, a well-dressed lady came up to me and asked whether I would send her a letter or card because she had never received a piece of personal mail in her life.

Another thing that amazed us immediately was the overwhelming preponderance of indigenous people in the population. It was evident everywhere. We were told that more than 85 percent of the population of the whole country is full-blooded Native American. Most of them are poor peasants in the countryside and working-class people in the cities. The poverty of the native population was extreme. The wealth of the country was controlled by a fraction of the 15 percent of the nonnative population. The rich were very content to maintain the status quo and were doing so. It was a provocative situation in which to study again some human relation problems. We were told that at that time only one native person in the whole country had risen to a professional position: he was a lawyer in Quito. We got in touch with him and had him spend a day with us at the workshop. His story was an interesting one. His father had saved and saved to get money to send him to grade school. When the boy learned that this is what his father planned for him, he ran away from home rather than go to school. Native people did not go to school; for him to go would have been a betrayal of his "Indianness" to his native confreres. Besides, to go to school he would have had to put on shoes, and that also would have been a betrayal of his ancestry. But the father captured his son, put shoes on him, and kept him at his books through grade and high school. The son did extremely well, so well, in fact, that he won a scholarship to Yale, where he did his college work and then remained to get a law degree. He returned to Quito to practice his profession, but he told us that up to the time we were there, he had never had a Native American client. The native people thought that Native Americans had no business being lawyers, so low was their self-image. All of his clients were from the upper class, which meant they were nonnatives.

To see that kind of severe division in society was something of a shock to all of us, but it led us to reexamine the prejudiced race relations in our own history that for so long segregated such a large part of our African American population from the rest of American society.

If the racial prejudice in Ecuador was a shock, the chicanery of the bishops there was an outright scandal. We learned that the people in the country who were assigned to run the International CARE Program at the time were the Catholic bishops, but we also learned that they were selling some of the CARE packages and using the money to build themselves a center in Quito for their biannual meetings. This scandal had come to Pope John XXIII's attention. To remedy it, he had appointed a young diocesan priest from Cicero, Illinois, who had a doctorate in sociology, to come to Quito and administer the program, which so irritated the bishops that they tried to have the priest's visa canceled by the government. When that failed, they planned to have him assassinated. That certainly sounds like an intrigue right out of the High Renaissance. This nefarious plan also failed, and the priest from Cicero was successfully administering the program when we were there. We had this information, not by hearsay, but from the lips of the priest himself. He spent a day with us and provided many of the historical and sociological background of the country and the sorry history of the Roman Catholic Church there. The Church had become thoroughly identified with the monied upper class, to the neglect of the indigenous population.

Having seen firsthand this scandalous neglect of the poor by the Church from the top down made the later turnaround of the bishops from all over Mesoamerica and South America at the post–Vatican II meeting at Puebla, Mexico, so remarkable. At that meeting, all the bishops signed a resolution to make the rights and welfare of the poor, especially the poor indigenous peoples, in their dioceses a major concern. Such an about-face had to be the effect of the divine inspiration of the Holy Spirit. A similar resolution came out of the bishops' later meeting at Medellín, Colombia. Admittedly, making a resolution is easier than carrying it out, but many churchmen have made remarkable progress since Vatican II in defending the rights of the poor. Some clerics became literal martyrs to the cause, including Bishop Romero of Salvador, who was shot down while saying Mass because of his outspoken defense of the rights of the native population. Several nuns were murdered in Salvador for working in the cause of the native peoples. And the whole world was genuinely shocked by the cold-blooded murder of the six Jesuits and two of their servants in San Salvador for their bold defense of indigenous rights and for calling attention to the injustices of the powers that be.

Our next foreign site for a workshop was Bogotá, Colombia. Here, too, we were to see the abysmal contrast between the riches of the few and the poverty of the many. And the many were the native peoples. We held our classes on the campus of our own Jesuit Universita Javeriana. It was situated at the edge of the city of Bogotá and practically abutted on the mountains that arose to the rear of the campus. As is frequently the case in South American cities, the luxury homes were in the valley, and the homes of the poor were on the mountainside. Some of the worst slums I have seen anywhere climbed up the mountain a little to the rear of the Javeriana campus. Makeshift shacks made up the village, many without electricity and all of them without running water. In fact, many of the residents had to come down to the valley to get any water at all. We would see young children all day long coming down from the mountain leading burros with tin oil cans flung over their backs to get the necessary water for drinking, cooking, and occasional washing. The city of Bogotá was notorious for children who had tired of life in the slums and who had bunched together in packs and spent their time thieving in the daytime and sleeping in odd corners of the city at night.

We also had an opportunity of observing firsthand the sharp sense of class distinction that still obtains in some quarters there. On one weekend, we visited a coffee plantation and the famous salt mine in which they have created a whole underground cathedral with altars and sculptures, all carved out of solid salt. We went to a nearby restaurant for lunch and invited the bus driver to come in and have lunch with us. The two students from the Jesuit Universita Javeriana, who had come along on the trip as our guides, refused to sit down at table with a bus driver. But again, before being too shocked, we had to remind ourselves of the many generations of strict racial segregation in our own country.

While we were in Colombia, we also had two very positive experiences that left us with a better impression of what the Church has done or at least what some churchmen have at times done for the underprivileged in Colombia. We went one weekend to Cartagena, on the northwest coast. It is a charming old colonial city and has the distinction of having the only truly walled fortress in the Western Hemisphere. It was an important harbor city, and Sir Walter Raleigh is said to have put into its harbor on one of his maritime excursions. But Cartagena was particularly interesting to me for an entirely different reason. It was the place where one of my Jesuit brethren of the seventeenth century, St. Peter Claver, spent his life working among the African slaves as they were being disembarked in the harbor. We visited his room in the Jesuit residence, now a chapel in honor of St. Peter, from the window of which he had a view of the harbor and could see when the slave ships arrived. When they did, he was off immediately to meet them, greet the slaves, feed them, clothe them, administer medicine to the sick, and, in the process, instruct them in the faith and baptize them. St. Peter and his helpers were the only bright spot in the lives of these poor slaves. As a result of his ministrations and missionary work among the slaves, almost all the African Colombians today are still Catholics. Their heaviest concentration remains in the coastal area, where they were kept to work in the cotton and corn fields.

It was a source of pride to me as a Jesuit to recall that it was one of my confreres who had made such a difference in the lives of the poor slaves in Colombia. As I offered Mass for our students at the altar in St. Peter Claver's room and thanked God for his life, I could not help thinking of the life of another of my Jesuit confreres, who by his simple and humble life of piety had inspired the successful young Peter Claver to leave his worldly career, join the Jesuits, and eventually dedicate his life to an apostolate among the slaves of Colombia. There are many roads to sanctity. The Jesuit lay brother Alphonsus Rodriguez, who spent most of his life working as porter at the Jesuit community house in the Spanish Island of Majorca, also became a saint doing it. He is known today as St. Alphonsus Rodriguez. It was his simple piety and his unfailing graciousness and courtesy to guests in the porter's lodge at Majorca that first attracted the go-getter Peter Claver to the Society. The poet Gerard Manley Hopkins was struck by the heroic fiber and saintly achievement that can go into such a seemingly unnoticed life as that of the humble porter. The point he makes, of course, is that it is not unnoticed by God. Here is Hopkins's poem:

*In honor of*
*St. Alphonsus Rodriguez*
*Laybrother of the Society of Jesus*

Honour is flashed off exploit, so we say;
And those strokes once that gashed flesh or galled shield
Should tongue that time now, trumpet now that field,
And, on the fighter, forge his glorious day.
On Christ they do and on the martyr may;
But be the war within, the brand we wield
Unseen, the heroic breast not outward-steeled,
Earth hears no hurtle then from fiercest fray.

Yet God (that hews mountain and continent,
Earth, all, out; who, with trickling increment,
Veins violets and tall trees makes more and more)
Could crowd career with conquest while there went
Those years and years by of world without event
That in Majorca Alfonso watched the door.

On a later occasion, I offered Mass at the altar in the Majorcan chapel where the porter's lodge had been in which Alphonsus spent most of what he would think of as a very unheroic life. It was a life very different from that of the servant of the slaves, Peter Claver, on the other side of the world. I tried to realize, in that little Majorcan chapel, the truth of what Hopkins had said: that God "Could crowd career with conquest while there went / Those years and years by of world without event / That in Majorca Alfonso watched the door."

The second very edifying experience we had in Colombia was a visit to the Barrio del Minuto de Dios. Along a public highway, not far from Bogotá, we encountered a sign that read EL BARRIO DEL MINUTO DE DIOS, the Barrio (Suburb) of the Minute of God. The sign bore public witness to what is perhaps one of the most constructive and hopeful social projects in all of South America. It is the result of the foresight and dedicated Christian charity of a priest of the Eudist congregation, Father Rafael Garcia Herreros.

Some years ago, touched by the appalling conditions of the thousands of poor people who were forced to live, without proper food and clothing, in wretched adobe huts or hovels pieced together from fragments of cardboard, scrap tin, and packing cases, Father Garcia began a television program in which he appeared on the screen for precisely one minute with a particular family that was in need of immediate help. He used the minute to describe the family's need and to make a plea for help in the name of Christian charity. He always received the help from some of the TV audience. But even more important than that, this minute of God began to call attention dramatically to the terrible social problem eating at the heart of so many countries in South America and elsewhere—the wealth of the few and the poverty of the many.

As response to the program grew, it occurred to Father Garcia that he might do something more genuinely and permanently constructive than just aiding individual families when they were in dire straits. Why not try to build a new community on genuinely Christian principles for these people? Why not demonstrate to the poor that the Church can do for them what the communists are forever promising but never actually doing? It was the attempt to answer these questions that had brought the Barrio del Minuto de Dios into being. And a marvelously effective answer it is.

Father Garcia began the development with a simple but adequate three-room house that he built with his own hands. He moved in a family from a ramshackle hut and began to teach its members how to live in their new surroundings: how to cook, how to sew, how to clean. Other poor families began to show an interest, and the Barrio del Minuto de Dios began to grow. From the beginning, the project was a cooperative one. Support continued to come from the audience of the TV program *El Minuto de Dios*. The prospective citizens of the barrio contributed the skills they had: carpentry, masonry, electrical work, painting, and so on.

To qualify for residence in the new barrio, a family had to be in dire need, and its members had to be willing to cooperate with the neighbors. They also had to show a willingness to improve their way of life physically, intellectually, and morally. From the beginning, there never were restrictions of race or creed, and as the barrio developed, natives and nonnatives, Germans and Spaniards, Mohammedans and Christians settled side by side in peace and harmony. Seven hundred families were living there when we made our visit.

What struck us almost at once as visitors to the Barrio del Minuto de Dios was the quality of the social planning that had gone into its development. It is very unlike a great many of our own lower-income housing projects, which are mere warrens into which poor families are moved without any education or help to teach them to live in a new environment. Not so the Barrio del Minuto de Dios. Here, everything, it seemed, had been thought of and provided for. Families were at first moved into houses that were not in *every* way unlike those from which they had come. They were neat and clean, and they had modern plumbing and electricity, but the kitchen stove was a coal stove with a brick oven. This similarity was deliberately planned as a link with the new residents' past experience.

The community also contributed work. If a man was an electrician, for example, he contributed his services to his neighbors, but the barrio was not communistic. Interest in private property was deliberately fostered. From their arrival, families paid a nominal rent, something between $10 and $16 a month, depending on the size of their house, and if the family paid this rent for five years successively, they would own the house. Provision was made for some mobility, too, within the community. When a family had met its rent and had demonstrated its ability to live peacefully, honestly, and constructively in the community, it might move into a more commodious house or apartment that compared well in conveniences with middle-income houses and apartments in the United States. The rent here was slightly higher, but, again, five years of rent established ownership.

The social planning was not merely on the level of housing. Much was being done in the barrio to teach all age levels how to live a new life. There was a complete school system from kindergarten through high school, and attendance at school was obligatory. Besides this, there were classes for adult men and women. They were taught to read and write, if they could not already do so; there were also classes in practical things, such as sewing and cooking for the women, and carpentry and various other skills for the men. In and out of class, the dignity of labor and the necessity of honesty and charity in dealing with one's neighbors were constantly stressed. Although none of the doors were locked, there had been no thievery in the community in the ten years of the barrio's history.

One of the most interesting details of the community was the constructive attitude toward work inculcated by signs everywhere and by precept and example. The honesty and diligence of the residents of the barrio had become so well known that neighboring factories were anxious to have them as employees, and factories were beginning to locate in the neighborhood to benefit by this source of excellent labor. It was part of the plan to attract enough factories into the neighborhood so that all barrio residents could be within walking distance of their work, thus eliminating transportation costs. It looked as if this would soon be accomplished. Men who had not yet been able to get jobs in factories were hired in the barrio's own shops, where they used a skill that they already had or learned a new one. The carpenter shop, shoe shop, and bakery were particularly well developed. Boys from the seventh grade on went to school in the morning and worked in one of the neighboring factories in the afternoon, so that when they had finished their schooling, they would be assured of a job. Meantime, they helped augment the family income.

The residents themselves did much of the work of constructing the barrio's houses, streets, and workshops, and they took immense pride in doing it. On the day we visited the barrio, a bricklayer and his young son were laying the bricks in the beautiful plaza in front of the new church. The father was justly proud of his work, and he was obviously enjoying showing his son how to do the job. Wherever the residents went in the barrio, they saw some of their own handiwork. And there was a good deal of rivalry among them in the development of the little flower gardens fronting each house. As a result, the barrio had none of that colorless monotony usually associated with public housing projects. Another manifestation of the spirit of the barrio was the cooperative stores in which groceries of all kinds were sold at considerably reduced prices.

Nor had recreation been neglected. There was a fine community hall, in which movies, dances, public lectures, and various other types of communal recreation were provided. Playing fields for children of all ages were either already being used or being planned. One of the problems with the poor in Colombia has always been that the men frequently spend what little money they earn on excessive quantities of beer. Beer was not outlawed in the barrio. There was a tavern, but no man could be sold more than two drinks. Drunkenness was practically nonexistent.

Mexico City's new housing developments Santa Fe and Independencia are as well or better planned than the Barrio del Minuto de Dios in Bogotá. In one important respect, they are vastly different, however: the projects in Mexico City are entirely inspired, financed, and executed by the government, and religion has been deliberately and systematically excluded. They are entirely secularist in spirit. In contrast, the very title of the development in Colombia, Barrio del Minuto de Dios, is proof that here God and religion are not excluded. In fact, Christian principles of social justice and charity are the motivating forces that consciously permeate the whole project. It is a deliberate attempt to demonstrate that the Church is genuinely interested in the poor and is willing to do something constructive for them.

A visible sign of the central importance of religion in this social project was the beautiful new church that had just been dedicated before we saw it. Simple but imaginative, it is one of the most beautiful in all of Bogotá and its environs, and it dominated the whole barrio. It is perhaps symptomatic of the new spirit operating in the barrio, however, that the schools were built before the church. Too often in the past history of Latin America, thousands of dollars were spent on elaborate churches but nothing on schools. Latin America may yet awaken to the importance of literacy and universal education in the fight against poverty and communism.

The communists in Colombia had not been slow to see that this project was robbing them of the basis of their constant propaganda— what they call the indifference of the Church and the wealthy toward the poor. They recognized Father Garcia as their worst enemy in Colombia. On at least two occasions, they had tried to kidnap or kill him, but, in spite of the great contribution Father Garcia had made to this unique social experiment, he had deliberately seen to it that its future was not dependent on him alone. The barrio was managed by a very capable layman, who had as his counselors a group of men from the barrio itself. Every ten families elected a chairman of their group. These chairmen formed a central council and constituted the governing body of the barrio. Father Garcia, perhaps too modestly, said: "They could eliminate me tomorrow, and the barrio would continue."

As we walked through the streets of El Barrio del Minuto de Dios, the effects of this social experiment in Christian living were perhaps most in evidence in the many clean, well-dressed, and well-behaved children whom we encountered everywhere. These children were always wreathed in smiles, a striking contrast to the usual rather sober-faced citizen of Bogotá and to the furtive, starved look on the faces of the droves of dirty, ill-clad children who wander the streets of the waterless shack towns that circle Bogotá and other Colombian cities.

One of the major social disgraces of South America has been the lack of a sense of social responsibility for the poor on the part of the small group of the vastly wealthy. Father Garcia's work had begun to do something about that, too. He could not have achieved what he had, of course, without the support of people of means, but more significant than their financial support was the social responsibility he was beginning to awaken in many of them. They were beginning to involve themselves in a constructive way in the welfare of the poor. One of the imaginative ways in which he had done this was by his annual Cena de Millionarios (Dinner of the Millionaires). The dinner cost $100 a plate, and the diners were served a cup of soup, a hard roll, and a glass of milk. This dinner had begun to awaken many Colombians to the social problem of the poor.

Father Garcia's project was at first branded as communistic, even by some of the hierarchy, but it had come to be recognized as the most positive bulwark against communism. In fact, in a manifesto by the Colombian bishops, his work at the Barrio del Minuto de Dios was held up for emulation everywhere in Colombia. A similar project has been begun outside of Tunja. And it is said that when the major cities of Colombia and South America have been ringed by such barrios, some of the major social ills of these countries will have been eliminated.

The substance of this account of the social experiment near Bogotá appeared in the January 1963 issue of *America* (vol. 108, pp. 95–99) in an article entitled "A Barrio in Bogotá." The editor made the following comment on it: "The history of the social planning from Plato's city-state to our day, has featured a number of Christian experiments. The newest one is described here by the Chairman of the English Department, St. Louis University, who has first-hand knowledge of it. As a deterrent to Communism, it may be something the Alliance for Progress should foster."

The firsthand experience of this marvelously successful social experiment was very uplifting for all of us. It showed us that one individual can make a difference. We could not help contrasting it with some of the dismal failures in housing projects in the United States. St. Louis is notorious for some of the worst failures, notably the Pruitt-Igoe project, consisting of some thirty-two large, low-income, high-rise residential units. But no provision whatever was made for assisting the residents to live a decent, humane life there. There were no handy markets, no shops, no schools, no recreational facilities, no cultural amenities, and, it goes without saying, nothing to take care of the residents' religious needs. As would be expected, the buildings soon deteriorated, and they became so unlivable and crime infested that they all had to be evacuated. They were later imploded simultaneously.

The next St. Louis housing fiasco took place in the Mill Creek area in the central part of the city. On a seven-hundred-acre area that was all cleared at one time, a new kind of housing for low-income families was constructed. It was made up of family townhouses, not high-rise warrens, which was supposed to give the residents a new sense of dignity and solve the problems seemingly inherent in high-rise, low-income apartment buildings. For a time, it did. The Mill Creek area was at first a dignified, well-integrated residential area for families of lower income. But gradually, through unbelievably bad management, it became so crime infested that it, too, became practically unlivable. As I write this, it has been completely demolished. We seem to be incapable of learning from our own past mistakes or from the good example of such successful developments as the Barrio del Minuto de Dios.

In neither Ecuador nor Colombia did we have the opportunity of experiencing much of the remains of the pre-Columbian cultures. We of course saw the spectacular collection of pre-Inca gold work that one of the Bogotá banks has on display: fine specimens of all the kinds of gold work in which the pre-Columbian people of South America were so adept—hammered embossed work, cast gold work, and filigree. But we saw little else of the architectural and artistic achievements of the pre-Columbian cultures in South America. We were told the best place to experience these achievements was in Peru, so we decided to go to Peru for our postworkshop bus tour. We flew to Lima. The several pre-Columbian museums there gave us ample opportunity to see firsthand the marvelous diversity and artistic achievement in ceramics of the various pre-Inca, pre-Columbian cultures. The Inca, which was the culture in control when the Spanish arrived, were, like the Aztecs in Mexico, Johnny-come-latelies on the scene. Like the Romans, they were not originators; much of what they achieved in architecture, sculpture, ceramics, gold work, and textiles was borrowed from their predecessors. The really great creativity of pre-Columbian cultures in South America was manifested in the work of such pre-Inca tribes as the Chavin de Huantar, Mochica, Paracas, Nazca, Tihuanaco, and the Chimuchancay. The diversified work of all of these cultures is beautifully illustrated in the extensive collection of ceramics in the Lima museums.

In one of the Lima museums, we were surprised to find that one whole building was devoted to a display of pornographic ceramics. Every conceivable form of sexual aberration, including bestiality, is relentlessly represented in these ceramics. The same kind of detailed artistry went into these pornographic subjects as was expended on the representation of religious mythology and on the rendering of genre scenes from ordinary life. Other cultures have also made pornography the subject of some of their art, but nowhere else have I seen such an obsession with the subject as here in these South American pre-Columbian cultures. Why this should be so, I have no idea. I am afraid I will have to leave the explanation to the anthropologists and sociologists.

What the museum exhibits also revealed, however, was the extraordinary skill these cultures had achieved in textiles. Peru is divided very sharply into two areas: the flat coastal land along the Pacific and the highlands and Andes Mountains to the east. The flat plains never receive any rain. The clouds form over the Pacific drift inland over the plains and do not release any of their moisture until they reach the mountains. The rains fall there, and the runoff creates rivers that flow through the plains to the ocean. Many of the most important pre-Inca cultures grew up in the plains. The inhabitants there devised a marvelous system of irrigation with water drawn from the rivers. The land was fertile, and the plainsmen raised sufficient crops and caught sufficient fish from the rivers and the ocean not only to feed themselves but also to help feed those dwelling in the highlands and mountains. The highlanders grazed llamas, alpacas, and vicunas

Professor Clarence Miller and Sister Una Hayes. Both were pupils of mine.

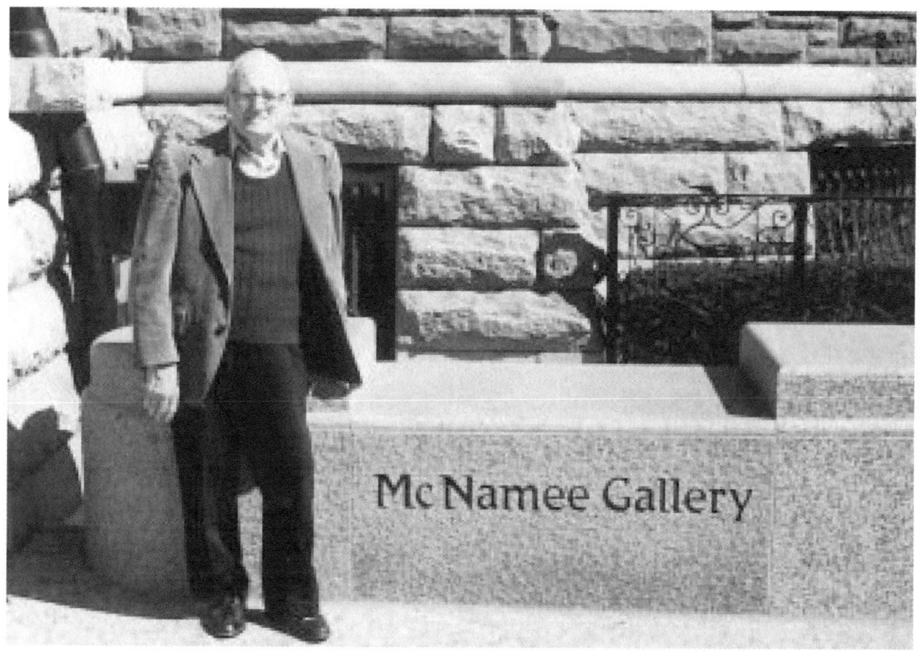

At the entrance to the McNamee Gallery in Cupples House.

On the front steps of Cupples House, which I restored.

Admiring part of the Glass Collection donated to Cupples House by Mrs.
Eleanor Turshin.

At my desk in Cupples House.

Cupples House board members, 1995. First row (from left): Peter Ambrose, Pamela Ambrose, Father Terrence Dempsey, S.J., Dr. Cynthia Stollhans, Eleanor Turshin, me, Gail Evans, Geraldine Kessler, Georgine Hartigan, Angela Breidenbach, Bill Winzerling. Second row: Robert Morrissey, Paul Martin, Eugene Mckay, Richard Hermann, Margaret Anthony, Bridget Flood, Jean La Fata, Harold Stahl, Father John Padberg, S.J.

Members of the English Department when I was
Chairman, at my ninetieth birthday party. Front row: Dr.
Mandeville, me, Father Ong, Dr. Benoit. Back row: Dr.
Fournier, Dr. Miller, Dr. Dougherty, Dr. Scott.

Miss Mary Bruemmer and Kathleen and Tyron Winter at the reception
in Cupples House in honor of my ninetieth birthday.

Father Ray Tully, me, and Father Paul Reinert, classmates at the 1999 convocation.

Charles Cuttler, me, Carolyn Valone, and Terry Dempsey at a presentation in honor of my ninety-first birthday.

Margaret Anthony and Ginny Bartling at ease at my ninety-first birthday party.

Sherry Linquist and Peter and Pamela Ambrose, lively participants in a conversation at the dinner in honor of my ninety-first birthday.

Above: Dale and Carol Boggs sharing the celebration of my ninety-first birthday. Carol was my first secretary in Cupples House. At left: with Trudy Busch at the party she hosted at Grant's Farm on the occasion of my ninety-first birthday. I spoke on the subject of "The Last Judgment" by Rogier Van der Weyden.

that produced marvelously fine wool. The llamas served as pack animals that helped carry materials to and fro between the lowlands and the highlands. The highlanders also worked the gold mines. So the two areas complemented one another.

The supply of wool from the llamas, vicunas, and alpacas soon prompted the art of spinning, dyeing, and weaving the wool into beautiful textiles that are the wonder of the world. Fine silk weaving may have up to six hundred threads to the inch; some of the fine woolen pre-Columbian textiles may have as many as fifteen hundred threads to the inch. Garments made out of vicuna wool were reserved for the Inca kings and their nobles. One of the uses of these fine textiles was connected with the pre-Columbian manner of handling the bodies of some of their important leaders. They were mummified in a seated position and wrapped and bound in a bundle. The bundle was in turn enfolded in an elaborately woven cloak that looked like a beautiful paisley shawl, and on top was placed a black felt hat. The bundle was then preserved in a tomblike room, where reverence continued to be shown to the dead leader. On special festival occasions, the bundle might be trundled out in a procession as if the dead leader were still blessing his people. Because the climate in the plains is so dry, many of these funeral robes have been very well preserved. This form of artistic achievement was specific to the South American pre-Columbian cultures because of the presence of the llama, alpaca, and vicuna there.

The Lima museums do provide fine examples of the artwork of most of the important pre-Inca cultures of South America, but we were particularly interested in seeing some of the actual Inca sites, the culture that was still flourishing when Pizarro and the other Spanish conquistadors arrived. We were told that the two best places to see these sites were Cuzco and Machu Picchu, so we flew to Cuzco high in the Andes—and I mean high. It is more than two miles above sea level, a mile higher than Denver. The air is extremely thin, and, for those not accustomed to it, it can be rather uncomfortable. Many of us felt very short of breath and developed headaches while we were there. We were told that the native people had developed a lung capacity a third larger than nonnatives to adapt to the lack of oxygen.

Cuzco had been the capital of the Inca Empire. It was a genuine empire, embracing all that is now Colombia, Ecuador, Chile, and

Bolivia—and the only real political empire in the pre-Columbian Americas. The Aztecs did not create an empire. They had a city-state that constantly warred on all neighbors to get victims for its human sacrifices. The Maya were far-flung geographically with important city centers in what is now Guatemala, Belize, Chiapas, and Yucatán. These centers were all independent city-states that were frequently at war with one another. The Incas, in contrast, developed a genuine political empire with absolute power resting in the person of the Inca (or emperor) himself. The geographical capital of that vast empire was Cuzco.

To create a real empire, several things are required. In the first place, there has to be the absolute power of the emperor at the center, and it helps if the emperor is divine: just as the Romans divinized their emperors, so did the Incas. A well-trained standing army is also necessary because the first step in building an empire is the conquest by war of the territories that will eventually make it up. Next in importance is the means of easy communication between the physical parts of the empire, which requires roads connecting those parts.

The Incas were past masters in all these steps of empire building. They concocted a mythical divine origin for the Incas—a brother and sister sent from the gods to the area of Lake Titicaca in Bolivia, who were given a mandate to found a new people with its political center at Cuzco. They were to conquer their neighbors, establish a new culture and regime, and see to it that their power and control be handed on through their offspring. Thus, for the Incas, imperial authority, conquest of one's neighbors, and empire building were mandated by the gods. The Incas took the mandate seriously. They built up a strong, well-equipped army that gradually conquered all that is now Colombia, Ecuador, Chile, Peru, and Bolivia, and imposed their myths, their language, and their customs on everyone they conquered. To maintain control of all these vast territories they had to build a system of roads. The only other ancient people to have constructed anything like this extensive and efficient road system were the Romans. Roads averaging twenty-four feet in width stretched to every major center of the whole Incan empire, and they all connected with Cuzco, the capital. They were all edged by low stone walls. Many were unpaved trampled soil; in swampy land, they became raised causeways paved with stone; in precipitous mountain areas, they were carved out of the mountainside. Rivers and gorges were spanned with all sorts of ingeniously constructed bridges. The emperor or Inca at Cuzco thus had easy access to any part of his far-flung empire. If trouble occurred anywhere, he could get a contingent of his army there quickly to quell the disturbance before it got out of hand. The roads were first built and later maintained by local labor. Roadwork was one of the ways that the populace paid its taxes. All along these roads, at distances a day's journey apart, rest stations were built and stocked with sufficient supplies to accommodate soldiers traveling to trouble spots or the Inca himself and his entourage making ceremonial visits to outlying parts of the empire. These stations were kept stocked by yearly contributions from residents along the road. The roads were also used to accommodate an ingenious courier system, with small courier stations at about five-mile intervals, that kept the Inca in Cuzco informed of what was going on all over the empire. A courier starting, for instance, in Quito, Ecuador, with a message to the Inca would run the first five miles to the first courier station, where he would pass on the message to the courier stationed there, who would run it on to the next station, and so on, until it reached the Inca at Cuzco. By this method, the message would arrive in Cuzco from Quito (thousands of miles) in about five days. As we learned about this amazingly efficient method of quick communication among the Incas, we could not help contrasting it with the astoundingly inefficient communication we had experienced in the modern Quito, with no mail delivery at all within the capital city of Quito itself.

To guarantee a local government loyal to the central Inca, the sons of local rulers in the conquered areas were taken to Cuzco, where they were heavily indoctrinated with the Inca worldview, myths, customs, and languages. Eventually they were sent back as government officials to their places of origin in the hope that they would be loyal to the new order they had been taught at Cuzco. Another means of winning the loyalty of the conquered was the tax levied on all citizens of the empire. A certain percentage of their produce—largely corn, of which the South American indigenous people had developed more than seventeen varieties—was put into common storage to be withdrawn by any citizens of the empire in dry seasons or when other disasters struck. This way, no one had to go hungry. It was actually a rather sensible kind of insurance. The throbbing heart of all this empirical activity was the capital Cuzco. And, as in the Roman Empire it was said that all roads led to Rome, it could be said here that in the Inca Empire all roads led to Cuzco.

We were able to sense that organization physically when we got our first glimpse of the city. On our way from the airport, we stopped at the site of the walled citadel that topped a hill outside Cuzco, Sacsahuaman, which was meant to guard the main city. From that eminence, we could get a view of the whole city in the valley. The modern city follows pretty much the plan of the old Inca city, laid out in the gridiron pattern that the Incas favored and imposed on every city they conquered all over the empire. They certainly followed it exactly in every city they planned from scratch. At the center of the Cuzco plan is a very large plaza. In Incan times, the Temple of the Sun, the most important god in the Incan mythology, would have been where the present cathedral is; across the square would have been the palace of the Inca, where a Dominican monastery now stands. A closer view of this monastery reveals that it is actually built on the massive stone foundation of the last Inca imperial palace. Thus, the palace of the Inca was given equal status to that of the temple—not by accident, because the Inca himself was considered to be divine and every device possible was employed to remind the populace of that fact. The plaza is large enough to accommodate a crowd of thousands. It was here that the Inca often harangued the public to impress on them his power and authority.

As we looked down from the eminence of the fortress Sacsahuaman, we could imagine the Inca haranguing the multitudes there much as Hitler harangued the crowds in Berlin, Stalin those in Red Square, or Mussolini those in the square in front of the Palazzo Venetia in Rome. Haranguing always goes with empire building. From our perch on the fortified hill, we could see the roads leading into the city from every direction. We could see the white line some of them cut into the side of the mountain on the northern edge of the city.

Before we left Sacsahuaman for our hotel in the heart of the city, we took a good look at the fortress itself. It is really one of the great architectural wonders of the world. It is a walled-in and fortified city. The walls, thirty or forty feet wide, are cyclopean structures made up of huge stones—some weighing more than twenty tons apiece. They are of uneven size and shape, and yet they are so neatly fitted together that you can hardly put a knife into the interstices. With no metal tools and no domestic draft animals, it is a constant source of wonderment how these immense pieces were fashioned and put in place. Enough of the outline of the buildings that made up the fort within the walls are extant to enable you to see that it was meant to be a place to which the whole city could retreat if necessary in case of an attack—with accommodations and supplies sufficient to sustain them through a fairly lengthy siege. There were barracks, too, for the permanent garrison that manned the fortress. All of this, of course, proved futile against Pizarro and his cohorts on horseback, who were equipped with superior weaponry.

When Pizarro and his men looked down from the fortress on the city below, two buildings in particular on the city square would have caught their eyes—all plated with gold and gleaming in the sun. When the Inca died, it was the custom to mummify his body in the seated position, wrap it in the funereal bundle, enshroud it in a beautiful hand-woven cloak, and install it in his palace permanently, thus making it a shrine housing this relic of the divine Inca. The exterior of the house was then covered with gold plate, and either everything on the interior was plated with gold, or objects made of pure gold replaced the ordinary ones. In one of these Inca shrines, when the Spanish arrived, they found even the bushes of the garden had been replaced with bushes of solid gold, and in the garden there was a life-size llama of pure gold. The Spaniards could hardly believe their eyes because it looked like Eldorado. Of course, they lost no time in stripping the Inca shrines of their gold and in shipping it all back to Spain.

We could get some vague impression of what the Inca capital looked like from our vantage point on the fortress hill of Sacsahuaman and from our meandering in the narrow gridiron streets of the city, but we were told a place to see a much better preserved Inca city was at Machu Picchu. It was a small fortified city built along one of the Inca roads into the jungle. It was so securely tucked away in the jungle that the Spaniards never knew it was there. It continued to function as an Inca center more than eighty years after the Spanish conquest and then mysteriously ceased to function. Its existence was not known until its ruins were discovered in the twentieth century. The only way to get to the site when we were there was by a bus mounted on railcar wheels that went on railroad tracks weaving through the jungle. The little stone-built Inca city perches precipitously on top of a mountainous promontory almost five thousand feet high. Mountains tower up almost perpendicularly on three sides of the promontory topped by the city of Machu Picchu. A swift mountain stream flows in a gorge it has cut through the mountains, and it circles the foot of the Machu Picchu promontory. This is one of the most awesome sites I have experienced anywhere in the world. Edmund Burke would have called it truly sublime.

A little commuter bus awaited us to take us up a narrow road cut into one end of the mountainous perch of Machu Picchu. As we wove our way up the dizzying hairpin curves, we noticed that the whole side of the Machu Picchu mountain had been cut into terraces firmly contained within man-made stone walls. The terraces had been filled with soil from the valley and were watered through stone pipes that carried water down to the terraces from the mountains above. Planted with corn, beans, squash, tomatoes, and potatoes, they provided food enough, especially when combined with fish from the river and game from the mountain forests, for the city dwellers on the hill the year round. The small city would have accommodated at most about eight hundred people. The bus dropped us at a stone gateway, through which we made our way up steep stone steps carved in the solid rock, along which stone drainage troughs had been built. Climbing up the hill on either side of the steep steps was what remained of the city's dwelling places, intact except for the thatched roofs. The houses, which usually consisted of two rooms, were constructed of stone with gabled stone ends. There were some larger buildings, also with gabled stone ends, that were evidently used for meetings of some kind. There were no temples or religious structures. The closest thing to a religious structure was a large sundial in a little public square at the very highest point of the city. The sun god was the central focus of the Inca religion, and it is said that these sundials, which figure prominently in many Inca sites, were meant to function as hooks to ensnare the benevolent influence of the sun god on the people. The site has never been invaded or plundered because it was previously completely unknown. Hence, the well-preserved stone ruins here do give a good impression of what a small remote Inca fortress city looked like. But the site itself is so awesomely placed among majestic mountains, above a roaring mountain stream coursing through a precipitous mountain gorge, and almost always wreathed with floating clouds that it would make a believer out of an atheist.

In the morning, we flew back to Lima and then to the States. This trip ended our workshops in human relations in Mesoamerica and South America. Looking with a critical eye at the human relations problems, they enabled both students and faculty to examine in a new light the many problems that face us at home. A particular advantage for me personally in these treks south of the border was that they introduced me to two new exciting areas of learning—pre-Columbian and South American colonial art. I have pursued the pre-Columbian area avidly ever since and have regularly taught a course in pre-Columbian art.

Because I had experienced firsthand so many pre-Columbian sites in both Mexico and South America, it was somewhat embarrassing to me to realize that I had never visited the impressive pre-Columbian site in my own back yard—the Cahokia Mounds, located a few miles northeast of East Saint Louis. When I finally did so, I was utterly amazed that the site compared so well with some of the important sites in Mexico. It had been a city of some twenty thousand people, oriented around a huge pyramid with smaller pyramids (some of them burial mounds), forming an impressive central plaza. Residences stretched out in all directions from the central plaza, and beyond them were many little ponds that had been created when the soil was dug up to construct the central pyramid and smaller mounds. Beyond these ponds were the cornfields that helped feed the population. The inhabitants were also evidently adept at astronomy. They had a Woodhenge, similar to England's Stonehenge and apparently related to their study of the heavenly bodies. The whole city was enclosed in a stockade of vertical logs for protection. There were signs in the pottery and obsidian remains in the mounds that the city might have traded with sites as far distant as Teotihuacán in Mexico. Originally, satellite sites were strung out from the Cahokia central city on both sides of the Mississippi River. A good many mounds were once located on the site of the city of St. Louis, all of which have been leveled. Because of these formations, St. Louis was once called "The Mound City."

# 14

# European Vignettes

THE SUCCESS of the Human Relations Workshops in Mesoamerica and South America prompted us to think of Europe as a site for other such workshops. We eventually held them in Lisbon, Majorca, Salzburg, Athens, and on a mail boat sailing from Bergen up the Norwegian coast to the Russian border. Our postworkshop tours included Spain, Italy, Switzerland, England, Egypt, and the Holy Land. Each of these workshops and subsequent bus tours provided remarkable educational opportunities for the students who participated, but, in retrospect, I do not think they were as successful as the Human Relations Workshops in Mesoamerica and South America. The extreme poverty and misery we encountered south of the border stimulated much more consideration of and pointed discussions of social justice and problems of individual human relationships than did the European setting, where conditions are comparable to our own. We all were enriched by the firsthand contact with countries and cultures that have contributed greatly to the formation of our own, but there were not as many surprises as those provided by our living for a time in Mexico and South America.

We chose Portugal as the site of our first European venture because we suspected it might be a little different from other European countries. We were right. The workshop was at Lisbon. I had thought of Portugal as a kind of accidentally roped off area of the Iberian Peninsula. We found that not to be the case. There is a small range of mountains on its eastern border that naturally separates it geographically from Spain. All its rivers run westward from these mountains, and the Tagus, which originates deep in central Spain, runs to the sea through the center of Portugal, terminating at Lisbon in a mighty expanse of water more than six miles wide. It provides an excellent natural harbor that can accommodate the largest seagoing ships even today. All of these geographical features turned Portugal away from the rest of the peninsula toward the sea. As a result, it became one of the most important maritime powers in the world, developing a rich trade all over the then known world, especially with China and Japan. It also developed flourishing colonies in India, Africa, and South America. Brazil, the largest of the South American countries, is thoroughly Portuguese, even in its language.

We had our workshop in Lisbon the year of the five-hundredth anniversary of Henry the Navigator, who did so much to make Portugal a maritime power. That fact was memorialized in an impressive new monument on the banks of the Tagus in Lisbon: a huge prow of a ship thrusting up from the bank of the river, with a heroic figure of Henry the Navigator at its point followed by other figures prominent in the maritime history of Portugal, including Vasco da Gama and Christopher Columbus, who sailed from the Tagus harbor at Lisbon.

Immediately behind the park that contains the memorial to Henry the Navigator is the Naval Academy, which has through Portugal's history trained the country's great navigators. And situated there, too, is the beautiful chapel and cloisters of San Hieronymo, where Portugal's great navigators always stopped to ask God's blessing on their seafaring ventures. Vasco da Gama, one of their greatest, is buried in the chapel. The chapel and cloisters are both examples of the Portuguese *manuelo* style, which is an adaptation of English perpendicular Gothic embellished with all kinds of maritime details in the stone carving, including a lavish use of maritime rope design, in places woven into sailor's knots, and a generous variety of sea shells.

Our group attended a sound and light performance one evening in the cloisters, in which scenes from the maritime history of Portugal were reenacted for us, framed by the beautifully carved cloister arcades on which constantly shifting colored lights played throughout the performance. It was a remarkably pleasant way of getting a first impression of how vitally important seafaring was in the history of Portugal, made all the more impressive by the fact that the performance was given a few yards from the spot where so many of the Portuguese explorers, colonizers, and traders embarked on their far-flung sea voyages.

The effect of Portugal's widespread trade relationships, especially those with China, are evident in much of its architecture. When you drive through villages in the countryside, you get the impression that you are in China because there are so many buildings with the turned-up tile roofs that are so typical of Chinese architecture. Another feature that strikes you in the countryside is its extreme tidiness. There is a law that all houses have to be painted every three years. They are usually whitewashed, and the shutters, window frames, and doors are painted bright blue, red, or yellow. Another distinctive detail in the Portuguese countryside are the cork trees. When they are stripped of their cork bark, the trunks are a bright orange. Their twisted trunks and branches alternating with the equally twisted contours of ancient olive trees give the impression that the natural countryside is afflicted with arthritis. Van Gogh caught some of that feeling in his paintings of olive orchards in southern France.

Portuguese is a Romance language somewhat comparable to Spanish, but it does not sound a bit like Spanish. There is a kind of swishing sound in its pronunciation that almost seems Russian. The Portuguese people are also very different from the Spanish: they have little verve and sparkle, and seem a bit dour. This sadness shows up in particular in the *fada,* their most typical vocal musical expression. The *fada* are sung by vocalists dressed completely in black, and the lyrics of the *fada* always tell a sad story. It is rather ironic that the Portuguese listen to this kind of music in their dinner clubs. The guests themselves, like the singer, are frequently dressed in black. This somberness contrasts sharply with an evening out in Spain marked by lively flamenco dancers who sing to the sound of castanets and the clicking of their heels.

Lisbon, where we had our workshop, is an attractive city, hilly like San Francisco, so much so that Alexandre Gustave Eiffel, the famous French engineer, experimented with the use of structural steel here to build an elevator to connect the lower with the upper town; only later did he use steel again to construct his famous tower in Paris. When we were there for our workshop, the only connection with the south bank of the Tagus was by ferry, which is again reminiscent of San Francisco before the construction of the Golden Gate Bridge. I have been back to Lisbon since a bridge was built across the river, adding another point of resemblance to San Francisco, and, incidentally, the same engineer who designed the Golden Gate Bridge designed the bridge at Lisbon. Still another way in which the history of Lisbon parallels that of San Francisco is the fact that it was almost totally destroyed by an earthquake in the eighteenth century. Hence, Lisbon today is a comparatively modern city as European cities go, but there are some few sections that remained fairly intact after the earthquake. One of them is the fortified citadel perched on top of one of the hills overlooking the harbor. Halfway up the street leading to the citadel is the old Romanesque cathedral, which was left unscathed after the quake. I was surprised to find a plaque in it commemorating the fact that Anthony of Padua was baptized in the cathedral. I had never thought of St. Anthony as Portuguese because he is so thoroughly identified with Padua and with the impressive basilica there where he is buried.

Portugal is smaller than Missouri, so we were able to see a great deal of it on weekend excursions during the workshop. We had very interesting experiences on those excursions. I am recording here my impressions of only the most memorable. One of our first jaunts was to Sintra, north of Lisbon, an area that Lord Byron said deserved to be called "Paradise Regained." He lived there for a time and wrote some of his *Childe Harold's Pilgrimage* there. He was right; the original Eden could not have been much lovelier than Sintra. It benefits from the warm tropical current that bathes the shores of Portugal and hence can support tropical plants along with the evergreens of a more northerly clime. The place is ablaze with bougainvillea vines and oleander bushes; vines and palm trees grow next to dark-green pine and cypress trees. The architecture is all done in the white stucco style much favored by the Portuguese, with the usual garnish of bright blue, red, or yellow balconies, shutters, and doors. Inside and out the buildings are also lavishly provided with beautiful tile work. Portugal is a rival of Holland and Spain in its widespread use of tile as an integral part of its architectural decor, probably an inheritance from the Moors, who occupied Portugal for centuries, as they did Spain. The ruins of their fortified castles can still be seen topping strategic hills all over the country. The beautiful little mountain that towers above Sintra on the north is today topped by a fantastic castle built by a German baron in the nineteenth century. It is so fantastic that it might have been designed by Walt Disney or by the architect who designed the Hearst mansion in California. But from a distance, it adds a romantic note to what already is a fantastically romantic natural landscape.

Nazare was our destination on another weekend trek. Nazare is a typical Portuguese fishing village on the sea. Its narrow streets of little whitewashed houses climb up the hillside just beyond the broad sandy beach. But it is not only the houses that are whitewashed; everything is—the streets and the precipitous steps that climb up the hill here and there are all completely whitewashed. The village looks very much like some of the Greek Island towns, such as Mykonos, with its blaze of all-white buildings. But, of course, the white is relieved here with the bright accents of its blue, red, and yellow shutters and doors. The most fascinating part of the village is the activity on the beach itself, all gyrating around the main focus of the village, fishing. The beach itself is beautiful, as are all the beaches in Portugal, made up of some of the most pure white sand I have seen anywhere in the world. They are so white that they almost look at a little distance as if they are made up of powdered sugar. These broad beaches at Nazare are always alive with the activity of fishermen either preparing their boats to put out to sea or unloading their boats after returning from a fishing excursion on the high seas.

The fishermen themselves add to the picturesque quality of the scene. They are dressed from head to foot in plaid woolen garments with a plaid stocking cap that hangs down to their waists and ends in a little tassel. The woolen clothes are a necessary precaution against the cold winds they will encounter for several days out on the high seas. The stocking cap is long enough to wind around the neck like a muffler to protect them from the cold sea gusts. Their boats are as picturesque as the fishermen themselves. They are sizable, about thirty feet long, have large gracefully curved prows, and are painted in very bright colors. Resting on the white beach, they look like bright tropical blossoms tossed up on the sand. Van Gogh compared similar boats he had seen on the coast of southern France to such blossoms and made them look like that in one of his famous paintings. When we were there, another picturesque note was added to the scene by the presence of whole pigskins, painted bright blue and hanging on racks ready to be loaded on the outgoing boats. They were being filled with fresh drinking water. One of the legs of the pig had a spigot inserted in it. The fishermen favor the pigskin container because the slight evaporation that takes place through the skin keeps the water cool. The glimpse of this very ancient container summoned up echoes of Christ's remarking that you don't put new wine into old skins. I also recalled having seen a hawker in the bazaar at Casablanca with a goatskin of water thrown over his shoulder, selling brass cups full of water to the bargainers in the bazaar.

When the fishing boats return, all the women of the village, dressed in black, descend the white expanse of the village streets to the beach, where they all pitch in with their husbands to pack the fish in ice crates to be shipped by truck to city markets in Portugal or to the airport, from which they are flown immediately to markets around the world. When the fish-laden boats arrive at the beach, preferably at high tide, they are guided right up to the water's edge. Tractors then pull them up onto the beach itself. At low tide, they are completely free of the water, and a flurry of activity ensues to empty them and reequip them for another trip at sea. At the next high tide, they are gently eased back into the water. I sometimes think of this scene when I order a special fish in a fine restaurant and recall all the flurry of activity that has gone into getting that fish on my plate. I marvel again at how long that activity has been going on in pretty much the same way around the world as it has at Nazare, but perhaps not everywhere in quite so picturesque a manner.

I think one of our most memorable excursions took us to Tomar on the day when a procession was in progress that reaches back to the earliest beginnings of the Portuguese people. These beginnings are actually Celtic, as are those of the Welsh, the western-most inhabitants of Britain. The procession is a tradition derived from the Druids in the earliest period of Portugal's history. It is really a harvest festival occurring in August. As it is celebrated today, it is a strange mixture of details dating back to Druid times and some details that are distinctly Christian. On the day of the procession, couples from neighboring villages gather at Tomar to participate in the procession. Both the men and women are dressed in their own very colorful local costumes, but the most striking feature of the procession is the headpiece that the women wear. Each headpiece is made up of four long loaves of bread, similar to the French baguettes, about a yard long, which are woven together with grapevines and garlanded with flowers, terminating at the top with an openwork white crown surmounted by a cross or the figure of a dove, both Christian symbols. The men and women walk in pairs, but it is the women's impressive headpieces that are most conspicuous. In the middle of the procession (of more than two hundred couples the day we saw it) appears a team of oxen pulling a large two-wheeled cart carrying a large wine barrel. The oxen, the cart, and the wine barrel are all painted a bright gold. The procession moves through the main street of the city and through the main plaza, past the cathedral. On the steps of the cathedral, a priest in full liturgical garb blesses the procession as it passes. Every detail of the procession comes from the old Druid harvest festival except the cross and the dove on the top of the women's crowns and this blessing by the priest. The procession finally ends in the city park, where barbecued lamb and sausages have been prepared. The crowns of bread are taken apart; the bread is broken up and served with the barbecue. The golden barrel of wine is broached, and Portuguese port adds sparkle to the fall festival.

There is one more Portuguese excursion I would like to recall because it turned out to be so hilarious. Father Maher and I had a particular reason for wanting to get a glimpse of Coimbra. It was a place that had impressed itself on our consciousness as young Jesuits because we were told that very early in the history of the Society of Jesus a group of young Jesuit scholastics at Coimbra had become rather insubordinate and refused to cooperate with their superiors. Word of this insubordination came to St. Ignatius in Rome, and he wrote a long, detailed letter to the obstreperous scholastics at Coimbra on the virtue of obedience, detailing at large the nature of the virtue, the necessity of it for the successful working of any society, and the special importance of it for members of the Society of Jesus. The letter was considered so important and so definitive of the Jesuit ideal of obedience that it was read publicly in Jesuit houses of training at least once a year during the evening meal. We thought it would be interesting to see the place where these young Jesuit colts had kicked over the whippletree. I had another personal reason for seeing Coimbra. The Jesuit College eventually built a library there that was said to be an outstanding example of baroque design. So one weekend Father Maher and I and the other four regular workshop faculty members arranged to rent a couple of Volkswagens and drive up to Coimbra. We were told in Lisbon that if we were going to Coimbra, we ought to arrange to stay at Busaco, a very nice little place in the woods outside of the city. The Schwartz couple made the reservations, but they made them in Father Maher's and my names. We pictured "the nice little place in the woods" as a rustic little chalet. We enjoyed the visit to the city of Coimbra, and we were all unquestionably awed by the splendor of the baroque Jesuit library. Late in the afternoon, we proceeded to find our little retreat in the woods.

We started on the designated road and soon realized it was beginning to climb a mountainside beautifully covered with that strange mixture of tropical palm and evergreen trees that we had come to expect in Portugal. But the farther up the road we drove, the more formal everything became with clipped hedges along the roadside. We finally made a last turn in the road, and, instead of the little woodland chalet we were expecting, we were in the presence of the country palace of the last king of Portugal, which had been turned into a hotel. We were quite unprepared for this splendiferous abode. We had nothing with us but the casual sports clothes we were wearing, and the only luggage Father Maher and I had was one red TWA bag between us. We made our way to the reception desk in the grand lobby of the hotel to check in. Very dignified English guests were seated about the lobby having afternoon tea. They looked rather startled by our invasion of their staid hideaway. We learned that the king and queen's suite had been reserved for "the fathers" in whose name the reservations had been made. (As an aside, I note that the cost of the suite for a night was eight dollars, an indication of how cheap it was to travel in Portugal at that time.) The porter in tails picked up our TWA bag, held it at arms length as if it might contaminate him, and proceeded to conduct Father Maher and me up to the Royal Suite. We entered a drawing room large enough to accommodate a convention. On a center table was a fresh bouquet of hydrangeas in a huge brass bowl that towered over our heads. The porter showed us the royal bedroom, with canopied beds on a dais and a bathroom in which you climbed marble steps to get into a bathtub that looked almost like a swimming pool. But when the porter departed and we decided to take a bath, we found there was no soap. We rang the maid's bell, and when we had put in our request, she returned shortly with a tiny bar of soap on a silver tray.

At dinner time, when we appeared at the dining room door in our sport shirts, we were told we could not be seated in that condition, but, not to worry, they had jackets and ties we could don and be properly vested like the other wedding guests. The dinner was excellent and served, of course, with the greatest finesse. After strolling through the beautiful gardens after dinner, which was served at a quite late hour as it was in Spain, we retired to the royal beds. In the middle of the night, a quite violent mountain storm blew up, and when it awakened me, I saw that the curtains were being blown straight out almost all the way across the room, and the rain was pouring in. I got up quickly to shut the great French windows a story and a half high, but I forgot that I was sleeping on a dais. I went crashing to the floor, and the disturbance wakened Father Maher. He switched on the lights and saw me wrapped around one of the queen's chairs. I told him what had happened. His rejoinder was precious: "For God's sake," he said, "don't break your leg. I can't write home to our provincial and tell him that you broke your leg falling out of the queen's bed." The whole situation was so incongruous that we both laughed ourselves sick before I had the gumption to get up and close the window to keep out the rain. The storm died down, and we had a good night's rest in royal luxury before gathering up our TWA bag and departing Busaco, the "little chalet in the woods," for Lisbon. As we were getting into our cars, we noted a whole caravan of burros with bright saddles on their backs, all lined up in front of the hotel. For what reason I will never know, they were all wearing plaid woolen leggings. They were assembled to take the English guests on rides up the mountainside. I'm sure the guests were glad to see the departure of us vulgar Americans.

We decided to have our next workshop in Athens. We chose to go to Greece by boat and booked passage on a venerable old ship of an Italian line, the *Saturnian.* It was actually in the last year of its life at sea and looked its age, but it was a remarkably smooth-riding ship because of the massive expanse of its hull. What it lacked in graciousness it made up for in friendliness. The crew was unusually obliging; many of them had worked on the ship for more than a dozen years. The Italian Catholic chaplain had been on board for twenty-five years. Although he had always had many English-speaking passengers aboard, he never learned a word of English. He looked exactly like Mussolini and had some of Mussolini's traits about him. The chapel was off the same deck as the swimming pool. At a benediction every afternoon, he would come to the pool in cassock, surplice, and cope, ringing a bell to herd some of the sunbathers into benediction just as they were. When he got them in the chapel, he conducted the prayer part of the service from the back of the chapel so his congregation could not slip out the back door.

The trip across was almost like a cruise. From New York, we had stops at Casablanca, Lisbon, Gibraltar, Palermo, and Naples. The ship went on eventually to Trieste, but we disembarked at Petra on the west Greek coast and took the bus from there to Athens. Athens was, of course, all that we hoped it would be—a marvelous setting under the shadow of the Acropolis to discuss, among so many other things, the contribution of the Greeks to our Western culture. We could look out of the hotel room in which we had our workshop sessions to the Acropolis, crowned by the Parthenon and the Erychtheum and the Temple of Nike, the goddess of victory.

We had a marvelously sensitive guide in Athens, a native of the city, a sculptor who also acted as a guide. He had the love of a native for what he was talking about and the sensitivity of an artist. I can still see him seated on the steps of the Parthenon, explaining to us why the architects who designed it made the floor rise up about eight inches higher in the middle than on the sides. All the pillars lean slightly inward, and they are all slightly plumper at their center than they are at the base—a phenomenon called *entasis*. Our guide pointed out to the hills that surround Athens and to the rough curve of the Acropolis itself, on which the Parthenon stands. He said it was the architects' intention to harmonize the building with its natural environment, in which there are many curves and sharp angles. If the Parthenon had been constructed in exact upright verticals and without the subtle curves of the foundations and the *entasis* in the pillars, it would have seemed to jar with its setting instead of harmonizing with it, and harmony was, he insisted, one of the great objectives of high-Hellenic, fifth-century art. I had never heard that precise explanation of the subtle aesthetic variations in the Parthenon. But standing there on the Acropolis with this native artist as our guide, we could see that he was right. He was so impressed with the interest of our group in what he had to say that he volunteered to be our guide throughout our stay in Greece. We took him up on the offer, and he guided us insightfully through Corinth, Delphi, Mycenae, and Epidaurus.

We had the workshop in Athens in the year that the Olympic Games were held in Tokyo. We were able to attend the inaugural ceremonies in Athens. They are held in the stadium, which, incidentally, is built on the foundations of the ancient Greek circus in which foot and chariot races were held. The ceremonies took place in the evening in a packed stadium. A small marble altar had been erected in the middle of the stadium, and King Constantine II (Greece still had a king then) presided behind it in a flowing ceremonial robe. To the sound of music from the Royal Band, the torch bearer on the last relay from Mount Olympus ran into the stadium bearing the flaming torch that had been lighted at Mount Olympus. The king put incense on the coals smoldering in a brass brazier on the altar. Clouds of incense rose to what god or gods I have no idea. The king then put his hands on the shoulders of the kneeling torch bearer—in a gesture of blessing, I presume. The torch bearer rose and started his run with the flaming torch to the airport; he and the torch were picked up there for the flight to Tokyo, where the Olympic Games would be initiated. I never inquired how the flaming torch was accommodated on the plane, but it somehow got to Tokyo. Meantime, the scene at the stadium turned into a band concert. The Royal Band provided the music and accompanied a troupe of Greek dancers performing for the crowd. It was interesting to me to note that there were none of the familiar soft drinks we are accustomed to at home on such occasions. Imports were forbidden at the time, therefore no Coca Cola or Pepsi. The only liquids served were native citrus orange and lemon drinks. There were no hot dogs, either. The food served was various kinds of tasty breads. On later visits to Greece, after it had been democratized, I discovered it had also become somewhat Americanized. Coca Cola and Pepsi were on sale everywhere and with them came the public billboards advertising their presence.

This inauguration ceremony reminded all of us what an important part athletics played in Greek culture. The modern Olympic Games are somewhat patterned on the original Greek athletic contests that took place every year at Olympia. Young Greek men spent a great deal of their time training and preparing for the contests there. All the contests were between individuals in ancient Greek times. There were no such things as team contests anywhere in Europe until hundreds of years later, when Europeans learned about team sports from the ball game that was so central to the pre-Columbian cultures of Mesoamerica and South America. When one recalls that two-thirds of the population of Athens were slaves (all the physical and craft labor was done by slaves), one realizes that the free youth had plenty of leisure time in which to improve their minds and train their bodies. The art of the Greeks gives some indication of how central athletic achievement was to them. When you visit the National Gallery in Athens, you can't help being impressed with the fact that whole galleries are devoted to the heroic-size *kouroi,* the idealized figures of young athletes. They are not portraits of individual athletic heroes, but idealized athletic figures executed to honor them. They are a bit archaic in style with their self-satisfied smile. The more realistic but still somewhat idealized Greek figures of later periods include very many allusions to athletic achievement. Witness, for instance, the bronze *Charioteer of Delphi,* the *Discus Thrower* by Myron, the *Spearbearer* by Polyclitus, the *Apoxyomenos* (an athlete scraping off sweat and dust from his body) by Lysippus, the *Boxer* by Apollonius, and the *Wrestlers.* Even the humanized Greek gods were often represented as athletes. The famous Apollo Belvedere once held a spear. Homer calls Apollo the spear-darter, which meant that he could throw a spear farther than any human being. And Poseidon, the god of the sea, was often represented actually casting a spear. Athleticism was definitely a dominant element in Greek life and culture, a fact that we were reminded of in the ceremonies associated with the inauguration of the Olympic Games.

After the workshop in Athens was over, we flew to Cairo, spent a few days touring Cairo and the lower Nile, then flew to Beirut and bussed from there to Jerusalem for a brief tour of the Holy Land. I had never really wanted to go to the Holy Land because I was afraid the reality might shatter the images of the land of Jesus as I had conjured it up in my mind. I was very surprised that this disillusionment did not happen. Much, of course, has changed there since Christ's time, but places and epiphanies still exist there in which you feel very close to Christ. Father Lukaschewski, a great photographer, was traveling with us that summer, and we were rooming together in the Jerusalem hotel just outside the Golden Gate of the Old City and not far from the Garden of Olives. We had just begun the Liturgy of the Word in our private Mass in our room one morning when very distinctly we heard a cock crow three times. That sound in that place almost tore us apart; we could hardly go on with the Mass. Another day, Father Maher and I had woven our way through the unremitting confusion that reigns in the Basilica of the Resurrection, built over the site of the tomb in which Christ was buried. We found ourselves absolutely alone kneeling in the tomb. The sudden full realization of where we were came over both of us. This was where the angel sat on the tomb and announced the resurrection to the faithful women. It was in the vicinity of this tomb that Mary Magdalene had mistaken Christ for the gardener; it was to this tomb that Peter and John raced to find not the risen Christ, but an angel announcing that Christ had risen. The sudden realization of the sacredness of this place flooded in on both of us, and we dissolved in tears of real joy. We had all had a similar feeling on our bus trip into the city of Jerusalem. In the evening, just a mile or so outside Jerusalem, we arrived at Bethany, the home of Mary, Martha, and Lazarus. It was and still is a peaceful place. We could understand why Jesus liked to return there to the home of his friends for a quiet weekend. As we knelt in prayer in the little chapel, just a few feet from the tomb from which Jesus summoned the dead Lazarus, I think all of us were suffused with peace that might have approximated the welcome calm that Jesus felt on those occasions when he weekended there. As most Christian visitors do when they visit Jerusalem, we made the "Way of the Cross" as a group, roughly on the route that Jesus would have taken from the praetorium where he was condemned to Calvary. Father Maher was leading the prayers.

Suddenly a workman dressed in a long cloak went across the narrow street ahead of us, dragging a long plank loaded with boxes on his shoulder. Just as Father Maher said "Jesus falls under his cross for the third time," the workman ahead of us stumbled and fell beneath his plank and boxes. It was as if the ninth station were being reenacted for us before our very eyes. That again, happening in that precise place where Christ may have originally fallen, was an extremely moving experience for all of us. Another place where I felt particularly close to Jesus was at the River Jordan, where he was baptized. Nothing had changed much there since Jesus' time. We could still look across the Jordan to an open desert land. We could imagine St. John, dressed in his camel's hair cloak, coming forward to the river to baptize Jesus, knee deep in the water. The visit to the Holy Land had not shattered my illusions; it enriched them.

But there was one experience I had while in Jerusalem that pointed up the acute problem of the conflict between Israel and Jordan (as the conflict was framed at that time) as nothing then or since has. Father Luke and I were strolling around the Old City of Jerusalem on the Jordanian side of the wall that then divided the city. It was only about nine o'clock in the evening, but the streets were practically abandoned. The only activity we could detect was in several bakeries in the basements of some buildings, which were operating full tilt to get the bread baked for the next day. We dropped into one of them to observe the bakers at work. Dropping into a bakery in

Jesus' time could not have been much different. Young teenage apprentices were mixing the dough in big wooden tubs and then kneading it by hand in long wooden troughs. When the dough was properly kneaded, it was shaped into big round loaves and allowed to rise for a time on long wooden paddles. Some of these loaves were pretty well risen when we came in. When they had risen enough, the whole paddle on which they rested was thrust into an open stone oven heated by a wood fire below. The finished golden loaves were allowed to cool on their wooden paddles. It was an interesting step back into an almost scriptural experience.

As we left the bakery, a young boy joined us—a Christian Jordanian. He spoke relatively good English so that we had no trouble communicating with him. It turned out that his home was an apartment built right on top of the Old Jerusalem wall. His parents at the time were out of the country on business in Belgium, so he invited us to have a look at his home. When we got there, he pointed out a house in the no-man's-land on the other side of the recently constructed ugly wall that divided the city into Jordanian and Jewish areas. He said: "That's our house, but I have never been in it. It is on the Jewish side of the wall." That little episode was a kind of capsule experience that symbolized the confused conflict in the Middle East. The house was taken from the Jordanian family. Until some reparation is made to them, there can be no basis for a harmonious relationship between that family and the Jewish confiscators. Likewise, until some justice is rendered the Jordanians from whom the land of modern Israel was taken, there can be no basis for real peace in the Middle East. There are hopes as I write this that some adjustments are being made between the two peoples to bring about that peace. At the time we were in Jerusalem looking at the Jordanian house in no-man's-land, in which our little Jordanian guide had never been, we felt that the day seemed distant indeed when any such reconciliation might come about.

Before we left Jerusalem, we made an excursion into the Israeli section of the city beyond the dividing wall and were impressed with the improvements that had been made there. But the experience that was a veritable epiphany was our visit to the monument to the Holocaust. It is just a flat plaza made of rough-surfaced granite, surrounded by a raised walkway on all sides made of the same rough-hewn granite. From that raised walkway, you look down at the plaza floor, which is punctuated by a series of living flames—one for each of the Nazi extermination camps. Each flame is framed by a bronze ring set in the granite. In front of each flame, the name of one of the extermination camps appears in bronze letters with the number of individual Jews exterminated in that camp. The numbers total up to more than six million. As we stood there, we realized that behind each one of these numbers was an individual human being, with his or her own name and identity, country, family, and friends, who was unceremoniously eliminated in the gas furnaces or died of disease or neglect in one of the camps. The sheer simplicity of the monument, with its stark statement of the number of victims and the place of their extermination, reveals dramatically the extent of the atrocity. Not a one of us looked dry-eyed at that monument that day. And I think we each felt some sense of guilt that the world, including our own country and our Church, had been so indifferent as to let this atrocity happen. The experience also helped us to understand later the compulsive drive of the Jewish world community to create the State of Israel, a country that they can truly call their own. That drive, of course, does not justify the displacement of other peoples to bring it about. Until the just claims of both parties can be recognized and adjustments made to meet them, there can be no peace in the Middle East.

Another very interesting site for one of our workshops was Salzburg, situated on the lively Salz River and ringed by gentle mountains. You can't be in Salzburg without thinking of Mozart and *The Sound of Music*. The Salzburg Music Festival was in full swing while we were there, so we had ample opportunity to enjoy great symphony and chamber music concerts performed by world-famous orchestras, and choral and solo recitals by great choirs and individual singers. We attended a recital one evening by Marian Anderson, who at the time was at the height of her singing career. We enjoyed several Mozart programs of chamber music, one presented in the Mirabelle palace and the other in the apartment of Mozart himself, in which he actually composed one of the concertos we were hearing. On Sundays, we had a choice of attending Mass at the cathedral or at one of the several other churches in the city in which great world choirs would be singing a Mass by such world-famous musicians as Mozart or Schubert or one sung in Gregorian chant.

But one of the most impressive presentations to me was the production of *Jederman*, a German version of the morality play *Everyman*, on an elaborate stage that stretched across the whole west facade of the cathedral. The production was staged and directed by the world-famous impresario Max Rinehart. Salzburg was actually Rinehart's home; he lived in a villa on the outskirts of the city. *Jederman* was presented with all the flare that characterized all of Max Rinehart's productions. I remember particularly the elaborate banqueting scene in which the elite of state and church in their full regalia were seated at a table groaning with gold and silver appointments and exotic foods. It resembled the elaborate banquet scene in the January calendar illumination *Tres Riches Heures*, in which the duc de Berri, who commissioned the work, is pictured at an elaborate banquet table; he is accompanied at his right by a cardinal in his full cardinal's regalia. The duke at Rinehart's banqueting table in *Jederman* was also accompanied by a cardinal in his full regalia. At the high point of the banqueting scene, when everyone at the table had his glass raised in a toast to the presiding duke, the skeletal figure of death stepped through the parted curtains at the back of the stage, moved up behind the cardinal, took his glass, put it down on the table, and quietly led him off through the curtains to his death, much to the consternation of all the guests at the table.

The point of the play *Everyman* or *Jederman*, of course, is that *every man*, be he high or low, rich or poor, is equally subject to the cold hand of death. Another memorable scene in the presentation involved the death of the duke himself. Rinehart's staging of it owed something to the famous painting *The Death of the Miser* by Hieronymus Bosch. As the scene opened, the indisposed duke was revealed in his beautiful canopied bed surrounded by tables of exotic golden treasures that he had accumulated through his lifetime, representing the vastness of his wealth. The room was alive with his friends who were there to pay him their respects. The whole point of the play is that no matter how much wealth you may have accumulated and how many friends you may have gathered about you, you can't take any of them with you in death. That fact was acted out in the play we saw. First the duke's golden treasury disappeared. Mysterious characters entered the room and one by one walked off the stage with the treasures. With his wealth gone, the noisy friends lost interest in the duke; one by one, they also departed. The duke was left to himself. The only person remaining was a personification of his "good deeds": a thin, emaciated, and undernourished person. The duke had not been prodigal in his good deeds, but "Good Deeds" was the only one whom he could take with him into the beyond. Meantime, his life powers were also failing. His senses, represented by personifications on the stage, began to leave him, too. First to go was hearing, then taste, sight, and finally consciousness. He slipped into a coma. Appearing on one side of the bed was a black devil with long black fingers like the tentacles of an octopus, who tried to claim the duke's soul, but an angel appeared on the other side of the bed and drove the menacing devil away. Just then the skeletal figure of Death stepped out from behind the head of the bed and slowly pulled a gray comforter up over the unconscious duke—a symbol of his death. "Good Deeds," guided by an angel, moved off stage at the same time. Though weak, he was all that could accompany the duke into the next life. This is the old everyman theme, but it was given a marvelous dramatic flare by the histrionic skill of Max Rinehart.

These marvelous musical and dramatic opportunities in Salzburg were, of course, a delight to all of us, but one other experience fitted in much more closely to our workshop on human relations.

Kurt von Schussnigg, the former chancellor of Austria, had come to St. Louis University after the Second World War to teach in the Department of Political Science. We had gotten to know him very well there. He functioned quite naturally in the academic environment and did whatever any of the other faculty members were expected to do. One of those things was to be available at a departmental table in the gymnasium on registration day to help students resolve conflicts in their schedules. On one registration day, von Schussnigg was seated at a table next to mine working on solving scheduling conflicts for some of the political science students. It was a source of admiration to me to see this man who had been forced to make world-shaking decisions about the fate of a whole nation sitting there puzzling over how the student at his desk might shift his schedule so he could work in the courses he needed.

Professor von Schussnigg was spending the summer in Austria when we were there and was living in a villa outside of Salzburg, so we invited him to spend a day with us in the workshop. During the day, he recounted the very difficult decision he had to make about Austria in the Hitler era: Was he to make the *Anschluss* with Germany and join Austria with Hitler's cause or hold out against him and almost certainly induce a bloody takeover of Austria? After much soul searching, von Schussnigg chose what he considered to be the lesser of two evils—the *Anschluss*. He arranged to go to Berchtesgaden, Hitler's Alpine hideout, to make the surrender. When he arrived, he was made to kneel before Hitler to make that surrender. Hitler was at pains to make it as humiliating and painful as possible. Von Schussnigg saved his country the violent takeover that a refusal would have precipitated, but his decision brought him several years as a prisoner in a war camp. He spent the day with us in a frank discussion of the whole Hitler phenomenon as he had experienced it. One of the students asked him whether he thought the German people in general had any responsibility for the horrors of the Holocaust. He remained silent for a while and then replied resolutely that he indeed thought they did. He said it never could have happened without the cooperation of thousands of German people immediately involved in the horror and without the indifference of thousands more who felt deep in their hearts that it was a "solution" to what they considered the Jews' disproportionately large influence in Europe. He said he thought there was some guilt there because he himself had had some deep-down feelings of that kind about the Jews, which he regretted. We were all somewhat surprised and, at the same time, rather edified at the public avowal of some sense of guilt in this great man.

During the workshop, we had the opportunity of visiting Berchtesgaden, just across the German border from Salzburg. It was the site of Hitler's Eagle's Nest, his modern dwelling and headquarters above ground, and the complex of bunkers two hundred feet underground that were supposed to provide an absolutely impregnable hideout. I remember seeing photos in the newspapers of Hitler standing at the picture window in the Eagle's Nest silhouetted against a beautiful view of the towering Alps in the background. The Belgian artist Magritte painted that view in one of his famous satirical works. In his painting, the mountain in the background terminates in the form of an eagle, symbol of Hitler's power, conquest, and empire. On the sill of the picture window is an actual eagle's nest with eggs in it, but beside it is a green apple, alluding, of course, to the apple of the Fall and suggesting that the Fall is the source of Hitler's false ambition and vanity, which had already cost the world so much agony. When we visited Berchtesgaden, there was no trace whatever left of the

Eagle's Nest. The underground bunkers were still there but unmarked. They were there as empty monuments to the futility of imperial power built on violent conquest.

I was later to see the site of the other bunker Hitler had built in Berlin just east of Checkpoint Charlie in the nefarious Berlin Wall. It was where Hitler, with his illusions of imperial grandeur, had committed suicide, when he knew that the Allied troops were closing in on bombed-out Berlin. The only indication of the place of the bunker was a broken broomstick rising out of the no-man's-land that separated West from East Berlin. These unmarked spots in Berchtesgaden and Berlin, once associated with the *Wehrmacht* and Hitler's vaulting ambition, reminded me of the poem "Ozymandias" by Percy Shelley, which speaks of another vain conqueror who left little trace of his power behind:

> I met a traveller from an antique land
> Who said: Two vast and trunkless legs of stone
> Stand in the desert . . . Near them, on the sand,
> Half sunk, a shattered visage lies, whose frown,
> And wrinkled lip, and sneer of cold command,
> Tell that its sculptor well those passions read
> Which yet survive, (stamped on these lifeless things,)
> The hand that mocked them and the heart that fed:
> And on the pedestal these words appear:
> "My name is Ozymandias, king of kings:
> Look on my works, ye Mighty, and despair!"
> Nothing beside remains. Round the decay
> Of that colossal wreck, boundless and bare
> The lone and level sands stretch far away.

But for Hitler at Berchtesgaden and Berlin, there weren't even "trunkless legs of stone" to remind us of his past "glory": at Berchtesgaden nothing and in Berlin only a broken broomstick stuck in the sand. *Sic transit gloria mundi.*

Father Trafford Maher, identified for years with work and publication in the human relations area, had planned and organized all of our foreign workshops in human relations. He had for a long time conducted full-semester courses on the subject at St. Louis University and workshops all over the country. The foreign workshops were just an extension of this interest. Father Maher had always put special emphasis on the interplay between the Christian and Jewish communities in his work in human relations. He had always actively cooperated in the work of the Conference of Christians and Jews and, over the years, had developed a fine rapport with the Jewish community in St. Louis. He shared that interest in the Jewish community with Pope John XXIII. Pope John had put the improvement of the relationship between the Christian and Jewish communities high on his agenda for Vatican II. In fact, he had assigned Cardinal Bea, a Jesuit, the task of spearheading that item in the agenda. American artist Frederick Frank became something of an official artist for Vatican II and published wonderful pen studies of all the main personalities in the council, and we asked him to do a portrait sketch of Cardinal Bea for our art collection at St. Louis University. He obliged with a very fine profile sketch of the cardinal, which I hung in one of the rooms in Cupples House at the university. I eventually sent the artist a snapshot of the portrait as it is hung in the Cupples mansion, which elicited the gift of a marvelous original lithograph of Pope John and this delightful letter from the artist:

Dear Father McNamee,

Thanks for the splendid catalogue raisonné of Cupples House which itself is such a jewel. I am most grateful that my Bea drawing is part of it. I enclose a lithograph I call "Pacem in Terris," and that is a vision of John XXIII flanked by the Dove as it came to me on the night of April 12, 1963, when the promulgation of the Encyclical came over the radio, and I threw down this image on the paper. No pen being at hand it flew out of the pipet of my ink bottle. Subsequently it was used for the cover of "America" and an indignant reader accused me of making the Pope look like a truck driver and the Dove like a plucked chicken. The only defense was that I saw Angelo Roncalli, then deadly ill, as a man full of vigor, and, as to the Dove, it was not the first time that it had not been recognized.

When later I brought a copy to the Pope's brother Xaverio in Sotte il Monte, he was very pleased with it, studied it carefully, and said: "Yes, we Roncallis have very big noses . . . but not *that* big, do we?"

With warm regards, as ever,
Yours,
Frederick Frank

I highlight this little aside on Pope John because it reveals his interest in the Christian-Jewish relationship. Ultimately this interest impinged very directly on the life of my good friend, Father Maher. As part of Pope John's plan to improve the relationship between the Catholic and Jewish communities, he decided to ordain a bishop for each country whose chief responsibility would be to work on this improvement. He planned on ordaining three such bishops in the United States, because of its size, one in the East Coast and one on the West Coast, and one in the Midwest. He evidently consulted the local hierarchy for suggested candidates for these positions. At least I know that he asked Cardinal Ritter in St. Louis to suggest a candidate for the Midwest. Because of Father Maher's years of work in the human relations area and his special rapport with the Jewish community, Cardinal Ritter suggested his name. The pope acted on the suggestion and sent a letter designating Father Maher. Traf was astounded at the suggestion and wrote a letter in which he tried to outline the reasons why he thought he should not accept the appointment. The pope did not think they were valid reasons and told Cardinal Ritter to tell Traf so. When we arrived back in the States from one of our foreign workshops, a letter from Cardinal Ritter awaited Traf. The cardinal told him that he was a Jesuit and that Jesuits had the reputation of responding willingly to requests for special assignments from the holy father. The holy father was asking him to take this special assignment, so he ought to take it and get on with it. With this push from the cardinal, Traf wrote his letter of acceptance. He and the other two candidates from the two coasts (I never did know who they were) gathered in Atlanta, where they were consecrated bishops and were given the commission by his holiness to set up offices in the three sites whose sole function would be to promote a better relationship between the Roman Catholic Church and the Jewish community.

Traf came back to St. Louis and began to plan to set up such an office. He first began to plan a staff. I know that he had engaged a Jesuit, Father Robert Shanahan, to be part of the team, as well as a Jewish gentleman with whom Traf had worked for years in the local Conference of Christians and Jews. He had already also begun to negotiate for a building in St. Louis that would house the office. The building he was considering was the old St. Louis Club Building on Lindell and Grand just across from the St. Louis University campus. (Incidentally, that building was recently purchased by the university and now houses a museum of art.) Traf had also made arrangements for some of the accouterments that go with being a bishop. He had commissioned an artist friend, Thea Ramsey, to design a simple pectoral cross and a bishop's ring. Thea did so and had them fabricated in silver by native craftsmen in Mexico with whom she had worked for years. At this point, Pope John died and was succeeded by Pope Paul VI, whose chief interest was strengthening ecumenical relationships and possibly even working toward a reunion of the Eastern Orthodox Churches and Rome. For whatever reason, he did not think Pope John's very public push for improved relationship with the Jewish community would help his eastern ecumenical project, so he simply canceled the Johannine program, leaving a good many newly consecrated bishops, including Traf Maher, without a function. Most of them became auxiliary bishops. Traf was offered such appointments a couple of times, but he always turned them down. He was convinced that his training and background had not prepared him to function well in that capacity. He spent the rest of his life in giving retreats to religious and laity, and, in fact, died suddenly of a heart attack while giving one of these retreats at the White House, the Jesuit retreat house near St. Louis. It was a strange ending for Traf's career. I have detailed this denouement here because, as far as I know, it has been recorded nowhere else. Why, I do not know, but what I do know is that what I have recorded here are facts. I witnessed all of them.

# 15

# In Pursuit of Angels

WHEN CRITICS of the medieval Scholastics wished to highlight what they considered the exaggerated speculations of medieval theologians, they represented them as disputing about how many angels could dance on the head of a pin. Angels since then have come in for a great deal of neglect, but as I write this book, there seems to be a considerable revival of interest in angels in this country. Fine curio shops are stocked with figures of angels in various media—crystal, glass, porcelain, wood and stone carving, and cast brass and bronze. In a recent visit to a major local bookstore, I noted a whole shelf of books devoted to angels. Many modern artists are including them in their works as well. The lead article in a recent (late 1990s) Christmas issue of *Time* magazine was recently devoted to a serious discussion by Nancy Gibbs of this renaissance in the interest in angels. The cover of the issue carries a full-page illustration of an angel and this caption: *"The New Age of Angels.* Sixty-nine percent of Americans believe they exist. What in heaven is going on?" The article concludes that what is going on in this very materialistic age in this very materialistic country is the expression of an instinctive hunger for something that transcends the mere material. Angels, it seems, provide that something. Nancy Gibbs concludes her article with these words:

> The act of looking for angels is an exalting gesture. To the degree that this search represents the triumph of hope over proof, it may be a good and cheering sign of our times. For all those who say they have had some direct experience of angels, no proof is necessary; for those predisposed to doubt angels' existence, no proof is possible. And for those in the mystified middle, there is often a growing desire to be persuaded. If heaven is willing to sing to us, it is little to ask that we be ready to listen.

I believe in angels. You can hardly read Scripture, either in the Old or New Testaments and not be a believer. Many of the most important events in both testaments involve the action of angels. But my pursuit of angels has been an academic one. I have pursued only liturgically vested angels as they exist and function in Early Netherlandish painting, but that circumscribed pursuit actually introduced me to a whole new area of learning, research, publication, and teaching that has substantially changed the direction of my life. How that came about is what I wish to recollect and record in the rest of this chapter.

I always had an interest in art and had always integrated it into my teaching of English literature and in my graduate students' research. The very first master's thesis I directed involved color symbolism in the medieval romance *Sir Gawaine and the Green Knight*. As time went on, I worked up graduate courses on the baroque elements in *The Faerie Queene* by Edmund Spenser, on mannerism as manifested in the work of the metaphysical poets, and on the narrative techniques of modern writers such as James Joyce and William Faulkner. In each case, I analyzed the parallels between the verbal and visual modes of expression in these various styles. I eventually directed doctoral theses in these areas. One of the most fascinating studies of this kind of parallelism between the arts proved to be the dissertation Sister Una Hayes wrote on the dramatic technique of Sean O'Casey. Sister was from Ireland and had relatives active in the Abbey Theatre in Dublin and was very interested in the theater. One of the focuses in her study was the rather unique theatrical feature of some of O'Casey's plays in which he presents a theme on a double stage: the theme is enacted on one side of the stage in a tragic manner and simultaneously in a comic manner on the other side. The effect on the audience of experiencing the same theme simultaneously as tragic and comic is that the tragic elements in the theme seem less tragic and the comic side of it less comic because of its tragic potential. The suggestion is that the truth of the situation falls somewhere in between the merely tragic or comic. O'Casey seems to have been the only dramatist to have tried this kind of double simultaneous exposure of a dramatic theme. Sister Hayes was hard put to come up with what might have inspired him to employ this dramatic device. I did not know any other dramatist who had employed anything like it. Shakespeare sometimes treats a theme in a serious tragic manner in the main action of the play and then treats the same theme comically in a subsequent scene, but he does not present the two modes simultaneously. It occurred to me that there might be an analogy to what O'Casey was doing on the stage in what the contemporary impressionists were doing with paint.

Painters such as Monet and Pissaro, in their attempts to catch the fleeting momentary effect of the play of light on an object, had learned to apply strong broken brush strokes of color side by side, which the eye at a little distance combines into colors that are not actually on the canvas. This technique, it seemed to me, had some analogy to what O'Casey was doing in presenting the same theme in the two contrasted tragic and comic modes, with the result that the theme or episode seems to be neither completely tragic nor comic, but in part both. I suggested that Sister Hayes look into whether O'Casey had any interest in or knowledge of the impressionist artists and their painting technique. When she did so, she found that O'Casey not only knew the impressionists but had a real passion for their work. His study and dining room were practically wallpapered with color prints of their works—especially works by Monet. So it is highly probable that the impressionists' painting technique had some influence on his developing his idiosyncratic stage technique in some of his plays.

All of this was just a peripheral excursion on the outskirts of art history for me, but I had an experience in my European travels that eventually drew me into a serious and permanent engagement in a genuine art history project. On several of my trips, I visited Florence and, of course, always enjoyed the incomparable treasures in the Uffizi Gallery. You cannot help being awed by the galaxy of Italian masterpieces there: some of the great enthroned Madonnas of Duccio, Cimabue, and Giotto that greet you in the very first gallery; and then a procession of masterpieces by Gentile da Fabriano, Leonardo da Vinci, Raphael, Botticelli, Michelangelo, Andrea del Sarto, and Parmigianino. And yet, amidst all the great masterpieces by these top Italian artists, the painting that most captured my attention in the Uffizi was not by an Italian artist at all, but by an Early Netherlandish painter. Perhaps it was the size of the painting—a huge triptych, the central panel of which measures ten feet by eight and four-tenths feet—that impressed me. By its sheer size, it dominates the gallery in which it is displayed, even though two of Botticelli's greatest paintings, *The Primavera* and *The Birth of Venus,* are displayed in the same gallery. The painting also commands attention by the intensity of its color, the almost miraculous rendering of detail, and the complexity of its iconography. I simply could not tear myself away from the painting. The painting I am referring to is the *Portinari Altarpiece* (c. 1476) by the Early Netherlandish painter Hugo van der Goes.

At this time, I knew almost nothing about the Early Netherlandish painters, but my fascination with this impressive triptych motivated me to learn something about them. When I began looking into the history of this school of painters of the thirteenth through the sixteenth centuries, I discovered it was a school about which almost nobody knew anything about for a long time. Early surveys of the history of art almost entirely neglected it. About the only attention paid to it was the inaccurate remark that the van Eyck brothers were responsible for inventing the oil medium. Later scholarship has shown that this statement is entirely incorrect. Modern scholars pretty well agree that Hubert van Eyck was probably an invention of overpatriotic Ghentians and that the famous polyptych *The Adoration of the Lamb* in St. Bavo's Cathedral in Ghent is entirely the work of Jan van Eyck. And Jan van Eyck did not invent the oil medium, though he did exploit it and demonstrated its remarkable versatility as a medium of expression as compared to the traditional tempera medium. The total disregard of the Early Netherlandish school of painting in the early histories of art may have been occasioned by the fact that the artists in the school were for various reasons so wholeheartedly committed to religious subject matter in their work. The early development of the discipline of art history corresponded to the early development of the history of the Renaissance, which saw the main thrust of that historical movement as a return to classical antiquity and the freeing of the world from what was represented as the smothering religious influence of the Middle Ages. Early art historians probably looked on the dominant religious subject matter of the Early Netherlandish painters as part of what was considered benighted medieval religiosity. If this shift in emphasis does not explain the neglect of this school of painting, the fact of the matter is that the whole school *was* for some reason simply ignored in early surveys of art history. I found it very interesting to discover how the school was brought into the consciousness of the art historical world. It is almost entirely the result of the work of one scholar, Max Friedlaender.

Max Friedlaender was the director of the Kaiser Friedrich Museum in pre-Nazi Berlin, which contained some outstanding paintings by Early Netherlandish painters, including *The Madonna in a Church* by Jan van Eyck, the Pierre Bladeline triptych *The Adoration of the Magi* by Rogier van der Weyden, two other major triptychs by the same artist—one the *Miraflores Altarpiece* (representing three episodes from the life of the Blessed Virgin) and the other the *St. John Altarpiece* (representing three episodes from the life of St. John the Baptist), and *The Adoration of the Magi* by Hugo van der Goes. Although no attention was being paid at that time to any of these paintings in surveys of art history, Friedlaender was intrigued by them and began to look into the background of the painters who did them. He had little help from printed material, but the more he worked on the paintings, the more curious he became about the painters behind them. He began to explore paintings elsewhere that seemed to have been done by the same painters. His conclusions were largely based on stylistic analyses of the works in various museums that seemed to show common authorship. This comparison started a long process of research in museums all over Europe that finally resulted in the publication of sixteen volumes that included a discussion of the painters whom Friedlaender considered at the time to be the major Early Netherlandish painters, with black-and-white photographs of their major works identified largely by stylistic analyses. In some instances, Friedlaender had not identified specifically who the individual painters were, so he gave them a name. An instance in point is the painter he called "the Master of Flemalle." He identified several paintings in the Staedelsches Kunstinstitut in Frankfurt as well as important paintings in other European museums as having come from this painter's hand. He gave the painter the name of a monastery in Germany with which he was supposed to have been connected. Later scholarship has actually identified the painter as Robert Campin of Tournai, but Friedlaender's identification of this body of work as coming from the hand of the one artist stands up pretty well. In a later edition of his pioneering work, which reproduces the original text exactly but provides new and better illustrations of the works from the Institut du Patrimoine Artistique and the Centre National de Recherches "Primitif Flamands" in Brussels, the editors add supplements that provide corrections, based on later scholarship, of some of Friedlaender's mistaken attributions. But a perusal of this later edition cannot help but prompt admiration for the general accuracy of Friedlaender's attributions.

It was Friedlaender's publications, especially his one-volume condensation of his longer work, that gave me my first introduction to the Early Netherlandish painters and their major works, including those of Hugo van der Goes, whose *Portinari Altarpiece* had so captivated me in the Uffizi.

I noted, however, that the author's concentration on the stylistic characteristics of the painters, which was so helpful in identifying the individual artists in this northern school, did not seem to reveal the full religious significance of the individual paintings or do justice to their rich religious symbolism. It was then that I first encountered the two-volume monumental work by the Princeton scholar Erwin Panofsky, *Early Netherlandish Painting: Its Origin and Character.* Panofsky's focus in this work is precisely on the rich religious symbolism that suffuses all the work of the Early Netherlandish painters. His work practically initiated iconography as a legitimate part of art history. He introduced the contrasted functions of *iconography*, which chiefly sets out to identify what the images employed by an individual painter in a specific painting are, and *iconology*, which goes on to determine the actual significance of these symbols in the precise context of the painting in which they occur. In his volumes on Early Netherlandish painting, Panofsky does both: he identifies the specific images and explains their religious significance in the various works in which they occur, *and* he shows how the very realism of the details of much of this northern Netherlandish painting somewhat disguises their symbolic meaning. He calls this phenomenon "disguised symbolism," yet he insists that almost every realistic detail of these paintings is suffused with a symbolic religious meaning. His two-volume work, in which he identifies the significance of most of these symbols in Early Netherlandish paintings, was a revelation to me, as it was to most bona fide art historians. Seeing how much Panofsky's iconographic and iconological analyses of these Netherlandish paintings contributed to an understanding of the religious significance of these works, I was amazed to discover that both he and Friedlaender were Jewish. When I first read Panofsky, I took for granted that he was a Roman Catholic, so thoroughly had he immersed himself in the theology, the history, and the liturgical implications that lay behind the paintings he was analyzing. His analysis of the *Portinari Altarpiece* certainly showed some of the reasons why that particular painting, of all the treasures in the Uffizi, had so intrigued me.

In looking into the background of the painting, I learned that it had been commissioned by Tommaso Portinari, the representative of the Medici bankers at Bruges. He sent it to the Medici, and they had it installed over the main altar of the Church of Sant 'Egidio. Professor Fred Harrt points out that although the Florentine artists had seen some smaller paintings executed in the medium of oil perfected by the northern Netherlandish painters, they had never before seen a work of this size rendered in the new medium and one that so beautifully illustrated its marvelous potentiality. Nor had they seen a work that so perfectly exemplified the northern penchant for religious symbolism. So the impressive new triptych in Sant 'Egidio had an extraordinary influence on Florentine artists. Domenico Ghirlandaio's *Adoration of the Shepherds* in the Sassetti Chapel of Sanctissima Trinita, for instance, shows obvious adaptations of the symbolic details of the *Portinari Altarpiece*. Panofsky was the first to point out most of the symbolic details in the *Portinari Altarpiece*. The central panel represents a nativity scene. The setting in the rear left background is an impressive, massive Romanesque castle half in shadow. Panofsky was also the first to comment that the Early Netherlandish painters used Romanesque architecture, frequently in a semiruined condition, to symbolize the receding Old Testament. Romanesque architecture at the time was receding in popularity, and Gothic was taking its place. The Netherlandish artists frequently used Gothic details to symbolize the New Covenant. The shadowed Romanesque castle in the *Portinari Altarpiece* symbolizes the Old Testament. Panofsky points out that it also symbolizes the House of David, of which both Mary and the Christ child are members. David's harp is carved on the tympanum over the Romanesque door in the background. The New Testament is represented in the brightly lighted figures in the foreground, not *in* the castle. They are actually visually inaugurating the New Covenant. The suggestion of the ruined stable in the right rear of the picture also symbolizes the receding Old Testament. The contrast between the Old and the New Covenant is symbolized in still another way. The ox in the shadows of the castle is looking out intently on the scene in the foreground, while the ass is munching hay at the manger, ignoring Mary and the Christ child. The ox is meant to symbolize those who accepted Christ as the Messiah and the ass those who ignored Christ. This symbolic meaning was based on a scriptural passage in Isaiah, where the prophet speaks of the ox who recognized his master and of the ass who recognized his master's hay. Incidentally, the manger at which the ass is busily munching hay resembles a stone tomb, an allusion to the death and burial that is ultimately facing the Christ child.

Panofsky also calls attention to the bundle of wheat that confronts the viewer in the forefront of the panel. It has a double symbolism: *Bethlehem* in Hebrew means "House of Bread," and so the bundle of wheat is thus an allusion to the place where Christ was born, but it also alludes to the Eucharist, in which the faithful receive the Body of Christ under the appearance of bread.

It should also be noted that there is a parallel eucharistic allusion in the grape-laden vines that adorn the *albarello* containing the floral still life in front of the bundle of wheat. Panofsky points out some of the symbolism of the flowers, but another scholar from Princeton, Robert A. Koch, discusses this symbolism in greater detail in an article that appeared in the *Art Bulletin* in 1964 (vol. 46). The blue-and-white iris symbolizes the passion or suffering of Christ but in particular that of the Blessed Virgin. The iris came to have that meaning from two sources. The Latin name for iris is *gladiolus*. It means "sword flower" and got that name from the fact that its leaf is shaped like a sword. But it came to symbolize Mary's suffering from the occasion of the presentation of the child in the Temple. When the ancient Simeon took the child in his arms and prophesied that the child would be the occasion of the rise and fall of many in Israel, he looked intently at Mary and said: "And a sword of sorrow shall pierce your heart." Hence the iris, the "sword flower," became the symbol of Mary's participation in the passion of her Divine Son. Hugo van der Goes particularly associates it with Mary the Mother of Sorrows in his paintings, as he does here in the *Portinari Altarpiece*. There is also a red lily in the *arbarello* that signifies the sacrificial shedding of Christ's blood to come and the great love Christ had for the whole human race. The Venetian glass vase next to the *albarello* contains sprays of purple columbine and purple carnations. Both flowers symbolize Christ's passion in their purple color; the five petals of the columbine also symbolize five wounds and the nails of the Crucifixion, as do the petals of the carnation (they are shaped like nails).

The columbine also traditionally supplied a healing medicine in the Middle Ages, so here it symbolizes the healing power of the coming sacrificial death of Christ. Strewn around the whole forefront of the floral still life are white and purple violets, symbols of humility—the humility of the Second Person of the Blessed Trinity, who was humbled to the condition of a human being in order to suffer and die for our redemption, and the humility also of the Blessed Virgin, who submitted herself to the will of God when she said to the angel at the Annunciation, "Behold the handmaid of the Lord, be it done unto me according to Thy Word."

Very conspicuous in the lower left-hand corner of the panel is an empty sandal, which Panofsky sees as a symbol of the reverence one should feel in the presence of the sacred—a symbol based, of course, on the Old Testament episode in which Moses was asked to remove his sandals out of reverence for God's appearing in the burning bush. A real sense of reverence is also induced in the onlooker by the arrangement and attitude of all the figures in the panel. Friedlaender long ago said that the arrangement is so formal that it suggests that the figures are all engaged in some kind of liturgical ritual. He was actually more right than he knew. The scene is organized around the image of the Infant Jesus, who is completely nude and lying in an open space in the middle of the composition. Ranging in a broad circle around him, beginning on the left, are two kneeling angels, Joseph and Mary, two more kneeling angels, three shepherds framed by the sketchy stable, and a group of five kneeling angels completing the circle on the right. Five angels hover above the scene at the top of the panel. All the angelic and human figures are equally intent on expressing their reverence and adoration of the Christ child in the center.

Anyone observing the painting cannot help noticing the strange contrast of scale between the human and the angelic figures in the central panel. The human figures (Joseph, Mary, and the three shepherds) are twice the size of all the angelic figures. One would expect that it would be the other way round, but what the artist is saying here is that all human beings now have a dignity that surpasses that of any angel because in the Incarnation the Second Person of the Blessed Trinity became a man, not an angel. It is obvious that it is to express this greater dignity of human beings as compared to angels that the artist employs this great contrast of scale in the figures of the

Nativity panel because in the side panels in which he represents the donor and his son and their sainted patrons on the left and the donor's wife and his daughter with their sainted patrons on the right, a similar contrast of scale is employed. The patron and his family are represented in very small scale but their patron saints in large scale.

In my long perusal of the painting, I noticed some details that neither Panofsky nor anyone else had called attention to. All the angels in the scene are dressed in liturgical vestments, but not just any liturgical vestments. They are all wearing some variation of vestments worn by subministers at a Solemn High Mass. None of them is wearing the chasuble, the vestment reserved for the celebrant of the Mass in Roman Catholic practice. It was perhaps my early experience as a sacristan, in which I became very familiar with all the vestments, and my later years as master of ceremonies, in which it was my duty to train participants for liturgical ceremonies, that made me more sensitive to van der Goes's employment of the liturgical vestments in his painting. Before Vatican II, the nature and use of every liturgical vestment was strictly prescribed. It struck me that van der Goes had garbed his angels here in every possible variation of vestments worn by subministers of a Solemn High Mass and had rendered all of the vestments with utmost accuracy. The two angels kneeling at the front left of the circle are wearing amices and albs. The foremost one is also wearing a stole crossed diagonally on his breast as a deacon wears it. His alb has a rectangular embroidered apparel stitched on the rear above the hemline, a decorative device added to the alb to commemorate the pointed pegboards that were hung from the waists of those condemned to be crucified to add to their torture as they carried their crosses to the site of crucifixion. Hence, the device on the alb here is a symbol of Christ's passion. The two angels kneeling in the rear are wearing simple amices and albs. Two of the angels in the group of five in the right foreground are clearly wearing dalmatics, the sleeved vestment with slits up the sides worn by deacons and subdeacons at a Solemn High Mass. The most visible angel of the group is wearing an elaborate damask cope, a vestment frequently worn by a master of ceremonies at a Solemn High Mass, but never worn by the celebrant of the Mass in Roman Catholic practice. All the angels hovering above are garbed in a similar variation of liturgical vestments.

Because Panofsky had shown that almost every other detail of the composition is suffused with a religious meaning, I was convinced that the very careful and exactly correct vestments of the angels also had a religious significance. They really amount to a eucharistic symbol, along with the bundle of wheat and the grapes on the *albarello*. They signify the sacrifice of the Mass in which Christ is both the priest offering the sacrifice and the victim being offered. The Christ child is represented as the priest with his hands raised in an offertory gesture and wearing what some patristic writers called "the Chasuble of His Flesh." It is to emphasize that fleshly chasuble that the Christ child is represented entirely nude, but his supine position on the bare ground also represents him as the victim being offered. This eucharistic allusion is also highlighted by the fact that there are stalks of wheat strewn over the whole area where the Christ child is lying. Christ as the celebrant of the Eternal Mass is being served by angelic ministers vested in all the possible variations of vestments worn by subministers of a Solemn High Mass. And to cap the eucharistic allusions, the words *Sanctus, Sanctus, Sanctus* (Holy, Holy, Holy) are stitched prominently on the band of the cope of the kneeling angel on the right. They are the words that open the hymn of praise sung immediately after the preface in the Mass, just before the actual eucharistic liturgy begins.

All of these details convinced me that the vested angels in this painting constitute an additional eucharistic symbol. I wrote a brief article in which I made that suggestion. I had made a quick survey of the works of other Early Netherlandish painters and found that many of them used liturgically vested angels in a similar way. To suggest that fact, I included in my introductory article an illustration of one of the *Enthroned Madonna* paintings by Hans Memling now in the National Gallery in Washington. In it, the nude Christ child is seated on the enthroned Madonna's lap as on an altar. He rests on a white cloth that is meant to suggest the white linen corporal on which the eucharistic body *(corpus)* of Christ rests in the Mass. The child is riffling through a book of Scripture with his left hand and is reaching with his right hand for an apple proffered by an angel on his right. The apple, of course, is a reminder of the guilt of the Fall in Eden, which Christ is assuming in order to make the sacrificial offering of himself on the Cross and in the Mass, which will redeem the human race from the consequences of the Fall. The two angels are garbed in liturgically correct vestments: the one on the left in an amice and alb, and the one on the right in amice, alb, and dalmatic—again, all vestments of subministers of a Solemn High Mass. As in the *Portinari Altarpiece* by van der Goes, the Christ child is completely nude, wearing the chasuble of his flesh. He is both the priest and victim being offered in the Eternal Mass, assisted by angels properly vested as assistant ministers.

The mere suggestion in this painting that the linen cloth on which the Christ child is resting is meant to be the corporal of the Mass is made completely explicit in the charming little *Nativity* by Stephen Lockner, now in the Alte Penakothek in Munich. Lockner simplified van der Goes's nativity panel in the *Portinari Altarpiece* to just the figure of the Blessed Virgin kneeling in adoration of the Christ Child, lying on what is unquestionably a corporal of the Mass. The identification is made explicit by crosses stitched into the corners of the cloth where they frequently occur in actual corporals. Lockner has a ruined stable in the background of his painting, suggesting the receding Old Covenant. The new one is represented by the figure of Mary and the Christ Child in the foreground. The ox and the ass are here, but not as symbols of the Old and New Covenants. They are both behind the manger, and they are very devoutly regarding the infant in the foreground. A bevy of little angels is adoring Christ from above the stable. They are wearing liturgical albs but of a bright blue color that matches the bright blue of Mary's garments—both symbolic of the hope of redemption. They may be intended to symbolize the angelic subministers of Christ as priest and victim lying on the corporal below, but they actually look like blue butterflies flitting above the stable.

I was so convinced of the validity of my interpretation of the vested angels as eucharistic symbols that I decided to send the article in which I made the case for the idea to the *Art Bulletin,* the most prestigious art history journal in the United States. Its editor at the time was Professor Horst Janson. I had met him thirty years previously when he was on the art history faculty at Washington University. In fact, when I was a student, he had lectured to the little seminar that continued the introductory art history survey at St. Louis University after our professor died in 1932. But he had obviously forgotten me because, when he received the manuscript of my little article, entitled "Further Symbolism of the *Portinari Altarpiece*," he called me and asked if I were an art history graduate student they had not heard about at the *Bulletin.* He said if I were, I should be given a reward that the *Bulletin* was then offering each year to the author of the best article submitted by a graduate student. I told him I did not qualify because I was chairman of the English department at St. Louis University. He then went on to say that he was very much impressed with the case I had made for the vested angels as eucharistic symbols in the *Portinari Altarpiece.* After reading my article, he had quickly fingered through some of his books on Early Netherlandish painting and could see that vested angels were a pretty consistent phenomenon in very many of those paintings. He said that my suggestion of their eucharistic significance would change the interpretation of a great many of these works and wondered why he and other art historians had not noticed them before. He then said that the idea was so important that the extent of its use and its origin ought to be explored, and that if I did not feel confident enough to do that on my own as a nonart historian, I ought to team up with an art historian and get the job done. I was, of course, delighted with his positive and enthusiastic reaction to my article and began to give his suggestion some thought. The article was published in the June issue of the *Art Bulletin* in 1963. It received favorable comment from many art historians immediately and especially from Professor Frederick Harrt, who said it provided the missing link in his analysis of the iconography of a tomb sculpture he was working on at the time. He also suggested that I pursue the subject further— the extent of its use in Early Netherlandish painting and its origins. I told him about Horst Janson's suggestion that I team up with an art historian to do the job. He saw no reason for my doing that: "You know how to read; you know research procedures; you have a record of publication. Do it yourself." After a little self-examination, I decided to give it a try. Professor Harrt also suggested that I apply for a Fulbright research fellowship, take a sabbatical, and go to Brussels, where the extensive photographic indices of Flemish painting at the Institut du Patrimoine Artistique and the Centre National de Recherches "Primitif Flamands" would be most helpful tools with which to trace the extent and consistency of the vested angel as a eucharistic symbol in Early Netherlandish painting. I took his advice, made the application for the Fulbright, and, I am sure, as a result of both Professor Horst and Professor Harrt's recommendations, I received it for the year 1965.

Professor Harrt was right. It was relatively easy to check the frequency and consistency of the use of vested angels in Early Netherlandish painting in the photographic indices at the institute and research center. I examined every photograph in both indices and found that once Robert Campin had established the vested angel in panel painting as a eucharistic symbol, almost every major artist in the Early Netherlandish school from the thirteenth well into the sixteenth century used it extensively. And they all used vested angels consistently. The angels always wear a variation of vestments worn by subministers of a Solemn High Mass, never the chasuble, which is the vestment reserved for the celebrant of the Mass in Roman Catholic practice. Of the hundreds of examples I found of paintings employing vested angels, I found only one artist vesting an angel in a chasuble. The painting was by a minor German artist in the sixteenth century, the Master of the Aachen Altar. The painting is *Mary with the Divine Infant and Angels* now in the Alte Pinakothek in Munich. He was obviously imitating the practice of the Netherlandish painters of garbing angels in liturgical vestments, but he did not understand the significance of the angels' wearing only the vestments of subministers who are serving the Christ figure in the composition as the celebrant of the Eternal Mass wearing the chasuble of his flesh. So he put a chasuble on an angel. No Netherlandish painter ever did that.

A point that my broad survey of Netherlandish painting in the photographic indices revealed is that vested angels as eucharistic symbols were employed in episodes from the entire life of Christ, from the Annunciation to the Last Judgment. The significance of this ubiquity of vested angels throughout the pictured life of Christ is that each and all of the episodes of that life were part of what he offered up to his Heavenly Father as part of his redemptive sacrifice at the Last Supper and on Calvary, and of what he bade us continue to offer in the holy sacrifice of the Mass. I recalled that it was this very notion of the Mass that Father Maurice de la Taille had discussed in his monumental *Mysterium Fidei* and that Father Dismas Clark had elaborated for a select group of us Jesuit scholastics on the plains of Kansas in the hot summer of 1933. I dug out the *Mysterium Fidei* and found that Father de la Taille had actually used the Netherlandish painters as witnesses to the antiquity and continuity of that particular theory of the Mass. He even had an illustration of Jan van Eyck's *Adoration of the Lamb* in his book, with a brief schematic interpretation that showed how the concept of the Mass corresponded to the theory he had expounded in his entire treatise. A eucharistic allusion is appropriate in representing any and all the mysteries from the life of Christ precisely because what Christ offered at the Last Supper and bade us continue to offer in the Mass was his entire self from his Incarnation to the Last Judgment. That is what justifies the Flemish painters' use of vested angels as eucharistic symbols in the rendering of any of the mysteries of the life of Christ.

The photographic indices were very helpful in finding an answer to the first part of my inquiry: how persistent and consistent the presence of the vested angels in Early Netherlandish panel painting actually is. But to determine how they got there I had to go farther afield than the photographic indices. I decided I would have to start at the beginning of Christian art and discover how angels were actually garbed in various places and successive times, and when and why they began to be dressed in liturgical vestments.

I began with the Byzantine period, the earliest period of sustained Christian art. By examining early Byzantine book illuminations and other Byzantine works of art, I discovered that angels participated in the general Byzantine tendency to emphasize Christ's divinity rather than Christ's humanity and to represent Christ as the Pantocrator, the Ruler of the Universe and the Authoritative Teacher. Angels accompanying him in the book illuminations are represented as his courtiers or royal guards sometimes wearing armor and carrying swords or spears. But I also discovered that a very common motif in the decoration of Byzantine church interiors represented what was called "the Eternal Liturgy" or "the Eternal Mass." In this motif, Christ is presented standing behind an altar wearing the *phelonian*, the Byzantine equivalent of the chasuble in the West. He is accompanied by angels wearing the *orarion*, the Eastern equivalent of the deacon's dalmatic in the West. So here you have a representation of Christ functioning as the celebrant of the Eternal Mass, assisted by angels functioning as deacons. This representation was an anticipation, if not the origin, of Christ functioning as the celebrant of the Eternal Mass, assisted by angels wearing the liturgical vestments of subministers of the Mass. It may not have been the general *conscious* origin of the use of vested angels as eucharistic symbols in Western art, but in at least one instance it probably did have a direct influence. In the upper range of Jan van Eyck's *Adoration of the Lamb,* the central majestic, enthroned figure of Christ represents him as ruler, teacher, and priest, assisted in two panels by angels, all but one of whom are garbed in vestments of subministers of the Solemn High Mass. Lotte Brand Philip has argued rather persuasively in her book *The Ghent Altarpiece* that this section of the famous polyptych was almost certainly influenced by the Byzantine tradition of the Eternal Liturgy.

My survey of how angels were garbed in the West eventually revealed what I think was probably the more general and immediate source of the vested angels in Western art in general and in Netherlandish art in particular. I had to examine book illuminations because they considerably antedate panel painting. To do this, I had to go where the manuscripts are, so this pursuit eventually brought me to the Bibliothèque Royale in Brussels; the Bibliothèque Nationale, the Bibliothèque de l'Academie Française, and the Musée Jacquemart-André in Paris; the Musée Condé at Chantilly outside of Paris; the British Museum in London and the Bodleian Library in Oxford; and the Metropolitan Museum (Cloisters) and the Morgan Library in New York.

What I found in an exhaustive examination of illuminated manuscripts—largely illuminated Bibles, Psalters, and Books of Hours—in all these places was that in Italy angels were traditionally garbed in a modification of the Roman toga, and in France in a cinctureless tunic resembling the garb generally worn by ordinary men in the Middle Ages. But I found that gradually in France, in the representation of one scene from the life of Our Lord—the visit of the Marys to the tomb—the angel seated on the tomb came to be represented as wearing an amice and a liturgical alb, even though all the other angels in the manuscript are represented in tunics or togas. I recalled from my work in the history of drama that the dramatization of this very scene of the visit of the Marys to the tomb initiated the development of Western drama. The little Latin liturgical drama—in which the angel's question *"Quem quaeritis in sepulcro?"*—opened the dialogue that became the seed of the whole development of drama in the West. This was also the first of a whole series of Latin liturgical dramas, acted by clergy in close association with the Liturgy itself, that would evolve into rather sophisticated dramatic compositions of dialogue and music that would continue to be performed in the church, by clergy in connection with the Liturgy, from the ninth down to the middle of the sixteenth century. I recalled that Karl Young had made a thorough study of this Latin liturgical drama and had published the texts of many of these plays in his impressive two-volume work *The Drama of the Medieval Church*. It occurred to me that the texts of these Latin liturgical plays might provide directives for garbing the angels in the plays. My suspicions were right. Many of the texts do include detailed directives for vesting the characters in the little playlets. The directives for the costumes of the angels are always variations of vestments of subministers of the Solemn High Mass—albs, dalmatics, or copes. There may not have been any intention on the part of the authors of these texts to make a eucharistic allusion in these prescriptions for the angels' garb, but it is interesting that the vestments prescribed are always those of subministers of the Solemn High Mass, but never the chasuble, the vestment of the celebrant.

These Latin liturgical playlets were developed for many of the important liturgical feasts of the year. A particularly interesting one was developed for the Feast of the Annunciation. This little play was called the *Missa Aurea* because gold vestments were used by the characters and by the ministers in the Mass itself. The directives of the *Missa Aurea* text suggest that two little *aediculae* be constructed on either side of the altar and be closed off from the congregation by curtains in front. In the *aedicula* on the right, a cleric dressed as the Blessed Virgin is to be placed, and in the other a cleric vested as the announcing angel. The directives for the garb of the angel again vary: a simple alb, an alb with a stole as the deacon wears it, a dalmatic, or a cope—again, all vestments of subministers of a Solemn High Mass. The directives indicate that when the deacon of the Mass intones the narrative of the Annunciation, the curtains are to be drawn back exposing the Angel Annunciate and the Blessed Virgin in their *aediculae*. They are to sing the lines ascribed to them in the Gospel, thus creating a little dramatization of the Annunciation itself.

In light of the very ancient tradition of these Latin liturgical dramas performed every year on the appropriate feast days, I discovered that it was precisely in the book illuminations of these two episodes in the life of Christ that the garb of the angels gradually became the liturgical vestments prescribed for the Latin liturgical plays. The artists evidently just transferred to their illuminations the garbs that for all of their lives they and their public had seen the angels wearing in the liturgical plays. The French representations of the Annunciation in these book illuminations are particularly interesting because they increasingly represent the scene as taking place in little *aediculae* similar to those fabricated for the presentation of the scene in the *Missa Aurea*. And the Angel Annunciate in these book illuminations are dressed in the vestments prescribed in the directives of the Latin liturgical play the *Missa Aurea,* so it is highly likely that the Latin liturgical plays enacted each year inspired the illuminators to so vest the angels in their illuminations of the scene of the Annunciation. Hence, later, when panel painters such as Robert Campin were looking for an additional eucharistic symbol for their panel paintings, they found it in the angels garbed in vestments of the subministers of the Solemn High Mass as they had been represented in the Latin liturgical drama and later in the book illuminations. Thus, we find the angel in Robert Campin's *Merode Altarpiece* vested in amice, alb, and a stole worn diagonally across the breast as the deacon wears it. In the same panel, the Christ child is represented as coming on the scene above as a nude infant carrying his cross. That image looks ahead to Christ's Crucifixion in which his sacrificial offering of himself, actually begun here at the Incarnation, will be consummated. But the nude infant also represents Christ as the priest celebrant of his Eternal Mass in which he continues to offer himself as a redemptive sacrifice for the salvation of humankind. And he is being assisted in that eternal eucharistic sacrifice here by the angel properly vested as a deacon.

Robert Campin's use of the vested angel here and in several other of his paintings may be the first conscious use of the vested angel as a eucharistic symbol in Netherlandish panel painting. I have concluded that a rather good case can be made for the medieval Latin liturgical drama as the immediate source of the convention of the vested angel in book illuminations and of the conscious use of the vested angel as a eucharistic symbol in Netherlandish painting. It took me the greater part of my Fulbright year to pin down that conclusion. I eventually published evidence for the Byzantine Eternal Liturgy motif and the Latin liturgical drama as sources of the vested angel as a eucharistic symbol in a lengthy article entitled "The Origin of the Vested Angel as a Eucharistic Symbol in Flemish Painting," in volume 59 (1972) of the *Art Bulletin.*

The Fulbright grant and the sabbatical leave from my duties at St. Louis University in 1965 had given me the leisure and the financial support to devote my full time to researching the topic of the vested angel, but it also provided a wonderful opportunity to immerse myself in a foreign culture, meet some very interesting people, and enjoy some rather unique experiences. All of this began at the reception given for all the Belgian Fulbrighters on our first Sunday in Belgium, arranged by Madame Dorothy DeFlandre, the director of the Fulbright program in Belgium. She had the reputation of running the best Fulbright program anywhere, and we soon learned that she deserved that reputation. She was American by birth but had married a native Belgian and spent the rest of her life in Belgium. It was her purpose as director of the Fulbright program to make the experience as enriching as possible for each participant. She devised many ways of bringing that about, one of them already conspicuous at our first reception. She had gone to the trouble of inviting prominent Belgian guests who were related to the specific backgrounds and interests of each of the Fulbright grantees to enable us to get in touch with important people who could be of help to us in our various projects. For those of us interested in art history, she had invited Mademoiselle Conmblen-Sonks, the director of the Centre National de Recherches, and Mademoiselle Jacqueline Folie, an editor and administrator at the Institut de Patrimoine Artistique. Because I would be doing most of my work at these two institutions during the year, it was tremendously helpful to make these important contacts immediately. Mademoiselle Conmblen-Sonks at the Centre National de Recherches could not have been more helpful in putting the resources of the center at my disposal. Jacqueline Folie took a very personal interest in my project, gave me important leads in my research, and read and critiqued some of my writing; she has also been endlessly encouraging ever since.

Just a few years ago, when I was revisiting Jacqueline at the institute in Brussels with a good friend of mine, Father Terry Dempsey, she looked intently at me and said: "What you ought to do is pull together some of the articles you have written on Netherlandish painting, flesh them out, add other things you are working on, and bring them out as a book. If you don't do it, it will not get done. And nobody else can do it because no one else has the background in theology and the Liturgy to do it." Then she looked at Terry and said:

"And you ought to see that he does it." She kept urging the same point in later correspondence. I really had no intention of doing a book on the subject, but at Jacqueline's and Terry's urging I set about doing it. The resultant book was published in 1997 by Peeters of Louven, Belgium, and is entitled *Vested Angels: Eucharistic Symbolism in Early Netherlandish Painting*.

In her last Christmas note, Jacqueline called my attention to some very recent new scientific photography that has been done on the panels of the *Ghent Altarpiece* by Jan van Eyck. The photography confirms a hunch I had about the original garb of the angel seated at the organ in the right angel panel in the upper range of the composition. The angel is now garbed in an elaborate damask secular cape rather than in the liturgical vestment in which all the other angels in both angel panels are garbed. I suggested that originally the seated angel may have been wearing a liturgical alb. The new photography proves that to have been the case. I cite all of this to illustrate what fruitful contacts Dorothy DeFlandre made for us Fulbrighters from the moment we arrived. This kind of helpfulness was to perdure through the year.

The Fulbright grant provided funds for a French tutor. Madame DeFlandre showed her resourcefulness and thoughtfulness in assigning me to Madame Jeanne Rousseau for my tutoring in French. Madame Rousseau was an art historian research assistant who worked with art historians in their research and publication projects. While she was tutoring me in French, she was working with Professor Bob Claesens on a book on Pieter Bruegel, which gave us a common area of interest on which I could practice my French, but it also immersed me in the life and work of Bruegel. One evening when I came to her apartment for my French lesson, she had the entire galleys for the book on Bruegel on which she and Professor Claesens were working. It was being published by the Mercatorfonds Press in their usual handsome format. Every work of Bruegel was being reproduced in full color. Madame Rousseau had done so much work on the research for the book that it was appearing as *Our Bruegel* under the joint authorship of Bob Claesens and Jeanne Rousseau. Madame Rousseau sent an autographed copy of the book to me when it finally appeared. Facilitating this very special contact for me was just another example of the kind of solicitude Madame DeFlandre had for every one of her Fulbrighters.

A great surprise awaiting me at the opening Fulbright reception was the discovery that one of the Fulbrighters that year was none other than Professor Charles Cuttler. I knew him, of course, by reputation for his publications about the northern Renaissance field and as the author of the only college textbook at the time on the northern Renaissance. He had read my article on the vested angels in the *Portinari Altarpiece* and said how important he thought the notion was and how glad he was to know that I was here to pursue the idea further. Of course, that kind of a greeting could not help endearing him to me. I got to know Chuck very well during the year. We made many art historical excursions together and spent hours discussing art historical subjects. I learned a great deal of art history from him, and he said he learned a lot of theology from me. I was surprised again to learn that Chuck was Jewish. It is not clear to me why so many of the greatest scholars in the Early Netherlandish field have been Jewish: Max Friedlaender, Erwin Panofsky, Lotte Brand Philip, and Charles Cuttler. This fact made me all the more admire the objectivity of their scholarship. Chuck and I became and remain close friends. He has always been most supportive of my efforts in the area in which he has an international reputation.

Another gracious arrangement Madame DeFlandre made for the Fulbrighters was to have each of us adopted into a Belgian family for the year, which enabled us to observe closely how a Belgian family lives and to experience some of their local traditions. I was adopted by a Flemish doctor and his family. I was invited to several of their family gatherings, including their celebration of the Feast of the Bean, a local custom dating far back in the Flemish tradition. It is celebrated in the winter. On some evening within the octave of Epiphany, the family gets together to celebrate the Feast of the Bean. My adoptive family invited me to be a part of their celebration. On the evening of the feast, three young children of the family, decked out as the Three Magi, came knocking at the door carrying a cake baked in the form of a crown. They arrived at dessert time. They were welcomed, and the cake was cut up for dessert. A bean had been put in the cake when it was baked, and the person who got the piece of cake containing the bean was crowned king of the feast and ruled absolutely everyone at the festivity for the rest of the evening. Part of the fun, of course, consisted in watching the participants carry out some of the crazy commands of the newly crowned king. Drink flowed freely during the festival, and, judging from some of the artistic renderings of the festival, it must have flowed with abandon at times in the past. The revelers in my adopted family were much more restrained, but the festival as I experienced it did bring back memories of the Jacob Jordaens's depiction of it entitled *The Festival of the Bean.*

Everyone in this painting, including the fat old king, is high as a kite, and everyone is still drinking. The table, laden with an excess of half-eaten food, is an indication that the whole affair has encouraged excess in both eating and drinking. In the front of this picture of human indulgence sits a big cat sober as a judge, staring out at us from the canvas, with a look of utter disdain on his feline face, as much as to say: "What fools these mortals be." This particular painting by Jordaens, the great disciple of Rubens, was one of the many famous paintings that Hitler and Goebbels confiscated and stored in a salt mine to await installation in the museum they planned to build in Berlin when the war was over. When the Allies found this stash after the war, many of the paintings were sent on a tour to museums all over the world while the damaged museums from which they had been stolen could be prepared for their return. Thus, Jordaens's *The Festival of the Bean* was one of the paintings displayed in the St. Louis Art Museum during that world tour. I was fascinated and amused with this painting at the time, but I little suspected then that I would one day participate in an actual Festival of the Bean, admittedly considerably more restrained than Jordaens's representation of it.

Madame DeFlandre was at great pains to make all of us visiting Fulbrighters realize that we were living in a bicultural country. There was actually hardly any way of escaping that fact. Brussels is a bilingual city—all the signs appear in both French and Flemish. The whole country is divided into French- and Flemish-speaking areas, and there seems to be little love lost between the two peoples. Both French and Flemish languages are prescribed by law in the schools. The Flemish learn both languages and continue to use them. The French learn them and try to forget the Flemish. One result of this situation is that in Brussels, the bilingual capital, most of the service positions are held by the Flemish because they have a deliberate fluency in both languages. There is a feeling on the part of the French that the Flemish language and culture are somehow inferior to the

French. When we were there, this antipathy between the two cultures had become so strong at the famous University of Louvain, which is located in the Flemish-speaking part of the country, that it resulted in student riots between the Flemish- and French-speaking students. During the riots, two students were actually killed in the courtyard of the Jesuit College at the university. A few years later, this animosity between the two elements at the university became so intense that the French-speaking faculty and student body simply picked up their books and founded a new university, Louvain Nouveau, in the French section of the country. The new campus was built in the countryside, and a new city, Louvain Nouveau, has gradually grown up around it. I'm not sure that this split has helped either university particularly. The old, now Flemish-speaking, Louvain, recognizing the relative nonutility of foreign students' learning Flemish, has introduced an entire English curriculum to try to continue to attract foreign English-speaking students to the institution. They are, of course, right in doing so. There is no real incentive to learn Flemish as a foreign language because there is so little important Flemish literature to which it would open the door. That fact actually motivated my taking up residence at the French-speaking Jesuit Collège St. Michel in Brussels rather than at the Gesu, the Flemish-speaking Jesuit residence, and my taking French lessons rather than Flemish. French would be a much more useful investment for me. Flemish is really a variant of Dutch, and my fair knowledge of German enabled me to read with some ease the Flemish documents I needed for my work.

Because of this rather low estimate of the usefulness of my mastering the Flemish language for my purposes, an innate irony in the uncomfortable Flemish-French interrelationship became glaringly apparent to me. It was the Flemish side of the component that had made the greatest cultural contribution to the history of art. It was the Flemish artists who had perfected the oil medium that had changed the history of art. It was also the Flemish artists who had developed the most profoundly religious and symbolically rich school of art in the history of art. I was here in Belgium to study the achievement of this school of art. The French side of the Belgian equation had made no such contribution to world culture, and yet the French definitely looked upon themselves as the superior side of the equation. This cultural split in the country was a firsthand experience of the kind of cultural and linguistic differences that are a problem in many parts of the world. In America, we have not confronted this issue in exactly the same way, even though such a split has taken place on the West Coast and in the Southwest, with their considerable Latino and Asian populations.

To be sure that all of us Fulbrighters experienced firsthand the linguistic and cultural differences of the various parts of Belgium, Madame DeFlandre arranged daylong and weekend trips to cities in the different linguistic areas. We made such trips to Liège and Tournai in the French-speaking area. Tournai was particularly interesting to me because of its impressive cathedral (a mixture of the Romanesque and Gothic) and for the fine collection of brass and silver reliquaries in the cathedral treasury. One of the most famous of these reliquaries is the beautifully painted one Hans Memling designed for the relics of St. Ursula for the chapel of the Hospital of St. John in Bruges. It is still displayed there along with other famous Memling paintings commissioned by the same hospital. One of our weekend excursions took us to Luxembourg, the German-speaking province that is loosely associated with Belgium politically.

But the most interesting of these ventures to me was our trip to Antwerp, the most important city in the Flemish-speaking part of Belgium. It became that when the river silted up at Bruges and that city ceased to be the mercantile, banking, and cultural center of the country. Time has just stood still in Bruges since then, and for that reason it is a fascinating city to visit because it has remained in every way exactly as it was when representatives of the Medicis such as Portinari and Arnolfini as well as great Flemish artists such as Jan van Eyck and Hans Memling walked its streets. When Bruges ceased to be the commercial and cultural center, Antwerp took its place.

Antwerp is a great harbor city, the largest after Rotterdam in all of Europe. That accounts for its remarkable economic success and its ability to replace Bruges as the cultural center of the country in the late sixteenth and seventeenth centuries. It is still a very thriving center. The signs of its past and present prosperity are in evidence everywhere. We started our tour of the city in the great square south of the cathedral. That square had interesting associations for me. I had taught Thomas More's *Utopia* for years to the honors students. More wrote the *Utopia* in Antwerp while serving there as an ambassador of King Henry VIII. He opens the *Utopia* with an account of his attending Mass in the Cathedral of Antwerp and then stepping out into the square, where he noticed a mariner in the company of his good friend Peter Giles. Peter introduces him to Raphael Hythlodaye, a mariner just back from a journey to the ideal kingdom of Utopia with some of the companions of the famous explorer Amerigo Vespucci. For me, it was a thrill to be standing in the very square where More places this imaginary encounter. But as I was musing on my hero, Thomas More, whom I admire just short of idolatry, and his fictional hero, Raphael, our guide was pointing out the bronze statue of Peter Paul Rubens in the square, a very historical Antwerpian hero. We were to learn before the day was over that Antwerp is as much the city of Rubens as Toledo is of El Greco.

We moved from the square into the cathedral, which, with its original vaulting of warm red brick laced with gray ribbing, is very characteristic of Belgian Gothic. (After restoration, it was all painted a uniform white.) But the great experience for any visitor to the cathedral is seeing several of the most famous paintings by Rubens. One of his most beautiful versions of *The Assumption* graces the main altar, and the massive triptychs *The Raising of the Cross* and *The Descent from the Cross* are displayed on either side of it.

Perhaps as a favor to me as a Jesuit, our next stop was the Jesuit Church of Saint Charles Borromeo, the elaborate baroque facade of which was designed by Rubens. Rubens also did more than two dozen paintings for the interior, all except two of which were destroyed in a disastrous fire in the eighteenth century. The two surviving canvases, *The Miracles of St. Ignatius* and *The Miracles of St. Francis Xavier,* are now on display in the Kunsthistorische Museum in Vienna. The visit to the Jesuit church reminded me that the Jesuit community at St. Borromeo's had commissioned Rubens to do a painting of St. Ignatius on the occasion of his canonization, and they insisted in the contract that the whole painting had to be done by the artist himself. He obliged with the great full-length portrait of St. Ignatius vested for Mass and looking up to a divine light shining in from above. The painting for a long time hung in Warwick Castle in England, but the Earl of Warwick eventually sold it to the Norton Simon Museum in Los Angeles. It is now one of the most important Rubens paintings in the United States. Another Jesuit community in Antwerp commissioned the seventeenth century Flemish artist, Jan van Luyten, to make a copy of the Rubens painting for their community. It eventually became part of the collection of fifty-two paintings, mostly Flemish, that Father Pierre De Smet brought from Belgium to St. Louis University in the 1830s. It now hangs in the entranceway to the Jesuit residence at the university.

Very prominent in the history of the Renaissance in the north is the Plantin-Moretus family because of the printing press they established in Antwerp. Many of the most important ancient classical texts and new editions of Scripture and the writings of the church fathers, which formed such an important part of the new Christian humanistic movement, were printed on the Plantin press. Erasmus, one of the greatest of the Christian humanist scholars of the time, had a room in the Plantin home, where he lived and worked as he was seeing some of his works through the Plantin presses. Both the Plantin mansion and the wing housing the presses remain today just as the Plantin-Moretus family left them. They were the next stop on our tour. Some of the books that came off this prestigious press are always on display in one of the corridors of the mansion. The presses remain just as they were and are still functional. Occasionally, special pamphlets, posters, and maps are still printed on the old presses and are sold as mementos. I bought a copy of an antique map of Antwerp printed on one of the presses. I later had it framed and hung it in the Flemish room in Cupples House at St. Louis University. I'll have more to say about that room in a later chapter.

After delving into the Renaissance past of Antwerp at the Plantin-Moretus Museum, we moved into modern Antwerp by hiking a few blocks down to the docks and taking a quick boat tour of the vast harbor. You cannot help being awed at its size. The docks literally stretch for miles, and they are all lined up with merchant ships from all over the world. There is no better way of getting an idea of the importance of Antwerp as a marine and merchant center than to take this tour of the harbor. When it was over, we settled into one of the many charming cafés along the docks for a typical Belgian lunch. It began with an endive salad, and the main course was eel, served with a green sauce made from green endive, and heavily buttered boiled potatoes. It ended with a rich apple tart, laden with thick whipped cream. And, of course, it was all washed down with a stein of good Belgian beer—after German beer, the best in Europe, and there is a lot of it made. It is said that the per capita consumption of beer by Belgians is the highest in all Europe.

Lunch finished, we bussed to the Royal Museum of Art, which has a fine collection of mostly Flemish paintings. Three works were particularly interesting to me. The first one was the triptych by Rogier van der Weyden called *The Seven Sacraments.* The three panels create the interior of a Gothic church, the nave in the center panel and the side aisles on the side panels. A huge crucifix dominates the foreground of the center panel, with the grieving figures of Mary, St. John, Mary Madgalene, and other grieving women. But in the rear, in front of a choir screen, Mass is in progress with the priest at the altar elevating the Host after the consecration. This whole scene, of course, represents the Eucharist. This juxtaposition of Christ elevated on the Cross and the eucharistic Body of Christ elevated by the priest at the altar is the artist's way of reminding us that the offering that the priest is making at the altar is the same as the offering of Christ on the Cross. This work was of particular interest to me because it was another visualization of the point about the Eucharist that I was finding so many of the Flemish artists made in different ways in their works. The other six sacraments were represented as being administered in side chapels of the overall cathedral setting. On the left from front to rear are baptism, confirmation, and penance; and on the right, from rear to front, ordination, marriage, and extreme unction. Above each of these scenes, a typical van der Weydenish fluttering angel is represented holding a banderole with a text appropriate to the sacrament being administered below. But what was particularly interesting to me was the color of the garments they are wearing (all, incidentally, liturgical albs). The color changes to suit the sacrament: white for baptism; gold for confirmation; red for penance; purple for ordination; blue for marriage; and black for extreme unction. This obvious shift in the color of the angels' garb with varying spiritual significance induced me later to examine more closely the shift in the color of the vestments of angels in all the Flemish paintings I was studying. I found that neither here nor elsewhere were these shifts just arbitrary. They are clearly a planned part of the spiritual significance of the paintings where they occur. In later study, I was to determine what that significance is.

The second painting that literally transfixed me was by Rubens—his *Longinus Piercing the Side of Jesus.* I had forgotten that this painting was in this museum. I had used a reproduction of it for years in my introductory course in art history to teach students the baroque manner of handling a subject matter in contrast to the classical or High Renaissance manner. To illustrate the latter, I had always used the central panel of *The Crucifixion Triptych* by Perugino now in the National Gallery in Washington. In it, Christ hangs on the Cross square in the front center of the composition accompanied by Mary on the left and St. John on the right. All three are lined up front stage like a posed tableau. There is little evidence of Christ's passion and suffering. His body looks like that of an idealized Greek god. And there is only the mildest expression of grief in the vertical figures of Mary and St. John at each side of the Cross. The whole scene is flooded with a uniform golden light, with little contrast of light and shadow. Everything is presented on a closed space within the frame, and all the figures are arranged symmetrically across the front of the space as on a stage of which we are not a part. This arrangement invites not emotional reaction or identification, but rather a quiet contemplation of the fact of the Crucifixion in the manner of a classical, intellectual, or High Renaissance treatment of a subject.

Rubens's completely baroque treatment of the same subject in his *Longinus Piercing the Side of Jesus* could not possibly be more different. It was one thing to pick out all the baroque elements of this composition on a slide with my students. It was another thing entirely to be standing before the original painting itself. In the first place, slides and illustrations in books never prepare you for the scale of the originals, even though their measurements may be given. I had never imagined this particular painting as big as it actually is, in part because one of the fifty-two paintings that Father De Smet brought to the university is an anemic version of the painting done by one of Rubens's less-talented assistants. It is only one-eighth the size of the original. So when I walked into the gallery where the original hangs, I was transfixed by it. The figures are almost life-size and throb with all the dynamism of Rubens at his best. No neat symmetrical arrangement of the figures across the forefront of a stage here. The figures of the bad thief, Christ, and the good thief are arranged on a violent diagonal that thrusts into the depth of the composition. It is an open composition, and some of the figures, such as Longinus on his horse, flow outside the frame into our space and pull us into the action of the scene. The whole scene is spotlighted, not floodlighted, which brings out the figures of Christ and the good thief into highlight and throws the figure of the bad thief into shadow. The colors are tense and vibrant, adding an emotional intensity to the picture. The painting is full of conflicting diagonals and flowing curves, which create a dramatic, dynamic, and emotional quality in the scene in contrast to the dominant verticals that create a calm and sober feeling in the Perugino *Crucifixion*. But most of all, there is a deliberate emphasis on the physical agony of the scene and on the emotional reaction to it on the part of Mary, St. John, and the grieving women. The whole presentation was devised to invite us to enter into the action and to *feel* the emotional intensity of it, not merely to *think* about it. And standing before this original baroque creation, I certainly *felt* what Rubens put into it in a way I never had in my many discussions of the slide projections of it. That one painting was an epiphany for me that day.

But in a neighboring gallery, my attention was arrested by another work that fascinated me for another reason. It was a very large triptych by Hans Memling. It caught my attention for two reasons: its large size and the fact that all three panels are exactly the same size, which is very unusual in Early Netherlandish painting. It is simply entitled *Christ with Angels*. The central panel represents Christ with six singing angels (three to each side), and each side panel merely pictures five angels playing musical instruments. But what riveted my attention was the fact that Christ in the central panel is wearing liturgical vestments, and the angels in all three panels are garbed in every possible variation of the vestments of subministers of a Solemn High Mass. Because the pursuit of vested angels was my special preoccupation for the year, I knew that here was a painting that I would have to study more thoroughly. In it, I had captured a whole bevy of vested angels.

The painting had to signify more than its noncommittal title expressed—*Christ with Angels*. I knew that I would have to come back to this gallery to determine precisely what Hans Memling was doing in the painting. Antwerp is only about thirty miles north of Brussels, so I could actually get back to the city easily whenever I wanted to by train. I spent a great deal of time studying the painting carefully during the year and did pry open its meaning. The process of my prying and its results are interesting enough to get some attention at the end of this Antwerpian adventure, which was all occasioned by the brief Fulbright tour of this very fascinating city.

The tour ended, as it should have, in Rubens's city, with a lecture on "Rubens as a landscape painter" by a professor from the University of Ghent and a reception, both in the house of Rubens. Rubens was a world traveler. In his early career, he spent several years in Italy at the court of the duchess of Mantua. He acted as a kind of court painter to her and counseled her in developing her impressive art collection. When he returned to Antwerp, he bought a large, Flemish-style, step-gabled mansion but immediately added a wing on the rear for his studio and an L-shaped wing in the Italian Renaissance style that enclosed a large landscaped courtyard, in the center of which he built a large baroque triumphal arch. The scale, furnishings, and style of the house, which is still pretty much as Rubens left it, are indices of Rubens's luxurious lifestyle. He was very successful financially, fulfilling commissions for kings, princes, and princesses in Italy, Spain, France, England, and at home in Belgium. He lived like a prince himself. As we wandered through the home, it was interesting to imagine Peter Paul grandly entertaining royalty and admirers there from all over the world.

The lecture on the artist as a landscape painter touched on the final years of the artist's life, when he retired for months at a time to Steen, the country house he had purchased, where he devoted himself to painting very sensitive and placid landscapes very different from the dynamic baroque works of his high maturity. Both the lecture and the reception that followed it took place in Rubens's studio, a story and a half high, which the artist himself had designed to accommodate his huge canvases. In one corner, a narrow door runs up the full story and a half to facilitate moving his heroic-size paintings in and out. Out the windows, you can see the large baroque triumphal arch that he painted in the backgrounds of some of his paintings.

Most of Rubens's paintings were very much cooperative projects. He always did the small preliminary studies himself, but these studies were then enlarged on the canvas by some of the bevy of apprentices and assistants he maintained to help him execute his many commissions. These assistants would also frequently do a great deal of the actual painting itself; the master would then add the final touches and work especially on finishing the face and the hands. This was so much his custom that if a client wanted a work entirely executed by Rubens himself, it had to be specified in the contract. I remarked above that the Jesuit community at St. Charles Borromeo had made that specification when they commissioned the painting of St. Ignatius, so presumably the painting now in the Norton Simon Museum in Los Angeles is entirely from Rubens's own hand. I said Rubens maintained a stable of apprentices and assistants to help him in his work. *Maintain* is the right term, because they actually lived on the premises. The large hall above the entire studio, now a gallery for the display of some of the artist's sketches and studies for his paintings, was actually a dormitory where his apprentices and assistants slept. Some of his apprentices, such as Jacob Jordaens and Anthony Van Dyck, went on to become first-rate painters in their own right, but most of them remained anonymous helpers. They sometimes ventured out on their own but not often with very noticeable success. A set of *The Apostles* on wood panels, which were part of the collection of fifty-two paintings that Father De Smet brought to St. Louis University, were designed by pupils of Rubens. Rubens himself touched up the faces of the Apostles, and you can certainly detect the contrast in the skills of the two hands. But, on the other hand, a painter such as Jan van Balen, who certainly did not reach the heights of such painters as Jordaens and Van Dyck, nevertheless showed real skill and a happy absorption of the qualities of his master. A beautiful signed rendering of *The Holy Family* by Jan van Balen is part of the De Smet collection at St. Louis University. It is a very competent painting showing the Christ child seated in his mother's lap, accepting a large bunch of grapes from her with St. Joseph looking on in the background. It clearly shows the influence of Rubens—especially in the plump proportions of the Christ child and in the quality of the flesh tones in the Rubens manner. Rubens had developed a method of doing the underpainting of flesh areas in red and adding flesh tones over the red, which gives his rendering of flesh a very lifelike appearance. That quality is very much in evidence in the flesh tones of the Christ child in our van Balen *Holy Family*. All these Flemish and Rubens associations in our own art collection at St. Louis University made this first excursion into Rubens's city, home, and studio a particularly fascinating experience for me.

I wish to pause here before leaving Antwerp to record my pursuit of the vested angels in the Memling triptych *Christ with Angels* that had so caught my attention on our first scurry through the museum on our Antwerp tour. I was convinced that the angels had a story to tell me if I would let them speak, so I made several trips back to

Antwerp and spent a considerable amount of time examining every detail of the painting carefully. Christ is pictured in the center of the central panel wearing a crown and holding a gemmed cross in his left hand, the base of which rests on a crystal globe representing the world that he redeemed by his death on the Cross. That fact is also suggested by the form of a cross created on the crystal globe by the reflection of a window mullion. Christ has his right hand raised in the traditional Byzantine gesture of the teacher. But what I was particularly interested in is how he is garbed. He is wearing a purple alb with a gold neckband, a stole crossed on his breast as the celebrant wears it, and an elaborate purple cope—all liturgical vestments. But a close scrutiny revealed Greek lettering stitched into the gold neckband on his alb. It reads in Greek: *Agyos O Theos.* Those words rang a bell for me because of the long years in which I functioned as a master of ceremonies for liturgical functions. They are the first words of the lamentations that are sung during the Ceremony of the Exaltation of the Cross as part of the Liturgy for Good Friday. Good Friday is the only day of the year on which Mass is not said. There is a ceremony called the Mass of the Presanctified that takes place, but it is not really a Mass because no consecration takes place in it; it is really only a Communion service in which the celebrant consumes the extra Host that was consecrated in the Holy Thursday Mass celebrating the institution of the Eucharist. This Host is reserved in a special tabernacle for the veneration of the public, until it is taken to the main altar and consumed by the celebrant in the Good Friday Liturgy.

Immediately following the Mass of the Presanctified, the Ceremony of the Exaltation or Veneration of the Cross takes place. The crucifix, which had been veiled in purple all during Lent, is gradually unveiled and then venerated first by the ministers at the altar and then by the whole congregation. While this is in progress, the choir sings the lamentation beginning with the line in Greek: *Agyos O Theos, Agyos Ischyros, Agyos Athanatos, eleison imas* (O Holy God, Holy Strong One, Holy Deathless [Immortal] One, have mercy on us). The first words of this lamentation, *Agyos O Theos,* are inscribed on the neckband of Christ's alb in the central panel of Memling's triptych. They are, it seems to me, the key to the artist's intention. The whole composition is a representation of the Ceremony of the Heavenly Exultation of the Cross. Memling indicates that the scene is taking place in a heavenly setting first by the fact that the figures are represented against a gold background, which in the Byzantine tradition had always indicated a heavenly realm, and second by the fact that the scene in both the central and the side panels is enwrapped in purplish clouds similar to those that Memling's mentor, Rogier van der Weyden, had used in his *Last Judgment* polyptych at Beaune to indicate a heavenly region for the figures in the upper range of his painting.

The *Agyos O Theos* cue from the Good Friday Ceremony of the Exaltation of the Cross also prompted me to take another look at the vestments Christ is wearing: a purple cope. I recalled then that before Vatican II in the Good Friday Liturgy the celebrant wore a black chasuble during the Mass of the Presanctified, but before the Ceremony of the Exaltation of the Cross, he removed that chasuble and donned a purple cope. So the Christ figure here is wearing the same vestment for the Heavenly Exaltation of the Cross that his earthly equivalent used to wear in the worldly Good Friday Exaltation of the Cross. This insight also explains the vestments that the assistant angels wear in both the central and side panels. They are wearing all the variations of vestments of subministers at liturgical ceremonies. Reading from right to left they are: (1) in the right panel, amice, alb, and cope; amice and alb; amice and alb; amice, alb, dalmatic, and maniple; and amice, alb, and dalmatic; (2) in the central panel, all six are wearing amices, albs, and dalmatics, and the one on the extreme right whose left arm is visible also a maniple; (3) in the left panel, amice, alb, and stole as the deacon wears it diagonally across the chest; amice and alb; and finally, amice, alb, and a broad purple stole worn as the deacon wears it. This last unequivocally relates the scene to the Lenten season and more specifically to Holy Week because it is only then that deacons wear the broad purple stole. Most of the vestments the angels wear are purple, another association of the representation with Lent and Holy Week. So I think there is no doubt that what Memling is representing in this unusual triptych is the Heavenly Exultation of the Cross. As the Byzantine artists had transplanted the Mass itself to the heavenly realm in their motif of the Eternal Liturgy or Eternal Mass, Memling is here similarly transplanting the Good Friday Ceremony of the Exaltation of the Cross to an eternal heavenly realm.

I eventually worked up my case for this interpretation of the triptych into an article and submitted it to the editor of the *Journal of the Warburg and Courtauld Institutes* in London. He replied immediately and said he thought that I had made such a convincing case for this interpretation of the triptych and that the interpretation gave the painting so much more significance, the editors of the *Journal* thought my article should be published immediately. The journal at the time had a backlog of articles he had agreed to publish eventually; it is published only once a year in an almost book-length format. My article on the Memling triptych, entitled "The Good Friday Liturgy and Memling's Antwerp Triptych," appeared in volume 37 in 1974. I received very favorable comments on it almost immediately from art historians in Rome, Paris, London, Belgium, and here in the States. I sent a copy of it to the director of the Royal Museum in Antwerp, where I first encountered the original. He was very appreciative of my interpretation of the painting and said he would change the title of the painting in the next edition of the museum catalog from *Christ with Angels* to *The Heavenly Exaltation of the Cross*. That was certainly a happy consummation of my pursuit of this particular bevy of vested angels.

The most extended excursion planned for all the Fulbrighters from Belgium, Holland, and Germany during the year was a full week's seminar in West Berlin. We were to gather in West Berlin at the Fulbright program's expense and participate in a discussion led by West Berliners on the relationship between East and West Germany and specifically on the function of West Berlin itself. It was really meant to justify for us why the Bonn government was expending so much money subsidizing West Berlin. Actually it did not justify it, but the experience was very worthwhile and educational in many ways not particularly planned by the West Berliners. In the first place, it was very amazing to see firsthand the extent of the destruction rained on the city in the bombings of the war. The city was practically wiped out. West Berlin had been largely rebuilt, but we could see relics of what the city had been before the bombing. All that remained of the great central railroad station was half of one massive arch standing on the edge of the no-man's-land that separated West from East Berlin. The ruins faced Checkpoint Charlie, the passage point to East Berlin. Across the wall, we could see some of the trees of the great Unter Den Linden Boulevard, one of the great boulevards of the world, now leading up to the ugly wall. And on the other side of the wall was what remained of the Brandenburg Gate—again, one of the great civic world landmarks, now emphasizing the closed passage between the two parts of the city. But perhaps the most astounding sign of the extent of the devastation of Berlin was the hill outside of it on which Berliners now ski in wintertime. It was built on the rather flat terrain that surrounds Berlin with the rubble hauled out of the devastated city. The Berliners call the hill Teufelsdroech, Devil's Dung. I'm not sure whom they are thinking of as the devil, Hitler or the Allies who bombed the city. But we did have a feeling, when we realized the extent of the destruction, that the devil had a hand in it.

Millions had been spent on the rebuilding of West Berlin, and it had been done well. It was a spanking new city. There was very little left to restore. There were fine well-stocked shops and cafés, and the city was ablaze at night with neon lights. The city was supposed to be a spectacular display, far within the borders of communist East Germany, of what a successful capitalist center should look like. It was also supposed to show to the East Berliners and the East Germans in general what a wonderful recovery capitalist West Germany had made. For a while, of course, it did demonstrate that fact and so successfully that the communist East German government knew that it had to veil the spectacle from the less-fortunate East Berliners. So the wall became a necessity. But given the wall and the effectiveness of its prevention of any movement from east to west, the tremendous expense of subsidizing this demonstration city really did not make much sense. And nothing in the presentations that several leaders from the West German government made convinced us that there was much sense to it. We also gathered from the West Berliners to whom we talked that they thought pretty much the same thing. They were almost sure that communism was so much in the ascendancy that West Berlin would eventually be assimilated into the East and that there was not much future for West Berlin. Young people were leaving, and the city was taking on the appearance of an old folks' home. No one back there in 1965 would have suspected that by 1992 communism would have collapsed from within, the Berlin wall would be torn down, and the Germanies would be reunited. But all of these things have happened. The existence of West Berlin, I think, had little to do with the collapse of communism. It is only now that the world fully realizes how tremendously different the two Germanies had become. It will take a very long time, a great deal of patience, and a lot of money to level those differences.

Chuck Cuttler, the prominent northern Renaissance scholar, and I had a great time exploring both East and West Berlin together. The Kaiser Friedrich Museum in Old Berlin was where the study of Early Netherlandish painting had originally begun. The rich holdings in the museum of works by Early Netherlandish painters had piqued the curiosity of the director Max Friedlaender and had prompted him to begin the study of Early Netherlandish paintings that resulted in his determining for the first time who the Early Netherlandish painters were and what were their major works. The Kaiser Friedrich Museum had very rich holdings from most periods before the war. Hitler was convinced that Berlin would never be taken and did not permit the evacuation of the museum's treasures early in the war. When it looked as if Berlin might fall, he reluctantly allowed a quick evacuation. Many of the museum's small artifacts were stashed in villas and farmhouses outside the city, the bulk of them to the west of the city. The very large paintings were stowed, of all places, in the basement of the headquarters of the Luftwaffe. That building and everything in it was simply bombed out of existence, so that all the large paintings that once graced the museum were completely destroyed. Some of the larger monumental architectural pieces such as *The Altar of Zeus* from Pergamum and *The Ishtar Gate* from Babylon were sandbagged. Although the building itself was badly damaged, some of these large sandbagged monuments remained unscathed. When we were there, restoration of some of the building had been completed since the war, and art objects that had been stashed in safe places on what ended up in East German territory had been replaced in the museum.

Chuck and I wanted to see what had been done, so we worked our way through Checkpoint Charlie, spent an afternoon in the sadly denuded museum and strolled around East Berlin—a depressing experience. Practically none of the old buildings had been restored. They remained blackened and burned-out hulks in the devastated city, and the new housing built by the communist regime was the boxy, prisonlike barracks that the communists were building everywhere. The only old building that at that time had been restored to anything like its former splendor was the opera house. The operas produced there provided some cultural relief to the East Berliners' drab existence. Chuck and I stayed for the performance of *Carmen* that evening, and when the performance was over, we dropped into the opera café off the lobby of the opera house. The only refreshment available was German bread and butter and some ersatz coffee. We could not help contrasting that with the tasty German pastries available in the many cafés back in West Berlin just on the other side of the wall. As we walked back through Checkpoint Charlie with spotlights glaring at us from the ugly wall and machine guns aimed our way from the watch towers, we were glad to be back in the freedom and plenty of West Berlin, luxuries that we very much realized the East Berliners we had just left could not enjoy.

Chuck and I spent a great deal of our free time in the days we had in Berlin in the new Dahlem Museum erected there to house the artwork that had been stashed in what became West Berlin. That stash fortunately included practically all the Early Netherlandish paintings that had so fascinated Max Friedlaender in the old Kaiser Friedrich Museum. It was a marvelous opportunity for me to be seeing these great masterpieces of Jan van Eyck, Rogier van der Weyden, and Hugo van der Goes through the eyes of one of the outstanding authorities on Early Netherlandish painting. This treat alone would have made the whole week's visit to West Berlin a very rewarding experience for me.

The Fulbright program had arranged many interesting contacts for us during the year, but I also managed to make a few of my own. Madame Rousseau, my French tutor, had told me about the small but select collection of Early Netherlandish painting in the possession of Baron Coppe in Brussels, which she said was particularly rich in the works of one of the sons of Pieter Bruegel, Jan, who came to be known as "Velvet" Brueghel because of the delicacy of his still-life and narrative paintings. I wrote to the baron, told him of my work on Early Netherlandish painting, and asked whether I might have the pleasure of seeing his collection. He replied that he would be happy to show it to me and invited me to come to dinner with his family and look at his collection. On the evening he suggested, when I appeared at his substantial mansion, the maid told me to take the elevator to the fourth floor, where the baron and his family were waiting for me. I had no idea what to expect, but I had envisioned the baron as an elderly, white-haired gentleman. I was surprised to find a vigorous person in his early fifties, an engineer with a degree from MIT in the States, married to a woman who was the direct descendent of Jodocus Veyt and Isabel Borluut, who had commissioned Jan van Eyck to do *The Adoration of the Lamb* in Ghent. The baron and his wife had nine children, most of whom were assembled around the dining room table awaiting my arrival. The baroness spent much of her free time as a volunteer social worker. This image of the baron and his family was not the one I had conjured up in my imagination.

The dinner conversation was a pleasant exchange of the baron's experiences in the States and my work and my impressions of Belgium. He said my seeing his art collection that evening would be somewhat delayed because his mother, the widowed Baroness Coppe, who lived downstairs in the main part of the mansion, was preoccupied with her favorite television program. Her television set was in the main grand salon where most of his collection hung, and Mother would not take kindly to having her program interrupted to allow an American interloper to gawk at the paintings. So we continued our chat upstairs until Mother's program was over, and she had retired to her private rooms. The baron and I then went down to the salon, turned up the lights, and I was greeted with an extensive collection of very fine Flemish paintings, not by the top masters but by very reputable artists. The strength of the collection did lie in the impressive array of works by Jan "Velvet" Brueghel, both his still-life works and his delicate and imaginative renderings of mythological and scriptural subjects. They were all done on Jan's usual rather small scale. I had never before seen so many together and enjoyed them and the other paintings in the company of their collector, who obviously took great pride in possessing them and seemed really delighted in sharing them. It was a very memorable evening.

My second comparable encounter with a private collector was not in Brussels but in London. I had been working on Robert Campin's use of the vested angel and had the impression that he first introduced one in *The Entombment,* which was in Count Antoine Seilern's private collection in London. I had never seen a colored illustration of it and felt I needed to see one, so I wrote to the count and asked him whether there was one available. He replied promptly, saying that he had never allowed colored reproductions to be made of any of the paintings in his collection because he thought they always distorted the color of the originals. He would send me a good black-

and-white photograph, but if I really had the need of seeing the color of the original, he would be glad to have me come to London to see it and the rest of his collection. Because he had one of the most extensive and important collections of Early Netherlandish paintings in private hands anywhere, this was an invitation I could not turn down. I arranged to go to London and meet him at his large town-house in the Kensington area. He greeted me warmly on my arrival. He had arranged for the director of the Warburg Institute to be there so we could all three tour his collection together. The catalog of the collection filled two hardcover volumes. It was a delight to be seeing this extraordinary assemblage of Early Netherlandish treasures through the eyes of the collector and assisted by the comment of the director of one of the outstanding art historical research centers in the world.

A good many of the paintings included vested angels, and I found myself trying out my theory about their eucharistic significance on these two very important authorities in the field. I was surprised to see how interested they were in what I had to say and how encouraging they both were that I proceed with my research. Count Seilern had a noon appointment at the Warburg Institute, but he had arranged with his maid to serve me lunch and gave me free run of his house and his whole collection for the whole afternoon. I spent a great deal of my time studying the Campin *Entombment* that I had come especially to see, but also reveled in ranging through the whole collection.

I did not expect then that I would ever have the opportunity of seeing the collection again. However, Count Seilern died a few years later. He had willed his entire collection to the Courtauld Institute, which is the Department of Art History of the University of London. The institute has a remarkable collection of modern art of its own, including such world-renowned paintings as *The Bar at the Folies-Bergère* by Edouard Manet. With much crowding, they installed the Seilern collection in their gallery on the premises of the University of London, where I saw it on a later visit. But it became imperative that the whole Courtauld collection be accommodated in more spacious quarters, so it was moved to more ample space in Somerset House on the Thames, where I saw it on my last visit to London. It has more spacious quarters there, but the French Louis XV flavor of the rooms does not provide the proper atmosphere either for their significant modern collection or for Count Seilern's distinctive Flemish collection. Neither collection is very well lighted. I am sure these deficiencies will be corrected. The great Seilern collection is more accessible to the public here than it ever was in the count's private home, but I am grateful that I saw it there in the company of the man who put it together with so much love and enthusiasm.

The most fascinating personal excursion of the year for me was the one that took me to I Tatti, Italy. My good friend, Frederick Harrt, who had supported my application for the Fulbright, had himself received a Fulbright grant for the year. He was spending it at the research center of I Tatti outside of Florence. I Tatti was the villa built by the famous scholar Bernard Berenson. He got his start as a world-renowned authority in art history, especially in the history of Tuscan art, when as an art history student at Harvard he had become Isabel Gardiner's art advisor as she was developing the fabulous collection in the Gardiner Museum in Boston. When Berenson became well known as an authority on art, he became associated as a consultant for the fabulous art dealer Joseph Duveen and accumulated considerable personal wealth in the process. He settled at Florence and built the beautiful villa I Tatti in the hills outside the city. He developed an impressive art historical library there as well as a respectable collection of mostly Tuscan art. The entire art history world gravitated to I Tatti. When he died, he left the whole establishment to Harvard, his alma mater, as an art history research center. Fred Harrt had worked with Berenson at I Tatti as an art history student and actually became something of a fair-haired boy of the great scholar. Harvard runs I Tatti now and grants a certain number of scholarships for study there each year. Because of Fred Harrt's special relationship to Bernard Berenson, he was allowed to spend his sabbatical year with his Fulbright grant on the I Tatti premises. The guest house, a thirteenth-century Tuscan farmhouse in the middle of an olive orchard that Berenson had converted into a guest house, was made available to Fred for the year. He invited me down to spend a week with him there—a rare opportunity I could not pass up. Fred was an authority on Tuscan art; he had studied it all his life and had Berenson's direction in doing so as a young man. He had just purchased a new Mercedes Benz, and he promised to show me many little-known Tuscan works of art in situ in little Tuscan hill towns I had never heard of. So I packed myself off to I Tatti for a week.

With the thirteenth-century farmhouse-turned-guesthouse came a Tuscan couple who did Fred's housekeeping and cooking. Fred knew that they would never be able to wrap their Tuscan tongues around my name, so he introduced me to them as Monsignore Mauritio degli Angeli, a sobriquet I had won by my interest in and pursuit of vested angels. It was an unforgettable experience to be expanding my knowledge of Tuscan and Italian Renaissance art in general with the help of such an authority in the field as Frederick Harrt. He was unbelievably generous with his time. He had a kind of possessive attitude toward all the art of Florence because he had studied it for so long and had written so extensively on it. He regaled me with stories about his work in the Second World War after the Allies had taken over Italy. Because of his knowledge of the art of Florence, he was assigned the task of seeing that the art that had been evacuated from the museums in Florence into all sorts of hideaways in the Tuscan hills was not being damaged. He was assigned a jeep and a sergeant driver, and he roamed the hills constantly checking the well-being of the masterpieces in their hiding places. He said it was an amazing experience to wheel up to a country villa and peer into a lean-to shed to see how Michelangelo's *Dawn* or *Dusk* from the new sacristy of San Lorenzo was doing. So it was no wonder that he looked on much of the art of Florence as, in a special way, his own.

My stay with Fred that week also gave me an opportunity to talk over with him my own project and get his reaction to some of my conclusions. He was most helpful and encouraging. I was eager to discuss with him one particular notion about the liturgical vesture of angels in Early Netherlandish painting. I noticed that in many paintings where there were more than one or two angels, the albs they wore were not all white, which by definition they should be (*alba* in Latin means "white"). Actual albs are always white. But in the Netherlandish paintings some of them were frequently also blue, green, gold, or red. Almost always the mixture of colors included all three: white, blue or green, and red or gold. The regular reoccurrence of these colors in the angels' vestments reminded me of the study I had directed years earlier on the color symbolism in the medieval romance *Sir Gawaine and the Green Knight*. I recalled that in Dante and later in Spenser's *Faerie Queene* these colors were associated with the three supernatural virtues of faith, hope, and charity: white for faith, blue or green for hope, and red or gold for charity. I

suspected that the Early Netherlandish painters might be symbolizing the three same supernatural virtues of the New Covenant, which
they symbolized in several other ways in their paintings, by their
rather consistent habit of vesting the angels in these three colors.

I discussed the idea with Fred, and he said he thought I was exactly
right and that he knew at least one Italian painter who had used the
three colors in connection with angels in exactly the same way. The
painting was *Enthroned Madonna with Angels* by Ambrogio Lorenzetti. It was commissioned for the town hall in the west coast city
Massa Marittima. I eventually went there to examine the painting.
Fred was right. The painting pictures an enthroned Madonna on a
three-step dais. On each step, a pair of angels stands on either side
of the Madonna. They are wearing modified albs. The albs of the pair
on the first step are white; those of the pair on the second step are
blue; and those of the pair on the third step are red. To clinch the
association of these colors with the three supernatural virtues, the
names of the three virtues are chiseled into the steps on which the
angels are standing—faith, hope, and charity in Italian. This presentation definitely was a parallel to what I thought the Early Netherlandish painters had done in consistently garbing their angels not in
white albs only, but in white, blue/green, or gold/red albs. It was a
way of reminding the public that the mystery of the New Covenant
being represented was part of the new supernatural order in which
*faith* gives a new knowledge of God, ourselves, and our destiny; a new
*hope* for a more dignified life here and for a life of eternal happiness
hereafter; and a new *love* that binds us more intimately in the life
and love of God in time and for all eternity. It was a way of reminding
the viewer of the three supernatural virtues that Paul speaks of when
he says: "There remain these three, faith, hope, and charity; and the
greatest of these is charity." Faith and hope are virtues of time; they
will not perdure into eternity. When we see God face to face, we will
not need faith; and when we possess God in the beatific vision, we
will not need hope. But we will always have charity or love; in eternity, we will know more clearly the God whom we love and who loves
us. So it is all this complex of values in the supernatural virtues that
the Early Netherlandish painters are reminding us of in their consistently garbing their angels in the colors of faith, hope, and charity. My
conversation with Fred Harrt on this point gave me the confidence to
say so in some of my publications.

I mentioned earlier that Fred had been an intimate associate of Bernard Berenson as a young student and had kept up the connection until Berenson died. He was also well acquainted with Nicky Mariano, Berenson's secretary and close companion through the many years of the scholar's productive life. For many years, she had occupied the guesthouse in the olive orchard in which Fred was living during his sabbatical year. When Berenson died, he left Nicky a house in the village, where she was still living at the time I was there. Fred invited her up to the guesthouse for lunch one day, and it was utterly fascinating to listen to her reminisce about her work and life with Berenson. The whole art history world had come to Berenson, and it was interesting to get her version of Berenson's relationship with Joseph Duveen, the great art dealer, who became so important in the art-dealing world, and of Berenson's estimate of himself. Duveen made such great collectors as Mellon and Morgan believe that unless they purchased a painting from him, it was not quite authentic. He thought of himself as not so much selling a Rembrandt painting as selling a Duveen painting, which Rembrandt happened to have painted. It was particularly interesting to hear her account of how Berenson as a Jew had avoided Hitler's net. He sat out most of the war in a quiet mountain village, where he went on with his work unmolested. Nicky was with him all through this period as his amanuensis.

She was engaged, at the time I met her, in writing her memoirs in which she recalled the long years with Berenson. It was published the next year (1966) by Alfred A. Knopf under the title *Forty Years with Berenson.*

Fred also arranged for a dinner one evening in the main villa, where we dined in Berenson's dining room. The research center at that time was being managed by Professor Myron R. Gilmore of Harvard. Fred had invited the great scholar of Tuscan art George Kaftal to the dinner and arranged that I sit next to him to give me the opportunity of coming to know him and his work personally and also to give me the chance of telling him what I was doing and get his reaction to it. I did both. I did get a good idea of the work he was engaged in at the time on the saints in Tuscan painting. I have enlarged that knowledge since by reading his *Saints in Italian Art* and *Saints in Tuscan Painting.* I told him about my work on the vested angels, and he was very interested. We talked about the Italian artists' lighthearted use of the convention of the vested angel once they had come to know it from the Early Netherlandish artists. The Italians sometimes vested their angels in modified albs and add stoles to their costume, but they frequently made them merely decorative arabesques floating off into space rather than any serious liturgical or theological symbol. I asked Dr. Kaftal why this should be so. His answer was an intelligent one. He said that in Italy there was not the necessity pressing on the artists to be reasserting the fact of the Mass and Christ's eucharistic presence because these truths were not being denied in Italy as they were so strenuously in the north, especially in what is now Holland and Upper Germany. So the Italian artists took the interesting convention of garbing angels in liturgical vestments and turned it into a decorative device with no very serious theological or eucharistic implication. He pointed out many examples of this practice in the work of Italian artists such as Fra Angelico, the Lorenzettis, and Botticelli. His explanation made sense.

The sabbatical year supported by the Fulbright grant did provide me the opportunity and time to pin down the origins of the vested angel as a eucharistic symbol. I found that there was a precedent for it in the divine Liturgy motif of the Byzantine tradition. Some Netherlandish artists, such as Jan van Eyck in the upper section of *The Adoration of the Lamb* and Rogier van der Weyden in the heavenly section of his *Beaune Last Judgment,* actually drew on that tradition. But I found that the more immediate source of the vested angels in the West was the long tradition of the Latin liturgical drama, the texts of which gave specific directions on how to vest the angels. I made a specific detailed study of the Latin liturgical drama as the source of the iconography in *The Annunciation Triptych of the Master of the Aix-en-Provence Annunciation,* entitled "The Medieval Latin Liturgical Drama and *The Annunciation Triptych of the Master of the Aix-en-Provence Annunciation."* It was published in the *Gazette des Beaux-Arts* (volume 83) in 1974 in Paris. And I showed in a study of *The Adoration of the Magi* by Rogier van der Weyden that the ciborium in the hands of one of the Magi in that painting is a eucharistic symbol derived from the Latin liturgical play for the Feast of the Epiphany. The study was published in *Studies in Iconography* (volume 2) and was subtitled "An Additional Eucharistic Allusion in van der Weyden's Columbia Triptych."

As you now know, it was not only through the Latin liturgical drama that brought vested angels into iconographic detail in Early Netherlandish painting. Sometimes they got there by direct transfer from the Liturgy itself. Such was the case in Memling's famous triptych in the Antwerp Museum, which the director of the museum retitled *The Heavenly Exaltation of the Cross* because of my published study of the triptych in *Journal of the Warburg and Courtauld Institutes* (vol. 37, 1974). Here there was a direct transfer from the liturgical Ceremony of the Exaltation of the Cross in the Good Friday liturgy to painting.

I have kept working on the subject of the vested angel steadily since 1965, the year of the Fulbright grant. Some years ago, Dr. Barbara Lane of Queens College in the Bronx, who has published widely in the area of Early Netherlandish painting, organized a northern Renaissance session for the College Art Association Convention in New York. She invited me to read a paper in the session. Because I had been working for some time on the eucharistic implications in the van der Weyden *Beaune Last Judgment,* I decided to work up a paper on that subject. It had become a fascinating subject to me. What van der Weyden did in that painting changed for some time the manner in which the Last Judgment was handled in Early Netherlandish painting. Traditionally, Last Judgment paintings in Flanders and elsewhere pay considerably more attention to the hordes of the damned being plunged into the torments of hell than to the blessed being conducted into paradise. That was certainly the case with the sculptures of the subject that often appeared in the tympanum of the main door to cathedrals in the Middle Ages. It was there also in the Last Judgment by van der Weyden's predecessor, Jan van Eyck. In van Eyck's fairly small vertical rendering of the subject, the whole lower half of the panel is a tangle of the damned being plunged through the skeleton of death into hell, where the lowering figure of Satan awaits them. Above the skeletal figure of death spread out like a bat over the pit of hell stands Michael the Archangel, in full armor with raised sword, driving the damned into the pit of hell. You eventually do get to the upper part of the panel, where you see the dead arising from the earth and sea and some of the blessed being led into the heavenly court by a vested angel. Christ the Judge is seated there with Mary on the right and St. John the Baptist on the left. But as you look at the entire composition, it is the damned being thrust into hell that leaves the most lasting impression.

When we come to *The Last Judgment* by Rogier van der Weyden, however, the whole mood changes. It is much more optimistic, which is partly the result of the circumstances that accompanied the commissioning of the painting. Chancellor Michael Rollins of Burgundy had built a hospital at Beaune, a short distance from Dijon, the capital of Burgundy, and he commissioned Rogier van der Weyden to do a panel of the Last Judgment for the altar of the combination hospital ward and chapel in his new hospital. It is no longer used as a chapel or hospital ward today, but it remains very much as it was originally designed. The Gothic timber-roofed chamber had hospital beds in small wooden cubicles all along both walls. At one end, there is an openwork wooden Gothic screen curtained on the rear. This screened off the sanctuary, where the altar was originally situated, from the hospital ward. In the morning, the curtains were drawn back, revealing the altar so the patients could assist at Mass from their beds. It was above this altar that van der Weyden's *Last Judgment* was to go. (The triptych is still in the hospital but not in the ward-chapel. It has been moved to another room, where it is protected by proper air and moisture control.)

It was probably the special circumstance of its placement that prompted van der Weyden to render the Last Judgment in a little more optimistic manner than had usually been the case in the past. He used vested angels to help him do so. The painting is a long horizontal polyptych that stretches almost halfway across the end of the ward-chapel. At the top of the central panel, Christ as Judge, in a purple cope, sits on the arch of a rainbow, itself a symbol of God's covenant with man and therefore also a symbol of hope. On the right is his Blessed Mother and on his left St. John the Baptist. This is actually an adaptation of the Byzantine *deësis* motif—an arrangement of figures including Christ in the center accompanied by Mary on the right and St. John the Baptist on the left. In smaller upper side panels are groups of angels garbed in white liturgical amices and albs, carrying the instruments of Christ's passion. Christ is pointing to the wound in his naked side, so here we have an allusion to Christ's sacrificial offering of himself on the Cross, and, in the vested angels and in Christ as Priest wearing the chasuble of his exposed flesh, an allusion to Christ's continuous offering of himself in the Eternal Liturgy or Mass. This is an adaptation of the Byzantine motif of the Eternal Liturgy in which Christ continues to offer himself in an eternal sacrifice in heaven, assisted by angels garbed in the vestments of subministers of the Mass. The artist alerts us to the fact that the action is located in heaven by the ring of clouds that completely circles Christ, the angels, and the other figures of Christ's heavenly court, and also by the fact that all the figures are thrown against a gold background, the Byzantine way of suggesting a heavenly locale.

In the lower section of the central panel appears the colossal figure of St. Michael standing firmly on the earthly terrain below but rising up to the heavenly scene above. He has been completely stripped of his armor and sword, and instead is garbed in the impeccably correct liturgical vestments of subministers of a Solemn High Mass: amice and alb, the stole crossed on his breast as the deacon wears it, and an elaborate damask cope that a master of ceremonies might wear. It is his figure and that of the Christ figure above that would have been most visible to the patients in their beds when the curtains of the screen were drawn back for Mass. Michael, rising in his liturgical vestments of the Mass just above the altar where the Mass was offered every morning for the patients in their beds, would have reminded them that if they united themselves with Christ offered in the holy sacrifice of the altar, they would have nothing to fear in death. Michael is holding a scale. The scale pan on our right is weighed down by the weight of an unrepentant sinner. He is probably destined to join those other unrepentant sinners who are moving toward the flames of hell suggested in the extreme right panel. The flames of hell are there, but in van der Weyden's treatment there is no display of the tortures of the damned. In the scale pan on the left (Christ's right), a figure of one of the blessed is rising heavenward in the rising pan. He will join the blessed moving toward the left panel, where an angel, garbed in exactly the same vestments Michael is wearing in the central panel, is leading one of the blessed through the gate of paradise. This scene must have made the sick in their beds feel that they were already hearing the words sung as the body of the deceased is carried from the church to the cemetery in the dismissal ceremony after a funeral Mass: *"Deducant te angeli in paradisum"* ("May the angels of God lead you into Paradise"). This is certainly a more hopeful and optimistic meditation on death and the Last Judgment than the more traditional treatment of these subjects in medieval sculpture and in medieval and contemporary Renaissance painting. It was the figure of St. Michael in his liturgical garb reminding the sick in the hospital ward of the redeeming effect of the eucharistic sacrifice of the Mass that helped create this more optimistic and more hopeful feeling.

This is the substance of what I said and illustrated in my presentation at the northern Renaissance session of the College Art Association Convention. Barbara Lane had invited Professor Robert A. Koch from Princeton University to respond to my presentation. I knew him from his insightful publications on the religious symbolism of flowers in Early Netherlandish painting and especially for his analysis of the floral still life in Hugo van der Goes's *Portinari Altarpiece*, the painting in which I had first noted the presence of vested angels as eucharistic symbols. Professor Koch was most positive in his comments. He said he thought I had made a good case for the more optimistic tone of van der Weyden's *Last Judgment* and that I had shown rather convincingly how the changed vestment of St. Michael had helped create that more optimistic view. He went on to say that my presentation also illustrated the importance of including the special circumstances and place of the commission of a given work of art to come to a fuller understanding of its meaning. He also thanked me publicly for the help that my publication on the liturgically vested angels in Early Netherlandish painting had been to art historians in coming to a better understanding of the eucharistic focus in that work. In conclusion, he said he hoped, as a reward for my past and present contributions to the better understanding of some aspects of Early Netherlandish painting, that vested angels would one day conduct me into paradise. Well, I hope so, too, but I will settle for the angels getting me there whether they are vested or not.

The northern Renaissance session at that New York convention was a gathering place for several outstanding scholars in the field. My good friend Chuck Cuttler was there to cheer me on, and another scholar whom I had not met before, James Snyder, was there as a commentator on one of the papers delivered in the session. Professor Snyder had a few years previously published a new text for the northern Renaissance entitled *Northern Renaissance Painting, Sculpture, the Graphic Arts from 1350 to 1575*. I had used it in some of my classes because it took a new approach and had integrated more of the recent scholarship on the field into its discussions than Chuck

Cuttler's text had done. (Chuck has since revised his very fine text to accomplish the same thing.) I introduced myself to Professor Snyder before the session began and told him how useful I had found his text. He thanked me and said—way too modestly—that what he had done in his textbook was summarize and synthesize the existing scholarship in the field, but that it did not compare with what I had done in my few articles. He said my work had really added a new dimension in the interpretation of many Early Netherlandish paintings. It was startling to hear this statement from a scholar of Dr. Snyder's eminence in the field. It made me seriously think again about Jacqueline Folie's suggestion that I pull together the articles I had published in the field, expand them, add new studies in the area, and publish it all as a book. I subsequently returned to serious work on the project and included in it an expanded version of the paper on the eucharistic implications of van der Weyden's *Last Judgment* that I read at the convention.

Another nudge in the same direction had come from Lotte Brand Philip's response to an article I had written on her book *The Ghent Altarpiece and the Art of Jan van Eyck* when it first appeared. I was very impressed with the case she had made in it for the original physical structure of the *Ghent Altarpiece,* with her conviction that the painting itself had all come from the hand of Jan van Eyck alone, but in particular with the case she made for the influence of the Byzantine tradition of the Eternal Liturgy in the panel of the upper range of the polyptych. Her discussion of the eucharistic implications of the whole work was the most sustained treatment of that aspect of the work I had yet seen. It was so important, I thought, that it deserved more than a brief review. I wrote an article on the subject and sent it to the *Review for Religious* because I thought its readers would be very interested in her discussion of how this great artist had embodied so much of the theology and history of the Eucharist into van Eyck's complicated polyptych. The article was published, and the readers did seem to be stimulated by it. I sent a copy of it to Lotte Brand Philip herself, and the following letter was part of her response to me:

February 7, 1975

My most cordial thanks for sending me the offprint of your wonderful *Art Bulletin* article ["The Origin of the Vested Angel as a Eucharistic Symbol in Flemish Painting"] and the very interesting new issue of *Review for Religious.* I knew of course your essay in the *Art Bulletin.* It contains the first kind words published about my van Eyck book, a fact which makes me very proud. For it is your article on the Portinari Altarpiece which is, in my opinion, the most important scholarly contribution in the field of the Northern Renaissance after Panofsky's great book appeared in print. All my students, undergraduates as well as graduates, always had to read this article.

I am very happy about your essay on the Eucharist in *Review for Religious.* A masterly summary of my reconstruction and iconographical analysis of the Ghent Altarpiece, your article stresses precisely those points which I myself felt to be the most important ones. How very nice that you quote exactly those lines of my preface which are closest to my heart but could of course not be accepted by many of my colleagues in art history.

That is probably an exaggerated estimate of the importance of my modest ventures into art history, but to be mentioned even in the same breath with Panofsky, one of the outstanding scholars in the field of Early Netherlandish painting, is high praise indeed.

This is the passage from the preface of her book that Lotte Brand Philip refers to in her letter:

> It is this isolated work of art which art historians have often sought to put into a broader context by linking its form and content to modes and trends of the period which were known to them from other fields. But while it may be instructive to see art in a general framework of *Geistesgeschichte* or sociology applied to it, as it were, artificially from without, we should not forget that for each individual work there had once existed a specific and natural "framework" quite palpable and concrete and supremely "sociological" in essence. Perhaps the simple and direct method of placing a work of art back into the very context of its own original setting and practical purpose can supply important new insights on the nature and meaning of a masterpiece. (*The Ghent Altarpiece and the Art of Jan van Eyck,* viii)

I think that by applying this method to *The Adoration of the Lamb,* Lotte Brand Philip came up with many new insights into the fuller meaning of *The Adoration of the Lamb.* For one thing, she brought the discussion back to its eucharistic significance. It is unquestionably the most complete treatment of that theme in the whole history of art. The arguments about the possible double authorship of the work got most art historians, including Panofsky, buried in disputes about who painted what in the painting, to the neglect of the true meaning of the painting in its specific setting in St. Bavo's Cathedral. The reason some art historians have not reacted kindly to Professor Philip's book on the great *Adoration of the Lamb* (to which she refers in her letter to me) is that she indulges in some personal surmises about the work for which she does not give sufficient evidence. These surmises do not, however, detract from the real insights she provides about the central eucharistic import of the work, especially the relevance of the Byzantine tradition of the Eternal Liturgy or Mass in understanding the upper range of the polyptych.

One experience I had in working on *The Adoration of the Lamb* by Jan van Eyck illustrated vividly to me the truth of Lotte Brand Philip's contention that much is to be gained by examining a work of art in the context of the place for which it was intended. Professor Philip herself and Elizabeth Dhanens have given convincing proof that the dominant theme of the upper range of the polyptych is the Eternal Liturgy or Mass, with the enthroned figure of Christ functioning as the celebrant assisted by the vested angels in the two angel panels. But I never was convinced that the lower panels represented either merely the Lamb of the apocalyptic vision, which Panofsky suggested, or the heavenly Jerusalem, which was Lotte Brand Philip's suggestion. I felt that van Eyck did everything possible to indicate that these panels represent the offering of the Mass not in any heavenly Jerusalem but very much here on earth. In the first place, very real, earthly land- and cityscapes stretches throughout all the panels. The landscape is made up of very realistically observed and rendered botanical specimens, dozens of which have been identified by botanists. The altar on which the Lamb stands is a very real liturgical altar, and the chalice into which He is shedding His blood is a very real Mass chalice. The whole point of the central panel is to emphasize that the blood being poured into the chalice by the Lamb and about to be offered to God in the sacrifice of the Mass is the very same blood that is eternally offered to God by Christ in heaven in the Eternal Sacrifice of the Mass. This is precisely what the Protestants were denying at the time, and it's precisely what van Eyck is reasserting in this polyptych.

He is at further pains to reassert in these lower panels that this truth has always been held in the Church, and he does so by visualizing the argument of St. Vincent of Lerins, a theologian who died in 450. Vincent was an early defender of tradition as well as of Holy Scripture as a legitimate source of theological truth, a tenet that Protestants contemporary to van Eyck were also denying. Vincent's famous *dictum* or canon concerning the legitimacy of tradition as a source of theological truth occurs in his *Commonitoria.* It reads: *"Quod semper, quod ab omnibus, quod ubique creditum est (est verum)"* ("What has been believed always and everywhere by all the faithful is true"). If this were not the case, Christ's promise of the indefectibility of his Church would have proven to be vain and unfulfilled. Part of what van Eyck is doing in the lower range of his polyptych is giving visible form to that canon or *dictum* of St. Vincent as it touches the sacrifice of the Mass and the Eucharist. A long procession of confessors and virgins from all periods of the Church in the upper part of the central panel; groups of prophets and Old Covenant figures on the lower left; apostles, popes, bishops, priests, and laity from the New Covenant on the lower right; knights and just judges (representing the active life) in the lower outermost panels; and pilgrims and hermits (representing the more contemplative life) on the lower right are all pictured as moving in procession in a common landscape and converging on the Lamb of God, who is shedding his blood into a liturgical Mass chalice on a liturgical altar. They are *all* expressing, in St. Vincent's phrase, *semper ubique* (always and everywhere) their faith in the reality of the Mass as a sacrifice and in the real presence of Christ in the eucharistic species. The Old Testament figures did so by preserving the prescribed ritualistic sacrifices of the Old Law, which looked forward to the sacrifice of Christ on the Cross and to the sacrifice of the Mass, of which the sacrifices of the Old Law were but a prophetic symbol. All the other figures in all the lower panels are professing their faith in the present reality of the sacrifice of the Mass here on earth in the New Covenant.

All of these ideas hold for the procession of sainted confessors and virgins in the upper reaches of the central panel as well. Every Mass is offered by the whole mystical Body of Christ, the Church Triumphant in heaven as well as the Church Militant on earth. Because in the doctrine of the mystical Body of Christ all the faithful are one with Christ, it is also true that in every Mass all the faithful on earth and those triumphant in heaven become a part of what is offered to God the Father. The place of the elect in heaven as witnesses to the

sacrificial offering of the Mass and as an actual part of what is offered
is recognized in some of the prayers in the canon of the Mass itself.
A prayer recited just before the consecration reads as follows:

> *Tibique reddunt vota sua, aeterno Deo, vivo et vero, communicantes
> et memoriam venerantes, in primis gloriosae semper Virginis Mariae,
> Genetricis Dei et Domini nostri Jesu Christ: sed et beati Joseph, eius-
> dem Virginis Sponsi, et beatorum Apostolorum ac martyrum tuorum,
> Petri et Pauli, Andreae, Iacobi, Ioannis, Tomae, Iacobi, Philippi, Ba-
> tholomaei, Mattaei, Simonis et Thadaei: Lini, Cleti, Clementis, Xysti,
> Cornelii, Cypriani, Laurentii, Chrysogoni, Ioannis et Pauli, Cosmae et
> Damiani: ut in omnibus protectionis tuae muniamur auxilio. Per eun-
> dem Christum Dominum nostrum.*

> (And we offer this sacrifice due unto the eternal God, living and true,
> in holy fellowship and venerable memory in the first place of the glori-
> ous and ever Virgin Mary, Mother of Jesus Christ our Lord and God:
> and St. Joseph her spouse; we also honor the Blessed Apostles and
> Martyrs, Peter and Paul, Andrew, James, John, Thomas, James, Philip,
> Bartholomew, Matthew, Simon and Thadeus; we honor, too, Linus,
> Cletus, Clement, Sixtus, Cosmas, and Damien, and all your saints. May
> their merits and prayers gain for us your constant help and protection,
> through Christ our Lord.)

In this prayer, the offering here on earth to God the Father is recognized as being made in communion with the Blessed Virgin and all
the saints in heaven.

The point that van Eyck is making in these lower panels is that the
saints in heaven and the faithful on earth are all at one in their common faith in the Mass and in the Eucharist. Both the Mass and the
Eucharist are part of a visualization of the famous theological argument of St. Vincent: *"Quod semper, quod ab omnibus, quod ubique
creditum est (est verum)."*

And there is another way in which van Eyck very subtly makes the
same point, which to my knowledge has never been clarified. It consists in the way in which he has represented the verdure in the background of these panels. Panofsky and others have called attention to
the very obvious presence of trees and shrubs that are clearly Mediterranean: cypress, umbrella pine, palm trees, and citrus fruit trees,
none of which grow in the north. We also know that these trees were
added by the artist after his sojourn in Spain. But no one has noted
the precise way in which he has distributed these southern imports.
It probably would not have occurred to me either if I had not made

a very careful study of the whole polyptych in the summer of 1985, the last time I would be able to see it in the precise chapel setting for which it was created. Because St. Bavo's is liturgically oriented, the facade faces west, and the apse is on the eastern extremity. *The Adoration of the Lamb* was placed on the eastern wall of the Veyt Chapel, which meant that the left panels were on the north, and the right panels on the south. With that in mind, it becomes significant that the Mediterranean verdure (cypress, umbrella pine, date palm, and citrus trees) are presented prolifically in the south panels, but not at all in the north panels. In the north panels, only verdure native to the north is represented. Northern and southern botanical varieties, however, commingle in the central panel, where the Lamb on the altar appears. This combination may very well be another way in which the artist subtly calls attention to the universality of faith in the Eucharist. The saints and faithful are represented converging from all four corners of the universe on the Lamb on the altar. In the verdure, the artist is saying that north and south also converge on it. It is another way of underlining the argument *"quod semper, quod ab omnibus, quod ubique."* But the possible placing of the southern verdure only on the right and central panels would not be apparent unless the polyptych were experienced in the Veyt Chapel, where the right panels were to the south and the left panels to the north. In their new placement, they are no longer experienced that way. Lotte Brand Philip was right. Experiencing a painting in the exact setting for which it was intended can sometimes substantially contribute to a better understanding of the work.

I think I have been relatively successful in my long pursuit of vested angels. The pursuit itself has been very rewarding, and I have been encouraged and pleased that so many professional art historians have been interested in my pursuit and have accepted the results of it. None of them had noticed the existence of the vested angels in Early Netherlandish painting or their importance as eucharistic symbols. I probably would not have done so either had I not functioned for years as a sacristan and a liturgical master of ceremonies. Both assignments had made me very familiar with all kinds of liturgical vestments and their specific uses. It is another manifestation of the truth of Maurice Baring's statement to which I referred at the beginning of these recollections. It has frequently been true that "In my end is my beginning."

# 16

# The House that Mac Built

AN ARTICLE on the early restoration of Cupples House at St. Louis University in one of the local papers was entitled "The House That Mac Built." Mac did not really build the house, but he did save it from being torn down and has spent many of his later years restoring and refurnishing it. Let me begin the story of Cupples House by recounting something about those who did build it. Samuel Cupples commissioned it and the prominent St. Louis architect, Thomas Annan, designed and built it.

The life of Samuel Cupples is a kind of Horatio Alger story. He was the thirteenth child of a couple back in Harrisburg, Pennsylvania, who hailed from Northern Ireland. They were devout Methodists and so was Sam all his life. At the age of seventeen, he caught the wanderlust and decided to go west. He went first to Cincinnati, where he was employed by a woodware company that made such utensils as axe handles, broom handles, and butter churns—all kinds of useful implements made out of wood. He turned out to be a phenomenally successful salesman. He was making only $25 a month and asked for a raise. He was refused the raise, but his employer suggested that he take a load of the woodware to St. Louis and open a distribution shop for it there because St. Louis was more central and fast becoming one of the most important railroad centers in the Midwest, actually surpassing Chicago at the time. Sam leaped at the suggestion, loaded a flatboat with the woodware, and started poling his way down the Ohio River. He tied up at night in towns along the river and sold some of his wares to pay his way. By the time he reached Cairo, he had sold all of it, so he went back to Cincinnati, got another load, and kept it intact as he poled his way back to St. Louis. On his second day in the city, he opened a little shop on the riverfront in a rented store (just where the south leg of the arch now stands).

That was the beginning of a very profitable venture in St. Louis. Sam was in the right place at the right time. Like Henry Shaw, he benefited by the steady trek of thousands going west to populate the central plains or push on to the West Coast. There was a great demand for Sam's woodware. He soon had salesmen hawking his wares all the way to the West Coast. The most successful of those salesmen were the Brookings brothers, who, like Sam himself, had come west to seek their fortune. They were actually so successful as salesmen that they decided to go into business for themselves. When Sam got wind of their plans, he called them in one day and said: "Boys, you can't do this; from now on you are half partners with me."

That was actually the shrewdest business decision Sam ever made. Robert Brookings was in many ways a business genius. It was largely through his acumen that Sam's business continued to flourish and became so fabulously successful. The bulk of the business had increased so much that distribution became a problem. It was Brookings who came up with the idea of building warehouses right next to the railroad tracks into which the freight cars could be shunted to cut down on handling. Eventually twenty-two such warehouses were built. This method of handling and distributing goods was so efficient that the Cupples Center became the distributor of everything that came to the city, and everything came by railroad in those days. That is chiefly how Samuel Cupples made his fortune, and it was eventually an immense one, amounting to something like $82 million in 1913 currency when he died.

He was entirely a self-made man. Both he and Brookings had only a grade school education. Like many self-made men of the time, Sam built a monument to his success. He resembled Silas in Dean Howell's *The Rise of Silas Lapham,* who built a huge mansion in the Back Bay area of Boston as a monument to his success. Sam built Cupples House.

The house is in every sense of the word a monument. It is huge, containing more than forty-two rooms, and is built in the Richardsonian Romanesque style. The architect, Thomas Annan, one of the most prominent architects in St. Louis at the time, had been greatly influenced by Richardson. In fact, Cupples House is more Richardsonian than anything Richardson designed himself because Annan borrowed details, both on the exterior and interior, from many of Richardson's buildings. The house cost $500,000 in 1889 currency, which would translate into something like $16 million today. I get some appreciation of how much was put into this private mansion when I recall that

Dubourg Hall, the administration building at St. Louis University, a five-story building a block long, with very good detailing both on the exterior and interior, cost $250,000 at the same time. And the most expensive mansion in the Westmoreland and Portland Places, which were built ten years later, cost only $250,000. Later, when I discuss the detailed architectural features of Cupples House, you will see where the money went.

It was both Mr. Cupples and the architect's intention that the house dominate its neighborhood. It did that at first by its location at the highest point in the city, by its size, and by the fact that the area was very sparsely populated when it was built. The thickly populated part of the city ended at Jefferson, and there was only a sprinkling of houses in the area of Grand and Lindell. Grand Avenue was then only a country road. And none of the scattered houses in the area remotely compared in size and grandeur to the Cupples Mansion. As the city moved westward and the whole area between Union Station and Grand Avenue was built up and became the luxury residential area, Cupples House still remained the most impressive residence in the area. All the other houses were modifications of the old stone-front town houses with a fine stone facade but plain brick side and rear walls. I call them houses with a Queen Anne front and a Mary Anne back. Cupples House was distinctive in being constructed of fine stonework on all four sides.

It was distinctive in many other ways as well. It sat on a little open piece of property surrounded on the sides and rear with a high stone wall made of the same stone as the house. All the other houses sat on narrow lots with just a driveway separating them. Those were horse-and-buggy days; houses were not built on huge properties that would have uncomfortably increased the distance between home and down-town. Another unusual feature of Cupples House was the location of the stables. They were not behind the house but on their own lot across the street facing the house. They were immense, with room for half a dozen horses and a great array of carriages, buggies, and sleighs. On the second floor of the stables were rooms for twenty-six servants. The Cupples family managed to get along with thirty-one live-in servants. Five of the top echelon, including the butler, the head maid, the chambermaid, the chauffeur, and the French chef, lived in rooms up the backstairs of the mansion itself. To feed all this help, Mr. Cupples eventually widened an open, covered back porch that stretched across the rear of the house, filled it in with windows, added an outside door to the space, and thus created a dining room for the servants. The hierarchy of servants is reminiscent of the TV *Masterpiece Theatre* production of *Upstairs Downstairs.* I can see the butler and head maid presiding at the head of the long table in the back porch dining room of the Cupples Mansion. There was plenty to keep the thirty-one servants busy. Just keeping the twenty-two fireplaces operating in winter took a lot of doing. Two laundresses washed every day in the basement laundry room, doing the washing on rubbing boards and hanging the clothes up to dry over the lanes of the bowling alley, which, incidentally, was another distinctive feature of the house. The exclusive duty of one servant was to drive out to Jennings every day, where Mr. Cupples had a farm, to bring in milk, cream, butter, eggs, and vegetables for the family.

Mr. Cupples was a great lover of horses and prided himself on his carriage and buggy steeds. It took a fleet of servants to care for the horses and riding equipment. He so loved horses that, years after he had invested in a fleet of automobiles, he still drove down to his office in Cupples Center in a horse and buggy. The stables were across the street from the mansion, so Sam could sit in his library, his favorite room in the house, and watch one of the servants curry his favorite buggy horse in front of the stables. The space behind the mansion, ordinarily occupied by the stables, was here taken up by a turn-around for carriages. Guests could be dropped under the massive porte cochere over the side door, and then the carriages could be driven around the circle in the rear to exit. And, incidentally, in the middle of this circle was the only tree on the premises. People at this time, even those living in such a luxurious mansion as Cupples House, did not seem to go in for much landscaping.

Cupples House for many reasons did dominate its neighborhood and continued to do so in the early 1900s, when luxury residences were built along Lindell and West Pine all the way to Forest Park before the 1904 World's Fair. These houses were more pretentious and situated on slightly larger properties than those that had been built east of Grand, but none of them approached the glory of Cupples House.

But one unexpected thing happened right on Grand and Lindell just east of the Cupples mansion that did somewhat overshadow it. St. Louis University, which had been located downtown at Ninth and

Washington Streets, bought the property between Lindell and West Pine along Grand Avenue and built the College Church and Dubourg Hall there, which forever spoiled Sam's view to the east and somewhat diminished his mansion's dominance in the area. He never forgave the Jesuits. In fact, he made a statement during his life that he never wanted the house ever to be sold to the Jesuits. And it wasn't; it was sold to the Brotherhood of Railroad Telegraphers after his death. They occupied it for forty years, and the university ultimately bought it from them. As I write this *in* Cupples House, I fancy I can see Sam twirling in his mausoleum in Bellefontaine Cemetery at the thought of a Jesuit infesting his mansion. But then I think that he might be happy if he could come back and see what a Jesuit has done in the last twenty-two years to bring his impressive mansion back to its former splendor.

Mentioning Sam's mausoleum reminds me of the odd fact that Sam is buried there with only women: his mother, his two wives, and his three daughters. And that, in turn, reminds me of another fact about Samuel Cupples. In spite of his immense wealth, his life was punctuated with death and sorrow. His first wife, Margaret Amelia Kells, died four years after they were married. She never lived in Cupples House. Sam then married her sister, Martha Sophia, and they had three daughters. All three children, under the age of four, died of diphtheria in the same year. Sam and his wife Martha immediately adopted a niece, Amelia Loman, who was raised in the house, was married in the house, and lived there with her husband until Sam built them a house of their own.

When Sam's second wife died, he took in the adopted niece's widowed mother, Harriet, with Harriet's two sisters, Martha and Mary. Martha and Mary were still quite young, so Sam added the round solarium on the rear of the mansion, which he used as a playroom for the children until they outgrew it. It originally had a glass dome, the metal framework for which still exists above the present ceiling of the room. (The dome can and will eventually be restored.) When the two nieces grew up, they were also married in the house, and all four families lived there for a time until Sam built homes for each of the nieces.

Sam was a devout Methodist and was very generous with his money for Methodist causes. He largely financed the building of St. John's Methodist Church on Holy Corners on Kingshighway and taught Sunday school there all his life. He built a Methodist orphanage here in St. Louis and a library for the Methodist college at Fayette, Missouri. His adopted partner, Robert Brookings, got him interested in educational causes. He established the first technical school in the city and built two engineering buildings at Washington University. And most important of all, he and Brookings donated the entire Cupples Warehouse Center to Washington University before they died. This center for many years was a very important part of that institution's endowment. Sam is quoted as saying of his many benefactions: "I have had great pleasure in accumulating my fortune, and I want also to have the pleasure of seeing where some of it goes while I am still alive." Cupples House was and remains a monument to his success.

But when Sam died in 1913, none of the family was interested in living in the house. It was too big, and there was difficulty in getting the servants necessary to maintain it. It was put up for auction in 1919 and was sold, as I mentioned above, to the Brotherhood of Railroad Telegraphers, who used it for forty years as their headquarters and offices. They were a dignified lot and never abused it. They actually made no structural changes in it whatever. But during their sojourn in the house, the neighborhood declined terribly. The area between Grand and Union Station became one of the worst slums in the United States, and most of the homes in the immediate neighborhood east of Grand were broken up into boarding houses. St. Louis University began to buy up some of this property for the future expansion of its campus, so that eventually it owned property on all sides of Cupples House.

I first knew the house in the mid-1930s, when I was a Jesuit scholastic at the university. I was always fascinated by it. It sat there in the middle of the campus, a massive, many-turreted, many-chimnied, lowering hulk, absolutely pitch black from top to bottom from decades of St. Louis soot. It had a mysterious air about it and reminded me of Hawthorne's "House of Seven Gables." I little dreamed then that, thirty some years later, I would be involved in saving the lowering monster from the headache ball and would work for more than twenty years restoring it. But that is what happened. A word on how that came about.

In the early 1950s, the Railroad Telegraphers built new headquarters for themselves on the corner of Lindell and Vandeventer, which left Cupples House available for sale. Because it was then almost entirely surrounded by St. Louis University, the university was the only interested party and bought it for a song—$50,000. It turns out that with the renewal of interest in Tiffany windows in recent years (the nine Tiffany windows in the house are alone worth several million dollars), the university got the house at a bargain price, to say the least. And what did the university use the house for? For many things, but chiefly as a student union for thirteen years. That fact renews my faith in the supernatural. It was used day and night for student-related meetings and activities, and not one initial was carved in the beautiful woodwork, and no damage was done to the priceless stained glass windows, nor did any other vandalism occur in the house. To me, such preservation approaches the proportions of a miracle. But during the Vietnam War the house just barely avoided being destroyed by fire. At that time, the ROTC offices on the third floor were the focus of an antiwar movement among the students, some of whom threatened to burn down the building. A similar group of dissident students did burn down the building that housed the ROTC offices at Washington University. During the disturbance on our campus, I looked out the window of my office (I was chairman of the English department at the time) and saw that one of my graduate fellows and one of my senior faculty members were leading the pack to set fire to the mansion. Fortunately, the university cordoned off the building for two days and nights, spirited the ROTC officers out the back door and off the campus, calmed down the students, and saved Cupples House from the flames.

It continued to be used as a student union building for several years, and various other organizations had offices there, including the theater department, the Night School, and the burgeoning art department. The presence of the latter department saved it from another disaster. I eventually taught art history courses as well as English courses. The slide library for the art history department was on the second floor of Cupples House. One day when I came to the building to prepare slides for one of my classes, I found janitors with their ladders, drop cloths, and brushes ready to paint the incomparably beautiful, hand-carved woodwork white because the dean of the Night School, who had his office on the first floor, found the wood paneling depressing. Although I had no authority to do so, I told them to stop, and I raised such a fuss with the powers that be that the woodwork was not painted white.

The bookstore was quartered in the basement for a while, but eventually that space became the Campus Club, the only fast-food operation on campus. Because the offices for the dean of men and the dean of women were on the second floor, the offices of the student newspaper and the archives on the third floor, and the only student meeting rooms on campus on the first floor, all the students came to know Cupples House very well and to visit it often. For a time, the university FM radio station, WEW, was also located on the rear of the first floor with a 535-foot radio tower poking up in the backyard.

The mansion continued to be so used until the new Busch Memorial Student Union was built on the new campus east of Grand. Then the question arose: What to do with Cupples House? The answer appeared on a blazing headline in the *University News:* "CHOUTEAU HOUSE TO BE RAZED." The building had been renamed Chouteau House when it was turned over to student use because the first student at St. Louis University was Charles Chouteau.

When I read that headline, I was in shock because in my many comings and goings in the house over the years I had come to admire the delicate workmanship throughout the house, especially the marvelous wood carving on the interior in at least nine imported woods and the equally impressive stone carving on the exterior. I realized that nothing like this work would ever be done again, and I thought it would be a crying shame to destroy such a unique example of architecture and the decorative arts. I finally persuaded the administration to hold off the headache ball. They gave me a reluctant permission to try to do something with it as an art center.

I had permission, period—no money and no physical help. But that is all I needed. By this time, I had retired from the English department. The university was cutting back on faculty; retirements were welcomed, and no replacements were made for retiring faculty. I continued to teach courses in art history, however. Some of the art history offices, including the slide library, were located on the second floor of Cupples House. I moved my office into the back porch space Mr. Cupples had created as a dining area for the servants. This was in late May. Because I had no money and no help, I donned my overalls and started to work myself. The university had respected the place, and as I remarked above, so had the students. No structural changes had been made. Some glass partitions had been added to create additional office space in the great hall on the second floor, but they had been so installed that when they were unscrewed, the woodwork was intact. I unscrewed them and hauled them to the dump myself. The biggest eyesore was the miles of ancient and less-ancient surface telephone wire that ran everywhere in the building, some of it relics of the Railroad Telegraphers' occupancy, but most of it from the thirteen years of university usage. A couple of university offices still functioned on the third floor, and there was no way of tracing how their phones connected through the maze of wire that networked the whole house. As long as the phones were operating, the phone company would not do anything about it. So one Saturday I took a pair of clippers and snipped the telephone wires arbitrarily. Monday morning, the offices had no phone service, so the phone company had to put in a temporary line to these offices, which gave me a free hand to rip out the telephone wires with abandon. I hauled away literally two truckloads of telephone wire. When I was finished, the walls everywhere looked pretty pockmarked, and I realized that if I was going to use the place in any public way, the walls would have to be painted. It looked like a daunting task—more than thirty public rooms—but I had done a lot of painting in my youth and was not intimidated. In my end is my beginning, but I really did not expect that that part of my beginning would show up in my ending. By the end of the summer, I had painted every room in the house a neutral buff. It was just a preliminary cleanup. In the basement area, benches had been built into the walls in all four rooms for the Campus Club. I ripped them out and did persuade the university maintenance department to replaster the walls. I painted the walls and hung a selection from our modern paintings and lithograph collection.

The house itself was almost entirely empty of furniture. All the original furniture had been designed by Thomas Annan, the architect, and was all made of the same wood as the woodwork in each room. Most of it had been taken by family members or had been sold at auction when the house was sold. There were a few items left that were probably too large and cumbersome to be used anywhere else. They included a beautiful hand-carved English settle with a curved top to catch the heat that was placed in front of the fireplace in the Grand Hall on the main floor, a huge hand-carved double desk of

English oak in the library, and two large *casapanca* (combination storage boxes and benches) in a Florentine pattern. But in spite of the lack of furniture, we thought the public might be interested in just seeing the house. My own work on it during the summer had revealed to me for the first time the superior workmanship throughout the house. We advertised an open house for a Sunday afternoon in October. We thought we might get a hundred or so visitors. Actually, more than three thousand trekked through the house on that first day. It was an eye-opener to both me and the administration to learn how much interest there might be in a restored Cupples house, and the first step in the restoration was to give it back its name: Cupples instead of Chouteau House.

One of the three thousand visitors at that first open house was a lady carrying two large photo albums. She turned out to be Mrs. Rumsey Ewing, the great-granddaughter of Mr. Cupples (through the adopted niece Amelia Loman Cupples). The albums she was carrying contained photographs of the exterior of the house and of the rooms in the house as they appeared in 1890. The albums had been in the possession of her aunt, Mrs. John Overall, a granddaughter of Mr. Cupples. Mrs. Overall had recently died, and her children seemed to have no interest in Cupples House. They had thrown the photo albums in a trashcan. When Mrs. Ewing saw the notice in the paper that we were planning restoration of the house, she fished the albums out of the trash and came to the open house bearing gifts. Mrs. Overall also had the original furniture from one of the second-floor bedrooms and Mr. Cupples's Steinway Duo Musica player piano—all slated for Goodwill. Mrs. Ewing persuaded the family to give it to Cupples House instead. The furniture, all made of chestnut matching the chestnut woodwork of the bedroom for which it was made, is now back in its original place and enables visitors to see how the house was originally furnished with furniture all designed by the architect. Thomas Annan anticipated Frank Lloyd Wright in that practice. The Steinway piano has been restored and is used for recitals in the house. The player mechanism is also being restored.

The photo albums proved in many ways to be a real windfall. In the first place, they did give pictorial evidence of what each room looked like in 1890. In my careful cleaning of the house, I had come to admire the exquisite and creative craftsmanship that prevailed in every detail of the house. I was determined that any restoration work had to respect that beautiful workmanship, enhance it, and not distract from it. The photographs of the rooms showed that much of the furnishings added by Mr. Cupples and the incidental decoration had often not enhanced the architect's original exquisite detailing. They frequently clashed with his work or covered it up with a Victorian clutter. Unquestionably, the most attractive feature of the interior is its fine woodwork, all hand-carved in delicate detail, even on the edges of the window frames. Much of this carving had been covered up by massive Victorian drapery. Even the fine Tiffany transom windows in the library had been hidden behind heavy drapery, and an elephantine overstuffed sofa in the library had obscured the fine English oak built-in bench in the room.

The photos convinced me that my objective in working on the house would not be a historical restoration, in which you choose a point in a building's past history and try to bring it back as nearly as possible to that historical moment in the past. I really could not see myself spending my old age building a monument to somebody else's bad taste, so what I determined to make my objective was what the experts call rehabilitation, not historical restoration. In rehabilitation, you respect the building itself and try to bring it back close to its original prime condition, but you use the building for a different purpose than the original one. It would, therefore, be my purpose to restore the house itself, as far as possible, to its original condition, but furnish it differently because we would have very little of the furniture designed by the architect. The house is not a fussy Victorian design; the rooms actually have fine, restrained classical lines. Hence, we could do almost anything we wanted within them as long as we kept some consistency within the individual rooms. As things worked out, because of the diversity of fine gifts that eventually came our way, we have been able to furnish the rooms with fine antique pieces that amount to a kind of history of furniture and the decorative arts.

The more I worked on the house the more I came to admire the talent of the architect, Thomas Annan, but I also came to see how profoundly he had been influenced by Henry Hobson Richardson, so I set about learning as much as I could about Richardson. His story was fascinating. He came from a family in New Orleans, but he went to college in Harvard, where he studied architecture and met his future wife. He won a scholarship to the Academie des Beaux-Arts in Paris, where he immersed himself in the European tradition of architecture. While he was there, the Civil War broke out at home. His family in New Orleans told him to stay in Europe until the war was over, which he did. He became an integral part of the architectural scene in Paris and traveled widely throughout Europe sketching architectural monuments wherever he went. He became particularly fascinated with medieval Romanesque architectural monuments and sketched them in detail. One of his sketches of the cathedral lantern in Granada was to inspire a similar lantern in Trinity Church in Boston, which is considered his masterpiece. When the war was over, he came back to the States, settled in Boston, married his college sweetheart there and spent the rest of his relatively short life in the Boston area. He is almost single-handedly responsible for the Romanesque revival in this country in church, civic, and domestic architecture. There are many of his own buildings in the Boston area, but churches, town halls, and private dwellings designed by him are found throughout the East and the Midwest.

Romanesque architecture, which developed in the early Middle Ages, had a fortress quality about it, whether it was a church, a castle, or a civic building. No matter what their chief purpose was, buildings in the period frequently had to function as fortresses against the constant incursions of the northern barbarian tribes. Hence, the walls had to be heavy and thick, and the windows high off the ground, some of them mere slits from which arrows could be shot. Round towers were placed strategically on the corners to provide lookouts in all directions. The tower over the main entrance frequently terminated at the second floor and overhung the entrance to enable the besieged to pour hot water or boiling oil on the invaders below. Added protection for castles were moats and drawbridges that could be raised to prevent unwanted entry. Where arches occurred in the buildings, they were the massive Roman arches. Much of the decorative sculptural detail is actually derived from eastern and Nordic sources.

Much of this fortresslike quality shows up in Richardson's buildings, and Thomas Annan certainly borrowed much from these buildings for Cupples House. There isn't any question about the massiveness. Wherever possible, Richardson favored the use of stone for his domestic architecture, and he liked a contrast between two colors of stone in his buildings. Annan has done that in Cupples House. The main walls of the building are of purple Colorado sandstone, but they are contrasted with the light-pink granite foundation stones and the massive pink granite pillars of the front entrance. The pink granite came from the Elephant Rock quarries in southern Missouri. The watchtowers that were such an important feature of Romanesque buildings and that were so often emulated by Richardson in his buildings were also picked up by Annan in Cupples House. The larger west tower reaches down to the ground; the smaller east one terminates at the second floor above the main entrance. Annan was not expecting Mr. Cupples to have to defend himself against unwanted guests with a caldron of boiling oil, but it is another Romanesque feature that he borrowed from Richardson. Asymmetry, another feature of Romanesque architecture, is a dominant element in Annan's design of Cupples House. The two towers are not the same size; the main entrance is not at the center of the building but at one corner, and it projects not outward but into the depth of the building. Many of the heavy Roman arches that are a feature of the decoration of the building are asymmetrically placed. No two capitals of the columns on the massive pillars on the front entrance are alike, and the multiple sculptural detail of the exterior is a melange of fantastic design characteristic of Romanesque architecture.

It was obvious that any serious restoration work on Cupples House would have to include the exterior. It would be a very public show of our seriousness about restoring the building and would reveal again many of its most distinctive Richardsonian Romanesque features, which had been very much obscured by the coat of St. Louis black soot that entirely obliterated the beautiful contrast between the purple Colorado sandstone and the pink Missouri granite. It was also imperative that the building be made completely weather and leak proof before extensive restoration work was undertaken on the interior, which would involve repairing the purple slate roof that was leaking in places; completely renewing the copper flashing, guttering, and down spouts; and tuck-pointing the entire building. But before tuck-pointing, the whole exterior would have to be cleaned.

All of this repair work meant money, and quite a bit of it, which I did not have. Early in my work on the house, I set up a legal foundation that had tax-exempt status. I organized a board of trustees to run it. The first president was Curt Engler, married to Robin Ewing, the daughter of Mrs. Rumsey Ewing, and therefore the great-great-granddaughter of Mr. Cupples. Curt Engler remained on the board, but was succeeded by George Conant as president. It was in George's presidency that we began the work of restoring the exterior. It occurred to us that we might be able to get some financial help for the project from the main Cupples Company. Its president at the time was John Wallace. George, Curt, and I got together with him, and he kindly pledged $35,000 toward the project. That amount was less than half of what we needed, but at the time we were considering selling two paintings from our modern art collection—one by Pousette D'Art and the other by Arshile Gorky. Both were painted in a very heavy impasto that was beginning to crack, and we would be soon losing paint from both of them. This kind of loss is almost impossible to repair. We had experts from Christie's look at them. They told us that the situation would not improve and that both of these painters were currently bringing good prices, especially Gorky, who was enjoying a retrospective in New York at the time. We were told that if we were thinking of selling them, this was the time to do it, before they had so seriously deteriorated that their value would be diminished and while the paintings of the artists were bringing good prices. We sold them through Christie's. They brought about $75,000, which provided the money we needed to do the entire exterior restoration. We first tried a chemical cleaning process on the stone, but the penetration of the soot was too deep. We had to sandblast the whole exterior lightly, which brought to light again the wonderful contrast of the dark-purple sandstone and the light-pink granite as well as all the sculptural detail everywhere on the building, all executed by stone carvers from England. This detail made very evident to everyone what an excellent example of Richardsonian Romanesque architecture Thomas Annan's mansion really is and what a good decision Samuel Cupples had made in choosing him as his architect.

When you step inside Cupples House, the architect's good taste and inventiveness become even more manifest. The glory of the interior is its woodwork, done in nine imported woods and all beautifully hand carved on the site by wood-carvers from England. A great deal of the woodcarving decorates the mantels of the twenty-two fireplaces, which originally were the only source of heat. They are completely different from one another, and they combine the beautiful wood carving with excellent Italian marble and mosaic, Delft tile, Puebla onyx, and St. Louis cast brass and wrought iron work.

Some restoration work was begun on the first floor before the work on the exterior because it was safe from the leaks that affected only some rooms on the third floor. We began with the restoration of the library, Mr. Cupples's favorite room. We had Mr. Cupples's original desk, a fine oil portrait of him, and photographs of his second wife and the niece he adopted, so we were able to create a Samuel Cupples presence in the room. We learned that one of his granddaughters was still alive in California, so we got in touch with her and asked her for a contribution to help restore the library, her grandfather's favorite room. She made a contribution of $10,000. Her son by her first marriage, René de Rosa, wrote the following inscription for the bronze plaque in the library, which her gift helped restore. It sounds like a bit of prose out of the nineteenth century and succeeds in capturing some of the flavor of the period.

> Maude Scudder Conner, whose generous gift helped to restore this library, recalls that as a small girl she would often visit her grandfather here.
>
> Then retired from day-long business chores, SAMUEL CUPPLES might seat himself near the bay window. From here he could watch his two matching chestnut horses, along with "Roanie" his tireless buggy steed, being scrubbed down in front of his coach stables across Pine Street.
>
> At other times, later in the evening, eyes fatigued, a companion would read to him from Dickens, Thackeray or another author whose works lined the library shelves.
>
> With its leisurely pace, this library became, for a small girl, a warm and special refuge. Here she could crawl up into the chair beside her loving "Grandpie" and feel quite secure.
>
> This plaque is affectionately given to the library by Maude Conner's son [René de Rosa] for whom a world of this security does seem distant; yet with a value of its own. And sadly for the casual visitor, the joys, the lively music of life, the sorrow and the rewards of the family, which flourished here are now quiet, silenced by time and change.

December 1976

The library still has the fine oak double desk that the architect designed for it. The two Tiffany windows in the room are decorated with the fleur de lis of St. Louis, and the three transom windows in the bay window show the coats of arms of the kings Louis XII, XIII, and XIV. In three spaces above the Romanesque niches on either side of the massive oak mantel are carved figures representing the three muses, but in the fourth space is a figure of St. Jerome—a tribute, no doubt, to Mr. Cupples's devotion to the Bible. Mr. Cupples had a Bible reading here in the library for his whole family every night before dinner. The inscription above the mantel reads: *Vita hominis sine litteris mors est* (The life of man without literature is death)—no doubt a contribution of Thomas Annan, the sophisticated architect of the building, but one with which Sam Cupples may have come to agree. He had only a grade school education, but, as René de Rosa says in the bronze plaque now in the library, in his old age, when his eyesight was failing, he had a reader read to him every evening here in his library. He read through all the novels of Dickens and Thackeray that he had missed as a boy.

As the renovation and restoration proceeded slowly, room by room, the project was greatly facilitated by the generosity of a few major benefactors. For the most part, their donations were not money, but significant gifts in kind that have enabled us to furnish all the rooms of the house completely in authentic antique furniture, paintings, and objets d'art that now make the house an outstanding showplace in the city and perhaps in the country. It was placed on the National Register of Historic Places in 1976 and was cited in 1989 by the National Victorian Society as an outstanding example of preservation and restoration. It is included in *The Smithsonian Guide to Historic America: The Plains States* and is appearing in a volume being published in London on *Great Homes in America*. All of this was made possible through the generous gifts of our benefactors. The cost of the restoration to date exceeds $3 million. A very large part of that amount has come from the sale of gifts in kind that we have not been able to use in the house but that we sold either in special sales in the house itself, at Sotheby's or Christie's in New York, or at Selkirks's here in St. Louis. The major renovation expenses were for rewiring the whole house, upgrading its plumbing, and installing a central heating, cooling, and moisture-control system, as well as a security system.

The story of some of our benefactors and their benefactions is an interesting one that deserves some attention in these recollections. It provides some of the most interesting elements of this second career for me. One of the most generous benefactresses has been Ms. Carolyn Skelly Burford. Carolyn's first contact with Cupples House was rather accidental. She lived at the time in a large mansion in Portland

Place but decided to move to a large thirty-five-acre estate on South Lindbergh Boulevard. The house on the estate was in the Italian villa style but somewhat smaller than her large mansion in Portland Place, so she decided to dispose of some things before she made the move. She was widowed by this time, but she still had her physician husband's extensive library, which she decided to donate to the Pius XII Memorial Library at St. Louis University. When the librarian went out to arrange for moving the books, Carolyn showed him a beautiful eighteenth-century English double secretary desk and asked him whether he would have any place for it in the library. He said he didn't think so, but that I might like to have it for Cupples House, which I was in the process of restoring. That was Carolyn's introduction to Cupples House. She became very interested in the project and over the years has donated distinctive antique furniture and objets d'art evaluated at more than $2 million. The antique double secretary desk provides the centerpiece for one of the sitting rooms on the second floor.

I cannot record here all the fine gifts she has made to the house, but I want to call attention to two of them because of their distinctive quality and because of the interesting circumstances that surrounded Carolyn's donation of one of them. The first is the beautiful commode that dominates the music room. It is the only room in the house in which the woodwork was painted white. It was meant to be more feminine because it was the room to which the women retired after dinner when the men went to the billiard room for a smoke. The woodwork is designed in classical Renaissance detail, and there is a lovely Italianate plaster-molded frieze above the light damask walls. We decided to furnish the room with French furniture, which would nicely harmonize with the decor of the room. Carolyn's commode fitted very well with that decorating scheme. It is an exact nineteenth-century copy of the original commode commissioned by King Louis XVI for his bedroom at Versailles. It is not in Louis XVI style, but in the elaborate Louis XV style. The original was designed by the famous furniture designer Jean Henri Riesener and is now on display in the Musée Condé at Chantilly outside of Paris. Ours is an exact copy, reproducing the fine ormolu decoration, the beautiful marquetry in several rare woods, and a fine marble top. It is so well done that even though it is a nineteenth-century copy, it has been appraised at more than $120,000. It unquestionably dominates the room, which is graced with other very valuable antique original period French furniture, including a love seat with two matching arm chairs in the authentic, more severe Louis XVI style and a fine rococo vitrine cabinet and two rococo marble pedestals. The light French quality of the room is augmented by the exuberant Dresden clock and candelabra on the mantel (also Carolyn's gifts), and by an elaborate Dresden urn and two Old Paris vases on Carolyn's commode.

There is hardly a room in the house that is not graced by one or two gifts from Carolyn, but I want to call particular attention to her gift for the dining room. Two of Mr. Cupples's great-granddaughters, Mrs. Rumsey Ewing and Mrs. Thomas McPheeters, gave the money to finance the restoration of the room. By the time we were engaged in that project, Carolyn had bought a mansion in Newport, Rhode Island, and was spending most of her time there. She heard that we were in the process of restoring the dining room and called to inquire whether we would be interested in having a new dining room set. She had already given us three Empire vitrine cabinets for the room, one of them antique and the other two fine nineteenth-century reproductions; we also had an Empire clock and candelabra on the mantel. I had seen Carolyn's dining room set, a beautiful antique Empire set, in her Lindbergh home in St. Louis. I presumed that is what she was offering us, so I sat down and wrote her an enthusiastic letter of acceptance immediately. I told her we were decorating the walls of the room with fine green silk moiré (her dining room set was upholstered in green silk); that we already had a number of Empire pieces in the room, including the vitrine cabinets she had given us; and that her Empire dining room set would beautifully complement what we already had. The only problem was that it wasn't her Empire set she was offering to us. She had another much less distinguished set on a truck back in Newport ready to send to us. When she got my letter, she called her accountant in St. Louis and told him: "Father McNamee wants the dining room set in the house; give it to him." What Father McNamee wanted and got was a very distinguished Empire dining room set (including the table, twelve chairs, a sideboard, and mirror) designed and signed by Desmalter, considered the prince of French Empire furniture designers. It does marvelously complete the room all in French Empire. That was one time I was very glad that I got my acknowledgment letter off with dispatch.

A gift from another quarter helped to complete the distinctly

French aura of the room. In the handsome, massive, built-in sideboard designed by the architect is displayed a set (more than ninety pieces) of beautiful eighteenth-century Baccarat crystal stemware—the gift of Mr. and Mrs. James Milton Ingham, neighbors to Mr. and Mrs. Curt Engler, in memory of their four-year-old daughter who died as the result of a minor operation that went bad. Mrs. Engler is the great-great-granddaughter of Mr. Cupples. Her daughter's tragic death is one of the afflictions that seem to haunt the Cupples family. Her brother was seriously injured as a teenager by a freak accident during a picnic when a stone pulled loose in the area where they were picnicking, hit him on the head, and permanently damaged his mental development. More recently, Veronica, René de Rosa's wife, was killed in an accidental fall in the Swiss mountains. And you probably recall the early death of Mr. Cupples's first wife and the deaths of all three of his children of diphtheria under the age of four. That does seem to be more tragedy than one family should be asked to bear.

Another very distinctive gift from Carolyn Skelly is a Dutch seventeenth-century bombé desk completely covered with beautiful inlaid marquetry work. It, like the dining room set, marvelously complements the room in which it is placed. The room originally was the billiard room, but we have made it into a Flemish room. There are several reasons why a Flemish room is particularly appropriate in Cupples House at St. Louis University. The university was founded by eleven Flemish Jesuits. Portraits of two of them, Father Jan van Asshe and the famous missioner and explorer Father Pierre De Smet, hang in the room. And four of the fifty-two paintings, mostly Flemish, that Father De Smet brought to the university from Belgium also hang in the room: *Scenes from the Crucifixion* by Jan van Rillaert; two genre paintings, *The Cobbler* and *The Scissors Grinder,* by David Teniers; and *Rest on the Flight into Egypt* by a seventeenth-century mannerist painter from Antwerp.

The most commanding painting in the room, and probably the finest painting in the whole university collection, is *The Adoration of the Magi* by the sixteenth-century painter Pieter Coecke van Aelst. Pieter was the son of Pieter Coecke van Aelst the elder of Antwerp, who inaugurated the Antwerp mannerist school. There are mannerist qualities about his son's painting of the Magi, but it also shows the influence of his several years sojourn in Italy, where he especially learned to master perspective, as this painting shows. Pieter eventually married Pieter Bruegel's daughter, so he was at the heart of the development of Flemish painting. The provenance of our painting is interesting. At a reception at Cupples House for some occasion, Elizabeth Benoist, of the old Benoist family in the city, said she had a painting she would like to give Cupples House if I were interested. It was the painting *St. Francis of Assisi* by the Italian painter Lodovico Cardi da Cigoli (1559–1613). Coming over to the States, her father had bought it from an emigrating Italian family who needed additional money when they arrived. It is a fine painting, and, of course, I wanted it. It now hangs in one of the second-floor sitting rooms. When I was at Elizabeth's home examining the Cigoli, she told me she had another painting in the basement that I might be interested in looking at. She said they had removed it from its frame because they wanted to use the frame for a portrait of their grandfather. She gave me a flashlight, and I groped my way through the basement and came upon the painting. My eyes almost popped out of my head. Flemish painting is the area in which I have specialized, and I could see at a glance that this was an important painting from that school. When I returned to the living room, Elizabeth had dug out photographs of a triptych in the Princeton University Museum that very much resembled her painting. She had acquired the photograph when some research had been done on her painting when she had offered it to the St. Louis Art Museum some years previously. The Art Museum, for some unknown reason, had turned down her offer. I was very interested in the painting, and Elizabeth and the Benoist family finally made a gift of it to Cupples House. The painting may have been the central panel of a triptych similar to the Princeton triptych. The cut-off corners at the top suggested that connection, but it had been framed in an elaborate Italian frame, which did not fit these sheered corners, and someone had filled in the corners with wood (the painting is on a wood panel) and had rather crudely extended the background details into these in-fills. The frame it had been in was in every way wrong for the painting. After I got it, I turned it over to Mr. Clement Robertson, the very good official restorer at the Art Museum at the time. He removed the in-fills and cleaned the entire painting, which revealed the rich and intense color so characteristic of Flemish painting at its best. Recall that it was the Flemish painter Jan van Eyck who perfected the oil medium. The painting needed very little retouching, only a tiny bit along a crack that had developed over the years in the panel. Just from stylistic elements, we were pretty sure that the painting was from the hands of Pieter Coecke van Aelst. A later photographic study was made of the panel by Professor Molly Faries from Indiana University, who was doing a study of Coecke van Aelst. Her infrared photography and study of the underdrawing proved conclusively that it is indeed by him, so this painting in our Flemish room, rescued from a potato cellar, is now possibly the most treasured possession in the whole of Cupples House.

The most distinctive piece of furniture in the Flemish room is a massive seventeenth-century baroque Flemish breakfront of hand-carved walnut with green-marble inserts from Port Sory in eastern Scotland. It is a magnificent example of seventeenth-century Flemish baroque woodcarving. The scenes carved on it are taken from the *Aeneid*. But, as is the case of many objects in the house, its provenance is almost as interesting as the object itself. It was owned by a Jewish gentleman in Vienna, a Mr. Otto Dukes, who got out of Austria just before the Nazis took over. He shipped many of his belongings to St. Louis because he had a friend on the faculty of our dental school. He eventually settled in New York, but the breakfront was too large to be accommodated in his New York apartment, so he loaned it to St. Louis University. It was a treasured heirloom, and he could not bear the idea of relinquishing ownership of it. For a long time, we had it on display in one of the parlors in Dubourg Hall, when the Jesuit community still lived there. Whenever Mr. Dukes came to town to visit his friend, he used to come to the parlor and commune with it for a while; it was a very important part of his memories. But he finally got the courage to donate it to us. It was then moved into the community dining room and used for the purpose for which it was made—a storage place for flat silver and linen in a dining room. I used to cringe when I saw the help yanking the doors open to get at the linen. It was a happy day when I persuaded the administration to transfer it to the Flemish room in Cupples House, where with the Flemish paintings, Flemish-style chairs, the Dutch bombé desk, and wallpaper that simulates the red and gold leather with which Flemish interiors were often decorated, the whole room succeeds in creating a real Flemish ambiance.

Other significant gifts from Carolyn Skelly Burford grace the greensward east of Cupples House. The first is a beautiful Carrara marble statue of Ganymede being swept up by Zeus, in the form of an eagle, to become the cupbearer of the gods. It is by the nineteenth-century French artist Jean Alexandre Joseph Falguiere. A fine statue by him is on display in the new D'Orsay Museum in Paris devoted to nineteenth-century French art. The second gift is two bronzes—representing the drunken god Silenus and a Faun—with a very interesting history. Carolyn had purchased them from an estate in Long Island and had them on display in the garden of her estate on Lindbergh, but eventually decided to give them to us. The appraisal papers that came with them described them as eighteenth-century baroque Italian works, but a Jesuit scholastic, Joseph Venker, traveling in California one summer, visited the Getty Museum in Malibu. He sent me photographs of the identical statues in the reflection pool of the main court of the museum. I wrote to the director and asked where the statues came from. He wrote back to tell me that they were nineteenth-century copies of the original bronzes in the Naples National Museum that had been found in the excavations of the ancient Roman city of Herculaneum on the outskirts of Naples. A bronze caster in Naples in the nineteenth century had been given permission to cast five copies of the originals. One of the set was the one in the Getty Museum. The director said he knew where three other sets were but did not know where the fifth one was. Ours turned out to be the fifth one. The bronzes, of course, were most appropriate for the Getty Museum reflecting pool because the museum itself is a copy of the villa in Herculaneum, covered by the ashes of Vesuvius, where the originals were found. So Carolyn's gift to us of the two bronzes provides an interesting conversation piece in our Cupples House garden.

One of our other major benefactors came to us in a way about as casual as our first contact with Carolyn Skelly Burford. One day, Mrs. Maurice Mendle, a perfect stranger to me, called and said she had a painting that she would like to donate to Cupples House if I were interested in having it. She said she had just gone through a divorce proceeding, was breaking up her household, and was moving into an apartment that would not accommodate all the things in her house. The painting turned out to be a fine oil by the Italian mannerist painter Francesco Maria Parmigianino (1505–40) entitled *An Apotheosis*. It represents, in typical mannerist fashion, a group of nude nymphs engaged in a fantastic dance in a garden setting. It is a very good example of Italian mannerism; I was certainly interested in adding it to our collection. Mrs. Mendle told me the only problem was that her brother-in-law, Milton, had the papers on the painting, and because of a family tiff at the time, they were not speaking, but she said that perhaps if I would contact her brother-in-law, he might give the papers to me. So I called Milton Mendle, introduced myself as a Jesuit professor of art at St. Louis University, and told him about his sister-in-law's gift. He said the situation was interesting. He had given the painting to his sister-in-law as a wedding present on the condition that if she ever wanted to dispose of it, she was to return it to him because it was one of a pair. But he went on to say that he and his wife Roberta were in the process of moving from their huge apartment into somewhat smaller quarters and would have to dispose of some of the contents of their old apartment. He wondered whether I would be interested in having the twin to the painting that his sister-in-law had offered. When I said I would, indeed, he asked where it was going to be placed at the university. When I told him it would be hung in Cupples House, which I was restoring, he burst into an exclamation over the phone: "My God," he said, "I've had a love affair with that house all my life!"

He went on to explain that he was really a frustrated architect. That was what he wanted to be as a young man and had begun to make preparations educationally to do so when his father died prematurely. Milton had to drop his ambitions to become an architect and come home to help run his father's printing business. He had spent the rest of his life doing that, but he had never lost interest in architecture and had made studying the interesting architecture of St. Louis his hobby. He had always been fascinated by Cupples House. He said he used regularly to switch over to Pine Street from Lindell when driving to or from downtown just to go by it and admire it, but had never been in it. So he packed up his second *Apotheosis* by Parmigianino in his car, brought it down, and toured Cupples House from cellar to garret. That was the beginning of a permanent and warm friendship between Milton and me, which ultimately resulted in very important donations in kind and monetary support for the house. One of his gifts was the important full-length *Portrait of Mrs. Battle* by the well-known English portrait painter Sir John Hoppner (1758–1810). It had been a wedding gift to his wife Roberta. It now graces the first landing on the grand stairwell in Cupples House. Another significant gift they made to the house is the huge French crystal chandelier in the dining room, which came originally from the library in Roberta's home in the old Vandeventer Place. Her father was Mr. Thomas Murray Pierce, a very successful lawyer. The Pierce mansion was the most impressive one in the whole of Vandeventer Place, so the beautiful crystal chandelier in the dining room is an interesting historical link with the famous old Vandeventer Place, now replaced by Cochran Veterans' Hospital.

Milton eventually joined the Cupples House board and almost immediately insisted that something had to be done to replace the ugly brick entrance to the basement gallery, which the university had added when the basement was used as a snack bar for the students. Verner Burks, a well-known St. Louis architect, was commissioned to design an entrance to the gallery that would be more suitable to the house. He came up with a beautiful design that replicated some of the massive granite details of the front entrance and the curve of the large neighboring bay window. He also picked up the original design of the iron railing on one of the balconies and duplicated it on the new entrance railing. Executing the design was estimated at about $65,000. Milton said he would be happy to pick up the bill on the condition that the gallery to which it gave entrance be named after me and that my name be inscribed on the entrance as an acknowledgment of what I had done in saving and restoring the house. That is why the inscription on the new granite entrance to the gallery reads "McNamee Gallery."

Milton also thought that the glass block windows that the university had installed in the east gallery were inappropriate and that stained glass windows should replace them. Robert Frei was commissioned to design them. He picked up the design of the Tiffany windows in the main stairwell and replicated them in variations of textured glass very similar to that used in the Tiffany windows, so they look as if they had been there from the beginning. Milton also financed the fabrication and installation of these windows.

So I may be forgiven, I think, for having a special affection for the two mannerist paintings by Francesco Maria Parmigianino that threw Milton and me together, but I would have treasured his friendship even if it had not resulted in any monetary benefit to Cupples House.

The next major benefaction to Cupples House was a little more stormy in its arrival. Mr. Arthur Drefs had for years been on the President's Council at the university. He and his wife, Artemesia, had no children, and he had assured Father Reinert that he intended to leave all his substantial fortune to the university because he had become very interested in the future of the university while on the board. But he died suddenly of a heart attack before he had made that stipulation in his will. He had intended to leave his fortune in trust to Artemesia during her lifetime with the stipulation that, at her death, the capital would come to the university. Artemesia knew what his intentions were, and she made out her will to correspond to her deceased husband's intentions. She informed Father Reinert of that fact.

All her life Artemesia had collected antique furniture. Her house, Number 2 on the St. Louis County Club grounds, was filled with it. One day, while talking to Father Reinert about the arrangements she had made in her will, she asked him whether there was any place at the university where her antique furniture could be used. Father Reinert suggested that I might be able to use some of it in Cupples House, which I was restoring. He told her he would have me come out and look at it, which I did. I had never met Artemesia, but I certainly had heard of her. Before I joined the English faculty, she had come down to the university in midlife to get an undergraduate degree in English because she had never finished college. Father Dreyfus, the chairman of the department at the time, told me she would arrive for classes in her Pierce Arrow with a chauffeur and a footman and then take her place in class with the undergraduate youngsters. When she finished her degree in English, she went out to Washington University and took classes in painting and ballet dancing. She continued both avocations and had both a painting and a dance studio on the top floor of her home. By the time I met her, she was in her late eighties but was still painting. When I called at her home, we had sherry and crumpets in the library, and I naturally cast my eye on some of her impressive antiques. I told her that I certainly thought we could use some of the items in Cupples House. She said: "That's not the idea. I want you to have everything in the house." I was staggered by the notion. She went on: "To be sure that you get it, I want to go through the house with you, make an inventory of its contents, and tell you about the provenance of some of the items. I'll put the inventory in my will so there can be no mistake about my intentions." We spent the rest of the day making the inventory. When we were finished, I asked her whether she had any relatives who might be interested in any of these things. She said, "No." Her only living sister was married to Mr. Mamoulion (the famous director of films such as *Oklahoma*) and was not interested in antiques. She went on to say that she had not been close to her nephews in the East (sons of a deceased sister) and that, anyway, none of these things had any family connections. She said she had bought them herself with her husband's money. This was the only time I ever saw Mrs. Drefs. She lived four more years and died in her early nineties.

I went out to the funeral parlor to pay my respects. When I arrived, the only person in the room was the wife of one of the nephews from the East. She was swathed in deep-black mourning from head to foot. The first thing that went through my mind was: "Artemesia's will will be contested—'The lady doth protest too much.'" And I was right; in due time, one of the nephews contested the will. The contention was that Father Reinert and I had alienated Artemesia's affections from her family. The truth was that neither Father Reinert nor I had had anything to do with Artemesia's making out her will the way she did. In fact, I had raised the question of her family when we made the inventory of the contents of her house. I told the lawyer that this occasion was the only time I had ever seen Artemesia, but he was determined to make me out a liar. In one inquisition, he brought in a whole stack of photographs of objects in the house, chosen at random. He asked me whether I recognized them and could remember where they were in the house. Since we had spent a whole day inventorying everything in the house I recognized all of them and recollected pretty much where they were as well. The lawyer said: "You have a very good memory. Now do you remember this?" He handed me a letter I had written Artemesia inviting her down to see Cupples House, where some of her things might end up. I had said in my previous deposition that I had seen her only once. The letter was to prove that I was obviously lying. I wasn't. Artemesia had become ill and was never able to make the visit to the house. Thus, we exploded that particular ploy, but others were tried. Depositions and counter-depositions went on for more than a year. The nephew finally settled out of court for $600,000, to which the university was willing to agree in order to avoid having the whole thing aired in the papers. The university got the bulk of Mr. Drefs's estate, and Cupples House got the contents of the house of Number 2, St. Louis Country Club. Artemesia's sister expressed an interest in having her sister's silverware, to which we readily agreed. She was not interested, as Artemesia suspected she would not be, in any of the antiques. An interesting twist in the situation was the fact that the second nephew in the East, who had refused to get involved in the original suit against the university although urged by the lawyer to do so, now sued his brother for some of the $600,000 awarded him. Money does make strange things happen.

The contents of the house had been in storage during the lawsuit. When it was released, we discovered that much of the antique furniture had been badly damaged by the high level of heat that Artemesia had maintained in her house in her later years. It could be restored, but it would cost more than we could afford to pay. And much of it, although important antique specimens, was unsuitable to what we were doing in Cupples House. We sorted out what we could use, which was a considerable amount, and then arranged to have a public sale of the rest. Florence Thatcher conducted the sale in the gallery in Cupples House, netting a profit for the house of more than $120,000.

By happy chance, Artemesia's gift of the contents of her house netted much more for us. I mentioned above that Artemesia had become a devoted amateur painter. Part of the contents of her house was more than fifty of her paintings. They were nicely framed, but Florence Thatcher said the paintings themselves were not good enough to interest buyers. She said we would stack them up and, on the last day of the sale, sell them for the frames. We stacked them up in the rear of the gallery, but one day I riffled through them just to see for myself what kind of a painter Artemesia was. She would not have won any prizes, but while riffling, I came upon a painting of some obvious merit. It pictured a woman seated under an umbrella. It was signed Henri Lebasque. I did not know much about the painter at the time, but I liked the painting. I took it out of the pile and ultimately hung it in one of the rooms in Cupples House. Then one day, when I was doing some more riffling, this time through one of Christie's auction sales catalogs, I ran into a photograph of a painting by Lebasque that had a high estimate of $120,000. My eyes popped.

We were at the time trying to raise money for the rewiring of

Cupples House, a very important precaution against fire because some of the wiring was still the old porcelain knob-and-wire type. The estimated cost of the rewiring was in the neighborhood of $120,000. I thought that safeguarding the whole house against fire was more important than this one painting, which, incidentally, might have been sold for $10 for the frame if my riffling had not detected it among Artemesia's productions. I sent a photograph of it to Christie's; they asked that we send on the painting. They were pleased with it and put it up for sale. It brought $120,000 at auction, almost the complete cost of our rewiring. What a happy riffle.

Some of Artemesia's furniture can be found in many rooms in Cupples House. She was particularly fond of Oriental work and many of her favorite Oriental pieces grace the southwest Oriental Room on the third floor, where there is a bronze plaque commemorating her benefactions.

Gifts in kind continue to be made to the house, and they *seem* just to fall into our laps. A very significant collection of fine glassware (more than five hundred pieces from more than twenty American manufacturers and nine foreign countries) recently came our way almost by chance. The collection had been put together by Ms. Eleanor Turshin from St. Louis and Douglas Archer, a retired army engineer from Kernersville, North Carolina. Their paths had met in St. Louis. Douglas was assigned to the Federal Map Center here in St. Louis after the war. Their mutual interests in glass brought them together, and they decided to develop a glass museum. Douglas had an antique shop back in Kernersville, and he said he would put his engineering skills to work on building cabinets for the collection if Eleanor would finance the purchase of the glass. The deal was made, and the museum was developed. But Douglas eventually had a heart attack and could no longer manage the museum. At first, their inclination was to sell the glass, but they had put so much energy and money into the project that they could not bring themselves to do it. They decided to try to find a home for it. Eleanor said: "If we are going to do that, I will bring it back to St. Louis and find a home for it there because that's where I live." She began looking for the new home. She offered it to the St. Louis Art Museum, the Missouri Botanical Garden, the Junior League, and a fourth party, all of whom expressed an interest in the collection but said they could have only a few pieces on display at any one time. One of Eleanor's very good friends is the dean of our Nursing School, Joan Hrubetz, who suggested to Eleanor that she offer the collection to Cupples House. Eleanor said: "What's Cupples House?" She had never been in it, but she now came down, had a look, and was delighted with what she saw. I flew to Kernersville to have a look at the glass and was equally delighted with what I saw. The upshot of it all was that the glass collection came to us, and we have installed about two-thirds of it on the third floor of Cupples House. The rest we will display as periodical changing shows of glass in one of the cabinets. Much of the collection is contemporary with Cupples House itself and is thus a significant addition to the house.

As I write this chapter, two other very significant collections have been added. The first is a collection of beautiful Staffordshire china (more than sixty pieces), a gift of Warren Lorella and Jay Cross. Many pieces bear an illustration of an episode from early U.S. history. The other collection consists of more than one hundred pieces of Wedgwood porcelain in all the colors that occur in the style, a gift of Mrs. Margaret N. Lange. Both gifts make handsome additions to the treasures in Cupples House.

So benefactions do continue to be made to Cupples House, the house that Mac did not *build,* but that he did *save* for posterity.

17

# An Excursion into Iconography

ON THE ITINERARY of our first visit to the city of St. Louis back in 1928, a group of us Wisconsinites who were headed for the Florissant Jesuit novitiate had visited the New Cathedral. I was awed by its immensity. I had never seen a Byzantine-style church before with its awesome march of great domes towering to the heavens. Most of the interior of the cathedral at that time was still raw concrete. There were mosaics in all four side chapels and on the lower arcades of the building. The great baldachino was in place, but the vestibule and all three of the main domes were still bare concrete. The semidomes in the transepts and the soffit arches in front of them were covered with temporary paintings done by a German artist, Gotthard Bauer from Munich, representing the Resurrection and Ascension in a rather conventional style. They simulated mosaics, but they were actually paintings on papier-mâché superimposed on chicken wire and were meant to be temporary until they could be replaced by mosaics. But even in its unfinished condition, the vast domed space of the cathedral was truly awe inspiring. I little thought then that I would live to see every inch of these vast concrete areas covered with glorious mosaics—when the St. Louis Cathedral could boast that it possesses the largest assemblage of mosaics in one building in the whole world. Nor could I, in my wildest dreams, ever have thought then that I would one day be involved in the planning of the iconography of the final mosaics to be installed.

The installation of the mosaics went on steadily in the post–World War I years, but was interrupted by the Depression and World War II. Under Cardinal Ritter, work was resumed, and the mosaics were installed in all three domes with their adjacent arches and pendentives. When Archbishop May arrived, the only sections left unfinished were the two apsidal semidomes, whose temporary paintings on papier-mâché were beginning to crumble, and the two flat walls in the rear historical bay, which recounted the history of the Roman Catholic Church in the St. Louis area. Archbishop May determined to complete the mosaic project. He formed a committee, of which I was a member, to plan the iconography for these mosaics in these final spaces.

I presume the reason I was brought on the committee was the fact that some time previously I had prepared a booklet on the cathedral discussing all the mosaics already installed. How I came to do so is interesting. I was offering Mass at the cathedral some time in the late 1950s, and Monsignor Gannon, the pastor of the cathedral at the time, mentioned that they were in need of a booklet on the mosaics in the cathedral to help visitors better understand what they were viewing. I told him I would be happy to work one up for him. His response was: "Do you know anything about the mosaics?" My reply was: "Not a lot, but I can learn it." He took the risk and told me to go ahead. I *did* learn a lot. I spent the better part of one whole summer with binoculars in hand studying the mosaics and identifying the iconographical details of every one of them.

I started by looking into the background of Byzantine architecture in general and of Eastern theology and liturgy to which the Eastern Byzantine architecture was closely linked. I read everything I could get my hands on about all of these areas. I learned that it was the Eastern theological emphasis on the divinity of Christ rather than on his humanity that affected both Eastern architecture and liturgy. The easterners thought of Christ particularly as the supreme ruler and authoritative teacher. Hence, they usually represented him seated on a throne in regal fashion, the Pantocrator (Ruler of All), they called him. And they always gave him the gesture of the teacher—pointing and middle fingers raised, with the thumb touching the ring and little fingers. The gesture had become the symbol of the rhetorician or teacher in classical times and was taken over in the Byzantine East as a symbol of Christ the Ruler and Teacher. They frequently also gave it to the four evangelists as teachers. In keeping with this regal and authoritative concept of Christ the Pantocrator, the easterners thought of the physical church as the throne room of Christ the King, hence the awesome domes and rich mosaic decorations. They frequently decorated the lower walls of their churches with horizontal stripes of marble in alternating colors to suggest the earth below and filled the arches and domes above with glorious mosaics worked in gold to create a sense of a heavenly vision. All of this, of course, is beautifully illustrated in the interior of the St. Louis Cathedral. But I had a problem about a Byzantine cathedral sitting in the center of a midwestern American city. I wondered why Archbishop Glennon had chosen the Byzantine style for his new cathedral when everyone else all over the country was building in the Romanesque or Gothic styles.

A possible answer to that question came from a very unlikely quarter. A Mrs. Betty Farris was working for her degree in art history in our department at St. Louis University. She eventually became our slide librarian in the department, an instructor in the history of American art, and a very dear friend of mine. She is a Methodist and belongs to Grace Methodist Church on Skinker, where she was engaged on the side in writing a history of the church. While she was doing this, she discovered some details of its history that I believe may have influenced Archbishop Glennon to choose Byzantine as the style of his new cathedral. Grace Methodist Church was originally located on the southeast corner of Lindell and Newstead, diagonally across from where the New Cathedral now stands. At that time, a good many members of the very successful business community in St. Louis were Methodists, and a great many of them lived in fine homes along Lindell Boulevard east of Kingshighway. As I remarked in a previous chapter, Samuel Cupples was a devout Methodist and prominent in St. John's parish on Kingshighway. Bishop Kenrick had wanted to locate the New Cathedral on the corner of Lindell and Kingshighway, where the Chase-Park Plaza Hotel now stands, but the property was owned by a Methodist family who would not sell it to the archbishop, so he eventually bought the property where the New Cathedral now stands. The Methodists said: "There goes our neighborhood. It will become an Irish slum." So they literally picked up Grace Methodist Church stone by stone and moved it out to Skinker, where it remains today. They were going to avoid being caught in an Irish slum, so I think this attitude was in Archbishop Glennon's mind when he came to build the New Cathedral on the Lindell property. He decided on a style of architecture and built on a scale that would in one step yank the Catholic community out of the slums. A grand Byzantine structure would do that, so Byzantine it was. The New Cathedral is actually totally Romanesque on the exterior, but in very grand proportions; its Byzantine quality is entirely a matter of its interior.

The neighborhood did eventually greatly deteriorate, but not because of the cathedral's presence. As a matter of fact, whatever respectability the neighborhood retained in the years of its decline was the result of the cathedral's being there. And in the present revival of the neighborhood, the cathedral remains its central jewel, a world-class structure visited by awe-struck tourists from all over the country and in fact from all over the world. As an index of some of the improved relationships between the religious sects that have taken place over the years, I was invited a few years ago by the pastor of Grace Methodist Church to give a Lenten series of lectures at his church on the influence of religion on the history of art.

In working on the subject matter of the mosaics that had already been installed, I came to realize how carefully the overall iconography had been planned. All the mosaics in the sanctuary have to do with the Eucharist. The great central dome, which in a typical Byzantine church would have been completely filled with an awesome figure of the Pantocrator or Supreme Ruler, is here filled with a kind of heavenly vision cast against a unique red background. It contains an image of the Trinity in what is known as the vertical Trinity design, with the enthroned God the Father holding the Son hanging on the Cross and the Dove of the Holy Spirit. Three other heavenly visions are represented: the prophet Ezekial with his mysterious wheels; Elijah being carried up to heaven in his golden chariot; and the woman of the Apocalypse, a prevision of the Blessed Virgin. In the great triangular pendentives are images of angels, representing the synagogue with its partial vision of revealed truth (the figure is blindfolded); the Roman Catholic Church, full visioned and carrying a cross and a chalice; ecclesiastical law; and finally civil law. The mosaics on the four great arches supporting the dome represent the days of creation; the sanctification of the human race under the inspiration of the Holy Spirit; the Last Judgment; and, finally, the glorious reign of the just in heaven. The rear bay represents the spreading of the faith in the St. Louis area. It includes a representation of the first baptism in the area and the first wedding. It also includes representations of the educational thrust of the Church in the St. Louis area through the work of various religious orders of men and women and also the social work of the Church in hospitals, orphanages, and other institutions, again achieved through the work of men and women from various orders. One section is devoted to the special work of the Vincentian Order in the diocese because of that order's long history of service to the diocese. The pendentives under the dome represent the first four canonized saints who worked in America. One of them, Saint Philippine Duchesne, worked, died, and is buried here in the St. Louis area. The others are Saint Isaac Jogues, a Jesuit martyred by the native people in upper New York; Saint Elizabeth Anne Seton, founder of the Daughters of Charity in the United States; and St. Frances Xavier Cabrini of the Missionary Sisters of the Sacred Heart, who worked among the Italian immigrants in the New York area and is buried there.

The task assigned the committee appointed by Archbishop May was to decide on the subject matter for the replacement of the papier-mâché paintings in the transept apses and neighboring soffit arches and for the two unfinished flat side walls in the historical bay. Some members of the committee and some not on the committee suggested that we just reproduce in mosaic the representations of the Resurrection and Ascension that the German artist, Gotthard Bauer, had worked out. It was argued that the public was familiar with them and that they harmonized fairly well with the existing mosaics. But the majority of the committee felt that because of the dominant place these apsidal transept spaces had in the cathedral, we ought to take the opportunity of choosing a subject matter and a style for them that would be a better expression of contemporary theological emphases in the Church and be somewhat more modern in style, rather than a mere reproduction of stylistic patterns of the past. The committee insisted, however, that the style not clash with the more traditional design of the existing mosaics but harmonize with them. But because the mosaics of the Last Judgment and the Triumph in Heaven on the soffit arches in front were already in place, the committee also urged that the designs for the remaining two soffit arches in front of the transept apses, then covered with Gotthard Bauer's paintings on papier-mâché, be closely related in design. Archbishop May agreed completely with these recommendations and cooperated closely with the committee in working out the subject matter for the new mosaics.

The artist chosen to do the work was Mary Reardon from Hingham, Massachusetts. She had done very fine mosaic work for the National Shrine in Washington, D.C., and came highly recommended by Arno Heuduck, who with his father had fabricated almost all the mosaics already installed in the cathedral. After much discussion, it was decided that the subject matter of the eastern apse should be *not* the actual Resurrection of Christ but one of Christ's apparitions after the Resurrection. That was what contemporary resurrection theology was emphasizing. No one actually saw the Resurrection itself, but what the Risen Christ was at pains to demonstrate was what his resurrected life was like. Christ came and went at will, passed through locked doors; but also ate with his disciples—in fact, he prepared a fish fry on the shore for them one day and participated in the fry to prove that he was not a mere ghost but had a body like theirs. He made doubting Thomas put his hands in the wounds in his side and hands to have physical evidence that it was really the Christ they knew that was appearing to them. So in the light of all this emphasis in modern resurrection theology, the committee thought that what should be represented in the apse was one of Christ's apparitions. But what apparition? Another central subject of contemporary theology is the place of women in the economy of grace and in the Church. Christ gave some paradigm for thought on the subject by appearing first to the women at the tomb and alone to Mary Magdalene, whom he sent as an apostle of the Resurrection to the Apostles, who, incidentally, were locked in the Upper Room in fear of their lives while the Marys were out at the tomb. We all agreed that this was an important statement to be making at this precise time, and that is why the apparition of Christ to Mary Magdalene became the central motif of the east apse.

But modern discussions of the Resurrection emphasize that it is meaningless unless there was an actual death. Christ actually did die and was buried. We are reminded of that fact in the apsidal mosaic on the right by the scene of the empty Cross and the carrying of Christ's dead body to the tomb. And much is made in contemporary theology of the fact that both the death and the Resurrection of Christ is what we commemorate in the Eucharist. Some of the ritual prayers of the Eucharist itself call attention to that. In a prayer shortly after the consecration, we are reminded that what we are commemorating in the Eucharist sacrifice are the death, Resurrection, and Ascension of Christ. To remind us of that eucharistic commemoration, the scene at Emmaus in which the disciples finally recognized the Risen Christ in the breaking of the bread is represented.

This combination of death and resurrection is symbolized at the apex of the soffit arch by the combination of the Cross and the crown. The resurrection motif is alluded to again in the soffit arch by scenes representing Christ raising Lazarus on the right and Doubting Thomas declaring his faith in the Risen Christ on the left.

The subject matter chosen for the west apse was not the Ascension of Christ but the descent of the Holy Spirit on Mary and the Apostles in the Upper Room on Pentecost. The reason for this choice again was the emphasis being placed on the function of the Holy Spirit in the Church and in the lives of individual Christians in modern theological thinking. This emphasis has been so central in modern theorizing and life that our age has sometimes been called "the Age of the Holy Spirit." To catch some of that spirit, the artist came up with a design that represents a huge tongue of flame that almost fills the whole apse. It embraces the figures of Mary and the Apostles, upon each of whom a tongue of fire is descending. This is Pentecost, the actual birthday of the Church. Out of the Upper Room, inspired and emboldened by the Holy Spirit, the Apostles went forth and preached the Word of God to the whole world. The artist has represented that fact in the figure of St. Peter preaching to the Jews first on the right. But the message of Christ was meant for the gentiles as well, which the artist suggests by the figures of St. Paul and St. Barnabas preaching to the gentiles on the left.

On the apex of the soffit arch, in a combination of a tongue of flame and the movement of the wind, the artist has included a symbol of the action of the Holy Spirit in the life of the Church and in the lives of individual Christians. "The spirit," Holy Scripture says, is mysterious, "and moveth where it will." Before the Ascension, when Christ was about to leave his Apostles, he told them he would not leave them orphans but would send them the Holy Spirit who would continue to teach them all the things that he had taught them. The Ascension is represented on the right side of the soffit arch. One of the chief things Christ taught his followers was a knowledge of the Trinity, that full triple personal life within the Godhead. The first visible manifestation of these three divine persons was on the occasion of Christ's baptism, when the Divine Son made man was manifest in Christ being baptized, the Divine Father in the voice from heaven saying: "This is my beloved Son." The Holy Spirit was manifest in the symbolic form of the dove hovering over the head of Christ being baptized. This great manifestation of the Trinity is represented on the left side of the soffit.

People studying the cathedral mosaics a hundred or two hundred years down the line (and they will be) will know by the contents of these particular mosaics that they were installed in the 1980s, not in the 1930s. These mosaics express what was going on in the Church at that time. The style of the mosaics is also a little different from those that had been previously installed, which were heavily dependent on the Byzantine style of the past. Both in content and style, these mosaics speak of their own age. One of the interesting features of many church buildings in Europe is that they do represent theological and stylistic emphases that correspond to the time periods when additions were made. In experiencing them, you can almost march back through time in content and style and experience the changing pageant of the past. We believe that future generations will be able to do the same thing in experiencing the mosaics of the St. Louis Cathedral.

The subject matter for the two flat walls in the historical bay was to relate to the history of the Church in the St. Louis area. St. Louis is known in history as the Gateway to the West, a fact beautifully commemorated in the Saarinen Gateway Arch. It was also actually the missionary gateway to the West. The Jesuit missioner from France, Père Marquette, had come here from Canada to evangelize the native Mississippi people, and Father Pierre De Smet had begun here his exploration of the West and his evangelism of the native people all the way to the West Coast. The committee agreed that a good subject for one of the panels in the historical bay would be St. Louis as a missionary gateway. The subject was given to the artist, Mary Reardon, and she came up with a design showing Marquette and a companion landing in a canoe at St. Louis, and in the center the figure of Pierre De Smet, wearing a buckskin jacket that the native people had given him and preaching to a group of them.

The St. Louis diocese was the first diocese in the United States to adopt a foreign mission. It is in Bolivia. The artist commemorated that fact with the figure of a diocesan priest conversing with a group of Bolivian native people accompanied by a llama. This mosaic was actually the final one to be installed. It completed the entire mosaic program in the cathedral. Arno Heuduck, who installed it, was suffering from a terminal cancer when he was working on it and died three months after it was finished. He and his father had fabricated approximately 90 percent of all the mosaics installed in the cathedral. Over the years, some twenty artists provided designs for the mosaics.

The second of the last two mosaics to be installed in the historical bay appropriately commemorated the work of Cardinal Ritter. He is represented in the center of the mosaic in his cardinalational robes. At his left is a group of integrated school children led by a nun. The scene commemorates Cardinal Ritter's integration of all the schools in the diocese ten years before the federal law of integration was passed. At his right is a group of clergy in conversation with one another—a Jewish rabbi, two Protestant ministers, and a priest— meant to commemorate Cardinal Ritter's interest in ecumenism and his work in shaping the Document on Religious Liberty in Vatican II that so strongly recommends better understanding between the various religious denominations and greater tolerance for various faiths. These two mosaic panels nicely round out the story of the Church in the historical bay. They are made to harmonize well with the other historical mosaics in the bay designed by Hildreth Meiere.

With the mosaics completed, two other things remained to be done to enhance their beauty. The windows in the upper gallery were glazed in a rather bright white glass that admitted entirely too much light, which blinded the viewer and prevented a proper experience of the mosaics themselves. At some point in the history of the cathedral, colored stained glass in an abstract pattern had been installed in the gallery windows on either side of the sanctuary, which cast colored tones on the gold mosaic in the sanctuary area, completely falsifying and actually cheapening the effect of the mosaics. In Byzantine churches, the windows were always glazed with a neutral amber glass or often with thin layers of alabaster, which shed a neutral golden light on the mosaics rather than a distorting foreign color. One day when Archbishop May was with us in the gallery inspecting the installation of some of the final mosaics, I remarked that now that the mosaic program was almost finished, we would have to start on the gallery window problem. He looked at me in consternation and said, "What window problem?" I called attention to the two problems of the windows and said that if we did not remedy them, we would be greatly diminishing the proper experience of the mosaics into which so much effort and money had been poured. He saw the point immediately and commissioned the Emil Frei Company to design windows with neutral amber tones that would cut down on the bright light and remove the distraction of false colors emanating from the colored windows in the sanctuary onto the gold mosaic. Robert Frei designed and installed the new windows, which have very much enhanced the appreciation of all the mosaics in the cathedral.

I had one other suggestion for the archbishop. Most people have a very hazy idea of what goes into the making of mosaics. With the largest collection of mosaics in one building in the world and an ever-increasing number of visitors from all over the world coming to see them, I thought it would be helpful to develop a museum in the basement of the cathedral that would show the whole process of making mosaics, including the artist's preliminary designs and to-scale magnifications of the design; the fabrication of the mosaics in the mosaicist's studio, in which the artist's design is translated into the mosaic medium; and finally the actual installation of the finished mosaic on the wall. The archbishop thought it was a capital idea and gave us the go-ahead on creating the museum. The architect, Verner Burks, designed the cabinetry and exhibition space, and I worked out the details of the exhibition itself. Arno Heuduck's widow donated much of the equipment and mosaic material from Arno's studio, so visitors can now follow the whole process of making mosaics, through the design, fabrication, and installation processes, which gives them a much better understanding of what lies behind the marvelous mosaics they experience in the cathedral itself.

We included in the museum display a beautiful series of professional photographs by John Nagel of many details of the mosaics in the cathedral with companion photographs of mosaics in Europe—especially those in Istanbul, Rome, Venice, and Ravenna—that inspired the artists who worked in the St. Louis Cathedral.

The museum also includes a display of liturgical vestments and vessels. Many of them have historical association in the diocese, and some of them are no longer used since the changes in the Liturgy after Vatican II. It is another way of keeping the public aware of our historical and liturgical past.

A half-hour video covering the history of the cathedral is available for visitors to the museum. The video shows the process of making mosaics, gives a brief overview of the mosaics in the cathedral, and shows the cathedral in actual use in some of the liturgical events of the year. The museum is thus a great help to visitors to get the most out of their visit to what is unquestionably a world-class architectural monument.

The booklet on the mosaics, which Monsignor Gannon originally commissioned me to do, went through two editions in black and white. In the third edition, I have added a section on the making of mosaics and colored photographs by John Nagel of all the mosaics in the cathedral. This edition will be a much more informative and beautiful guide to and memento of the cathedral for visitors.

I was also drawn into another architectural project closer to home than the cathedral—the restoration of the Chapel of the Crucified King at the University Hospital on the occasion of its fiftieth anniversary. I was actually slightly involved in its beginning. I was master of ceremonies at its dedication liturgy in 1932. I had just come to the university from Florissant to begin my philosophy studies. As I indicated previously in these recollections, Father Preuss had gotten me hooked on the study of medieval architecture in general in his evening sessions on Romanesque and Gothic European architecture. I had read Ralph Adam Cram's book *The Spirit of the Gothic,* which had intensified my enthusiasm for the subject. I was particularly excited when I discovered that the architect for the University Hospital Chapel was none other than Ralph Adams Cram.

The Desloge family had given the money to finance the building of the hospital. As a bow to the French background of the Desloge family, the hospital is topped off with a very Frenchified copper roof. The roof has been dramatically lit in recent years and is now a beacon landmark in the city at night, advertising French associations of the University Hospital. In 1933, the Desloge family made an additional gift to finance the construction of a hospital chapel dedicated to the memory of Firmin Desloge. They stipulated that Ralph Adams Cram be the architect and that he design it in the French Gothic style. That, of course, was most agreeable to Cram because he, more than any other, is responsible for the Gothic revival in this country. The design he came up with vaguely resembles the Sainte Chapelle in Paris on the exterior, but differs from it on the interior in that it has side aisles and a low clerestory. It is a beautifully proportioned stone-vaulted structure, and all the stone vaulting is functional. There are no steel supports in the building. The Desloge funds, however, were not ample enough to commission the stained glass windows. The windows were glazed with a neutral-colored glass in a uniform diaper pattern. The chapel was a beautiful structure, but a Gothic stone structure without its stained glass windows is a rather colorless and cold entity. The Desloge chapel remained that way for fifty years.

The focal point in the chapel had always been the impressive stone sculpture over the altar by the English sculptor John Angell. It represents Christ on the Cross, but not a suffering Christ. He looks regal and triumphant over death—a reminder of his Resurrection—a happy thought for a hospital chapel, where death or the fear of death is such a familiar subject. Mary and John are not sunk in grief but stand as witnesses of Christ's triumph over death. The figures are life-size, and so the sculpture dominates the chapel.

But through the years, the chapel fell on hard times. Like everything else in the city, it was smudged by the decades of St. Louis soot, and after Vatican II it was frightfully mishandled. In some places, as a result of a misapplication of the council's urging a more real participation of the congregation in the liturgy of the Mass, some churches and chapels were turned upside down to make the Mass more "homey." The Communion service of the Mass was so overemphasized that the sacrificial offering of Christ as the gift of adoration, thanksgiving, petition, and reparation to our Heavenly Father was nearly lost sight of. The almost excessive emphasis on the Communion element in the Mass and the attempt to make it a "homey" experience resulted at times and in certain places in a rather bizarre rearrangement of the church interior, which happened at the Desloge University Hospital chapel. The altar with its splendid sculpture of Christ the Crucified King was simply ignored. A plain plywood table was set up in the middle of the nave. It looked like a rustic picnic table you might find in a park, and actually the idea was to make the Communion service a kind of picnic. The pews were grouped around the picnic table in a "chummy" fashion. There was nothing about the arrangement that would induce any kind of reverence in the presence of the divine or suggest that part of what was going on at the altar was a sacrificial offering of the Body and Blood of the Risen Christ to our Heavenly Father. And this arrangement, of course, was a desecration of the beautiful Ralph Adams Cram chapel, which, even without its stained glass windows, had such a feeling of quiet reverence about it, all focused on the beautiful sculptured image of Christ the Crucified King.

The chapel remained in this condition until Father Thomas Kelly was made chaplain at the hospital in the 1970s, and he decided to do something about it. The fiftieth anniversary of the chapel was approaching, and he persuaded the powers that be to undertake a thorough cleaning of the chapel inside and out to remove the fifty years' accumulation of soot, to redo the interior to accommodate the new liturgy, but in a little less "chummy" way, and above all to commission the stained glass windows that would finally bring the chapel up to the level of beauty and dignity that the architect had intended. Surprisingly, Father Kelly got the go-ahead from the administration for the whole project. He engaged Verner Burks to plan the cleaning, restoring, and redesigning of the chapel to meet the new liturgical needs. He engaged Rodney Winfield to design the windows, which the Emil Frei Company would fabricate. Father Tom asked me to act as design consultant with Verner Burks and as a consultant with Rodney Winfield in working out the iconographic program for the windows. Both were marvelously congenial people.

Verner from the beginning insisted that the focus should return to the beautiful English sculpture of Christ the Crucified King and that hence the pews should be restored and repositioned to face the altar. The beautiful stone altar table would be retained with its tabernacle, but a platform would be extended out into the nave, supporting an exact duplicate of the original altar for the Mass facing the people. This arrangement would put the offering priest at the new altar on an exact axis with the figure of the Crucified Christ the King above making his offering of himself on the altar of the Cross and suggesting by his demeanor his Resurrection and triumph over death. Warm red carpeting was added around the altar and down the aisle, which added some color that had been lacking in the chapel before. Verner also designed a beautiful outdoor meditation garden just outside the chapel.

The main addition to the refurbished chapel was to be the windows. Because of the fine Gothic ambiance of Cram's structure, Rodney Winfield decided that the windows should be designed to emulate the medieval windows in the Sainte Chapelle in Paris and those in the Chartres Cathedral. He asked me to suggest the iconographic program. Because we were working in a hospital chapel where patients and guests alike are apt to be preoccupied with the subject of death, I thought it appropriate that the iconography of the windows should touch on that subject and express the Christian perspective on it. In that perspective, death is not the end but the beginning of eternal life, and with it goes the promise of the final resurrection of the body itself. That sequence of death-life-resurrection is imaged for us in the lives of both Christ and his Blessed Mother. So I decided that in the three windows on each side of the chapel a sequence of panels representing scenes from the lives of Christ and Mary would point up this positive and hopeful view of death for any visitor to the chapel. The two sequences would climax in the death of Christ on the Cross, but the one would terminate in the Resurrection of Christ and Pentecost, and the other in the Assumption of Mary into heaven. The two small windows facing the congregation of the south wall on either side of the altar would carry the same message: the one on the left would picture Christ in his agony in the garden, the one on the right his Resurrection.

There is a tall lancet window on either side of the sanctuary. Because the Angell sculpture of Christ the Crucified King really represents Christ on the Cross as the eternal priest, vested in the chasuble of his flesh, as some of the church fathers described him, offering himself as the eternal victim to his Heavenly Father, I thought that in these adjacent windows it would be appropriate to represent angels vested in dalmatics, the vestments of deacons at a traditional Solemn High Mass. The combination of the Angell sculpture and the windows would constitute an image of the Eternal Mass or Liturgy being offered forever in heaven by the Risen Savior, which would be echoed in the chapel by the Mass offered at the chapel altar below. This eucharistic allusion is carried out also by the grapes in the window on the left and the bundles of wheat in the window on the right.

Rodney Winfield worked out this whole program with very great sensitivity and a feeling for the medieval style that graces the windows of the Sainte Chapelle in Paris. He added many symbolic details throughout the scheme to augment the meaning of the panels they accompany. The whole renovation program resulted in a hospital chapel that is marvelously prayerful, very respectful of the original design of the architect, and at the same time a fine adaptation to the needs of the new Liturgy.

Earlier in my life, I had been involved as master of ceremonies in the dedication Liturgy at the opening of the chapel; then I was involved in its restoration as a consultant to the architect and the stained glass artist; and now I was involved as the homilest of the Mass in the Mass of rededication at the completion of the restoration. I remarked at the end of my homily that after fifty years they had found it necessary to give the Desloge chapel a face-lifting, but that I feared that after fifty years they could not do anything for me. The president of the university, Father Fitzgerald, remarked at the reception afterward that indeed they could. The hospital has a plastic surgery department, and he could ask them to give it a try. But because it was not a Ralph Adams Cram treasure we were talking about, I passed up his offer.

Since Father Lawrence Biondi has become president of the university, more has been done to expand and beautify the campus than was done in the previous one hundred years. Part of the beautification has been the restoration of some of the university's oldest and most distinctive buildings. One of the oldest is Dubourg Hall, the administration building. It was designed by the distinguished nineteenth-century architect Thomas Walsh in the English Collegiate Gothic style. It had deteriorated badly over the years; the red sandstone trim was in especially bad condition. The building has now been thoroughly restored inside and out, and the very distinctive former library, with its many balconies with wrought iron and brass-trimmed railings and its impressive hammer-beam ceiling, has undergone restoration. It provides a beautiful assembly, reception, and concert hall with a great deal of old-world charm. I was asked to suggest an iconographic program for the windows that Rodney Winfield would design and Stephen Frei would install. I took the preservation and dissemination of the Word as a theme. It begins, in the west apsidal windows, with a figure of Christ the Pantocrator, the Teacher, associated with an image of St. Ignatius, whose Society of Jesus, through its educational ventures, is engaged in disseminating the Word. The side windows bear images of the four evangelists, also disseminators of the Word. All of these figures employ the Byzantine gesture of the teacher. The four panels of windows on the north side visualize the various ways in which the Word has been preserved and disseminated: by scrolls, by illuminated manuscripts, by the printed book, and by the computer.

Father Biondi suggested the addition of representations of Teilhard de Chardin, Gerard Manley Hopkins, St. Catherine of Sienna, and St. Philippine Duchesne, in their various ways also disseminators of the word, human and divine; and of the seals of all the Jesuit colleges and universities in the United States, which through education also are engaged in disseminating the human and divine word.

But perhaps the most important restoration project in this renewal program at the university was the restoration of St. Francis Xavier (College) Church. Like Dubourg Hall, it was originally designed by Thomas Walsh, but only the basement was built in his lifetime. After his death, the work was taken over by Henry W. Switzer of Chicago, who made minor changes in the design. Thomas Walsh's design was a very conscious adaptation of the design for the Cathedral of St. Colman in Cobh, Ireland. Father Henry C. Bronsgeest, the Belgian pastor of the College Church at the time, requested that Walsh use it as his model. That design really ties the College Church into the very heart of the Gothic revival in England in the nineteenth century, a movement sparked and promoted by Augustus Welby Pugin, who himself contributed the designs for much of the interior decoration of the Houses of Parliament in London; for the main altar of the Jesuit church on Farm Street, also in London; and for the entire Catholic Cathedral in Killarney, Ireland. The Cathedral of St. Colman's in Cobh was designed by his son, E. W. Pugin. The cathedral is perched on a bluff above the harbor of Cobh (formerly Queenstown) and would have been the last thing that the thousands of emigrants leaving Ireland would have seen from the tender that took them out to their ship anchored in the harbor. I thought of that with some emotion when I visited Cobh because one of those emigrants was my grandfather.

When you see the cathedral at Cobh after you have seen the College Church in St. Louis, you can't help noticing the many similarities: the one tower positioned asymmetrically on the right of the facade and especially the march of great red granite pillars on the interior transformed above the capitals into Gothic columns moving out into fan vaulting at the top. There is much of St. Colman's in the College Church, but Walsh and Switzer refined the design, and, although smaller, the College Church succeeds in being a more harmonious design.

Like everything else in St. Louis in the smoke era, the College Church became very blackened inside and out over the years. A thorough cleaning and renovation were in order, as well as changes on the interior to adapt it to the needs of the new Liturgy.

Kurt Landberg, a local architect well known for his outstanding restoration work, was engaged to direct the restoration. Several committees made up of members of the parish were appointed to check on different aspects of the project. I was on the arts and liturgy committee that was to check on the aesthetic and liturgical correctness of every aspect of the project. We met every two weeks for two years and checked on every element of the project before, during, and after each thing was done. Sylvia Efken, a specialist in design at the Monsanto Company, chaired the committee. Every member of the committee brought his or her expertise to the task, and we worked very well together, with the result that the finished restoration created a very pleasant and prayerful atmosphere for the new Liturgy.

The project began with a thorough cleaning of the exterior, which brought out the beautiful limestone structure with its multiple sculptured saints on the facade and tower, but the major work took place in the interior. Much of the work was not visible because it involved putting in a completely new heating system, a cooling system, which the church did not have previously, and sophisticated new lighting and sound systems. But the renovations that can be seen really enhance the Gothic quality of the building. The whole interior had been painted a uniform gray to simulate stone, which did not bring out the beautiful pattern of the fan vaulting—vaulting that comes closer in appearance to the wonderful fan vaulting of Exeter Cathedral in England than any vaulting I have seen anywhere else in the States. A subtle contrast of color between the flat part of the vaulting and the ribs brings out the fan pattern of the ribs as they had never been seen before. All along the side walls a heavy dark-purple marble dado had been installed, supermounted with innumerable bronze plaques commemorating the donors to the church. That dado and the line of confessionals in between with Gothic frontals, whose varnished wood had darkened almost to a black, created a very heavy dark horizontal that almost entirely destroyed any Gothic vertical lift on the side walls. The marble dado was removed, and the Gothic frames on the confessionals were painted to match the frames of the Gothic windows above them. The result was a lightening of the walls and a definite vertical Gothic lift upward.

The windows themselves had been designed by Emil Frei Jr., who considered them his masterpiece, but they had been darkened by some fifty years of St. Louis soot. Cleaned inside and out, they now sparkle and create the ever-shifting shafts of colored light in the interior that stained glass windows are meant to create. The floor was completely replaced, with the wiring for the new acoustical system installed in it, and the new floor was finished in a parquet pattern. The old, rather uncomfortable pews were discarded. The new ones retained the carved Gothic ends of the old ones but were shortened to expose the bases of the impressive granite columns.

The old organ in the loft had not been designed for the church, and its bulk obscured two-thirds of the beautiful rose window. The organ was discarded, but some of its Gothic framework was refashioned to make an attractive framing for the beautiful rose window. When a new organ is installed, it will be bracketed, as organs are in many traditional Gothic churches in Europe, on either side of the altar in the sanctuary end of the church.

A new baptismal font, an octagonal structure of white and purple marble, large enough for baptism by partial immersion, was placed at the rear of the main aisle just inside the door of the vestibule. The original chalice-shaped white marble font is incorporated into one side of the larger font. From it, a steady steam of water flows into the larger font below. The smaller font can be used for infant baptisms and also serves as the Holy Water font. The position of the font here, of course, is meant to remind the faithful, as they enter the church, of their baptism, which was the means of their birth in the faith. Stretching from the baptismal font all the way up to the foundation of the altar at the other end of the church is the main aisle finished in a basketweave parquet pattern of three different colors of wood. The same woods are used in the steps to and the platform of the altar itself, which is meant to remind the faithful that they, and not just the officiating priest, are participating in the sacrificial offering being made at the altar. We tried to suggest the same thing by having the artist who fabricated the new wooden altar, the pulpit, and the lectern incorporate into their decoration the large Gothic arcades formed by the massive granite columns and by the Gothic arches they support, as well as the smaller arcade of the clerestory gallery above. This brings the nave into the sanctuary as the faithful in the nave are brought into the sacrificial offering made at the altar in each Mass.

The old main altar was a large Gothic structure with a high reredos above the altar table. The first suggestion was to remove it entirely and supplant it with a space for the choir. Our committee opposed the idea. We suggested removing the old altar table and tabernacle, and leaving the superstructure of the altar as a reredos background for the choir below and for the new altar, which would be farther forward on the island platform constructed for it. The suggestion was acted upon with the result that, besides preserving this interesting architectural link with the past, the very significant symbolism of the iconographical details of the old sanctuary and reredos were also preserved.

The iconographic program begins with the beautiful stained glass windows in the upper apse. Emil Frei Jr. considered them his masterpiece, and well he might. They are the closest approximation in the United States to the famous stained glass windows in the apse of Chartres Cathedral. They represent the Trinity in heaven: God the Father and God the Son as enthroned figures, and God the Holy Spirit represented as a dove in the central octagonal window at the top. The trinitarian figures are arced by a glorious rainbow and are surrounded to the right and left with adoring angels. As you move down to the altar reredos itself, you encounter first a Carrara marble full-length figure of Christ, the incarnate Son of God, at the highest niche of the central spire—the translation of the eternal, ineffable Word of God into human flesh accessible to all of us. In lower niches at each side are the figures of St. Ignatius Loyola, founder of the Society of Jesus, and St. Francis Xavier, patron of the College Church. Large bas-relief sculptures appear lower still on the reredos that represent the miracle of the multiplication of the loaves and the wedding feast of Cana, where Christ turned water into wine, both seen as allusions to the Eucharist, in which the bread and wine are turned into the Body and Blood of Christ in each sacrifice of the Mass. And still lower are sculptures of the symbols of the four evangelists, whose writings preserved and disseminated Christ's saving truth in the world. It would have been a pity to have lost all this rich symbolism by the complete removal of the old reredos of the main altar. A beautiful new gold and red enamel cross (not crucifix) designed by the artist Rodney Winfield graces the old throne in the center of the reredos screen, and an exquisitely wrought processional crucifix in gold and silver repoussé by the same artist is on permanent display near the new altar.

In the old sanctuary, there were four side altars dedicated to the Blessed Virgin, St. Joseph, the Sacred Heart, and the young Jesuit saints, St. Aloysius and St. John Berchmans. The new Liturgy prescribes that there be only one altar, the altar at which Mass is celebrated, so all four side altars were removed. But the exquisite and unique bas-relief sculptures *Our Lady, the Comforter of the Afflicted* and *The Death of St. Joseph* were retained in their niches where the two main side altars were. The sculptures were carved by the German-born artist Joseph Sibbel. He considered these sculptures his masterpieces. Dramatically lit, they provide beautiful termini to the two side aisles.

Our committee came into conflict with the architect and the central committee over the placement of the tabernacle for the reservation of the Blessed Sacrament. It is no longer supposed to be on the main altar. The architect and central committee were for placing it in a room by itself, to which there would have been access by a door where the old Sacred Heart altar had been. But if that were done, there would have been no evidence whatever of Christ's presence in the Blessed Sacrament in the main body of the church. Our committee objected strongly. We suggested that a eucharistic tower tabernacle be constructed where the old Sacred Heart altar had been, using the central spiral niche of the Sacred Heart altar itself and the beautiful tabernacle from the old main altar with gold-embossed adoring angels on its doors to construct the new tower tabernacle. Such tabernacles from the Middle Ages still exist in places in Europe. There is a notable example in the College Church of St. Peter in Old Louvain. Both the architect and the central committee were persuaded, and we got our tower tabernacle. We placed two adoring angels in white Carrara marble on pedestals at each side, suspended a fine white crystal tabernacle light in the upper niche of the tower, and thus had a very visible sign of the eucharistic presence of Christ in the body of the church.

I have never visited the church since when there are not some of the faithful kneeling in reverent prayer before the tabernacle. It was interesting to discover that the iconography of the little stained glass window, previously obscured by the old Sacred Heart altar, has a definite eucharistic content. It contains a chalice and a host, two adoring angels, and the words *Sanctus, Sanctus, Sanctus,* and *Venite Adoremus.* It was almost as if the window had been waiting for the eucharistic tower tabernacle.

The very beautiful and prayerful atmosphere created by all the cleaning, restoration, and thoughtful additions has made very much worthwhile the hours that several committees spent working on the project. The result is that the full beauty of one of the finest Gothic revival churches in the country has been enhanced and, with the help of very efficient and modern lighting, has been made a model setting for the beautiful liturgies that take place there.

So hurrah for Father Biondi, who has done so much to restore and enhance some of the treasures of the campus and to expand and beautify the whole campus. These contributions are all very visible. But hurrah to him, too, for other contributions to the well-being of the university that are less visible: the addition of many endowed professorships, a great increase in student scholarships, upgraded faculty salaries and benefits, and expanded library holdings.

18

# A Touch of Mortality and a Thought for the Future

WHEN YOU HAVE REACHED the age of ninety-one, you have to remind yourself of your mortality, especially when you read the obituaries and see how few of the deceased have reached ninety-one. If your health is relatively good, you simply don't think of death as waiting for you. That reminds me of some powerful lines in Gerard Manley Hopkins's "Wreck of the Deutschland" on this very subject.

> We dream we are rooted in earth—Dust!
> Flesh falls within sight of us, we, though our flower the same,
>     Wave with the meadow, forget that there must
> The sour scythe cringe, and the blear share come.

As usual, Hopkins chooses remarkably effective imagery from everyday life to express our forgetfulness about the inevitability of death for each of us. He chooses his images from the farmland. They are particularly vivid and effective to me because I myself have wielded the scythe and mower in a meadow and the plow in the fields.

We had a very pleasant marsh or meadowland on the farm that grew lush natural hay that we always mowed in midsummer. The meadow was a spot I always enjoyed. Amid the wild grass, very special beautiful wildflowers flourished that did not grow elsewhere. I remember especially the waxy golden-yellow marsh marigolds, the jack-in-the-pulpits, and the deep purple–fringed gentians. They were always at the height of their bloom at haying time. As I started mowing, I could see these beautiful flowers waving in the breeze and falling before my mower. As I cut one swath, I could see the blossoms waving carelessly in the wind that would be felled in my next round with the mower. The sudden death of flowers seemed even more aggressive when they fell before the hand scythe. When "the sour scythe cringed."

It was the same when I was plowing the fields, which were frequently spangled with wild daisies or bright orange paintbrush blossoms. I knew as I passed them by in the first furrow that I would catch them on the next one: "the blear [plow]share would come." Yet the fringed gentians in the meadow and the daisies in the field did keep waving gleefully, oblivious of the crunch of the scythe or the destructive plowshare that was about to fell them. That, Hopkins is saying, is the way most of us put off the thought of the grim reaper.

But sometimes the reaper gets so close to us that we can't ignore him. Some twelve years ago, he brushed my shoulders. I had had my general physical examination from my regular doctor and was given a clean bill of health, but in a routine examination my heart doctor for some reason decided he wanted a general physical repeated. The X-rays of that examination showed that there seemed to be a spot on my left lung that looked suspicious. Dr. Thurman said he was not a lung specialist and that I better go to the hospital and have a scan taken to check out that spot. The scan showed that the spot on the left lung was just a shadow of old age, but that there was a suspicious spot on the right lung. Dr. Thurman sent me to a lung specialist with the scan, and when the specialist examined it, he said: "You are going into the hospital tomorrow. The spot on your right lung is almost certainly cancerous."

There was that dreaded word—CANCEROUS—which sounded like a death knell. I had been waving with the meadow, oblivious that the "blear share" would come. After further examination, the doctors operated, removed the upper lobe of the right lung, and found that the spot was indeed cancerous. They were so sure, however, that they had gotten all the cancerous cells that they did not even prescribe postoperative therapy. I guess they were right. That was some twelve years ago, and the cancer has not reoccurred.

But the experience was a close brush with death, and it forced me to stop waving with the meadow and give some thought to death. When you do that from a Christian perspective, death loses some of its terror because you really come to appreciate the fact that death is not an end but a beginning. John Donne puts it forcefully in his famous sonnet on death in which he really takes some of the grimness out of the grim reaper.

> Death be not proud, though some have called thee
> Mighty and dreadfull, for, thou art not soe,

> For, those, whom thou think'st, thou dost overthrow,
> Die not, poore death, nor yet canst thou kill mee;
> From rest and sleepe, which but thy pictures bee,
> Much pleasure, then from thee, much more must flow,
> And soonest our best men with thee doe goe,
> Rest of their bones, and soules deliverie.
> Thou are slave to Fate, chance, kings, and desperate men,
> And doth with poyson, warre, and sicknesse dwell.
> And poppie, or charmes can make us sleepe as well,
> And better then thy stroake; why swell'st thou then?
> One short sleepe past, wee wake eternally,
> And death shall be no more, death thou shalt die.

My little brush with death prompted me to think about my own mortality and about the fact that although the grim reaper's scythe had missed me on his last round, I know he'll be back. That realization led me to think more seriously about preparing for a successor to take over the direction of Cupples House. I thought I had provided for a successor in the person of Father Terry Dempsey, but as things worked out, his taking over eventually became impracticable. Burns was right: "The best laid plans of mice and men / Oft gang agley."

Terry had come to St. Louis University originally from Painesville, Ohio, to work on a doctoral program in English. I was chairman of the department at the time and got to know Terry well. He also took some art history courses, some of which I taught. He completed all the course work for the doctorate in English, but then his widowed mother became ill, and he had to get work to help support her. He began teaching English at the Jesuit De Smet High School in St. Louis. He continued his interest in art by including it in some of his teaching there and by mounting shows in the school library with paintings that he borrowed from our collection at St. Louis University. Eventually, his mother became so ill that he had to go home to help care for her. He taught English for a while in his hometown high school in Painesville. Eventually he joined the Jesuits and, following his novitiate, came back to Fusz Memorial Jesuit Seminary at St. Louis University to study philosophy. While there he continued to pursue his interest in art and in Cupples House specifically and decided that he really would like to continue his studies in art history rather than in English literature. Because that was his decision, I asked him whether he would be interested in getting a degree in art history and then coming back to the art department at the university with the idea of eventually taking over the directorship of Cupples House. The idea appealed to him, and that was what he decided to do. The provincial agreed with the plan, and because Terry had already had so much high school teaching experience, the provincial suggested that, instead of the usual regency teaching, Terry do a year of apprenticeship at Cupples House before going on to theology in Berkeley, which is what he did. He also did some teaching during the year at De Andreis High School, but spent most of his time helping out at Cupples House. He did his theology at Berkeley and took courses in art history. In two additional years after completing his program in theology, he finished all the requirements for the doctorate in art history.

The degree was conferred by the Theological Union, but he had taken the bulk of his course work at the University of California. One of the members of his board was Peter Selz of Berkeley University, formerly curator of modern art at the Museum of Modern Art in New York. The other two members were John and Jane Dillenberger of the Theological Union. Terry wrote his doctoral dissertation on the religious dimension in modern art. In the course of his research, he interviewed more than 150 artists of various faiths who had a compelling interest in a religious or spiritual element in their art. Ironically, that subject matter and a suggestion I ultimately made to Terry was to result in his elimination as a viable prospect for succeeding me in the directorship of Cupples House. This is what happened.

When the Jesuit seminarians moved out of Fusz Memorial, the building became a university dormitory. Father John Waters asked me to make an inventory of the art objects in the ten chapels in the building because it was not likely that it would continue to be used as a chapel. As I was doing so, it occurred to me that the chapel would make a fine space for a religious museum. I had seen former chapels and churches used that way in Europe, especially a very successful one in Cologne. I wrote to Terry at Berkeley suggesting the idea. He at first reacted very negatively because he seemed to have unpleasant memories of the place.

But he had offered his First Mass in the Fusz chapel, so he dug out some of his pictures of the event and began to see that the space did have real possibilities as a museum. He came up with the idea of making it a gallery in which the works of any artists of any faith who had a religious dimension in their work might be exhibited. When he came to the art history faculty at the university, he began to implement that idea. By careful planning, he has turned the chapel space into one of the most impressive display galleries in the city. His contact with artists all over the country has enabled him to inaugurate a series of exhibits of work of modern artists with a religious dimension in their works that have been most impressive. The museum goes under the acronym MOCRA—the Museum of Contemporary Religious Art. It has been so successful and so time- and energy-consuming that Terry could in no way now take on the added burden of managing Cupples House. My little suggestion of a religious museum in the former Fusz chapel has so fructified under Terry's guidance that I was left without a designated successor in the directorship of Cupples House. Everybody, including Terry, recognized that fact, and, as I write, Pamela Ambrose from New York, who has had wide experience in museum and gallery work, has been appointed director to take Cupples House into the future it deserves.

I do not see what remains of my own future as idling my time away, however. I really feel a little bit like Tennyson's Ulysses, who said:

> I am a part of all that I have met;
> Yet all experience is an arch where through
> Gleams that untraveled world whose margin fades
> Forever and forever when I move.
> How dull it is to pause, to make an end.
> To rust unburnished, not to shine in use
> As though to breathe were life! Life piled on life
> Were all too little, and of one to me
> Little remains.

But in the life that does remain to me, I have no intention of "rust[ing] unburnished." There is plenty left for me to do to keep what remains of the old machine burnished.

I will continue my Scripture group, eleven men who have been meeting every month for more than a dozen years to read and discuss Scripture and share a Liturgy together.

As I write, an article I composed for the revised text of Dr. John Morley's book on gerontology is in the press. It has to do with the shift of style manifest in the work of long-lived artists who move from a rather reserved and classical style to a more expressive, even mannerist or surrealistic style as their own experience broadens and deepens with age. I illustrate the point with the work of Michelangelo, Titian, El Greco, and Marc Chagall. Some of the best work of all of these artists was produced when they were older than seventy. I conclude my discussion of these great masters with the remark that the world would have been greatly impoverished if they had all retired at sixty-five.

For the last few years I have been working on a book-length study of the *Vested Angel* as a eucharistic symbol. The book has finally been published by Peeters of Louvain, Belgium. It demonstrates the ubiquity of this symbol in Flemish painting and the source of the symbol in Byzantine theology and art and in the more proximate sources of the medieval and Renaissance Latin liturgical practice.

I am at present working on the text of a publication called "The Jesuits and the Baroque." I still have some photography to do to illustrate the text.

I have projects in mind also that will help better exploit Cupples House and its contents for the public. They include minicourses organized around the contents of the house and related subjects. I am working as a consultant on a video introduction to the house for visitors and individual audio guides to make the tours of individuals through the house more interesting and memorable. As long as my health holds, I do not intend to "rust unburnished," but to "shine in use."

And should I become disabled, I will take consolation with Milton in the realization that "they also serve who only stand and wait."